THE NEW INTERPRETER'S® BIBLE

NEW TESTAMENT SURVEY

THE NEW INTERPRETER'S® BIBLE

NEW TESTAMENT SURVEY

ABINGDON PRESS
Nashville

THE NEW INTERPRETER'S® BIBLE
NEW TESTAMENT SURVEY

Library of Congress Cataloging-in-Publication Data

The new interpreter's Bible. New Testament survey.
p. cm.
Includes bibliographical references and index.
ISBN 0-687-05434-6 (978-0-687-05434-3 : alk. paper)
1. Bible. N.T.--Introductions. I. Title: New Testament survey.

BS2330.3.N49 2006
225.6'1--dc22
2005032593

The HebraicaII® and GraecaII® fonts used to print this work are available from
Linguist's Software, Inc., PO Box 580, Edmonds, WA 98020-0580.
Tel (425) 775-1130. Web www.linguistsoftware.com

PUBLICATION STAFF
President and Publisher: Neil M. Alexander
Editorial Director: Harriett Jane Olson
Reference Unit Director: Paul Franklyn
Reference Project Manager: Marianne Blickenstaff
Development Editor: Heather R. McMurray
Editorial Consultant: Kathy Chambers
Production and Design Manager: Ed Wynne
Composition Specialist: Brenda Gayl Hinton
Print Procurement Coordinator: Paul Shoulders

MANUFACTURED IN THE UNITED STATES OF AMERICA

Publisher's Foreword

> "While it is appropriate to distinguish historical and literary explanation of the text as a work of the past from reflection on its import in various situations today, it is also necessary to ground the later in the former. The fact that most writers of the *NIB* are professional Bible scholars reflects the conviction that what effective and imaginative interpretation needs most is solid grounding in an explanation of the text that engages the religious and moral content of scripture."
>
> —Leander E. Keck,
> General Editor of *The New Interpreter's® Bible*

The success of *The New Interpreter's® Bible* (12 volumes) as a standard of contemporary biblical scholarship prompts the creation of two surveys based on the introductory materials included in this commentary set. The *Old Testament Survey* and *New Testament Survey* are easily accessible to students who are seeking an expert overview of every book of the Old or New Testament. These volumes can be used as primary texts alongside the Bible, or as supplements to other textbooks.

The New Interpreter's® Bible New Testament Survey provides the introductory content for each book of the New Testament. As an added bonus, the *Survey* also provides introductions to genres of literature contained in the Bible. The articles in the *Survey* cover essential historical, socio-cultural, literary, and theological issues, which are illustrated with maps and charts. For students interested in key points related to the original languages of the Bible, we have provided the Hebrew, Aramaic, and Greek languages along with transliterations and translations. Each chapter includes an updated list of suggested readings.

The New Interpreter's® Bible line is committed to providing balanced coverage of critical issues for seminary and church audiences. Perhaps the best reason to consider the *New Testament Survey* as a textbook is that it represents a collection of noteworthy biblical scholars, each writing in their own field of expertise. Moreover, these collections represent a diversity of scholarship that includes perspectives of women and men, racial and ethnic minorities, Protestantism and Catholicism.

Contributors

DAVID L. BARTLETT
Lantz Professor of Preaching and Communication
The Divinity School
Yale University
New Haven, Connecticut
(American Baptist Churches in the U.S.A.)
1 Peter

C. CLIFTON BLACK
Otto A. Piper Professor of Biblical Theology
Princeton Theological Seminary
Princeton, New Jersey
(The United Methodist Church)
1, 2, & 3 John

M. EUGENE BORING
I. Wylie and Elizabeth M. Briscoe Professor of New Testament, Emeritus
Brite Divinity School
Texas Christian University
Fort Worth, Texas
(Christian Church [Disciples of Christ])
Matthew

Fred B. Craddock
Bandy Distinguished Professor of Preaching and New Testament, Emeritus
Candler School of Theology
Emory University
Atlanta, Georgia
(Christian Church [Disciples of Christ])
Hebrews

R. ALAN CULPEPPER
Dean
McAfee School of Theology
Mercer University
Atlanta, Georgia
(Southern Baptist Convention)
Luke

JAMES D. G. DUNN
Lightfoot Professor of Divinity, Emeritus
Department of Theology
University of Durham
Durham, England
(The Methodist Church [Great Britain])
1 & 2 Timothy; Titus

CAIN HOPE FELDER
Professor of New Testament Language and Literature
The School of Divinity
Howard University
Washington, DC
(The United Methodist Church)
Philemon

RICHARD B. HAYS
George Washington Ivey Professor of New Testament
The Divinity School
Duke University
Durham, North Carolina
(The United Methodist Church)
Galatians

Morna D. Hooker
Lady Margaret's Professor of Divinity, Emerita
The Divinity School
University of Cambridge
Cambridge, England
(The Methodist Church [Great Britain])
Philippians

LUKE T. JOHNSON
Robert W. Woodruff Professor of New Testament and Christian Origins
Candler School of Theology
Emory University
Atlanta, Georgia
(The Roman Catholic Church)
James

ANDREW T. LINCOLN
Portland Chair in New Testament Studies
Department of Humanities
University of Gloucestershire
Cheltenham, United Kingdom
(The Church of England)
Colossians

GAIL R. O'DAY
Associate Dean of Faculty and Academic Affairs and Almar H. Shatford Professor of Preaching and New Testament
Candler School of Theology
Emory University
Atlanta, Georgia
(United Church of Christ)
John

PHEME PERKINS
Professor of New Testament
Boston College
Chestnut Hill, Massachusetts
(The Roman Catholic Church)
Mark; Ephesians

CHRISTOPHER C. ROWLAND
Dean Ireland's Professor of the Exegesis of Holy Scripture
The Queen's College
Oxford, England
(The Church of England)
Revelation

J. PAUL SAMPLEY
Professor of New Testament and Christian Origins
The School of Theology and The Graduate Division
Boston University
Boston, Massachusetts
(The United Methodist Church)
1 & 2 Corinthians

ABRAHAM SMITH
Associate Professor of New Testament
Perkins School of Theology
Southern Methodist University
Dallas, Texas
(The National Baptist Convention, USA, Inc.)
1 & 2 Thessalonians

ROBERT C. TANNEHILL
Academic Dean and Harold B. Williams Professor of Biblical Studies, Emeritus
Methodist Theological School in Ohio
Delaware, Ohio
(The United Methodist Church)
The Gospels and Narrative Literature

CHRISTOPHER M. TUCKETT
Fellow and Tutor in Theology
Pembroke College
University of Oxford
Manchester, England
(The Church of England)
Jesus and the Gospels

ROBERT W. WALL
Chair and Professor of Christian Scriptures
School of Theology
Seattle Pacific University
Seattle, Washington
(Free Methodist Church of North America)
The Acts of the Apostles; Introduction to Epistolary Literature

DUANE F. WATSON
Professor of New Testament Studies
School of Theology
Malone College
Canton, Ohio
(The United Methodist Church)
2 Peter; Jude

N. THOMAS WRIGHT
Bishop of Durham
Bishop Auckland, United Kingdom
(The Church of England)
Romans

Contents

PART ONE: THE FOUR GOSPELS AND ACTS

THE GOSPELS AND NARRATIVE LITERATURE

ROBERT C. TANNEHILL

The Gospels and narrative literature can be studied on several levels, e.g., the level of complete Gospels and the level of the short narrative episodes that they contain. These episodes follow recognizable patterns, and those that follow the same pattern may be classed as examples of the same literary type. This article will first examine types of short narratives in the Gospels and then will discuss the Gospels themselves as extended narratives containing these short narrative forms.

TYPES OF NARRATIVE IN THE GOSPELS

Certain stable patterns of short narrative are found within the Gospels and the surrounding culture. The repetition of these patterns is evidence that they were found to be effective and worthy of imitation. Within first-century Mediterranean culture, the development of literary skill consisted, in part, in the mastery of these narrative patterns. The patterns were seldom used rigidly; they could be adapted to the content of the story, and skillful storytellers could employ these patterns creatively.

Patterns of short narrative may be studied by form critics, who will ask about the function of each type within a community's life; by rhetorical critics, who will ask how each type is able to affect an audience; and by literary critics, who will ask how these short patterns enrich the larger narrative, helping to create a complex communication that deepens our experience of humanness.[1]

Short narrative types include pronouncement stories, parables, wonder stories, and promise and commission epiphanies. Before considering complete Gospels as narratives, one needs to note several longer narrative sequences within the Gospels in which scenes are linked by clear plot developments. These represent narrative at an intermediate level between the short episode and a complete Gospel.

Pronouncement Stories. Within the Gospels are a number of short narratives in which Jesus responds to a person or situation, and this response is the main point of the narrative. These narratives may be called pronouncement stories. Matthew 18:21-22 provides an example:

> Then Peter came and said to him, "Lord, if another member of the church sins against me, how often should I forgive? As many as seven times?" Jesus said to him, "Not seven times, but, I tell you, seventy-seven times."

A pronouncement story is a brief narrative in which the climactic (and often final) element is a pronouncement that is presented as a particular person's response to something said or observed on a past occasion. Pronouncement stories have two main parts: the pronouncement and its setting—i.e., the response and the situation provoking that response.[2] In some cases an expressive action, making a point without speech, or a response combining speech and action may substitute for the pronouncement.

The pronouncement story is closely related to a form widely used in the Greco-Roman world, the *chreia.* An ancient educational textbook, Theon's *Progymnasmata,* defines the *chreia* as "a concise statement or action which is attributed with aptness to some specified character or to something analogous to a character."[3] Although a *chreia* may sometimes simply indicate the person who is the source of the statement or action, it often provides a brief setting, presenting the statement or action as a response in a particular situation. It is then equivalent to a pronouncement story. One of Theon's examples shows how concise a *chreia* can be: "Alexander the Macedonian king, on being asked by someone where he had his treasures, pointed to his friends and said: 'In these.'"[4] Most examples of pronouncement stories in the Gospels are significantly longer, yet retain the same basic structure. Furthermore, Theon required his students in their exercises to take a concise *chreia* and expand it.[5] Thus there is some flexibility in the length and amount of detail among them.

The pronouncement story is generally equivalent to Rudolf Bultmann's *apothegms* and overlaps to some extent Martin Dibelius's *paradigms*.[6] The pronouncement story is very selective in what it presents; it is not to be confused with a full report of a dialogue. Where there are two parties in the scene, they are generally not given equal attention. The scene is rhetorically shaped so that the concluding response makes the chief impression, due to its climactic position, and often due to the forceful language used in the pronouncement. Thus the little scene serves to display the wit and wisdom of a particular person, whose pronouncement or significant action is presented for admiration and often for emulation. When these stories present persons and highlight values that represent the cultural heritage, they maintain cultural continuity. Yet pronouncement stories may also have a sharply critical edge, undermining confidence in accepted values and seeking to replace them.

The pronouncement stories in the Gospels often present two contrasting attitudes to a situation, one in the setting and the other in the response. As the brief scene unfolds, there is a sharp shift from one attitude to the other. The setting, by expressing one attitude, makes it available for challenge. The hearer or reader is invited to make the shift traced in the scene or, at least, to reaffirm a previous decision of this kind. It is easy for persons of a different time and culture to lose a sense of the challenge in many of these pronouncements, since we may not have an investment in or attraction to the position being challenged. Yet the reason for emphasizing the climactic pronouncement and contrasting it with an initial attitude is best understood when we recognize that a significant shift in attitudes and values is being advocated.[7]

The pronouncements featured in these stories seem designed to be provocative and memorable rather than to present reasoned arguments for a position. Nevertheless, a response may include a rationale (a brief supporting reason, attached with "for" or "because"). Furthermore, there are some scenes, especially controversy scenes, in which arguments are developed. Burton Mack has studied an ancient school exercise called the "elaboration" of the *chreia* (a prescribed way of developing arguments in defense of a *chreia*), and he and Vernon Robbins have found traces of similar argumentative patterns within some Gospel pronouncement stories.[8]

Pronouncement stories are numerous in the synoptic Gospels, and they contribute much to the impression of Jesus and his message that we receive there. In spite of their brevity, many of these scenes have a dramatic quality, as Jesus interacts with other parties. The dramatic setting helps to make the climactic saying of Jesus impressive and forceful.

The nature of the dramatic interaction can be clarified by dividing pronouncement stories into subtypes. Below I present a typology of pronouncement stories based on the relation between their two essential parts, the setting and the response. Viewed from this perspective, there seem to be five subtypes of Gospel pronouncement stories.[9]

1. Correction Stories. In the dialogue between Peter and Jesus quoted above, Peter proposes that he might forgive up to seven times and Jesus corrects him by saying, "Not seven times, but . . . seventy-seven times" (Matt 18:21-22). In correction stories, the response corrects the views or conduct of another party. The response may be prompted by something observed, or it may be caused by a statement, request, or question. In the case of requests or questions, the response does not grant the request or answer the question but corrects an assumption on which the request or question was based, turning the encounter in a new direction. By word or action the person encountering Jesus has taken a position, and Jesus responds with a correction. Among the other correction stories in the synoptic Gospels are Matt 8:19-20 par. (the homeless Son of Man); 8:21-22 par. (let the dead bury the dead); Mark 9:33-37 par. (who is greatest?); 9:38-40 par. (the strange exorcist); 10:35-45 par. (request of James and John); 13:1-2 par. (the great temple buildings); Luke 9:61-62 (plowing and looking back); 11:27-28 (blessing of Jesus' mother); 14:7-11 (places at table); 17:20-21 (God's reign among you).

There is always tension in a correction story. This tension does not appear until the corrective response, for the person who encounters Jesus is neither criticizing nor testing him, and the attitude expressed in the setting may seem quite acceptable. The corrective response introduces tension and opens up distance. The response challenges commonly accepted thought and invites change. These stories are useful where crucial decisions are being ignored and where there is a tendency to reduce the vision of Jesus to the ordinary.

Discussion of Gospel pronouncement stories has been strongly influenced by controversy dialogues (called "objection stories" below), in which Jesus responds to critics. The correction stories, however, are equally important, and they are addressed not primarily to critics but to Jesus' followers and other persons attracted to him.

2. Commendation Stories. Commendations are similar to corrections, except that Jesus responds by commending what he has seen or heard. Pure commendation stories are rare in the synoptic Gospels, but in Matthew, Peter's confession has been turned into a commendation story, for the emphasis now falls on Jesus' laudatory response to him (Matt 16:13-20).

As in correction stories, often there is an element of tension in commendation stories. There may be a surprise in the commendation, for Jesus may praise someone or something commonly ignored or despised. The tension with another standard of judgment may be dramatized in the story by introducing a third character (who may be an individual or a group) whose words or actions express a contrasting view. The result is a "hybrid" story in which the response will probably have a double function: to commend one party and correct another, or to commend one party and respond to the objection of another. This feature of the stories expresses tension with other views in the social context. Thus there is an indication that these stories, too, attempt to cause or reinforce a shift of attitude on the part of hearers or readers. An example of a hybrid story is Mark 10:13-16—Jesus' blessing of the children—in which Jesus both corrects the disciples and commends the children by associating the reign of God with them. In this case Jesus' affirmation of the children is expressed both in words and in action. Other examples of hybrid correction-commendation stories are Mark 3:31-35 par. (Jesus' true family); 12:41-44 par. (the poor widow); and 14:3-9 par. (the woman who anoints Jesus). Hybrid objection-commendation stories are found in Matt 21:14-16 (the children's praise) and Luke 10:38-42 (Mary and Martha).

Many Gospel pronouncement stories indirectly praise Jesus, since they present his responses for admiration. Commendation stories show, however, that Jesus is not the only representative of positive values. The neglected and despised people praised by Jesus also represent positive values. Thus these people function as models for the hearer or reader.

3. Objection Stories. In a number of stories, Jesus must answer an objection. These stories frequently have three parts, moving from description of an action to an objection to that action, and then to the response. The first element, however, may appear only in the objection itself. In Mark 2:15-17 the three elements appear in sequence: the meal with tax collectors and sinners is described, the scribes object, and Jesus responds with sayings that first draw an analogy with a physician and then disclose the fundamental principle that guides his ministry.

The objection is often expressed as a demand for justification, using a question beginning with "Why?" In these scenes, which are often called "controversy dialogues," tension is introduced not by Jesus (as in correction stories) but by the party expressing the objection. Here the tension focuses on Jesus, for he is being challenged. (This is true even if the disciples are addressed, for the teacher is responsible for his disciples.) The response may consist of a rhetorical question, an analogy, or a fundamental statement of principle.

Although disciples may sometimes object, as in Mark 8:31-33, many of the objections come from the scribes and Pharisees. The formation and transmission of these stories doubtless reflect the need of the early church to defend the distinctive practices and perspectives of the Jesus movement within its historical context. The apologetic needs of the church are probably reflected in a tendency to expand Jesus' response into a series of arguments. This does not mean that these stories function only to support the early church against outside critics. Followers of Jesus would seldom be as clear and deeply committed to a position as Jesus is in these stories. They continue to be a challenge to Jesus' followers to clarify and deepen their commitment.

Some additional objection stories in the synoptic Gospels are Mark 2:18-22 par. (question about fasting); 2:23-28 par. (plucking grain on the sabbath); 3:20-30 par. (the Beelzebul controversy); 7:1-15 par. (eating with defiled hands); and Luke 2:41-51 (the boy Jesus in the Temple).

There is an overlap of objection stories with wonder stories (discussed below) in the sabbath healing stories. The objection-response sequence is primary when the story ends with Jesus' response to the objection, as in Luke 13:10-17 and 14:1-6. It may still be very important when the scene ends with the healing, as in the story of the man with a withered hand (Mark 3:1-6 par.), where the healing is part of Jesus' response to the implied objection of the opponents.

4. Quest Stories. These stories tend to be longer and more complex than most pronouncement stories and may include features of the other types. Jesus responds to an issue raised in the scene, but now this response is part of a story in which someone is in quest of something important for human well-being. This quest is sufficiently important that we are told its outcome. In other words, the scene does not end simply with Jesus' impressive response, as in many pronouncement stories. There is some resolution, positive or negative, to the other person's quest. As a result, the person coming to Jesus receives more attention in the narrative than in many pronouncement stories. In a sense it is this person's story, for the scene is shaped by his or her desire, expressed at the beginning, and ends when this desire succeeds or fails. Since we are asked to look at events in the light of this person's need and desire, sympathy for him or her is encouraged, although the social standing of the person may hinder this.

An obstacle, sometimes expressed as an objection or a difficult condition, may surface within the scene, and Jesus' response will be crucial at this point. The objections that may occur in quest stories make them similar to the objection stories just discussed, but here the objection functions as an obstacle within a quest. Several of these stories involve healing or exorcism and are similar to other wonder stories. If we simply group them with wonder stories, however, we will ignore their structural similarity with quest stories that lack healing or exorcism. An interesting example of a quest story that includes both an objection and an exorcism is that of the Syrophoenician woman (Mark 7:24-30), who seeks the exorcism of an unclean spirit from her daughter. The exorcism itself is reported very briefly, however. The main emphasis is on the dialogue between the woman and Jesus. The story is unusual in that Jesus himself objects to the woman's quest and even more unusual because the woman is able to change the mind of Jesus, who normally is viewed as the final authority. The woman's daring rejoinder enables the quest to move to a successful conclusion. The prominent role she plays and the way in which the quest shapes the whole story show that this is something more than an objection story. It is a quest story. The social status of the questers is a significant factor in quest stories. The one quester who fails is from high social rank (Mark 10:17-22 par.), while successful questers—like the Syrophoenician woman, the centurion (Matt 8:5-13 par.), the sinful woman in the Pharisee's house (Luke 7:36-50), the Samaritan leper (Luke 17:12-19), Zacchaeus (Luke 19:1-10), and the crucified criminal (Luke 23:39-43)—are aliens and outcasts. Thus these stories reverse social judgments and undermine prejudices; they both invite the outcasts and help to create openness for them in the community.

5. Inquiry Stories. These scenes move from a question or request for instruction to the answer. Questions may also be found in other types of pronouncement stories, but the inquiry story lacks the distinctive characteristics of the other types. The responder does not correct an assumption behind the question, as in a correction story, nor does the question express an objection, as in an objection story. There is a straightforward movement from question to answer, which means that attention tends to focus almost entirely on the content of the answer. Examples are Luke 11:1-4 (the Lord's Prayer); 13:22-30 (enter through the narrow door); and 17:5-6 (increase our faith). There is generally less dramatic tension in these scenes than in other pronouncement stories.

There is dramatic tension, however, in one subgroup, the testing inquiries, for in these scenes Jesus is being tested by a hostile or skeptical party. The tension focuses on Jesus, who is put in a difficult situation. Failure to give an impressive answer would result in loss of influence and might be dangerous in other ways. On the other hand, an impressive answer is all the more impressive in a situation of risk. Matthew 22:34-40 (the greatest commandment); Mark 11:27-33 par. (by what authority?); and 12:13-17 par. (paying taxes to Caesar) are examples of testing inquiries.

Parables. Parables are figurative language. They are imaginative narratives composed in order to illuminate a subject that lies beyond the literal subject matter of the story. Scholars commonly distinguish three subtypes: the similitude, the parable proper, and the example story.[10] We may speak of the first two as metaphorical narratives, for they refer indirectly to a sphere of meaning that is normally distinct from the literal content of the story, suggesting a connection between the two. The similitude (e.g., the mustard seed, Mark 4:30-32) is brief and focuses on an event that happens repeatedly, such as the growth of seed. Even so, it has the basic components of a narrative: events happening to one or more participants in a setting. The parable proper (e.g., the prodigal son, Luke 15:11-32) is a more fully developed story that narrates a unique and sometimes surprising sequence of events. It may have several scenes and tends to have a larger number of characters. The example story (e.g., the rich fool, Luke 12:16-21) is different in that the second level of meaning does not pertain to another sphere (as in metaphor) but to the sphere of meaning of which the story itself is a part. The example story still works as a trope; it suggests much more than its literal meaning. But the trope is not metaphor but synecdoche, in which the story is a part standing for a larger whole that must be imagined.

Metaphors often have bundles of associations and, therefore, are capable of complex development. Just as a poem may draw repeatedly from the image field suggested by a root metaphor, so also a parable may develop the image field of a metaphor through narrative. Thus linking a mustard seed metaphorically to the reign of God may lead to a narrative development from sowing to growth of the seed to the mature bush, all in some way suggestive of God's reign. In a similitude the brief narrative recalls what everyone would expect in the situation. The new element arises from the metaphorical transfer of meaning to a different sphere. In the parable proper the course of the narrative is not predictable at the beginning; indeed, some surprising things happen. Yet these stories make use of stereotypical associations, which bring with them an initial set of expectations and identifications. Thus first-century hearers would expect that a king (Matt 18:23), a father (Luke 15:11), or a landowner (Matt 20:1) might represent God. This sort of identification need not be an allegorical misreading of the parable. Stereotypical associations establish a set of expectations that the parable can use. Hearers, having made the initial identifications, discover that the parable is using traditional associations to produce unexpected results. The parable can set the traditional associations in motion, in part by reinserting them into the human sphere from which they were drawn and using fresh human experience to reimagine how God as father or owner might act.

The parables inhabit a different narrative level from that of other stories being discussed in this article. The narrator is Jesus, a participant in the events of the larger narrative. Thus we are dealing with embedded narrative, an act of narration that occurs within the narrative world being constructed by the Gospel narrator. Techniques of narrative analysis are useful at both levels.

Narrative analysis is especially helpful in interpreting parables that are more complex. It is useful to ask whether the parable builds up to a climax at which a decisive event or crucial decision takes place. Then the prior narrative will prepare for this climax, and anything that follows will clarify its results. If the parable story can be understood according to this or some other pattern, it can be apprehended as a whole, and the function of each part within the whole becomes clear. This approach guards against the tendency to isolate an element of the story in order to derive some special meaning from it. Interpretation must concentrate on the climax of the story, to which the rest of the story contributes, if it is to do justice to the parable as a whole. Thus an interpretation of the parable of the vineyard workers (Matt 20:1-16) as primarily a call to missionary work in God's vineyard would be inadequate because it ignores the climax of the parable, which focuses on the unusual way in which the wages were paid.

The parable of the vineyard workers also exemplifies a common narrative technique: the narration of a series of events in parallel form, with a difference that will prove to be significant. The parallelism makes the difference stand out so that its significance can be considered. In the case of the vineyard workers, we have parallel accounts of hiring workers. Those hired at midday fade out of the story at the time of payment so that the story can concentrate on those showing the greatest difference, the workers hired at the beginning of the day and those hired one hour before the end. The parables avoid unnecessary descriptive detail. This encourages the comparison of persons who are essentially alike except for one characteristic, which is thereby isolated for consideration.

Through construction of such contrasts, the narrator controls the issues that are brought to the hearer's attention. In a story of a man with two sons, we may guess at the beginning that the two sons will differ in some way that will be important to the story. Such is the case in the parable of the prodigal son (Luke 15:11-32), but this parable also presents two contrasting responses to the younger brother's homecoming. Here the contrast is between the father and the older brother, who remain in conflict at the end of the story. The development of two major contrasts adds to the complexity of this parable.

There are other ways in which the narrator guides the hearer's focus of attention. For instance, a moment of crucial decision may be emphasized by reporting a person's deliberation as internal speech (cf. Luke 16:3-4 in the parable of the dishonest steward). Here the progress of the narrative has slowed in order to give detailed attention to this moment. In other cases expansion of direct discourse between two parties may highlight a central issue. In the parable of the talents the expanded dialogue between the third servant and the master is where the main issue is clarified and resolved (cf. Matt 25:24-30).

The parables are attractive and interesting as stories, which serves their goal of persuasion. Some parables explicitly ask for a verdict from the hearer, as in the ones that begin "Which one of you . . . ?" (e.g., the lost sheep, Luke 15:4-7). In other cases Jesus is depicted as rendering a verdict himself (e.g., the parable of the Pharisee and the tax collector; cf. Luke 18:14). Some parables are open-ended because there is an unresolved conflict at the end (e.g., the prodigal son, Luke 15:11-32). Nevertheless, the story makes clear where the narrator's sympathies lie. The parables may be even-handed in allowing conflicting perspectives expression within the story. This does not mean, however, that these views are given equal value. The workers who labor all day in the sun express their objection strongly, but the owner of the vineyard has the last word (Matt 20:11-15).

Although in the Gospel of John parables are not characteristic of Jesus' teaching, as they are in the synoptic Gospels, John does contain some related forms. We find, for instance, the short simile of the grain of wheat that dies but is fruitful (John 12:24). In John 10:1-5, Jesus speaks figuratively of the shepherd, the sheepfold, and sheep. This is called a *paroimia* (παροιμία), a "figure of speech" (10:6). It describes customary activities, like the synoptic similes, yet a greater variety of details appears. The figurative language is then interpreted, and Jesus specifically identifies himself with the gate of the sheepfold and the shepherd (10:7-18). This section of John is rather similar to the parable of the sower (Mark 4:3-8, 14-20) in its movement from figurative language to allegorical interpretation.

Wonder Stories. Although these scenes are usually called miracle stories, the term *miracle* is best avoided because it means to many an act of God that violates the laws of nature. Nature itself was understood differently by those who told the Gospel wonder stories, for it was widely assumed at that time that the physical world was open to the operation of divine and demonic powers. Nevertheless, there was a strong sense, then as now, of the difference between the usual and the wonderful. The indications of amazement at the end of many of these stories attest to that difference. The wonder stories tell of occasions when God's power surprises people whose expectations are limited to normal human experience. In the Gospels the wonder is almost always a gracious act of help from God, although wonders of punishment are also possible (see Mark 11:12-14, 20-21; Acts 5:1-11). Thus the wonder stories attest to the belief that, unusual as it may be, God's grace is available even for bodily needs and dangers.

In the synoptic Gospels these wonders are sometimes called *dynameis* (δυνάμεις), literally "powers"—i.e., manifestations of divine power or "mighty acts" (cf. Matt 11:20-23; Mark 6:2, 5). The Fourth Gospel prefers to speak of Jesus' "signs" (σημεῖα *sēmeia*; see John 2:11; 12:37).

In the early Gospel tradition, Jesus' wonders were an integral part of the outburst of hope for overcoming evil associated with the coming of God's reign. Jesus' healing ministry is summarized in words that recall scriptural prophecies of salvation (Matt 11:5 par.; cf. Isa 35:5-6; 61:1), and the continuation of that ministry through the disciples is associated with the approach of God's reign (Luke 10:9). Jesus' exorcisms, especially, reveal the conquest of evil power through the appearance of God's reign (Matt 12:28-29 par.).

Most Gospel wonder stories can be divided into six types (although some of the stories have affinities with more than one type).[11] Discussion of these six types will help us to recognize common patterns and themes, although the point of emphasis will vary among stories of the same type.

1. Exorcism Stories. In this type of wonder story, Jesus encounters a person possessed by a demon and forces the demon to leave, enabling the person to return to a normal life. The demon is evil, but the possessed person is not, for the demon is an alien force that can be expelled. When the exorcism takes place, the story focuses on the interaction between Jesus and the demon (or unclean spirit). It is the demon who speaks with Jesus; the possessed person is so controlled by the demon as to be incapable of independent thought or action. Jesus addresses the demon directly and powerfully, forcing it to submit and depart.

The exorcism in the Capernaum synagogue (Mark 1:21-28 par.) presents such an encounter in brief form. The exorcism of the Gerasene demoniac (Mark 5:1-20 par.) and of the possessed boy (Mark 9:14-29 par.) are more complex examples of this type. In the former, Jesus' interaction with the demons goes through several steps. There is also considerable interest in depicting the original condition of the possessed man and the change that takes place in him. In the latter story, the father of the boy assumes a major role, especially in the Markan version. The father requests help, and his faith is important; both features draw this story close to healing stories, which will be discussed next. However, the workings of the evil spirit and Jesus' command for it to depart are also vividly depicted. Perhaps we should speak of the story of the possessed boy as a mixed form. It is distinctly different from the story of the Syrophoenician woman (Mark 7:24-30 par.), where, even though the woman's daughter is possessed by an unclean spirit, no attention is given to Jesus' confrontation with the spirit. Therefore, the Syrophoenician woman's story should not be included among the exorcisms.

2. Healing Stories. In this type of wonder story, Jesus responds to the bodily need of another person, and the principal interaction is between Jesus as healer and the person in need (in some cases also the representative of this person, such as a mother or father). Normally the healing story presents an encounter with Jesus, together with indications of the type of illness or disability a person suffers (sometimes with emphasis on its severity), then reports the healing itself. This is often followed by an action demonstrating that the healing has taken place or a response of amazement or praise from witnesses. Frequently the action begins when persons address Jesus with a request for healing, either for themselves (blind Bartimaeus, Mark 10:46-52 par.) or for another (Jairus's daughter, Mark 5:21-24, 35-43 par.). In some episodes, however, Jesus takes the initiative. This is the case in two of the four Johannine healing stories (John 5:2-9; 9:1-7). Also in the raising of the widow's son (Luke 7:11-17) there is no request for Jesus' help; rather, Jesus' action is due to his compassion (7:13). The healing stories are the largest group of wonder stories in the Gospels.

In the story of the hemorrhaging woman (Mark 5:25-34), the cure takes place relatively early in the scene (v. 29). This is a sign that a physical cure is not the sole concern. The story continues for five more verses as Jesus searches for the woman and the woman reveals herself with fear and trembling. How will Jesus respond to an unclean woman who has violated purity laws by touching him? The healing (which responds to her social isolation as well as to her physical need) is not complete unless she is free of social condemnation for violating religious taboos.

Jesus does not condemn her but commends her for her faith (Mark 5:34). Faith is an important theme in the healing stories. Sometimes Jesus asks for faith from those who come for healing (Matt 9:28-29; Mark 5:36 par.; John 4:48-50). Most striking are the cases in which Jesus commends someone's faith. These people become models of the faith that others should show in similar situations. Such people persist in reaching out to Jesus for help when blocked by the crowd or separated by a social barrier (e.g., the hemorrhaging woman;

blind Bartimaeus, who is at first rebuked by the crowd, Mark 10:46-52 par.). The same kinds of people demonstrate faith in quest stories involving healing (e.g., the centurion, Matt 8:5-13 par.; the Canaanite woman, Matt 15:21-28; the Samaritan leper, Luke 17:12-19). These stories, however, differ from healing wonders in that the questing persons raise problems other than their physical afflictions that Jesus must resolve with an authoritative pronouncement. Faith is presented in these healing and quest stories as resolute action that, in spite of society and its taboos, reaches out to Jesus as the source of help. It is the opposite of resigned acceptance of suffering.[12]

Healing stories, as well as other types of wonders, may take on symbolic meaning. This is especially characteristic of the Gospel of John (note that John 9 begins with the healing of a blind man and ends with climactic statements about spiritual sight and blindness), but it is also true of some scenes in the other Gospels. For instance, it is significant that healings of a deaf man and a blind man surround Jesus' harsh words about the disciples' deafness and blindness in Mark (see 7:31-37; 8:18, 22-26).

3. Provision Stories. Some wonder stories can be called provision stories because Jesus provides food or drink for a crowd in a surprising way. In the Gospels we find not only stories of Jesus feeding crowds in the wilderness (Mark 6:34-44 par.; 8:1-10 par.), but also stories of Jesus providing wine for a wedding (John 2:1-11) and great catches of fish (Luke 5:4-7; John 21:1-14). The great catches of fish in Luke and John are elements within commissioning stories focusing on Simon Peter. The provision stories tend to attract symbolic significance. Thus the feeding stories recall the feeding of Israel with manna in the wilderness and suggest the formation of a new people under God's care. When the great catch of fish in Luke 5:4-7 is followed by Jesus' call to share his work of "catching people," the catch of fish becomes a symbolic promise of success in the future mission. The imagery of wedding and abundant wine in John 2:1-11 suggests the new time of fulfillment that is replacing the old order.

There are three provision stories in John (2:1-11; 6:1-15; 21:1-14) but only four healing stories and no exorcisms.

4. Controversy Wonders. Stories of this type are actually a mixed form, for they follow the pattern of pronouncement stories involving controversy (called "objection stories" above) as well as wonder stories. The emphasis may not fall on the wonder. In two sabbath healing stories special to Luke (the bent woman, 13:10-17; the man with dropsy, 14:1-6), Jesus' principal pronouncement follows the healing, taking climactic position. In the case of the bent woman, the cure takes place early in the scene and is the cause of the controversy, a subordinate position. I would classify these two stories as objection stories, not wonder stories. Even in the stories of the paralyzed man (Mark 2:1-12 par.) and the man with the withered hand (Mark 3:1-6 par.), which do end with a healing, Jesus' interaction with his critics is very important, and the point being scored has more to do with Jesus' authority and insight into God's will than with his power to heal. In these two stories the wonder is significant not only for the person healed and as a disclosure of the power of the healer but also because it speaks to the issue of controversy. The healing is itself part of Jesus' answer to his opponents.

Classification of literary types is not an end in itself. It is a means of calling attention to various patterns in stories so that we can understand each story better. When a story does not fit easily into a single category, it is useful to compare it to several types, for this may show that several important developments are taking place at the same time.

The story of the paralyzed man is a case in point. It has features of healing stories, quest stories, and objection stories. The ending is typical of a healing story, but this story is more complex than most healings. The striking action of digging through the roof shows a determination that makes the paralyzed man's party stand out as remarkable people, giving them the importance typical of quest stories, and the controversy over forgiveness functions like the obstacle that appears in other quest stories. But the controversy with the scribes is also like objection stories, and the proclamation that "the Son of Man has authority on earth to forgive sins" (Mark 2:10 NRSV) is clearly a central feature of this scene. Thus this scene is both the story of a successful quest, which involves healing, and a revelation of Jesus' authority within a controversy wonder. The tension of desire in the quest and the tension of challenge in the objection are resolved at the same point, for Jesus' answer to the objection requires both words and healing action (2:9-12). Classification of the story is less important than recognizing both of these developments.

In John 5 and 9 also, Jesus' healings are connected with controversy, but John develops the controversies not within the healing scene but through lengthy dialogue and monologue following it.

5. Rescue Wonders. These relate how someone in danger (especially from a storm at sea or imprisonment) is rescued through altering natural forces or physical objects, such as the wind, chains, or prison doors (see Acts 12:1-11). Probably the stilling of the storm in Mark 4:35-41 par. belongs in this category, although Jesus addresses the sea as if he were exorcising a demon, and the concluding question ("Who then is this?") suggests that the scene is also an epiphany. Rescue wonders encourage the belief that God's power can intervene in situations of danger.

6. Epiphany Wonders. These are stories in which the wonder primarily demonstrates Jesus' divine power and authority. This can be an aspect of the other wonder stories, but I will reserve this term for stories in which epiphany is the primary concern, for exorcism, healing, provision, controversy, and rescue are absent or secondary. The transfiguration story is a clear example (Mark 9:2-8 par.). We should probably also include Jesus' walking on the water, for the rescue of the disciples from the wind is secondary to the revelation concerning Jesus, at least in Mark 6:45-52 and John 6:16-21.

We should not assume that each type of wonder story has a single function. Even brief stories are often more complex than that, and their functions may shift with social setting. Perhaps we may say, however, that the wonder stories were told to elicit the praise of God and wonder at Jesus' power, often depicted at their end. Through presenting Jesus as the mediator of God's saving power, these stories could both call new people to trust Jesus as healer and rescuer and reinforce such faith within the church. In particular, these stories encourage belief that God's saving power extends to those who are suffering physically and those who are socially excluded because of demonic possession and uncleanness. These stories call people out of resigned acceptance of their physical and social limits by providing examples of liberation from evil powers and models of daring faith—a faith that goes beyond expected behavior in order to reach out to the power that saves.

Promise and Commission Epiphanies. In addition to the wonder stories of Jesus' earthly ministry, there are stories that report the surprising appearance of God or a messenger of God (in the Gospels, an angel or the risen Christ) who brings a message containing a promise or a commission (or both). The promise and commission will refer to events beyond the scene itself. The best examples in the Gospels are the annunciation scenes in the birth narratives and some of the resurrection appearances.

Benjamin Hubbard has called attention to a series of "commissioning stories" in the Hebrew Bible and the New Testament.[13] In discussing some of the same stories, I have chosen a longer title in order (a) to limit consideration to stories that report an epiphany and (b) to call attention to the fact that the message may contain a promise as well as authorization and instruction to do something (a commission). Thus in the Lord's appearance to Isaac in Gen 26:23-25 (a brief example of the form) the message consists entirely of reassurance and promise. The message for the future concerns what God will do rather than commanding Isaac to do something. In some cases the message announces the future birth of a child. Raymond Brown has called attention to the precedents in the Hebrew Bible for the Gospel annunciations of birth.[14] These scenes are a subtype of the promise and commission epiphanies.

Hubbard has analyzed the commissioning stories into seven components: the *introduction*, which sets the scene; the *confrontation* (God or God's messenger appears); the *reaction*, in which the person addressed responds, often expressing fear or unworthiness; the *commission* (the core of the message, which, as I explained above, may emphasize the divine promise as much as or more than the human task); the *protest* (the person addressed may claim that the promise or commission is impossible); the *reassurance*, which may occur after the reaction of fear, the commission, or the protest; and the *conclusion*, which rounds off the scene.[15] Not all components are found in every example. The appearance of God's messenger and the message delivered are the essential elements.

The annunciations of birth in Luke 1:5-38 are examples of the full form. Following the introductions, we are told of the confrontation with the angel (vv. 11, 28), Zechariah's and Mary's disturbed reactions (vv. 12, 29), the angel's reassurance ("Do not be afraid," vv. 13, 30), the promise and commissioning (vv. 13-17, 31-33), and the protest (vv. 18, 34), followed by reassurance (or reinforcement) through additional signs of divine power (vv. 19-20, 35-37). The annunciation in Matt 1:18-25 lacks a reaction and protest from Joseph, but the situation and content of the message closely resemble other examples of the birth announcement subtype.[16]

Many of the Gospel resurrection scenes follow a similar format. In Mark's depiction of the empty tomb (16:1-8), the story moves from introduction (vv. 1-4) to confrontation with the messenger (v. 5); reaction ("They were alarmed," v. 5); reassurance ("Do not be alarmed," v. 6); message, including commission and promise (vv. 6-7); and conclusion (v. 8). Matthew's version of this scene is followed by an encounter with Jesus in which the sequence of confrontation, reaction, reassurance, commission, and promise is quickly repeated (Matt 28:9-10). The final scene in Matthew (28:16-20) concentrates on Jesus' speech, but the following elements are still clear: introduction, confrontation ("When they saw him," v. 17), reaction (v. 17), reassurance (v. 18),[17] commission, and promise (vv. 19-20).

Not only Matthew but also Luke and John contain appearances of the risen Jesus to groups of disciples, and these scenes follow the same basic pattern. In Luke 24:33-49 the reassurance following the disciples' fear is greatly expanded, so that we have these divisions: confrontation (v. 36), reaction of fear (v. 37), reassurance (vv. 38-43), commission, and promise (vv. 46-49). In John 20:19-23 the confrontation is described at the end of v. 19. The repeated "Peace be with you" probably functions as reassurance, not just greeting, and Jesus' showing of his hands and side has a similar function. The reaction of the disciples is joyous, not fearful, in this scene. The scene ends with the commission (vv. 21*b*-23).[18]

These stories present the holy God and the risen Christ as the source of the promise and mission that guide the church. They also seek to suggest the awesomeness of human encounters with this transcendent source. Borrowing the Hebrew Bible's pattern of epiphany scenes serves to support this sense of awe. The focus of the scenes is on the message of promise and commission that is delivered.

Longer Narrative Sequences. Despite the episodic quality of much of the Gospel material, there are portions of the Gospels in which we find clear plot developments through a series of interrelated scenes. These narratives are significantly longer than the small units we have discussed to this point and represent an intermediate level between the short episode and a complete Gospel narrative. As examples I will briefly discuss the Markan passion narrative, the Lukan birth narrative, and the Samaritan narrative in John.

Although some parts of Mark 14–15 might be told as separate stories, the significance of each scene is enhanced by its place within the larger narrative, and there are a number of indications of careful literary construction binding the sections of these chapters together.

There are at least two complementary approaches to the literary study of the Markan passion narrative (Mark 14–15). First, one may seek to understand this story as a representative of a story genre with a relatively fixed plot and set of characters. Thus one can discuss the Markan passion narrative as a variation on Jewish stories of the persecuted righteous one or of the wise person who is the object of a conspiracy but is vindicated.[19] This approach may help us to sense some of the echoes of familiar stories of the endangered Joseph, Esther, Daniel, etc., that first-century readers might have heard in the passion account and also help us to understand some of the significant points of difference from the common pattern. Second, one may study the literary composition of the Markan narrative itself, seeking to understand its plot lines, characterization, and rhetoric. I will briefly discuss the Markan passion narrative from the second perspective.

The Gospel of Mark, like other narratives, can be studied in the light of its overall plot. Such study would show that the passion narrative is the climax of Mark because each of three important plot lines is brought to a dramatic point of decision, as three continuing participants interact with one another.[20] I am referring to the plot lines centering on (1) Jesus, who has received a commission from God and must fulfill that commission; (2) the disciples, who have received a commission from Jesus and should fulfill that commission; and (3) Jesus' opponents, who want to destroy him. From one perspective, the passion story is a narrative of how Jesus' opponents succeed in carrying out their desire to shame and kill him. From another perspective, it is a narrative of Jesus' fulfilling his commission from God, which since 8:31 is known to include rejection and death. From a third perspective, it is a narrative of the disciples who have been called to follow Jesus, taking up their own crosses and losing their lives (8:34-35), but who instead desert Jesus in order to save their lives. Each of these plot lines is prepared in Mark 1–13, and each is carefully developed in the passion story, resulting in significant characterization of all three parties.

The narrative's rhetorical shape begins to appear when we note the techniques used to highlight certain events so that they will make a strong impression on readers. Jesus predicts his betrayal by Judas (Mark 14:18-21), the flight of the disciples (14:27), and Peter's denial (14:30), thus calling readers' attention to these events before they happen. This is part of a strong emphasis on the disciples' failure in the passion story. The narrative also reinforces Jesus' experience of rejection by repeated mocking scenes (14:65; 15:16-20, 29-32), placed after each of the main events following Jesus' arrest (the Sanhedrin trial, the Pilate trial, and the crucifixion). These mocking scenes are also important because they contain ironic testimony to Jesus' true status. The narrative also contrasts Jesus' bold confession, which leads to his death, and Peter's denial by inserting Jesus' interrogation by the Sanhedrin into the story of Peter's denial (14:53-72).

Furthermore, dramatic moments are used for significant disclosures about Jesus. The Sanhedrin trial builds to a climax with the high priest's direct question about Jesus as Messiah. In this setting of official interrogation, Jesus publicly reveals the messianic secret, even though it costs him his life (Mark 14:61-62). At an equally dramatic moment, Jesus, approaching death, cries out, "My God, why have you forsaken me?" (15:34). This cry epitomizes the meaning of the passion events for Jesus. He has been rejected by the leaders of Israel and deserted by his own disciples. Rejection by humans raises sharply the question of divine abandonment, since with his death Jesus' mission comes to nothing. This cry, of course, also seeks an answer from God, which comes not as rescue from death but as resurrection. The Lukan birth narrative (Luke 1:5–2:40) also shows signs of careful literary construction. We find, for instance, balanced scenes and motifs used in connection with John the Baptist, on the one hand, and Jesus, on the other (note especially the parallels between the two annunciation scenes in 1:5-25 and 26-38). The angelic announcements in these scenes share connecting themes with the prophetic hymns that follow (1:46-55, 68-79; 2:29-32; see also 2:10-14). These announcements and hymns gradually disclose the Lukan understanding of the purpose of God to be realized through John and Jesus, providing a basis for interpreting the rest of the Gospel narrative. Full understanding comes only through considering these revelatory scenes together. They come to a climax with the presentation of Jesus in the Temple, where Simeon's oracle (2:29-32) announces God's salvation in its full scope (encompassing both Israel and the Gentiles), and where his warning to Mary (2:34-35) provides the first indication of the resistance that Jesus must face.

The Lukan birth narrative, especially through the angelic announcements and prophetic hymns, interprets the future work of John and Jesus in the context of the divine purpose, providing a preview of the later narrative and a basis for understanding its importance. Other peoples will share in the salvation, but the birth narrative emphasizes the fulfillment of promises of salvation for Israel. Because of this emphasis, the rest of the narrative is not a simple story of success, for the expectations aroused at the beginning are not fully realized. Much of Israel, in fact, rejects salvation through Jesus, creating tension between the hopes and expectations aroused at the beginning and the actual course of the narrative. This twist in the plot carries a tragic effect.[21]

The Samaritan narrative in John 4:1-42 is a unified dramatic dialogue in which persons other than Jesus have important roles and in which each section contributes to a significant development, leading to a conclusion. Thus it is useful to analyze the statements of participants as actions within a plot and as disclosures of character. Setting is also important, for the location in Samaria is appropriate to the dialogue, and Jacob's well provides the initial topic (water) for the conversation.

To be sure, this narrative, like other sections of John, contains some shifts that, at first, are puzzling. Part of the time Jesus is talking with the Samaritan woman; part of the time with his disciples. The conversation begins with the subject of water (4:7-15), then shifts to the woman's husbands (4:16-18), to worship (4:20-24), to food (4:31-34), and to the harvest (4:35-38). Yet each part contributes to the forward movement of the narrative. To some extent the woman and the disciples balance each other as Jesus' conversation partners. While one occupies the foreground, the other is in the background. Nevertheless, we are made aware of the absent party's activity. The woman struggles to understand the water that Jesus offers; the disciples struggle to understand the food that Jesus is eating. All are led through a revelatory process that begins with ironic misunderstanding. The woman comes to recognize who Jesus is, and Jesus teaches the disciples about his mission and their place within it. This teaching includes helping the disciples to understand and accept Jesus' mission among the Samaritans, for the brief discourse about the harvest (4:35-38) is a commentary on Jesus' encounter with the Samaritan woman and the people of her town.

On the one hand, the narrative portrays a revelatory process in which Jesus carries out the mission to which he refers in 4:34 and discloses to the disciples their role in it. On the other hand, the narrative portrays the Samaritan's coming to faith, with each stage of dialogue and movement making its contribution. The Samaritan woman not only comes to faith (her progress indicated by her reactions to Jesus) but also becomes Jesus' witness, the founding missionary for her community. Through the indirect language of symbolism and irony, and through the text's narrative form, we are invited to participate in a "revelatory dynamic." It is the text as narrative that presents revelation as dynamic process. Thus the narrative form of the text is not an accidental feature that can be ignored.[22]

Even when the Samaritans come to Jesus, the narrative of this process is not quite ended. The narrative quickly draws a distinction between secondhand faith, based on the woman's testimony, and firsthand faith, based on encounter with Jesus himself. Then the narrative sequence closes with a confession of faith suitable to the missionary breakthrough that it presents.

THE GOSPELS AS NARRATIVES

Form criticism is accustomed to study a small unit of tradition apart from its Gospel context, and the liturgical reading of the Gospels also conditions us to focus on isolated units within the Gospels. Yet these small narrative units are found within a larger narrative frame, consisting of the Gospel itself. Compared to modern narrative, the synoptic Gospels seem very episodic, consisting, in part, of short scenes placed in a sequence with few connecting threads of plot. Nevertheless, attentive reading of a Gospel as a unitary narrative can help us to understand the functions of the parts within the whole.

In studying the Gospels as wholes, it is also appropriate to ask whether they belong to a larger literary genre. Much of the material within the Gospels conforms to generic types. Is this true also of the Gospels themselves? Until recently it was the conviction of many scholars that the Gospels are a unique kind of literature. In part this was due to the belief that they, as "popular" writings, could not be compared with contemporary Greco-Roman literature. This belief has been waning, and now a number of scholars argue that the Gospels belong within the genre of ancient biography.[23]

The Gospels share with ancient biography some general similarities of content, form, and function. In content, they focus on the life of one person, especially that person's public career. In form, they fit, to various degrees, the pattern of ancient biographies that frame a person's public career with narratives of origin and youth, at the beginning, and death, at the end. In between, biographical presentation could be chronological, but not necessarily so. The subject's words and deeds were used to illustrate character, and various short genres, such as the pronouncement story, were incorporated into the biography for this purpose. In function, many ancient biographies were concerned with praising their subject as an exemplar of the virtues to be honored and emulated in the community. The Gospels have a similar function for the Christian community, while serving other functions as well.

The genre of the Gospels continues to be a subject of debate. Adela Yarbro Collins, for instance, denies that Mark is a biography. Although it may be concerned with the identity of Jesus and presents him as a model, these are not its main purposes. Basically, it records events that changed the world—eschatological events. Thus she classifies it as apocalyptic history.[24]

Luke, too, might be regarded as history, for it is part of a two-volume work that includes Acts. This could make some difference in our understanding of Luke, for biography presents a person's deeds and words as illustrations of character, while history is interested in a person's achievements in so far as they had consequences for society. Yet "during the late Hellenistic period history and biography moved closer together with the increasing emphasis on character in historiography. Biography and history became more and more difficult to distinguish."[25] The fact that one genre can be embedded in another might also suggest that Luke can be regarded as a biography even if Acts, and Luke–Acts as a whole, is placed in another category.

Narrative criticism of the Gospels frequently distinguishes between a Gospel as story (the basic events and characters that provide the content of a narrative) and as discourse (the particular perspective from which this story is told and the rhetorical means of expressing that perspective). As Seymour Chatman writes, "The story is the *what* in a narrative . . . discourse the *how*."[26] This distinction calls attention to a narrative's discourse. We are encouraged to recognize that a narrative is always being told from some perspective and that particular techniques are being used to shape it to that perspective. In other words, the distinction encourages us to consider a narrative's rhetoric.

Studying how a story is told calls attention to the voice telling the story, the voice of the narrator. The Gospel narrators seldom speak in the first person, choosing to efface themselves in order to focus attention on their story. Yet the narrator of a Gospel is the voice through which a particular set of interests, norms, and values is presented.

The interpretive role of the narrator is most obvious when the narrator provides explanations in narrative "asides" and gives "inside views" of the characters. The narrator assumes the privilege of interpreting the inner working of human hearts and making judgments about them, as when the narrator of Mark, following the disciples' encounter with Jesus walking on the sea, states that the disciples' "hearts were hardened" (6:52). An interpretive perspective shapes the narrative in many other ways. Someone has decided which character is most important, deserving to be put in the center of the narrative. Furthermore, certain characters are presented as trustworthy and insightful. They are "reliable characters" in the sense that they become spokespersons for the perspective that is being expressed by the writing as a whole. In the Gospels, of course, Jesus is not only given central importance but also functions as the most reliable character. The underlying perspective of the narrative need not be fully and directly expressed by the narrator because it can be conveyed through Jesus' words and actions. Jesus can provide commentary on the narrative, including norms for judging persons and events, through his parables, for instance.[27]

The small narrative units discussed above are placed in a sequence in the Gospels. As a result, one scene influences our understanding of another. One factor in this process is the "primacy effect," which suggests that material placed early in the narrative takes on special importance.[28] We need to orient ourselves at the beginning of a narrative. The perspective established there will continue to influence our understanding of characters until we are told something that indicates a change in them or requires us to change our opinion of them. This observation should help us to recognize the importance of the promise and commission epiphanies (annunciation scenes) in the birth narratives of Matthew and Luke. They serve to connect Jesus to the purpose of God, provide initial statements of that purpose, and disclose the commission from God that Jesus must fulfill. The narrative that follows is to be interpreted in the light of these initial disclosures. We are guided in interpreting Jesus' ministry not only by the birth narratives in Matthew and Luke but also by such key scenes as Jesus' announcement in the Nazareth synagogue (Luke 4:16-19). We should expect complications to develop, for the beginning of a narrative will not disclose everything. In the Gospels, Jesus encounters hardened hearts and deaf ears, not only in other religious leaders but also in his own disciples. Such conflict adds suspense to the narrative and raises the question of how Jesus' commission can still be fulfilled. The conflict leads to a crisis in the passion story. In this and other ways individual units of tradition become part of a developing plot that moves through conflict to a crisis and its results.

Thus the order of events in a Gospel is important. A Gospel's narrative rhetoric, however, also appears in variations of frequency and duration.[29] Repetition (an increase in frequency) and extended duration (a slowing of narration to give greater attention to a scene) indicate emphasis. When an event is emphasized in these ways, we must seek to understand how it is being understood and why it is important. Some types of repetition provide stability to the story by contributing, for instance, to characterization. If a person does something once, we may take note but reserve conclusions about the person. If the person does it twice or more, we conclude that it is characteristic of this person. Thus we are told twice that the disciples have failed to understand about the loaves (Mark 6:52; 8:17-21) in boat scenes following the two feedings of multitudes. This repetition suggests that the problem is not minor and temporary but arises from the basic character of the disciples.

The narrator may repeat the same type of event, as in the example above, or may repeatedly refer to a single event. We may be told about an event in advance (a preview), told about it as it happens, and then be reminded of it later (a review). In Luke, Jesus begins to announce his coming rejection and death in 9:22. The repeated previews lead up to the passion story itself. Then the messengers at the tomb and the risen Jesus remind his followers of his words and their fulfillment because they have not been properly understood (24:6-7, 25-27, 44-46). The emphasis on this theme through repetition not only indicates its importance but also prods the reader to consider why Jesus' death was "necessary" (24:26) and how it fulfills Scripture (24:27, 44-46).

Although they have not been discussed in this article, it should be noted that the sayings of Jesus—and the extensive discourses that may be composed of these sayings—are part of the narrative. To speak is a narrative action, and what Jesus says may be studied for what it reveals about him, for the norms that it establishes in judging the behavior of others, and for its intended and actual effect on later events in the narrative.

Studying the Gospels as narratives (a literary approach) does not conflict with an interest in their historical and social settings. A narrative not only creates a narrative world, but it also depends on and comments on a preexisting social world. Our understanding of how a text functioned within a past social context can make an important difference in our view of that text's significance.

Scholars attempt to reconstruct the social contexts of the Gospel tradition, thereby providing additional contexts for the sayings and stories beyond the literary context of a Gospel. As a result, important issues may emerge. If, as Burton Mack has argued, some of the pronouncement stories arose from the disappointing experience of a group of Jesus' followers who had sought to bring synagogues to faith in Jesus, an early function of these stories may have been to justify the Christian side of a bitter conflict, reinforcing a negative stereotype of scribes and Pharisees in the process.[30] We should note the hypothetical character of such historical reconstructions and the fact that the Gospel traditions passed through several stages of use, during which their functions may have changed. Even at a particular time and place, a tradition may have had multiple functions. Nevertheless, such historical reconstructions are valuable, not because they specify, once for all, the significance the material must have, but because they suggest ways in which the material might have been employed and help us consider whether it should be used in the same way today.

Telling the stories of Jesus did and will have a function within a social context, producing results that are good or evil. Retelling and interpreting these stories is an act for which we must take ethical and religious responsibility, with as much awareness of the consequences as possible. The Gospels reveal their original social contexts only in a general way. Through intense labor and some guesswork, scholars attempt to be more specific, with results that force us to think in new ways. Nevertheless, the fact that the Gospels themselves do not specify these social settings may, if we choose, be viewed as a gift. Thereby the Gospels free themselves, and the stories they contain, to function in various ways in different historical and social contexts. This is not to say that any narrative unit will fit any situation; rather, many texts have more possibilities of social significance than is commonly recognized. Furthermore, it is right to remember that in reading the Gospel narratives we are reading about another time and place. While we may affirm the continuing relevance of these words, a story about the past does not decide for us how it is relevant to the present.

That involves ethical and religious decisions for which we must take responsibility.

FOR FURTHER READING

Bultmann, Rudolf. *The History of the Synoptic Tradition.* Rev. ed. New York: Harper & Row, 1976.

Moyise, Steven. *The Old Testament in the New Testament: Essays in Honor of J. L. North.* JSNTSup 189. Sheffield: Sheffield Academic Press, 2000.

Powery, Emerson B. *Jesus Reads Scripture: The Function of Jesus' Use of Scripture in the Synoptic Gospels.* Biblical Interpretation Series 63. Boston: Brill, 2003.

Rhoads, David M., and Kari Syreeni. *Characterization in the Gospels: Reconceiving Narrative Criticism.* JSNTSup 184. Sheffield: Sheffield Academic Press, 1999.

Rhoads, David, and Donald Michie. *Mark as Story: An Introduction to the Narrative of a Gospel.* Philadelphia: Fortress, 1982.

Robbins, Vernon K., comp. and ed. *Ancient Quotes and Anecdotes.* Sonoma: Polebridge, 1989.

Scott, Bernard Brandon. *Hear Then the Parable: A Commentary on the Parables of Jesus.* Minneapolis: Fortress, 1989.

Theissen, Gerd. *The Miracle Stories of the Early Christian Tradition.* Philadelphia: Fortress, 1983.

ENDNOTES

1. See Carl R. Holladay, "Contemporary Methods of Reading the Bible" in *NIB* (Nashville: Abingdon, 1994–1998) 1:125-49.

2. See Robert C. Tannehill, "Introduction: The Pronouncement Story and Its Types," *Semeia* 20 (1981) 1.

3. See Ronald F. Hock and Edward N. O'Neil, *The Chreia in Ancient Rhetoric, vol. 1 The Progymnasmata* (Atlanta: Scholars Press, 1986) 83.

4. Hock and O'Neil, *The Chreia in Ancient Rhetoric,* 91-93.

5. Hock and O'Neil, *The Chreia in Ancient Rhetoric,* 101-3.

6. See Rudolf Bultmann, *The History of the Synoptic Tradition,* rev. ed. (New York: Harper & Row, 1976) 11-69, and Martin Dibelius, *From Tradition to Gospel* (New York: Charles Scribner's Sons, 1934) 37-69.

7. See Robert C. Tannehill, "Attitudinal Shift in Synoptic Pronouncement Stories," in *Orientation by Disorientation,* ed. Richard A. Spencer (Pittsburgh: Pickwick, 1980) 183-97.

8. See Burton L. Mack and Vernon K. Robbins, *Patterns of Persuasion in the Gospels* (Sonoma: Polebridge, 1989).

9. For further discussion and examples, see Robert C. Tannehill, "Introduction: The Pronouncement Story and Its Types" and "Varieties of Synoptic Pronouncement Stories," *Semeia* 20 (1981) 1-13, 101-19; idem, "Types and Functions of Apophthegms in the Synoptic Gospels," in *Aufstieg und Niedergang der Römischen Welt,* eds. Hildegard Temporini and Wolfgang Haase, vol. II.25.2 (Berlin: Walter de Gruyter, 1984) 1792-1829.

10. In the Gospels the term for "parable" (παραβολή *parabolē*) is used more broadly, being applied even to short aphorisms. My discussion is confined to narratives.

11. This typology is my adaptation of Gerd Theissen, *The Miracle Stories of the Early Christian Tradition* (Philadelphia: Fortress, 1983) 85-112.

12. A point emphasized by Antoinette Clark Wire, "The Structure of the Gospel Miracle Stories and Their Tellers," *Semeia* 11 (1978) 106-8.

13. Benjamin J. Hubbard, *The Matthean Redaction of a Primitive Apostolic Commissioning: An Exegesis of Matthew 28:16-20* (Missoula: Scholar's Press, 1974); idem, "Commissioning Stories in Luke–Acts: A Study of their Antecedents, Form and Content," *Semeia* 8 (1977) 103-26.

14. Raymond E. Brown, *The Birth of the Messiah* (Garden City, N.Y.: Doubleday, 1979) 156-59.

15. Benjamin J. Hubbard, "Commissioning Stories in Luke–Acts," 104-5.

16. See Brown, *The Birth of the Messiah,* 156.

17. Also in Luke 1:19 the speaker emphasizes his authority in order to reassure someone who is doubtful.

18. Jerome H. Neyrey understands John 20:24-29 as the protest and reassurance that commonly follow a commission. These are presented, however, as a separate scene. See Neyrey, *The Resurrection Stories* (Wilmington: Michael Glazier, 1988), 27, 76-78.

19. See George W. E. Nickelsburg, "The Genre and Function of the Markan Passion Narrative," *HTR*

73 (1980) 153-84, for comparisons of Mark's passion narrative to Jewish literature; see also Burton L. Mack, *A Myth of Innocence: Mark and Christian Origins* (Philadelphia: Fortress, 1988) 249-69.

20. See Robert C. Tannehill, "The Gospel of Mark as Narrative Christology," *Semeia* 16 (1979) 60-62, 76-77.

21. See Robert C. Tannehill, *The Narrative Unity of Luke–Acts: A Literary Interpretation*, vol. 1, *The Gospel According to Luke* (Philadelphia: Fortress, 1986) 15-44; and "Israel in Luke–Acts: A Tragic Story," *JBL* 104 (1985) 69-85.

22. See Gail R. O'Day, *Revelation in the Fourth Gospel: Narrative Mode and Theological Claim* (Philadelphia: Fortress, 1986) 89-96; see also 49-89.

23. See, e.g., David E. Aune, *The New Testament in Its Literary Environment* (Philadelphia: Westminster, 1987) 17-67. The following paragraph is also based on Aune's work.

24. Adela Yarbro Collins, *The Beginning of the Gospel: Probings of Mark in Context* (Minneapolis: Fortress, 1992) 1-38.

25. David E. Aune, *The New Testament in Its Literary Environment*, 30.

26. Seymour Chatman, *Story and Discourse: Narrative Structure in Fiction and Film* (Ithaca, N.Y.: Cornell University Press, 1978) 19.

27. See Mary Ann Tolbert, *Sowing the Gospel: Mark's World in Literary-Historical Perspective* (Minneapolis: Fortress, 1989) 148-59, 233-39. Mary Ann Tolbert has studied the implications of the parable of the sower (Mark 4:3-9, 14-20) and the parable of the wicked tenants (Mark 12:1-12) when understood as commentary on Mark's narrative as a whole.

28. On the primacy effect, see Menakhem Perry, "Literary Dynamics: How the Order of a Text Creates Its Meanings," *Poetics Today* 1 (1979) 53-58.

29. Gérard Genette discusses narrative time in terms of order, duration, and frequency. See his *Narrative Discourse: An Essay in Method* (Ithaca, N.Y.: Cornell University Press, 1980) 33-160.

30. Burton L. Mack, *A Myth of Innocence: Mark and Christian Origins*, 192-207.

JESUS AND THE GOSPELS

CHRISTOPHER M. TUCKETT

THE NATURE OF THE GOSPELS

The four books in the New Testament that now bear the title *Gospel* are clearly similar at one level. They all purport to give an account of events in the life of Jesus of Nazareth; further, they all give a detailed narrative of the course of events leading to his death by crucifixion, and they all conclude with some account of Jesus' tomb being found empty and/or Jesus appearing again alive after his death to some of his followers. As such, then, our Gospels are clearly different from, say, the book of Acts, which gives an account of the life of the later Christian community, and from the letters of the New Testament, which act as communications between individuals and various groups in the first-century Christian communities. By contrast, our Gospels appear to be, at least on the surface, "lives of Jesus"; hence, it has been assumed by many that they provide our primary source of information about the life of Jesus; indeed, they can and should be used in a relatively straightforward way to provide such information.

Such claims, however, need to be treated with some care. Few would doubt that our Gospels provide us with our primary sources of information about Jesus. On the other hand, we should not ignore contributions that other sources, both inside and outside the New Testament, may make in giving us knowledge about Jesus. Further, and perhaps more important, we must be aware that our Gospels do not provide us with information about Jesus in a straightforward way. Moreover, we should not forget that using the Gospels to provide information about Jesus is not the only way in which they may be read with profit today. The purpose of this article is to bring out some aspects of the many ways in which scholars today seek to come to grips with the phenomenon of "Jesus and the Gospels."

On almost any showing, our Gospels are highly unusual literary documents. We regularly label them as "Gospels," though even that name is strange in many ways; and the process that led to their having this name is by no means clear. Some have sought to establish that these writings were first called "Gospels" very early; however, "very early" in this context cannot be much before the end of the first century or the early part of the second century. It is unlikely that the evangelists themselves regarded their own literary works as "Gospels." Rather, in the first century, "gospel" was something proclaimed, heard, and believed (cf. Mark 1:14; 1 Cor 15:3); it was not something written or read. It was, moreover, unique; there was one and only one gospel (cf. Gal 1:6), which, for someone like Paul, was supremely concerned with the significance of the death and resurrection of Jesus but, as far as we can tell from Paul's few references, had little to do with the life and teaching of Jesus prior to his crucifixion. The use of the word *gospel* as the general term of a literary text describing the life of Jesus thus represents a very large semantic shift.

Further, it is clear now that our Gospels were not the only texts in early Christianity claiming to be "gospels." We now know of several texts that call themselves "gospels." Some of these texts are available to us, especially since the discovery of the Nag Hammadi library.[1] These include the *Gospel of Thomas*, the *Gospel of Philip*, the *Gospel of Truth*, and others. We know of the existence of other texts because they are quoted by early Christian writers, even though we do not ourselves have the full texts. For example, Jerome cites a passage from the *Gospel of the Hebrews*, giving an account of an appearance of the risen Jesus to James; yet we possess no copy of this gospel. One suspects that other texts were in existence about which we now know nothing. Eventually, of course, the church excluded these other gospels from its canon of Scripture and included only the four Gospels of Matthew, Mark, Luke, and John. We need not go into the details of canonization here, but the question of how far these non-canonical texts are important for giving us information about Jesus will be considered later. We should, however, note that many of these non-canonical gospels are rather different from our four canonical ones. The *Gospel of Thomas* is a string of over a hundred sayings of Jesus with virtually no narrative at all and certainly no account of Jesus' death or resurrection appearances. The *Gospel of Truth* is an extended meditation on aspects of God and the world with scarcely any mention of Jesus explicitly (though with a number of possible allusions to traditions of Jesus' sayings). Thus the assumption that a literary text called a "gospel" is a document giving a connected narrative of the life and death of Jesus is not justified by these other so-called gospels. Nevertheless, such an assumption does apply to the canonical Gospels, and these will be our primary focus.

Genre. If one does restrict attention to the canonical Gospels, then the question arises, What *kind* of documents are they? To what literary category, or "genre" (to use the technical term), do they belong?

The problem of classifying the genre of the Gospels has been much debated in critical scholarship over the years. In one way it is easier to say what the Gospels are not: They are not letters; they are not plays; they are not (probably) apocalypses. In fact, the Gospels are in many ways *un*like almost anything else in ancient literature. Thus for many years, the Gospels were said to be *sui generis*—i.e., of a genre peculiar to themselves—indeed, many today would still argue that this is the case.

As others have pointed out, however, such a claim is extremely odd in literary terms. Some understanding of the genre of a text is essential if the text is to be understood at all. We have to know that a text is a poem or a play or a detective story or an obituary if we are to be in any position to understand it. Indeed, a writer could scarcely write a text without some prior notion of the kind of writing he or she was attempting to produce. Hence the idea that a text is *sui generis* is, in literary terms, an extremely odd claim.

Therefore, in recent years there has been a number of attempts to place the Gospels within the context of other literary products of the ancient world, above all within the category of a "biography." It is recognized that the Gospels are not biographies in any modern sense of the word. Above all, there is nothing in them about Jesus' childhood and origins (at least in what is probably the earliest Gospel—namely, Mark; see below), nor about Jesus' psychological development (see below on form criticism and Jesus). Nevertheless, it is now becoming clear that such features did not always characterize ancient biography, which is now seen as a very broad literary category, so that it is possible that the NT Gospels could be placed within the wide parameters that accommodate ancient biographies. Such a procedure would resolve the problems, from a literary point of view, of asserting that the Gospels are *sui generis*. But the very breadth of the category of biography in turn means that simply calling a Gospel a "biography" does not necessarily help very much in interpreting the text.

The Gospels as Christian Texts. The unusual nature of the gospels—and their fascination—arises in part from the fact of their being written by people who were not neutral about the person they were describing and whose life they were purportedly reporting. The gospel writers were all "supporters" of Jesus; they were all Christians. Indeed, we have very little literature anywhere near contemporary with Jesus from someone who was either neutral or hostile to Jesus.

Further, the gospel writers shared the belief, held throughout the Christian church, that the Jesus about whom they were writing had in some way or other triumphed over death. Hence, Jesus' death on the cross was not the end of his story; Jesus had been raised by God from death to a new form of life. Jesus was thus now alive again from the dead and, as such, was present in and with his community. Therefore, he continued to speak to and to guide the community in the period after his death on the cross. This guidance could be described in different ways by different people. Some could speak of Jesus' being directly with his people (cf. Matt 28:20); others could use the language of the "Holy Spirit's" directing and guiding the church (Luke; John); others, such as Paul, could speak of Christians' being "in Christ" in some sense. But there was a common belief that the presence and influence of Jesus was not confined to a period in the past and terminated by his crucifixion. Hence, any teaching ascribed to Jesus was not regarded as necessarily *only* that of a figure in the past, not perhaps even primarily that. Rather, it was above all the teaching of one who was now alive and guiding the Christian community as its Lord. Thus any sharp distinction that we might wish to make between a pre-Easter and a post-Easter situation would probably have been rather unreal for first-century Christians, including the gospel writers. For them, the teaching of Jesus was that of the person who had lived and taught and died in Palestine around 30 CE, but who was now alive and reigning at God's right hand, leading and guiding his followers in the present.

The net result was that Christians felt free to adapt and change the teaching of Jesus as it had come down in the tradition in order to apply it to their own situations. What was important about Jesus' teaching was that it was applicable in the present, not merely a relic from the past. Some traditions may have been preserved simply because they were from a revered past; but one assumes that the bulk of the tradition was preserved because it was believed to be relevant to the needs of the present. Certainly, we see this in the case of Paul, who occasionally refers to Jesus' teaching precisely because it is relevant to the situation he addresses. Thus in 1 Cor 7:10, he cites Jesus' teaching on divorce when discussing divorce in Corinth; in 1 Cor 9:14, Paul refers to Jesus' teaching on support for missionaries in his own discussion about the rights of apostles to receive financial backing. Moreover, Paul evidently felt quite free in relation to this teaching. For example, in the latter case he claims the right to be able to ignore Jesus' teaching in this respect (see 1 Cor 9:15). In part this may arise from Paul's own claim to be an apostle and hence to be in a peculiar position of authority; however, at least in Paul's eyes, the basis for his authority derives from his possession of the Holy Spirit (see 1 Cor 7:40), and this was common to all Christians.

This freedom to adapt the teachings of Jesus, no doubt conditioned above all by the church's resurrection belief that Jesus was still alive and speaking to his followers, leads to the peculiar problems our Gospels provide in relation to the issue of "Jesus and the Gospels." The precise extent to which this freedom was felt by early Christians is debated. However, the fact remains that, on any showing, the Gospels are not identical. They report incidents in the life (and death) of Jesus that do not agree. At times these reports appear to clearly refer to what is a single incident in the life of Jesus. Yet the fact that the reports differ indicates that someone somewhere has changed things to a certain extent. Thus the *differences*, or perhaps better the combination of similarities *and* differences, among the Gospels give rise to many of the problems faced by critical scholarship.

Differences Among the Gospels. Among the canonical Gospels, the most obvious differences exist between John's Gospel and the other three. Matthew, Mark, and Luke are in many respects very close to one another. They recount many similar incidents, often in the same order—indeed, they are so similar that it is both possible and often profitable to view them alongside one another in parallel and look at them together—i.e., "synoptically." (The Greek preposition *syn* means "with"; *optic* has to do with seeing and looking; hence, *synoptic* means looking at each Gospel with the others.) Hence, the designation of these three Gospels as the synoptic Gospels.

John's Gospel differs famously at many levels from the Synoptics. In terms of time and space, according to John, Jesus has a longer ministry (three years), spending much time in Jerusalem as well as Galilee; in the Synoptics his ministry appears to last for only one year, with Jesus spending only one final week in Jerusalem. Apparently similar stories appear differently: Jesus' action in the Temple, driving out those buying and selling, takes place very early in John (2:13-22), but a few days before Jesus' death in the Synoptics (Mark 11:15-19). Some important events are missing in John; for example, there is no institution of the Eucharist in John's account of the last supper. Conversely, other equally important events recorded in John are not mentioned in the Synoptics (e.g., the raising of Lazarus from the dead). So, too, the categories and methods used by Jesus in his teaching differ. In the Synoptics, Jesus teaches mostly in small units, focusing on the kingdom of God, using parables extensively and saying little about himself directly; in John, Jesus teaches in long discourses, focusing on such themes as eternal life and, at times, speaking quite explicitly about his own identity (cf. the great "I am" sayings).

These differences have, of course, been noted for a long time. In the days prior to critical scholarship, attempts were made regularly to harmonize the different Gospel accounts. One way to do this was to argue that, if two different accounts appear in our Gospels, then they must reflect two different incidents in the life of Jesus. Hence, for example, the different accounts of Jesus' action in the Temple show that Jesus drove people out of the Temple twice; two different accounts of Jesus' teaching about the double love command (Mark 12:28-34; Luke 10:25-28) reflect two different events in Jesus' ministry. Jesus, like any good teacher, may have sought to get his message across by raising important aspects on more than one occasion. Other differences between John and the Synoptics might be explained by differences in the audience: Jesus chose to teach the crowds in ways other than the methods he used to speak to the disciples.

It is now widely recognized that such attempts at harmonization can solve the problems raised by differences among our Gospels only in a very superficial way. Doubling up incidents in the life of Jesus may solve things occasionally (Jesus may have discussed the importance of the double love command on more than one occasion), but in the end the process becomes absurd. Are we to believe that Jesus entered Jerusalem on a donkey three or four times in almost (but not quite) identical circumstances and each evangelist recorded a different occasion accurately? And such an idea becomes even more ludicrous with other events; we cannot really have two last suppers (one with an "institution" of a eucharist, as in the Synoptics, and one without, as in John), let alone three separate last suppers with similar, but slightly different, forms of institution at each one with each accurately recorded in one of the three synoptic Gospels! Least of all can we have Jesus dying more than once! Much more plausible, then, is the view that these different accounts in our Gospels represent different reports of the *same* incident, and the differences may reveal something more about the way in which a tradition was told and used later.

As far as the problem of Jesus and the Gospels is concerned, it is widely agreed that our primary evidence for recovering information about Jesus' own life and teaching is to be found in the synoptic Gospels, rather than in John. This is not to deny that John may preserve valuable historical data at times, and some of that we shall consider later. But for the most part, the considerably developed presentation of John, with the greatly heightened christology, is thought to reflect primarily a remolding of the Jesus tradition by a later Christian writer. Such remolding undoubtedly reveals the work of a Christian writer of extraordinary depth and profundity. But it is primarily the evangelist's own grasp of the truth of the Christian claims about Jesus that we see reflected in the Fourth Gospel and not so much the teaching of the pre-Easter Jesus. For the latter, we must turn to the Synoptics.

When we do so, however, we rapidly discover that the phenomenon of disagreements is not confined to a comparison between John and the Synoptics. The synoptic Gospels themselves display a pattern of agreement and disagreement. I have already referred to the extraordinary measure of agreement among the Synoptics—so great, indeed, that they are called "Synoptic." Nevertheless, the Gospels also exhibit considerable disagreement. Some items I have already noted in passing or by implication; e.g., the different versions of the story of the double love command in Mark 12 and Luke 10, or the three similar, but different, versions of the institution of the eucharist by Jesus in Matthew 26, Mark 14, and Luke 22. Many of the differences among the Synoptics are minor; they involve small differences in wording and less difference in substance. Yet the smallness of the differences is significant precisely because it makes it correspondingly difficult to ascribe them to separate events in the life of Jesus. Jesus would then need to have been repeating himself in triplicate constantly!

The nature of the agreements among the Gospels raises the possibility that these agreements might be explained by the existence of common sources used by the evangelists. Much effort has been devoted to this area of gospel studies, which is usually known as source criticism.

SOURCE CRITICISM

The close relationship among the synoptic Gospels and the rather more distant relationship between John and the Synoptics makes it sensible to consider the synoptic Gospels separately in this context. We shall, therefore, consider first the problem of the sources and the relationships of the synoptic Gospels, a problem usually referred to as the "Synoptic Problem."

The Synoptic Problem. The agreements among the synoptic Gospels are so extensive that it is now widely believed that the three Gospels are in some kind of *literary* relationship with one another. It is sometimes argued that the agreements among these Gospels could be based on common dependence on oral tradition, or on underlying Aramaic traditions, but the close verbal agreement between the Greek texts of our present Gospels—an agreement that is at times almost verbatim (cf. Matt 3:7-10/Luke 3:7-9) and that goes far beyond what one would normally expect from common oral tradition—makes this unlikely. For example, in Mark 2:10, there is a grammatical break in the narrative, as Mark has Jesus turn from talking to the crowds to address the paralyzed man. Precisely the same switch occurs in exactly the same way at exactly the same point in Matthew and Luke in their parallel accounts. Agreements of this nature and this detail are scarcely what one would expect from common dependence on oral tradition alone. The evidence thus demands a literary relationship at the level of our Greek texts: Either one Gospel has been used by the writers of the others as a source, or the evangelists have had access to common sources.

The most widely accepted solution to the synoptic problem today is the so-called "two-source theory." This theory argues that the earliest synoptic Gospel is Mark and that it was used as a source for Matthew and Luke; this, then, accounts for the agreements among all three Gospels in the material they have in common. Matthew and Luke in addition share a further body of material that, in the two-source theory, is explained by both writers' having access to another source or body of source material that is no longer extant but is usually known as "Q."[2] Matthew and Luke also have access to material that is peculiar to each, and this is usually known as "M" and "L" material, respectively (whether M and L constitute separate "sources" is less clear).

There is not enough space here to discuss the synoptic problem in detail or to offer a full defense of the two-source theory. Some loose ends in the theory remain. For example, the precise nature and extent of Q remain unclear. Was Q a single document? Was it available to Matthew and Luke in precisely the same form? How far are M and L separate sources? There is also a potentially embarrassing number of places where Matthew and Luke must have changed Mark in identical ways (the so-called minor agreements), a fact that is rather surprising on the two-source theory if Matthew and Luke did not know each other. Thus the whole theory has been questioned by some. For example, a strongly held minority view today has sought to revive an older solution to the synoptic problem associated with the nineteenth-century scholar J. J. Griesbach, who argued that Matthew's Gospel came first; that Luke wrote second, using Matthew; and that Mark wrote last, using both Matthew and Luke as sources. Others have argued for different modifications of the two-source theory; for example, some accept the priority of Mark but question whether one needs a lost Q source to explain the Matthew-Luke agreements, arguing that the latter can be fully explained by Luke's direct dependence on Matthew. Still others have pleaded for more complex solutions to the problem, postulating a number of intervening stages in the growth of our Gospels with intermediate stages.

Certainly the contemporary debate has highlighted the weak and inconclusive nature of some of the arguments in the past that have been used to promote the two-source theory. This applies especially to some of the more "formal" arguments, referring to global patterns in the overall set of agreements and disagreements. For example, in arguing for Markan priority, some have appealed to the fact that nearly all of Mark is paralleled in Matthew or Luke or both. Yet all this shows is that some literary relationship exists; it does not prove that the only possibility is that Mark's Gospel was the *source* of Matthew and Luke. Similarly, the much discussed appeal to the failure of Matthew and Luke ever (or hardly ever) to agree against Mark in order and wording does not prove that Matthew and Luke independently used Mark as a source; it only shows that Mark is some kind of a "middle term" between the other two in any pattern of relationships.

Probably the most important kind of arguments are based on concrete comparison of individual texts, asking which way the tradition is most likely to have developed. For example, the words of Peter's confession at the scene at Caesarea

Philippi are recorded by Mark as "You are the Messiah" (8:29 NRSV), and by Matthew as "You are the Messiah, the Son of the living God" (16:16 NRSV). It seems more likely that Matthew has expanded Mark's shorter version in a way that is characteristic of Matthew by adding a reference to Jesus as Son of God, than that Mark has abbreviated Matthew's longer version. It would be entirely in keeping with Matthew's interests and christological concerns if Matthew has added a reference to Jesus as Son of God here. However, Matthew's reference to Jesus as Son of God would have been very congenial to Mark had he known it, since Mark too has a keen interest in Jesus as Son of God; hence it is less likely that Mark omitted the phrase if it had been in a source available to him at this point. Thus Markan priority seems to account for the development of the tradition here better than any theory that makes Mark dependent on Matthew.

In the case of the Q tradition, advocates of the two-source theory would claim that neither Matthew nor Luke consistently gives the earlier form of a tradition they share in common. Sometimes Matthew is more original, sometimes Luke. For example, Matthew is probably more original in his version of the woe about cleansing the inside and outside of cups, where Luke suddenly and extraneously brings in an exhortation to "give alms" (Matt 23:26; Luke 11:41). But Luke is probably more original in his version of the Beatitudes in having Jesus say that the "poor" and the "hungry" are blessed, rather than the "poor in spirit" and those "hungering after righteousness" as in Matthew (Matt 5:3, 6; Luke 6:20, 21). Such examples would have to be multiplied many times over to make a fully convincing case for any one theory, and the reader is referred elsewhere for such treatments (see the bibliography below).

Great stress is laid by some, especially supporters of the Griesbach hypothesis, on the value of patristic statements about the Gospels. It is true that these are often discounted by advocates of the two-source theory, and they certainly give little (if any) support to a theory of Markan priority, asserting almost uniformly that Matthew was the first Gospel to be written. However, it is uncertain how reliable this evidence is. Much of it is relatively late, and it all may go back to one early (i.e., 2nd cent.) statement of Papias. Further, the antiquity of this statement does not establish its reliability. Hence the majority of modern scholars would prefer to rely on the evidence of the Gospel materials themselves to establish the nature of the relationship among them.

Sources of John. The problem of the sources used by John is a more difficult one in some respects. Several scholars have argued that John is using source material, especially in the miracle stories. John may have had access to a so-called Signs Source ("sign" [σημεῖον *sēmeion*] is the word used regularly in John to refer to Jesus' miracles). In this respect, scholars refer to the numbering of the first two miracles in John as the "first sign" (John 2:11) and the "second sign" (John 4:54), and also the reference in 20:31 to the "many other signs which Jesus did." Some, too, have sought to distinguish between the viewpoint of the miracle stories themselves (where Jesus' miracles are seen as stupendous feats) and the rest of the Gospel (where what is crucial is faith in Jesus himself). Nevertheless, the theory has been criticized by some, and the issue is a very open one in contemporary Johannine scholarship.

There is also the problem of the relationship between John and the synoptic Gospels. Despite the differences between them, John does share a number of features with the Synoptics, including at times some striking verbal agreements (e.g., the common mention of a sum of 200 denarii in the story of the feeding of the 5,000 in Mark 6:37 and John 6:7). At one time it was thought that John was quite independent of the Synoptics, but in recent years there has been a strong revival of support for the view that John may have known and used one or more of the synoptic Gospels. If he did, he must have exercised considerably more freedom than say Matthew and Luke did with Mark. Furthermore, there is considerably more material in John that cannot have been derived from the Synoptics, so that any theory of John's dependence on the Synoptics may have only limited use.

Source Criticism and the Quest for the Historical Jesus. In relation to the problem of discovering information about Jesus, it should be clear that a solution to the synoptic problem may be an important step in the process. Given three parallel (but not identical) versions of a saying of Jesus in our synoptic Gospels, the likelihood is that these are not three independent witnesses; rather, they represent one tradition subsequently used by the other two Gospel writers. Thus the secondary versions do not tell us anything about Jesus: rather, the earliest version must be our primary source. Assuming the two-source theory, then, Mark's Gospel will normally give us a more accurate account of Jesus' teaching than either Matthew or Luke when all three are parallel. Thus when Mark 9:1 has Jesus predict that some persons standing by him will not taste death "until they see that the kingdom of God has come with power," and Matt 16:28 has "[until] they see the Son of Man coming in his kingdom," the two-source theory would suggest that Matthew's version is secondary to Mark's and so Jesus did not refer to the Son of Man at this point. Any theories about the (very complex) problem of what *Jesus* meant by the term *Son of Man* could not then use this verse in Matthew as part of the evidence.

Yet while Mark's Gospel may be more accurate than Matthew's and Luke's, we must beware of proceeding too far too fast and deducing too much from the evidence. It would be tempting to assume (as some have!) that since Mark and Q are the earliest sources, they should provide the primary evidence about Jesus. We cannot, however, assume that M and L material is ipso facto less useful in this respect. An M tradition may well be as early as a Markan (or Q) tradition. For example, the M tradition in Matt 16:17-19, where Jesus pronounces the famous blessing on Peter, may well be very ancient (even if it may not have originally belonged in its present context of Peter's confession). So, too, many of the best-known parables of Jesus appear in the L tradition of Luke—yet that does not of itself make them less valuable as sources for discovering Jesus' teaching.

Despite these caveats, it remains true that Mark and Q (on the two-source theory) still provide sources that are earlier than the present Gospels of Matthew and Luke. Nevertheless, we cannot simply assume that Mark and Q, although perhaps more reliable as sources of the life of Jesus than Matthew and Luke, are necessarily absolutely reliable. We cannot simply take Mark's Gospel, say, as an accurate transcript of the life of Jesus. On most conventional datings of the Gospels, Mark was probably written at some point in the decade 65–75 CE. (There is considerable debate about whether Mark was written before or after the fall of Jerusalem in 70 CE.) The date of Q is very uncertain, though most would probably date the "final" version of Q (if it is indeed appropriate to talk in such terms) not much earlier than the mid 50s.

Matthew and Luke are, of course, later still. Nearly all scholars would agree that verses such as Matt 22:7 and Luke 21:20 clearly presuppose the fall of Jerusalem in 70 CE. Hence, between the end of Jesus' life (c. 30 CE) and the writing of our Gospels there is a period of probably more than 35 years, and between the end of Jesus' life and Q there is a gap of 25 years or more. Further, it is now becoming more and more clear that the earliest Gospel sources, Mark and Q, are just as much influenced by post-Easter Christian ideas as are the later Gospel writings of Matthew and Luke. The process of changing and adapting the Gospel traditions about Jesus in the light of subsequent events is not confined to Matthew and Luke. W. Wrede's work on secrecy in Mark's Gospel in 1901 has made scholars aware of this in relation to Mark; and recent studies of Q have shown how much Q has its own characteristic and distinctive features in handing on traditions about Jesus. Thus in order to discover reliable information about Jesus, we must try to reach back behind the Gospel accounts to try to bridge the gap of a generation or more over a period when the Gospel tradition was probably being handed on primarily in oral form. This attempt is usually known in scholarly circles as form criticism.

FORM CRITICISM

Forms and Setting. Form criticism (the standard English "translation" of the German word *Formgeschichte*) has many aspects. Its name (*form* criticism) derives in part from one aspect of its activity that seeks to identify the common "forms" of individual units of the tradition. One of the basic assumptions of much contemporary Gospel study is that the individual stories (pericopes) of the tradition are the basic units; the evangelists worked as editors to put these individual stories into a connected sequence. Hence, in order to reach back behind the evangelists, one needs to look at the individual units. Further, several of these units seem to display a common structural pattern, or form, in the way the stories are told. Moreover, it was believed that, on the basis of such common forms, one might be able to deduce the kind of situation, or setting, in which stories were told in such a way. It was assumed that similar settings would give rise to stories being told in similar ways or forms. In turn, given common forms, one might be able to deduce the settings in which such stories circulated. (The technical phrase used for such a setting is the German *Sitz im Leben*, "*setting in life.*")

Early New Testament form critics devoted considerable time and effort to such classification of the units of the gospel tradition. There was by no means universal agreement, either in the categories or forms identified, or in the proposed *Sitz im Leben* for each form. Some (such as Dibelius) thought of quite broad categories with a correspondingly general *Sitz im Leben*. Others (such as Bultmann) attempted far greater precision in the proposed forms, with many different categories and hence a correspondingly more precise proposal for the *Sitz im Leben* of each category. So, too, the way in which a *Sitz im Leben* was assigned to each form varied. Dibelius thought in general terms, with somewhat preconceived ideas about what such settings might be (e.g., preaching, teaching, the cult). Bultmann was far more specific, very often deducing the setting from the story itself; for example, controversy stories about debates between Jesus and the Jewish authorities were seen as reflecting similar debates between Christians and their contemporaries. Both approaches are open to criticism. The detailed suggestions of Bultmann are in danger of producing rather circular arguments: Do we know that Christians were involved in debates of the same nature as Jesus, apart from the Gospel evidence? The more general approach of Dibelius is open to the charge of producing rather preconceived ideas of what the activity of the early church was, as well as being very general. (Was preaching central to the life of the early church? What did preaching constitute?) Further, the whole approach may be questioned if it is assumed that a single form could arise from one and only one setting. One *Sitz im Leben* may have given rise to a variety of forms. Conversely, one story in a single form may have been used in a variety of settings. Hence the attempt to correlate form and setting in a neat one-to-one relationship may not be satisfactory.

This is, however, not the only or the most significant aspect of form criticism. Form criticism, at least as practiced by German scholars, has always been regarded as a more wide-ranging exercise. In part this is reflected in the German word for the discipline: *Formgeschichte*. *Geschichte* is one of the German words for "history," and so *Formgeschichte* has been seen as including not only the analysis of the "forms" of the units of the tradition, but also an attempt to analyze their history.

Tradition History/Criticism. This aspect of form criticism tries to determine how the tradition developed in time and also to say something about its ultimate origin. The concern is thus with the tradition-history of the material, and this whole approach is sometimes referred to as "tradition criticism." In this respect, form criticism has often had rather bad press in some quarters, since many form critics are regarded as having been extremely skeptical about the historicity of much of the tradition. For some this is regarded as straying outside the proper boundaries of form criticism, since questions of form and *Sitz im Leben*, on the one hand, and historical reliability or authenticity, on the other, are separate.

On the one hand, this distinction is valid, and certainly the two aspects should not be confused. To assign a particular *Sitz im Leben* to a tradition—i.e., to make suggestions about where or how a tradition was handed on within the life of the early church, is quite separate from the question of its historical authenticity. To claim that Gospel stories of Jesus' debating sabbath observance with the Pharisees reflect early church debates about whether Christians should observe sabbath is really quite independent of whether these stories are authentic. Christians could have invented them to justify their own behavior; equally, the stories could reflect real conflicts in which Jesus was involved with the same issues continuing into the post-Easter situation.

On the other hand, to raise the question of authenticity is not in itself illegitimate, and it is not an illegitimate part of form criticism if the latter is understood as *Formgeschichte*. How skeptical some of the form critics actually were is another matter. Whatever the results proposed, the questions posed by form critics are valid and indeed vital for anyone concerned with the phenomenon of Jesus and the Gospels.

Authenticity. The validity of raising questions of authenticity would be denied by few scholars today. Very few would claim that every tradition about Jesus in all the Gospels is as it stands an authentic transcript of an event in the life of Jesus. We have already seen this in relation to parallel accounts in the Gospels themselves. Parallel, but not identical, versions in two or more Gospels do not represent accurate reports of multiple events in the life of Jesus but rather, in part at least, later Christian adaptations of earlier traditions.

Moreover, the process is unlikely to have started only when Matthew and Luke used Mark (and Q). Within Mark's Gospel itself, some traditions probably reflect later Christian adaptations of earlier traditions. A classic example is to be found in Mark 2:18-22 (esp. v. 20). Jesus is asked about the legitimacy of fasting (v. 18) and replies in vv. 19*a* and 21-22 in terms that appear to suggest that fasting is quite inappropriate in the new situation of the present, which is in radical discontinuity with the past; a new situation has arisen comparable to a wedding where one does not fast (v. 19); and the new and old situations seem to be quite separate (cf. the imagery of the patch and the garment and wine and wineskins in vv. 21-22). But v. 20 introduces a quite different note: The period of non-fasting will be only temporary, for the time will come when the bridegroom will be taken away from them and fasting will be reintroduced. Verse 20 seems somewhat out of place in the context and looks very much like a later Christian attempt to adapt the teaching of Jesus in the light of Christian practice of fasting again.

In other instances in Mark's Gospel too it seems most likely that a Christian (Mark or a pre-Markan editor) has rewritten and adapted the tradition in the light of subsequent events. For example, the very detailed passion prediction in Mark 10:32-33, which corresponds so precisely to the events of Jesus' passion (a Jewish trial with a death sentence followed by a Gentile trial and mockings, spitting, and scourging) is implausible on the lips of Jesus in quite such detail. (If Jesus had really predicted everything in such detail, why were the disciples apparently so overwhelmed with surprise when it all happened?) More plausibly, a Christian has written up the prediction in the light of subsequent events, though perhaps adopting a more general prediction of coming suffering and death (as, e.g., in Mark 9:31) that came from Jesus himself.

In both these instances, we may have examples of Christians taking up authentic sayings of Jesus and adapting and expanding them in the light of later events. How far Christians actually *created* sayings of Jesus *de novo* is hard to say (though any distinction between "adapting" and "creating" is at best a thin one). Few NT scholars would deny that it never happened. For example, the saying in Matt 18:20 ("where two or three are gathered in my name, I am there among them" [NRSV]) presupposes an ongoing presence of Jesus in the post-Easter community, together with a position ascribed to Jesus comparable to that of the Shekinah of God (cf. the well-known Jewish parallel in *m.'Abot* 3:2, which talks of God's Shekinah being present whenever two or three meet to study the Law). Both factors make it hard to ascribe the saying to Jesus himself in the pre-Easter situation. It is, therefore, probably a "creation" of the early church. Similarly, the saying three verses earlier in Matt 18:17 ("if the offender refuses to listen even to the church, let such a one be to you as a Gentile and a tax collector" [NRSV]) puts on the lips of Jesus a command for exclusion from the community, which seems incompatible with Jesus' general openness to all; it also uses terms presupposing that "Gentiles" and "tax collectors" are archetypes of people beyond the pale, which again hardly squares with Jesus' well-attested openness and welcome to tax collectors. (Jesus' attitude toward Gentiles is more difficult to assess, though it is hard to see his attitude as anything other than, at least in principle, one of equal openness.) Thus the saying in Matt 18:17 is hard to credit to the historical Jesus. Hence at times it is clear that sayings that are not authentic have been attributed to Jesus by later Christians.

Criteria of Authenticity. How, then, can we distinguish authentic from inauthentic sayings? A number of possible criteria have been proposed, and these have been discussed extensively. In part, the whole exercise depends on one's starting point and where one thinks any "burden of proof" lies. Is a tradition to be assumed authentic until it is shown to be otherwise? Or is a tradition to be assumed a Christian creation until it is shown to be authentic? For many more "skeptical" critics (i.e., those who would answer yes to the second question), a very important criterion is that known as the "criterion of dissimilarity." This argues that a tradition about Jesus is authentic if it shows Jesus to be dissimilar to both Judaism and the early church. This criterion is perhaps the one that has aroused the fiercest and most intensive debate. Few would deny that, insofar as it allows anything through its net, this criterion does establish authentic Jesus traditions; traditions not derived from Judaism, and not creations of the early church, are as likely as anything to be genuine sayings of Jesus.

However, the criterion has been heavily criticized. It is in danger of producing a very distorted picture of Jesus. (Was Jesus always "dissimilar" to the early church? Or to Judaism?) It also presupposes that our knowledge of both "Judaism" and "the early church" is sufficiently comprehensive for us to be able to determine what is "dissimilar" to either entity; and it is now quite clear how fragmentary our knowledge of both Judaism and early Christianity really is. Hence, on its own this criterion cannot be the only one used.

Criteria have been proposed appealing to "coherence"; what coheres with material established as authentic by other means could be accepted. But good fiction is "coherent" as well! Some scholars appeal extensively to Aramaic idioms, or to Semitic or Palestinian presuppositions, in individual traditions as indicating authentic material. For example, the use of the passive voice in the Beatitudes probably reflects a Semitic "divine passive," avoiding mentioning God. Other sayings are constructed in parallelism, perhaps reflecting a Semitic idiom. Elements of the parables presuppose social structures that place the tradition firmly within Palestinian society. All this has value. However, the problem with all such arguments is that, while such considerations may show that a tradition reflects the Aramaic language and/or a Palestinian environment, Jesus was not the only person to live in Palestine and speak Aramaic! Thus the fact that a tradition reflects a Semitic milieu may only show that the tradition is to be traced back to an Aramaic-speaking, or Palestinian, community.

Some, too, have appealed to a criterion of "multiple attestation," claiming that a tradition attested in more than one of the major strands of the Gospels (Mark, Q, M, L) or in several different forms may be authentic. Again this has value, but the criterion is less useful in practice since so few of the individual traditions are multiply attested. Nevertheless, such a criterion does have value in relation to general themes of the tradition.

It is probably fair to say that none of the criteria proposed is foolproof. None should probably be considered in isolation. Very often, too, they point in different directions. For example, Jesus' love command is drawn from Jewish Scripture (Deut 6:5; 11:1); yet it is quite consistent and coherent with his radical openness to all members of his society and his apparent disregard for other parts of the Jewish law in the interest of love. Hence it could be authentic. Each tradition has to be considered on its merits, with a judicious and careful assessment of all the factors and criteria involved. A radical skepticism about the historicity of the tradition is probably out of place. Few would argue that nothing of the historical Jesus is preserved in the Gospels. Several facets of Jesus' teaching in broad terms are in some respects unlike Jewish teaching of the time and also are not carried forward in early church teaching (e.g., preaching about the kingdom of God). Conversely, many facets of the life of the early church are *not* read back into the Gospels: The widespread confession of Jesus as "Lord" is rare in the earliest gospel traditions; the debates about circumcision, which were so pressing in the Judaizing disputes in Pauline communities, are not reflected in the Gospels at all; language about Christians' possessing the Holy Spirit is also rare in the gospel tradition. Hence a radical skepticism about the authenticity of the tradition as a whole is probably out of place. Nevertheless, one cannot deny that some degree of Christian adaptation of Jesus traditions has taken place in the Gospels, and so the question of authenticity is a very real one.

Form Criticism and the Quest for the Historical Jesus. Where do the results of form criticism leave us in any search for the historical Jesus? The basic presupposition of form criticism—that the individual pericopes are the basic building blocks of the tradition, and the activity of putting them into a connected narrative is due to a later editor—means that the detailed ordering of the material in the Gospels cannot tell us anything about the chronology of the life of Jesus. The evidence is simply not available to us to reconstruct an exact sequence of events. Hence we cannot distinguish stories that belong to an early part of Jesus' ministry from those stemming from a later part, and we cannot trace any chronological development in the life of Jesus. Thus older-style "lives of Jesus" (very prevalent in the 19th cent.) written on this basis are simply non-starters in the light of form criticism. (One exception may be provided by the passion narrative where in any case an ordered chronological sequence is in part demanded by the nature of the events concerned; the sequence arrest-trial-death-resurrection appearances could not occur sensibly in any other order!)

Nevertheless, most scholars today would agree that a total skepticism about recovering information about Jesus would be far too one-sided. Even if we cannot put the events of the ministry of Jesus into a connected series, there are still a number of general themes that one can with confidence trace back to Jesus' own ministry. These would include Jesus' preaching about the kingdom of God; his use of parables in his teaching; his openness to the outcasts of religious society, including tax collectors and "sinners"; his arguments with Jewish leaders, including probably the Pharisees; and perhaps his use of the term *Son of Man* (although this is a much-debated issue). In the case of any one individual tradition, there will be doubts and arguments about its authenticity. But few would deny that in broad terms, important facets of the life and ministry of Jesus are available to us through critical use of the NT synoptic Gospels.

NON-SYNOPTIC EVIDENCE FOR JESUS

So far I have considered primarily the synoptic Gospels in discussing the problem of seeking to recover reliable information about the pre-Easter ministry of Jesus. What of other possible sources?

John. One obvious candidate to consider here is the Fourth Gospel. As we saw earlier, most scholars today would regard the Fourth Gospel as primarily evidence of the beliefs and thought of the evangelist we call John and not very easily usable for giving us information about the historical Jesus. This assessment is, of course, a large generalization. Many have argued that John does preserve elements of tradition that may be historical. These vary in nature. They include features such as the fact that Jesus may have had a ministry longer than the single year implied by the Synoptics, and that he worked in Jerusalem for more than one final hectic week; moreover, it is possible that Jesus may have worked alongside John the Baptist, perhaps even baptizing people (John 4:1). John's dating of the last supper and the crucifixion as all taking place on the eve of Passover (rather than Passover itself, as implied by the Synoptics) has had its defenders. So, too, some sayings embedded in the Fourth Gospel may be authentic sayings of Jesus, albeit now elaborated and developed by the evangelist in the discourses in which they are placed: for example, the saying in John 5:19 ("the Son can do nothing on his own, but only what he sees the Father doing" (NRSV) may reflect an earlier, perhaps less christologically developed, parabolic saying of Jesus himself about ordinary sons learning from their fathers.

Despite all these possibilities, however, it is questionable how much independent value John provides in giving information about Jesus. The question of chronology may be important (though, as we saw above, scholars today would not wish in the light of form criticism to place much weight on any synoptic chronology; and, in any case, many of John's chronological time references may be heavily theologically charged and influenced). Further, the value of possibly authentic sayings of Jesus being preserved in John is unlikely to enhance our actual knowledge of Jesus himself very significantly. Those who argue for the possibility of such traditions in John usually do so because the saying in John is similar to the sayings tradition in the Synoptics. Sayings in John that offer a radically different presentation of Jesus from the synoptic picture are, precisely because they are so different, rejected as being inauthentic. Hence the result of such research will inevitably produce merely a few more sayings that basically support the picture of Jesus already established from the Synoptics. Thus the overall picture obtained is unlikely to be significantly altered by the addition of a few Johannine sayings. A synoptic Jesus, with a few synoptic-like sayings from John added, will still be a synoptic Jesus! Certainly there may be elements in John that do significantly change our picture of Jesus, or perhaps fill what would otherwise be puzzling gaps. (For example, the possibility that Jesus worked alongside John the Baptist, perhaps baptizing as well, might explain better the extraordinarily privileged position given to John the Baptist in the Synoptics, and also explain why a water baptism rite was adopted in the early Christian church, apparently without any discussion at all.)

Overall the evidence provided by John is unlikely to alter our picture of Jesus from the Synoptics significantly. Generally the Fourth Gospel gives us primary insight into the beliefs of the great Christian writer behind it, rather than direct information about Jesus himself.

Paul. For other sources of information about Jesus, one should not forget the letters of Paul in the New Testament. Paul rarely cites the teaching of Jesus but does so occasionally, notably in 1 Corinthians 7, 9, 11 on divorce, financial support, and the Eucharist respectively. There is also possibly an appeal to the teaching of Jesus in the "word of the Lord," cited in 1 Thess 4:15 (though it is not entirely clear that Paul is referring here to a saying that he knows as that of the pre-Easter Jesus). Other possible allusions to Jesus traditions occur elsewhere in Paul, although there is no explicit reference to Jesus (e.g., Rom 12:14: "Bless those who persecute you; bless and do not curse them" [NRSV]; cf. Matt 5:44; Luke 6:28). The amount of data is very limited. Nevertheless, its date should not be forgotten. Paul wrote his letters in the mid-50s, whereas the Gospels all date from at least 10 to 15 years later. Paul is thus our earliest witness to Jesus. Thus in seeking to find Jesus' original teaching on, say, the issue of divorce, we should not confine attention to the sayings in the Gospels (Mark 10:11-12 and par.) but must take seriously the evidence of 1 Cor 7:10-11 as well. And the somewhat freer attitude reflected in the latter (e.g., in v. 11*a*, especially if this is to be regarded as part of the quotation Paul is actually citing here and not, as it is often taken, Paul's own comment) may then throw a different slant on Jesus' attitude to divorce. However, as already noted, the extent of the data we can extract from Paul is very limited, since Paul (for whatever reason) cites the teaching of Jesus so rarely.

Non-Canonical Evidence. The question of the value of other evidence for Jesus is much disputed today. As I noted earlier, several other documents calling themselves Gospels purport to give information about Jesus. None of these, of course, is now part of our New Testament. That does not of itself necessarily negate their value in possibly providing information about Jesus. Thus the question needs to be asked: Can our knowledge of Jesus be extended by these writings?

For the most part, the majority view is that these non-canonical texts are not very useful for providing information about Jesus. For the historian of early Christianity, they are of immense interest in letting us see how later writers responded to the events of Jesus' life and how traditions about Jesus developed. But for the most part these gospels are probably to be dated much later than our canonical texts and are not of great historical value in preserving reliable traditions about Jesus. This cannot, however, be taken as a cast-iron rule. In particular, one or two of the non-canonical gospels may be early, or if not themselves early, may preserve very primitive traditions. For example, the *Gospel of Peter* exists in fragmentary form, the extant text giving us an account of the passion of Jesus. Some have argued that this gospel may preserve a very primitive early account of the passion (even if in its present form the *Gospel of Peter* is relatively late). Others would argue that the entire gospel is late and simply represents a legendary rewriting of the passion narratives of all our present canonical Gospels.

The one non-canonical text in which the issue of possible authentic Jesus traditions is most keenly debated today is the *Gospel of Thomas.* This gospel, known in fragments for the last one hundred years, is now available to us in full in Coptic as one of the texts discovered in 1945 in the Nag Hammadi library. This "gospel," as already noted, does not conform to the genre of the canonical Gospels: It contains no narrative, no account of the passion or resurrection, but simply has a list of over one hundred sayings of Jesus loosely strung together and introduced by the very brief note "Jesus said. . . ." Some of the sayings are very similar to sayings preserved in the synoptic Gospels; others are very different. Ever since its discovery, there has been much debate about whether the sayings in *Thomas* represent a line of tradition independent of the Synoptics and so provide an independent source for the teaching of Jesus, or whether *Thomas* depends on our Gospels and thus is primarily a witness to the development of the synoptic tradition after the time of the writing of the canonical Gospels. There is no scholarly unanimity at present, and very different views are held. For some, the fact that *Thomas* presents its synoptic-like sayings in an order that seems to bear no correlation at all to the order in which these sayings come in our synoptic Gospels suggests strongly that *Thomas* is independent of our Gospels. Moreover, many would claim that the synoptic-like sayings in *Thomas* show none of the redactional features (i.e., elements attributed to the final editor of the Gospels) that the parallels in the synoptic Gospels have. Hence the sayings in *Thomas* go back to a stage at least as early as, if not earlier than, our present Gospels. Other scholars have argued that the *Gospel of Thomas* does show some features that are redactional in the canonical Gospels and, hence, presupposes the synoptic Gospels in their finished form, so that *Thomas* is post-synoptic and primarily a witness to the post-synoptic development of the tradition. It is probably fair to say that the issue of *Thomas* and the synoptics is hotly debated with scholarly opinion evenly divided on the matter.

Yet, as with the Fourth Gospel, it is uncertain how far the evidence of *Thomas* will radically alter our picture of Jesus. Almost all students of *Thomas* would agree that not *all* the sayings in that document can be traced back to Jesus. Some of the sayings reflect secondary expansions of the Jesus tradition in a quasi-"gnostic" direction. (The question of whether the *Gospel of Thomas* itself is gnostic is hotly debated, but few would deny that, at least in its present form, it reflects tendencies that are on the road to later Gnosticism.) As with John, the criterion often implicitly used to distinguish early from late sayings in *Thomas* is related to their similarity to the synoptic picture; synoptic-like sayings are more likely to be early than others. Thus the picture of Jesus that emerges is likely simply to reinforce the synoptic picture already available. It is true that some details may change; indeed, the fact that *Thomas* at times offers versions of sayings that are closely parallel to synoptic traditions may then provide us with extremely valuable information in assessing the detailed wording of individual traditions (*if*, of course, *Thomas* is judged to be independent of the synoptics). But the very similarity between these sayings implies that the overall portrait of Jesus emerging from *Thomas* will probably simply reinforce the synoptic picture rather than radically change it.

It thus appears likely that our primary source of evidence for information about the historical Jesus remains the synoptic Gospels. Other sources may provide some ancillary evidence and important snippets of information regarding details, but the prime source remains the synoptic tradition.

REDACTION CRITICISM

So far I have considered the subject of Jesus and the Gospels with the question of the historical Jesus very much to the fore, looking at the ways in which the Gospels (and other evidence) can be used to provide information about Jesus. However, this is not the only purpose for which the Gospels may be used. As with any historical text, a gospel can tell us just as much (sometimes more) about the person who has written it as about the events purportedly being described. We have seen this already in passing in relation to form criticism and in relation to the Fourth Gospel. Form criticism (in part) seeks to discover something about the early Christian groups who preserved and handed on the individual stories in the Gospels. And critical study of the Fourth Gospel is aimed primarily at discovering something about the thought and situation of the evangelist. Such an approach, which has dominated study of the Fourth Gospel ever since the rise of critical scholarship, is now being increasingly applied to the synoptic Gospels. This branch of study is usually known as "redaction criticism."

Redaction criticism as a self-conscious discipline applied to the synoptic Gospels was first developed after the last World War in the works of such scholars as G. Bornkamm on Matthew and H. Conzelmann on Luke. Earlier form critics had held a rather "low" view of the synoptic evangelists themselves. Attention had been focused on the earlier stages in the development of the tradition, and the evangelists themselves were seen as simply collectors, "scissors-and-paste" editors, putting the units of the tradition together in a relatively unstructured way. Such a view of the evangelists' work has changed in more recent study, and the evangelists are now seen as much more purposeful agents in their use of the traditions available to them. Hence the focus of attention has been much more on what the Gospels may tell us about the evangelists themselves, the communities for which they were writing, the situations and conflicts they were engaged in, etc., quite as much as anything to do with the history they are describing. In the early days of such study, attention was focused primarily on the changes that one evangelist had made to the tradition. In the case of Matthew and Luke, the situation was (in part) relatively straightforward. On the assumption of Markan priority, one of the sources used by Matthew and Luke is directly available to us: the Gospel of Mark. Hence it is possible to look at Matthew and Luke alongside Mark and identify the ways in which the secondary evangelist has changed Mark. (The technical word for this changing is *redacting,* hence the name "redaction criticism.") Thus, for example, by looking at the ways in which Matthew has introduced a number of changes into Mark's story of the stilling of the storm, G. Bornkamm was able to show how Matthew has introduced some distinctive, characteristic ideas into the story; the account of the disciples in a boat during a storm becomes an account of Christians in the church facing turbulent times in their own day.

Such a procedure is relatively easy with Matthew and Luke using Mark, simply because Mark is directly available to us. In the case of the Q tradition, the procedure is more complex, since Q is not extant and hence the reconstruction of the Q tradition and the consequent identification of changes made by Matthew/Luke to Q is a rather more delicate operation. Nevertheless, it is not impossible. For example, it seems likely that the Q version of the Beatitudes pronounced Jesus' blessing on the "poor" and the "hungry" (Luke 6:20-21). Matthew has probably "spiritualized" these by changing the "poor" to "poor in spirit" and the "hungry" to those "hungering after righteousness" (Matt 5:3, 6). Certainly the last change reveals Matthew's own concern for "righteousness," which is a key concept in Matthew's Gospel and one that he is very keen to promote. Thus a redaction-critical approach shows us something of the evangelists' own ideas and the issues they wished to highlight and to emphasize for their communities.

Redaction criticism in general terms, in the sense of seeking to discover the concerns of the authors of the Gospel texts, has come to dominate modern gospel studies. Yet one should also note that within the broad rubric of redaction criticism, the method of approach has changed somewhat over the years. In the early days, attention was focused very much on the actual changes made by a Gospel writer to the source used. (Hence the name *redaction* criticism.) Places where the tradition was left unaltered tended to be ignored. Such an approach, however, is in danger of giving a rather lopsided, or skewed, impression of an evangelist's concerns. It may well be that there were times when an evangelist agreed strongly with a tradition and so preserved it unaltered. Indeed, the very fact that a tradition has been preserved and repeated by a later writer implies a strong measure of agreement on the part of the latter. (If a writer disapproves of a tradition, there is always the option of simply leaving it out—an option sometimes exercised by Matthew and Luke [cf. Mark 7:31-37 and 8:22-26, which are not present in the later Gospels.]) Hence, if redaction criticism is aimed primarily at rediscovering something of the characteristic ideas and concerns of an evangelist, one must take seriously the *whole* of the evangelist's work, the whole Gospel, and not merely focus on redactional changes made by a gospel writer to an earlier source.

Thus in recent years there has been a trend to move away from an exclusive, narrow focus on the changes, or emendations, made by an evangelist (sometimes called "emendation criticism") and to look quite as much at the Gospel as a whole, as a unified literary work, to see what that may tell us about an evangelist. Thus as well as looking at detailed changes in wording made by an author to the tradition, one may wish to look at the way in which the whole narrative is now structured and the way in which different parts of the narrative relate to other parts. Such an approach has been variously called "composition criticism" or "literary criticism" or "narrative criticism" (though each of these probably represents different nuances and approaches).

Thus, for example, as well as looking at detailed changes in wording by Matthew on his sources (e.g., adding a reference to "righteousness" in Matt 5:6), one can take seriously the way in which Matthew appears to have structured and arranged the material into five great "blocks," starting with the Sermon on the Mount in Matthew 5–7 and ending with the eschatological teaching in chaps. 24–25. The precise significance of such an arrangement is much disputed. (Are the five blocks meant to correspond in some way to the five books of the Torah?) But at the very least, the arrangement highlights the importance of Jesus' teaching for Matthew and shows Matthew's concern (evidenced elsewhere, cf. Matt 28:19-20) to stress the abiding validity of Jesus' teaching for the post-Easter Christian community, a concern that makes Matthew different from, say, Paul (who very rarely cites Jesus' actual teaching) and perhaps even Mark (for whom the question of *who* Jesus is may be more important than *what* Jesus actually teaches).

In recent years, some scholars have gone even further along these lines and have adopted an even more rigorously "literary" approach, bracketing off the question of sources and redactional changes completely. On this view, the text of one Gospel is to be taken as the author's own work in its entirety and is to be analyzed on its own, independently of the history of its traditions. The problem of the extent to which the history of the tradition is relevant to the interpretation of a Gospel is much disputed. Most scholars today would probably take a middle path and not want to bracket off an older type of emendation criticism completely. But the more recent literary approaches have convinced everyone of their intrinsic value. Moreover, in the case of the Gospels of Mark and John, where the identification of possible prior sources used by the evangelists is much more difficult (simply because there is no independent attestation for such sources), a more "unitary" approach, taking the Gospel text as a whole, is to a certain extent essential in the light of the available evidence. Thus in order to discover something about one evangelist, one must take the whole of the Gospel into account (and, of course, in the case of Luke, the book of Acts as well).

CONCLUDING REFLECTIONS

For some the approach of redaction criticism (however defined) is a worrisome development and seems prejudicial to what is regarded as the most "obvious" and "straightforward," indeed the theologically most valuable, way of reading the Gospels—i.e., to obtain information about the life of Jesus. The aim of this article has been in part to place some severe question marks against such claims, although there is more than one issue at stake here.

Simply at the level of facts, such a way of reading the Gospels is certainly not a straightforward exercise. The Gospels do not give us simple transcripts of the life of Jesus. Our four canonical Gospels are very different and give four different presentations of the life of Jesus. Discovering the historical Jesus from these sources (and bearing in mind other possible evidence as well) is a complex business. We have to account for the differences between John and the Synoptics, for those between the Synoptics themselves, and then use any theories and results in these areas to discriminate within our Gospels between what can confidently be traced back to the pre-Easter Jesus and what represents later Christian editing and activity. And one must bear in mind that any such later editorial activity took place within the context of the common Christian belief that the Jesus who had taught and worked in Galilee and died in Jerusalem was now alive in a new way, raised by God from the dead, and was guiding and still speaking to his church in the present. Any distinction that we might wish to make between authentic Jesus tradition and later Christian editing would have probably been totally unreal to a first-century Christian; the later Christian editing would no doubt have been assumed to be voice of the risen Jesus speaking to his church, and this risen Jesus was precisely the same person who had taught and worked in Galilee. All this indicates that the use of the Gospels to recover information about the pre-Easter Jesus is by no means straightforward.

More important, one should note that such a use of the Gospels is not necessarily the only one with any theological value. Undoubtedly for Christians, the person of Jesus has central theological significance. But equally, responses to the whole Christ-event by Christians also have theological significance. And this is especially the case in relation to the earliest responses to Jesus: Precisely because they are the first responses, they stand as the fountainhead of all subsequent Christian tradition and directly influence all later Christian theologizing. Hence the importance of a figure like Paul. (Such a significance is, of course, closely related to, but not quite identical with, any ideas we might wish to hold of biblical authority.) The evangelists and their Gospels fall into this role as well. If at times we regard their Gospels less as sourcebooks giving us direct information about Jesus, and more as sources enabling us to see early Christians struggling to come to terms with their convictions about Jesus and to make these relevant to their own day, this will for some positively enhance, rather than detract from, their theological significance.

For Christians, the primary theological task is undoubtedly the same as that of the Gospel writers: to make beliefs and traditions about Jesus relevant to the present and to the situations we all face. Part of this process will, of course, involve the constant effort to ensure that the "Jesus" who is central to Christian faith is none other than the historical Jesus of Nazareth; hence the crucial importance of the critical effort to recover, and constantly check the accuracy of, information about Jesus that the available sources afford us. But the hermeneutical task is no less vital, and in this respect the Gospels also have much to teach us. If in some ways of studying the Gospels and considering the phenomenon of Jesus and the Gospels we see less of "Jesus" and more of the "gospels," their authors and their communities, that is no loss but a profound gain as we see, and seek to learn from, Christians engaged in struggles that are very similar to our own.

FOR FURTHER READING

General:

Allison, Dale C. *Jesus of Nazareth: Millenarian Prophet.* Minneapolis: Fortress, 1998.

Crossan, John Dominic. *The Birth of Christianity: Discovering What Happened in the Years Immediately after the Execution of Jesus.* San Francisco: HarperSanFrancisco, 1998.

Greenspoon, Leonard J., Dennis Hamm, Bryan F. Lebeau, eds. *The Historical Jesus Through Catholic and Jewish Eyes.* Harrisburg, Pa.: Trinity, 2000.

Harrington, Daniel J., S. J. *The Gospel of Matthew.* SP 1. Collegeville, Minn.: Liturgical Press, 1991.

Holladay, Carl R. "Contemporary Methods of Reading the Bible." In *NIB.* Nashville: Abingdon, 1994. 1:125-49.

Marshall, I. H., ed. *New Testament Interpretation.* Exeter: Paternoster, 1977.

Newman, Carey C. *Jesus and the Restoration of Israel: A Critical Assessment of N. T. Wright's Jesus and the Victory of God.* Downers Grove, Ill.: InterVarsity, 1999.

Powell, Mark Allen. *Jesus as a Figure in History: How Modern Historians View the Man From Galilee.* Louisville, Ky.: Westminster/John Knox, 1998.

Sanders, E. P., and M. Davies. *Studying the Synoptic Gospels.* Philadelphia: Trinity Press International, 1989.

Stanton, G. N. *The Gospels and Jesus.* Oxford: Oxford University Press, 1989.

Stefemann, Wolfgang, Bruce J. Malina, and Gerd Theissen. *The Social Setting of Jesus and the Gospels.* Minneapolis, Minn.: Fortress, 2002.

Tuckett, C. M. *Reading the New Testament.* Philadelphia: Fortress, 1987; London: SPCK, 1987.

Vermes, Geza. *Jesus in His Jewish Context.* Minneapolis, Minn.: Fortress, 2003.

Wright, N. T. *The Contemporary Quest for Jesus.* Facets. Minneapolis, Minn.: Fortress, 2002.

Genre:

Aune, D. E. *The New Testament in Its Literary Environment.* Philadelphia: Westminster, 1987.

Burridge, R. A. *What Are the Gospels? A Comparison with Greco-Roman Biography.* Cambridge: Cambridge University Press, 1992.

Source Criticism:

Synoptic Problem:

Bellinzoni, A., ed. *The Two Source Hypothesis.* Macon: Mercer University Press, 1985.

Farmer, W. R. *The Synoptic Problem.* 2nd ed. New York: Macmillan, 1976.

Fitzmyer, J. A. "The Priority of Mark and the 'Q' Source in Luke." In *Jesus and Man's Hope.* Vol. 1. Pittsburgh: Pittsburgh Theological Seminary, 1970.

Hoffman, Paul, John S. Kloppenborg, and James M. Robbinson, eds. *The Critical Edition of Q: Synopsis Including the Gospels of Matthew and Luke, Mark and Thomas with English, German, and French translations of Q and Thomas.* Hermeneia. Minneapolis, Minn.: Fortress, 2000.

Labahn, Michael, and Andreas Schmidt, eds. *Jesus, Mark and Q: The Teaching of Jesus and its Earliest Records.* JSNTSup 214. Sheffield: Sheffield Academic Press, 2001.

McKnight, Scot and Matthew C. Williams. *The Synoptic Gospels: An Annotated Bibliography.* IBR Bibliographies 6. Grand Rapids, Mich.: Baker, 2000.

Streeter, B. H. *The Four Gospels.* London: Macmillan, 1924.

John:

Fortna, R. *The Fourth Gospel and Its Predecessor.* Philadelphia: Fortress, 1988.

Lindars, B. *Behind the Fourth Gospel.* London: SPCK, 1971.

Smith, D. M. *Johannine Christianity.* Columbia: University of South Carolina Press, 1984.

Form Criticism:

Barbour, R. S. *Traditio-Historical Criticism of the Gospels.* London: SPCK, 1972.

Bultmann, R. *The History of the Synoptic Tradition.* Oxford: Blackwells, 1968.

Dibelius, M. *From Tradition to Gospel.* New York: Scribners, 1934.

McKnight, E. V. *What Is Form Criticism?* Philadelphia: Fortress, 1969.

Non-Synoptic Evidence:

Koester, H. *Ancient Christian Gospels.* Philadelphia: Trinity Press International, 1990.

Redaction Criticism:

Perrin, N. *What Is Redaction Criticism?* Philadelphia: Fortress, 1969.

Petersen, N. R. *Literary Criticism for New Testament Critics.* Philadelphia: Fortress, 1978.

Powell, M. A. *What Is Narrative Criticism?* Minneapolis: Augsburg Fortress, 1990.

ENDNOTES

1. In 1945 a cache of thirteen ancient books (codices) written in Coptic was discovered just across the Nile River east of Nag Hammadi, Egypt. The codices, which date to the fourth century CE, reflect a combination of Christian and gnostic influences.

2. Q stands for *Quelle*, the German term for "source."

THE GOSPEL OF MATTHEW

M. EUGENE BORING

The gospel was a message before it became a book. *Gospel* (εὐαγγέλιον *euaggelion*) is the term used by the early church for the good news of the saving act of God in Jesus Christ. The books called "Gospels" are in the New Testament canon because they mediate this saving message and because, with the rest of the canonical books, they are the norm for its continuing proclamation and interpretation.

Matthew was the "favorite" Gospel of early catholic Christianity. Although New Testament books, including the Gospels, were arranged in a variety of orders in the early manuscripts, Matthew was always first, just as it was the most-quoted by the Church Fathers. The modern reader can readily understand the several reasons for this favored position. Matthew is carefully structured to facilitate memory. Even today, it is likely that Christian readers acquainted with the location of key texts that occur in more than one Gospel (e.g., the beatitudes, the Lord's Prayer, Peter's confession, parables) will know the *Matthean* location. Moreover, it was believed that Matthew was written first and, unlike Mark and Luke, that it was written by an apostolic eyewitness. Besides, Matthew begins with a genealogy—distancing and forbidding to many modern readers—which served the ancient reader as a bridge connecting the Gospel with the story of salvation in the Hebrew Bible.

Responsible interpretation of the Gospel must correspond to the nature of the Gospel itself. The Gospel of Matthew, like all the New Testament Gospels, was composed as a *literary* work to interpret the *theological* meaning of a concrete *historical* event to people in a particular historical situation. An appropriate interpretation of the Gospels in the church will, therefore, be at once historical, literary, and theological. These approaches are not mutually exclusive, but correspond to the nature of the Gospel.

MATTHEW IN HISTORICAL PERSPECTIVE

Historical Criticism: Interpreting a Stratified Text. The Gospels are historical documents in the sense that each was concerned to interpret the theological meaning of a particular historical figure and was composed to address a concrete historical situation. The specific contours of Matthew's historical context will be discussed below. The concern here is to remind the contemporary reader that the Gospels were not written as a collection of general timeless truths, and that they were not written to us, but were directed to another historical situation in another time and place.

The historical nature of the Gospel means that authentic interpretation should be concerned with the meaning of the text in its original setting. Matthew, like all New Testament documents, should first be allowed to speak to the people of its own time in their conceptual framework, addressing their concerns. Then, if found also to speak to our concerns—and this is the conviction of the church in all ages and the reason for biblical study and preaching in the church—it will be the authentic word of the Bible speaking to us, not the reflection of our own desires, ideologies, and concerns. The subjective element in all interpretation prohibits any absolute distinction between the ancient meaning of the text and its contemporary meaning. Yet the quest for "what it meant" cannot be ignored in any responsible effort to discover "what it means" for our own time and place.

The Christian reader's concern to hear and understand the specific word of Matthew to his situation is a by-product of the particularity of the Christ-event. Just as Jesus of Nazareth was not humanity in general but a specific, time-conditioned historical individual, an Aramaic-speaking Jew of first-century Palestine, so also all of the canonical documents that mediate the meaning of this event are specific, time-conditioned historical documents. This fact is not to be lamented, but celebrated. While the doctrine of the advent of the Messiah affirms, to be sure, a christological truth about Jesus, it also makes an affirmation about the world and human life—namely, that God is present not only in the eternal absolutes of the transcendent world, but is manifest also in the historical ambiguities of this world and this life.

Historical interpretation is appropriate to a historical revelation, a historical Jesus, and a historical Bible. This means that every interpretation is finite, fragmentary, and inevitably involved in the relativities of history and human finitude. We interpreters are always involved in making finite judgments, and "probably" is often the best we can do. Historical study does not traffic in absolutes. This, too, is not to be lamented as a necessary evil; it is to be celebrated as the way the Word of God is mediated by a historical revelation in historical documents by historical interpreters. The following sections deal with particular dimensions of historical interpretation in the case of Matthew.

The Text of Matthew. Every student of Matthew reads a text that has been reconstructed because the original manuscript, like that of all New Testament documents, has been lost.[1] However, text critics have been able to establish the best text of Matthew (the one closest to the original text) with a great, but not absolute, degree of certainty. The two most widely used editions of the Greek New Testament have the same set of editors and hence the same text.[2] The critical apparatus for *The Greek New Testament, Fourth Edition*[4] (*UBSGNT*) gives data for 160 sets of variant readings in Matthew, selecting only those deemed most important for translation into other languages, while the 27th edition of the *Novum Testamentum Graece*[27] ("*Nestle-Aland*") gives data for more than a thousand variant readings in Matthew, likewise only a selection of the variations considered most important for exegesis. The reconstruction of the text in Matthew by Heinrich Greeven differs from that of *UBSGNT*[4] and *Nestle-Aland*[27] in 160 places.[3] This means that about six times per chapter, two of our standard editions of the Greek text of Matthew disagree as to the original wording of the Gospel. The NRSV is based on the standard *UBSGNT*[4]/*Nestle-Aland*[27] text, departing from it only very rarely, while the NIV is based on an eclectic text constructed by the translators. Thus the differences between the NIV and the NRSV are not necessarily variant translations, but reflections of the translators' differing judgment on the wording of the original Greek text.

Source Analysis. Sometimes still called "literary criticism," this approach attempts to determine which sources were used by the author, their nature and extent. During the nineteenth and early twentieth centuries, a scholarly consensus emerged that Matthew used Mark as a major source, along with a collection of sayings of Jesus (with a minimum of narrative) called "Q." This majority viewpoint has recently been challenged, and the whole question has been thoroughly reexamined in the last three decades.[4] There is less unanimity and dogmatism than previously, and simplistic solutions are now avoided, but the opinion of the great majority of scholars continues to be that Matthew used Q (in a slightly different form from the version used by Luke) and Mark (perhaps in a slightly revised form from canonical Mark) as his major sources, along with materials peculiar to his own stream of tradition ("M"). The two-source hypothesis, so understood, remains the best working hypothesis for study of the synoptic Gospels.

Form Criticism. Matthew's written sources depended on living oral tradition. For some decades after the Easter events, the materials from and about Jesus were transmitted orally in the life of the Christian community as individual stories and sayings, and collections of the same. During this period, each story or saying was communicated and heard not as part of a "life of Jesus," but as a witness to the meaning of the Christ-event as a whole in the church's preaching, teaching, worship, conflicts, and clarification of its own understanding of the meaning of Christ and the Christian life. Each unit of the tradition was thus a theological witness to the meaning of the Christian faith and was subject to continual expansion, modification, and reinterpretation in order to communicate the meaning of the faith to changing situations.

As the church passed on the traditions from and about Jesus, the individual units of tradition assumed a number of forms, which the church had adopted and adapted from its Jewish and Hellenistic environment. The following list, based on the work of Rudolf Bultmann, supplemented with recent developments, shows the major types of materials, many of which have subtypes:

I. The Sayings Material
  A. *Apothegms* (pithy sayings of Jesus that serve as the "punch line" for a brief narrative context; also called "pronouncement stories" and paradigms). The *chreia* is a related form with even less narrative framework.
  B. *Dominical Sayings* (sayings of Jesus that circulated independently in the tradition—i.e., without a narrative framework).
    1. *Logia,* also called "proverbs" or "wisdom sayings" (Matt 6:27-28; 7:6; 10:10*b*).
    2. Prophetic and apocalyptic sayings (Matt 5:3-9; 10:32-33; 11:21-24; 16:28).
    3. Legal sayings and church rules (Matt 6:2-4, 5-6, 16-18)
    4. "I" sayings (Matt 5:17)
    5. Similitudes and parables (Matt 13:3-9; Mark 4:3-9)

II. The Narrative Material
  A. Miracles Stories (Matt 8:23-27; 9:1-8).
  B. Historical Stories and Legends (Matt 3:13-17; Mark 1:9-11)[5]

The Structure of the Sermon on the Mount

Introduction: Setting of the Sermon	4:23—5:22	Mark 1:39; 3:7-13/Luke 6:12, 17-20*a*
I. Triadic Pronouncements That Constitute the Disciples as the Eschatological Community, 5:3-16		
A. The Beatitudes: Character and Destiny of the Disciples	5:3:12	Luke 6:20*b*-23
B. The Disciples as Salt	5:13	Luke 14:34-35/Mark 9:49-50
C. The Disciples as Light and a City on a Hill	5:14-16	Luke 8:16; 11:33/Mark 4:21
II. Tripartite Instructions on the Way of Life in the Eschatological Community, 5:17–7:12		
A. Part One: "The Law"	5:17-48	
1. The law and the "Greater Righteousness"	5:17-20	Luke 16:16-17
2. Three Antitheses Modeling the Greater Righteousness, 5:21-32		
a. Anger	5:21-26	Luke 12:57-59/Mark 11:25
b. Lust	5:27-30	Mark 9:43
c. Divorce	5:31-32	Luke 16:18/Mark 10:3-4; 11:12
3. Three Antitheses for the Disciples' application, 5:33-48		
a. Oaths	5:33-37	M
b. Retaliation	5:38-42	Luke 6:29-30
c. Love	5:43-48	Luke 6:27-28, 32-36
B. Part Two: "The Temple Service": Three Acts of Righteousness Before God, 6:1-18		
1. Giving to Charity	6:1-4	M
2. Prayer, 6:5-15		
a. Not like the hypocrites or the Gentiles	6:5-8	M
b. The Lord's Prayer	6:9-13	Luke 11:2-4
c. The condition of forgiveness	6:14-15	Mark 11:25(-26)
3. Fasting	6:16-18	M
C. Part Three: "Deeds of Loving Kindness": Additional Instruction in Authentic Righteousness, 6:19–7:12		
1. Serving god or Mammon	6:19-24	Luke 12:33-34; 11:34-36; 16:13
2. Anxiety	6:25-34	Luke 12:22-32
3. Judging	7:1-5	Luke 6:37-43/Mark 4:24-25
4. Pearls Before Swine	7:6	M
5. Asking and Receiving	7:7-11	Luke 11:9-13
6. Concluding summary: The Golden Rule	7:12	Luke 6:31
III. Three Eschatological Warnings, 7:13-27		
A. Two Ways	7:13-14	Luke 13:23-24
B. Two Harvests (False Prophets)	7:15-23	Luke 6:43-46; 13:25-27
C. Two Builders	7:24-27	Luke 6:47-49
Conclusion off the Sermon	7:28-29	Mark 1:22

Form criticism studies the form, setting, function, and meaning of these individual units of tradition during the period of oral transmission. Since the form of the material is inseparably bound to both its function and its meaning, determining the form of a passage and perceiving how it functioned in its early-church setting is one of the steps of sound exegesis. Form-critical studies give the contemporary interpreter a sense of the dynamism of the early Christian community, which both maintained continuity with the past by faithfully handing on the traditions and creatively modified them to address new situations. This perspective is particularly appropriate to Matthew's theological perspective, in which the living Christ accompanies his church through history as its Teacher (see 1:23; 18:20; 28:20).

Redaction Criticism. The study of how the authors of the Gospels selected, arranged, modified, and added to the tradition in the composition of the Gospels is called redaction criticism. In the case of Matthew, this means especially attending to how he has incorporated and sometimes rewritten Q and Mark. As source analysis had concentrated on the sources behind our present Gospels, and form criticism had concentrated on the individual units of tradition behind all our sources, redaction criticism returned to a concern for the meaning of the final form of the whole document. Special attention was paid to the theological tendencies of the evangelist, seen in the additions, omissions, and modifications in the sources. As the evangelists were increasingly recognized to be composers and not merely editors, this discipline was sometimes called "composition criticism," and tended to modulate into the kind of literary criticism discussed below.

Tradition Criticism and the "Three Levels" of Historical Gospel Study. For the sake of a clearer understanding it will sometimes be important to consider what a particular story or saying might have meant in its pre-Matthean setting, whether in the life of Jesus or the life of the church prior to Matthew. However, also important is disclosure of the meaning of the text as Matthew composed it for his own time and place. The distinction between the pre-Easter life of Jesus and the post-Easter meaning in Matthew's church is especially important in this regard.

However, perceiving the sweep of tradition from Jesus to the written Gospels is important for understanding the nature and meaning of the final form of the canonical text. "Tradition criticism" is often used as an umbrella term for studying the whole course of the tradition from Jesus to the completed Gospels. This should be thought of as a dynamic process, as the stories and sayings from and about Jesus were preached, reinterpreted, and handed on in the various streams of early Christianity.

Of every saying or story represented by a Gospel pericope, one may ask three sets of historical questions: (1) Does this unit of tradition tell us something about the actual life of Jesus of Nazareth? If so, what did it mean in that setting? (2) Was this unit of tradition transmitted by the church between the time of Jesus and the time the Gospels were compiled orally, in written sources, or both? If so, what changes did it experience in that period, and what did it mean in that setting? (3) What contribution did the evangelist make in composing the final form of the text, and what is the meaning of this text in the evangelist's context?

In practice, historical method requires that one begin with the final form of the text, work backward through the layers to the historical Jesus, and then forward again through the history of the tradition to the final form of the text in the Gospels. Assuming that Jesus' ministry can be dated about 30 CE and that Matthew was written about 90 CE, this means that in every Matthean text the historical interpreter should try to distinguish the 30 CE Jesus meaning(s), the 30–90 CE church meaning(s), and the 90 CE meaning(s) in Matthew's own text and situation.

But such analysis should not be misunderstood as though the only "authentic" materials are those that "go back to Jesus." Matthew, like the other evangelists and those prior to him who handed on the oral tradition, interpreted by retelling, modifying, omitting and expanding, including the creation of new stories and sayings. Matthew stands in a long biblical and Jewish tradition in which such creative midrashic retelling was the legitimate means of reinterpretation, as illustrated, e.g., by Deuteronomy's retelling of the exodus story, or the Chronicler's retelling of the David story, in each case with modifications and expansions, including the creation of new sayings and speeches for the characters in the story.[6]

Despite the value of such historical study of the developing tradition "behind" the text, the object and norm of the church's study, teaching, and proclamation is the text of the Bible in its present canonical form. All of Matthew is to be taken seriously as the church's Scripture, not simply, or even particularly, the relatively more "historical" elements, for the text as a whole mediates the church's message of the meaning of the Christ-event.

MATTHEW'S REINTERPRETATION OF SACRED DOCUMENTS AND TRADITIONS

Although Matthew was influenced by and makes use of religious ideas that were in the air in the Hellenistic world, his Gospel reflects no direct literary influence from pagan writings. His reading seems to have been limited exclusively to Jewish and Christian religious documents.

Jewish Sources. The one set of documents that we may be certain was present in Matthew's community and exercised a profound influence on the composition of his Gospel is the Septuagint (LXX), a Greek translation of Hebrew Scripture. Matthew's tensions with the Jewish community did not result in any lessening of his interest in the Jewish Scriptures. On the contrary, he was concerned to show that the Jewish Scriptures find their fulfillment in Jesus and the church.

Matthew contains no direct quotations from the apocryphal/deuterocanonical books or any other literature outside the Hebrew canon. The fact that Matthew was acquainted with many of the ideas and phrases used in both the deuterocanonical and pseudepigraphal writings seems to be clear, however, from the fact that the Gospel has 78 allusions to them (58 to the apocrypha, 20 to other extra-canonical texts, such as 4 Maccabees and *1 Enoch*).[7]

Importance of Scripture for Matthew. Matthew directly quotes the Scripture forty times with an explicit indication, such as "it is written" (e.g., Matt 4:4 = Deut 8:3). Matthew also contains several other direct citations not explicitly so identified (e.g., 27:46 = Ps 22:1; their exact number depends on how strictly one distinguishes between quotation and allusion). The *Nestle-Aland* identifies twenty-one such quotations, making a total of sixty-one direct quotations in twenty-eight chapters. In addition to direct quotations, Matthew's text contains a plethora of biblical paraphrases, allusions, and imagery, the exact number again depending on how strictly one determines the criteria for identifying an allusion. The count of such allusions varies from 294 in the *Nestle-Aland* to thirty in the list provided for translators by the American Bible Society.[8]

On any analysis, Matthew's mind and text are thoroughly steeped in the Scriptures, containing considerably more such quotations and allusions than any of the other Gospels.

Distribution. Of the sixty-one quotations, twenty-four are taken over from Mark and nine from Q. Twenty-eight quotations, however, are peculiar to Matthew. Ten of these quotations are Matthean additions to Markan contexts, three are added to Q contexts, and fifteen are in peculiarly Matthean material. Thus Matthew introduces almost as many quotations as he takes over from his sources, and often adds quotations to his sources. Matthew never omits a biblical quotation from the Markan or Q material he incorporates, and he preserves most of the allusions as well.

Practically all of the direct citations belong to two categories: either Jesus quotes the Scripture to other characters in the story (43 times), or the narrator quotes the Scripture to the reader (13 times). The remaining quotations are divided among the high priests and scribes (2:5-6), the Sadducees (22:24), the devil (4:6), and the crowds (21:9), with one quotation being shared by the scribes, the disciples, and Jesus (17:10-11). Neither the disciples nor the Pharisees ever quote the Scripture directly.

The following books from the Hebrew Bible are quoted. The first figure indicates the number of quotations distinctive to Matthew; the second figure indicates the total number of quotations from the book: Genesis 0/3; Exodus 3/5; Leviticus 2/3; Numbers 0/1; Deuteronomy 2/8; Psalms 4/12; Isaiah 5/10; Jeremiah 2/2; Daniel 2/5; Hosea 3/3; Jonah 1/1; Micah 1/2; Zechariah 2/3 (cited as "Jeremiah" in 27:9); Malachi 0/2; and the unknown reference cited in 2:23. As in the other Gospels and the New Testament as a whole, Matthew cites most often the Psalms, Isaiah, and Deuteronomy. No direct citations are taken from apocryphal and pseudepigraphical books, but there may be allusions to them (e.g., Matt 11:29/ Sirach 6:24-25, 28-30; Matt 27:43/ Wis 2:13, 18-20; Matt 5:5/1 Enoch 5:7; Matt 25:31/1 Enoch 61:8; 62:2-3).

In Matthew's time the text of the Bible was in the process of standardization by the rabbinic/scribal leadership emanating from Jamnia. This is dramatically illustrated by the difference in the biblical texts from Qumran (hidden 70 CE), which manifest great variety, and those from the time of the Second Revolt in 132–135 CE, found in the Wadi Murabba'at, which are uniformly of the Masoretic type, indicating that the standardization of the text was effectively accomplished during that period. Since in Matthew's time the text had not yet been standardized, a variety of text forms in both Hebrew and Greek existed in the Judaism of Matthew's day.

The OT citations in Mark are consistently from the LXX, and the few direct quotations in Q are almost as consistently from the LXX. Matthew's incorporation of Mark and Q material retained their citations in LXX form, sometimes even adjusting them slightly to make them closer to the LXX. Some of the quotations peculiar to Matthew, or introduced by him into Markan or Q contexts, also are of the LXX type. The LXX was thus a familiar and respected translation in Matthew's community; it seems to have been the primary version of the Bible used by Matthew himself. Sometimes the point of the quotation is absent from the Hebrew text and depends on the Greek translation, including quotations placed in Jesus' mouth (e.g., 21:16 = Ps 8:3 LXX).

The Formula Quotations. A special category is formed by ten "formula quotations," sometimes called "reflection citations" (*Reflexionszitaten*) or "fulfillment quotations" (see 1:22-23; 2:15; 2:17-18; 2:23; 4:14b-16; 8:17; 12:18-21; 13:35; 21:4-5; 27:9-10). All are introduced by Matthew into their contexts. Except for the four formula quotations in the birth narrative, all are triggered by a Markan context. Apart from the citation of Zech 9:9 in Matt 21:4-5, none are cited elsewhere in the New Testament. They thus seem not to belong to a standard repertoire of early Christian proof texts, but exclusively to Matthew and/or his own tradition. They are distinguished from the other quotations, including the others peculiar to Matthew, (a) by their introductory formula identifying an event in Jesus' life as the fulfillment of Scripture; (b) by the fact that all are spoken not by a character in the story to other characters, but by the narrator to the reader; and (c) by their text type. The full introductory formula is found in the first quotation, "All this took place to fulfill what had been spoken by the Lord through the prophet" (1:22), and is repeated with minor variations in all the others.[9] "To fulfill" translates ἵνα πληρωθῇ (*hina plērōthē*), which may mean "result" rather than "purpose." While Matthew generally follows the LXX, these ten quotations are distinctive in that they diverge from the LXX and from all other known text types. It is debated whether this means that they represent a lost text type, or are the products of a Matthean Christian scribal exegetical "school," or represent Matthew's own hermeneutical work on the text. In any case, they seem to represent the result of a kind of Christian scribal activity. They are not as arbitrarily placed as they may seem to us, but within the first-century Jewish context represent a sophisticated and subtle approach to Scripture. This form of interpretation, which adapts the text to fit more closely the presupposed fulfillment, was practiced in other streams of first-century Judaism, and bears some resemblance to the *pesher* mode of interpretation practiced at Qumran. It has sometimes been argued that the fulfillment quotations represent a pre-Matthean Christian collection of proof texts, or testimonia, but this is unlikely since they are all integrated into their contexts and can hardly be thought to have existed as a collection apart from their present contexts. Since they reflect Matthean themes, they seem to be the product of the same school within which the Gospel was formulated or, more likely, to have been arranged by Matthew himself.

Matthew's Theology of Fulfillment. It has often been thought that Matthew's use of Scripture is apologetic, that he is concerned to prove the messiahship of Jesus to the Jews using their own Scripture. This is a mistaken notion for two reasons: (1) The Gospel of Matthew is not directed to outsiders in order to convert them, but to insiders to express, clarify, and strengthen their faith. In particular, Matthew is not directed to Jews outside the Christian community—though Matthew's church has a strong Jewish-Christian element and a long tradition within Judaism. (2) As "proof," Matthew's use of Scripture is not convincing. If he is thought to be assembling scriptural evidence for Jesus' messiahship, his Christian interpretation of the texts in contrast with their obvious original meaning, along with the changes he makes in the text itself, make him subject to the charge of manipulating the evidence in a way that would be unconvincing to outsiders.

What Matthew's use of Scripture reflects is not apologetics directed to outsiders, but confession directed to insiders. The conviction that Jesus is the Christ is the presupposition of his use of Scripture, not the result of it. From the earliest times, the idea that the Christ is the fulfillment of Scripture was the universal conviction of early Christianity. At first this was a general conviction, without specific elaboration, as in the early Christian creed cited by Paul in 1 Cor 15:3-5. The traditions that came to Matthew were already permeated with this conviction, illustrated by specific OT texts. In particular, Mark had repeatedly referred to specific events in Jesus' life as unfolding in accordance with Scripture (but without the fulfillment formula), and at the end of the story Mark has Jesus say, "But let the scriptures be fulfilled" (Mark 14:49). Matthew seems to have taken up this Markan hint and elaborated it into his ten fulfillment citations. (Cf. his emphatic rewriting of Mark 14:49 in Matt 26:56.) It is Matthew's conviction that, as the Messiah, Jesus is the fulfillment of the Scripture as a whole is expressed in his interpretation of individual texts.

Given Matthew's presupposition that the Christ is the fulfillment of Scripture, and his view that the Scripture as a whole (esp. the Prophets) predicted the eschatological times, which Matthew saw as dawning with the advent of Christ, it is understandable that he uses Scripture to add details to his story of Jesus. We can see this happening also in non-canonical documents, such as Justin Martyr's version of the story of Jesus' triumphal entry into Jerusalem, in which the colt on which Jesus rode was found "bound to a vine."[10] This detail is not found in any early Christian story, but comes from Gen 49:10-11, which Justin took to be a prophecy of Christ. Likewise, in Matt 27:42-43, the words of the chief priests, scribes, and elders at the cross are taken from Mark 15:32 and then augmented with the words of Ps 22:8. Since we can observe the growth of the tradition on the basis of Christian exegesis of the Old Testament in passages we can check, the question arises whether, in those places where we have no direct control, the Matthean scribal community, and Matthew himself, created narrative elements or even whole narrative units as an expression of their faith that the Scripture was fulfilled in Jesus. It may well be that the correspondence of "prediction" and "fulfillment," from Matthew's point of view, fits so well because elements of the narrative were generated by hermeneutical interaction with the scriptural text.

This hermeneutical phenomenon went both ways. The fact that Jesus came from Nazareth generated a "prediction" in 2:23. This would also explain why many modern interpreters have difficulty seeing the OT as a "prediction" in the first place, since they no longer share Matthew's hermeneutical presuppositions and methods. The hermeneutical task for the contemporary interpreter of the Gospels is to share Matthew's conviction that the Christ came as the fulfillment of Scripture, expressed in his theology and illustrated and communicated by his own interpretative techniques. Contemporary readers may take seriously and appropriate Matthew's theology, without being bound to adopt Matthew's hermeneutical methods as our own. An aspect of the historical conditionedness of biblical revelation is that Matthew interpreted Scripture in a way appropriate to his own time. We do not belong to that time, and so we must interpret Scripture using the methods appropriate to our own time. It is precisely our own historical method that allows us to see and appreciate Matthew's interpretation, to understand his witness to Christ in his own terms, and to be challenged to share his faith.

Christian Sources. *Pauline Letters and Traditions?* It has sometimes been suggested that Matthew is responding directly to Paul or Pauline Christianity (e.g., in 5:19), or even that Matthew had read Paul's letters and was influenced by them.[11] While the Gospel seems to have been written in Antioch or its environs (see below) where Paul had been active (Gal 2:11; cf. Acts 13:1; 14:26; 15:22), Paul's lasting influence in Antioch seems to have been minimal, hardly affecting the Matthean stream of Christianity. There are no indications of direct literary influence from the Pauline corpus.

The Sayings-collection Q. (Quelle, "Source") From the early history of the Matthean church, probably from the time of its founding, Q had been a revered document of the community's sacred tradition. Presumably, it was often read in the worship of the Matthean congregation(s), and shaped and expressed the ethos of Matthean Christianity. Q was not merely a source for the evangelist

Matthew; it was a part of the history of the community of which he was a part. Q assumed the continuing validity of the law characteristic of early Jewish Christianity (cf. Q 16:17 = Matt 5:18).[12] Matthew's respect for Q may be seen in the fact that when Mark and Q overlap, Matthew often prefers the older and more rigorous Q version (see 10:10 = Luke 10:4; cf. Mark 6:8-9). Matthew set forth a major reinterpretation of Q not only by the (relatively minor) modifications he made in this document, which was part of the sacred tradition of his church, but also primarily by incorporating it within the narrative structure of the Gospel of Mark. In its original form, Q tended to be a growing, unstable document, too readily amenable to expansion by new "sayings of the risen Jesus" spoken by Christian prophets. By inserting it into the pre-resurrection framework of Mark's narrative, Matthew was able both to preserve the continuing address of Jesus to his church through Q and to prohibit its continued expansion by grounding it in the history of the pre-Easter Jesus.[13]

The Gospel of Mark. Some time after 70 CE the Gospel of Mark arrived in the Matthean community, was accepted as part of the community's own sacred tradition, and was used in its life and worship. Mark had been written in and for a Gentile Christian community no longer living under the rule of Torah (Mark 7:1-23). Matthew's Jewish-Christian community carried on a mission to Gentiles and was open to the insights of Gentile Christianity. The narrative of Mark became a fundamental part of the Matthean church's way of telling the Jesus-story, along with its characteristic emphases: Jesus the miracle worker, Jesus the crucified and risen one, Jesus the inaugurator of the Gentile mission. If the Gospel of Mark was already associated with Peter, this strengthened the emphasis on Peter as the leading apostle, already present in the Matthean stream of tradition, and facilitated Mark's acceptance as a normative Christian text for Matthew's church. Matthew did not merely "combine" Q and Mark. He made the Markan narrative basic, inserting his Q and M materials into the Markan story line, to which they were subordinated. Matthew is an elaboration and new interpretation of the Markan narrative, not of the Q sayings collection.

The Special Matthean Materials and Traditions ("M"). In addition to Q and Mark, Matthew followed traditions and materials peculiar to his own community. "M" was not a separate document, but represents the body of peculiarly Matthean traditions. Since these traditions were formed or handed down by the local churches that also helped form Matthew's own theological perspective, it is at times difficult to distinguish M tradition from Matthew's redaction. M may have contained collections of Scripture quotations particularly relevant to Matthean theology, (*testimonia*), Christian scribal interpretations of such quotations, midrashic comments and developments of Q and Markan texts and other items of Christian tradition, as well as sayings and stories from and about Jesus unique to the Matthean tradition. Although a few of these materials could have been written down prior to Matthew, most, if not all, were handed on orally for a generation or more prior to Matthew. It is often the case that they had already been adapted, modified, and expanded to address new situations; sometimes they preserved earlier forms of the tradition with remarkable fidelity, especially traditions affirming earlier Jewish Christianity's adherence to the Torah.

Matthew and His Community's Use of This Sacred Tradition. Matthew, steeped in all of his community's sacred texts and traditions, treated them all with great seriousness and respect without being slavishly bound to any of them. Just as Matthew was familiar enough with the Jewish Scriptures to make scores of allusions to it without specifically calling attention to it, so also Q, Mark, and M formed part of the warp and woof of his mind. His use of Q and Mark is at the farthest pole from a "cut-and-paste" use of them as "sources." Matthew's mind is so saturated with Q and Mark that he can allude to them even in sections where he is not "using" them. Markan phrases creep into a Q passage, and vice versa. A phrase from Q becomes a favorite "Matthean" phrase, used repeatedly in non-Q passages.[14] It is important to note that these texts had been used for decades in Matthew's church, and not only Matthew himself, but also his intended hearers/readers were intimately familiar with them.[15] Matthew does not write for naive readers.

Redaction criticism's careful attention to the interpretative changes Matthew made in his sacred tradition represented by Q and Mark is not merely a modern academic exercise, but represents the experience of the hearers/readers of the

Matthean community who were already familiar with Q, Mark, and M, and who needed a new way to read them in a changed situation. Like the Chronicler's retelling/interpretation of the story of Samuel and the monarchy in 1–2 Chronicles, Matthew retells the familiar story with respect, skill, and midrashic imagination.

This reinterpretation did not happen in a vacuum. Thus one must determine the settings—social, political, religious, ecclesiastical—within which the Gospel of Matthew emerged.

Matthew's Christian Community. The Gospel of Matthew is not the product of an isolated author, but reflects the life and concerns of a particular Christian community. Matthew has long been known as the most ecclesiastical Gospel, the only Gospel to use the word *church* to describe the community of believers (16:18; 18:17). Matthew's church has obviously been involved in an intense relationship with the surrounding dominant Jewish community, and it cannot be defined, as it did not define itself, apart from that relationship.

Relation to the Jewish Community. *Matthew as a "Jewish" Gospel.* The Gospel of Matthew has traditionally and popularly been known as the Jewish Gospel, sometimes over against Luke or John as the Gentile Gospel. Matthew does, of course, have interests that are distinctively Jewish (e.g., concern for the law, Sabbath, Temple). He feels no need to explain Jewish customs, as did his Markan source (cf. Matt 15:1 to Mark 7:1-4). Matthew's Gospel contains texts that suggest that his community is still subject to the disciplinary measures of the synagogue authorities (10:17-23; 23:2), and perhaps that it still keeps the sabbath (24:20). And Matthew does sometimes make *Gentiles* synonymous with *pagan* (5:47; 6:7, 32; 18:17; 20:25). But some features traditionally designated "Jewish" are manifested in the other "Gentile" Gospels (e.g., genealogy, fulfillment of the Scriptures). In particular, it must be pointed out that Matthew's interest in the Scripture, including his allusions to it, which assumes that his readers were biblically literate, does not establish the "Jewishness" of Matthew, since, e.g., the Gospel of Luke and Paul's Letter to the Romans display a similar use of Scripture, and since all our Gospels preserve traditions from Jewish Christianity and manifest varying degrees of Jewishness.

Jewish Christianity was not a monolith, but a spectrum of groups with a variety of stances toward the law. It is thus somewhat simplistic to think of Matthew as *the* Jewish Gospel, particularly since it has considerable elements that reflect an alienation from Judaism. We may mention, for example, references to "their" synagogues (4:23; 9:35; 10:17; 12:9; 13:54; 23:34),[16] to "their" scribes (7:29), and a final reference to "the Jews" as though they were another group (28:15). There are also instances where Matthew has a *less* Jewish version of a saying than its Lukan parallel (Matt 10:37// Luke 14:26; Matt 10:28//Luke 12:4-5; Matt 5:18//Luke 16:17). In Matt 18:15-20, problems of discipline come before the church, not before the synagogue. Furthermore, Matthew has some (strong!) pro-Gentile tendencies, not only Jewish ones (e.g., 28:18-20).[17] Thus Matthew is "both deeply Jewish and painfully anti-Jewish."[18]

Matthew's church saw itself as the messianic community, the eschatological people of God, distinct from all—Jew or Gentile—who did not believe in Jesus as the Messiah. Matthew continued the Jewish practice of using *Gentile* in the sense of "outsider." Thus both his anti-Jewishness and his anti-Gentile bias are, in effect, expressions of his sense of belonging to the Christian community distinct from the non-Christian world, both Jewish and Gentile. The Gospel draws the line between believers and non-believers in Christ; it is Christ, not Jewishness, that divides people (10:21-22, 32-39). But even this division, though affirmed, is also transcended (see 25:31-46). Designations of one Gospel as "Jewish" and another as "Gentile" or "universal" are misleading and should be abandoned.

Ambiguity of Data About Judaism. Our data for assessing Matthew's relation to Judaism is not clear. There was no monolithic Judaism of Matthew's time that can serve as a fixed point of comparison. Like early Christianity, Judaism in the late first century was itself in a process of flux and development, seeking its way forward after the catastrophic war of 66–70 CE. Neither is there any unambiguous contemporary source. Pharisaic and developing Rabbinic Judaism of Matthew's time must be reconstructed from later Jewish sources, which tend to reflect later issues and situations. Thus, on the one hand, we lack a clear picture of "the" Judaism of Matthew's time.

On the other hand, the Gospel contains traditions from various periods and situations, so that it is not always clear what represents Matthew's own situation and what represents a time when the pre-Matthean community may have been more rigorously Jewish than Matthew's own church had become.[19] Thus some data in the Gospel can be interpreted in opposite ways. For example, Matthew is not concerned with the issue of circumcision for Gentile converts, which we know was important for the first-generation Gentile mission (see Acts 13–15; Galatians 1–4). In theory, this datum could mean either that Matthew's church was still within a thoroughly Jewish context where circumcision was assumed, or that the church had become so thoroughly oriented to the Gentile mission that circumcision was no longer an issue.

This means that the traditional way of posing the question of whether Matthew's church was still "Jewish" and "in" the synagogue or "Gentile" and already "out" of the synagogue is no longer adequate. Rather than representing Judaism and the synagogue as static entities, with a post-70 "council" of Jamnia making decrees for an established Judaism, we should think rather of an extended period after the 66–70 war, stretching to the time of the codification of the Mishnah (about 200 CE) as the period of "formative Judaism." During this time, the pre-70 Pharisaic party, although now dominant, still competed with other Jewish groups that had survived the war (priestly, scribal, apocalyptic, Christian, to some minor extent even Sadducean and Zealot) and finally established itself as the definitive element in that kind of Rabbinic Judaism that became "normative."[20] Within this mix, the Matthean community was apparently a movement still related to formative Judaism, a group that regarded itself as the authentic people of God, experiencing itself as a persecuted minority at the hands of the dominant Pharisaic leadership (see, e.g., 5:13-16; 10:23, 32-33, 40-42; 25:31-46). Historically, although there were instances of Jewish persecution of some early Christians—i.e., of Jewish Christians who were still within the synagogue structure and subject to its discipline—there was no extensive or systematic persecution by Jews of Christians as such. Jewish persecution of early Christians should neither be magnified as fuel for anti-Semitism nor denied altogether in the interest of contemporary Jewish-Christian relations. Such instances of Jewish persecution of Christians were not a matter of one religion or race oppressing another, not a matter of outsiders interfering in the religious practices of another group (and not at all like the later Christian pogroms against the Jewish community). Such texts as 10:17 and 23:34 reflect an internal struggle of Jew vs. Jew, analogous to the internal conflicts among Christians in the Reformation period.

Results: Clear Affirmations and Continuing Questions. As a result of recent studies, we may make the following clear affirmations as a basis for further interpretation of the Gospel of Matthew:

The Gospel of Matthew does not understand itself to represent a new religion, Christianity, over against a different religion, Judaism. Nor does it regard the church as the "new Israel" that replaces the "old" Israel. Matthew regards the Christian community of Jews and Gentiles as the continuation of the people of God, to come to eschatological fulfillment at the time when "the twelve tribes of Israel" are regathered. Both Israel and the church must undergo the judgment of the Son of Man.

Matthew does, however, see those Jews who had rejected Jesus as the Messiah, especially their leadership (scribes, Pharisees, Sadducees, high priests), as having forfeited their claim as the people of God (21:43). Thus in Matthew's view empirical Israel is henceforth one nation among others, called along with them to constitute the continuing people of God by confessing Jesus as the Messiah and living by his teaching (10:32-33; 28:18-20).

The Jewish elements in the Gospel do not mean that it was written for the Jews in the sense that it was directed to Jewish outsiders to convince them that Jesus is the Messiah. Matthew wrote his Gospel for members of his own community to instruct them in their own faith and to clarify it over against misunderstandings, not as an evangelistic or apologetic writing directed to outsiders.

Matthew was in some kind of continuity, intense dialogue, and debate with formative Judaism. Developments in contemporary formative Judaism, including especially what was going on at Jamnia and its effects in the synagogues in Matthew's own environs, are of deep concern to him. He had the developing Pharisaic leadership and its program for all Judaism in view as the chief opponents and alternatives to his own understanding of the way forward for the people of God. His Gospel includes traditional Jewish-Christian materials that are in some sense superseded, but were important enough for him to include, and in some sense to affirm. While such texts as 10:16-25 express Christians' alienation from "their" synagogues, the fact that Christians could be beaten in these synagogues and brought before local Jewish courts (sanhedrins) indicates that the victims of such abuse were still in some sense considered within the Jewish community. In this sense, Matthew's church was "Jewish."

Although Matthew's church and/or the Q community from which it sprang had previously carried on an unsuccessful mission to the Jewish people, it now abandoned a specifically Jewish mission, no longer seeing itself as a renewal movement in Judaism, and engaged in a mission to the Gentiles—i.e., the "nations," of which Israel is now one (28:18-20). Matthew understood the present and future of his church to be oriented to the Gentiles, and thus regarded developing non-Christian Judaism only as a competitor and opponent. In this sense, Matthew's church was "Gentile."

Questions remain. In particular, the question of the "*Birkath ha-Minim*" ("Blessing [Curse] Against the Heretics") is unresolved. At the newly founded academy and rabbinic court at Jamnia, which was assuming leadership in the reconstitution of Judaism after the 66–70 war, one of the synagogue prayers was reformulated to include a curse against the "*minim*" (separatists, heretics). The later Church Fathers understood this to be directed against Christians, and thus claimed that Christians were cursed in the Jewish synagogues.[21] It has sometimes been argued that this prayer served as a tool in ferreting out Christians in the synagogue (who, of course, could not participate in this part of the liturgy) in order to force them out of the synagogue.[22] The wording of the prayer changed over time, in part due to fear of Christian reprisals, so that the original wording is disputed. It is not clear that it originally included a reference to Christians, but may have been directed against any group considered heretical by the Jamnian leaders.[23] Nor is it clear that in Matthew's time the Jamnian leadership had authority to regulate the synagogue liturgy. It is thus an oversimplification to regard the *Birkath ha-Minim* as proof that Matthew and his community had been officially excluded from formative Judaism, and to regard Matthew's Gospel primarily as the response of an excommunicated group to Jamnia. Thus the *Birkath ha-Minim* cannot be made the basis of an interpretation of Matthew's situation. Nonetheless, the evidence is clear that there were deep tensions between developing Judaism and Matthew's church, which had its own sense of identity, structures, and procedures for excommunication and promulgating new authoritative teachings over against formative Judaism.

Was Matthew's church a sect? Certainly not in the sense that Qumran was, a community that withdrew from the rest of society, for Matthew's church did not passively withdraw and turn inward, but carried on an active mission to the world. Yet there are sectarian features of Matthew's church,[24] in that it claimed to be the true people of God, appropriating the traditions of the parent body as its own and claiming itself as the sole legitimate heir (cf. 10:16; but this attitude had already developed in the Q community).

Is the Gospel of Matthew anti-Semitic? In view of the use of certain Matthean texts through the centuries in support of racism and anti-Semitic statements and actions (especially 21:43 and 27:25), this question must be faced honestly, especially by Christians who wish to take Matthew seriously as canonical Scripture. To pose the question in terms of anti-Semitism, however, is anachronistic, for the issue in Matthew is not racial prejudice, but religious conflict.[25] The historical situation from which the Gospel of Matthew emerged was filled with tensions not only between Jews and Gentiles, but also with internal strife among various Jewish groups (of which the Matthean church was one). The Matthean Christian community, itself partly or even predominantly Jewish, felt itself to be persecuted by the Jewish leadership.[26] In the conflict, sharp words were exchanged, so that from Matthew's side negative caricatures of Jewish leadership and religious practice were presented as a part of the polemic (see 21:43; 23:1-36; 27:24-26).[27] While it is absurd to accuse Matthew of anti-Semitism—he pictured Jesus and the disciples as Jewish, was himself a Jew, and wrote for a church with a Jewish tradition and membership—lamentably, it is true that the sayings and imagery deriving from the conflict of Matthew's church and the Jewish leadership have been used to fuel the fires of anti-Semitism. Just as modern interpreters must be on guard that Matthean texts not be used to encourage anti-

Semitism, so also legitimate modern sensitivities about anti-Semitism must not obscure a historical understanding of Matthew's negative and polemical stance toward the formative Judaism of his own time.[28]

Change and Development. We may picture Matthew himself and numbers of his community as Jews who had grown up before the war of 66–70 with the synagogue as their spiritual home. Prior to the destruction of the Temple, they had encountered early missionaries of the "Jesus movement," probably related to or identical with the missionary prophets of the Q community, with their eschatological message of Jesus' return as Son of Man. They had been converted to faith in Jesus as the Son of Man, the fulfillment of their hopes for the coming Messiah, without ever dreaming that this would eventually alienate them from their religious and cultural home in Judaism. Then tensions developed, and those who had become disciples of Jesus found themselves an isolated group within the synagogue. Following the beginnings of the reformation of Judaism at Jamnia, Matthew's group found not only itself but the synagogue as well in the process of change, and tensions increased. When the Gospel was written, Matthew and his community were alienated from these developing structures. They refer to their own gathering as the "church" (ἐκκλησία *ekklēsia*; the word is found only in Matthew in the Gospels [16:18; 18:17]; 18:15, 21 in the NRSV are translations of *adelphoi* (ἀδελφοί), usually translated "brothers and sisters"). In some ways they now found themselves more oriented to the Gentile world than to the emerging shape of Judaism, while continuing to affirm their Jewish past, of which they considered themselves the legitimate heirs. Matthew and his church had lived through a period of rapid change; the Gospel of Matthew has much to say to a community experiencing social change to which it wants to adapt while being faithful to its Scripture and tradition.

Structure and Leadership. Since the plotted story line of Matthew extends from Jesus' birth to his resurrection appearance to his disciples, but does not continue into the post-Easter period of the church, Matthew's characterization of church life is communicated indirectly, in two ways. (1) The pre-Easter Jesus predicts and describes the situation of the post-Easter church, and (2) the story of Jesus and his disciples is narrated at two levels simultaneously, so that the pre-Easter narrative framework sometimes intentionally becomes transparent to the situation of the post-Easter church and its faith in Jesus as the risen and exalted Lord.

Peter, Apostles, Disciples. The disciples are often transparently addressed as the post-Easter Christian community (e.g., 10:17-42; 18:15-20). Matthew thought of the disciples as the whole group of those who had committed themselves to follow Jesus (8:21; 9:14; 10:25, 42; 12:49; 27:57; 28:19). Within this group was a central, symbolic core of twelve who represent the present leaders and future judges of the people of God (19:28). *Apostle* is not an important word for Matthew; he uses it only once (10:2), as a synonym for *disciple* (10:1). Except for 10:2, Matthew always refers to this central group as "the twelve disciples" (10:1; 11:1; 20:17) or simply "the twelve" (10:5; 26:14, 20, 47).

Within this group of twelve, Peter plays a distinct, symbolic role. Matthew modifies and adds to his tradition to emphasize the special role of Peter (10:2; 14:22-33; 15:15; 16:16-19; 17:24-27). Just as Peter is representative of the Twelve, so also the Twelve are representative of the larger body of disciples, and there are many times when the picture becomes transparent to the whole body of post-Easter disciples, so that the reader may identify with Peter and the other disciples. Yet Peter's significance in Matthew cannot be reduced to that of a cipher for the twelve or for the church as a whole. He is called first and is designated as the "first," (10:2, added to Mark). He plays a unique role in the founding and maintenance of the Christian community, and receives a special christological revelation from God, a unique pronouncement of blessing by Jesus, and a special (and unrepeatable) responsibility in the founding of the church (see 16:17-19). Peter had himself been in Antioch (Gal 2:11), the probable provenance of the Gospel, and in later tradition was considered the patron apostle of the church in that city and then its first bishop.[29] Petrine traditions and Petrine Christians may have played a role early in the history of Matthew's community, which may have regarded some of the M traditions as deriving from Peter or being especially associated with him. If the Gospel of Mark was already associated with Peter when it was accepted by the Matthean community, this would have both facilitated its reception and strengthened the prominence of Peter. In Matthew's stream of tradition, Peter was looked upon as the representative apostolic figure, as was Paul in the Deutero-Pauline stream, the Beloved Disciple in the Johannine stream, and James in yet other circles. The Matthean church was "Petrine" rather than "Pauline" or "Johannine" or "Jacobite."[30] (Matthew is distant from Pauline and Johannine Christianity, and James the brother of Jesus plays no role at all in Matthew's story.) Later Petrine Christianity as represented in the *Apocalypse of Peter* from Nag Hammadi appeals to Matthew as its authority, and uses Matthean vocabulary to describe itself ("little ones").

"Official" Order of Ministry? It may seem surprising that the "most ecclesiastical" Gospel has no references, direct or indirect, to formal ministerial structures. There is no mention of a bishop or deacons, which is particularly surprising if the Gospel was written in Antioch or its environs, since only a few years later Ignatius of Antioch made a strong case for the monarchical episcopate as the norm of church government, and apparently stood in the Matthean tradition and used the Gospel of Matthew (Ign. *Eph.* 19:1-3; Ign. *Smyrn.* 1:1 = Matt 3:15; Ign. *Phld.* 3:1 = Matt 15:13; Ign. *Pol.* 2:2). Likewise the *Didache*, also in the Matthean tradition, reflects the transition from earlier charismatic ministry to the formal structures of bishops and deacons. Matthew seems to be earlier in the same historical trajectory that led to Ignatius and the *Didache*, but prior to the development of formal ecclesiastical offices. The fact that some members of Matthew's community were beginning to claim the offices and titles that formative Judaism was beginning to use and invest with more formal authority than before ("rabbi," "father," "instructor,") seems clear from the Gospel's protest against such tendencies (23:8-12).

Leadership in the Matthean Church. The Matthean community seems to have had prophets among its leadership, probably as its principal leaders, as in the earlier days of the community reflected in the *Didache* (cf. Matt 5:12 to Luke 6:23; Matt 10:41; 23:34; even 7:21-22 presupposes there were "good" prophets in the community). These prophets were charismatic figures who received and transmitted revelations from the exalted Lord, and who had other leadership roles. They were at home in the life of the community, but some of them also made missionary journeys (10:41). Matthew valued such prophets and saw them as a model for all church leadership and the Christian life as such (5:12), but also saw the danger of such charismatic leadership (7:15, 21-22; 24:11, 24).

Matthew also understood the risen Lord to have sent sages and scribes to function as leaders in the church (13:52; 23:34). The exact functions of these ministers is not clear, but they apparently served in roles analogous to surrounding Judaism. Sages would have transmitted and interpreted the wisdom traditions of the community, but differently than in Judaism, since Matthew not only understood Jesus to be the messenger of Wisdom, but also utilized the figure of transcendent Wisdom as a christological category for understanding the status of the risen and exalted Christ.[31] Scribes not only would have worked over and transmitted biblical materials and provided midrashic interpretations and fulfillment quotations, but presumably would have done the same with the other sacred traditions of the community as well—namely, Q, Mark, and some of Matthew's special materials. This means that Matthew has some Q and Markan traditions that already had received Christian scribal interpretation. Matthew himself might have been such a Christian scribe who brought out of his accumulated traditional treasure both old and new things for the edification of the community (13:52). Sages and scribes (like prophets) no doubt participated in the teaching ministry within the community, but the exact roles and how they were related to each other can no longer be determined.

Matthew also used the terms *righteous* and *little ones* to designate members of his community (10:41-42; 13:17, 49; 18:6, 10, 14). It has been suggested that both are semi-technical terms for church leaders. "Righteous" or "Just" was the title given the leader of the Jerusalem church, "James the Just," so it is sometimes supposed that leaders in Matthew's church were called "righteous." "Little ones" is sometimes thought to be a special name for wandering missionaries. However, since Matthew does not use a specific title such as "Christian" to designate the members of his community, it is probably better to understand both "righteous" and "little ones" as general names for all authentic members of the community (like

Coins in the Gospels

By New Testament times coins had been in use in Palestine for over six hundred years. The Jews struck currency of their own from the Persian era (fifth century BCE) until the end of the Bar Kochba revolt (135 CE). The currency circulating at Jesus' time would have been a mixture of various denominations of gold, silver, brass, and bronze coins from all parts of the Roman Empire and beyond.

"They paid him thirty silver coins."

Because they were made of the highest grade of silver, shekels and half-shekels struck at the mint at Tyre were accepted by the Jews as the official standard for payments specified in the Bible. Thus the Greek word *argyria* ("silver"), used to describe the money paid to Judas for betraying Jesus (cf. Exod 21:32; Zech 11:12), is believed to refer to the silver Tyrian shekel, worth approximately four denarii. This same coin is probably what Jesus refers to as a *stater* (Matt 17:27), which Peter used to pay the temple tax for Jesus and himself. The coin shown here, struck in 60/59 BCE, pictures the Phoenician deity Melkart as Heracles; the reverse pictures an eagle and reads "Tyre, Holy and Inviolate." The *didrachma*, or "two drachma" (Matt 17:24), a silver coin used to pay the half-shekel temple tax (Exod 30:13), may refer to a silver half-shekel struck at Tyre, essentially the same design as the shekel but half the weight. Shekels and half-shekels of this type were struck at the mint at Tyre from 126 BCE until about 70 CE.

"Render unto Caesar the things that are Caesar's."

The *denarius*, a Roman silver coin, was the typical day's wage. The coin shown, first issued c. 19 CE, pictures Emperor Tiberius (14–37) and reads "Tiberius Caesar, son of the Deified Augustus and himself Augustus." The reverse shows Livia, mother of Tiberius, represented as Pax, goddess of peace, and reads "High Priest." The *denarius* is mentioned in Matt 20:2; 22:19; Mark 6:37; 12:15; 14:5; Luke 7:41; 10:35; 20:24; and John 6:7; 12:5

"What woman having ten drachma. . . ."

The *drachma* (Luke 15:8), a Greek silver coin, was approximate in value to the Roman denarius. The coin shown here, from Parthia, has the bust of Orodes I, the Parthian emperor (57–37 BCE) who briefly drove Herod I from Jerusalem; the reverse shows a seated Arsaces (founder of the Parthian empire) and reads "King of Kings; Arsaces, Benefactor, Righteous one, God Manifest, Lover of the Greeks."

"Take nothing for the journey except a staff– no bread, no bag, no money [*chalkon*] in your belts."

The Greek term *chalkon* ("copper"; Mark 6:8) could refer to any midsize copper coin.

"Are not five sparrows sold for two *assaria*?"

Assarion (Matt 10:29; Luke 12:6) is the designation of various copper coins struck outside of Palestine. In NT times, sixteen *assaria* equaled one *denarius.* The obverse of the coin pictured here shows Augustus and reads "Deified Augustus, Father"; the reverse shows an altar between the letters S(ENATVS) C(ONSVLTO), meaning "By the Consent of the Senate," and reads "Providence."

"A poor widow came and put in two *lepta*, which are worth a quadrans."

The *quadrans* (Mark 12:42) was a small bronze coin; four *quadrans* normally equalled an *assarion*, sixty-four a *denarius.* The coin pictured here was struck in Rome about 5 BCE, during the reign of Augustus. The obverse (not pictured) shows an altar; the reverse contains the legend "Apronius Gallus [the overseer of minting operations], maker of gold, silver, and bronze coins." A *lepton* (or "thin piece" [Mark 12:42; Luke 21:2]), also called a *perutah* by the Jews, was a small copper coin, the coin of least value in circulation. These coins varied greatly in size and value; normally, two *lepta* equaled one *quadrans.* The coin pictured, struck in either 8 or 12 CE, shows a palm tree with clusters (obverse), and a wheat head with the legend "Belonging to Caesar" (reverse).

"brothers and sisters," "sons of God," "servants," "slaves," "disciples"), for those who were neither prophets, sages, nor scribes.

Social Status. Matthew seems to reflect a relatively wealthy urban community. The "poor" and "hungry" in the Q beatitudes become in Matthew "poor in spirit" and those who "hunger and thirst for righteousness" (Matt 5:3, 6// Luke 6:20-21). References to small-denomination copper coins are replaced by references to gold and larger-denomination coins (Mark 6:8// Matt 10:9; Luke 19:11-27//Matt 25:14-30), and stories are told of high finance (e.g., 18:23-35) and lavish dinner parties (22:1-14). Matthew specifically adds to Mark the fact that Joseph of Arimathea, who buried Jesus, was both a disciple and a wealthy man (27:57).

Place of Origin. Several locations for the Matthean community have been argued: Palestine (Galilee, Caesarea, Jerusalem), Syria (Tyre or Sidon, Antioch), Egypt (Alexandria), Transjordan (Pella). The majority of scholars favor Antioch, for the following reasons: (1) Internal evidence of the Gospel points to some Greek-speaking urban area where Jews and Christians were in intense interaction. Greek was the dominant language of Antioch, which probably had the largest Jewish population in Syria. Matthew seems to breathe a more urbane air than either Q or Mark. Whereas Mark refers to cities eight times and villages seven times, Matthew has twenty-six references to cities and only four references to villages. (2) Peter is prominent in both Matthew and in Antiochene tradition, which made him the first bishop of Antioch. After the encounter between Paul and Peter in Antioch (Galatians 2), Paul seems to have lost popularity there. (3) Jerusalem seems out of the question, since James plays no role. (4) Matthew introduces "Syria" into his sources (4:24), perhaps as a pointer to his own church and to ground it in the saving history. (5) The contacts with Ignatius of Antioch and with the *Didache* point to this area as the origin of the Gospel of Matthew. (6) Only in Antioch did a stater equal exactly two drachmas (17:24-27). (7) Situating Matthew in Antioch fits the situation described in Acts, where Palestinian Christians started the Antiochene church, which then developed a Gentile mission, not without tensions. (8) The early and widespread acceptance of the Gospel implies "sponsorship" by a major church. There is no evidence for Rome or Ephesus as the sponsor; Antioch is the best remaining possibility.

Date. Matthew's community stretched over an extended period, developing and changing as it confronted and adapted to new situations. But the Gospel itself represents a cross-section of this growing tradition at a particular time, a "freezing" of it in the theological composition of one particular scribal leader of the community at a specific moment in its history. Since the Gospel contains no specific chronological data to identify its time of composition, that date cannot be pinpointed, but there are indications of a general period.

(1) On the two-source hypothesis, Matthew must have been written after Q and Mark. There are good reasons for dating Mark a few years either side of 70 CE, so Matthew must be enough later for Mark to have become the sacred tradition of the community.

(2) The war of 66–70, and the consequent destruction of Jerusalem, is almost certainly reflected in 22:7. Yet Matthew does not seem to be overwhelmed by the catastrophe, which seems some distance away in both space and time.

(3) Matthew seems to be intensely concerned with the developments in formative Judaism in the generation after 70. It is difficult to determine whether he reflects the specificity of the Birkath ha-Minim, which was apparently promulgated in the 80s (see above).

(4) Matthew, and not merely Matthean tradition, seems to have been used by both the *Didache* and Ignatius (see above). The *Didache* is difficult to date, but Ignatius wrote c. 110. Thus it seems that the Gospel of Matthew was composed in the period 80–100, for which 90 may serve as a good symbolic figure.

Authorship. Two of our oldest and best MSS (X, B) entitle the document simply "according to Matthew" (ΚΑΤΑ ΜΑΘΘΑΙΟΝ *KATA MATHTHAION*). Later MSS have "The Gospel According to Matthew," "The Holy Gospel According to Matthew," and other minor variations. Since the oldest MSS of the other Gospels also have the simple form "according to Mark," "according to Luke," "according to John," these titles apparently were added to the Gospels at the same time, with the common title "Gospel" uniting them all. The titles of our earliest MSS thus derive from the period when the fourfold Gospel canon was formed about the middle of the second century CE.[32]

The form and content of these titles is the church's testimony that there is only one gospel, the good news of Jesus Christ, but "according to" four different evangelists. It was important to early Christianity to attach apostolic names to its key documents, not as a matter of consciously falsifying history, but as a way of claiming theological adequacy and legitimacy for their contents, for which some kind of normative status was claimed. Thus most canonical and non-canonical documents for which some normative status was claimed received secondary apostolic titles (e.g., *Gospel of Thomas, Gospel of Philip, Gospel of Bartholomew*). In the case of the canonical Gospels, the value and significance of such titles is that they express the church's claim that these writings represent legitimate and authentic interpretation of the meaning of the Christ-event. It is also possible that in some cases the titles may transmit some authentic tradition with regard to the actual author.

Matthew itself, like the other New Testament Gospels, is anonymous. The issue is whether the title in this case, in addition to its primary theological function, also has historical value. Uncritical interpreters have always simply taken the tradition at face value, but a few recent critical scholars have also argued for apostolic authorship by the eyewitness Matthew.[33] Practically all critical scholars consider the evidence against apostolic authorship to be overwhelming: (1) The Gospel itself is anonymous. Apostolic authorship is a claim made for the book, not a claim made by the book itself. The case is thus different from the Deutero-Pauline letters. (2) The use of Mark and Q as sources undercuts its claim to eyewitness testimony. (3) The Greek language in which the Gospel was composed was the native language of the author and is of higher quality than the relatively unpolished Greek of Mark. Given the author's setting and background, he may have known enough Hebrew and Aramaic to work with texts, but there is no evidence that he was fluent in these languages. (4) The claim to apostolic authority, implicit in the title, is sufficiently accounted for by the historical and theological factors discussed above. (5) Evidence used to support authorship by the publican Matthew—e.g., the numerical patterns of the narrative, supposedly pointing to a tax collector's facility with figures—are fanciful and unconvincing. Rather, the real points of contact are with Haggadic and scribal composition. The argument that Matthew was a relatively minor character in the story and would not have been chosen as the purported author if he had not actually written the Gospel runs aground on the fact that practically every character in early Christianity, major and minor, had Gospels attributed to him, as the long lists of Gospels in the New Testament Apocrypha make clear.[34] The apostle Matthew conceivably may have been associated with Q or some of the M materials, so that there would be a genuine historical connection between Matthew and the Gospel, however indirect. More likely, the ascription to Matthew was made on the basis of the shift from "Levi" in Mark 2:14 to "Matthew" in Matt 9:9 and the consequent identification of the Matthew of Mark 3:18 as "the publican" in Matt 10:3.

For convenience, I will continue to use the traditional name "Matthew" to refer to the anonymous author of the Gospel of Matthew. Although we do not know the author's name, from the document he has given us we can surmise that he was of Jewish background, but must have grown up in a Hellenistic city (presumably Antioch) and spoke Greek.[35] The Septuagint (LXX) was his standard Bible. He may have been able to handle Hebrew well enough to facilitate biblical study, and enough Aramaic for informal communication. He knew the traditions and methods of the synagogue, but had never had the formal training that was becoming standard for scribes in formative Judaism. He was likely some kind of teacher for his community, although it is difficult to describe in "official" terms what kind of teacher that was. He may have drawn a cameo self-portrait in 13:52 of the "scribe who has been trained for the kingdom of heaven," but *scribe* is not intended in the technical sense here.

MATTHEW IN LITERARY PERSPECTIVE

Literary Criticism. The Gospel of Matthew is neither a record made by a reporter nor a collection assembled by an editor, but a narrative composed by an author. Thus literary criticism in biblical studies today connotes something more comprehensive than analysis of language and style—namely, the study of the rhetorical techniques used by the author in composing the narrative.[36] Matthew did not compose *ex nihilo*, but certainly used sources and traditions grounded in the actual events of the life of Jesus and the early Christian movement. Yet the final composition is the literary creation of an author, who made authorial decisions about (1) which literary genre to adopt or adapt for his composition (see below); (2) where and how to begin and end the story; (3) how to structure the narrative so that its movement communicated the meaning he wanted to evoke (see below); (4) what kind of narrator would tell this story;[37] (5) from what point of view the story would be told;[38] (6) how the narrative was to be plotted; (7) who the characters would be and how they would be characterized; and (8) the implied reader—i.e., the ideal reader presupposed by the way the document is written, the intended readers in Matthew's church, who may or may not correspond to actual readers.[39] The interrelations of these dynamics make a story communicate meaning. The analysis of how meaning is communicated through its literary forms is the concern of a number of related and overlapping disciplines, which may all be considered aspects of literary criticism: narrative criticism (narratology), rhetorical criticism, and reader-response criticism.

Just as source criticism dominated Gospel studies of the late nineteenth and early twentieth centuries, so also form criticism prevailed in the period between the two World Wars, and redaction criticism became foremost during the 1950s and 1960s. So in the last two decades literary criticism, without replacing the other approaches, became a prominent and indispensable method of Gospel interpretation. Instead of attempting to reconstruct sources and earlier forms of the text in order to look through it as a window to the events that lay behind it, current literary criticism strives to look at the final form of the text as a whole, to enter into the story world it creates, and to be addressed by the message of the story itself. While the redaction-critical approach permitted the interpreter to state the message of the Gospel in a series of abstract statements summarizing the main points of the "theology of the evangelist," illustrated by the redactional changes he had made, literary criticism insisted on the inseparability of the message and the story form in which it is embodied, which is not a disposable container for the "message" or "theology" of the evangelist. Literary criticism reminds us that the Gospel form, the story about Jesus, is in continuity with the form of communication used by Jesus himself: the parable. In the Gospel, the teller of stories becomes himself the principal character in a story.

Genre. The issue of literary genre is a fundamental and indispensable *hermeneutical* concern. What kind of document one supposes one is reading is decisive for the question of meaning. Theoretically, one could think of Matthew as biography, history, fiction, midrash, lectionary, and other genres, or some hybrid of two or more of these. While a case can be made for each of the above, indicating that the Gospel genre has elements of and resemblances to more than one genre, recent scholarly debate has centered on whether the Gospel should be interpreted as a type of Hellenistic biography of Jesus, or whether the Gospel genre was an original form of narrative devised by the early church to communicate its faith in Jesus.[40] The Gospel genre, while not utterly discontinuous from the available genres of literature, is a distinctive new departure fashioned to express in narrative form the christological convictions of early Christianity.

The following points are important for considering the genre of Matthew:

(1) Matthew is a narrative whole. It is neither a collection of individual stories nor a series of discourses with appended narrative sections. As a story, its mode of communication is indirect. Thus Matthew as a whole is to be interpreted as a story is interpreted, with the perspectives and tools of literary criticism.

(2) Because Matthew adapted and modified Mark, without a fundamental change in genre, the Gospel of Matthew is whatever Mark was. Two features distinguish Matthew (and Mark) from Hellenistic biography: (a) The Gospel is a community narrative, not an individualistic writing. The material for the story comes from the community tradition, a tradition that is already theologically charged. The story itself is intended for reading (aloud) in community worship and study, not for private, individual reading. Oral traits abound. (b) The narrative is permeated by christology. It is not only christological narrative,

but it is christology in narrative form as well. Although it is the story of a historical figure who appears in almost every scene, and although it uses historical (and other) materials, the Gospel's purpose is not biographical but christological. (Especially in the case of Matthew, this means that it is also ecclesiological, since there is no christology without a corresponding understanding of discipleship.)

Three essential features characterize the narrative christology of the Gospels. (1) The story holds together in one narrative portrayals of the Christ that reveal both the transcendent power of God and the weakness of the fully human Jesus. The Gospel genre narrates the earthly career of a recent historical figure who is now the exalted and present Lord who continues to act and speak.[41] Within the narrative, Jesus is portrayed both as divine Lord and as truly human servant who suffers and dies. Prior to Mark, these two christologies struggled against each other. Mark saw the value of both and devised a way of presenting them together in one narrative, with the "messianic secret" as a primary literary-theological device. Matthew adopted Mark's product, but no longer needed the messianic secret, which he minimizes and includes in only a vestigial manner.

(2) The "life of Jesus" is portrayed as the definitive segment of the line of redemptive history. That is, the story of Jesus is not related as complete in itself. The narrative world of the Gospel is much larger than the plotted narrative, stretching from creation to eschaton. The story of the Christ is not the whole story of God's saving acts, but it is the definitive segment of that story. Within history, within one life, the meaning of the whole of history is disclosed, an advance picture of the eschatological victory of the kingdom of God. This is fundamental to the confession "Jesus is the Christ." The kind of narrative appropriate to this confession is the Gospel. (3) The central figure of the narrative is at once the there-and-then Jesus of Nazareth as a figure of past history and the risen Lord who continues to speak and act in his church of the readers' present. Faith in the resurrection of Jesus is fundamental to this double perspective. As christology has implications for ecclesiology throughout, so here too the simultaneous double perspective on Jesus includes a double perspective on the other actors in the story. The disciples are not only the pre-Easter followers of Jesus, but are transparent to the Christian readers of Matthew's own time. The Pharisees are not only figures in a story about what happened to the historical Jesus, but represent the opposition to the church in Matthew's time.

The Gospels are different from Hellenistic biographies in that they presuppose and mediate a christological understanding of their central character that is different from the Hellenistic heroes and gods. This perspective on the nature of the Gospels is important for interpretation, whether or not one considers the Gospel genre unique.

Structure. Meaning is communicated not only by what is said, but also by the strategy of communication built into the text as its rhetorical structure. We must, therefore, distinguish between outlines imposed upon the material by the modern reader and the document's own rhetorical structure built into it by the author and discovered by the interpreter. Matthew himself calls attention to the structural features of his opening section 1:1-17, from which it is clear that he is an author of considerable literary skill who does not compose randomly or casually. There are many indications of structural patterns that may be clues to the overall structure of the book.

Chronology. The Gospel is a narrative in chronological order, from Jesus' ancestry and birth through his baptism, ministry in Galilee, final journey to Jerusalem, conflict, arrest, crucifixion, resurrection, and concluding commissioning of the disciples. Matthew tightens the chronological connections of his sources, making many of Mark's paratactic connections (clauses that are parallel instead of subordinated each to the other) with "and" (και *kai*) or "next" (εὐθύς *euthys*) more explicitly into a chronological narrative. This results in a more tightly knit story. Yet, it is clear that the historical chronology of Jesus' life is not Matthew's structuring principle, since he does not hesitate to rearrange the chronology of his sources and shows no interest in integrating the narrative into the chronology of the history external to the story world (cf. Luke 3:1-2), with the result that the reader is unable to designate the date or duration of the events portrayed in the narrative.

Geography. As in Mark, "Galilee" and "Judea" play important structural roles in the composition. Prior to the beginning of Jesus' ministry, he is something of a wanderer, the storyline proceeding from Bethlehem to Egypt, back to Nazareth, then to the Jordan to be baptized, into the wilderness to be tempted (which involves trips back to Jerusalem and to a "very high mountain"), then back to Nazareth before finally settling in Capernaum as "his own city" (4:12-13; cf. 9:1). Matthew pointedly locates the beginning of Jesus' ministry in "Galilee of the Gentiles," underscoring the location with one of his formula quotations (4:14-16; on formula quotations, see Excursus "Matthew as Interpreter of Scripture," 151-54). Although Jesus makes journeys across the lake of Galilee and into Tyre and Sidon, Matthew seems to picture all of Jesus' ministry as being in Galilee until 19:1. From this point on, Matthew thinks of Jesus as being in Judea, including the territory on the east bank of the Jordan (Perea, Transjordan). Geographically, one could think of three sections of the narrative:

I. Pre-Galilean Preparation (1:1–4:16)
II. Galilean Ministry (4:17–18:35)
III. Judean Conflicts, Death, Resurrection, Return to Galilee (19:1–28:20)

Summaries. Q had no narrative summaries, and Mark had only two that picture Jesus traveling and that summarize an extended period of preaching and healing (Mark 1:14-15; 6:6*b*). In addition, Mark had a number of summary statements that picture Jesus healing and teaching on individual occasions, without narrating the details (Mark 1:32-34; 3:7-12; 6:32-33, 53-56; 10:1). Matthew takes over all of the Markan summaries, uses them as transitions, and even elaborates them. Mark 3:7-12 and 6:6*b* are used in Matt 4:23-25 and 9:35 as important structural brackets for a key Matthean unit. Otherwise, however, the summaries do not play major structural roles in Matthew's composition.

Speeches. Five times Matthew concludes a major speech of Jesus with almost identical formulae, "Now when Jesus had finished saying these things" (7:28 NRSV; cf. 11:1; 13:53; 19:1; 26:1). The formula acts not merely as a conclusion, but as a transition, pointing back to the completed speech and forward to the continuing narrative, relating Jesus' words to his deeds and binding speech and narrative together. Although perhaps derived from the transitional statement in Q (Luke 7:1), they are all redactional, representing part of Matthew's own structural pattern. The outline of the speeches, and their location in the narrative, represent Matthew's own compositional decisions (see the Outline below). Each speech represents a major theme of the Gospel: (1) The Sermon on the Mount (5:1–7:29) presents the authoritative teaching of the Messiah, who has come not to destroy the Law but to fulfill it. (2) The Missionary Discourse, 10:5*b*-42, is Christ's address to his disciples, who are sent forth in mission as representatives of Christ and with his authority. (3) The parable collection, 13:1-52, portrays the hiddenness of the kingdom of God in the present, in conflict with the evil kingdom of this age, but ultimately triumphing over it. (4) The discourse of 18:1-35 concerns the internal life of the church, addressing its need of both rigorous discipline and profound forgiveness if its members are to live together as Christ's disciples. (5) The concluding Judgment Discourse, 23:1–25:46, corresponds to the initial paradigmatic Sermon on the Mount, placing the life called for there in a specific eschatological context of universal judgment and triumph of God's kingdom.

Already in the second century Matthew was regarded as structuring his Gospel in five "books" in imitation of the Pentateuch and as an alternative to the Jewish understanding of Law.[42] This view was made popular by B. W. Bacon in the early twentieth century and has since been adopted with variations by several leading Matthean scholars.[43] The speeches are an important structuring device, but the Gospel should not be regarded as a structure of five speeches with a narrative framework. The narrative is primary with the speeches inserted into it.

Repeated Formulae and Framing Devices. Two examples of repeated formulae as structural markers are:

1. "From that time Jesus began to . . . [ἀπὸ τότε ἤρξατο ὁ Ἰησοῦς + infinitive, *apo tote ērxato Iēsous*]" (4:17/16:21). The first occurrence of the formula introduces Jesus' public proclamation of the kingdom of God, leading to conflict and rejection. The recurrence of the formula in 16:21 introduces the period of Jesus' private instruction of his disciples concerning his suffering, death, and resurrection. If these are considered the primary structural markers, the following outline results:

I. The Presentation of Jesus (1:1–4:16)
II. The Ministry of Jesus to Israel and Israel's Repudiation of Jesus (4:17–16:20)
III. Jesus' Journey to Jerusalem and His Suffering, Death, and Resurrection (16:21–28:20)[44]

2. The Sermon on the Mount and the following collection of miracle and discipleship stories are bracketed with almost identical summary formulae (4:23/ 9:35). The fact that the reader is encouraged to think of chapters 5–9 as a unit, "the messianic teaching and the messianic acts of power," seems to be clear from the narrator's reference to the collection of miracle stories in chapters 8–9 as "what the Messiah was doing" (11:2) and from Jesus' statement that follows in 11:4, "Go and tell John what you hear [chaps. 5–7] and see [chaps. 8–9]" (NRSV). Matthew has altered Q at 11:4 in order to get this pair.

Chiastic Structures. Chiasm is an elaboration of this framing technique in which pairs of units are arranged to form a series of corresponding frames arranged around a central focus—e.g., in the pattern ABCBA. This rhetorical pattern was fairly common in the ancient world. Both Peter F. Ellis and C. H. Lohr[45] see the entire Gospel arranged according to this chiastic structure, an arrangement correlated to the "five-books" scheme discussed above:

A 1–4 Birth and beginnings	Narrative
B 5–7 Blessings, entering the kingdom	Discourse
C 8–9 Authority and invitation	Narrative
D 10 Mission discourse	Discourse
E 11–12 Rejection by this generation	Narrative
F 13 Parables of the kingdom	Discourse
E´14–17 Acknowledgment by disciples	Narrative
D´18 Community discourse	Discourse
C´19–22 Authority and invitation	Narrative
B´23–25 Woes, coming of the kingdom	Discourse
A´26–28 Death and rebirth	Narrative

Chiastic structure is clearly a part of Matthew's technique and represents one of his favorite structuring devices, especially in 1:1–12:21, where Matthew is most freely creating his own structure. The neatness of such charts is beguiling, however, and fitting the whole Gospel into a single chiastic pattern requires some forcing.

Triadic Patterns. Matthew's tendency to compose in triads has often been noted, most recently in the work of W. D. Davies and Dale C. Allison, Jr.[46] Matthew himself calls attention to his triadic structure of the initial unit, the genealogy (1:2-17). There are numerous other triadic constructions (e.g., three temptations in 4:1-11), especially in the early part of the Gospel, where Matthew is creatively composing. However, this pattern disappears as soon as Matthew begins to follow the Markan order at Matthew 12:22/Mark 3:22. Triadic composition as a Matthean feature seems to be confirmed by the fact that the Matthean additions to the Markan speeches are consistently triadic, while the material adopted from Mark is not.

A Single, Comprehensive, Mono-Level Outline? Some of the patterns noted above coincide and reinforce each other. For instance, the geographical turning point at the beginning of the "Galilee" section coincides with the "from that time Jesus began . . . [infinitive]" formulae of 4:17 and 16:21. Other patterns seem to be independent of each other. Some patterns may have belonged to Matthew's sources rather than reflecting his own composition. This means that it is not possible to integrate all of the structural patterns that can be observed in Matthew into one flat-surface, one-dimensional linear outline that the reader can see as *the* outline of Matthew. The structure of Matthew should be thought of in a more dynamic, interactive way, as a complex of interlocking structures with more than one movement present in the text at the same time, as though there were multiple layers of outline; as a result, any one element may be involved in the dynamics of more than one movement. That the "outline" is not neat and obvious may not necessarily mean that Matthew is casual or spontaneous, but that the writer was somewhat constrained by his materials. It may also be that Matthew the writer excelled at storytelling and that, therefore, he kept the outline inconspicuous, not allowing it to intrude in such a way that the story can be "summarized." The outline below is an effort to attend to and respect the different levels of structural dynamics in Matthew's story, yet present a linear, flat-surface outline to help the reader grasp the Gospel as a whole.

Matthew's Sacred Tradition (Mark and Q) as the Key to His Structure. Matthew was deeply influenced by the structures of both of his major sources. Although he rearranged several items in order to get similar material together, he maintained the rough outline of both Q and Mark, following Q more closely in the earlier chapters and Mark more closely from 12:22 on. Since both Matthew and his intended readers were thoroughly familiar with the story line of Mark, Matthew made the Markan narrative fundamental for the structure of his own story. After extracting material from later sections of Mark for his creative structure of 1:12–12:21, he never deviated from the Markan order of pericopes from Matt 12:22//Mark 3:22 to the end of the Gospel. In the first part of the Gospel, the original readers would recognize Markan and Q materials, but rearranged and amplified to produce an entirely new story world. From 12:22 (Mark 3:22) on, the reader would be in familiar territory, but would have been given a new framework within which to interpret it. In Matthew's restructuring of the story, the kingdom of God became the key theme of the whole. Matthew's Gospel should thus be thought of as being structured in two main parts oriented to his treatment of Mark, with the kingdom of God as the comprehensive theme uniting the whole.

The Structure of Part One, "The Conflict of Kingdoms Initiated and Defined" (Matthew 1:1–12:21). Matthew chose the conflict scene in Mark 3:22-30 as the key point at which to join his own composition to the Markan story line (Matt 12:22). Matthew's choice seems to have been influenced by the fact that this scene is one of the few that appears in both of his sources (for Q, see Matt 12:22-24//Luke 11:14-15). The primary reason for choosing this section where his two sources converge, however, is the conflict it pictures between the kingdom of Satan and the advent of the kingdom of God proclaimed by Jesus. This conflict between the evil of the present world represented by the "kingdom of Satan" and the coming kingdom of God already present in Jesus is fundamental to understanding both the plot and the theology of the Gospel of Matthew. The explosive conflict in this scene is ignited by the charge that Jesus has Beelzebul—i.e., that he is in league with Satan and works by Satan's power (12:24, 26). This accusation, attributed by Matthew specifically to the Pharisees (Mark 4:22, "scribes"; Luke 11:15 "some") was very important to Matthew. Members of his own community, and perhaps he himself, had faced this charge from the emergent Pharisaic leadership (cf. 10:25). Matthew had obviously reflected deeply on this theological indictment, found in both his major sources, and made it central to the own structure of his work.

With his eye on this scene in the Markan narrative, and using materials from Q, Mark, and the traditions of his own community, Matthew composed an extensive section, the entire first part of his narrative, that builds toward this key scene of conflict in Mark. Already this is a clue that conflict is key to the plot of Matthew's story.[47] The story begins with the announcement of the advent of a new "King of the Jews" (1:1-25). But this proclamation is made in a setting where a king already represents the ruling power of that age. In the conflict that necessarily results, the Jewish leaders side with the earthly ruler, while the king sent from God is worshiped by Gentiles (2:1-23). John the Baptist appears with the message of the near advent of God's kingdom, and Jesus begins his ministry only after being baptized by John (3:1–4:17). Jesus then calls disciples (4:18-22), who are witnesses to the word and works of the messianic king (4:23–9:35). The disciples are called to follow Jesus, who empowers and equips them for their mission to represent him, but they still live in this age and are tempted to waver (9:36–11:1), as is John the Baptist himself (11:2-19). Thus the conflict continues (11:20–12:14), even though the new king is a servant figure who, when the Jews reject him, will fulfill Scripture by bringing salvation to the Gentiles (12:15-21). Using a chiastic pattern, Matthew has carefully arranged, rewritten, and expanded his traditional materials into the following structured narrative.

A Jesus as Messianic King, Son of David and Son of God	1:2-25
B Conflict with the Kingdom of This Age	2:1-23
C The Ministry of Jesus in Relation to John the Baptist	3:1–4:17
D The Disciples Called	4:18-22
E The Authority of the Messiah in Word and Deed	4:23–9:35
D´The Disciples Authorized and Sent	9:36–11:1
C´The Ministry of Jesus in Relation to John the Baptist	11:2-19
B´Conflict with the Kingdom of This Age	11:20–12:14
A´The Servant King	12:15-21

This chiastic structure is formed "from the inside out"; thus it may be thought of as a series of concentric circles (see Fig. 2). The section 4:23–9:35 is clearly marked off by Matthew himself, by more than one signal: (1) 4:23 is a bracket with 9:35; (2) 11:2, "what the Messiah was doing" (NRSV), points back to chapters 8–9, continued by the disciples in chapter 10; (3) 11:4, "hear and see," refers to chapters 5–7 ("hear") and 8–9 ("see"); and (4) 11:4*b*-5 describes the content of chapters 5–9. Thus "the Messiah in word and deed" as the central defining core is surrounded by discipleship sections: 4:18-22, the disciples called, and 9:36–11:1, the disciples authorized and sent. The Messiah is not thought of as an individual (a "great man"), but as the generator of the messianic community. So 4:18–11:1 embrace the Messiah/disciples. There are clear structural markers at these two points in the narrative.

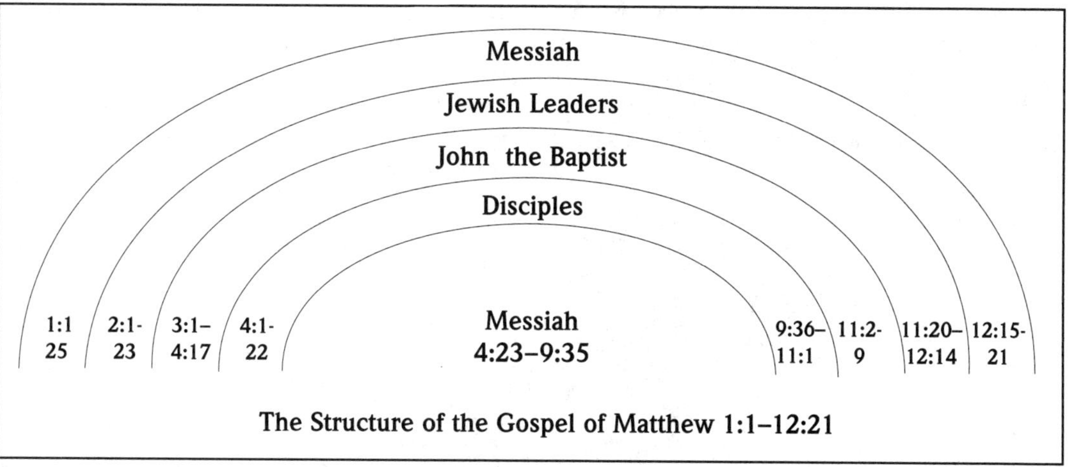

The Structure of the Gospel of Matthew 1:1–12:21

The next concentric circle comprises the sections presenting John the Baptist. John is located between "the disciples" and "the opponents." On the one hand, he is honored as a true prophet of God, the greatest "among those born of women" (11:11 NRSV), whose message anticipates and is identical with Jesus' (3:2/4:17) and whose ministry marks the turning point of the ages (11:12). On the other hand, he never becomes a disciple, nor do his disciples transfer their allegiance to Jesus but continue as an independent group (9:14); after 3:17 the logic of Matthew's theology and story requires that they should do so. Matthew's story comes to terms with this historical reality by locating John and his disciples as neither disciples nor opponents, though they play important roles in God's saving plan on the border between disciples and opponents; therefore, they are allied with Jesus.

The next circle is represented by the Jewish leadership, who are portrayed as flat characters consistently opposed to Jesus, antithetical to the kingdom proclaimed and made present by him. They are, in fact, the representatives of the kingdom of Satan. They struggle with Jesus for allegiance of "the crowds" and finally win them over (27:20-25).

The outermost bracket surrounding the whole, as well as the central core, is filled by Jesus, the king who redefines kingship. The lines that indicate the correlated sections are not intended to separate them as though they were discontinuous with each other, just as the diagram that distinguishes Part One from Part Two is not intended to divide the book into two discontinuous halves. The book as a whole is a continuous narrative, in which each section both builds on the preceding and prepares for the next. In particular, Matthew's creative Part One is not discontinuous from Part Two, but prepares the reader for it and leads in to it.

In this framework, Jesus himself as messianic king is central, filling not only pivotal central section 4:23–9:35 (E), but the beginning and ending units that frame the entire section as well (A, A'). Note that the conflict is not ultimately between Jesus and the Jewish leaders; the narrative unfolds as the earthly, historical segment of a cosmic story. The this-worldly conflict with which the narrative is concerned has a cosmic, mythological backdrop and points beyond itself. Thus God is the hidden actor in the story throughout, and Satan is the hidden opponent. The conflict with Satan is woven into the structure throughout as an underlying theme (exorcism stories); thus it is not to be localized only in the "temptation" passage (4:1-11), which is only one incident among others, not a major turning point in the outline. The repeated charge of collusion with Beelzebul in 9:32-34 and 10:25 keeps the conflict alive in an ironic way, and prepares the reader to rejoin the Markan story line at 12:22 (= Mark 3:22) on the note of conflict with Israel. The reader now knows that Satan, though already defeated by Jesus, is in the background of this conflict. The original readers were aware from their own experience that the conflict continues through the narrative and into the reader's own time, even among Jesus' disciples (16:23).

The Structure of Part Two, "The Conflict of Kingdoms Developed and Resolved." This narrative picks up the Markan story line at 12:22 (= Mark 3:22), and the conflict continues. Matthew's church, previous hearers/readers of Mark's Gospel and Q, have now been given a new framework for interpreting their sacred tradition. From 12:22 on, the narrative sections simply follow the Markan outline and order. Matthew imposes his own stamp on it by inserting his own traditions and compositions into the narrative sections and by developing the Markan speeches into major compositional units to correspond to the Sermon on the Mount and the Missionary Discourse in Part One. The resulting series of five speeches thus forms the interlocking structure between Parts One and Two.[48]

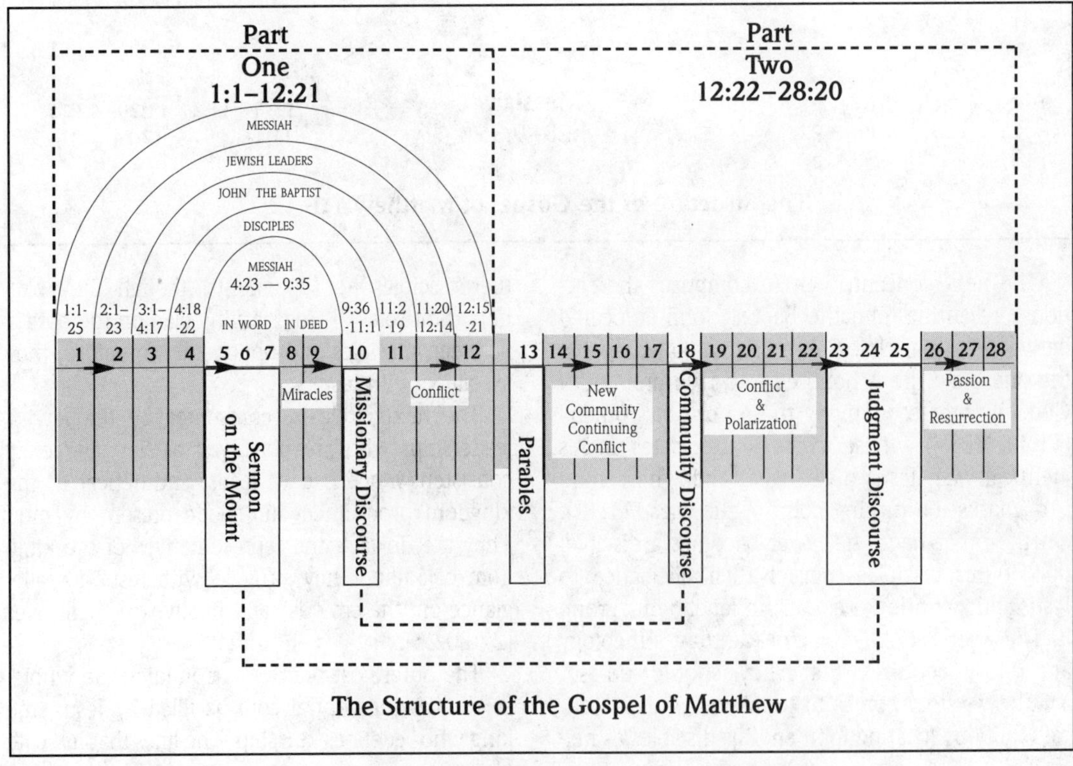

The Structure of the Gospel of Matthew

MATTHEW IN THEOLOGICAL PERSPECTIVE

The Gospel of Matthew is a theological document. The subject matter is God's saving act in Christ, with Jesus appearing in almost every scene. Thus while Matthew may also be used as a source from which to glean historical and sociological data about early Judaism and Christianity, the Gospel itself is a theological document that must be understood theologically. This means, in the first place, one needs to make an effort to apprehend the Gospel in Matthew's theological categories: God, kingdom of God (vs. kingdom of Satan), christology, church, history, fulfillment and eschatology, ethics, law, and discipleship. This is the theological minimum, necessary even to describe Matthew historically. For the contemporary interpreter who approaches the Gospel as canonical Scripture, theological interpretation also involves the hermeneutical task of translating Matthew's theological affirmations into categories meaningful to one's own age.

Although the Gospels were not originally written to us, there is another, equally valid, sense in which it is true and important to say that they were written to us. The Gospels were all addressed to the church to help the Christian community understand, clarify, and share its faith in Jesus as the Christ. The contemporary church is in historical, organic, theological unity with the Christian communities to which the Gospels were originally addressed. The life of the church through the centuries is the living theological link through which the Gospels have been transmitted and continually reinterpreted to the present day. The fact that the New Testament is the church's book means that the interpretative task already under way in the composition of the Gospels continues in the hermeneutical task of making theological sense of the Gospels' message in our time and place. The original message must first be heard in its own context and categories. To become a live option and address of the Word of God to us, it must then be translated into contemporary theological categories. The interpreter's task is not only to uncover the theology of the ancient writer in his terms, but to make it hearable in contemporary terms as well.

Historical study of the Gospel of Matthew is an ally in this task. Matthew was himself an interpreter, standing in the living streams of tradition, interpreting the meaning of the Old Testament into the new situation by looking back on the advent of the Christ, his ministry, crucifixion, and resurrection. In particular, Matthew stands in a Christian hermeneutical stream interpreting the sacred texts of Christian tradition revered in his church (namely, Q and Mark) and the M traditions unique to the Matthean community. Matthew's own interpretation represented in the Gospel of Matthew then entered into the living stream and has been the object of interpretation in the church for nineteen centuries. The contemporary interpreter stands with Matthew in this continuing stream, heir to Matthew's Bible and his Christian traditions (Q, Mark, M), the Gospel of Matthew itself, and the church's continuing interpretation of them all. Matthew is not the passive object of our interpretive work. He is a fellow interpreter who speaks not only to us, but also with us.

FOR FURTHER READING

Aune, David E., ed. *The Gospel of Matthew in Current Study.* Eerdmans, 2001.

Carter, Warren. *Matthew and the Margins: A Socio-Political and Religious Reading.* Sheffield: Sheffield Academic Press, 2000.

Clark, Howard B. *The Gospel of Matthew and its Readers: A Historical Introduction to the First Gospel.* Bloomington, Ind.: Indiana University Press, 2003.

Cousland, J. C. R. *The Crowds in the Gospel of Matthew.* NovTSup 102. Leiden: Brill, 2002.

Davies, W. D., and Dale C. Allison, Jr. *A Critical and Exegetical Commentary on the Gospel According to Saint Matthew.* 3 vols. ICC. Edinburgh: T & T Clark, 1988, 1991.

France, R. T. *Matthew: Evangelist and Teacher.* Grand Rapids: Zondervan, 1989.

Hagner, Donald. *Matthew 1–13.* WBC 33A. Dallas: Word Books, 1993.

________. *Matthew 14–28.* WBC 33B. Dallas: Word Books, 1995.

Keener, Craig S. *A Commentary on the Gospel of Matthew.* Grand Rapids, Mich.: Eerdmans, 1999.

Kingsbury, Jack Dean. *Matthew as Story.* 2nd ed. Philadelphia: Fortress, 1988.

Levine, Amy-Jill and Marianne Blickenstaff, eds. *A Feminist Companion to Matthew.* Feminist Companion to the New Testament and Early Christian Writings 1. Sheffield: Sheffield Academic Press, 2001.

Long, Thomas G. *Matthew.* Westminster Bible Companion. Louisville, Ky.: Westminster John Knox Press, 1997.

Luz, Ulrich. *Matthew 1–7: A Commentary.* Minneapolis: Augsburg, 1989.

———. *Matthew 8-20.* Hermeneia. Minneapolis, Minn.: Fortress, 2001.

Meier, John. *Matthew.* Volume 3 of the New Testament Message series. Collegeville, Minn.: Liturgical Press, 1980.

Overman, J. Andrew. *Church and Community in Crisis: The Gospel According to Matthew.* The New Testament in Context. Valley Forge, Penn.: Trinity, 1996

Saldarini, Anthony J. *Matthew's Christian-Jewish Community.* Chicago: University of Chicago Press, 1994.

Stanton, Graham N., ed. *The Interpretation of Matthew.* Edinburgh: T&T Clark, 1995.

Works About Matthew's Use of the Old Testament:

Gundry, Robert H. *The Use of the Old Testament in St. Matthew's Gospel.* Leiden: E. J. Brill, 1967.

McCasland, S. Vernon. "Matthew Twists the Scripture," *JBL* 80 (1961) 143-48, responded to by James A. Sanders, "The Gospels and the Canonical Process." In William O. Walker, Jr., ed. *The Relationships Among the Gospels: An Interdisciplinary Dialogue.* San Antonio: Trinity University Press, 1978.

Soares-Prabhu, G. M. *The Formula Quotations in the Infancy Narrative of Matthew.* AnBib 63. Rome: Biblical Institute, 1976.

Stendahl, Krister. *The School of St. Matthew and Its Use of the Old Testament.* ASNU 20. Lund: C. W. K. Gleerup, 1954; reprinted with a new Introduction by the author, Philadelphia: Fortress, 1968.

Works About the Sermon on the Mount:

Augustine, "Our Lord's Sermon on the Mount." In volume 8 of *The Nicene and Post-Nicene Fathers.* Grand Rapids: Eerdmans, 1979.

Barth, Karl. *Church Dogmatics.* Edinburgh: T & T Clark, 1957. II.2.686-99.

Bonhoeffer, Dietrich. *The Cost of Discipleship.* New York: Macmillan, 1963.

Calvin, John. *Matthew, Mark, and Luke.* Volume 1 of *Calvin's Commentaries.* Edited by D. W. Torrance and T. F. Torrance. Grand Rapids: Eerdmans, 1972.

Guelich, Robert. *The Sermon on the Mount.* Waco, Tex.: Word Books, 1982.

Luther, Martin. "The Sermon on the Mount." In volume 21 of *Luther's Works.* Edited by Jaroslav Pelikan. St. Louis: Concordia, 1956.

Strecker, Georg. *The Sermon on the Mount: An Exegetical Commentary.* Nashville: Abingdon, 1988.

Works About the Kingdom of God:

Chilton, Bruce, ed. *The Kingdom of God in the Teaching of Jesus.* IRT 5. Philadelphia: Fortress, 1984.

Kingsbury, Jack Dean. "Matthew's View of the Son of God and the Kingdom of Heaven." In *Matthew: Structure, Christology, Kingdom.* Philadelphia: Fortress, 1975.

Ladd, George Eldon. *The Presence of the Future.* Grand Rapids: Eerdmans, 1974.

Perrin, Norman. *Jesus and the Language of the Kingdom: Symbol and Metaphor in New Testament Interpretation.* Philadelphia: Fortress, 1976.

Willis, Wendell, ed. *The Kingdom of God in 20th-Century Interpretation.* Peabody, Mass.: Hendrickson, 1987.

ENDNOTES

1. The oldest preserved fragment of Matthew is papyrus $\mathfrak{P}^{64/67}$ in Barcelona and Oxford, from about 200 CE, which contains fragments of chapters 3, 5, and 26. Sixteen other papyri contain parts of Matthew, but most are only a few lines. The most extensive papyrus fragment of Matthew is the third-century $\mathfrak{P}^{45}$ in the Chester Beatty collection in Dublin, containing a total of 55 verses from chapters 20–26. The oldest complete Greek text of Matthew is found in the great majuscule ("uppercase") codices of the fourth century, Sinaiticus (א) in the British Museum in London, and Vaticanus (B) in the Vatican Library in Rome. The complete Greek text of Matthew is found in an additional 13 majuscules from the fifth to the tenth centuries, and in 99 later minuscules (MSS written in lowercase, cursive letters) from the ninth to the sixteenth centuries, as well as in fragmentary form in hundreds of other manuscripts, mostly late minuscules. In addition, Matthew is represented in hundreds of MSS of ancient versions, lectionaries, and quotations in the Church

Fathers.

2. See Kurt Aland et al., *The Greek New Testament*, 4th ed. (Stuttgart: United Bible Societies, 1993); Kurt Aland et al., *Novum Testamentum Graece*, 27th ed. (Stuttgart: Deutsche Bibelgesellschaft, 1993).

3. See Heinrich Greeven, *Synopsis of the First Three Gospels with the Addition of the Johannine Parallels*, 13 ed. (Tübingen: J. C. B. Mohr [Paul Siebeck], 1981). Cf. Franz Neirynck, "Greeven's Texts of the Synoptic Gospels," in *Evangelica II: 1982–1991 Collected Essays*, ed. F. Van Segbroeck, BETL 99 (Leuven: Leuven University Press, 1991) 377-88.

4. For a discussion of the problem and issues raised below about form criticism, redaction criticism, and tradition criticism, see Christopher Tuckett, "Jesus and the Gospels," in *New Interpreter's Bible*, 12 Vols. Nashville: Abingdon, 8:71-86.

5. See Rudolf Bultmann, *History of the Synoptic Tradition*, trans. John Marsh (New York: Harper & Row, 1963; German ed., 1931).

6. *Midrash* is the term used for the rabbinic type of exposition of biblical texts. Halakhic midrashim were expositions of legal texts, while haggadic midrashim were commentaries on narrative texts. The latter often involved creative retelling of the biblical story.

7. These figures are derived from the indexes of Kurt Aland et al., *Novum Testamentum Graece*, 26th ed. (Stuttgart: Deutsche Bibelgesellschaft, 1979) 769-75.

8. Kurt Aland et al., *Novum Testamentum Graece*, 27th ed., Appendix IV, 770-806; Robert G. Bratcher, *Old Testament Quotations in the New Testament* (New York: United Bible Societies, 1961) 1-11.

9. Four additional citations are sometimes included in this group: 2:6; 3:3; 13:14-15; 26:56. Although 14 is a significant number for Matthew (1:2-17), the additional four do not meet the above criteria and are all of a different text type.

10. Justin *Apology* 32.

11. See Maurice Goulder, *Midrash and Lection in Matthew* (London: SPCK, 1974) 144.

12. This survey follows the convention of citing Q texts by Lukan versification. Cf. John Kloppenborg, *Q Parallels: Synopsis, Critical Notes, & Concordance* (Sonoma, Calif.: Polebridge, 1988) xv and *passim*.

13. For elaboration of this point and evidence for it, see M. Eugene Boring, *The Continuing Voice of Jesus: Christian Prophecy and the Gospel Tradition* (Louisville: Westminster/John Knox, 1991) 191-234, 242-46, 255-56.

14. For example, "little faith" (ὀλιγοπιστος *oligopistos*) occurs once in Q 12:28 = Matt 6:30, but is added to Markan contexts in Matt 8:26; 14:31; 16:8; cf. 17:20.

15. See Sir John Hawkins, *Horae Synopticae: Contributions to the Study of the Synoptic Problem*, 2nd ed. (Oxford: Clarendon, 1909) 170-71. He lists nineteen passages where Matthew reproduces phrases derived from his sources but used in a different context. Nils Dahl, *Jesus in the Memory of the Early Church* (Minneapolis: Augsburg, 1976) 40, gives data from the passion story, showing that both author and intended reader presupposed familiarity with Mark.

16. This contrast is not only in passages where the narrator is speaking. In 10:17 Jesus speaks of "their" synagogues (cf. 16:18 "my" church).

17. The 1947 article by Kenneth W. Clark, "The Gentile Bias in Matthew," *JBL* 66 (1947) 165-72, is still classic. More recently, see Georg Strecker, *Der Weg der Gerechtigkeit*, FRLANT 82 (Göttingen: Vandenhoeck & Ruprecht, 1962); and John P. Meier, *The Vision of Matthew: Christ, Church, and Morality in the First Gospel* (New York: Paulist, 1979) 17-25.

18. Daniel Patte, *The Gospel According to Matthew: A Structural Commentary on Matthew's Faith* (Philadelphia: Fortress, 1987) xi.

19. In addition, Matthew himself may not have been consistently clear, but retained an uncomfortable tension in his own thought, so that our own inability to derive unambiguous results may itself be an accurate interpretation of the text. See R. T. France, *Matthew*, Tyndale New Testament Commentaries (Grand Rapids: Eerdmans, 1985) 19.

20. For a variety of perspectives on this complex history, see Jacob Neusner, "The Formation of Rabbinic Judaism: Javneh (Jamnia) from A.D. 70 to 100," *ANRW* 11.19.2.3-42; E. P. Sanders, ed., *Jewish and Christian Self-definition*, vol. 2, *Aspects of Jewish Self-definition in the Greco-Roman Period* (Philadelphia: Fortress, 1981); J. Andrew Overman, *Matthew's Gospel and Formative Judaism: The Social World of the Matthean Community* (Minneapolis: Fortress, 1990); David L. Balch, ed., *Social History of the Matthean Community* (Minneapolis: Fortress, 1991), esp. the

chaps. by Anthony J. Saldarini, "The Gospel of Matthew and Jewish Christian Conflict," 38-61, and L. Michael White, "Crisis Management and Boundary Maintenance: The Social Location of the Matthean Community," 211-47. Anthony J. Saldarini, *Matthew's Christian-Jewish Community* (Chicago: University of Chicago Press, 1994); Graham Stanton, *A Gospel for a New People* (Edinburgh: T & T Clark, 1992), chapter 5, "Synagogue and Church" 113-145.

21. Justin *Dialogue with Trypho* 16, 47, 96, 137; Origen *Homilies on Jeremiah* 10.8.2; Epiphanius *Panarion* 29.9.1; Jerome *Epistula ad Augustanum* 112.13.

22. See W. D. Davies, *The Setting of the Sermon on the Mount* (Cambridge: Cambridge University Press, 1966) 275-77.

23. See Reuven Kimelman, "Birkath ha-Minim and the Lack of Evidence for an Anti-Christian Jewish Prayer in Late Antiquity," in E. P. Sanders, ed., *Jewish and Christian Self-definition*, vol. 2, *Aspects of Jewish Self-definition in the Greco-Roman Period* (Philadelphia: Fortress, 1981) 2:245-68; Klaus Berger, M. Eugene Boring, Carsten Colpe, *Hellenistic Commentary to the New Testament* (Nashville: Abingdon, 1995), on John 16:2 for the text of this "blessing" and notes on its history and interpretation.

24. See Graham Stanton, *Gospel for a New People* (Edinburgh: T & T Clark, 1992) 85-168.

25. See Shaye J. D. Cohen, *From the Maccabees to the Mishnah* (Philadelphia: Westminster, 1987) 46-49.

26. This did not, however, make Matthew superficially pro-Gentile. He portrayed critical, negative pictures of Gentiles as well as of Jews. In 24:9, he adds "the Gentiles" to Mark's "hated by all." In 25:32, at the last judgment "all the Gentiles" will be separated into saved and condemned. In 20:19, the high priests and scribes will hand Jesus over to the Gentiles, and in 27:1-56, it is the Gentile governor and Roman soldiers who actually condemn and kill Jesus.

27. See Luke T. Johnson, "The New Testament's Anti-Jewish Slander and the Conventions of Ancient Polemic," *JBL* 108 (1989) 419-41.

28. For a more negative view of Matthew's anti-Judaism than that presented in this survey, see Fred W. Burnett, "Exposing the Anti-Jewish Ideology of Matthew's Implied Author: The Characterization of God as Father," *Semeia* 59 (1992) 155-92.

29. Pseudo-Clementine *Homilies* 20:23; *Recognitions* 10:68-71; Origen "Homily on Luke 6" (GCS Origen IX, 32).

30. This is not to say that, for Matthew, Peter was only a local patron saint. Unlike the Beloved Disciple or even Paul, Peter had significance as an ecumenical symbol. In the appended chap. 21 of the Gospel of John, Peter becomes such a symbol for the Johannine community, depite the predominance of the Beloved Disciple in chaps. 1–20.

31. Cf. Matt 11:18-19, 25-30; 23:34 vs. Luke 11:49. See also M. Jack Suggs, *Wisdom, Christology, and Law in Matthew's Gospel* (Cambridge, Mass.: Harvard University Press, 1970).

32. This is the majority scholarly view. For a more conservative evaluation of the historical value of the titles and arguments for their earlier date, see Martin Hengel, *Studies in the Gospel of Mark* (Philadelphia: Fortress, 1980).

33. Robert H. Gundry, *Matthew: A Commentary on His Literary and Theological Art* (Grand Rapids: Eerdmans, 1982) 609-22, argues for Matthean authorship, even though he believes the eyewitness Matthew relied on the secondary Mark for much of his structure and content, including the account of his own call in Matt 9:9 (Mark 2:14).

34. See Wilhelm Schneemelcher, *New Testament Apocrypha: Gospels and Related Writings* (Louisville: Westminster/John Knox, 1990). His table of contents lists 63 titles, several of which are attributed to characters more "minor" than Matthew (e.g., Thomas, Philip, Matthias, Gamaliel).

35. A significant minority of scholars understand the strong Gentile orientation of the Gospel to mean that the author himself must have been a Gentile, attributing the Jewish elements in the Gospel to the evangelist's tradition rather than his redaction. See Strecker, *Der Weg der Gerechtigkeit*, John Meier, *Matthew*, New Testament Message 3 (Collegeville, Minn.: Liturgical Press, 1990; reprint of Wilmington, Del.: Michael Glazier, 1980).

36. From the recent bibliographical explosion on this subject, the following provide readable introductions related to interpreting the Gospel of Matthew, and further bibliography: Norman R. Peterson, *Literary Criticism for New Testament Critics* (Philadelphia: Fortress, 1978); Mark Allan

Powell, *What Is Narrative Criticism?* (Philadelphia: Fortress, 1990). See esp. Jack Dean Kingsbury, *Matthew as Story*, 2nd ed. (Philadelphia: Fortress, 1988); and the essays in *Interpretation* 46 (1992).

37. The Matthean narrator is omnipresent and omniscient in relation to the world of the story, allowing the reader to stand with the narrator as the silent observer of every scene. Temporally, the narrator is located after the resurrection but prior to the parousia, during the time of the church's duress in this world. The story world constructed by the author and communicated by the narrator is limited in time and space, however, not extending to the transcendent world of God or the demons or to pre-creation or post-parousia time.

38. The narrator's point of view corresponds to that of the main character, Jesus, whose point of view is identical with that of God. The reader thus sees and hears everything from God's point of view, to which the characters in the story are not privy.

39. For a concise discussion of all these aspects of literary criticism, see Jack Dean Kingsbury, *Matthew as Story*, 2nd ed. (Philadelphia: Fortress, 1988) 30-42.

40. During the period when form and redaction criticism of the Gospels was dominant (c. 1920–60), most New Testament scholars thought of the Gospel as a unique literary genre devised by the evangelists, as in the work of Rudolf Bultmann. More recently, scholarly opinion has tended toward "Hellenistic Biography," as argued most recently by Richard A. Burridge, *What Are the Gospels*, SNTSMS 70 (Cambridge: Cambridge University Press, 1992).

41. I have elaborated each of these points in Boring, *Truly Human/Truly Divine: Christological Language and the Gospel Form* (St. Louis: Christian Board of Publication, 1984) and in *Continuing Voice of Jesus: Christian Prophecy and the Gospel Tradition* (Louisville: Westminster/John Knox, 1991).

42. See the discussion of an unidentified Greek fragment from the second century CE in Peter F. Ellis, *Matthew: His Mind and His Message* (Collegeville, Minn.: Liturgical Press, 1974) 10.

43. Bacon's view was set forth in his *Studies in Matthew* (New York: Henry Holt, 1930).

44. See Jack Dean Kingsbury, *Matthew as Story*, 2nd ed. (Philadelphia: Fortress, 1988) 40; David R. Bauer, *The Structure of Matthew's Gospel: A Study in Literary Design*, JSNTSup 31 (Sheffield: Almond, 1988).

45. Peter F. Ellis, *Matthew: His Mind and His Message* (Collegeville, Minn.: Liturgical Press, 1974) 10-13; C. H. Lohr, "Oral Techniques in the Gospel of Matthew," *CBQ* 23 (1961) 404-27.

46. W. D. Davies and Dale C. Allison, Jr., *A Critical and Exegetical Commentary on the Gospel According to Saint Matthew*, ICC 3 vols. (Edinburgh: T & T Clark, 1988–91) 1:66-68. Already W. C. Allen, *A Critical and Exegetical Commentary on the Gospel According to St. Matthew*, ICC (New York: Scribners, 1910) lxv, gives a long list of Matthean triads.

47. See Mark Allan Powell, "The Plot and Subplots of Matthew's Gospel," *NTS* 38 (1992) 187-204.

48. For a more detailed rationale for the structure here proposed, see M. Eugene Boring, "The Convergence of Source Analysis, Social History and Literary Structures in the Gospel of Matthew," *JBL Seminar Papers* (Atlanta: Scholars Press, 1994) 587-611.

The Gospel of Mark

PHEME PERKINS

AN ORIENTATION TO MARKAN STUDIES

By the early twentieth century, most scholars accepted the hypothesis that Mark provided the basic narrative framework behind the Gospels of Matthew and Luke. These two Gospels, it was believed, had supplemented Mark with material derived from a collection of Jesus' sayings (designated Q, from the German *Quelle*, meaning "source") and with other traditional material unique to each evangelist. Although more complicated theories of the relationships among the Gospels are occasionally defended, this view still provides the clearest way of understanding the synoptic Gospels.[1] Initially, this insight, combined with the brevity and simple style of the Markan narrative, led commentators to assume that Mark's Gospel contains an early summary of what was known about Jesus.[2] This view seemed to agree with the ancient testimony in Eusebius's *History of the Church* (early fourth century CE) that Mark's Gospel derives from Peter's remembrances, recorded by Mark, who had been with him in Rome.[3]

Form Criticism. The simple view of Mark as someone who collected earlier traditions about Jesus did not survive further critical analysis of the Gospel. Form criticism taught scholars to analyze the individual units as examples of established patterns in the oral tradition. It also taught them that the use of particular types of material in the life of a community influences the form and content of what becomes traditional material. In some instances, Matthew and Luke may have taken a saying or parable of Jesus from a tradition that is less developed formally than the Markan version. The duplication of groups of miracle stories surrounding the feeding of the multitudes (Mark 6:30-44; 8:1-10) and the stilling of the storm (Mark 4:35-41; 6:45-52) suggests that Mark may have used two versions of the same cycle of miracles. Analyses of the types of miracle stories in antiquity raised questions concerning the function of such narratives. Stories of rescue at sea belong to the type of story in which the epiphany of a divine being delivers individuals from distress.[4] If the reason for reciting miracle stories in the early communities was to identify Jesus as a divine being, then stories about him could have been shaped to fit that type. No individual miracle story has an *a priori* claim to represent what happened in the life of Jesus. Form-critical analysis suggests that miracles, conflict stories, and even individual sayings had all been shaped by oral tradition before the evangelist composed his Gospel, which itself was composed with the listening audience in view.[5]

Determining which features of Mark's account represent theological concerns that are peculiar to the evangelist is more difficult than in the case of Matthew and Luke. With the latter, analysis of how each evangelist has treated Mark and the common material shared by them enables scholars to suggest literary and theological emphases unique to each evangelist. The storm at sea episode is one example. In Mark's version (4:35-41), the exchange between Jesus and his disciples is very harsh. They accuse Jesus of not caring if they perish. He replies that the disciples have no faith. In Matthew's version (8:23-27), the disciples' request is formulated as a petition in a rescue story that expects a divine being to act. Matthew's Jesus comments on the disciples' "little faith" prior to his calming the sea. One might conclude that the miracle then cured their deficiency in faith. Luke (8:22-25) keeps the comment on the disciples' faith after the miracle but moderates both the disciples' request and Jesus' comment on their faith. A survey of other passages involving the disciples would show that Matthew and Luke usually moderate the harsher elements in the Markan account.

"The Twelve" Identified in Matthew, Mark, Luke, and Acts*

Matthew 10	Mark 3	Luke 6	Acts 1
Simon, also known as Peter	Simon (to whom he gave the name Peter)	Simon, whom he named Peter	Peter
Andrew his brother	James son of Zebedee	Andrew his brother	John
James son of Zebedee	John the brother of James (to whom he gave the name Boanerges, that is Sons of Thunder)		
John his brother	Andrew	John	Andrew
Philip	Philip	Philip	Philip
Bartholomew	Bartholomew	Bartholomew	Thomas
Thomas	Matthew	Matthew	Bartholomew
Matthew the tax collector	Thomas	Thomas	Matthew
James son of Alphaeus	James son of Alphaeus	James son of Alphaeus	James son of Alphaeus
Thaddaeus	Thaddaeus	Simon, who was called the Zealot	Simon the Zealot
Simon the Cananaean	Simone the Cananaean	Judas son of James	Judas son of James
Judas Iscariot, the one who betrayed him	Judas Iscariot who betrayed him	Judas Iscariot who became a traitor	

*NIB 9:138

Treatments of Mark as a simple report of what was remembered often assume that negative images of the disciples are evidence of early tradition. The modifications in Matthew and Luke could then be described as part of the process of turning Jesus' disciples into heroes. After all, the picture of Peter in Acts shows no lack of faith or unwillingness to confront suffering. So if Mark, as an earlier source, says the disciples had no faith, he must be reporting what they were actually like. However, more careful analysis of the type of material Mark is using has led scholars to reject that simple solution. Based on the results of form criticism, many scholars now believe that the traditions from which Mark crafted his portrait of the disciples would not have carried such negative evaluations. For example, the usual point of a rescue miracle was to lead the audience to acknowledge the presence of the deity. A collection of miracles that leads to misunderstanding rather than confession does not make sense. Therefore, scholars began to suspect that Mark had created his picture of Jesus' disciples by altering the traditional conclusions of such stories. One controversial solution to the problem even suggests that Mark sought to counter the influence of a Christology of the "miracle-working Jesus" that had been associated with the Twelve,[6] a view that turns the ancient theory of Markan origins on its head. Not only was Mark not a follower of Peter, but also he thought that the Twelve had misunderstood the true significance of Jesus' life and death on the cross. Most interpreters, however, do not accept this understanding of Mark's depiction of the disciples. Mark's narrative highlights the dichotomy between the divine and the human. The disciples' failure highlights the fact that Jesus transcends the purely human.[7]

Since Mark's Gospel appears to have been the earliest written account, much of the discussion during the first half of the twentieth century centered on using Mark to draw up a picture of the historical Jesus. The fact that Jesus often commanded others to remain silent about his miraculous deeds (e.g., 1:34, 44) and told his disciples not to tell anyone that he was the Messiah (8:29) was thought to indicate a deliberate policy on Jesus' part. He did not wish to draw attention to himself as a populist, political leader. That apparently simple solution, however, does not account for the Gospel's persistent motif of Jesus' authority. Even though it is not an indication of perceptive understanding, astonishment and awe can be attached to Jesus' teaching (1:22, 27), exorcism (1:27), healing (2:12), nature miracles (4:41), public activity in general (6:2), and, finally, the angelic announcement of his resurrection (16:8). Markan summaries emphasize the size of the crowds pressing around Jesus (1:32-34, 45). Since the summaries are probably Mark's composition, he can hardly have intended to suppress the popularity of Jesus with the crowds.

Redaction Criticism. During the second half of the twentieth century, redaction criticism made scholars aware of the fact that the evangelist was more than a collector of traditional material. Mark writes from a consistent point of view. Keys to his intentions have been sought in the repetitions, summary passages, stories embedded within each other, and the narrative move from the miracle worker and authoritative teacher of the opening chapters to the crucified Son of God at the close. A common approach has been to discuss Markan redaction in terms of the christology of the Gospel. As soon as Jesus is acknowledged by the disciples as the Messiah, he begins to teach them the necessity of suffering (8:27-33). A select group sees Jesus transfigured and hears God declare him "Son," only to be warned not to tell anyone until after the death and resurrection of Jesus (9:2-13). These examples suggest that Mark wishes to qualify the theology of glory with the cross, because it is only in offering himself on the cross that Jesus is truly Son of God (15:39).

In recent decades, the same redaction-critical questions that were applied to Mark have been applied to the sayings source (Q) used by both Matthew and Luke. Scholars have isolated strata within Q that identify Jesus with divine Wisdom and as an eschatological prophet who anticipated the coming of God's kingdom. This latter stage is associated with the apocalyptic Son of Man. The Q collection appears to have taken its final, written shape by 60 CE, some years earlier than Mark. Comparisons between the two raise further questions about Markan redaction.[8] Q depicts Jesus as a prophetic figure, with controversy stories and miracles understood as evidence for his authority to speak as God's representative. Like John the Baptist, Jesus suffers the fate of prophets who offend the wealthy and powerful. Mark, on the other hand, has made the cross the key to Jesus' identity (although Jesus' prophetic role remains important). Q associates Jesus' disciples with his mission much more closely than Mark does. They take up the message and the fate of their master and participate in his apocalyptic glory. When the Son of Man judges the nations, he will be assisted by the Twelve (Luke 22:30//Matt 19:28). For Mark, the Twelve only accompany Jesus during his ministry. They are chosen to "be with him" (3:14) but fail to complete the journey because they flee when Jesus is arrested. Yet the judgment that their "flight" represents a complete failure from Mark's point of view must be nuanced. Jesus predicted their flight, which fulfills the prophetic word about the flock that is scattered when its shepherd is struck down (Mark 14:27-28, citing Zech 13:7).[9] Throughout the passion narrative, Jesus' prophecies are fulfilled.

Literary Criticism. Finally, as the analysis of sources, layers of tradition, and their editing becomes more complex and less likely to yield certain historical evidence, scholars have turned to other methods. Sparked by interest in literary criticism, especially questions of how a narrative shapes the responses of its readers, literary theories are invoked to describe the impact of Mark's narrative as a whole. Individual episodes cannot be treated apart from their place in the story. Mark teaches readers what to anticipate as the Gospel progresses. They share a perspective with the narrator that differs from that of any of the characters in the story. A number of puzzling features in the Gospel, especially the fact that it ends with the women fleeing the tomb and not telling anyone, can be resolved quite differently, depending on what assumptions an interpreter thinks Mark's reader will bring to the story from the earlier narrative. If they remember that Jesus' promise to see the disciples again forms the second half of the comment on their flight (Mark 14:28), then the readers know that they will be restored as a community. If they remember the prophecies concerning the future of believers in Mark 13 or the comment that the sons of Zebedee will share Jesus' baptism of suffering (Mark 10:39), then readers know that the disciples did take up the cross. If readers bring forward the negative examples of the disciples' behavior from the earlier narrative, then the conclusion heightens Jesus' abandonment by all his followers.

Pastoral experience shows that the insights gained from methods of narrative analysis are often the most useful for preaching and Bible study. One must contend with the fact that most parishioners encounter the text only in isolated fragments, however. All of the synoptic Gospels sound the same; therefore, people find it difficult to attend to the larger structural features in each individual Gospel. One of the most endearing features of Mark's narrative on the pastoral level is the evident weaknesses of Jesus' disciples. They seem to become more bewildered and frightened as the story unfolds. For many laypersons that depiction lends a consoling air of reality to Mark's vision of Christian discipleship. No ordinary person can be like Jesus, but Mark's description of Peter sets a standard that is within reach.

Social-Scientific Criticism. Another recent development in New Testament scholarship, social-scientific criticism, looks to the social sciences for categories of analysis.[10] Models of peasant societies developed in the twentieth-century cultural anthropology are applied to the New Testament evidence. How do such societies view charismatic leaders? What is the mechanism by which persons gain and lose honor? How are social boundaries drawn and maintained? What cultural and social values are maintained by religious groups in the society? Such questions about the social, economic, and political contexts of early Christian texts tries to locate Christianity's impact on the larger social structures of its time. Sometimes concrete details in the stories provide clues about the circumstances in which a tradition originated. Gerd Theissen has observed that Mark 2:13-14 speaks of tax collectors in Capernaum. That fact requires a boundary in the vicinity. After 39 CE there would not have been such a toll station, because the territory that had belonged to Philip was united to eastern Galilee. Therefore, storytellers familiar with the situation must have framed such stories before 39 CE. This observation shows that some of Mark's traditions came from ancient Palestine and may have been collected in written form within a decade of Jesus' death.[11] However, the Palestinian origin of its traditions does not demonstrate that the Gospel was composed in Palestine.

MARK'S AUDIENCE

Redaction criticism has fostered a number of attempts to reconstruct the situation of the church for which Mark wrote.[12] The traditional view that Mark wrote down remembrances of Peter in Rome either before Peter's death or shortly thereafter lead to a number of hypotheses. The emphasis on suffering was thought to depict the persecutions in Rome under Nero's rule. However, as we know from Paul's letters (e.g., 2 Cor 1:8-11; 1 Thess 2:14-16), Christians suffered persecution elsewhere in the empire. Other readers have noted the concern with false messianic prophecies and with the fate of the Temple in Mark 13. They also point out that the advice to flee (Mark 13:14-22) correlated with the promise that Jesus would go ahead of his disciples to Galilee (Mark 14:28; 16:7). Therefore, they suggest, Mark was written somewhere in Syro-palestine during the turmoil generated by the revolt against Rome. Because of their links to Judaism, Gentile Christians could not side with the other Gentiles in the region. Because they know that Jesus was Messiah and not any of the false prophets or leaders of the Jewish rebellion, Gentile Christians could not be associated with the Jewish resistance. The extent to which Mark 13 can be taken to refer to the community depends on whether the evangelist has employed earlier apocalyptic formulations.

Discussions of the social context that is presupposed by Mark now figure prominently on both sides of the debate. Demographic descriptions of the Roman house church congregations during the first two centuries provide a possible context for the Gospel.[13] The majority of Roman Christians were lower-class immigrants, both Jew and Gentile, organized in several quite diverse house church communities. Mark commonly portrays

Jesus explaining his public teaching to the disciples inside a house (1:29-33; 2:1, 15; 3:19; 7:24). This detail may have reminded readers of their own instruction in household churches. Christianity had emerged among the Jewish population in Rome by 48 CE. A few Roman Christians enjoyed higher status than the artisans, laborers, and tradespersons of the majority. Paul's letter to Roman Christians seeks to inculcate toleration and solidarity between the various factions (Rom 11:13-36; 14:1–15:13). By the time Paul wrote Romans (c. 57 CE), Gentile Christians were in the majority and had to be warned against lording it over the Jewish Christians who had founded the churches in the city. If Paul's comments on respect for governing authorities (Rom 13:1-7) address the concrete danger of rebellion against market taxes imposed by Nero, then Mark's insistance that Christians avoid the political turmoil in Palestine may address the Roman situation as well.

A number of details in the Gospel show that the author was not familiar with places referred to in his tradition; geographical mistakes occur at several points (5:1; 6:53; 7:31; 10:1). We also find Matthew correcting Mark's citations of Scripture. For example, Mark attributes a combination of Isa 40:3 and Mal 3:1 to Isaiah (1:2-3), but Matthew cites only the Isaiah section (Matt 3:3). Mark must explain Jewish customs to his audience, and often does so with some uncertainty (7:3-4; cf. Lev 22:1-16; 7:11, 19*b*). He retains a number of Semitic words from his traditions but must explain them to readers (5:41; 7:34; 14:36; 15:22, 34, 42). Replacement of external purity rules by emphasizing moral virtues (7:14-23) may be typical of Hellenized Jews as well as Gentiles, but the assertion that "all foods are clean" (v. 19*b*), made by the narrator, would not be typical of that environment. Nor would challenges to sabbath observance (2:23-28) be characteristic of a Jewish community. Matthew modifies both stories so that the generalizing conclusions that Mark draws from them are no longer present. Jesus, who is greater than David, suspends sabbath obligation in the interests of the mercy God commanded in the prophet (Matt 12:1-8). Matthew omits Mark's parenthetical comment that Jesus declared all foods clean (Matt 15:15-20). Those exegetes who agree that Mark's audience was Gentile Christians, but hold that Mark himself was a Palestinian Jew,[14] seem to ignore both the internal evidence as well as the evidence from Matthean corrections that Mark is not personally familiar with Jewish practice.

By the mid-first century CE, Christians were distinguishable from Jews, so the Christians were singled out as scapegoats for the great fire during Nero's reign.[15] Mark refers to persecution as the cause for many to fall away (4:17) and for fraternal betrayal (13:9). These comments might easily refer to the type of betrayal experienced by the Roman Christians during this persecution, which would cost both Peter and Paul their lives.[16] In 2 Tim 4:9-16, Paul injects this note of betrayal into Paul's last days, when those who should have defended the apostle abandoned him instead. None of these correspondences demand a Roman locale for the audience projected by Mark's narrative. The traditional assumption that Mark was written at Rome was based on the tradition that linked Mark with Peter. Early Christian writings from Rome contain no evidence of familiarity with Mark. Therefore, the best one can say for the traditional view that Mark's intended audience was the Roman house churches c. 70 CE is that the Gospel can be understood as reflecting that experience. The understanding of discipleship it projects would incorporate the situations faced by Christians in Rome.[17]

Other exegetes remain unconvinced by the claim that early Palestinian Jesus tradition, preserved among Roman Christians, accounts for the Palestinian elements in the Gospel of Mark.[18] They locate Mark's church among the Gentile communities of the eastern provinces, possibly in Palestine or Syria. With the number of Hellenistic cities in that area, such a change in venue may not contribute much to understanding the social context of the Gospel itself. The Latinisms found in Mark (12:42; 15:16) may have been commonplace anywhere Roman soldiers were quartered.

Those who think that Mark was written from a Syro-palestinian perspective, point to chapter 13 as their major evidence. Its prophecies of false prophets, war, denial, and betrayal (vv. 6-13) fit the turmoil associated with the civic strife that accompanied the Jewish war against Rome.[19] The focus on the Temple's destruction (13:1-2), as well as Jesus' condemnation of the Temple as a "house of brigands" (11:17), may allude to events at the end of that revolt. Zealot leaders had taken over the Temple as their headquarters (perhaps motivated by prophecies from Daniel[20]). Titus destroyed the Temple completely, leaving not one stone standing. The Jewish civil war created serious problems for Gentile Christians as well, who were easily caught up in the violence erupting between Gentiles and Jews in the Hellenistic cities of Palestine during the revolt. Josephus describes massacres by both Jews and Gentiles of each other.[21] Mark's emphasis on Jesus' positive stance toward Gentiles and its sharp attacks on Jewish leaders have been seen as responses to such violence.[22] Since Josephus describes the zealots who occupied the Temple as defiling it,[23] Mark's advice to flee when sacrilege occurs has been read as an allusion to that event (13:14). The Jewish leaders are seen as responsible for the destruction that has come upon the nation (Mark 12:9).

As in the case for a Roman provenance, the hypotheses of Palestinian origins provides a possible explanation for some of the details in the narrative. Josephus's own account of the Jewish war shows that it was possible for a Jew living in Rome to offer an account of those events some years after Mark's Gospel was written. Josephus's writing serves an apologetic function. Unlike the Zealots, whose excessive pride God punished by destroying the Temple, the Romans demonstrated reverence for Jerusalem as a holy place.[24] Mark need not have written his Gospel in immediate proximity to the events of the Jewish revolt to use them as evidence for the truth of Jesus' predictions concerning the Temple and the fate of Israel.

The difficulty in determining a concrete sociopolitical context for Mark's Gospel has been further complicated by the influence of narrative criticism. Literary critics have warned scholars against making quick judgments about the historical communities that lie behind a text. They point out that narratives can project an implied audience, which may be quite different from the actual readers. Unlike the apocalyptic visions of Daniel 7–12, Mark does not correlate prophecies, specific historical figures, and events. Therefore, Mark does not seem interested in providing an apocalyptic history to explain events in the recent past. Mark 13 remains subordinate to the larger framework of events that led to Jesus' death on the cross, since Mark has woven the discussion of the Temple's fate into the narrative of Jesus' death. Both occur according to God's plan.[25]

AUTHORSHIP AND DATE OF COMPOSITION

Since Mark must have been written before Matthew and Luke, and since the turmoil in Judea, which led to the destruction of the Temple, appears to have been in progress or recently completed by the time the Gospel was written, most scholars agree that Mark wrote his Gospel probably around 70 CE. Those who hold out for the tradition of a Roman origin prior to Peter's martyrdom opt for the earlier end of the spectrum, c. 62–64 CE. The tradition that Mark's Gospel was associated with Peter first appeared in the second century. Eusebius cites a statement by Papias (c. 120/130 CE): "Mark, who became Peter's interpreter, accurately wrote, though not in order, as many of the things said and done by the Lord as he had remembered."[26] Eusebius goes on to explain that Mark collected anecdotes from Peter, but did not possess an ordered account from the apostle. The Papias tradition does not actually affirm that Mark was in Rome when he met Peter, although most later authors presumed that was the case. Since the Papias tradition refers only to anecdotes, the statement could merely be a defense of the apostolic origin of the Gospel. However, when its traditions are compared with the other Gospels and with evidence for pre-Gospel tradition in Q, one finds that the anecdotes cannot be a collection of stories from a single source. Mark, itself, contains variants of a single tradition. Some of Mark's material had already been collected into larger units, and other episodes appear to be preserved in a more primitive form in Q.

Therefore, those scholars who do not wish to dismiss the ancient testimony completely presume that Papias correctly identifies the author of the Gospel as a second-generation Christian named Mark. Since "Mark" was a common name, that clue does not provide much help in locating the Gospel or its author. The New Testament refers to a Jewish Christian named Mark who was initially associated with Paul (Acts 12:12; 13:5, 13; Col 4:10; Philemon 1:24). First Pet 5:13 refers to Mark as an associate of the imprisoned Peter. Since 1 Peter speaks of its city of origin as "Babylon," a well-established code for Rome (cf. Rev 17:5),[27] later Christians would conclude that Mark received his material from Peter at Rome. Whether or not these references to "Mark" refer to one and the same person cannot be determined. First Pet 5:12 claims that the letter was written down by another Pauline follower, Silvanus (2 Cor 1:19; 1 Thess 1:1). Therefore, it appears that the author of 1 Peter seeks to assimilate Peter's image to that of Paul by including two figures from the Pauline mission. The Mark referred to in 1 Pet 5:13 is probably the "John Mark" associated with the Pauline mission, but that connection does not provide any significant information about the author of the Gospel of Mark.

The evidence clearly does not support one theory of authorship or social context over the other. Awkward explanations of Jewish customs do suggest that the community consisted of Gentiles (cf. Mark 7:3-4; 14:12; 15:42). Mark has inherited multiple versions of some miracles. Other units of the narrative, such as the discourse on parables (Mark 4:1-34), the apocalyptic discourse (Mark 13), and the passion narrative, seem to embody several levels of tradition. Therefore, the Gospel reflects a more complex history than the ancient tradition might suggest. Mark was not composed to record historical remembrances about Jesus. Mark 1:1 refers to what follows as the "beginning of the gospel of Jesus Christ." In Paul's letters, "gospel" (εὐαγγέλιον *euangelion*) refers to the message of salvation that the apostle preached (Rom 1:1, 16; 10:16; 11:28; 1 Cor 4:15; Gal 1:6-9). Mark 1:14-15 retains that sense of *gospel* as "preached message." Therefore, the opening words of Mark suggest that what follows fulfills the function of earlier preaching.

LITERARY GENRE

By attaching the noun *gospel* to the beginning of a narrative, Mark signals a transition from the oral form of "preached message" to the designation of a written account of Jesus as a "gospel." As scholars have come to appreciate the marked contrast between speech and writing in the dynamics of cultural transmission, that shift in meaning has taken on new importance. The privileged authority for the tradition shifts away from lineal descendents, charismatic prophets, or wise elders charged with remembering and restating the tradition. In the moment of speaking and hearing, the audience encounters directly the founding authority of its faith. Interpretation and personal communication are embedded in the oral performance quite differently from the way they are in writing.[28] Papias's version of the origins of Mark's Gospel suggests an attempt to recapture a world that is passing by looking for a tradition that links writing with having heard the apostles; the materials in Mark's narrative exhibit numerous characteristics of oral transmission.[29] Yet, the Gospel ends on a note of silence (16:8), which sets the oral world at risk.[30]

By recognizing the tension between the oral and written in Markan tradition, we can appreciate the difficulties built into the question of genre. The usual question posed by Mark 1:1 is whether the evangelist has created a new written genre, "the gospel." Since a genre cannot emerge without antecedents, what comparative experiences with texts would readers or hearers bring to the gospel? Or has Mark merely adapted a familiar genre, such as a Hellenistic biography, to the traditional material available? A century of vigorous debate saw the question of the gospels as ancient biographies eclipsed by form criticism, only to return to the former way of thinking when it became clear that the evangelists did more than collect and edit earlier complexes of tradition. The intentionality evident in the construction of the narrative poses the question of what conception of genre guided the process.[31]

In 1901 Wilhelm Wrede's book *The Messianic Secret in the Gospels* was published, a book that has played a critical role in discussions of gospel genre.[32] Wrede emphasized the tension between the confession that Jesus is Messiah and Lord and the pre-resurrection life and deeds of Jesus. He proposed that Mark took the idea of a "messianic secret" from his sources to combine his christological confession with a non-christological version of Jesus' deeds. The disciples are depicted as unable to perceive the truth about Jesus until after the resurrection. By making this combination, Mark provides a christological context for the Gospel's readers. Therefore, the gospel genre has a confessional shape, which distinguishes it from the common Greco-Roman biographies.

Ancient biographies emphasize the unusual birth, the childhood exploits that prefigure the heroe's later life, and the extraordinary nature of the characters. A life should end with triumph and honor. If the hero is condemned, like Socrates, then he should exhibit wisdom in fearless nobility and a wise saying. Biographies of Moses by Jewish writers like Philo and Josephus follow all the conventions of their time.[33] The Gospels, however, do not fit the model provided by such biographies. Some scholars have resolved the dilemma by arguing that Mark chooses to narrate history in an apocalyptic mode.[34] This hypothesis has its own difficulties, since Mark does not employ the symbolic or prophetic typologies to encode the account of Jesus' ministry and death into a cosmic vision of salvation.

The apocalyptic analogies do highlight an important element in the gospel genre: The truth about its hero cannot be divorced from a revelation of God's purposes. Without that post-resurrection perspective, the life of Jesus, unlike that of Moses, would not be sufficiently noteworthy to merit attention. Some scholars prefer to treat Mark as the foundation story for an early Christian community that had no interest in history or biography.[35] This view assumes that a non-messianic Jesus tradition can be reconstructed from Q, which reflects the original emphasis of Jesus' ministry. Consequently a narrative that depicted him as the suffering Son of Man could only be the product of extensive communal myth-making. Part of the difficulty in assigning a particular literary genre to the Gospel lies in the nature of its sources. The fact that Mark's literary skills do not approach those of most ancient biographers may indicate that he was unaware of the rhetorical conventions associated with composing the life of a famous figure. Mark also appears to have been constrained by his sources. They were not christologically neutral but had been shaped by emerging Christian beliefs.[36] Despite the elements of eschatology and the peculiar death of its hero, which stretch the boundaries of what was commonly thought to be a biography or a "life," Greco-Roman readers would have to conclude that Mark is an exercise in biography. Recent stage productions demonstrate that Mark's oral character makes it possible to envisage the entire Gospel's being performed before an audience.[37]

Wrede correctly pointed out that the Gospel has a confessional agenda to establish the fact that Jesus is the Son of God. Some scholars add to this emphasis the necessity of explaining how the Son of God came to be crucified. The scandal of the cross must be absorbed into the larger explanation of God's saving purposes. Both of these concerns have been embedded in the structure of the narrative itself.

Scholars generally agree that the Gospel of Mark can be divided between the initial account of Jesus' divine authority in miracles and teaching and the preparation for the passion, which begins at 8:27. There is less agreement about smaller divisions within the two halves of the Gospel. The evangelist often initiates an episode, interrupts it to recount another event, and then returns to the first episode (e.g., 3:20-21, 31-35; 5:21-24*a*, 35-43; 11:12-14, 20-25; 14:1-2, 11-10). By interlocking individual stories, Mark encourages the reader to interpret one episode in the light of the other. At the same time, the interruptions reflect typical patterns of oral storytelling. Another pattern of organization that makes it easy for hearers to follow the progress of the story is by geography. The Prologue contains John the Baptist's witness to Jesus as the "Coming One" in the desert (1:1-8). Prior to the turn toward the passion, Jesus' ministry takes place in and around Galilee (1:9–8:21). Then Jesus begins a journey that moves toward Jerusalem while he instructs the disciples about the cross (8:22–10:52). His passion and death conclude a series of events that take place in and around Jerusalem (11:1–15:41). Finally, a series of events take place at the tomb, ending with the angel's announcement and the flight of the women (15:42–16:8).[38]

EXCURSUS: REIGN OF GOD IN MARK

The phrase "reign" or "kingdom" of God (ἡ βασιλεία τοῦ θεοῦ *hē basileia tou theou*) frequently designates the subject of Jesus' message in the synoptic Gospels.[39] Although more common in Matthew and Luke, this phrase occurs fourteen times in the Gospel of Mark. In the Old Testament, God's rule over Israel would usher in the age of justice and peace. Isaiah 52:7 heralds good news, peace, salvation, and the reign of God to the nation. Since God's rule would also be the day of vengeance against the wicked (cf. Isa 61:1-2), the summons to repent implies the need to prepare the nation for the coming of the rule of God. However, the Hebrew expression "kingdom of God," or its Greek equivalent, appears only twice in the Old Testament (1 Chr 28:5; Wis 10:10). In the apocalyptic tradition, God's rule always exists in heaven. When that rule finally holds sway on earth, the kingdoms of earthly rulers will be destroyed (Dan 2:44; Rev 11:15).

Consequently, statements about entering the kingdom suggest conditions that persons must fulfill in order to be counted among the elect who are part of the kingdom God establishes (cf. Mark 10:23-24; Rom 14:17-18). "Entering" sayings suggest a future dimension to the kingdom. Those who fulfill the stipulated conditions now will belong to the kingdom that is to come. In the beatitudes the kingdom can be said to belong to particular persons (Matt 5:3, 10; Luke 6:20); the same expression appears in Jesus' saying about the children (10:13-16).

Mark's description of Joseph of Arimathea as one who awaits the kingdom of God (15:43) suggests that the kingdom's presence is not the direct result of human activity; God must be responsible for its approach. The crowd's acclamation in Mark 11:10 refers to the "kingdom of our father David that is coming." Reference to a "secret" associated with the kingdom (Mark 4:11) suggests that believers have an understanding of the kingdom that differs from expectations held by the crowd. Some of Jesus' sayings suggest that the kingdom is not yet present but can be anticipated by his disciples (Mark 9:1; 14:25). The parables, which are introduced as examples of the kingdom of God (4:26, 30), suggest a hidden presence of the kingdom's beginning. Its arrival appears both inevitable and somewhat beyond human control.

The juxtaposition of the critical time being fulfilled and the kingdom drawing near in the introduction to Jesus' ministry (1:4-15) creates ambiguity over how the kingdom of God is related to the ministry of Jesus. On the one hand, Jesus' preaching and ministry seem intended to make the rule of God present to those who believe. On the other hand, the cosmic judgment which will make God's rule over the world visible to all nations remains in the future. One solution is to treat the fulfillment as a reference to the promises in the prophetic quotation of 1:2-3, while the incompleteness of the kingdom looks toward the future. Jesus' ministry has inaugurated the coming of the kingdom.[40]

FOR FURTHER READING

Best, Ernest. *Mark: The Gospel as Story.* Edinburgh: T & T Clark, 1983.

Collins, Adela Yarbro. *The Beginning of the Gospel: Probings of Mark in Context.* Minneapolis: Fortress, 1992.

Donahue, John R. and Daniel J. Harrington. *The Gospel of Mark.* SP 2. Collegeville, Minn.: Liturgical Press, 2001.

Fowler, Robert M. *Let the Reader Understand: Reader-Response Criticism and the Gospel of Mark.* Minneapolis: Fortress, 1991.

Guelich, Robert A. *Mark 1–8:26.* WBC 34A. Dallas: Word, 1989.

Gundry, Robert H. *Mark: A Commentary on His Apology for the Cross.* Grand Rapids: Eerdmans, 1993.

Hooker, Morna D. *The Gospel According to St. Mark.* London: A. & C. Black, 1991.

Horsley, Richard A. *Hearing the Whole Story: The Politics of Plot in Mark's Gospel.* Louisville, Ky.: Westminster/John Knox, 2001.

Kingsbury, Jack Dean. *The Christology of Mark's Gospel.* Philadelphia: Fortress, 1983.

Levine, Amy-Jill and Marianne Blickenstaff, eds. *A Feminist Companion to Mark.* Feminist Companion to the New Testament and Early Christian Writings 2. Sheffield: Sheffield Academic Press, 2001.

Maloney, Elliott C. *Jesus' Urgent Message for Today: The Kingdom of God in Mark's Gospel.* London: Continuum, 2004.

Räisänen, Heikki. *The "Messianic Secret" in Mark.* Translated by C. Tuckett. Edinburgh: T & T Clark, 1990.

Sabin, Marie Noon. *Reopening the Word: Reading Mark as Theology in the Context of Early Judaism.* New York: Oxford University Press, 2002.

Taylor, Vincent. *The Gospel According to St. Mark.* 2nd ed. New York: St. Martin's, 1966.

Tolbert, Mary Ann. *Sowing the Gospel: Mark's World in Literary-Historical Perspective.* Minneapolis: Fortress, 1989.

ENDNOTES

1. For a detailed analysis of the argument for the two-source theory of gospel composition, see Joseph A. Fitzmyer, *The Gospel According to Luke I–IX*, AB 32 (Garden City, N.Y.: Doubleday, 1981) 63-97. For an analysis of the hypotheses concerning a possible pre-Markan passion narrative, see M. Soards, "The Question of a Premarkan Passion Narrative," in Raymond E. Brown, *The Death of the Messiah: From Gethsemane to the Grave. A*

Commentary on the Passion Narratives in the Four Gospels, vol. 2 (Garden City, N.Y.: Doubleday, 1994) appendix IX.

2. See Vincent Taylor, *The Gospel According to St. Mark,* 2nd ed. (New York: St. Martin's, 1966).

3. Eusebius *History of the Church* 3.39.5.

4. See Gerd Theissen, *The Miracle Stories of the Early Christian Tradition,* trans. F. McDonagh (Philadelphia: Fortress, 1983) 100-103.

5. See the extensive discussion of oral characteristics in Markan style by Christopher Bryan, *A Preface to Mark: Notes on the Gospel in Its Literary and Cultural Settings* (New York: Oxford, 1993) 67-151.

6. See T. J. Weeden, *Mark: Traditions in Conflict* (Philadelphia: Fortress, 1971).

7. See Philip G. Davis, "Mark's Christological Paradox," *JSNT* 35 (1989) 3-18.

8. See Dieter Lührmann, "The Gospel of Mark and the Sayings Collection Q," *JBL* 108 (1989) 51-71; *Das Markusevangelium,* HNT (Tübingen: J.C.B. Mohr [Paul Siebeck], 1987).

9. See Brown, *The Death of the Messiah,* vol. 2, 128-30.

10. See John H. Elliott, *What Is Social-Scientific Criticism?* (Minneapolis: Fortress, 1993); Gerd Theissen, *The Gospels in Context: Social and Political History in the Synoptic Tradition* (Minneapolis: Fortress, 1991); Bruce J. Malina and Richard L. Rohrbaugh, *A Social-Science Commentary on the Synoptic Gospels* (Philadelphia: Fortress, 1992).

11. Theissen, *The Gospels in Context,* 119-20.

12. See Joel Marcus, "The Jewish War and the *Sitz im Leben* of Mark," *JBL* 111 (1992) 441-62; C. Clifton Black, "Was Mark a Roman Gospel?" *ExpTim* 105 (1993) 36-40; Theissen, *The Gospels in Context,* 235-89.

13. On Roman Christianity see Peter Lampe, *Die stadrömischen Christen in den ersten beiden Jahrhunderten: Untersuchungen zur Sozialgeschichte* (Tübingen: J.C.B. Mohr [Paul Siebeck], 1987); J. S. Jeffers, *Conflict at Rome: Social Order and Hierarchy in Early Christianity* (Minneapolis: Fortress, 1991).

14. Such as Dieter Lührmann, *Das Markusevangelium,* 6-7; Robert A. Guelich, *Mark 1–8:26,* WBC 34A (Dallas: Word, 1989) xxviii.

15. Tacitus *Annals* 15.44.

16. *1 Clem* 5.4-7; 6.1; Ignatius. *Rom.* 4.2-3.

17. See Black, "Was Mark a Roman Gospel?"

18. See, e.g., Howard Clark Kee, *Community of the New Age: Studies in Mark's Gospel* (Philadelphia: Westminster, 1977); Dieter Lührmann, "The Gospel of Mark and the Sayings Collection Q" Marcus, "The Jewish War and the *Sitz im Leben* of Mark"; Theissen, *The Gospels in Context.*

19. For sociological studies of the situation in Judea during this period, see Richard Fenn, *The Death of Herod: An Essay in the Sociology of Religion* (Cambridge: Cambridge University Press, 1992); Martin Goodman, *The Ruling Class of Judea: The Origins of the Jewish Revolt Against Rome A.D. 66–70* (Cambridge: Cambridge University Press, 1987); for a discussion of Judea in the context of Roman policy in the Near East see Fergus Millar, *The Roman Near East 31 B.C.–A.D. 337* (Cambridge, Mass.: Harvard University Press, 1993).

20. See Marcus, "The Jewish War and the *Sitz im Leben* of Mark."

21. Josephus *Jewish Wars* 2.18.1-2; secs. 457-61.

22. See Marcus, "The Jewish War and the *Sitz im Leben* of Mark," 453. Theissen makes the more probable suggestion that Gentile Christians in these cities would have fallen victim to attack by both sides (*Gospels in Context,* 268-70).

23. Josephus *Jewish Wars* 4.6.3; sec. 388.

24. See Josephus *Jewish Wars* 5.362-74. See also Hans Conzelmann, *Gentiles, Jews, Christians: Polemics and Apologetics in the Greco-Roman Era,* trans. E. M. Boring (Minneapolis: Fortress, 1992) 203-11.

25. See Robert A. Guelich, "Anti-Semitism and/or Anti-Judaism in Mark?" in *Anti-Semitism and Early Christianity,* ed. C. A. Evans and D. H. Hagner (Minneapolis: Fortress, 1993) 92-95.

26. Eusebius *Ecclesiastical History* 3.39.15.

27. On the connection between Peter and Rome in Eusebius, see Pheme Perkins, *Peter: Apostle for the Whole Church* (Columbia: University of South Carolina Press, 1994) 41-43; on the Papias tradition, see Charles M. Nielsen, "Papias: Polemicist Against Whom?" *TS* 35 (1974) 529-35.

28. See the seminal study by Werner Kelber, *The Oral and the Written Gospel* (Philadelphia: Fortress, 1983) 90-139.

29. Kelber, *The Oral and the Written Gospel* 44-89; Christopher Bryan, *A Preface to Mark: Notes on the Gospel in Its Literary and Cultural Settings* (New York: Oxford, 1993) 67-84.

30. Kelber (*The Oral and the Written Gospel* 128-

29) insists that Mark deliberately destroys the hopes of the disciples to be representatives of the risen Lord.

31. See Theissen, *The Gospels in Context:* 235; David E. Aune, *The New Testament in Its Literary Environment* (Philadelphia: Westminster, 1987) 17-76; Adela Yarbro Collins, *The Beginning of the Gospel* (Minneapolis: Fortress, 1992) 1-38.

32. Wrede's book was translated as *The Messianic Secret* (Cambridge: Clarke, 1971).

33. See Louis H. Feldman, *Jew and Gentile in the Ancient World* (Princeton: Princeton University Press, 1993) 242-87; Aune, *The New Testament in Its Literary Environment* 27-66; Christopher Bryan, *A Preface to Mark: Notes on the Gospel in Its Literary and Cultural Settings* (New York: Oxford, 1993) 22-64.

34. So Collins, *The Beginning of the Gospel*, 4-38.

35. See Burton L. Mack, *A Myth of Innocence: Mark and Christian Origins* (Philadelphia: Fortress, 1988).

36. This notion is contrary to Wrede.

37. The videotape of the British actor Alec McCowan reciting the King James Version of Mark is distributed by the American Bible Society.

38. See Christopher Bryan, *A Preface to Mark: Notes on the Gospel in Its Literary and Cultural Settings*, 82-84.

39. See George R. Beasley-Murray, *Jesus and the Kingdom of God* (Grand Rapids: Eerdmans, 1986); Joel Marcus, "Entering into the Kingly Power of God," *JBL* 107 (1988) 663-75; J. C. O'Neill, "The Kingdom of God," *NovT* 35 (1993) 130-41; Roy A. Harrisville, "In Search of the Meaning of 'The Reign of God' " *Int* 47 (1993) 140-51.

40.Cf. Aloysius M. Ambrozic, *The Hidden Kingdom: A Redaction-Critical Study of the References to the Kingdom of God in Mark's Gospel*, CBQMS 2 (Washington, D.C.: Catholic Biblical Association, 1972) 19-25.

The Gospel of Luke

R. ALAN CULPEPPER

Each of the Gospels presents the story of Jesus in a different way, and much of their richness is lost if one tries to harmonize them into one consistent account. Each Gospel contains a different structure, develops different themes, and portrays the person of Jesus in its own unique way. The Markan Jesus is an enigmatic and tragic figure, misunderstood and abandoned. Being a disciple of the Markan Jesus means taking up the cross and following him. The Matthean Jesus is a new Moses who fulfills the Scripture and establishes the authority of his own words. Being a disciple of the Matthean Jesus, therefore, means keeping his teachings and making other disciples. The Johannine Jesus is the Word incarnate, the heavenly revealer who is not of this world but who was sent to reveal the Father. Being a disciple of the Johannine Jesus means responding to the revelation with belief, being born from above, imbibing living water and eating the bread of life, and fulfilling one's place and vocation in the community of the "children of God."

The Lukan Jesus is compassionate, a friend to outcasts. Luke also relates Jesus to the history of Israel, the Scriptures, contemporary world history, and the unfolding of God's redemptive purposes in human history. Jesus is the Savior sent to seek and to save the lost. For Israel, Jesus' ministry has ironic and tragic consequences. The religious leaders reject Jesus, and like those who killed God's prophets in the past, they hand Jesus over to be crucified. The people, however, are far more receptive to Jesus than are their leaders, and they are only temporarily implicated in his death during the trial before Pilate. The Gospel ends with the disciples being commissioned as witnesses for the mission they will undertake in the book of Acts.

In order to enter more deeply into the reading of this Gospel, one needs to consider its place among the Gospels, recognize its distinctive structure, sensitize oneself to its dominant christological emphases, and summarize its leading themes.

LUKE AMONG THE GOSPELS

Like the other Gospels, Luke's author is anonymous; it does not indicate who wrote it or where or when it was written. According to early tradition that can be traced to the second century, Luke, the physician and companion of Paul, wrote both Luke and Acts. The earliest manuscript of the Gospel $\mathfrak{P}^{75}$, dates from 175–225 CE and contains extensive portions of the Gospel. This manuscript contains the earliest occurrence of the title "Gospel According to Luke." How much earlier the titles of the Gospels may be traced is a matter of debate. The titles were apparently attached to the Gospels, however, when they began to circulate and it became necessary to distinguish one from another.

The New Testament provides meager information about Luke. Philemon lists Luke among Paul's "fellow workers" (Philemon 24). Colossians, which was probably written about the same time, names Luke among Paul's companions and identifies him as "the beloved physician" (Col 4:14). Second Timothy, which was probably composed later by one of Paul's associates, reports of Paul's final imprisonment, "Only Luke is with me" (2 Tim 4:11).

The "we" passages in Acts (16:10-17; 20:5-15; 21:1-18; 27:1–28:16) have contributed further to the tradition of Luke's association with Paul. In these verses the narrator in Acts shifts from third-person to first-person narrative. These passages have been interpreted in various ways: as evidence that the author was present with Paul on these occasions and wrote from firsthand experience (or, in a variation of this view, that he used his own diaries); that he drew from a diary written by one of Paul's companions and did not change the voice of the narrator to make it consistent with the rest of his account; or that he wrote in the first person at this point in the narrative to heighten interest or to follow a literary convention in the reporting of sea voyages.

Even if one takes the New Testament references to Luke at face value and agrees that Luke was the author of Luke and Acts and that the "we" sections report Luke's firsthand experiences, the New Testament does not tell us how much Luke was influenced by Paul's thought. Since Luke is listed among those who "send greetings" (Col 4:14; Philemon 24), one might presume that Luke knew of Paul's letter writing. Nevertheless, we do not know that Luke read Paul's letters; we do not know how long Luke was with Paul or how familiar he was with the patterns of Paul's theology and preaching. As a result, we must read the Gospel according to Luke on its own terms and not against the background of Pauline theology.

The earliest references to Lukan authorship in the writings of the Church Fathers appear in ancient prologues and in the writings of Irenaeus and Tertullian. The latter are easier to date than the former.

Irenaeus (c. 130–200), bishop of Lyon and defender of the fourfold Gospel, wrote *Against Heresies*, a lengthy apologetic work in five books, around 185 CE. At issue in the interpretation of Irenaeus's testimony is how much he knew of Luke and the composition of the Gospel beyond the New Testament references surveyed above. Irenaeus wrote: "Luke also, the companion of Paul, recorded in a book the Gospel preached by him."[1] Irenaeus, therefore, attributes to Luke a role in relation to Paul similar to the role that tradition from Papias accorded to Mark: "Mark, the disciple and interpreter of Peter, did also hand down to us in writing what had been preached by Peter."[2] Citing the "we" passages, Irenaeus claims further that "Luke was inseparable from Paul" and that he "performed the work of an evangelist, and was entrusted to hand down to us a Gospel."[3] In doing so, Luke, who was "not merely a follower, but also a fellow-labourer of the Apostles," learned from the apostles what they had learned from the Lord and delivered to us "what he had learned from them," as he himself testified in Luke 1:1-4.[4] Valuable as his testimony is, therefore, Irenaeus, our earliest witness, tells us nothing more than can be found in the New Testament references.

In his treatise *Against Marcion*, Tertullian (c. 150–c. 225, writing c. 207–208) attacks both Marcion's rejection of the other three Gospels and his abridgment of the Gospel according to Luke. Regarding the first, Tertullian insists on the succession of the Lord, the apostles (Matthew, John, and later Paul), and those who followed the apostles (Mark and Luke).

> Of the apostles, therefore, John and Matthew first instil faith into us; whilst of apostolic men, Luke and Mark renew it afterwards. . . . Luke however, was not an apostle, but only an apostolic man; not a master, but a disciple, and so inferior to a master—at least as far subsequent to him as the apostle whom he followed (and that, no doubt was Paul) was subsequent to the others. . . . Inasmuch, therefore, as the enlightener of St. Luke himself [Paul] desired the authority of his predecessors for both his own faith and preaching, how much more may not I require for Luke's Gospel that which was necessary for the Gospel of his master.[5]

Nevertheless, Tertullian affirms the authority of the Gospel and defends the credibility of its transmission prior to Marcion's proposed emendation of it. Marcion must have found it in its original form, since he argued that it had been "interpolated by defenders of Judaism."[6] Luke's Gospel, Tertullian affirms, "has stood its ground from its very first publication. . . . For even Luke's form of the Gospel men usually ascribe to Paul" and "Luke's Gospel also has come down to us in like integrity [as the other Gospels] until the sacrilegious treatment of Marcion."[7] Tertullian, therefore, attests the authority of Luke and the reliability of its original form, rejecting Marcion's argument for an abridged version of the Gospel.

The date of the Muratorian Canon, which survives in an eighth-century manuscript, is debated. It has been suggested that it comes from Rome around 200 CE, but more recently arguments for a fourth-century date and provenance have gained ground.[8] The introduction to Luke, at least, contains little that could not have been gleaned from the New Testament.

> The third Gospel book, that according to Luke. This physician Luke after Christ's ascension (resurrection?), since Paul had taken him with him as an expert in the way (of the teaching), composed it in

> his own name according to (his) thinking. Yet neither did he himself see the Lord in the flesh; and therefore, as he was able to ascertain it, so he begins to tell the story from the birth of John.[9]

The prologue to Luke in the ancient Gospel prologues contains further biographical information. The "Oldest Gospel Prologues" were once thought to have been composed together as anti-Marcionite prologues to the four Gospels, but they are now generally treated as independent documents. R. G. Heard concluded that the prologue to Luke in its present form dates from the third century. Nevertheless, he suggested that the first part of it "incorporates, if not an earlier and purely biographical Prologue, at least earlier and very valuable biographical data."[10] The first part of the prologue reads as follows:

> Luke is a Syrian of Antioch, a doctor by profession, who was a disciple of apostles, and later followed Paul until his martyrdom. He served the Lord, without distraction, unmarried, childless, and fell asleep at the age of 84 in Boetia, full of the Holy Spirit.[11]

The second part adds that he wrote the Gospel "in the regions of Achaea." While these biographical details are credible, they are also unsubstantiated, making it difficult to know how much value to assign to them.

As this brief survey of the testimony of the Church Fathers indicates, from late in the second century the tradition that Luke wrote the Gospel and Acts was widely accepted. Most of what we know about Luke, however, comes from the New Testament itself. By the third century, added details about Luke and the circumstances of the composition of the Gospel appear in the old Gospel prologues, but this data cannot be corroborated from other sources. In view of this impasse, scholars have turned to the Gospel of Luke itself and its relationship to the other Gospels for further information regarding the evangelist and the composition of the Gospel.

The Gospel of Luke is an independent composition with its own literary and theological integrity. Nevertheless, it is often instructive to note parallels (or a lack of them) in Mark or Matthew. Luke himself indicates that he knows of other written accounts (see 1:1). Luke does not number himself among the eyewitnesses, however, but among those who came later and learned the tradition "handed on to us by those who from the beginning were eyewitnesses and servants of the word" (1:2-3).

The Gospel of John is the result of a similarly complicated, but probably independent, composition history. Using the Two Source hypothesis (Mark and Q) one can derive the following rough outline of Luke's use of his sources.

Luke 1:1–2:52	L
Luke 3:1–6:19	Mark (and Q for material about John the Baptist and the Temptations)
Luke 6:20–8:3	Q and L
Luke 8:4–9:50	Mark
Luke 9:51–18:14	Q and L
Luke 18:15–24:11	Mark and L
Luke 24:12–24:53	L

The infancy narrative has no parallel in the other Gospels and is quite different from the birth account in Matthew 1–2. Whereas Matthew features Joseph's role in the birth of Jesus, Luke's account highlights Mary's role. The only elements common to the two accounts can be summarized in a confessional statement: Jesus was born of the virgin Mary in Bethlehem. Luke defers the genealogy of Jesus until after the baptism and temptations, and the genealogy is quite different from that found in Matthew 1:1-18, except that both are genealogies of Joseph and both trace the line of Jesus to David and Abraham.

Luke also brings forward Jesus' visit to Nazareth (Mark 6:1-6) and uses the scene in the synagogue at Nazareth (Luke 4:16-30) as the keynote for Jesus' public ministry. For the ministry in Galilee, Luke (4:31–6:19) follows Mark (1:21–3:19) until the Sermon on the Plain, which is not found in Mark but has parallels in Matthew's Sermon on the Mount.

Following the sermon, Luke adds a collection of miracles and teachings (7:1–8:3) that clarify Jesus' role in relation to John the Baptist and his identity as one greater than the prophets. This section, which is compiled from tradition drawn from Q and L, has been called the "little interpolation."

Through the rest of the Galilean ministry (Luke 8:4–9:50) Luke follows Mark (Mark 4:1–9:40). Curiously, Luke's account of the Galilean ministry skips sections of the Markan account: the so-called big omission (Mark 6:45–8:26 at Luke 9:17) and the "little omission" (Mark 9:41–10:12 at Luke 9:50).

The "big interpolation" follows (9:51–18:14). Luke fills nine chapters of the extended journey to Jerusalem with incidents and teachings drawn from Q and L. Luke, therefore, places most of the Q material in the little and big interpolations, whereas Matthew places it in five sermon blocks (Matt 5:1–7:27; 10:5-42; 13:3-52; 18:3-35; 23:2–25:46).

For the entry into Jerusalem, Jesus' ministry in the Temple, and the passion narrative, Luke again follows Mark, expanding and inserting material from one or more other sources. Scholars have often suggested that Luke drew from a separate passion narrative in addition to Mark, but the evidence for a second passion narrative is thin and can be accounted for by appeal to oral tradition and Lukan redaction.

Mark has no resurrection appearances of Jesus in its earliest form (which concludes with Mark 16:8), so Luke again goes his own way at this point, narrating the appearance to the two on the road to Emmaus and the appearance to the eleven back in Jerusalem (neither appearance has a parallel in Matthew). Throughout Luke 24 there are fascinating points at which Luke and John share common traditions.

Since the Gospel according to Mark is usually dated about the year 70, a date for Luke in the mid-eighties appears likely. Moreover, because the book of Acts makes no mention of Paul's letters or letter writing (as does 2 Pet 3:16), it also appears likely that Luke and Acts were written before Paul's letters were collected and circulated as a collection. Unless the prologue to the book of Acts was added later, it indicates that the Gospel was written first: "In the first book, Theophilus, I wrote about all that Jesus did and taught from the beginning until the day when he was taken up to heaven" (Acts 1:1-2 NRSV). A further factor in the date of Luke's composition of the Gospel is his handling of Jesus' predictions of the destruction of Jerusalem (esp. the embankments in 19:43-44 and the camps in 21:20). Without disputing that Jesus may well have forecast the destruction of Jerusalem, Josephus reports on the events leading to the destruction of the city and suggests that Luke has drawn from the tradition of Jesus' words, reflected on them in light of Old Testament prophecies of destruction, and set forth the predictions in such a way that readers in his own time could easily see that Jesus' words had been fulfilled in the bloody days at the end of the war of 66–70 CE. A date for the composition of the Gospel in the mid-eighties is based, therefore, on Luke's use of Mark, the absence of references to Paul's letters in Acts, and the Lukan form of Jesus' predictions of the destruction of Jerusalem.

Some definition of the character of the evangelist can be gleaned from the Gospel itself. Luke is a skilled writer who is adept with the Greek language, knows the conventions of Hellenistic historiography, demonstrates a remarkable knowledge of the OT, has been influenced by the style of the Septuagint, and has carefully compiled a full record of the ministry of Jesus and the development of the early church. Luke is both a miniaturist and a master designer. An individual story or pericope is a Gospel in miniature, artfully depicting Jesus' message, his ministry among the outcasts, or the central elements of the kerygma. Luke is a good storyteller. He knows how to use character and color and paints scenes vividly with his words. Luke is also a master designer in the sense that he gives structure to the whole of his work. Luke situates Jesus in the context of the history of his time and also in the long history of the purposes of God and God's redemption of Israel and of all people. Moreover, Luke expands the genre of Gospel writing by linking the story of Jesus more securely to the leading figures of Jesus' time, by narrating both the annunciations and the births of John and Jesus, by inserting a genealogy that traces Jesus' lineage back to Adam, "the son of God" (3:38), by including in his Gospel more of Jesus' teachings, and by tying the Gospel story to the events that followed in the Acts of the Apostles. Luke chronicles God's call for the repentance of Israel, Israel's rejection of the gospel, and the beginnings of the mission to the Gentiles. Luke's skills and artistry are evident, therefore, both from the examination of particular scenes and stories and from the design and thematic development of the two books.

Luke was probably a Gentile, but apparently one who was knowledgeable in the OT and had a working grasp of Jewish practices and institutions. His description of houses (5:19), cities, and social classes (e.g., 14:15-24) shows that he was familiar with the structure and social organization of a Hellenistic city like Antioch or Ephesus. The evangelist's deference to Theophilus ("most excellent Theophilus," 1:3) indicates that he himself was probably a member of the artisan class rather than the elite—Theophilus's subordinate, not his equal. Even if the tradition based on Col 4:14 is correct and the evangelist was a physician, that would not make him wealthy or a member of the elite. In the first century, physicians were artisans. Efforts have been made to show that Luke's descriptions of illnesses, afflictions, and healings in the Gospel are more precise than those in other accounts, but the evidence will not support the argument that the Gospel must have been written by a physician. Moreover, the theological differences between Luke and Paul mean that even if Luke was Paul's associate and companion for a period of time, the Gospel of Luke must be read on its own terms and not against the background of Paul's writings. One important step in the reading of the Gospel is the recognition of its design or structure.

STRUCTURE

Banal as it may seem to say so, the Gospel according to Luke is about Jesus. For that reason, it owes a great deal in form to ancient biography. It begins with a literary prologue that confirms the author's qualifications and guarantees the reliability of the biography. The events surrounding the birth of the hero serve as divine omens of his future greatness. An event from his youth foreshadows the work he will do in his maturity. Similarly, the events at the beginning of his public life characterize the significance of the work he is about to do. The heart of the work, then, is a record of his mighty acts and sage teachings. The narrative ends, appropriately, with accounts of the hero's farewell discourse, the manner of his death, the mysterious events that followed his death (appearances to his acquaintances and a translation into heaven), and his parting words to his followers. Distinctive as the Gospel is, each of these elements appears in other Jewish and Greco-Roman biographies.[12]

Some parts of the Gospel's structure are clearly discernible and universally recognized. At other points, the structure is open to various interpretations. The major units of the Gospel are often marked by transitions, introductions and conclusions, lapses in time, changes of geographical location, and the introduction of new characters. From such indications, the following structure emerges.

Luke 1:1-4	The Prologue
Luke 1:5–2:52	The Infancy Narrative
Luke 3:1–4:13	Preparation for the Ministry of Jesus
Luke 4:14–9:50	The Ministry in Galilee
Luke 9:51–19:27	The Journey to Jerusalem
Luke 19:28–21:38	The Ministry in Jerusalem
Luke 22:1–24:53	The Passion and Resurrection Narratives

The Gospel contains seven main sections. The prologue is distinguished both by its content and by its style. The first four verses of the Gospel follow the pattern of the prologues of other historical works and are written in some of the most polished and elevated Greek of the entire New Testament. With v. 5, the style changes dramatically, becoming much more Semitic.

Luke's infancy narrative is distinctive in that it constructs parallels and contrasts between the births and roles of John the Baptist and Jesus. Seven sections are clearly visible; the annunciation of the birth of John the Baptist to Zechariah in the Temple (1:5-25), the annunciation of the birth of Jesus to Mary (1:26-38), Mary's visit to Elizabeth (1:39-56), the birth of John the Baptist (1:57-80), the birth of Jesus and the visit of the shepherds (2:1-20), the presentation of Jesus in the Temple (2:21-40), and Jesus in the Temple at the age of twelve (2:41-52). Luke is also the only Gospel to report any event from Jesus' boyhood. Unlike the legends in the *Infancy Gospel of Thomas*, however, Luke's story of Jesus in the Temple points ahead to his ministry, and especially to his teaching in the Temple in Luke 19:47–21:38.

The elapse of years and the extended introduction to the historical context in 3:1-2 indicate the beginning of a new section of the Gospel, one that is devoted to the preparations for the ministry of Jesus. The individual units of this section are also clearly identifiable. The first three describe John's ministry, the second three Jesus' preparation for ministry: (1) the setting of John's ministry (3:1-6), (2) John's preaching (3:7-18), (3) the imprisonment of John (3:19-20), (4) the baptism of Jesus (3:21-22), (5) the genealogy of Jesus (3:23-38), and (6) the temptation of Jesus (4:1-13).

Luke divides the ministry of Jesus into three periods: the ministry in Galilee (4:14–9:50), the ministry en route to Jerusalem (9:51–19:27), and the ministry in Jerusalem (19:28–21:38). The primary ambiguity in the structure of Luke concerns the end of the journey to Jerusalem and the beginning of the ministry there. Most commentators regard Jesus' parable on kingship in 19:11-27 as the conclusion of the journey section and the transition to his entry into the city. Others, however, mark the end of the Lukan journey section at 18:14 (after which Markan parallels resume) or at 18:34 (after which the sequence of events and the geographical references become significant to the progress of the narrative), and the beginning of Jesus' ministry in Jerusalem at 19:41 (his weeping over the city) or at 19:45 (his entry into the Temple).

The structure of the journey section is also vigorously contested. Fitzmyer divides the journey into three parts using the references to Jerusalem as indications of the beginning of a new section (9:51-13:21; 13:22-17:10; 17:11-18:14, with a return to Markan material in 18:15-19:27), but he recognizes that this scheme is "a mere convenience, since the division at these points is otherwise insignificant and somewhat arbitrary."[13] Evans contends that the journey section is patterned on the arrangement of materials in Deuteronomy 1–26.[14] Others find lectionary cycles or chiastic structures as the basis for the organization of this section of the Gospel. The lack of consensus and the variety of approaches to solving the problem of the structure of the journey section underline the reality that Luke has neither related the material in these ten chapters to the journey motif nor made the basis for its organization clear.

Rather than attempting to fit the material into a consistent pattern on the basis of geographical references, the sequence of the parables, or perceived parallels with Deuteronomy, the interpreter can mark the internal linkages, organization, and subject matter of these chapters while despairing of achieving a neat, balanced, or consistent structure. For example, Jesus' visit to the home of Mary and Martha is coupled with the lawyer's question and the parable of the good Samaritan in 10:25-42. Luke 11:1-13 offers instruction on prayer. The debates and exchanges of 11:14-36 fit under the subject of responses to charges of deviancy. The extended unit in 12:1–13:9 collects instructions on readiness for the coming judgment. Luke 13:10-35 contains events and parables that concern the unexpected reversals brought by the kingdom of God (the stooped woman, the mustard seed and the yeast, the narrow door, and warnings for Jesus and Jerusalem). Luke 14 returns to the meal scenes that are characteristic of Luke. Luke 15 is a famous collection of parables on the joy of recovery and return (the lost sheep, the lost coin, and the prodigal son). Luke 16 contains two parables on rich men and lovers of money that are joined by a miscellaneous collection of sayings in 16:14-18. Luke 17 does not offer a thematic unity as readily as other sections, since it contains the demands of forgiveness and faith (17:1-10), the healing of the ten lepers (17:11-19), and sayings on the kingdom and its coming (17:20-37). Much of the travel section develops Luke's emphasis on Jesus' gospel to the rich and the poor, and this theme provides a unifying thread for the various paragraphs of Luke 18:1–19:27 (the unjust judge and the persistent widow, the Pharisee and the tax collector, the little children and the rich ruler, the blind beggar, Zacchaeus, and the parable of the greedy and vengeful king).

The structure of the rest of the Gospel falls in place more easily. Jesus' ministry in Jerusalem (19:8–21:38) is set in the Temple. After Jesus enters the city (19:28-40), he weeps over the city and drives the merchants from the Temple (19:41-46), preparing it for his ministry there and pointing ahead to its imminent destruction. Teaching in the Temple each day, Jesus is supported by the people and opposed by their leaders. First he is questioned by one group after another as they seek to trap him in his answers. Then he warns of the coming wars and persecutions, the destruction of Jerusalem, and the coming of the Son of Man.

The passion and resurrection narratives (22:1–24:53) report the preparations for the Passover (22:1-13), the last supper (22:14-20), and the Lukan farewell discourse (22:21-38). The events that lead up to Jesus' trial before Pilate follow in succession: Jesus is arrested (22:47-53); Peter denies Jesus in the courtyard (22:54-62); Jesus is challenged to prophesy (22:63-65) and is then brought before the Sanhedrin (22:66-71). Luke arranges the trial before Pilate neatly in five scenes in 23:1-25: Pilate's first declaration of Jesus' innocence, Jesus' appearance before Herod, Pilate's second declaration of Jesus' innocence, Pilate's third declaration of Jesus' innocence, and Pilate's capitulation to the crowd.

Parables in the Synoptic Gospels

Parable	Luke	Matthew	Mark
Patches and wineskins[1]	Luke 5:36-39	Matt 9:16-17	Mark 2:21-22
The blind leading the blind[2]	Luke 6:39-40	Matt 15:14*b*	
The log in your own eye[2]	Luke 6:41-42	Matt 7:3-4	
Producing good fruit[2]	Luke 6:43-45	Matt 7:16-20	
The two builders/building on a solid foundation	Luke 6:46-49	Matt 7:24-27	
The riddle of the children	Luke 7:31-35	Matt 11:16-19	
The two debtors	Luke 7:41-43		
The lamp	Luke 8:16	Matt 5:14-1	Mark 4:21-22
Seed and the soil/the sower	Luke 8:4-8	Matt 13:3-8	Mark 4:3-9
The good Samaritan	Luke 10:30-35		
The parable of a shameless neighbor	Luke 11:5-8		
The kingdom divided against itself[3]	Luke 11:17*a*	Matt 12:25*a*	Mark 3:24
The house divided against itself[3]	Luke 11:17*b*	Matt 12:25*b*	Mark 3:25
The return of the unclean spirit	Luke 11:24-26	Matt 12:43-45	
The rich food	Luke 12:16-21		
The returning master	Luke 12:36-38		
The thief in the night/the watchful owner	Luke 12:39-40	Matt 24:43-44	
The good and wicked servants	Luke 12:42-46	Matt 24:45-51	[Mark 13:33-37]
The going before a judge	Luke 12:58-59	Matt 5:25-26	
The barren fig tree	Luke 13:6-9	[Matt 21:20-22	Mark 11:20-25]
The mustard seed	Luke 13:18-19	Matt 1:31-32	Mark 4:30-32
The yeast	Luke 13:20-21	Matt 13:33	
The narrow door	Luke 13:24-30		
The choice of places at table	Luke 14:7-11		
The great supper/great banquet	Luke 14:16-24	Matt 22:1-14	
The fool at work	Luke 14:28-30		
The fool at war	Luke 14:31-32		
The lost sheep	Luke 15:3-7	Matt 18:12-14	
The lost coin	Luke 15:8-10		
The prodigal son	Luke 15:11-32		
The dishonest steward	Luke 16:1-9		
The rich man and Lazarus	Luke 16:19-31		
The servant who serves without reward	Luke 17:7-10		
The unjust judge and the persistent widow	Luke 18:1-8		
The Pharisee and the tax collector	Luke 18:9-14		
The talents/the greedy and vengeful king	Luke 19:11-27	Matt 25:14-30	
The wicked tenants/the Lord's vineyard given to others/vineyard tenants	Luke 20:9-18	Matt 21:33-44	Mark 12:1-11
The fig tree in bloom[1]	Luke 21:29-31	Matt 24:32-35	Mark 13:28-29
The weeds		Matt 13:24-30	
The hidden treasure and the pearl		Matt 13:44-46	
The net		Matt 13:47-48	
The owner of a house		Matt 13:52	
What can defile[4]		Matt 15:10-11	Mark 7:14-15
The unmerciful servant		Matt 18:23-35	
The laborers in the vineyard		Matt 20:1-16	
The two sons		Matt 21:28-32	
The bridesmaids		Matt 25:1-13	
The seed growing of itself			Mark 4:26-29
The watchful servants			Mark 13:33-37

[1]Although treated as a saying in Matthew and Mark, this passage is described as "a parable" by Luke.
[2]Although treated as a saying in Matthew, this passage is described as "a parable" by Luke.
[3]Although treated as a saying in Matthew and Luke, this passage is described as "a parable" by Mark.
[4]Described as "a parable" by both Matthew (15:15) and Mark (7:17)

Luke's artistry is also visible in his account of the crucifixion, death, and burial of Jesus (23:26-56). On the way to the cross, Jesus is supported by three individuals or groups (Simon of Cyrene, the people, including women from Jerusalem, and the two crucified with him). Following the crucifixion, Luke notes the responses of three other individuals or groups (the centurion, the crowds, and his acquaintances, including the women from Galilee).

The resurrection narratives in Luke 24 cluster in three sections: the discovery of the empty tomb (24:1-12), the appearance on the road to Emmaus (24:13-35), and the appearance to the eleven (24:36-53). The latter is composed of three subsections: proofs of the resurrection (24:36-43), Jesus' interpretation of the Scripture and commissioning of the disciples (24:44-49), and the blessing of the disciples and Jesus' departure (24:50-53), which also serves as the conclusion of the Gospel. Significant as the structure of the Gospel is, however, most of the freight is carried not by its structure but by Luke's christology and the various themes for which Luke is famous.

CHRISTOLOGICAL EMPHASES

Not only is Luke centered around the person of Jesus, but also it focuses the question of his identity so that it becomes part of the plot of the Gospel during the Galilean ministry. The scribes and Pharisees question, "Who is this who is speaking blasphemies?" (5:21). John sends two of his disciples to ask, "Are you the one who is to come, or are we to wait for another?" (7:20). Those at the table in Simon the Pharisee's house ask, "Who is this who even forgives sins?" (7:49). Then, Jesus' own disciples ask one another, "Who then is this?" (8:25). In the next chapter Herod asks the same question, "John I beheaded; but who is this about whom I hear such things?" (9:9). Shortly thereafter, Jesus asks his disciples the question of his identity: "Who do the crowds say that I am?" (9:18). The repeated question sustains the issue, and the characters search for an answer while the identity of Jesus, revealed from the annunciation of his birth, is confirmed and amplified for the reader. The Galilean ministry concludes, then, with Peter's confession, "The Messiah of God" (9:20) and the voice from heaven, which says, "This is my Son, my Chosen" (9:35).

While much of Luke's characterization of Jesus is conveyed by the biographical form of the Gospel and the presentation of the events and teachings that typified his ministry, the titles employed at various points in the Gospel also serve to characterize Jesus in various roles. The titles, however, are not static entities with consistent meanings. On the contrary, they are fluid, and their meaning develops and changes with the unfolding narrative, the interaction between context and title, and the tensions and complementarity among the different titles. The reader may find it helpful, therefore, to survey Luke's use of the leading christological titles in order to sensitize oneself to this aspect of the narrative.

1. Son of God. This title occurs surprisingly seldom in Luke—only six times, once in the annunciation (1:35), twice in the devil's temptations of Jesus (4:3, 9), twice in the outcry of the demons (4:41; 8:28), and once in the accusations of the chief priests, the scribes, and the council (22:70). The disciples never confess or worship Jesus as "Son of God," and where the centurion confesses that Jesus was the Son of God at his death in Mark, Luke has altered the confession so that the centurion says instead, "Certainly this man was innocent" (23:47). The difference between the roles of the title "Son of God" in Mark and Luke is all the more striking when one realizes that it appears in the first line of the Gospel (Mark 1:1) and then at the christological high point of the Gospel, which comes with the centurion's confession in Mark 15:39. Luke has neither of these. From such observations, one might conclude that Luke denies or diminishes the significance of this title for Jesus by using it to characterize the distorted perception of Jesus by the devil, the demons, and Jesus' adversaries.

On the other hand, the title also appears obliquely in very positive contexts. Jesus is first introduced in the annunciation with the words "He will be great, and will be called the Son of the Most High" (1:32). The only occurrence of the actual title in a positive context follows immediately (1:35). At his baptism, the voice from heaven declares, "You are my Son, the Beloved" (3:22), and at the transfiguration the voice from heaven says, "This is my Son, my Chosen" (9:35). Thereafter, Jesus himself appears to adopt the title in his words to the disciples, "No one knows who the

Son is except the Father, or who the Father is except the Son and anyone to whom the Son chooses to reveal him" (10:22). The last occurrence is even more oblique; in the parable of the wicked tenants Jesus echoes the language of the voice from heaven when he says that the owner of the vineyard resolves, "I will send my beloved son" (20:13).

In effect, the title is not part of the public discourse in the Gospel but part of the privileged communication to the reader. Only one who has heard the words of Gabriel at the annunciations and the voice from heaven at Jesus' baptism and transfiguration would understand the significance of Jesus' allusions to the title in 10:22 and 20:13. Jesus never uses the title directly with the crowds or his opponents and only indirectly ("the Son") with his disciples. Luke appears to endorse the title "Son of God" and uses it indirectly to define Jesus' relationship to God as Son to the Father, while treating it as a mystery known to the spiritual beings (Gabriel, the devil, and the demons) and a scandal to his adversaries. If the title was originally used metaphorically or suggested kingship (as in 1:32, "and the Lord God will give to him the throne of his ancestor David"), the virgin birth narrative affirms the literal sense rather than the metaphorical meaning of the title.

The heart of the issue is not whether Jesus is the Son of God (that is made clear at the annunciation, the baptism, and the transfiguration) but how Jesus will fulfill his identity. What is the role of the Son of God? The devil challenges him to turn a stone into bread or throw himself down from the Temple (4:3, 9). Ironically, eating with outcasts and feeding his followers, blessing, breaking, and giving bread will indeed characterize his ministry, as will his teaching in the Temple—but not in this way.[15]

2. Prophet—One Greater Than the Prophets. At least one aspect of Jesus' identity revolves around his role as a prophet. Jesus is a prophet who fulfills Moses and the prophets, but he is also one greater than the prophets.

Jesus' prophetic identity is tied to his relationship with John. The annunciation to Zechariah declares that John will possess the spirit and power of Elijah (1:17), and his work is described in terms that echo the OT prophets. By contrast, Jesus will be the Son of the Most High (1:32) and the "mighty savior" from the house of David (1:32-33, 69). Zechariah later affirms the angelic announcement concerning John when he says, "And you, child, will be called the prophet of the Most High" (1:76). John's prophetic role is confirmed in the accounts of his ministry (e.g., 3:1-6) and even by Jesus himself: "A prophet? Yes, I tell you, and more than a prophet" (7:26). Jesus is greater than John, who is the forerunner of Jesus; therefore, it follows that Jesus, too, is greater than the prophets.

Nevertheless, at significant points Luke portrays Jesus as a prophet and as one who fulfills the prophets. As a description of his ministry, Jesus reads from the prophet Isaiah (Luke 4:18-19). In the dispute that follows, Jesus characterizes the crowd's antagonism by saying, "No prophet is accepted in the prophet's hometown" (4:24); and he defends his interpretation of Isaiah by appealing to events in the ministries of Elijah and Elisha (4:25-28).

Jesus' Works in the Gospel of Luke as Fulfillment of the Prophets

	Elijah/Elisha	Isaiah	Luke
the blind	2 Kgs 6:17	29:18; 35:5; 42:18; 61:1 (LXX)	4:18; 7:21 (cf. 6:39-42) 14:13, 21; 18:35
the lame		35:6	14:13, 21
the lepers	2 Kgs 5:1-14		5:12-16; 17:12-19 (cf. 4:27)
the deaf		29:18; 35:5; 42:18	11:14
the dead	1 Kgs 17:17-24	26:19	7:11-17; 8:40-42, 49-56
the poor	61:1	4:18; 6:20; 14:13, 21; 16:19-31; 18:22; 19:8; 21:1-4	

The issue of Jesus' relation to John and the prophets takes center stage in Luke 7. Luke's account of the raising of the widow's son in 7:11-17 exhibits clear parallels with Elijah's raising of a widow's son in 1 Kings 17. The crowd perceives the significance of the event and responds, "A great prophet has arisen among us" (7:16). Such a confession is especially significant in view of the widespread notion that the spirit of prophecy had been taken from Israel and that there would be no other prophets until the end times (see, e.g., 1 Macc 9:27; cf. 1 Macc 4:46; 14:41).[16]

John's disciples come to Jesus to ask if he is "the coming one," an allusion to Mal 3:1; 4:5-6, but Jesus attributes that messenger role to John himself (7:27), while defining his ministry in terms of fulfillment of the prophets (esp. Isaiah and Elijah/Elisha). John fulfilled the role of the one who would prepare the way for the Messiah. Thus he was greater than the prophets (7:26, 28), but even the least in the kingdom is greater than he. This clarification opens the way for Jesus to assume other, more adequate titles while he fulfills the work of the prophets.

Simon the Pharisee mistakenly thinks Jesus is not even a prophet (7:39), while others think he is a prophet, or one of the prophets (9:8, 19; 24:19). At the transfiguration, Moses and Elijah appear with Jesus and talk with him about his "exodus" in Jerusalem (9:30-31). Perhaps elevating Jesus' authority over that of even Moses and Elijah, the voice from heaven then claims Jesus as "my Son" and admonishes the disciples to "listen to *him*" (9:35, italics added). As a prophet, and indeed the one who fulfills the prophets, it is appropriate that he die in Jerusalem (13:33). Finally, the resurrection narratives emphasize that Jesus fulfilled the prophets and that the gospel story must be understood in their light (24:25, 27, 44). While Luke recognizes that Jesus was more than a prophet, it also insists that he must be understood as "a prophet mighty in deed and word before God and all the people" (24:19).

3. Lord. The importance of the title "Lord" in Luke is evident first by its frequency. The term occurs 103 times in Luke, but in some forty of these instances it refers to God as "the Lord." In another 24 instances the term is used of persons besides Jesus (19:33) or characters in Jesus' parables (12:36, 37, 42-47; 16:3, 5; 20:13, 15). Of the remaining instances, when "Lord" refers to Jesus, eighteen are in the vocative, where others address Jesus as "Lord." In these instances, it is difficult to decide when the title means simply "sir" and when it carries the meaning "Lord" (as it seems to at least in 5:8; 6:46; 9:61; and 10:17). Most important, however, the narrator frequently calls Jesus "Lord" in the narration (7:13, 19; 10:1, 39, 41; 11:39; 12:42; 13:15; 17:5-6; 18:6; 19:8; 22:61; 24:3). Since the narrator's speech patterns carry great authority, it is significant that while the narrator refers to Jesus as "the Lord," the narrator does not commonly call Jesus "the Messiah" (see 2:26; 4:41), "the Savior," or "the Son of Man" (see 5:24).

Statistics do not tell the whole story, however, and the categories are neither as clear nor as static as they may appear. The repeated use of "Lord" to refer to God in the infancy narratives colors its use in reference to Jesus later in the Gospel. Fitzmyer suggests, further, that the title was first used of Jesus in reference to his status as risen Lord and then retrojected back into the ministry of Jesus.[17] The title was used of rulers and masters in the Greco-Roman world, and it apparently was used as a term of respect for teachers and great men and in an elevated sense in reference to God in pre-Christian Judaism.

Interesting subtleties become evident when Luke's use of "Lord" to refer to Jesus is examined systematically. After encountering the term in reference to God ten times in Luke 1:6-38, the reader hears Elizabeth ask, "Why has this happened to me, that the mother of my Lord comes to me?" (1:43). Then, at the birth of Jesus, the angels announce, "To you is born this day in the city of David a Savior, who is the Messiah, the Lord" (2:11). The uses of "Lord" in the vocative begin in Luke 5:8, and there the juxtaposition of "Lord" and "sinner" implies that the term means more than "sir": "Go away from me, Lord, for I am a sinful man!" Jesus uses the title in a Son of Man saying in Luke 6:5, "The Son of Man is lord of the Sabbath." Shortly thereafter, he asks his disciples, "Why do you call me 'Lord, Lord,' and do not do what I tell you?" (6:46). The narrator's references to Jesus as "the Lord" start in the next chapter (7:13, 19).

At points there are interesting relationships between the metaphorical use of "Lord" and the use of the title in the vocative or by the narrator.

For example, the term occurs nine times in 12:36-47. In Luke 12:36-37, Jesus speaks of a master or lord in a parable, where the master seems to represent the coming Son of Man. In 12:41, Peter asks, "Lord, are you telling this parable for us or for everyone?" and the narrator continues, "And the Lord said" (12:42), after which Jesus uses the term five more times in an explanation of the parable and in related sayings in 12:42-47. Similarly, the vocative occurs in 13:23, "Lord, will only a few be saved?" and Jesus gives a parabolic or metaphorical answer in which many seek entrance, saying, "Lord, open to us" (13:25), but the owner of the house will not let them in. The metaphorical and the absolute uses of the term are again difficult to distinguish in 16:8, where interpreters have debated whether the verse is part of Jesus' parable or a comment by the narrator following the parable. The precise connotations of the term are also difficult to determine in Luke 19:31, 34, where the disciples take a colt for Jesus to ride on and tell its owners, "The Lord [or its lord] needs it." By the end of the Gospel, the disciples use the term not only in the vocative but also in the absolute when they echo the Easter confession, "The Lord has risen indeed, and he has appeared to Simon" (24:34).

The title "Lord," therefore, subtly infuses the Gospel with the church's post-Easter confession of the risen Lord. Luke affirms the confession of Jesus as Lord. Even from his birth, Jesus is the Lord who would rise from the dead.

4. Messiah or Christ. Much like the title "Son of God," the title "Messiah" or "Christ" also belongs to the privileged knowledge of who Jesus is that is communicated by the Gospel. Literally, *Messiah* means "the anointed one" or "the Christ." The title first appears at the birth of Jesus, where the angels announce, "To you is born this day in the city of David a Savior, who is the Messiah, the Lord" (2:11). Of all the constructions using these titles in the New Testament, this verse is the only place where this one (χριστὸς κύριος *christos kyrios*) occurs, but it resembles the combination of the two titles in Luke 2:26, "the Lord's Messiah," and Acts 2:36, "know with certainty that God has made him both Lord and Messiah, this Jesus whom you crucified." Anointing was connected with kingship (cf. 1 Sam 24:6), and "the Lord's anointed" was the one anointed by God to serve as king.

The identity of Jesus as the Messiah is then treated as "inside information" known to the narrator, the reader, and the angels and demons, but not to the other characters. The Holy Spirit revealed to Simeon that he would not die until he saw "the Lord's Messiah" (2:26), and then guided Simeon to recognize Jesus as the Messiah. The people question whether John might be the Messiah (3:15), but the reader knows better. In an interpretive comment, the narrator explains that the demons also knew that Jesus was the Messiah (4:41).

The knowledge of Jesus' full identity as the Messiah breaks upon the disciples in 9:20 when Peter confesses that Jesus is "the Messiah of God." Even so, they do not understand the fate that awaits Jesus in Jerusalem. The superiority of the Messiah to David is explained in 20:41-44. Jesus' messiahship becomes the source of ironic mockery at his trial and crucifixion. The council of the religious leaders demands, "If you are the Messiah, tell us" (22:67). One of the three charges leveled against Jesus when he is brought before Pilate is that he says "that he himself is the Messiah, a king" (23:2). The charge may arise out of Jesus' words about the Messiah and the son of David in 20:41-44, but he does not openly claim these titles in Luke. The mockery of the leaders of the people at the cross connects the title with the words of the voice from heaven in 9:35: "Let him save himself if he is the Messiah of God, his chosen one!" (23:35; cf. Isa 42:1). Similarly, one of those crucified with Jesus challenges him, "Are you not the Messiah? Save yourself and us!" (23:39).

The title "Messiah," therefore, conveys the hidden identity of Jesus, as does the title "Son of God," but it also serves as a bridge to the more functional title "Savior" (see below). Further aspects of Jesus' role are conveyed by the title "Son of Man," and these must be examined before we turn to the title that defines the dying Christ in Luke ("Savior"). The title "Son of Man" appears repeatedly in the passion predictions, but in the resurrection narratives, "Messiah" replaces it in sayings where we might have expected to find "Son of Man": "Was it not necessary that the Messiah should suffer these things and then enter into his glory?" (24:26), and "Thus it is written, that the Messiah is to suffer and to rise from the dead on the third day" (24:46).

5. Son of Man. In Luke, Jesus speaks of himself as "the Son of Man" more frequently than with any other form of self-reference. The title "Son of Man" occurs 25 times in Luke (not counting the variant in 9:56). Moreover, with the possible exception of Luke 5:24, which may be a comment by the narrator, the term occurs only on the lips of Jesus in Luke. All three of the traditional categories of Son of Man sayings occur in the Gospel. The sayings that describe Jesus' earthly ministry (8 sayings) are the most diverse and the most like circumlocutions (where "the Son of Man" simply stands for "I"). The Son of Man has authority to forgive sins on earth (5:24); he is lord of the sabbath (6:5); his followers will be persecuted on his account (6:22); in contrast to John the Baptist, he came eating and drinking (7:34); he has no place to lay his head (9:58); those who speak against him will be forgiven (12:10); he came to seek and to save the lost (19:10); and Judas betrays him with a kiss (22:48). Five times the title "Son of Man" occurs in predictions of Jesus' suffering and death (9:22, 44; 18:31; 22:22; 24:7), and twelve times in sayings that refer to the future coming of the Son of Man in glory (9:26; 11:30; 12:8, 40; 17:22, 24, 26, 30; 18:8; 21:27, 36; 22:69). Moreover, Luke has added the title to sayings where it does not appear in Mark or Matthew (e.g., 6:22; 9:22; 12:8, 40; 19:10).

The background of the use of "Son of Man" in the Gospels is still vigorously debated. It occurs in Dan 7:13: "I saw one like a human being/ coming with the clouds of heaven" (NRSV), where it seems to refer to the exaltation of the holy ones of Israel to God. Use of the term to designate an apocalyptic figure (as in the parables of *1 Enoch*) is attested in later sources, as is the use of "the son of man" as a circumlocution in Aramaic. Jesus may have used the term in its generic sense ("a human being") or as a self-reference. Alternatively, he may have used the term because it was sufficiently ambiguous to force the hearer to discern its intended meaning. The various uses of the title in Luke, however, alternate between emphasizing Jesus' humanity and his future role as risen Lord. The lowly one seen in Jesus' ministry will suffer and die, but God will vindicate him and he will return in the future as the exalted Son of Man. One's response to the Son of Man who died on the cross determines the judgment that one will receive when the Son of Man comes in the future. Thus the title "Son of Man" serves an important role in the Gospel, because it links Jesus' ministry, his death, and the future judgment.

6. Savior. Luke is the only one of the Synoptics to call Jesus "Savior." Yet, as significant as the characterization of Jesus as the Savior is in Luke, the title occurs only twice in the Gospel, both times in the infancy narrative. In the first instance it is applied to God (1:47), and in the second the angel of the Lord announces to the shepherds: "To you is born this day in the city of David a Savior, who is the Messiah, the Lord" (2:11).

In this case, however, one cannot gauge the importance of a term merely by counting the frequency of its occurrence. Although the title "Savior" occurs only twice, Jesus is repeatedly identified as God's salvation or as the one who saves. Zechariah rejoices that God has "raised up a horn of salvation for us/ in the house of his servant David" (1:69; cf. 1:71, 77), clearly a reference to Jesus. When Simeon sees Jesus, after he had been promised that he would see the Messiah, he too gives thanks to God, "for my eyes have seen your salvation" (2:30; cf. 3:6).

During the course of his ministry, Jesus assures various ones that their faith has "saved" them or made them whole (7:50; 8:48; 17:19; 18:42). Then, in Jericho, he tells Zacchaeus, "Today salvation has come to this house. . . . For the Son of Man came to seek out and to save the lost" (19:9-10). Fittingly, the theme reaches its climax at the crucifixion of Jesus, where through the irony of the mockery Jesus is portrayed as the taunted Savior. First the leaders of the people scoff, "He saved others; let him save himself if he is the Messiah of God, his chosen one!" (23:35). Then the soldiers join the sport, introducing another title: "If you are the King of the Jews, save yourself!" (23:37). The third time it is one of the two crucified with Jesus who says, "Are you not the Messiah? Save yourself and us!" (23:39). The functional sense of the title has displaced the title itself while also defining the role of the Messiah, the King of the Jews. By the end of the passion narrative, the reader understands clearly the import of both the angelic announcement at Jesus' birth and Simeon's ominous words that a sword would pierce Mary's heart (2:35).

Other titles also serve to characterize Jesus: "servant," "master," and other titles.[18] Luke's characterization of Jesus is distinctive, however, not for the defining role of its titles but for the variety of themes that flesh out these confessions.

THEMES

Luke is noted for its richness of themes. No other Gospel develops so many themes as fully as does Luke. Seeing the relationship of a particular verse to others that develop a common theme is vital to gaining appreciation for any given passage in the Gospel. The reader is encouraged, therefore, to take the time to read the related verses in context. As an aid to such thematic study of the Gospel, the development of some of its principal themes is traced here.

1. God's Redemptive Purposes. Luke sets the life of Jesus both in its historical context and in a theological context. All that happens in the Gospel and in Acts is ultimately a part of God's redemptive plan for the salvation of all humanity. The phrase "God's purpose" occurs only once in Luke, but several times in Acts (Luke 7:30; Acts 2:23; 13:36; 20:27). Luke's development of this theme is evident in the Gospel's treatment of three related emphases: the sovereignty of God, the fulfillment of Scripture, and the scope of Jesus' redemptive work.

The sovereignty of God means that God's purposes direct events in human history. Some events "must" happen, and there is a divine purpose at work even in puzzling and tragic events. Jesus must be about his Father's business (or in his Father's house; 2:49). He must proclaim the kingdom of God (4:43) and suffer and die (9:22; 17:25; 24:7, 26). It was necessary in God's purposes that Jesus come to Zacchaeus's house (19:5). Even wars and insurrections must occur before the end (21:9). The Scriptures too must be fulfilled (22:37; 24:44).

Gabriel, God's emissary, inaugurates the new era chronicled in the Gospel by declaring first to Zechariah and then to Mary the births and the future work of John the Baptist and Jesus. From the beginning, they are to be understood as carrying out what God has purposed. All things are possible with God, even things that are not possible for ordinary mortals (1:37; 18:27). God is our Savior (1:47), and we are saved by God's mercy (1:78). If it were necessary, God could even raise up children to Abraham from the stones (3:8). In a manner reminiscent of the records of the prophets of old, Luke says that the Word of God came to John the son of Zechariah (3:2), and the Spirit of the Lord anointed Jesus for his ministry (4:18). It was "necessary" (δεῖ *dei*) that he proclaim the kingdom of God (4:43), so each of the succeeding references to the kingdom is to be understood in this light. Jesus' mighty acts are also transparently God's acts. For example, when he raises the son of the widow of Nain, the people respond: "God has looked favorably on his people!" (7:16). The Pharisees and the lawyers are characterized as those who rejected "God's purpose" (7:30). When Jesus exorcised the unclean spirits from the Gerasene demoniac, he instructed him to go and "declare how much God has done for you" (8:39). Such exorcisms are evidence both that Jesus acts "by the finger of God" and that "the kingdom of God has come to you" (11:20). God's providence extends even to sparrows that are sold at a rate of five for two copper coins worth only a sixteenth of a denarius each (12:6). God feeds even the ravens (12:24) and clothes the grass of the field (12:28). Consequently, God also "knows your hearts" (16:15) and will respond quickly to grant justice to the chosen ones who cry out night and day (18:7-8). In a sense, the whole Gospel declares what God has done and leads the reader to follow the example of the disciples in praising God in response (24:53).

Because God is sovereign, the Scriptures must be fulfilled (22:37; 24:44). In no sense can the Gospel according to Luke be pitted over against the OT in a Marcionite fashion.[19] Luke takes care to relate the events of the Gospel to the Scriptures, so that an attentive reader must constantly consult OT passages that are quoted or alluded to in the Gospel. Luke refers to "all that is written" three times (18:31; 21:22; 24:44) and to that which "is written" thirteen times (in various forms: 2:23; 3:4; 4:4, 8, 10, 17; 7:27; 10:26; 19:46; 20:17, 28; 22:37; 24:46). Jesus declares that "today" the Scriptures are fulfilled (4:21), and three times in the resurrection narratives Luke says that Jesus opened the Scriptures for his disciples (24:27, 32, 45). The Scriptures are an expression of God's purposes, so the roles of John and Jesus are characterized at the annunciation in allusions to Scripture; the disciples do not fully understand the events that have transpired among them until they understand them in the light of Scripture. The fulfillment of the Scriptures, consequently, is a further confirmation for the reader that the plan of God is being accomplished.

The plan of God reaches from the works of God among Moses and the prophets through the ministries of John and Jesus to the mission of the church in Acts. The preaching of the gospel to the Gentiles is a direct consequence and outworking of the purposes of God that guided Jesus, but will not be fulfilled until the coming of the Son of Man in glory. The plan of God in Luke and Acts extends temporally through the history of Israel, the ministry of Jesus, and the mission of the church; geographically, from the Temple to the ends of the earth; and ethnically, from the religious leaders to the outcasts, and from the Jews to all peoples. As a result, many of the themes that are treated below could be subsumed under the rubric of the fulfillment of God's redemptive purposes.

2. Salvation for All Alike. Perhaps Luke's most dramatic insight is his perception that Jesus announced salvation for all people alike. Although Jesus' initiatives toward all persons regardless of their social standing are a common feature of all the Gospels, no other Gospel is so clear and emphatic on this point. If Luke was influenced by Paul's mission and Paul's grasp of the gospel, it may have been at this point. Paul declares that the gospel is for "the Jew first and also to the Greek" (Rom 1:16 NRSV). In the blessing of John the Baptist, traditionally called the *Benedictus*, Zechariah praises God for fulfilling the covenant with Abraham and bringing salvation to Israel (1:68-79). Simeon, in the blessing traditionally called the *Nunc Dimittis*, declares that God has prepared this salvation"in the presence of all peoples,/ a light for revelation to the Gentiles/ and for glory to your people Israel" (2:31-32). Luke then extends the quotation from Isa 40:3, which is found at the beginning of Mark, reading also the next two verses:

> "Every valley shall be filled,
>   and every mountain and hill shall be made low,
> and the crooked shall be made straight,
>   and the rough ways made smooth;
> and all flesh shall see the salvation of God."
> (Isa 40:4-5; Luke 3:5-6)

At the synagogue in Nazareth, where Jesus interprets a later passage in Isaiah, he provokes the anger of his townsmen by reminding them that God sent the prophets Elijah and Elisha to a widow in Sidon and to a leper from Syria (4:24-30). The mighty works of God's deliverance were not for Israel alone. In his parables and teachings, Jesus emphasizes further that the inclusiveness of God's mercy knows no bounds: "Then people will come from east and west, from north and south, and will eat in the kingdom of God" (13:29). It will be like a master sending his servant out again and again, saying, "Go out at once into the streets and lanes of the town and bring in the poor, the crippled, the blind, and the lame" (14:21) and "Go out into the roads and lanes, and compel people to come in, so that my house may be filled" (14:23). At the end of the Gospel, Jesus commissions his disciples for this task, sending them out because the fulfillment of the Scriptures, the fulfillment of God's purposes, requires that "repentance and forgiveness of sins is to be proclaimed . . . to all nations, beginning from Jerusalem" (24:47; cf. Acts 1:8). The universalism of the gospel means that what God has done in Christ, God has done for all people, but it does not mean that all people will repent and accept God's mercy. The very proclamation of such a radical gospel leads some to exclude themselves from it. The people at Nazareth seek to kill Jesus (4:29). The patriarchs and the prophets will feast in the kingdom of God, but "you yourselves [will be] thrown out," Jesus warns those who took offense at his gospel (13:28), and the master of the banquet fills his house with nondescript guests so that "none of those who were invited will taste my dinner" (14:24). Tragically, the gospel of God's universal grace will not be universally accepted.

Luke's concern to present the radical inclusiveness of Jesus' ministry is evident in the numerous scenes in this Gospel in which Jesus reaches out to sinners, Samaritans, tax collectors, women, and outcasts. Both social and religious factors conditioned the prevailing attitude to the privileged toward these groups. A vital part of Jesus' proclamation of the new order of the kingdom of God, therefore, consisted in his challenge to the collusion of the religious authorities in the social prejudices of his day. Although the various groups of the oppressed and outcasts of society all illustrate this aspect of Jesus' ministry, by handling them separately we can see the role each plays in the Gospel.

Luke refers to *"sinners"* more than does any other Gospel (17 times). Interestingly, the term does not occur in the annunciations or the poetic sections of the infancy narrative, and the only reference in the passion and resurrection narratives is the echo of the passion predictions in Luke 24:7. Peter acknowledges that he is a sinner (5:8). The pattern of the majority of the references to sinners in the Gospel reveals that "sinners" are often associated with tax collectors. The term often emerges in the context of table fellowship and Jesus' practice of eating with those scorned by the religious authorities, and it often represents the viewpoint of the Pharisees and religious leaders. When Jesus' disciples are criticized for eating with "tax collectors and sinners" (5:30), Jesus responds that he has not come to call the righteous but sinners to repentance (5:32). In the Sermon on the Plain (6:17-49), Jesus challenges his disciples to do more than the sinners who love those who love them, do good to those who do good to them, and lend to those from whom they hope to receive (6:32-34). Jesus again refers to sinners when he quotes his critics as saying that "the Son of Man has come eating and drinking, and you say, 'Look, a glutton and a drunkard, a friend of tax collectors and sinners' " (7:34). The narrator identifies the woman who approaches Jesus in the house of Simon the Pharisee as "a woman in the city, who was a sinner" (7:37), and Simon refers to her as a sinner (7:39). When the Pharisees and scribes see the tax collectors and sinners coming to Jesus, they grumble and complain that Jesus "welcomes sinners and eats with them" (15:1-2). Jesus responds by telling the parables of the lost sheep, the lost coin, and the prodigal son. The first two of these parables end with the lesson, "Just so, I tell you, there will be more joy in heaven over one sinner who repents than over ninety-nine righteous persons who need no repentance" (15:7; cf. 15:10). In the parable of the Pharisee and the tax collector (18:9-14), the tax collector beats his breast and says, "God, be merciful to me, a sinner" (18:13), and Jesus assures his audience that "this man went down to his home justified" (18:14). Once more, when Jesus went to the home of Zacchaeus, the people complained, "He has gone to be the guest of one who is a sinner" (19:7). The only other references to sinners in Luke come in 13:2, where Jesus asks whether the Galileans who perished were worse sinners than others, and in 24:7, where the angel at the tomb recalls Jesus' warning that he would be "handed over to sinners." The contexts in which most of the references to sinners occur in Luke serve to define "sinners" primarily as those who were shunned by the Pharisees and scribes. They are the tax collectors, harlots, and others with whom Jesus ate and drank, thereby violating the social codes and prescriptions of the Pharisees.

The *Samaritans* were another stereotypical group of outcasts from the perspective of pious Jews. The Samaritans are shown in a positive light in each of the three instances where they appear in the Gospel. When the disciples want to call down fire on a Samaritan village, Jesus rebukes them (9:51-56). The "good Samaritan" (10:33) has become one of the most famous figures in Jesus' teachings, and when Jesus heals ten lepers only a Samaritan sees what has happened and returns praising God (17:11-19). To this one also Jesus gives the assurance, "Go on your way; your faith has made you well" (17:19).

Women play a significant role also, and Luke often features male and female characters in pairs. The infancy narrative features the role of Zechariah and Elizabeth, Joseph and Mary, and Simeon and Anna. In contrast to the Gospel of Matthew, Mary rather than Joseph is the principal character in Luke's account of the birth of Jesus. Later in the Gospel, Jesus exorcises an unclean spirit from a man in the synagogue in Capernaum and then heals Peter's mother-in-law (4:31-39). He heals a centurion's servant and then raises a widow's son (7:1-17). Jesus vindicates the sinful woman over Simon the Pharisee (7:36-50). Luke is also the only Gospel to note that Jesus was accompanied by a group of women who supported him and the male disciples (8:1-3). Jesus' mother and brothers are not dismissed but are held up as "those who hear the word of God and do it" (8:21; cf. 11:27-28). Jesus heals a woman with a hemorrhage and then raises Jairus's daughter (8:40-56). The account of Jesus' words to Mary and Martha, defending Mary's sitting at his feet and attending to his teachings like a disciple, is unique to Luke (10:38-42). The account of the healing of the crippled woman who could not stand up straight clearly declares Luke's understanding of Jesus' concern for the dignity and wholeness of the woman (13:10-17). The story has often been linked with the healing of the man with dropsy (14:1-6). Jesus draws his parables from the experience of women as well as from male experiences: The kingdom is like "yeast that a woman took and mixed in with three measures of flour"

(13:21). Elsewhere Jesus' parables feature both male and female characters: a shepherd who loses a sheep and a woman who loses a coin (15:3-10), an unjust judge and a persistent widow (18:1-8). Later, in the Temple, Jesus castigates the scribes who "devour widows' houses" (20:47) and praises the poor widow who gives two copper coins (21:1-4). When Jesus predicts the destruction of Jerusalem, he laments in particular the suffering it will inflict on mothers and infants (21:23). Only in Luke does Jesus call upon the daughters of Jerusalem to weep not for him but for the suffering that they will experience in the coming days (23:27-29). Luke again notes the role of the women from Galilee following Jesus' death (23:49, 55-56). At the tomb, the angel declares the Easter tidings to the women; they are not merely messengers to the male disciples (24:1-12).

The various references to women in Luke's Gospel demonstrate both Jesus' concern to extend God's mercy to women as well as to men and Luke's sensitivity to Jesus' radical departure from the social conventions of his time. Luke portrays Jesus associating freely with women and calling for a new pattern of relationships both by his actions and in his teachings. Recent interpreters have pointed out, however, that Luke distances women from the prophetic ministry and confines women to traditional roles: "prayerful, quiet, grateful women, supportive of male leadership, forgoing the prophetic ministry."[20] Luke remains grounded in the social context of the first century. Nevertheless, if its portrayal of Jesus' relationships with women falls short by contemporary standards, it was radical in a first-century context. Jesus permits a woman to touch his feet in public and to sit at his feet with male disciples, and he defends a woman from the scorn of Simon the Pharisee. While Luke's Jesus does not succeed in freeing women from the shackles of societal repression, he specifically includes women among those for whom the coming of the kingdom is good news and points to the inauguration of a new community in which freedom, dignity, and equality may be realized.

3. The Blessings of Poverty and the Dangers of Wealth. The poor are also prominent in Luke. Just as Jesus habitually associates with tax collectors and sinners, so he also declares God's vindication of the poor and divine judgment upon the rich. Popular theology held that the rich were blessed of God, but Jesus turned popular theology on its head, maintaining that God would lift up the poor and cast out the rich. From the time of the exile, poverty had come to be associated with humility and dependence on God. Whereas Matthew spiritualizes the beatitudes, "Blessed are the poor in spirit" (Matt 5:3 NRSV), Luke faces the economic realities of poverty, "Blessed are you who are poor" (6:20) and laments the condition of the rich, "But woe to you who are rich,/ for you have received your consolation" (6:24).

Luke's handling of the beatitudes and woes is part of the pattern of his characterization of Jesus' responses to wealth and poverty throughout the Gospel. Not surprisingly, Luke refers to the poor and the rich more than does any other Gospel. Modern readers must, therefore, guard against efforts to pull the prophetic sting from Luke or spiritualize poverty in spite of Luke's efforts to prevent us from doing so. The canticles of the infancy narrative announce the theme. The Lord has "looked with favor" on his lowly servant (Mary), "brought down the powerful from their thrones and lifted up the lowly," and "sent the rich away empty" (1:48, 52-53). In his opening address at Nazareth, Jesus reveals that he has been sent to "bring good news to the poor" (4:18), and he refuses to allow those in Nazareth to hear the Scriptures as promises of deliverance for themselves only. To John's disciples, Jesus responds that the preaching of good news to the poor is one of the signs that validates his ministry (7:22). Embarrassingly, Jesus exhorts the guests at a banquet to invite the poor, the crippled, the lame, and the blind when they give a banquet (14:13, 21). The rich fool thought he was fixed for life, that his future was secure, but the Lord demanded his life of him that night (12:16-21). "Life does not consist in the abundance of possessions," Jesus warned (12:15). Indeed, some of the seed is choked out by "the cares and riches and pleasures of life" (8:14). The poor man Lazarus, who lay at the rich man's gate, is carried to Abraham's bosom, while the rich man who feasted every day is condemned to perpetual torment. They are two men separated by a table, and in the hereafter the tables are turned (16:19-31). How hard it is, Jesus laments, for those who have wealth to enter the kingdom of God (18:24). His exhortation to the ruler who sought eternal life is to sell what he has and give to the poor (18:22), which is just what Zacchaeus pledges to do: "Half of my possessions, Lord, I will give to the poor" (19:8). When the poor widow gives all she has, however, she is praised above the rich who give great sums of money (21:1-4).

Contemporary interpreters face the temptation either to dismiss or to spiritualize Luke's teachings on the dangers of wealth on the one hand or to literalize and absolutize them on the other hand. The challenge is to deal seriously with this aspect of the Gospel in the context of individual life-styles and caring communities in a materialistic and technological society that has widened the gap between rich and poor.

4. Table Fellowship. One of the most characteristic settings for the ministry of Jesus in the Gospel according to Luke is the meal scene. Jesus eats with tax collectors and sinners, with Pharisees, with the crowd, and with the disciples. According to a perceptive quip, "Jesus is either going to a meal, at a meal, or coming from a meal."[21] The meals in Luke become a "type scene," a scene repeated at intervals with subtle variations. The importance of the meal scenes is suggested both by the significance of table fellowship in the first century and by the repetition and complexity of the meal scenes in this Gospel.[22]

Immediately after Jesus called Levi, the tax collector, to follow him, Levi gave a banquet for Jesus. For the first time, we hear the charge that Jesus eats and drinks "with tax collectors and sinners" (5:29-32). In chap. 7, Simon the Pharisee invites Jesus to a meal at his house, where a sinful woman weeps at Jesus' feet and anoints them (7:36-50). When the crowds follow Jesus to a deserted place, Jesus feeds the multitude with five loaves and two fish (9:12-17). When another Pharisee invites Jesus to a meal, Jesus scandalizes his host first by not washing before the meal and then by castigating the Pharisees for being more concerned about washing the outside of vessels than about inner purity (11:37-52). In chap. 14 Jesus is again invited to the house of a leader of the Pharisees (14:1-24). This time he challenges the guests to take the lower seats rather than the seats of honor and then admonishes the host not to invite friends and relatives to a dinner but to invite "the poor, the crippled, the lame, and the blind" (14:11). The parable of the great banquet follows (14:15-24).

Related to the meal scenes is the parable of the rich man and Lazarus, which features the offending table of the rich man (16:19-31). Against this background, the institution of the Lord's Supper (22:14-20) and the meal at Emmaus (24:13-35) take on a special significance. The meal is connected with Jesus' death. His breach of the social boundaries through his inclusive table fellowship fueled the opposition that led to his death. Whenever the Lord's supper is observed both his table fellowship with outcasts and his death for sinners is commemorated. The Table becomes the place where disputes over greatness are set aside and divisive barriers are overturned by means of voluntary servanthood (22:24-27). Table fellowship also characterizes both the eschatological promise and the experience of the church. The hope of the disciples and the promise Jesus offers is that they will eat and drink at Jesus' table in the kingdom (23:30). The risen Lord, moreover, is present with the believing community and makes himself known to them in "the breaking of bread" (24:35). Here then is *the heart of Luke's hermeneutic:* After investigating everything carefully (1:3), Luke has found that he recognizes "the truth concerning the things about which you have been instructed" when memory of the actions and teachings of Jesus' ministry is enlightened by the Scriptures and reenacted in the hospitality and table fellowship of the community of believers.

5. The Role of a Disciple. Christology and discipleship are always connected. How one understands the role of Jesus as the Christ shapes one's understanding of discipleship. Luke takes the hard edge off Mark's portrayal of the disciples, omitting the statement that the disciples' hearts were hardened (Mark 6:52), Jesus' rebuke of the disciples for their failure to understand about the loaves (Mark 8:17-21), Jesus' rebuke to Peter, "Get behind me, Satan" (Mark 8:32-33), and the disciples' final abandonment of Jesus (Mark 14:50-52). At other places Luke softens the critique of the disciples. At the transfiguration, when Peter asked if they could build booths and stay there, Luke adds "not knowing what he said" (Luke 9:33). In the Gethsemane scene, Jesus finds the disciples "sleeping because of grief" (22:45). The disciples are called not to die with Jesus but to take up their cross *daily* and follow him (9:23).

Jesus is the model to be imitated. He is empowered by the Spirit, he is compassionate toward the poor and oppressed, he heals and forgives, he prays, and he dies a model martyr's death. The disciples are called with an unconditional, absolute, person-centered call: "Follow me" (5:27; 9:59). Complementing the Gospel's emphasis on the dangers of wealth and possessions, Luke notes that the disciples "left everything and followed him" (5:11, 28). Those who offer to follow him but cannot leave other concerns behind are rejected (9:57-62).

Aspects of Luke's characterization of Jesus need to be explored further, therefore, as reflections of the model that Jesus offers for his disciples. Jesus' obedience to God's direction is a model for his followers. He "must" be in his Father's house, or "about my Father's interests" (see 2:49). Jesus rebuffs the devil's attempts to gain his allegiance or direct the course of his ministry; Jesus follows the direction of Scripture and chooses to worship God "and serve only him" (4:8). What the Lord has anointed Jesus to do (4:18), he faithfully accomplishes in the following chapters. His prayer at the end of his ministry, "not my will but yours be done" (22:42), is consistent with all that he has done to that point.

Related to both Jesus' empowerment by the Spirit and his obedience to God is the role of prayer in Luke's account of Jesus' ministry. The Spirit descends on Jesus "when Jesus also had been baptized *and was praying*" (3:21, italics added). Jesus regularly withdrew from the crowds to deserted places to pray (5:16). He prayed all night in the mountains before he chose the twelve disciples (6:12), then he taught the disciples to pray for those who abused them (6:28). Jesus' conversation with the disciples and Peter's confession that he was the Messiah occur while Jesus was praying (9:18). Similarly, the three disciples witness the transfiguration when they accompany Jesus on another of his retreats to the mountains for prayer (9:28). Jesus teaches the disciples the model prayer on another occasion when they have seen him praying (11:1-4). In addition, several of Jesus' parables are related to prayer: the parable of the neighbor in need at midnight (11:5-8; cf. 11:9-13), the parable of the widow and the unjust judge (18:1-8, esp. v. 1), and the parable of the Pharisee and the tax collector (18:9-14). In contrast to Jesus' practice and teaching regarding prayer, the scribes say long prayers for the sake of appearance (20:47).

Like various other themes, the emphasis on prayer as a facet of Jesus' character that is modeled for the disciples culminates in the passion narrative. Jesus prays on the Mount of Olives before he is arrested. He instructs the disciples to "pray that you may not come into the time of trial" (22:40, 46). Then, he kneels and prays for deliverance from the suffering he knows lies ahead, and in a textually dubious verse is strengthened by an angel. Later, when Jesus is dying, he dies praying: "Father, forgive them; for they do not know what they are doing" (23:34, which is absent in some MSS); and "Father, into your hands I commend my spirit" (23:46). Both of these prayers from the cross, moreover, are unique to Luke, and Jesus' role as a model of martyrdom is confirmed when in the book of Acts Stephen echoes the two prayers of Jesus as he dies (Acts 7:59-60). If following Jesus in Luke means doing as Jesus does, then prayer is a vital part of being a follower of Jesus.

The trial and death of Jesus also confirm his identification with the oppressed, and that he was innocent under the law—a righteous man. Just as it was characteristic of Jesus that he ate with tax collectors and sinners, so also at his death "he was counted among the lawless" (22:37) and died with criminals (23:33). The beginning of Luke's passion narrative makes it clear that the religious leaders were "looking for a way to put Jesus to death" (22:2) and that Satan facilitated their plot against Jesus (22:3-6).

Luke underscores the innocence of Jesus repeatedly throughout the trial and crucifixion scenes. The Gospel takes pains to ensure that the reader understands that the accusations against Jesus are false charges. Jesus did not forbid the payment of taxes (23:2; cf. 20:20-26). His role as the Messiah was diametrically opposed to that of an earthly king (23:2; cf. 19:11-27), and by the end of the trial Luke has shown that it is the leaders themselves who pervert the people (23:2; cf. 23:13-18). The trial before Pilate is structured around Pilate's three declarations that he finds no crime in Jesus (23:4, 14, 22). When Pilate sends Jesus to Herod, Herod returns him and Pilate reports that Herod found him innocent also (23:6-12, 15). Jesus' innocence is confirmed by two authorities, but Pilate nevertheless capitulates to the will of the leaders of the people (23:25). At the cross, the "penitent thief" crucified with Jesus also maintains that Jesus has done nothing wrong (23:41), and the centurion who witnessed Jesus' death "praised God and said, 'Certainly this man was innocent' " (23:47).

The function or functions of Luke's emphasis on Jesus' innocence can again be interpreted variously.

If Theophilus is a Roman official, Luke may be concerned to make the point that Jesus (and the disciples and Paul in Acts) was repeatedly declared innocent by the Roman authorities, confirming that from its inception Christianity was not an illegal religion and was not perceived as a threat to Roman authority. On the other hand, if (as seems more likely) the Gospel is intended for the believing community, the repeated declarations of innocence in the Gospel and Acts may serve to reassure believers of the rightness of their convictions and to give them precedents to which they can appeal when they too are "brought before kings and governors" (21:12).

The centurion's praise of God and affirmation that Jesus was δίκαιος (*dikaios*) moves the characterization of Jesus to another level. The term may mean "innocent," but Luke uses it elsewhere with the sense of "just" or "righteous." Among those whom Luke characterizes as "just" are Zechariah and Elizabeth (1:6), Simeon (2:25), and—in the same context as the centurion's confession—Joseph of Arimathea (23:50). In Acts, moreover, Jesus is called "the Righteous One" (Acts 3:14; 7:52; 22:14).

The prominence of *joy* and *the praise of God* in Luke defines the response of those who see God's power at work in John the Baptist and Jesus and hear the good news of the kingdom. The birth of John brought joy and gladness (1:14, 44, 58), and at the birth of Jesus the angels brought the shepherds "good news of great joy for all the people" (2:10). Some who receive the gospel with joy, however, are like seed sown in rocky ground: "They believe only for a while and in a time of testing fall away" (8:13). The seventy Jesus sent out on mission returned filled with joy at what they had seen (10:17), and Jesus reminds the scribes and Pharisees that there is joy in heaven over one sinner who repents (15:7, 10). Joy also characterizes the response of the disciples to the appearances of the risen Lord (24:41-52).

In Luke those who see the power of God at work or hear the good news are not only filled with joy, but their characteristic response is to glorify or praise God as well. This doxological undertone to the Gospel is evident in the response of the shepherds at Jesus' birth, who returned, "glorifying and praising God for all they had heard and seen" (2:20). Thereafter, both terms, "glorify" (δοξάζω *doxazō*) and "praise" (αἰνέω *aineō*), occur in various contexts, but not together. The more common term is "glorify" (*doxazō*). The paralytic and those who witness his healing glorify God (5:25-26). The raising of the son of the widow at Nain (7:16) leads the crowd to glorify God, and the crippled woman (13:13), the Samaritan leper (17:15), and the blind beggar in Jericho (18:43) respond to their healings by glorifying God. Then, when the centurion witnesses Jesus' death, another of God's mighty acts, he too glorifies God (23:47).

The other term Luke uses to describe responses of awe, penitence, gratitude, and worship is *aineō* ("to praise God"). The angelic host that announces Jesus' birth praises God (2:13), and then the shepherds answer the angels with their own praise of God (2:20). Later, the disciples add their antiphonal response, praising God (19:37) with a variation of the angels' words, saying, "Peace in heaven,/and glory in the highest heaven!" (19:38).

Significantly, the Gospel ends with the disciples' praising God (24:53). Here a third verb occurs: "blessing" God (εὐλογέω *eulogeō*). Codex Bezae (D) has the more common "praise" God (*aineō*; which also occurs in Acts 2:47; 3:8-9), but the idiom "to bless God" also occurs earlier in the Gospel when Zechariah praises God (1:64) and when Simeon takes Jesus in his arms and praises God (2:28). The choice of the verb in 24:53 may be due to the occurrence of the verb twice earlier in the same scene (24:50-51), where Jesus blesses the disciples. Appropriately, the Gospel ends on a note of blessing and doxology.

6. The Importance of an Accurate Witness. This theme is more important to Luke than a tallying of the frequency of its occurrence in the Gospel might indicate. The only occurrence of the verb "to bear witness" (μαρτυρέω *martyreō*) is in 4:22, where the people of Nazareth initially respond to Jesus by bearing witness to him. The two related words for the witness borne occur only four times (μαρτυρία *martyria*, 22:71; and μαρτύριον *martyrion*, 5:14; 9:5; 21:13). The Sanhedrin asks what further need there is for testimony after Jesus responds to their question as to whether he is the Son of God by saying, "You say that I am" (22:70-71). The disciples, however, are to be witnesses for Jesus and the gospel. Thus the term evokes a judicial context. When the disciples are persecuted and brought before kings and governors, "This will give you an opportunity to testify" (21:13). The concept of "witness" develops in the course of the New Testament writings from the role of an eyewitness, to one who can testify to the gospel, to one who dies for the sake of the gospel ("a martyr" [μάρτυς *martys*]). The special Lukan use of this term links two senses of it: The disciples can bear witness to the fact of Jesus' death and resurrection, and they can testify to its significance. Luke 24:48 links both senses. By the time we come to Paul (Acts 22:15), the sense has already shifted from the first to the second sense. Paul can bear a confessing witness, but he was not an eyewitness to the events of Jesus' ministry (Acts 1:22).

For their work as witnesses, the disciples will be empowered by the Holy Spirit. The Gospel of Luke plays an important role in shaping the biblical doctrine of the Spirit in that it affirms that the Holy Spirit was active before the birth of Jesus (1:35, 41, 67; 2:25-27), the Spirit rested upon Jesus during his ministry (3:22; 4:1, 14, 18; 10:21), and Jesus charged the disciples to wait in Jerusalem until the Spirit had come upon them (24:49; cf. 11:13). The witness of the disciples, therefore, is guided and empowered by the Spirit. Confirming this promise, the book of Acts notes that the Spirit guides the disciples and the early church in each of its major new ventures. The linkage between witness and Spirit is explicit in Acts 5:32: "And we are witnesses to these things, and so is the Holy Spirit whom God has given to those who obey him" (NRSV). The concern for an accurate and continuing witness also guided Luke in the writing of the Gospel, "So that you may know the truth concerning the things about which you have been instructed" (1:4).

READING THE GOSPEL OF LUKE

The study of the Gospel according to Luke is a richly rewarding experience. Luke is a good storyteller and has the penetrating insight of a prophet. As a result, the Gospel is engaging and offers a perspective on the redemptive events of Jesus' ministry. It continually calls the Christian community to model more fully Jesus' concern for the oppressed, the overlooked, and the outcast. The kingdom community is one in which the social barriers that divide and exclude are torn down and God's grace can begin to flow to and among the wealthy and the poor, the sick and the self-righteous, the powerful and the excluded. The study and teaching of such a Gospel can serve to actualize in individuals and in congregations the redemptive purposes of God that guided Jesus' ministry and resulted in his death and resurrection. If the Spirit empowered the witness of this Gospel, then by opening ourselves to it we may also be guided by God's Spirit to be a part of God's ongoing redemptive work. The study of the Gospel, therefore, calls us to see the sights and hear the words of Jesus' ministry as if we had been among the eyewitnesses, to grasp Luke's distinctive perspective on the person and work of Jesus, and to see the implications of the Gospel for the times and circumstances in which we live.

FOR FURTHER READING

Commentaries

Craddock, Fred B. *Luke.* Interpretation. Louisville: Westminster/John Knox, 1990.

Danker, Frederick W. *Jesus and the New Age: A Commentary on St. Luke's Gospel.* Rev. ed. Philadelphia: Fortress, 1988.

Ellis, E. Earl. *The Gospel of Luke.* NCB. Greenwood, SC: Attic, 1966.

Evans, Craig A. *Luke.* New International Biblical Commentary. Peabody, Mass.: Hendrickson, 1990.

Fitzmyer, Joseph A. *The Gospel According to Luke.* AB 28 and 28A. Garden City, N.Y.: Doubleday, 1981, 1985.

Johnson, Luke Timothy. *The Gospel of Luke.* Sacra Pagina 3. Collegeville: Liturgical Press, 1991.

Marshall, I. Howard. *The Gospel of Luke: A Commentary on the Greek Text.* NIGTC. Grand Rapids: Eerdmans, 1978.

Nolland, John. *Luke.* 3 vols. WBC 35A-C. Dallas: Word, 1989–93.

Schweizer, Eduard. *The Good News According to Luke.* Translated by David E. Green. Atlanta: John Knox, 1984.

Stein, Robert H. *Luke.* The New American Commentary, 24. Nashville: Broadman, 1992.

Talbert, Charles H. *Reading Luke: A Literary and Theological Commentary on the Third Gospel.* New York: Crossroad, 1982.

Tannehill, Robert C. *The Narrative Unity of Luke–Acts: A Literary Interpretation*, vol. 1: *The Gospel According to Luke.* Philadelphia: Fortress, 1986.

Tiede, David L. *Luke.* Augsburg Commentary on the New Testament. Minneapolis: Augsburg, 1988.

Other Studies

Bonz, Marianne Palmer. *The Past As Legacy: Luke-Acts and Ancient Epic.* Minneapolis, Minn.: Fortress, 2000.

Brown, Raymond E. *The Birth of the Messiah: A Commentary on the Infancy Narratives in the Gospels of Matthew and Luke.* New York: Doubleday, 1977.

———. *The Death of the Messiah: A Commentary on the Passion Narratives.* 2 vols. New York: Doubleday, 1994.

Conzelmann, Hans. *The Theology of St. Luke.* Translated by Geoffrey Buswell. New York: Harper & Row, 1961.

Darr, John A. *On Character Building: The Reader and the Rhetoric of Characterization in Luke–Acts.* Louisville: Westminster/John Knox, 1992.

Grassi, Joseph. *Peace on Earth: Roots and Practices from Luke's Gospel.* Collegeville, Minn.: Liturgical Press, 2004.

Karris, Robert J. *Luke: Artist and Theologian.* New York: Paulist, 1985.

Kingsbury, Jack Dean. *Conflict in Luke: Jesus, Authorities, Disciples.* Minneapolis: Fortress, 1991.

Kurz, William S. *Reading Luke–Acts: Dynamics of Biblical Narrative.* Louisville: Westminster/ John Knox, 1993.

Levine, Amy-Jill and Marianne Bliekenstaff, eds. *A Feminist Companion to Luke.* Feminist Companion to the New Testament and Early Christian Writings 3. New York: Continuum, 2002.

Maddox, Robert. *The Purpose of Luke–Acts.* Göttingen: Vandenhoeck & Ruprecht, 1982.

Malina, Bruce J., and Richard L. Rohrbaugh. *A Social-Science Commentary on the Synoptic Gospels.* Minneapolis: Fortress, 1992.

Moessner, David P. *Jesus and the Heritage of Israel: Luke's Narrative Claim Upon Israel's Legacy.* Luke the Interpreter of Israel 1. Harrisburg, Pa.: Trinity, 1999.

Navone, John. *Themes of St. Luke.* Rome: Gregorian University Press, 1970.

Neyrey, Jerome H., ed. *The Social World of Luke–Acts: Models for Interpretation.* Peabody, Mass.: Hendrickson, 1991.

Parsons, Mikeal C. *The Departure of Jesus in Luke–Acts: The Ascension Narratives in Context.* JSNTSup 21. Sheffield: Sheffield Academic, 1987.

Powell, Mark Alan. *What Are They Saying About Luke?* New York: Paulist, 1989.

Schaberg, Jane. "Luke." In *The Women's Bible Commentary.* Edited by Carol Newsom and Sharon H. Ringe. Louisville: Westminster/ John Knox, 1992.

Sheeley, Steven M. *Narrative Asides in Luke–Acts.* JSNTSup 72. Sheffield: *JSOT,* 1992.

ENDNOTES

1. Irenaeus *Against Heresies* 3.1.1 (ANF, 1:414).

2. Irenaeus *Against Heresies* 3.1.1 (ANF, 1:414).

3. Irenaeus *Against Heresies* 3.14.1 (ANF, 1:437-38).

4. Irenaeus *Against Heresies* 3.14.1-2 (ANF, 1:438).

5. Tertullian *Against Marcion* 4.2 (ANF, 3:347-48).

6. Tertullian *Against Marcion* 4:4 (ANF, 3:349).

7. Tertullian *Against Marcion* 4:5 (ANF, 3:350).

8. See A. C. Sundberg, Jr., "Canon Muratori: A Fourth-Century List," *HTR* 66 (1973) 1-41; and Sundberg, "Muratorian Fragment," in *IDBSup* (Nashville: Abingdon, 1976) 609-10.

9. Wilhelm Schneemelcher, ed., *New Testament Apocrypha*, rev. ed., trans. R. McL. Wilson (Louisville: Westminster/John Knox, 1991) 1:34.

10. R. G. Heard, "The Old Gospel Prologues," *JTS* 6 (1955) 11.

11. Heard, "The Old Gospel Prologues," 7.

12. See esp. Charles H. Talbert, *What Is a Gospel? The Genre of the Canonical Gospels* (Philadelphia: Fortress, 1977); and Richard A. Burridge, *What Are the Gospels? A Comparison with Graeco-Roman Biography* (Cambridge: Cambridge University Press, 1992).

13. Joseph A. Fitzmyer, *The Gospel According to Luke (I–IX)*, AB 28 (Garden City, N.Y.: Doubleday, 1981) 825.

14. C. F. Evans, "The Central Section of St. Luke's Gospel," in *Studies in the Gospels: Essays in Memory of R. H. Lightfoot*, ed. D. E. Nineham (Oxford: Blackwell, 1955) 37-53.

15. See further Martin Hengel, *The Son of God: The Origin of Christology and the History of Jewish-Hellenistic Religion* (Philadelphia: Fortress, 1976).

16. Josephus *Against Apion* 1.41.

17. Fitzmyer, *The Gospel According to Luke (I–IX)*, 203.

18. Fitzmyer, *The Gospel According to Luke (I–IX)*, 197-219.

19. Marcion, c. 140 CE, rejected the OT, deleted OT references from Luke, and held that only his edited version of Luke and ten Pauline letters were Scripture.

20. Jane Schaberg, "Luke," in *The Women's Bible Commentary*, ed. Carol Newsom and Sharon H. Ringe (Louisville: Westminster/John Knox, 1992) 275.

21. Robert J. Karris, *Luke: Artist and Theologian, Luke's Passion Account as Literature* (New York: Paulist, 1985) 47.

22. For an insightful analysis of the role of the Lukan meal scenes, see Craig Thomas McMahan, "Meals as Type-Scenes in the Gospel of Luke" (Ph.D. diss., Southern Baptist Theological Seminary, 1987).

The Gospel of John

GAIL R. O'DAY

In even the most cursory reading of the four Gospels, it is apparent that the story of Jesus in the Gospel of John differs from that found in the other three Gospels in significant ways. In the synoptic Gospels, Jesus' ministry is a one-year Galilean ministry; he leaves Galilee to go to Judea and Jerusalem only once, in the final journey that culminates in his death. John recounts a three-year ministry; three different Passover feasts are celebrated in the course of Jesus' ministry (2:13; 6:4; 11:55), as opposed to the one Passover celebrated during Jesus' final days in the Synoptics. Moreover, in John, Jesus' ministry alternates between Galilee and Jerusalem. He makes three trips from Galilee to Jerusalem in the course of his ministry (2:13; 5:1; 7:10), and, indeed, most of his ministry is concentrated in Judea and Jerusalem. The chronology of Jesus' trial and crucifixion is also different in John. All the Gospels agree that Jesus was crucified on a Friday, but in the synoptic Gospels that Friday is the first day of Passover and in John it is the Day of Preparation for the Passover (18:28; 19:14).

The Johannine Jesus uses some short parables and proverbs (e.g., 4:36-37; 8:35; 10:1-5; 12:24; 16:21), but there are no parables that begin, "The kingdom of God is like . . ." in John. There are few compact narrative units that make up much of the story of Jesus in the Synoptics,[1] and little of the ethical teaching material found in the other Gospels. Instead, the Gospel of John is characterized by a literary style that interweaves narrative, dialogue, and discourse to create lengthy drama-like scenes (e.g., 4:4-42; 6:1-69; 9:1–10:21;11:1-44). The centerpiece of Jesus' teaching in John is the Farewell Discourse and Prayer (John 14–17), a speech of unparalleled length compared with any in the other Gospels. The common scholarly nomenclature through which the Gospels are identified underscores the distinctiveness of John—Matthew, Mark, and Luke are grouped together as the synoptic (literally, "seen together") Gospels, whereas John is isolated as the "Fourth Gospel."

The liturgical life of the church heightens the sense of a divide between John and the Synoptics. Within the church's three-year lectionary cycle, each of the synoptic Gospels has its own year—Matthew (Year A), Mark (Year B), Luke (Year C)—but there is no year for John. The lectionary thus seems to reinforce for clergy and laity alike that John is somehow both different from the other Gospels and perhaps not as essential to the church's reflection on Jesus. Because John is not heard as often in the preaching of the church, John remains a strange and less familiar voice.

Yet if one studies the lectionary cycle carefully, looking not simply at the broad strokes of the three-year cycle but at the texts assigned to particular liturgical seasons, a different picture of the distinctiveness of the Johannine voice emerges. In each of the lectionary cycles, texts from John are read during the Christmas, Lenten, and Easter seasons. For example, the Christmas Day Gospel in each of the three lectionaries is John 1:1-18. Readings from John 3, 4, 9, and 11 form the heart of the Lenten lectionary in Year A, and the Gospel lessons during the Sundays of Easter in each of the three years are drawn from John. The fact that the church turns to readings from John to guide it through each of the critical turning points in its liturgical life—the celebration of the birth of Jesus, the preparation for Jesus' death, and the joy of Easter—highlights another distinctive quality of the Gospel of John.

Story and theological interpretation are inseparably intertwined in John. The "I am" sayings that are a trait of Jesus' speech in John; the Gospel's rich metaphors and images; the poetic language of the Prologue; the theological reflections of the Farewell Discourse; Jesus' repeated statements about his unity with the One who sent him into the world, the One who loves him; the repeated identification of God as Jesus' Father—all ask the reader to ponder who Jesus is and who God is.

The Gospel's various literary techniques have a common theological goal: to open up the world of the Gospel story to the world of the reader's own experience. Because the questions Jesus asks his conversation partners become questions for the reader, the Gospel's dialogues and conversations seem to draw the reader into the stories as a participant. The Gospel makes frequent use of irony and symbolism, literary devices that ask the reader to discover the deeper meaning of an expression. At times, the Gospel narrator comments directly on a story to ensure that the reader is grasping its significance (e.g., 7:39; 8:27; 11:51-52; 12:33; 18:32; 19:35). The confessional language of the Prologue, which affirms, "We have beheld his glory" (1:14), blurs the line between storyteller and reader, as it invites the reader to join in its affirmation. The Gospel of John opens up the story of Jesus to the reading community's own experience so that readers can discover the presence of God in Jesus for themselves.

John draws no lines between history and interpretation, story and theology. To try to separate what happened in the life of Jesus from its meaning is a false pursuit for this Gospel. That claim does not minimize or dismiss the possible historical value of the account of Jesus' life and ministry in John, but instead recognizes that, for John, the value of the events of Jesus' life and ministry lies in their theological significance—what they reveal about God—and not in the events in and of themselves. In order to understand *what* John says about Jesus and God, then, one must attend carefully to *how* he tells his story. The literary style of this Gospel works in partnership with its theology to invite the reader into a new world shaped by the revelation of God in Jesus.

The Johannine theological vision often differs from what many Christians assume to be normative for Christian faith. For example, the Johannine treatment of the eucharist, lodged in the metaphorical discourse of John 6, is radically different from the accounts of the last supper in the Synoptics (Mark 14:22-25 and par.) or the words of institution recorded in 1 Cor 11:23-26. The Johannine understanding of sin and the death of Jesus also brings an important alternative voice to conversations about sin, salvation, and atonement.

THE THEOLOGICAL WORLD OF JOHN

To understand the theological world of John, one must begin by recognizing the centrality of the incarnation to the Gospel. The theological significance of the incarnation is cogently expressed in two lines from the Prologue: "In the beginning was the Word, and the Word was with God and the Word was God" (1:1) and "the Word became flesh and lived among us" (1:14). These two claims are the foundation on which the rest of the Gospel is built: Jesus is the incarnate Word of God. That is, as 1:18 makes clear, Jesus provides access to God in ways never before possible, because Jesus' revelation of God derives from the most intimate relation with God. Jesus provides unique and unprecedented access to God because Jesus shares in God's character and identity; that is what 1:1 draws to the reader's attention. Yet, it is as the Word made flesh that Jesus brings God fully to the world (1:14). Jesus' revelation of God is thus not simply that Jesus speaks God's words and does God's works, although that is part of it (e.g., 5:19-20, 30; 10:25, 37-38; 12:48-49). It is, rather, that Jesus *is* God's Word. No line can be drawn between what Jesus says and what he does, between his identity and mission in the world. Jesus' words and works, his life and death, form an indissoluble whole that provides full and fresh access to God.

Theology and Christology. The pivotal role of the incarnation in John helps to clarify the relationship between theology and christology in the Gospel. The ultimate concern of this Gospel is with God. The good news is the revelation of *God* in Jesus. To focus exclusively on Jesus, as is often the case when verses from John are taken out of context in the contemporary church, is to miss the Gospel's central claim. What Jesus reveals about God comes through what Jesus reveals about himself. Christology redefines theology—that is, Jesus decisively changes how one talks about and knows God—but christology does not replace theology.

The interrelationship of theology and christology in John is clearly seen in the way to which God is referred. God is referred to as "the one who sent me [Jesus]" (e.g., 4:34; 5:38; 8:29) and as "the Father" (e.g., 5:17; 6:45; 14:16). Both of these ways of speaking of God highlight God's relationship with Jesus. "The one who sent Jesus" identifies God as the one from whom Jesus' mission in the world originates (e.g., 3:17). This identification of God points to the union of God's and Jesus' work in the world. By speaking of God as Father and Jesus as Son, John calls attention to the love and familial intimacy between them. Indeed, this familial intimacy is one of the central theological metaphors of the Gospel. At 1:12-13, for example, the Gospel notes that all who receive Jesus and believe in him become "children of God."

The use of father language for God is a painful issue for many women in the contemporary church because of the burden of patriarchy it frequently carries. Many women rightly note that an exclusive use of father language for God both flattens the richness of biblical images for God that sends disturbing messages about systems of power and authority. Yet the Gospel of John is an acute reminder that the elimination of father language is not the solution to this issue. "Father" is an essential name for God in John, and it is impossible to eliminate or even change the Father/Son language of this Gospel without seriously altering the Gospel's theological vision. The church's task, therefore, is to move beyond the assumption that *Father* is a generic synonym for "God." The Fourth Gospel itself argues against that claim, since God is identified as "the one who sends" with the same frequency as God is identified as "Father." The theological and pastoral task is to discover what the particulars of Father/Son language in John contribute to a fuller understanding of God, Jesus, and the Christian life. John does not use Father/Son language to reinforce the claims of patriarchy. Rather, he uses it to highlight the theological possibilities of intimacy and love that rest at the heart of God.[2]

Eccesiology. All of the Gospel's other theological concerns derive from its theology of the incarnation. For example, its eccesiology—its understanding of the life of the faith community—is expressed succinctly in Jesus' commandment of John 13:34-35: "Just as I have loved you, you also should love one another. By this everyone will know that you are my disciples, if you have love for one another." The full expression of Jesus' love is the gift of his life (see 10:11, 14, 17-18; 15:12-15), the crowning moment of the incarnation (19:30). For us to love one another as Jesus loves, then, is to live out the love of the incarnation, to show in one's own life the fullness of love that unites God and Jesus. The commandment to love as Jesus loves takes on added urgency in a community for which persecution and martyrdom were a social reality (cf. 16:2-3). John's image of the faith community, then, derives from his understanding of the relationship between God and Jesus.

Pneumatology. John's pneumatology, his understanding of the Spirit, also derives from his understanding of the relationship between God and Jesus. Jesus' death marked the end of the incarnation. If the revelation of God is lodged decisively in the incarnation, what happens after Jesus has died? Is the revelation of God so temporally bound that it is available only to those who knew the historical Jesus? The Paraclete is the Fourth Evangelist's solution to this theological dilemma. "Paraclete" is the transliteration of the Greek noun παράκλητος (*paraklētos*), the noun the Fourth Evangelist uses to speak of the Spirit. This noun has many meanings—for example, "the one who exhorts," "the one who comforts," "the one who helps"—all of which the Gospel seems to employ in its discussion of the identity and function of the Spirit in the life of the faith community. The Spirit/Paraclete will remain in the community after Jesus' death and return to God ("And I will ask the Father, and he will give you another Paraclete, to be with you forever" [14:16; see also 14:26]). The Spirit/Paraclete will continue the revelation of God begun in the incarnation, "He will glorify me because he will take what is mine and declare it to you" (16:14; see also 14:26; 16:13, 15). The Spirit thus makes it possible for succeeding generations of believers to come to know the God revealed in Jesus.

Eschatology. John's eschatology is also shaped by his understanding of the incarnation. Because God is fully revealed in Jesus, Jesus' advent into the world brings the world to a moment of crisis and decision (e.g., 3:16-21). One does not have to wait for a future revealing of the fullness of God's glory and God's will for the world or for eternal life to be bestowed. Both are available now in Jesus: "Very truly, I tell you, anyone who hears my word and believes him who sent me has eternal life, and does not come under judgment, but has passed from death to life" (5:24); "And this is eternal life, that they may know you, the only true God, and Jesus Christ whom you have sent. I glorified you on earth by finishing the work that you gave me to do" (17:3-4). In Jesus' death, resurrection, and ascension, his "hour," the world is judged. Jesus' death, the full expression of his love, judges the world because it reveals the character of God (e.g., 14:31; 17:24). Jesus' victory over death judges the world because it reveals the impotence of the ruler of the world (e.g., 12:31; 14:30; 16:11). Jesus' ascension judges the world because when he is reunited with God "with the glory that I had in your presence before the world existed" (17:5), his work is completed (e.g., 16:10).

The theological intensity of this Gospel can be discouraging to many readers. In the middle of yet another complex theological statement in the Farewell Discourse, one may long for one of the short, pithy narratives of the synoptic Gospels. Yet the theological intensity of this Gospel is its genius. The Fourth Evangelist held his faith deeply, and he clearly wanted his readers to share his passion for life shaped by the incarnation. He weaves together narrative and theology in an attempt to open up the wonder and mystery of the incarnation as fully as possible, so that the Gospel readers can know themselves to be the recipients of Jesus' gifts. The Fourth Evangelist loved God and Jesus deeply, and he invites his readers to share that love.

As a preliminary step in orienting the reader to the distinctive Johannine narrative and theological voice, it is important to review issues that illumine the historical setting of this document within first-century Judaism and the later life of the church.[3]

EXCURSUS: THE PARACLETE

The Farewell Discourse places a rich portrait of the Paraclete before the Gospel reader. The Paraclete is intimately tied to Jesus' preparation of his disciples for their life after his return to God. In none of the other Gospels does the Spirit play such a central role in the teaching of Jesus. Furthermore, by speaking of the Spirit as the Paraclete, the Fourth Evangelist seems to be attempting to free his portrait from early Christian preconceptions of the nature of the Spirit in order to get a fresh hearing for the role the Spirit plays in the life of the believing community. For example, John does not identify the presence of the Spirit in the Christian community with specific spiritual gifts (cf. 1 Cor 12:1-11, 27-28; 14:1-33; Acts 2:4). The Gospel does not portray the Spirit as actively directing the activities of the believing community (cf. Acts 8:29, 39; 10:19; 11:12; 13:2, 4), nor does it point to the role of the Spirit in baptism (cf. Acts 2:38; 8:16-17; 10:44-48). The portrait of the Paraclete in the Farewell Discourse is thus one of the most substantive and distinctive theological contributions of this Gospel, and it warrants the interpreter's careful reflection.

THE PARACLETE AS THE PRESENCE OF JESUS

It is impossible to overstate the crisis that the believing community faced as a result of Jesus' death. The shape and scope of this crisis can be illustrated by looking at the conversation between Jesus and Peter at 6:67-68. At 6:67, Jesus asked the Twelve whether they, too, wanted to leave him because of the difficulty of his teachings. In response, Peter replied, "Lord, to whom can we go? You have the words of eternal life" (6:68). Peter, speaking for the disciples, recognized the life-giving power of Jesus' revelation. At Jesus' death, the disciples face the inversion of the situation proposed at 6:67: Jesus is leaving them, and Peter's question becomes even more poignant, "Lord, to whom can we go?" Is Jesus' death the end of his "words of eternal life"?

Paraclete Passages in the Gospel of John (NIV)

14:16-17	"And I will ask the Father, and he will give you another Counselor to be with you forever—the Spirit of truth. The world cannot accept him, because it neither sees him nor knows him. But you know him, for he lives with you and will be in you."
14:26	"But the Counselor, the Holy Spirit, whom the Father will send in my name, will teach you all things and will remind you of everything I have said to you."
15:26	"When the Counselor comes, whom I will send to you from the Father, the Spirit of truth who goes out from the Father, he will testify about me.
16:7-11	"But I tell you the truth: It is for your good that I am going away. Unless I go away, the Counselor will not come to you; but if I go, I will send him to you. When he comes, he will convict the world of guilt in regard to sin and righteousness and judgment; in regard to sin, because men do not believe in me; in regard to righteousness, because I am going to the Father, where you can see me no longer; and in regard to judgment, because the prince of this world now stands condemned."
16:12-15	"I have much more to say to you, more than you can now bear. But when he, the Spirit of truth, comes, he will guide you into all truth. He will not speak on his own; he will speak

> only what he hears, and he will tell you what is yet to come. He will bring glory to me by taking from what is mine and making it known to you. All that belongs to the Father is mine. That is why I said the Spirit will take from what is mine and make it known to you."

It is important to be clear about the theological dimension of this crisis. In John, Jesus' revelation of God hinges on the recognition that Jesus is the incarnate Logos, the Son of God. Jesus' revelation of God is not a general, abstract revelation of the character of God. The essence of God cannot be abstracted from the incarnation and represented as some general notion of the "divine." Rather, the reality of the incarnation is the essence of Jesus' revelation of God. It is in the Word become flesh, in God's gift of his Son, that believers come to know who God is. That is, the incarnation has brought believers into new relationship with God and has opened up the possibility of their becoming children of God (1:12-13). Jesus' death and departure thus presented the disciples, and the church, with a crisis far greater than simply the loss of their teacher and friend. Jesus' death and return to God marked the end of the incarnation. If the revelation of God is lodged in the incarnation, what happens when Jesus is gone? Was Jesus' revelation of God possible for only the first generation of believers, available only to those who had physical contact with Jesus and his ministry? Was Jesus' revelation of God thus limited to one particular moment in history, or does it have a future?

It is the theological genius of the Fourth Evangelist to present the Paraclete as the solution to this crisis. Throughout Jesus' words about the Paraclete, the emphasis repeatedly falls on the Paraclete as the one who will continue Jesus' work after his absence, as the one who will make it possible for the experience of God made known and available in the incarnation to be known after Jesus' death. The description of the Paraclete is echoed by the Gospel's description of Jesus. For example, the verbs "to witness" and "to abide," both identified in the Gospel with the life and ministry of Jesus, are associated with the Paraclete in the Farewell Discourse ("witness" [μαρτυρέω *martyreō*], e.g., 3:32; 8:13-18; 15:26-27; "abide" [μένω *menō*], e.g., 14:17, 25; 15:4). The Paraclete is explicitly described as speaking the words of Jesus and reminding the disciples of Jesus' teaching (14:26; 15:13-15). The Paraclete's origins are explicitly linked to the agency of God and Jesus, and the Paraclete is described as being sent by God and given by God (14:16, 26), verbs that are also used to describe Jesus' advent into the world (e.g., 3:16; 4:34; 6:38; 12:44-45). The very language of these promises thus establishes the connections between the ministry of Jesus and the ministry of the Paraclete. The Paraclete is positioned as the link between the historical ministry of Jesus and the future life of the church after Jesus' death.

Through the promise of the Paraclete, the Fourth Evangelist is able to portray Jesus' death, resurrection, and ascension not as the end, but as the beginning of a new era in the life of the believing community. Indeed, in 16:7-8, Jesus goes so far as to speak of his departure as being for the disciples' good, so that they will be able to share in the advent of the Paraclete. Future generations of believers are not left alone, bereft of the experience of God made known in the incarnation, because the Paraclete takes that experience of God and extends it beyond the limits of Jesus' life and death. The Paraclete makes it possible for all believers to share in the good news of the incarnation, because the Paraclete makes Jesus present to believers, even though Jesus is now physically absent.

The promise of the abiding presence of the Paraclete highlights the interconnection of all aspects of the Johannine theological vision. In addition to clarifying the Johannine understanding of the Spirit (its pneumatology), the Paraclete passages also contribute to the Fourth Evangelist's portrait of Jesus and point to the writer's understanding of the nature of Christian community. As the Farewell Discourse is at pains to make clear, Jesus' death will not leave the disciples orphaned, because Jesus and God will send the Paraclete to the believing community. Jesus will leave the world, but the disciples will not (17:11, 15), and the promise of the Paraclete shows Jesus as one who will continue to support his followers for perpetuity. The promise of the Paraclete thus stands as a testament to the reliability of Jesus and his love, because Jesus has not ignored the future of those who will live on after he leaves them. It is a stunning portrait of Jesus that has at its heart a conviction about the abiding presence of Jesus with those whom he loves and who love him. Jesus is, indeed, the good shepherd who loves and cares for his own both in his death (10:17-18; 13:1, 35; 15:12-13) and beyond.

The promise of the Paraclete thus provides the ultimate definition of what Jesus means when he says, "Abide in me as I abide in you" (15:4). The presence of the Paraclete means that there are no temporal or spatial limits on Jesus' love and on believers' access to that love. The love of God made known in the incarnation continues into the life of the community through the gift of the Paraclete. What is critical about the promise of the Paraclete is that Jesus and God send the Paraclete to the *community*, not to individuals. Readings of the Fourth Gospel that emphasize the individual believer's mystical relationship to Jesus through the Spirit distort the Johannine picture of the Paraclete. The Paraclete is not a private possession, nor is its presence discernible as an internal experience of the individual believer. The Paraclete is given to and known in the community. Because the Paraclete is the presence of Jesus after Jesus' departure, it is not simply a subjective experience of "God," but is always linked to the revelation of God made known in the incarnation. The Paraclete keeps the community grounded in Jesus' revelation of God, not in an individual's private experience of God. The Paraclete is thus the unifying mark of Christian community, because it gives all believers access to Jesus.

THE PARACLETE AS TEACHER AND WITNESS

Jesus' teachings in the Farewell Discourse consistently depict the Paraclete as teacher and witness, and this depiction illuminates the role of the Paraclete in forming and shaping Christian community. Two passages are especially important in this regard. First, at 14:26, Jesus says that the Paraclete will "remind you of all that I have said to you." This verse points both to the connection between what Jesus said and what the Paraclete will say (see also 16:14) and to the nature of the Paraclete's teaching role. For the Paraclete, to teach is to remind the community of what Jesus himself said. Second, at John 16:12-13, Jesus says, "I still have many things to say to you, but you cannot bear them now. When the Spirit of Truth comes, he will guide you into all the truth." In these verses, Jesus points to the importance of fresh encounters with the words of Jesus, given at the time of need, not in advance of that time, and identifies the Paraclete as the medium of those encounters.

These descriptions of the Paraclete are pivotal for contemporary Christian communities of faith, because they point to the ways in which the Paraclete enables past, present, and future to converge in the life of the church. The Paraclete enables the words of Jesus to resound afresh in ever-changing circumstances. On the one hand, the Paraclete's role is essentially *conserving*. That is, the Paraclete enables the Christian community, at any time in its life, to reach back to the teachings of Jesus and "remember," to bring Jesus' teachings to life afresh with new understanding. On the other hand, the Paraclete's role as teacher is also *creative*. The Paraclete enables the word of Jesus to move forward from its moment in history to the present life of the church. The Paraclete gives new meanings to the teachings of Jesus as the changing circumstances of faith communities and the world demand.

The words of Jesus that community members are able to receive before a crisis are quite distinct from the words that the community is able to receive during or after a crisis. For example, if someone tried to tell an adolescent what he or she would need to hear from Jesus to endure what life will bring at thirty, fifty, or seventy years of age, the adolescent would not be able to "bear" them. The words of Jesus that a community will need to endure the destruction of a church building by fire would also be insupportable in advance of the event. The words of Jesus that the community needs to hear to make sense of the church's place in changing social and economic circumstances are likewise unbearable in advance, because there is no context for such words in advance of the situation of need. The Fourth Evangelist portrays the Paraclete as the guarantee that the words of Jesus will always be available as fresh words for any and all futures.

The Paraclete thus ensures that there is an ongoing communication between Jesus and contemporary communities of faith. As with the Gospel's emphasis on the abiding presence of the Paraclete, this interpretation of the Paraclete's role as teacher and witness is also a stroke of theological genius. This understanding of the Paraclete as teacher both honors the integrity of the historical ministry of Jesus and at the same time recognizes that Jesus' ministry must always be interpreted in order to keep its offer of God alive.

The Paraclete's teaching, witness, and interpretation can take many forms in the life of the faith community. The first place where the reader of the Fourth Gospel experiences the work of the Paraclete is in the Gospel narrative itself. In telling his story of Jesus, the Fourth Evangelist shares in the work of the Paraclete. He does indeed "remind" his readers of what Jesus said and did, thus carrying the teachings of Jesus forward from the past into the present. But in his reminding, he also places the story of Jesus into conversation with the circumstances in which his readers live, so that they are able to hear Jesus' words as if he were speaking to their own lives and needs. The two levels of many of the Gospel's narratives, in which Jesus' relationship to the Jewish authorities of his day melds with the Jewish controversies of the Evangelist's time (e.g., John 5:31-46; 7:11-13; 9:22-41), can be interpreted as the work of the Paraclete, to show that Jesus' story is both a past event and a contemporary story.[4] The Fourth Evangelist understands, perhaps better than any other evangelist, that story and interpretation, history and theology, are inseparably linked in the life of Jesus and the church and that is incumbent upon the faith community to engage in disciplined conversation between the story of Jesus and their own stories.

The contemporary Christian also experiences the Paraclete in the preaching of the church. Each time a preacher attempts to proclaim the Word of God in a new circumstance, he or she shares in the work of the Paraclete. At its heart, preaching belongs to the ongoing conversation among past, present, and future in the life of the church. Like the work of the Paraclete, preaching is both conserving and creative. It is at the same time both old and new, past tense and contemporary. The preacher is bound both to the traditions of the church, so that his or her work is an act of reminding, and to the present moment, so that his or her work is also an act of discovering how the Word of God speaks in a new day. The gift and presence of the Paraclete allows both the preacher and the congregation to share in a fresh experience of the Word of God.

AUTHORSHIP

Like all the other Gospels, John is an anonymously written document; its traditional title, "The Gospel According to John," first appears as the heading of second-century CE manuscripts. The "John" of this title is presumably John, the son of Zebedee, thus according apostolic authorship to the Gospel. The authorship of the Fourth Gospel was a subject of much debate in the second and third centuries. Christian Gnostics (e.g., Valentinus and Heracleon) who were drawn to the Fourth Gospel claimed apostolic authorship as a way of giving apostolic grounding to their faith perspectives. The opponents of Gnosticism, especially Irenaeus, the bishop of Lyons (c. 130–200 CE), claimed apostolic authorship as a way of refuting gnostic claims. Christian Gnostics drew on a wide spectrum of early Christian documents as sources and expressions of their theology and christology (for example, the *Gospel of Thomas*).[5] In *Against Heresies*, Irenaeus points to the apostolic authorship of Matthew, Mark, Luke, and John and insists on the authority of these four Gospels alone in his attempt to delegitimate the gnostic Gospels and other writings. This apologetic setting must always be kept in mind when one weighs the issue of apostolic authorship.

Beginning in the mid-second century, church theologians identified John, the son of Zebedee, with "the disciple whom Jesus loved," as this quotation from Irenaeus shows: "Afterwards John, the disciple of the Lord, who also had leaned upon his breast, himself published his Gospel, while he was living at Ephesus in Asia."[6] Despite Irenaeus's identification, there is no clear internal Fourth Gospel evidence to support linking John, the son of Zebedee, with the beloved disciple; the tradition of the apostolic authorship of the Gospel began to erode in the nineteenth century. The "disciple whom Jesus loved" is always identified by his relationship with Jesus, never by name. There is one passing reference to "the sons of Zebedee" at 21:2, the introduction to a scene in which the beloved disciple appears, but this verse also contains a reference to "two others of his disciples," so that no clear identification is possible.

The identification of John, the son of Zebedee, with the beloved disciple can be conjecture at best and is based largely on the desire to ascribe apostolic authorship to this Gospel. Yet this very understanding of apostolic authority runs counter to the Fourth Gospel's understanding of discipleship. The Twelve have a very minimal role in this Gospel (they are mentioned explicitly only at 6:69, 71; 20:24).

Therefore, it is not necessary to postulate that the beloved disciple was one of the Twelve in order for him to have had authority within his community.

In addition to the Gospel, four other NT books are associated with the name "John": 1, 2, and 3 John, and the Revelation to John. Like the Gospel, the three epistles are anonymous documents; their attribution to John the apostle derives from the manuscript tradition of the early church. The author of Revelation, by contrast, identifies himself as "John" at Rev 1:1, 4, 9; 22:8.

Although the tradition labeled the epistles and the Gospel as having been written by the same author, the internal evidence does not support that conclusion. The three epistles (particularly 1 John; 2 and 3 John are too brief to enable much comparison) do share some pivotal theological language and concepts with the Gospel of John (e.g., the commandment to love one another; the image of the faith community as children; light; life), but there are also many important differences. For example, the role of the Spirit/Paraclete, so pivotal to the picture of the life of the community in John (e.g., 16:8-11), has no similar role in 1 John, which is singularly concerned with community life. The understanding of sin and atonement (e.g., 1 John 1:7; 2:2; 4:10) is also quite different from that found in the Gospel. Most important, the situations addressed by the Gospel and 1 John are quite different. Whereas the Gospel is oriented toward the community's conflict with synagogal Judaism (see below), the epistle is primarily concerned with intra-Christian conflicts. The opponents with whom the author of 1 John debates are members of the Christian community (or have been).

It is, therefore, widely held that the epistles originated within the same faith community that produced the Gospel, but not from the same author at the same time. Much of the conflict to which 1 John is addressed seems to be generated by disagreement over the interpretation of the theology contained in the Gospel (e.g., the reality of the incarnation, 1 John 4:2-3; 5:6). This suggests that the epistles came from a later stage in the community's life.[7]

It is unlikely that the "John" of Revelation is the apostle John, the son of Zebedee, or the author of the Gospel or the Johannine epistles. He does not claim that identity for himself, but records that he was persecuted and imprisoned on Patmos for his faith (1:9; note also his reference to the "twelve apostles of the Lamb" at 21:14). The differences between the Gospel and Revelation are quite striking, beginning with the thoroughgoing apocalypticism that shapes Revelation. Yet behind these striking differences, the two books nonetheless contain some distinctive theological and imagistic echoes; Rev 19:3, like John 1:1, refers to Jesus as the Word of God; Jesus' gift of living water appears in both (John 4:13-14; 7:37-38; cf. 6:35; Rev 22:17). The invective toward "those who say that they are Jews" in Rev 2:9 is very similar to the language of John 8:44-47. These echoes suggest that the Gospel and Revelation may have originated within communities that shared some traditions about Jesus.

The key to any discussion of authorship of the Gospel is the Gospel's own evidence about the relationship between the beloved disciple and the author of the Fourth Gospel. The "disciple whom Jesus loved" first appears at 13:23 and plays a prominent role in the last chapters of the Gospel (19:26-27; 20:3-10; 21:1-14, 20-24; see also 19:35). It is difficult to imagine that the author of the Gospel, who is so insistent on maintaining the anonymity of the disciple, would nonetheless refer to himself as "the disciple whom Jesus loved." More important, there are two verses that explicitly distinguish the witness of the beloved disciple from the work of the author. Both 19:35 and 21:24 use a third-person pronoun to refer to the beloved disciple and his testimony and stress that this testimony is true. John 21:24 is especially important in this regard, "This is the disciple who is testifying to these things and has written them, and we know that his testimony is true." The author of the Gospel thus claims eyewitness authority for the accounts in the Gospel, but points to another, the beloved disciple, as the source of that witness. The beloved disciple, therefore, is not the author of the Gospel, but is presented as the authorizing voice of the traditions that are recounted in the Gospel.

The identity of the beloved disciple was probably known to the first readers of the Gospel. That is, he is not a fictional creation,[8] but a historical figure who played an important role as an eyewitness link to Jesus for the community out of which the Gospel arose (note the concern about his death in 21:20-24). That identity is no longer recoverable for contemporary readers, who must rest content with the information the Gospel supplies about this disciple. Yet the beloved disciple's significance is not limited to his role as eyewitness. Because he is never named and is instead always portrayed as the recipient of Jesus' love, this disciple also emerges as a symbolic figure who embodies the ideal relationship with Jesus that the Gospel hopes to make available to all its readers.

Thus the name of the author of this Gospel is unknown. What *is* known about the author, is that he understood himself to be connected to the traditions about Jesus through the eyewitness testimony of the beloved disciple, that he held the beloved disciple's testimony to be true, and that he regarded the transmission of that testimony to be an act of faith ("He who saw this has testified so that you also may believe" [19:35]).

JOHN'S USE OF SOURCES AND TRADITIONS

How is the reader to weigh the value and relative importance of source and composition theories for the interpretation of John? It is indisputable that the Fourth Evangelist drew on earlier traditions in the composition of his Gospel; he did not create the Gospel from whole cloth. It is critical, therefore, that the contemporary reader not be naive about the transmission of traditions in the first decades of the church, or about the composition process. Source and composition theories help the contemporary reader to recognize and remember that the development of NT literature did not move in one step from the time of Jesus to the written Gospels, but that there were many intermediate steps. It is the pivotal assumption of form criticism and all discussions of oral traditions that stories and teachings circulated in oral form to meet community needs—teaching, preaching, mission, worship, and probably also the entertainment value of telling good stories.

Such theories also stand as a caution to contemporary readers who may be tempted to perceive the faith traditions of the first decades of the church as monolithic or simplistic. Different communities had access to different streams of tradition. The Fourth Gospel, for example, draws explicit attention to the traditions that came to it through the distinctive witness of the beloved disciple. In addition, individual traditions were regarded as more helpful or essential to a community's life, depending on its social and religious setting and needs, much as in the preaching and teaching of the church today.

The most important source question is whether John knew and drew on the synoptic Gospels. A quotation from Clement of Alexandria offers the classic view of Johannine dependence on the Synoptics: "Last of all John, perceiving that the external facts had been made plain in the gospel, being urged by his friends and inspired by the Spirit, composed a spiritual gospel."[9] Clement recognized that the Gospel of John posed a decisive question about the interrelationship of history, theology, and interpretation. The solution that Clement proposed, and that remained the dominant view into the nineteenth century, was to assume Johannine use of the Synoptics. This solution confirmed the other canonical Gospels as the historical norm for the story of Jesus and rendered the differences between John and the Synoptics less problematic. John is simply exercising theological or "spiritual" freedom in his use of the other Gospels.

The most influential work to question the view that John depended on the other Gospels was that of Percival Gardner-Smith.[10] He carefully compared scenes held in common by John and the synoptic Gospels, and these comparisons led him to conclude that the interrelationship of the Gospels was best explained by the assumption that John used independent Jesus traditions that often resembled those in the Synoptics, not that John intentionally altered the synoptic Gospels.

The work that was begun in Gardner-Smith's brief study was completed by C. H. Dodd in *Historical Tradition in the Fourth Gospel.* Dodd does a careful analysis of all of the Johannine passages that have any synoptic parallels and concludes that "behind the Fourth Gospel there lies an ancient tradition independent of the other gospels, and meriting serious consideration as a contribution to our knowledge of the historical facts concerning Jesus Christ."[11] Both Gardner-Smith and Dodd gave a prominent position to oral traditions about Jesus rather than explaining all overlaps among the Gospels in terms of dependence on written documents. The work of Gardner-Smith and Dodd thus made it possible to examine and interpret the Johannine traditions about Jesus on their own terms, not as being derivative of the Synoptics. They also pointed to John as an independent resource for information about Jesus.

Johannine independence from the synoptic Gospels has become the majority position in Johannine scholarship. Of the major twentieth-century commentaries on John written after Dodd, only C. K. Barrett's work argues for Johannine dependence on Mark.[12] Johannine dependence on the Synoptics, especially Mark, has recently emerged as a fresh topic of debate,[13] but the exegetical evidence amassed by Dodd is difficult to overcome. John makes use of a stream of oral tradition that often overlaps with, but is nonetheless independent from, the traditions on which Mark and the other Gospels drew.

Another approach to source questions is to explain the distinctiveness of the Johannine traditions by appealing to other written sources. The classic lines of this approach to John were drawn by Rudolf Bultmann.[14] Bultmann understood the Fourth Evangelist to be a master literary craftsman who drew together three major sources in the composition of the Gospel: a passion-narrative source; a revelation-discourse source; and a signs source. The revelation-discourse source is Bultmann's most controversial proposal. It is the key to Bultmann's contention that a gnostic revealer-redeemer myth lies behind the Fourth Gospel's christology; the Prologue is the linchpin for this source. Bultmann maintained that John found this myth in the revelation-discourse source and rewrote it by making Jesus the redeemer. Bultmann's thesis of gnostic influence was very influential on German scholarship on John, although the suggestion of a revelation-discourse source has been largely rejected.

Bultmann's suggestion of a signs source as the source of the miracles recounted in John has received wider acceptance. The key elements in isolating this source are the occurrence of the noun "sign" (σημεῖον *sēmeion*) in the Gospel (e.g., 2:11; 4:54; 20:30), the enumeration of the two Cana miracles (2:11; 4:54), and the purported tension between the positive valuation of miracles in the source and the seemingly negative view of miracles in the Gospel (e.g., 4:48). Robert Fortna, for example, following Bultmann's suggestions, has worked diligently for several decades to reconstruct "the Gospel of signs."[15]

The signs-source hypothesis, however, runs counter to the insights about the role and diversity of oral traditions proposed by Dodd and also overemphasizes the differences between the Johannine and Synoptic miracles. When one identifies the miracles in John—the wine miracle at the Cana wedding (2:1-11); the healing of the royal official's son (4:46-54); the healing of a lame man (5:1-18); the feeding of the five thousand (6:1-14); Jesus' walking on water (6:16-21); the healing of a blind man (9:1-41); the raising of Lazarus (11:1-44), and the miraculous catch of fish (21:1-14), one notices that with the single exception of the wine miracle at Cana, each of these miracles has some analogue in the synoptic tradition. Therefore, it seems more credible to postulate the common oral traditions about Jesus as the source of these stories than a fully formed signs source. That is, it seems more likely that John had access to an oral tradition that grouped together a series of miracle stories about Jesus than that he drew on a written signs collection. In addition, the signs-source hypothesis plays down the interrelationship of miracle and discourse throughout the Gospel. Johannine scholars are divided on the hypothesis of a written signs source; some express skepticism about the viability of this hypothesis,[16] while others use the source as an exegetical tool in their commentary work.[17]

There was a final piece to Bultmann's source theory: an ecclesiastical redactor responsible for the final form of the Gospel. To this editor Bultmann attributed all sections of the Gospel that reflect later ecclesiastical issues, for example, the eucharistic section in 6:51-58. Although it is impossible to accept Bultmann's characterization of this editor and his concerns, because "ecclesiastical" concerns are not foreign to the theology of John, the thesis of a final editor or editors of the Gospel is shared by many Fourth Gospel scholars.

Raymond Brown, for example, proposes five distinct stages in the composition of John.[18] The stages are (stage 1) a body of traditional material; (stage 2) its development in the teaching and preaching of the Johannine community; (stage 3) its organization of this material into a Gospel narrative by the "evangelist" (perhaps the preacher of stage 2); (stage 4) a secondary edition by the evangelist; and (stage 5) a final editing by the redactor. Brown's theory has in its favor that it highlights the liveliness and fluidity of traditions about Jesus in early Christian communities and emphasizes the intersection of the formation of the Gospel with the developing religious and pastoral needs of a particular community. Yet the precision with which he classifies the stages; the distinctions he makes among stages 3, 4, and 5; and his attempts in his commentary to distinguish which parts of the Gospel belong to which stage of composition cannot be supported adequately by the evidence of the Gospel text.

Source and composition theories place their emphasis on moving behind the text, that is, on the history of the text. These theories are thus valuable tools in reconstructing early Christian history.

DATE OF COMPOSITION AND SOCIAL AND RELIGIOUS SETTING

𝔓[52], an Egyptian papyrus fragment that dates from the early second century, contains the text of John 18:31-33, 37-38, suggesting that the Gospel was known in Egypt by 100 CE. In addition, John appears to have been in wide circulation by the middle of the second century CE. Heracleon wrote the first commentary on John around 150 CE (excerpts from this commentary are preserved in Origen's commentary on John).[19] Among the second-century church fathers, Irenaeus (180 CE) and Melito of Sardis (175 CE), both in Asia Minor, show indisputable knowledge of the Fourth Gospel, as do Bishop Polycrates (190) and the Muratorian Canon (180–200) from Rome. Tatian's *Diatesseron,* a Gospel harmony composed circa 175 CE, draws on texts from John and treats it with the same authority as he treats the synoptic Gospels. Moreover, Ignatius of Antioch may have had knowledge of John as early as the beginning of the second century. The manuscript evidence and the evidence of early church tradition thus suggest that the Gospel was completed no later than 100 CE.

In addition to this external evidence, the Gospel points to the crisis that may have precipitated its composition and hence provides additional assistance in arriving at a date. At three places in the Gospel, the expression "put out of the synagogue" occurs (9:22; 12:42; 16:2). In a highly influential study, J. Louis Martyn proposed that this phrase refers to a practice of excommunicating perceived heretics from the synagogue. This practice was formalized in the Benediction Against Heretics (*Birkath ha-Minim*), a benediction introduced into the synagogue liturgy sometime after the destruction of the Jerusalem Temple in 70 CE and probably between 85 and 95 CE.[20]

There is considerable scholarly debate about the precise contours and dating of this benediction. Nonetheless, this benediction offers an important example of the religious conflicts within first-century Judaism. The destruction of the Jerusalem Temple in 70 CE, the cultic center, meant a radical reorientation of Jewish religious life. Pharisees, priests, and Jewish Christians (or perhaps less anachronistically, Christian Jews), among others, struggled over religious identity and power. The benediction was the attempt of the pharisaical/rabbinic branch of Judaism to assert its control in the face of alternative forms of Judaism. This branch of post–70 CE Judaism ultimately did assert its control, emerging from these struggles as the dominant religious group within later Judaism.[21]

EXCURSUS: JOHN 9:22 AND THE BENEDICTION AGAINST HERETICS

The Benediction Against Heretics can be found as the twelfth in a list of nineteen benedictions in the contemporary Jewish prayer book, but because the prayer book was heavily censored in the Middle Ages, this version is not a reliable version of the one introduced by the first-century rabbis. A more reliable text, although its exact age is difficult to determine, is a version of the Benediction found in the Cairo Genizah in 1896: "For the apostates let there be no hope and let the arrogant government be speedily uprooted in our days. Let the Nazarenes [Christians] and the Minim [heretics] be destroyed in a moment and let them be blotted out of the Book of Life and not be inscribed together with the righteous. Blessed art thou, O Lord, who humblest the proud!"[22]

Martyn's precise linkage of 9:22 with the benediction against heretics has been questioned on a number of points. The questions cluster largely around issues of the dating of the twelfth benediction and the reliability of the reference to Christians in the Cairo version of the benediction. Scholars have pointed out that the words of the benediction were not fixed by the late first century and that the prayer must be read in the context of the changes within late first-century Judaism itself. Prior to the destruction of the Jerusalem Temple by the Romans in 70 CE, Judaism had many avenues of expression, which included Pharisaic/rabbinic, Sadducean, apocalyptic, nationalistic (Zealot), and Christian.[23] After the destruction of the Temple, however, the Pharisaic/rabbinic branch moved into ascendancy and began to establish standards of Jewish orthodoxy along its lines. The original form of the prayer was probably directed against heretics in general—that is, all Jews who do not adhere to the Pharisaic/rabbinic line, rather than exclusively against Christians, with the explicit reference to Christians added after the first century.[24]

This does not mean, of course, that the community for which the Fourth Evangelist wrote could not have experienced the general malediction against heretics as directed specifically against them. What it does mean, however, is that one must be careful about how closely one links the social setting of the Fourth Gospel to one particular interpretation of the benediction. While the shape of the conflict between the Johannine community and the synagogue might not be explained point for point for correspondence between John 9:22 and the wording of the Benediction Against Heretics, Martyn's basic understanding of the social circumstances that gave rise to the Fourth Gospel holds true: This community experienced expulsion from the synagogue as a fact of its religious life, and it laid the responsibility for that expulsion on the Jewish authorities—i.e., the Pharisees.[25]

The religious turmoil within emergent Judaism after 70 CE is critical to the dating of the Fourth Gospel. In the Gospel's intense rhetoric about "the Jews" (see below) and its predictions of expulsion, persecution, and martyrdom for believers, this intra-Jewish conflict is visible. The Fourth Evangelist and those for whom he wrote understood themselves to be a persecuted religious minority, expelled from the synagogue, their religious home, because of their faith in Jesus.[26] The pain of this intra-Jewish struggle is fresh and real for the Fourth Evangelist; many of Jesus' words in the Farewell Discourse can be read as intended to uphold this community in its struggles (see 15:18–16:3).

The publication of the benediction c. 90 CE marked the formalization of an intra-religious struggle that had been going on in many local communities prior to this date. The Gospel of John may stem from one such community, in which the practice of expulsion from the synagogue began almost immediately after the destruction of the Jerusalem Temple. The intensity of the conflict with the Jewish leadership, and the pivotal role it plays in shaping the religious and social identity of the community that read this Gospel, suggests 75–80 CE as the earliest possible date of composition; the external evidence, as noted above, makes a date much later than 100 CE unlikely. Thus the Gospel of John is roughly contemporaneous with Matthew, which was written in response to the same intra-Jewish struggles.

John thus belongs to and derives from the complex and multi-faceted cultural and intellectual milieu of first-century Judaism. The influence of this diversity of Jewish traditions on the Fourth Evangelist is evident throughout the Gospel. From beginning to end, the Gospel is shaped by the language and images of the OT. The opening words of the Gospel ("In the beginning . . .") are clearly intended to echo Gen 1:1. What is most striking about John's use of the OT is that the references to it are uniformly positive. For example, Jesus' description of his gifts are couched in the language of Scripture (cf., e.g., 6:32-33; Ps 78:24). Jesus' self-designation as "I AM" echoes the use of the divine name in the Septuagint of Second Isaiah (e.g., Isa 43:25; 51:12; 52:6). Indeed, the Scriptures are pointed to as bearing witness to Jesus (e.g., 5:39, 46). John's animosity to the Jewish religious authorities thus does not extend to Jewish religious traditions. He is thoroughly saturated in and shaped by the Jewish Scriptures.

THE "I AM" SAYINGS IN JOHN

Absolute "I AM" sayings without a predicate nominative:

4:26 Jesus said to her, "I AM, the one who is speaking to you."

6:20 But he said to them, "I AM; do not be afraid."

8:24 "I told you that you would die in your sins, for you will die in your sins unless you believe that I AM."

8:28 "When you have lifted up the Son of Man, then you will realize that I AM, and I do nothing on my own, but I speak these things as the Father instructed me."

8:58 "Very truly, I tell you, before Abraham was, I AM."

13:19 "I tell you this now, before it occurs, so that when it does occur, you may believe that I AM."

18:5, 7 Jesus replied, "I AM." When he said to them, "I am," they stepped back and fell to the ground.

"I AM" sayings with a predicate nominative:

6:35 "I am the bread of life. Whoever comes to me will never be hungry, and whoever believes in me will never be thirsty."

6:51 "I am the living bread that came down from heaven. Whoever eats of this bread will live forever; and the bread that I will give for the life of the world is my flesh."

8:12 "I am the light of the world. Whoever follows me will never walk in darkness but will have the light of life."

9:5 "I am the light of the world."

10:7, 9 "Very truly, I tell you, I am the gate for the sheep."

10:11, 14 "I am the good shepherd."

11:25-6 "I am the resurrection and the life."

14:6 "I am the way, and the truth, and the life."

15:1, 5 "I am the true vine, and my Father is the vinegrower."

Jewish wisdom traditions in particular pay a prominent role in John. These traditions, found in both canonical and extra-canonical Jewish documents (e.g., Proverbs, Sirach, Wisdom of Solomon), personify Wisdom as the presence of God's Word in the world (e.g., Prov 8:22, 34; Wis 7:22-26) and draw attention to God's Word as a source of nourishment and life (e.g., Prov 9:5; Sir 15:3; 24:21). One hears echoes of the idioms of the wisdom traditions in the Prologue (1:1-18) and throughout Jesus' discourses in John (e.g., 6:35; 7:37-38).

The discovery of the Qumran material has contributed to a broader understanding of the diversity of early and mid–first-century Judaism. The sharp dualistic language in John—light/darkness; good/evil—has counterparts in the documents of the Qumran sectarians. While it remains unclear how far one can postulate direct influence, at the very least the similarities between John and Qumran solidly locate the Gospel within the religious diversity of first-century Judaism.

In the first-century Mediterranean world, it was impossible to draw a rigid line between Judaism and Hellenism. The most important example of the rich conversation between Jewish and Greek thought is in the work of Philo of Alexandria, an early first-century Jew who wrote in Greek and was equally at home in Greek philosophy and Jewish Scripture. Philo has important similarities with John.[27] For example, "word" (λόγος *logos*) and "light" (φῶς *phōs*) figure prominently in the thought worlds of both Philo and John, and both were concerned with reinterpreting the Jewish scriptural traditions in the light of the circumstances in which they lived. Again, while direct influence of Philo on John cannot be demonstrated, Philo broadens our understanding of first-century Judaism and helps us to see John more clearly in its variegated Jewish context.

The question of gnostic influence on John needs to be examined in the light of the diversity of first-century Mediterranean Judaism. Just as one cannot draw a sharp line between Judaism and Hellenism in the first century, so also one cannot draw a sharp line between Judaism and Gnosticism. Much of what emerged as definitional for later Gnosticism—dualistic language, the pivotal role of light/dark imagery, the emphasis on knowledge—is found already in less developed forms in Jewish wisdom literature, Qumran, and Philo.[28] The proto-Gnostic tendencies in the Jewish traditions closest to the Fourth Gospel, as well as in the Fourth Gospel itself, may account in part for the important role John played in the theology of later Christian Gnostics (e.g., Valentinus and Heracleon).

The Gospel of John was thus written by a Jewish Christian for and in a Jewish Christian community that was in conflict with the synagogue authorities of its day (represented in the Gospel as "the Pharisees" or "the Jews"). The traditional identification of Ephesus as the place of the Gospel's composition fits this description, because Ephesus had a large and active Jewish community (see Acts 18–19), but nothing tells singularly in its favor either. Antioch and Alexandria, two Mediterranean cities with large Jewish populations, have also been proposed as the location of the Fourth Gospel. Nor is it possible to rule out a location in Palestine for the Fourth Evangelist and his community.[29] The place of the Gospel's origin, like its author, must remain unnamed; what is critical to the interpretation of John is the recognition of its origins in the religious life of first-century Judaism.

Historical-critical work is essential to the interpretation of John, as it is of any biblical book, because each book was written in a particular social and historical context. John reflects and arises out of the struggles and celebrations of an actual faith community. To ignore the first-century social, religious, and historical environment opens up the danger of interpreting John as if it were spoken directly to twentieth-century Christians, when it is not. It was written for first-century Jewish Christians whose world was in crisis because of their faith in Jesus as the decisive revelation of God. The good news of John for twentieth-century Christians is always mediated through this first community of readers. The contemporary reader, therefore, must be willing to engage in acts of theological and historical imagination when reading John; the reader must be willing to envision the experience of the first readers and the meaning of the Gospel for them.

A crucial illustration of this is John's language about "the Jews." This language arises from conflicts between two different groups of first-century Jews: the community of the Fourth Gospel (Christian Jews) and the synagogue authorities. The intense enmity of this language is forged in the struggle for religious and community identity. And, most important, it is language spoken by one group of Jews to another, not by Gentile Christians about Jews. To recognize this social context is not to whitewash the problematic nature of much of this language. Rather, recognition of the socially determined nature and function of this language is essential for any responsible conversation about this language in a contemporary context. To appropriate this language into the modern situation of Jewish-Christian relations without attending to the inseparability of this language from the social world of Johannine Christians is unethical at best, tragic at worst. Awareness of the social, historical, and cultural contexts out of which John emerged, therefore, is essential not only for understanding what texts meant "then" but also for determining what texts mean "now."

THE STRUCTURE OF THE GOSPEL OF JOHN

It is conventional in Johannine scholarship to divide the Gospel of John into two parts: chaps. 1-12, commonly referred to as "the Book of Signs," and chaps. 13-20, commonly referred to as "the Book of Glory." John 21 is most often treated as an appendix or second ending to the Gospel. The reference to the arrival of Jesus' hour in John 13:1 thus serves as the dividing line between the two major sections, "Now before the festival of the Passover, Jesus knew that his hour had come to depart from this world and go to the Father." There is no question that John 13:1 marks a major turn in the Gospel narrative, because it initiates the enactment of the events of Jesus' hour, but this conventional division oversimplifies the contents of John 1-12 and the interrelationship of the events of Jesus' ministry and his "hour." This introduction proposes an alternative structure for John.

John 1:1-51, The Prelude to Jesus' Ministry. This section consists of two parts: a hymnic prologue (1:1-18) and a narrative prologue (1:19-51). Both of these sections function like the overture to an orchestral piece: They introduce a theme that will be developed throughout the remainder of the Gospel. Both sections have stylized structures that underscore their function as overture. John 1:1-18 begins the Gospel with a poetic celebration of Jesus' origin with God and his coming into the world. John 1:19-51, which narrates the witness of John the Baptist to Jesus (vv. 19-34) and the gathering of the first disciples (vv. 35-51), is composed as a series of four days that lay the groundwork for the unfolding of Jesus' ministry.

John 2:1–5:47, "The Greater Things": Jesus' Words and Works. Jesus' public ministry is narrated in two cycles: John 2:1–5:47 and John 6:1–10:42.[30] These chapters contain miracles and discourses by Jesus that point to the authority of Jesus' words and works—the wine miracle at Cana (2:1-11); the cleansing of the Temple (2:13-22); two healing miracles (4:46-54; 5:1-9); Jesus' conversations with Nicodemus (3:1-21) and the Samaritan woman (4:4-42)—and so fulfill his promise to his disciples that they would see "greater things" (1:50). Yet this cycle also contains the first story of Jesus' conflict with the Jewish authorities (5:9-47), a conflict that includes the decision to kill Jesus (5:18). This first cycle establishes the themes and tensions that characterize Jesus' public ministry in John—from the manifestation of Jesus' glory (2:1-11) to the rejection of that glory (5:9-47).

John 6:1–10:42, Jesus' Words and Works: Conflict and Opposition Grow. The second cycle of Jesus' public ministry follows the same pattern as the first—it begins with a miracle in Galilee, the feeding of the five thousand (6:1-15), and concludes with hostility to Jesus and renewed intention to kill him (10:31-39). The second cycle poses the same basic question as the first: Will people receive the revelation of God in Jesus? The difference between the two cycles is that the urgency of that question is highlighted as the hostility to Jesus increases.

John 11:1–12:50, The Prelude to Jesus' Hour. In most commentaries, John 11–12 is identified as the conclusion of Jesus' public ministry. This introduction proposes, however, that these two chapters form a unit in their own right in John. To read them simply as the conclusion of Jesus' ministry is to miss their narrative and theological significance in the overall development of the Gospel. Their primary function is to provide a bridge between the story of Jesus' ministry and that of his death (John 13–19). Just as John 1:1-51 stands as a prelude to Jesus' ministry, so also John 11–12 stands as the prelude to Jesus' hour. Many of the themes that will be developed fully in the narrative of Jesus' hour are anticipated here.

John 13:1–17:26, The Farewell Meal and Words of Jesus. John 13:1 signals a new orientation in the Gospel narrative; Jesus' hour, the time of his death, resurrection, and ascension, has arrived. From this point, the Gospel's focus will not waver from depicting and interpreting the events of Jesus' hour. John 13:1–17:26—which narrates the foot washing (13:1-20), Jesus' Farewell Discourse (14:1–16:33) and prayer (17:1-26)—provides the theological framework for interpreting the remainder of the Gospel.

John 18:1–19:42, "The Hour Has Come": Jesus' Arrest, Trial and Death. John 18–19 is the theological and narrative heart of the Gospel's depiction of Jesus' "hour." These chapters present the reader with the consummate portrait of Jesus as the one who willingly lays down his life for those he loves.

John 20:1-31, The First Resurrection Appearances. Jesus' hour consists of his death, resurrection, *and* ascension. John 20—Jesus' resurrection appearances, the gift of the Spirit, the ascension (alluded to, but not actually reported)—thus belongs to the narrative of Jesus' hour. It is not until Jesus' return to God (20:17) that his hour is completed.

John 21:1-25, Jesus' Resurrection Appearance at the Sea of Tiberius. This introduction proposes that John 21 be read as an integral part of the Gospel narrative rather than as an appendix or second ending. John 21:1-25 points toward the future life of the believing community and its continuing witness to Jesus.

JOHANNINE STUDY TODAY

The two most important figures in Fourth Gospel scholarship in the early and middle decades of the twentieth century were Rudolf Bultmann and C. H. Dodd. The contributions of Bultmann's work lay in the areas of source criticism and the literary history of the Fourth Gospel, history of religions (gnostic influence), and Johannine theology. As noted above, Dodd's major contribution was his investigation of the role of oral tradition in the shaping of the Gospel and his careful comparisons of John and the Synoptics. In addition to Dodd's demonstration of Johannine independence from the synoptic Gospels, Dodd was also a perceptive reader of Johannine literary and narrative technique, as the last third of *The Interpretation of the Fourth Gospel* demonstrates.[31]

In the decades since Bultmann and Dodd, the single most important work in Johannine studies is probably J. Louis Martyn's monograph *History and Theology in the Fourth Gospel.*[32] While others before Martyn had pursued the relationship of the Fourth Gospel to the synagogue, none had argued with such exegetical and methodological clarity. Nor had anyone so intentionally addressed the interaction between community and tradition in the formation of the Gospel. The task that Martyn sets for himself in the introduction to *History and Theology* makes this clear:

> Our first task . . . is to say something as specific as possible about the actual circumstances in which John wrote his gospel. How are we to picture daily life in John's church? Have elements of the peculiar daily experience left their stamp on the

> gospel penned by one of its members? May one sense even in the exalted cadences the voice of a Christian theologian who writes *in response to contemporary events and issues* which concern, or should concern, all members of the Christian community in which he lives?[33]

To meet his task, Martyn combines exegetical and historical analysis to conclude that many of the Gospel's dialogues and narratives are to be understood on two levels: (1) a witness to the time of Jesus and (2) a witness to the rearticulation of the tradition in response to events in the life of the Johannine community. As noted in the discussion above, the decisive event for this second level is the conflict of the Johannine community with the synagogue, perhaps in conjunction with the Benediction Against Heretics. In the preface to *History and Theology*, Martyn expressed his surprise that his research had led him away from previous convictions about links with Mandaean literature to the Jewish context he proposed.[34] When questions were asked about the everyday events with which the Gospel community was faced, the pivotal place of relations with Judaism reemerged.

Martyn's work decisively altered the landscape of Johannine studies in two ways. First, his analysis of the Jewish context out of which the Fourth Gospel developed remains the governing view of Johannine studies. Second, as a result of Martyn's work, and that of Raymond Brown in his commentary and subsequent monograph on the Johannine community,[35] the term "Johannine community" has become a commonplace in discussions of the Fourth Gospel. One need only survey dissertations of the 1970s and 1980s to see the prominence of studies that focus on the Johannine community.

In the decades since Martyn's and Brown's generative work about the Johannine community and its relationship to Judaism and early Christianity, two new areas of Johannine study have developed. One development was the move toward literary studies of the Gospel. In *The Anatomy of the Fourth Gospel*, the pioneer work in this field of Johannine scholarship, R. Alan Culpepper studies the literary characteristics of the Fourth Gospel and the narrative world created by them.[36] Literary-critical analysis asserts that the form and rhetorical devices of any given text must be taken with utmost seriousness and not regarded as incidental or extraneous. Studies of John's narrative structure, symbolism, irony, and imagery have enriched the encounter with the distinctive voice of the Fourth Gospel and have brought renewed vitality to exegetical work.[37]

A second important development in recent Johannine studies is the attention given to the social world of the Gospel. This approach to John builds directly from the community history approach of Brown and Martyn, but does so with a concern for the dynamics of social and cultural factors that shaped the life of the community out of which the Gospel grew, rather than for the reconstruction of the community's history. David Rensberger's work *Johannine Faith and Liberating Community* is an important example of this approach.[38]

FOR FURTHER READING

Commentaries

Barrett, C. K. *The Gospel According to St. John.* 2nd ed. Philadelphia: Westminster, 1978.

Beasley-Murray, George R. *John.* WBC 36. Waco, Tex.: Word, 1987.

Brown, Raymond E. *The Gospel According to John.* AB 29 and 29A. New York: Doubleday, 1966, 1970.

Bultmann, Rudolf. *The Gospel of John.* Philadelphia: Westminster, 1971.

Haenchen, Ernst. *John.* Hermeneia. 2 vols. Philadelphia: Fortress, 1984.

Hoskyns, E. C. *The Fourth Gospel.* Edited by F. N. Davey. London: Faber and Faber, 1947.

Kysar, Robert. *John.* Augsburg Commentary on the New Testament. Minneapolis: Augsburg, 1986.

Schnackenburg, Rudolf. *The Gospel According to St. John.* 3 vols. New York: Seabury, 1982.

Other Studies

Bieringer, Reimund, Didier Pollefeyt, and Frederique Vandecasteele-Vanneuville, eds. *Anti-Judaism and the Fourth Gospel.* Louisville, Ky.: Westminster/John Knox, 2001.

Bultmann, Rudolf. *The Theology of the New Testament.* New York: Scribner, 1955.

Culpepper, R. Alan. *Anatomy of the Fourth Gospel: A Study in Literary Design.* Philadelphia: Fortress, 1983.

Dodd, C. H. *Historical Tradition in the Fourth Gospel.* Cambridge: Cambridge University Press, 1963.

———. *The Interpretation of the Fourth Gospel.* Cambridge: Cambridge University Press, 1953.

Käsemann, Ernst. *The Testament of Jesus: A Study of the Gospel of John in the Light of Chapter 17.* London: SCM, 1968.

Kim, Jean Kyoung. *Women and Nation: An Intercontextual Reading of the Gospel of John from a Postcolonial Feminist Perspective.* Boston: Brill, 2004.

Levine, Amy-Jill and Marianne Blickenstaff, eds. *A Feminist Companion to John.* 2 volumes. Feminist Companion to the New Testament and Early Christian Writings 4 and 5. Sheffield: Sheffield Academic Press, 2003.

Martyn, J. Louis. *History and Theology in the Fourth Gospel.* Nashville: Abingdon, 1968; 2nd ed., 1979.

Moloney, Francis J. *The Gospel of John: Text and Context.* Biblical Interpretation Series 72. Boston: Brill, 2005.

Rensberger, David. *Johannine Faith and Liberating Community.* Philadelphia: Westminster, 1988.

Sloyan, Gerard S. *What Are They Saying About John?* New York: Paulist, 1991.

Smith, D. Moody. *The Theology of the Gospel of John.* Cambridge: Cambridge University Press, 1995.

ENDNOTES

1. See Robert C. Tannehill, "The Gospels and Narrative Literature," in *The New Interpreter's Bible* (Nashville: Abingdon, 1995) 8:56-70, and in this volume.

2. See Gail R. O'Day, "John," in *The Women's Bible Commentary*, ed. Carol A. Newsom and Sharon H. Ringe (Louisville: Westminster/John Knox, 1992) 303-4.

3. For a thorough overview of the historical and religious setting of the Gospel of John, see D. Moody Smith, *The Theology of the Gospel of John* (Cambridge: Cambridge University Press, 1995) 1-74.

4. J. Louis Martyn, *History and Theology in the Fourth Gospel* (Nashville: Abingdon, 1968; 2nd ed., 1979) 143-51.

5. See James M. Robinson, ed., *The Nag Hammadi Library in English*, 3rd ed. (San Francisco: Harper & Row, 1988).

6. Irenaeus *Against Heresies* III.11.2.

7. For the view that the epistles precede the Gospel, see Charles Talbert, *Reading John: A Literary and Theological Commentary on the Fourth Gospel and the Johannine Epistles* (New York: Crossroad, 1992).

8. Bultmann is the important exception to this view. He maintained that the beloved disciple was only a symbolic figure. See Rudolph Bultmann, *The Gospel of John: A Commentary*, trans. G. R. Beasley-Murray, R. W. N. Hoarse, and J. K. Riches (Philadelphia: Westminster, 1971) 484.

9. Quoted in Eusebius *Ecclesiastical History* VI.xiv.7.

10. Percival Gardner-Smith, *Saint John and the Synoptic Gospels* (Cambridge: Cambridge University Press, 1938).

11. C. H. Dodd, *Historical Tradition in the Fourth Gospel* (Cambridge: Cambridge University Press, 1953) 423.

12. C. K. Barrett, *The Gospel According to St. John*, 2nd ed. (Philadelphia: Westminster, 1978).

13. See especially the work of Frans Neirynck, "John and the Synoptics," in *L'Evangile de Jean: Sources, Redaction, Theology*, ed. M. de Jonge, (Louvain: Louvain University Press, 1977) 73-106; and "John and the Synoptics: 1975–1990," in *John and the Synoptics*, ed. A. Deneaux (Louvain: Louvain University Press, 1992). For a judicious review of the question, see D. Moody Smith, *John Among the Gospels: The Relationship in Twentieth Century Research* (Minneapolis: Fortress, 1992).

14. Bultmann, *The Gospel of John.*

15. Robert T. Fortna, *The Gospel of Signs: A Reconstruction of the Narrative Source Underlying the Fourth Gospel* (Cambridge: Cambridge University Press, 1970); and *The Fourth Gospel and Its Predecessor: From Narrative Source to Present Gospel* (Philadelphia: Fortress, 1988).

16. E.g., Barrett, *The Gospel According to St. John*, 2nd ed. (Philadelphia: Westminster, 1978), 18, 77; Raymond E. Brown, *The Gospel According to John (I–XII)*, AB 29 (Garden City, N.Y.: Doubleday, 1966) xxxi; (but see also 1:195); George R. Beasley-Murray, *John*, WBC 36 (Waco, Tex.: Word, 1987) xl.

17. Schnackenburg, vol. 1, 67; Kysar, *John*, Augsburg Commentary of the New Testament (Minneapolis: Augsburg, 1986) 12-13. See also Kysar, *John the Maverick Gospel*, rev. ed. (Louisville: Westminster/John Knox, 1993).

18. Brown, *The Gospel According to John (I–XII)*, AB 29 (New York: Doubleday, 1966) xxxiv-xxxix.

19. See Elaine Pagels, *The Johannine Gospel in Gnostic Exegesis: Heracleon's Commentary on John* (Atlanta: Scholars Press, 1972).

20. See J. Louis Martyn, *History and Theology in the Fourth Gospel* (Nashville: Abingdon, 1968; 2nd ed., 1979).

21. See Shaye J. D. Cohen, *From the Maccabees to the Mishnah* (Philadelphia: Westminster, 1987).

22. The first published translation of this text was in S. Schecter, "Genizah Specimens," *JQR* old series 10 (1898) 197-206, 654-59. This translation is the one quoted by Martyn, *History and Theology in the Fourth Gospel*, 58.

23. Daniel J. Harrington, "The Problem of 'the Jews' in John's Gospel," *Explorations* 8, 1 (1994) 3-4.

24. Steven T. Katz, "Issues in the Separation of Judaism and Christianity After 70 CE: A Reconsideration," *JBL* 103 (1984) 69-74.

25. David Rensberger, *Johannine Faith and Liberating Community* (Philadelphia: Westminster, 1988) 22-29.

26. See Rensberger, *Johannine Faith and Liberating Community.*

27. See, e.g., C. H. Dodd, *The Interpretation of the Fourth Gospel* (Cambridge: Cambridge University Press, 1953) 54-73; and Peder Borgen, "Philo," in *The Anchor Bible Dictionary* (New York: Doubleday, 1992) 5:333-42.

28. See Craig A. Evans, *Word and Glory: On the Exegetical and Theological Background of John's Prologue*, JSNTSup (Sheffield: JSOT, 1993).

29. See Martyn, "Glimpses into the History of the Johananine Community," in *L'Evangile de Jean, Sources, Redaction, Theologie*, ed. M. de Jonge (Louvain: Louvain University Press, 1977) 149-75.

30. Most commentaries identify John 2:1–4:54 as a distinct unit in Jesus' ministry, because it begins and ends with a "sign" at Cana. I propose that the Cana miracles are not a unit in themselves, but only part of the first narrative cycle of Jesus' ministry. See also Kysar, *John*, 22-23, who identifies 2:1–5:47 as a unit.

31. See C. H. Dodd, *The Interpretation of the Fourth Gospel* (Cambridge: Cambridge University Press, 1953).

32. J. Louis Martyn, *History and Theology in the Fourth Gospel.* See the comment by John Ashton, *Understanding the Fourth Gospel* (Oxford: Clarendon, 1993) 107.

33. Martyn, *History and Theology in the Fourth Gospel,* 18.

34. Martyn, *History and Theology in the Fourth Gospel,* 11-12.

35. Raymond E. Brown, *The Community of the Beloved Disciple* (New York: Paulist, 1979).

36. R. Alan Culpepper, *The Anatomy of the Fourth Gospel* (Philadelphia: Fortress, 1983).

37. See, e.g., Paul D. Duke, *Irony in the Fourth Gospel* (Atlanta: John Knox, 1985); Gail R. O'Day, *Revelation in the Fourth Gospel* (Philadelphia: Fortress, 1986); Jeff Staley, *The Print's First Kiss: A Rhetorical Investigation of the Implied Reader in the Fourth Gospel*, SBLDS 82 (Atlanta: Scholars Press, 1988); Mark W. G. Stibbe, *John's Gospel* (New York: Routledge, 1994).

38. See also Jerome Neyrey, *An Ideology of Revolt: John's Christology in Social-Science Perspective* (Philadelphia: Fortress, 1988); and Norman R. Petersen, *The Gospel of John and the Sociology of Light* (Valley Forge, Pa.: Trinity International, 1993).

THE ACTS OF THE APOSTLES

ROBERT W. WALL

The Acts of the Apostles is one of the most exciting and challenging books in the Christian Bible. Here we find a highly evocative story of the church's beginnings that traces its dramatic growth from sacred Jerusalem to imperial Rome. Because of its continuing importance in shaping the identity of today's church, Acts demands our most careful reading and thoughtful interpretation.

The importance of Acts for Christian formation is belied, however, by its sparse use in the church's lectionary, which assigns but a few of its most colorful episodes from the early chapters for use during the seven weeks leading from Easter to Pentecost. While liturgical practice reflects the book's keen stress on the Lord's resurrection and God's Spirit, Acts contains a much thicker portfolio of lessons to enhance the teaching ministry of the church.

In order to draw fully upon the resources brought forward from the book of Acts, especially in this postmodern era of Bible study when methodological imperialism has been replaced by methodological pluralism, the student of Scripture should examine every biblical text in the light of different interpretive interests and cultural sensibilities. What follows seeks to introduce readers to this methodological pluralism by considering various topics from the book's origins to its inclusion within the New Testament canon. Layers of the text's full meaning are found at each of four different locations where interpreters pause for instruction in guiding the church's reflection upon God's Word for today. The critical admission of a text's multivalency, or variety of meaning, need not imply that the meaning is relative to an individual interpreter. What must finally regulate a faithful reading of Acts at every location—whether "behind the text" or "in the text" or "in front of the text"—are those core convictions of Christian confession and those distinctive practices that mark out Christian κοινωνία (*kōinōnia*, "community"). When every element of Scripture study aims at theological understanding, the community of interpreters moves toward obedience to the divine will.

ACTS AS CONVERSATION: READING ACTS AS HISTORY

The Acts of the Apostles began its life as the written conversation between a storyteller (Luke) and his story's first reader (Theophilus). Modern commentaries on Acts are generally interested in reconstructing the circumstances of this correspondence as the most direct angle of vision to the text's intended meaning. To learn about the personal identities of the narrator and the first readers, their location, the circumstances that occasioned the writing of the book, and its date and communicative intention is not the disinterested pursuit of historians. Attending to such queries can make today's interpreters more aware of the book's continuing relevance and religious authority. To be sure, the historian's interest in the narrative of Acts does not necessarily supply us with accurate historical information about the origins of Christianity or of the narrator's purpose in telling his story. Such a presumption would be anachronistic, for Luke's task is to interpret and grant theological significance to past events rather than to describe them objectively or with factual precision suitable for his modern readers.[1]

Acts is an anonymous book. Even though the traditions of the ancient church assert that the evangelist Luke wrote both the Third Gospel and Acts—and there is no hard evidence to deny his authorship—knowing his identity or even that he was a sometimes traveling companion of Paul adds hardly anything to our understanding of his narrative. We can, perhaps, sketch the basic features of the nameless author of this narrative: He was an educated and well-traveled Greek who may well have converted to Judaism years before he became a Christian missionary; perhaps he was even an associate of Paul.[2] As a matter of literary fact, however, this narrator does not insinuate himself into his story, nor does he even bother to identify himself when joining Paul's company during the apostle's European mission (16:10-17; 20:5-16; 21:1-18; 27:1–28:16). Some modern scholars have come to base their historical judgment of Luke's authorship and the reliability of his story about Paul on these so-called "we" passages and the perceived intimacy they reflect between the narrator and the apostle.[3] The ambivalence of current opinion over both the reliability of Luke's sources and his authorship of Acts reflects the indeterminacy of these matters. In any case, the anonymity of Acts indicates that the narrator's focus is on the story rather than on his own identity.

The date and provenance of Acts, while important for determining its original social location, also cannot be determined with precision. Even if a date for Luke's Gospel from the mid-80s is likely and the narrative unity of Luke and Acts is presumed, this critical conclusion does not guarantee that Acts came from the same time and place as the Gospel. The argument that the same narrator must have written Acts with his Gospel depends largely on the claims that both the Gospel of Luke and Acts share (1) common language, (2) consistent theology, and (3) an ignorance of a second-century corpus of Pauline letters. Each of these claims, however, has been challenged; each is at day's end indeterminate.[4]

Once again the reader's sense of the time and place of Acts must arise from a close reading of the narrative. Luke probably wrote at a time when stressing the church's Jewish roots was necessary for both theological and political reasons. On the one hand, Rome should allow the church the same political freedoms it allowed Judaism; on the other hand, believers should retain their Jewish Scriptures and practices in order to be fully Christian. This later emphasis would have been especially pertinent if the theological tendency of Luke's church was toward supersessionism or some other theological expression that reflected the general failure of the church's mission to the Jews of the diaspora.[5] This would explain Luke's principal concern regarding the health of the church's Jewish legacy.

Perhaps we can discern more about the world behind Acts by considering the first reader, Theophilus (see 1:1; Luke 1:3), who is otherwise unknown to us. Evidently Theophilus is a new, although socially prominent, believer. Some have speculated that his name, which in Greek means "dear to God," is Luke's clever metaphor for every new Christian seeking theological instruction. However, it is more likely that Theophilus is a wealthy patron who has provided funds to enable Luke to write a detailed narrative of the church's beginnings for public consumption. Both his Greek name and his apparent spiritual immaturity (see Luke 1:4), especially when considered with the writer's honorific appellation "most excellent Theophilus" (Luke 1:3), suggest that Luke's first reader was an affluent Greek, perhaps a God-fearer before converting to Jesus,[6] who desires a useful story to confirm his faith in the face of mounting confusions and challenges. It is reasonable for us to imagine that he found the transition from one symbolic world to another profoundly difficult.

While the narrative unity between the Gospel and Acts links Luke's story of Jesus to the events that follow his departure, Acts is an independent biblical writing with its own literary, theological, and canonical integrity. While not disconnected from the purpose of his Gospel, Luke's reasons for writing a second book may be inferred from the distinctive theological emphases in Acts. Powell usefully summarizes these emphases in six categories: irenic, polemical, apologetic, evangelistic, pastoral, and theological.[7] His index catalogs those historical contingencies at the end of the first century that occasioned and helped shape this narrative as edifying communication from Luke for Theophilus.

(1) Acts was written to consolidate disparate faith communions. Luke's *irenic* ("promoting peace,") spirit is no doubt an idealized feature of his theological vision. At the same time, his ecumenicity is never divorced from the hard pragmatics of the first church's mission in the world (see 6:1-7; 11:1-18; 14:27–15:29). A religious movement that lacks solidarity within its diverse membership will be ineffective in advancing its claims. Moreover, in the wider Roman culture, riddled with conflict and controversy of all kinds, a community of shared goods (material and spiritual) would embody evidence for the transforming power of God's saving grace. Surely the historical referent of this narrative theme is intended to compel Theophilus to locate himself within a community that practices reconciliation as the way of God.

(2) Acts was written as a *polemic* against idolatry. Scholars have long argued that Luke wrote Acts to challenge certain heretical forms of Christianity or even formative Judaism. That is doubtful. Rather, Luke responds positively to the concerns voiced by James at the Jerusalem Council over the "gentilizing" of the church (see 15:20-21, 28-29). Agreeing with Paul's epistolary advice to the Corinthians (see 1 Corinthians 8–10), Luke's narrative sounds a cautionary note. Adding uncircumcised, uncatechized Gentiles to the church's rolls while the church's mission carries the Word of God farther and farther from the holy city may very well incline a pragmatic leadership (perhaps including Theophilus) to accommodate pagan religious practices and secular values that will corrupt its Jewish heritage.

(3) Acts was written as an *apologia* for Christianity. Read as a narrative about people, Luke's portrayal of Christian leaders underscores the authority and importance of their traditions for the future of the church. This is especially true of Paul, whose standing within the ancient church was contested into the second century. Luke does not locate Paul's religious authority in his apostolicity (see 1:21-22), as he does in his letters (e.g., Galatians 1–2). Rather, Paul's importance for the church is guaranteed by his prophetic vocation and performance (see 20:17-35).

Read as a political narrative, Luke's ambivalent depiction of Rome (and of Paul's Roman citizenship) in Acts may intend to define citizen Theophilus's relations with a non-Christian Roman world. While it is possible for a strong believer to be a good citizen (e.g., Paul), loyalty to the gospel or the church's missionary vocation must never be compromised by the obligations of citizenship.[8] Paul's defense speeches (see Acts 22–26; 28) are not concerned with his relationship to Rome; his *apologia* in Acts is funded by a rehearsal of his Jewish background and practices, along with a description of his prophetic vocation as a teacher of Israel. For this reason, neither repentant nor unrepentant Israel should have a problem with him or with the Christian congregations he has founded. Such a defense would be especially crucial if Theophilus belongs, as seems likely, to a congregation founded by Paul's mission. The Paul of Acts embraces his Roman and Tarsain citizenship without apology, and so should Theophilus when appropriate; the more important commitment, however, is to the church's Jewish roots. The Pauline legacy shapes a future that is closer to Israel than to Rome.

(4) Acts was written as a tool of the church's evangelistic *mission*. Clearly the literary theme that follows the triumph of the Word of God from Jerusalem to Rome testifies to the power and necessity of the proclaimed gospel. The prophetic boldness and effectiveness of the church's mission, superintended by God's Spirit, expresses this same theme. If the missionary episodes are read as indicating normative patterns of outreach for subsequent generations of Christians, then Acts may have been written for Theophilus to invigorate his congregation's missionary vocation or to teach him how to convert others in continuity with the missionaries of the earliest church.

The natural shift of the church's geographical epicenter from Jerusalem to Rome following the fall of Jerusalem would have instigated different concerns from those earlier between the Gentile mission and the Jewish church (see 11:1-18; 15:13-29; 21:17-26). The pressures on Luke's first readers would have been most keenly felt from the pervasive paganism of Roman cities. His response to this new missionary situation, however, is reactionary rather than progressive. When Paul finally arrives in Rome, he does not carry God's Word to its pagan population but first establishes his Jewish credentials (see 28:17-22) in order to convert religious Jews to Jesus (28:23-25). Luke does not perceive paganism as the church's principal threat; rather, the church's outreach is substantially weakened by the loss of its connection with the core beliefs and practices of repentant Israel.

(5) Acts was written to deepen the fragile faith of new believers such as Theophilus. Luke's *pastoral* intent for writing this narrative may have been to characterize Christian discipleship in response to his patron's particular struggles, with implications for all who share Theophilus's social status within the church. This motive underlies several narrative themes. For example, Acts provides a basic chronology of the religious roots of Christianity that may have enabled Theophilus and other new believers to locate themselves within space and time as participants of a real historical movement.[9] More important, Acts' distinct emphasis on the community of goods and description of well-known role models, such as Barnabas, may well have commended to affluent believers like Theophilus the sharing of their wealth with the community's poor as a Christian practice (see 2:42-47; 4:32-37; 11:27-30). This

and other distinctive resurrection practices envisage a counterculture that may have proved a difficult life-style for the empire's rich and famous. That is, Acts was written to encourage members of urban congregations, such as Theophilus, to spearhead the redistribution of wealth as the guiding principle of the church's welfare program (cf. 1 Timothy 5–6). Further, the content and narrative significance of the speeches in Acts may have reassured the well-educated Theophilus that the gospel has intellectual integrity (see 17:22-31).

(6) Acts was written in response to a *theological* crisis. It is only a slight exaggeration to say that every New Testament book is occasioned by a theological crisis—a confusion over or misappropriation of some core conviction of God's Word that threatens to subvert the audience's Christian formation and witness. Several important interpreters of Acts have considered the occasion of Luke's narrative from this angle of vision. For example, H. Conzelmann famously opined that Acts was written to correct the apocalyptic eschatology of a church troubled by an internal conflict over end-time fanaticism and doubt. For this reason, Luke edited out most eschatological speculation from his sources and creatively shaped a narrative that emphasizes mission and church growth in a "real" world.[10]

The theological crisis that occasioned the writing of Acts, however, is similar to that of Paul's Letter to the Romans; it concerns whether "there is any unrighteousness on God's part" (Rom 9:14) with respect to unbelieving Israel (Romans 9–11).[11] The rousing success of Paul's urban mission in the diaspora among God-fearing Gentiles, coupled with his relative lack of success among Jews who remained divided in their response to the risen Jesus (see 28:16-28), may have prompted some Jewish believers to wonder whether the church's mission actually subverted God's promise to restore historic Israel: "Has Israel stumbled so as to fall?" (Rom 11:11). The church's missionary reports, combined with the destruction of the Jerusalem Temple, the placing of Palestine to direct Roman rule by Roman governors, and the virtual cessation of the Jerusalem church by end of the first century, provided the necessary warrants for some believers in Luke's church to argue that the relevant symbols of covenant renewal between God and a "true" Israel no longer should include the traditional expressions of Jewish identity and holiness. These believers may have even appealed to Jesus' prediction of Jerusalem's destruction by Rome as the just deserts of Israel's rejection of him as Messiah (see 6:14; cf. Matt 24:1-2; Luke 19:41-48). The worrisome consequence was the attenuation of the church's Jewish legacy, without which the church could not be the church.

We should note that Luke's response in Acts is different from Paul's in Romans; Paul wrote a generation earlier when this internal threat was not so keenly felt. While both contend that only a remnant within Israel ever repented of sin and turned to God in faith (Rom 9:6-29), Paul is clearly dissatisfied with a divided Israel as a permanent solution. He, therefore, posits the full restoration of historic Israel at the return of Jesus following the Gentile mission (see Rom 11:25-36).[12] Acts does not register so sharp a dichotomy between the Jewish rejection of the gospel and the Gentiles embrace of it as found in Romans (see Rom 11:11-24). Rather, Luke is resigned to a divided Israel as a permanent feature of God's plan of salvation (see 3:19-23). The promise of a faithful God to restore Israel has *already* been realized in the church's mission to the entire household of Israel (Acts 2–8). For Luke, unlike for Paul, the return of Christ inaugurates a season of "universal restoration" (3:21); and for him, unlike for Paul, the promise of Israel's "refreshment" has already been fulfilled among repentant Jews (see 3:19-20). In the meantime, the pattern of God's faithfulness to Israel agrees with (rather than reverses) biblical prophecy: Israel is restored first and only when repentant Gentiles are "grafted in their place to share the rich root of the olive tree" (Rom 11:17).

This same difference is also reflected by the principal opponents of Paul's Gentile mission within the church. In the Pauline letters, Paul is opposed by "Judaizers"—Jewish Christians who stipulated that all Gentile converts must also be catechized and circumcised according to the traditions of the Judaizers' ancestral religion. As a working symbol of his opposition to this "Judaizing" movement within the church, he refused to circumcise Titus, a Greek convert (see Acts 15:1-2; cf. Gal 2:1-10). When Luke wrote Acts, however, the principal internal threat to the church's faith were "Gentilizers" who threatened to erase anything Jewish from the church's core identity. To mark this different context, Luke tells the story of Paul's circumcision of Timothy, who symbolizes the mission's resistance to the gentilizing of the church's Jewish legacy (see 16:1-5; cf. 15:19-21, 28-29; 21:25). Surely Luke was right to worry; the attenuation of the church's Jewish legacy led to Marcionism in the next generation and has cultivated the anti-Semitism that continues to debilitate our own.

ACTS AS COMPOSITION: READING ACTS AS LITERATURE

The principal interest of those interpreters who approach Acts as a composition is to construct the literary world within the text rather than to reconstruct the ancient world behind it. Some "in-the-text" readings of Acts are vitally interested with historical questions too—with those first-century exigencies and communicative intentions that contributed to the narrator's choice of literary genre and narrative aim. Other literary explorations into Acts detach the literary text from these historical moorings in order to consider its intertextuality, linguistics, or creative storytelling in ways that treat Acts' historical context as largely irrelevant to the theological points it scores.

For the majority of interpreters of Acts, the most important literary query concerns its *genre:* Is Acts a history, a biography, a novel, an apologia, or a variety of literature without ancient parallel?[13] The stakes in answering this question are large, since what one concludes about a book's genre influences what one concludes about its overarching purpose—that is, function follows literary form. The literary critic typically begins with the recognition that Acts is the second of two volumes whose interpretation requires a prior decision about its narrative unity with Luke's Gospel. Until recently most commentators have simply affirmed the unity of Luke and Acts and extended this unity to a common genre. In this case, the genre of "Luke-Acts" is introduced by the preface to Luke's Gospel (1:1-4), which is then alluded to in the preface to Acts (1:1-2). That is, Acts is the second volume of a continuous *diēgēsis*—a historical narrative of some sort—about "the things fulfilled among us" (Luke 1:1).

At the very least, however, this consensus must now be qualified in several ways. Simply put, Acts is not a gospel. Luke's Gospel is more like ancient biographical literature that tells the story of a person's life and career. This biography is "gospel" because it tells the life story of the Savior from conception to ascension. Acts, on the other hand, sketches the origins of a religious movement, itself full of miracles and magic but without telling the story of only one heroic character. Moreover, the narrative of this second volume is deliberately set within a chronological and geographical framework similar to historical monographs produced in antiquity (see 1:8). Acts is hardly "secular" history, since its narrator structures the progress of this movement as a commentary on biblical prophecy. Read from this literary perspective, the story of the successive missions of various prophets-like-Jesus who carry the Word of God from Jerusalem to Rome and from Jew to Gentile has been scripted by God according to Israel's Scriptures (see 2:14-21; 15:13-21; 28:25-28).

A number of studies have demonstrated that Acts is best read as a genre of ancient *historiography,* itself quite fluid in form and function. Luke's narrative is a selective account of what happened—a "history" shaped and signified according to his personal theological beliefs and pastoral purposes (see above, "Acts as Conversation"). History, whether ancient or modern, is almost always written with a language and within a framework that reflects the historian's discrete perspective on the meaning of events. In the case of Acts, then, Luke selects and arranges a series of events that he narrates for his reader(s) in order to give meaning to the church's mission and message as a history that accords with God's redemptive plans for Israel and the nations.

Since Luke was not himself an eyewitness to much of what he recounts and interprets, he depended upon sources for his relevant information.[14] The content and nature of these sources, whether oral or written; their identity; and Luke's reception and handling of them are all matters of considered and continuing speculation. Dibelius's verdict that Acts is largely the creative work of its author, whose access to reliable material was limited at best, has keenly influenced the modern discussion.[15] On this view, for example, the speeches of Acts are not based on notes taken by auditors but are Luke's literary creations. Even the "we" passages of Acts are not the accounts of an eyewitness but reflect the rhetorical artistry of a narrator who inserts himself into the narrative world in order to influence the reader's impressions of what is read (see 16:10-16). This older view has been substantially revised by new appreciation for the artistry of ancient historiographers, whose representations of a real event cohere not only with other literary elements of their composition but also with available information about that event as recalled by reliable (and often firsthand) witnesses. Many scholars, therefore, are inclined to accept Luke as one of Paul's team whose memory (or personal diaries) is the principal (but not the only) source he draws upon when shaping his story of Paul's mission and trials. While it remains another matter to assess the historical credibility of what is written in the first person or the nature of Luke's personal relationship with Paul, the narrator's presence as "credible witness" to events narrated in several passages has a measured rhetorical effect on the reader. Luke must have realized this, or else he would have surely erased every trace of himself from Acts. Instead, he chooses to address certain reservations about Paul or the results of his mission by placing himself unobtrusively in the story to help relieve the suspicions about a controversial Paul.[16]

In this light, another important interest of literary criticism is to determine how the various elements of Luke's story form a coherent plotline: How does Acts work as a narrative?[17] Simply stated, the plot of Acts unfolds in support of Luke's theological aim. On the one hand, he designs his story according to a specific geographical and chronological framework. The action begins in Jerusalem before moving beyond the holy city into the neighboring provinces of Samaria and Judea before moving into the nations and peoples beyond Palestine. Many have found this geographical outline indexed by Jesus' programmatic prophecy in Acts 1:8. In addition, Acts traces the key events with brief glimpses of the most important leaders of earliest Christianity to establish a general chronology of the church's origins. On the other hand, this historical conception provides the framework for two grand thematic movements ("conversion" and "consecration"), each scripted by extended citations of Scripture (see 2:17-21; 15:16-18) that narrate how the redemptive purposes of God are realized through the church's mission (see "Acts as Theology," below).

Among the many narrative elements that make up the plot of Acts, the speeches are especially important.[18] They make up roughly one-third of the composition and often signal programmatic movements in the plot while providing summaries of the narrator's core theological commitments. The speeches of Acts typically provoke further responses to the gospel that move the story's action from setting to setting in a "logical" manner. As such they supply an interpretive matrix by which the narrative's aim is made clearer. The most important and often debated of these speeches serve missionary ends. Peter's Pentecost sermon (see 2:14-41), the inaugural sermon of Paul's mission to the nations at Pisidian Antioch (see 13:16-41), and Paul's sharply stated Socratic retort at the Athenian Aeropagus (see 17:22-31) are good examples of missionary discourse that serve the narrator's programmatic concerns. Other speeches shaped according to the conventions of different rhetorical genre are important to the plotline of Acts. For example, Stephen's apologia as a prophet-like-Jesus stipulates the nature of the prophetic vocation that details the conflict between Christian preaching and Jewish tradition (see 7:1-53). Paul's so-called farewell speech defines the sort of person who best serves an orderly succession of future leaders in the fledgling church his mission has founded (see 20:18-35). Finally, the various defense speeches of the Paul of Acts at the book's end (see 22:1-21; 24:10-21; 26:2-23; 28:17-20) serve to defend his spiritual authority within emergent Christianity and within the Christian biblical canon of the Pauline letters that follow.

Even though reflecting different rhetorical conventions to serve different narrative settings, the speeches of Acts draw from a common pool of images and ideas.[19] The result is a profound sense of continuity both in the *content* of Christian proclamation from the risen Jesus (see 1:3) to the imprisoned Paul (see 28:30-31) and in the *vocation* of Christian preachers inspired by the Holy Spirit to perform competently, faithfully, and boldly all the tasks of the prophet-like-Jesus. Thus every speech in Acts—whether missionary, apologetic, or edifying—is centered by the non-negotiable content of God's saving word. Jesus performs signs and wonders as God's Messiah; he then suffers and is crucified; and finally he is resurrected and exalted by God to confirm that "there is no other name under heaven by which we must be saved" (4:12). To show that this messianic "event" conforms to the script of God's salvation, proofs from prophecy are layered into the speeches. Eyewitness testimony, whether of the risen Jesus (e.g., 2:32; 26:8, 15-16, 26), of personal experience of God's presence (e.g., 15:7-11, 12), or of an exemplary life (e.g., 20:18-21), complements Scripture's witness. Religious experience is glossed by Scripture's interpretation to prove the trustworthiness of the Gospel's claims about the Lord's messiahship and the faithfulness of God to promises of redemption. Other narrative elements, such as Luke's summaries (see 2:42-47; 4:32-35) and interludes (see 6:1-7), perform roles within Acts similar to the speeches. These elements underwrite the most important literary themes and provide a retrospective on previous events in preparation for the future.

Luke's use of repetition is another important literary convention of his narrative. For instance, the triadic telling of important episodes underscores their value in the narrative world (e.g., Paul's call, 9:9-19; Cornelius's conversion, 10:1-44). In addition, the repeated uses of prophetic catchwords (e.g., παρρησία *parrēsia*, "boldness") and phrases (e.g., σημεῖα καὶ τέρατα *sēmeia kai terata*, "signs and wonders" or ἔσχατος τῆς γῆς *eschatos tēs gēs*, "end of the earth"), of kerygmatic motifs (e.g., ἄφεσις *aphesis*, "forgiveness" or βασιλεία τοῦ θεοῦ *basileia tou theou*, "kingdom of God"), of literary themes (e.g., ἅπαντα κοινά; *hapanta koina*, community of goods) and narrative actions (e.g., mixed response to the gospel or mass conversions) are important for several reasons. The entire range of meaning unfolds by each repetition of a word or literary theme in new compositional settings. More important, the *intratextuality* within Acts invites a more reflexive or unified reading of the story. Through repeated words or images the reader is reminded of earlier episodes or texts that are then recalled and brought into a mutually informing dialogue with the current text or episode. For example, in the testimony that God did "signs and wonders" among the Gentiles (15:12), the reader recognizes that the use of "signs and wonders" recalls Joel's prediction concerning the last days (Joel 2:19). In this way, the reader recovers the theological subtext of Paul's (and Peter's) testimony: God's promise of salvation is extended to include everyone, Jew and now Gentile, who repents and turns to the Lord Jesus in faith. Luke's use of repetition forges a literary coherence that aims disparate pieces of the narrative toward a common theological purpose.

Similar to the phenomenon of intratextuality within Acts, the *intertextuality* between Acts and antecedent sacred tradition supports and adds an inherent depth of understanding to Luke's narrative aim.[20] Even a cursory reading of Acts reflects Luke's routine use of sacred tradition, both biblical (LXX) and kerygmatic. He needs only to mention a familiar biblical phrase or employ a familiar prophetic typology (e.g., God's judgment of unrepentant Israel) to evoke other biblical texts and stories where that phrase is used or follows a typological pattern. Sometimes these texts are actually cited (e.g., 2:17-21), but more often Scripture is echoed by reference to common words or narrative elements (e.g., people, places, events). The "diverse components of the biblical anthology share a common worldview, [where] innumerable strands link together the constitutive units [to form] a literary and ideological entity."[21] The anticipated result of finding these citations or hearing those echoes of an earlier text when reading another is to link these two texts together as partners in a reflexive, mutually informing conversation—hence, the label "intertextuality." Significantly, the cited or echoed text recalls not only a particular story or idea but also a history of reception (both within and external to Scripture) that adds still additional layers of information to the interpretive matrix. The result is that the reader is able to discern a fuller, richer meaning.[22]

While Luke's rereading of his sacred tradition is also shaped by the currents of his Greco-Roman world, his use of Scripture in Acts is essentially Jewish. Thus he employs tradition in a way consonant with the church's Jewish heritage. The idea of Scripture that lies behind its appropriation in Acts is that the cited or echoed text is produced by the Spirit of God. This same Spirit leads interpreters to render Scripture's divinely intended meaning in public proclamation (17:3). In this way, Scripture (or Jesus tradition) is rightly used to supply evidence that "these things that have happened among us" follow God's prophesied plan for Israel's promised restoration. That is, Luke does not use Scripture in defense of the faith ("proof from prophecy") but as integral to his story's theological meaning. This particular quality of Lukan composition is similar to Jewish midrashic literature.[23] Modern interpreters, alert to the principles of Jewish exegesis, will recognize, for example, that Luke's composition of Peter's Pentecost sermon is midrash-like: the citation of a relevant biblical text (Joel's prophecy, Joel 2:28-32 [LXX 3:1-5]) is followed by commentary on its contemporary meaning (see Joel 2:14-21, 22-41) and the inclusion of biblical commentaries (*midrashim*) on Pss 16:8-11 and 110:1. Luke's use of catchwords and phrases from biblical texts throughout his narrative suggests a sustained and reflexive dialogue with Israel's Scriptures—that is, between his text and the biblical text—that is characteristic of midrashic literature. The intent is to lead us into a fuller and more contemporary understanding of God's Word.[24]

No introduction to the literary fabric of Acts is complete without mentioning the artistry of Luke's storytelling. His effective use of romance[25] and dramatic episodes involving divine speech and action,[26] his use of local color to add realism to the most crucial episodes of Paul's mission (27:1–28:10), and the lively wit he brings to his storytelling (20:7-12), sometimes to mock the early church's competition (see 19:28-34), all contribute to a well-told story that entertains as well as edifies.

The book of Acts has a complex textual history.[27] R. Brown comments that "Acts has a textual problem more acute than that of any other New Testament book."[28] In addition to the standard set of textual variants, the ancient Greek manuscripts of Acts include a distinctive group best exemplified by the bilingual (Latin and Greek) Codex Bezae (D), known as "the Western text of Acts."[29] One must decide whether this Western text or another prominent family of manuscripts, the so-called Alexandrian text of Acts, most nearly represents the Acts written by Luke and thus the narrative used for this study. The majority of textual scholars believe that the most distinctive features of the Western text are scribal interpolations added long after Luke's death; for this reason such scholars prefer to use the Alexandrian text as the basis of modern translations (including both the NIV and the NRSV).

Some scholars, however, have proposed that both texts of Acts were put into circulation roughly at the beginning of the canonical process toward the end of the second century, when Luke's reasons for writing Acts were replaced or qualified by still other concerns of the emerging church catholic. Significantly, the Western text of Acts, which expands Luke's narrative (more than the speeches) to reflect the theological tendencies of this church, betrays its concern to distinguish Christianity from Judaism as two discrete religious and theological options. In doing so, this popular version of Acts became an "anti-Judaic" narrative. The hostility of unrepentant Jews and their leaders is intensified in the text, while the institutions and traditions of Judaism are diminished in importance. A large number of "Western" variants contribute to this negative impression; thus, in Epp's words, "the Jews come out rather poorly in the D-text."[30] Further, Western scribes added narrative materials to enhance Paul's already powerful profile. Not only are his deeds made even more spectacular and his character more virtuous, but also he is routinely protected by the Holy Spirit against the evil machinations of his Jewish opponents, who are powerless against him in any case. While these later interpolations may well reflect an early scribal commentary on Luke's Acts in the service of the canonical process,[31] they helped to foster a supersessionist theology and anti-Semitic prejudice within the church that remains to this day. For the contemporary church, reading the story of Paul in Acts in the light of Luke's original theological agenda may provide a necessary corrective to this dark side of the canonical project.

ACTS AS CONFESSION: READING ACTS AS THEOLOGY

The decisions one makes about reading Acts as literature influences one's reading of Acts as a theological narrative.[32] Biblical narrative envisages the narrator's confession of faith—his core Christian beliefs—in narrative form. B. Gaventa's salient point is worth keeping in mind: "Luke's theology is intricately and irreversibly bound up with the story he tells and cannot be separated from it. An attempt to do justice to the theology of Acts must struggle to reclaim the character of Acts as a narrative."[33] At the same time, the theology of Acts contributes to a fuller biblical theology that monitors and molds the church's confession of faith according to its rule of faith.[34] For this reason, reading Acts as theology is an important project for any interpreter whose faith seeks theological understanding.

The theological substructure of Luke's narrative world is an antecedent "master" story about what God has done to bring salvation to the world according to the Scriptures. The inner logic of this foundational narrative and the substance of its core themes are introduced into Acts by the story of the first Pentecostal outpouring of the Holy Spirit (2:1-47) and are then developed within the rest of Acts by subsequent stories of the church's mission and speeches of a succession of prophets-like-Jesus. That is, the theological coherence of Acts is not found in a system of propositions about God or the way of God's salvation, but in the integral elements of a Christian story about how God's redemptive promises, prophesied by Scripture, are fulfilled. The following outline of this master story is intended only to orient the reader to the principal elements of a more theological reading of Acts.

(1) *God, the only God, has a plan of salvation disclosed in Israel's Scriptures.* God's sovereign presence and God's saving activities, according to Acts, are inextricably linked to God's redemptive plan (see 2:23; 13:36; 20:27). While God is not a character in the narrative, the narrated events occur as a "divine necessity" (δεῖ *dei*; see 1:16; 3:18; 5:38; 13:27; 27:24), whether they result in great successes or puzzling tragedies. The narrative world of Acts is underwritten by a faithful God who works through an empowered church to fulfill promises made both to Israel and to all "the families of the earth" (3:25).

God promises to restore repentant Israel first of all (1:6). For this reason the church's mission begins in the holy city among devout Jews from "every nation under heaven" (see 2:5-11) and religious status (2:10*b*; 6:1-7; 8:4-25, 26-40). God is Israel's God, and God's salvation is promised to the "people" (λαός *laos*) of Israel and is first experienced by repentant Jews before moving out to include believers from every nation (chaps. 1–8; see esp. 3:17-26).[35] When the Word of God is finally carried beyond Palestine to the nations, the foundation of every new congregation is the church's Jewish legacy (15:19-21, 28-29; see also chaps. 16–28). Indeed, Israel's God is the sovereign Creator of all things (see 4:24) who alone determines the destiny of every nation (see 14:15-17; 17:22-31). It is this God who promised Abraham that all the nations would be blessed (see 3:25-26; cf. 7:5). For this reason the terms and aim of God's Word are never circumscribed by nationalistic or ethnocentric commitments, nor can any one sacred place domesticate a transcendent God or a people's covenant with such a God (see 7:44-50). The universal scope of God's salvation is predicated on the success of the church's mission among repentant Jews whose vocation is as "light to the nations to the end of the earth" (see 13:44-47). Repentant Gentiles who are added to the church membership rolls share in blessings promised to Israel, not because unrepentant Israel rejected the gospel but because a remnant of repentant Jews within Israel accepted its assertion that the resurrected Jesus is the Messiah of God.

The God of Acts orchestrates Christian history. The surety of God's redemptive purpose is central to the theology of Acts. Good planning not only envisions the prospect of what a people might become but it also implements and actively brings its purpose to realization in people's lives. Thus the God who makes promises also keeps them by carefully choreographing the events that accomplish redemption in the history of the repentant community. God's Spirit is poured out on this community as a gift of salvation, and, just as critically in Acts, the Spirit enables and directs members of the community in missionary activity according to God's plan.

This divine plan is revealed by the Scriptures of Israel, especially its prophetic texts and typologies. Jervell has famously asserted that "Luke is the fundamentalist within the New Testament,"[36] because Luke believes that Scripture vocalizes the intentions of God and predicts the history of God's salvation. God's Spirit and Israel's Scriptures are two parts of an integral whole in Acts. The Spirit can guide the church's mission and make its message effective only when witness is grounded in the wisdom of Scripture as rightly interpreted by Spirit-inspired prophets-like-Jesus (see 2:4; also, e.g., Peter, 4:8; Stephen, 6:3, 10; Philip, 8:4-6, 11-13; Paul, 13:4-12; James, 15:28). The conflict within Israel is essentially over which community is custodian of the christological interpretation of Scripture (see 17:2-3). In this sense, Scripture not only is interpreted by the Spirit-filled community in the light of the risen Jesus but also interprets and authorizes the community's mission in the Spirit's power and message about the Lord's resurrection.

(2) *According to prophecy's script, Jesus of Nazareth is God's Messiah, the only Savior, who realizes God's redemptive purpose as attested by his prophetic ministry and resurrection.*[37] The redemptive partnership between God, who takes complete responsibility for creation's promised restoration, and Jesus, who ushers its fulfillment into history, is at the epicenter of the theological conception of Acts. Jesus is God's Messiah, whose divine appointment as the world's Savior is at God's direction and according to God's plan as disclosed in Scripture (see 2:22-23, 36; 10:34-43). God alone can attest to Jesus' redemptive role and does so by the powerful deeds and persuasive word that God effects through him (see 2:22;

10:38). God's ultimate confirmation of Jesus' messiahship is disclosed in God's resurrection of him (see 2:36). God has made Jesus reigning Lord (2:36; cf. 1:9-11; 5:30-31); all must call upon his name for their salvation (see 2:21; 4:12).

God's faithful response to Jesus is reciprocal of Jesus' costly faithfulness to God, indicated by his suffering. The narrative of Jesus enshrined in the missionary speeches of Acts echoes both Jesus tradition and Scripture to render the Lord's suffering and death as faithful to God's redemptive purpose (see 5:30; 10:39). In this sense, God's resurrection of Jesus is more than a vindication of his messiahship; it is also symbolic of Christian mission and discipleship that demands bold obedience to God's divine purpose in order to participate in its forward movement to the end of earth and time (see 14:22).

The kerygmatic Jesus of Acts reflects a fairly robust christology. While the terms of the church's proclamation emphasize his suffering and resurrection, details of Jesus' entire messianic career are included (1:22; 10:37-38), as is his parousia, when he will come to restore (3:19-21) and judge (17:30-31) all humanity (10:42). Luke's profile is consistent with the Gospel's story about Jesus and clearly assumes his readers' familiarity with it (1:1). Luke's theology of the cross is more prophetic than salvific. That is, rather than emphasizing Jesus' death as a sacrifice for sin (= Pauline), Acts interprets the crucifixion as symbolic of unrepentant Israel's obduracy about Jesus' mission (3:22; cf. 7:37).

The question may well be asked, then, In what sense is the Jesus of Acts the Savior of the world? The profile given above suggests various activities at different stages of his messianic career: in his past as the prophetic carrier of God's saving word (see 3:22; 7:37); during his present as exalted Lord with divine authority to save all who call upon him (see 2:21; cf. 7:56, 60); and in his future as returning agent of God's final restoration and judgment of all people (see 3:20-21; 17:31). The departure of the living Jesus at the beginning of Acts is a condition for a mission that continues what he has begun to do and say (see 1:1-2, 9-11). His bodily absence, however, does not mean that his redemptive influence is effectively in the past or that he is experienced as exalted Savior only in the words of the proclaimed gospel. The emphasis on the Lord's resurrection in Acts underwrites his living presence and active participation in the church's mission.[38]

Thus, while Jesus does not dwell within the believer or the community "in him" (as in Pauline thought), he does exist beyond the church's kerygma. For instance, he reappears in visionary guise at strategic moments in the church's mission to disclose God's purpose for particular people (especially Paul) and places (see 7:55; 9:3-6, 10-16; 23:11), and the mere mention of his name revitalizes those who come into its power (see 4:8-12). It is incorrect, therefore, to speak of Jesus as a passive figure during the church's present mission. While God's Spirit has replaced God's Messiah as the principal agent of salvation during "these last days" (see 2:17-19), the exalted Lord continues as a sometimes participant in the church's mission.

(3) *All who earnestly repent and call upon the living Jesus will be saved, the Jew first and also the Gentile.* All who hear the gospel, whether Jewish or Gentile, are divided into two groups: the repentant and the unrepentant. Indeed, the common identifying mark of all who belong to Jesus is their positive response to the saving call of God issued in the proclamation of the gospel and their reception of the Holy Spirit (see 15:7-11). Likewise, the spiritual crisis facing Israel (most especially) and the nations is their ignorance of the gospel: People cannot convert to the light if they continue to live in darkness. The prophet's imperative is grounded in this practical reality (see 3:17; 13:27; 17:30).

Converting to Jesus means calling him "Lord" (see 2:21) and confessing that he is the promised Savior God has sent forth into the world to rescue us from our enemies and—especially—to forgive our sins (see 2:38; 3:19; 5:31; 13:38-39; 15:9) and so to liberate us from eternal death (see 13:46). But salvation also involves healing the sick (see 3:7-8; 4:8-12; 28:7-9), illuminating the ignorant (see 3:17; 13:27; 17:30), rescuing the vulnerable from political threat (see 12:4-11; 16:30-31) and material poverty/hunger (see 4:33-34), guarding against demonic powers (see 5:16; 16:16-18; 19:11-20; 26:17-18), and protecting from natural catastrophe (see 27:21-26, 31-44). Each expression of saving grace heralds God's commitment to keep the biblical promise of a "universal restoration" (see 3:21).

At the same time, each act of divine benefaction responds to a deliberate act of faith commensurate with need. Repentance is an intellectual reorientation—a change of one's mind—away from any ordering of one's life that opposes the reign of God and toward the truth claims of God's Word. The repentant Jews who asked Peter following Pentecost, "What shall we do?" vocalize the decisive question that is implied throughout Acts in different narrative settings: How shall a needy people respond to the gospel's invitation to enter into a new life with God? The answer comes in a series of imperatives: listen (2:22; 7:2; 8:6; 13:7, 16; 15:13; 19:10; 28:28); believe (3:16; 8:12-13, 37; 11:17, 21; 13:12; 14:23; 15:11; 18:8); be baptized (2:41; 8:38; 9:18; 16:15, 33; 19:1-5); turn to God (3:19; 9:35; 11:21; 20:21; 26:20); request instruction (8:31; 9:5; 10:30-33; 24:24; 26:17-18); show hospitality to strangers (16:15, 33-34; 28:7-10). Indeed, there are some who will respond more eagerly to the Word of God because of conscientious study (17:11) or faithfulness to Jewish training (15:21), both of which indicate readiness to receive God's truth.

The clear impression left by this glossary of salvation is its all-encompassing holistic nature. God's grace saves people from disease, disaster, demons, death, and destitution; and it also forgives people of sin. This penetration of divine grace into human life symbolizes the biblical conception of salvation—one that reroutes a broken and battered creation back toward the original intentions of its Creator, beginning with Israel's restoration (3:19-21).

(4) *Those who repent and belong to the Lord Jesus Christ receive the Holy Spirit and are initiated into a community of goods.* The third person of the Holy Trinity is disclosed at Pentecost as the Spirit of prophecy who empowers persons to bear a persuasive and insightful witness to the risen Jesus (see 2:4). As the reader of Acts should expect, this is not very different from the idea of God's Spirit in Israel's Scriptures.[39] However, the powerful influence of the Holy Spirit in Acts extends to all believers and reflects the characteristics of a personal deity. The Spirit speaks (8:29; 10:19; 13:2) and guides (13:4; 15:28; 16:6-7), and people can lie to (5:3), test (5:9), and resist (7:51) God's Spirit. The Spirit is not external to those it influences (cf. 11:15) but is "poured out" to "fill up" (2:4; 4:8, 31; 6:3, 5; 7:55; 9:17; 11:24; 13:9) those it empowers for ministry.

The Holy Spirit enables the Lord's successors to continue to do and say what he began during his messianic career (1:1-8). That is, the Spirit's presence within the community of believers provides the essential resource for obeying its missionary vocation (1:8; 2:1-4, 17-21). As Jervell notes, "the church does not lead and guide itself: God does through the Spirit."[40] In particular, the Spirit funds the religious authority of a succession of prophetic leaders (8:14-19) who interpret the prophecies of Scripture (2:4), speak the Word of God persuasively (4:8) and boldly (4:29-31; 9:27, 29; 19:8; 28:31; cf. 18:26), and perform mighty signs and wonders (5:12-16; 8:13; 14:3). All of these activities are in continuity with Jesus and the Old Testament prophets before him.

Peter's programmatic reference to the "gift of the Holy Spirit" at Pentecost (2:38) is important in two ways for filling out Luke's idea of the Spirit. First, the Spirit of prophecy is also the transforming Spirit of God, whose work is especially realized in the resurrection practices of the repentant community.[41] Second, salvation is marked out within history by a concrete experience of the Spirit's reception (see 8:14-17, 39-40; 9:17; 10:43-44; 19:5-6). Neither the protocol nor the experience of being filled with the Spirit follows a common pattern, and the narrator stresses different literary themes in each episode. Nevertheless, it is clear from Acts that God's salvation and the reception of God's Spirit are integral elements of any real experience of God's benefaction, to which the community bears witness in the manner of its life together (see 2:47).

The church of Acts is a community of goods. Its united witness to the Messiah's resurrection is not only proclaimed but is also embodied in its common life under the aegis of the Holy Spirit. The community's "resurrection practice" includes four discrete elements: economic, spiritual, religious, and social. As economic κοινωνία (*koinōnia*), the community reorders its possessions according to the principle of Jubilee (see Luke 4:16-18) so that its generosity toward the needy reciprocates God's generosity in the gift of salvation (see 2:44-45; 4:32–5:11; 6:1-6; 11:27-30). Likewise, the gift of God's salvation is embodied as the gift of God's Spirit. As with material possessions, the Holy Spirit is the common property of an inclusive community, so that its Pentecostal coming upon repentant Jews is repeated on repentant Samaritans (see 8:14-16) and Gentiles (see 10:44; cf. 11:17; 15:9). Living boldly under its powerful influence is a second resurrection practice of those who follow Jesus. The religious dimension of the community's solidarity is expressed most profoundly by a prohibition: Abstain from things polluted by idols (15:20; see also 15:29; 21:25). The concern of Acts is not so much the inward, spiritual purification of individual believers but the political purity of a community's identity. The sin of idolatry undermines Scripture's legacy as that which gives shape to a people's worship of and allegiance to God (see 7:38-44). Those who practice idolatry—who substitute alternative deities for worship of Israel's God, the only God—demonstrate their ignorance of God's redemptive purpose (14:14-18; 17:22, 24-29; 19:26). A prophetic community is a counterculture to the surrounding order. A sociology of external conflict requires all the more a sociology of internal unity. This is possible to maintain only by a carefully managed protocol of conciliation that forges unity between its disparate groups (see 6:1-6; 14:27–15:29). The solidarity of believers is emphatic within Acts: Believers are "together" when at worship and in mission.

The religious authority of the community's leadership team receives particular stress in Acts even as it does in the so-called Pastoral Letters of the Pauline corpus (1–2 Timothy and Titus). The emphasis is not on ecclesiastical orders so that a succession of male leaders is placed at the top of an institutional hierarchy/patriarchy. Rather, the religious authority of the Lord's successors is practical, prophetic, and personal. Further, it is ever adaptable to the changing landscape of the church's mission, for no one model of leadership is found in Acts. Yet Peter (4:32–5:16), Priscilla (18:1-28), and Paul (20:18-35) are surely the principal prophetic exemplars of Acts.[42] In particular, the similarities between Luke's portraits of the apostle Peter in the first half of Acts and the missionary Paul in the second half suggest that God grants spiritual authority predicated by a common prophetic vocation that is commissioned by and in continuity with the risen Lord. Moreover, the confirmation of this authority is by persuasive word and powerful deeds that are enabled by the Holy Spirit rather than by individual talent or education (see 4:13). Both Peter and Paul stand out as individuals. The moral value of their personal portraits in Acts should not be underestimated. Each embodies characteristics that are critical to the future leaders of the church: Their courageous and costly obedience to their calling, stewardship of possessions, theological perspicuity, religious observance, and personal piety are marks of the faithful disciple (see 20:18-35).

There are also real differences between the Twelve, represented by Peter, and their successors, represented by Stephen, Philip, James, and Paul. Although the matter remains contested among scholars of Acts, I want to emphasize the special significance of the Twelve—and Peter in particular—within the economy of God's salvation. They are close friends of the historical and resurrected Jesus and thus warrant being considered his apostolic successors (see 1:3-11, 21-22); and their commission to prophetic ministry and spiritual authority are glossed by Jesus' earlier prophecy that they would act as regents and judges of Israel (see chaps. 3–5; cf. Luke 22:29-30). Their inspired ministry is the medium through which the kingdom is restored to repentant Israel. Further, every decisive movement in the church's mission to the end of the earth is initiated or confirmed by apostolic authorization. While the Paul of Acts embodies most fully the vocation of repentant Israel as light to the nations, it is the Peter of Acts who both inaugurates (10:1–11:18) and confirms it (15:6-11). The continuity between Peter and Paul can function as an important element of Luke's apologia for Paul precisely because of Peter's key role in God's plan of salvation.

(5) *The community's resurrection hope during the last days is for the return of Jesus and the promised season of universal restoration he will fulfill.* Acts is a narrative about "the last days" (see 2:17; 3:19-26); in fact, every element of this "master story" is ultimately understood against an eschatological horizon. This theological conception may come as a surprise to those who note that while Acts opens in a resounding eschatological key (see 1:6-8, 10-11), the remaining narrative rarely sounds another futuristic note (see 3:19-21; cf. 7:31; 10:42; 17:30-31). Nowhere is there a discourse on the future as found everywhere else in the New Testament. Of course, Luke presumes a prior reading of his Gospel and knowledge of its prediction of the Lord's return, confirmed at Jesus' ascension. Further, Peter's reference to a future "time of universal restoration" (3:21) and Paul's prophecy of endtime judgment (see 17:31) point to God's cosmic triumph at the Lord's return to earth. Although scholars continue to debate the meaning of these texts, the narrator's theology is not shaped by a concern to correct some mistaken eschatology—for example, a perceived delay in Christ's return or an apocalyptic faction within his church. The focus of Luke's escha-

tology in both his Gospel and Acts is God's commitment to promises made according to Scripture. Therefore, the primary theological problem addressed by the book is *theodicy*, the vindication of God's justice.

Acts envisages both the Lord's return (1:10-11) and the outpouring of the Holy Spirit (2:17) as eschatological events. The central theme in Luke's reckoning of this eschatological moment, however, is neither a detailed chronology nor the apocalyptic cast of the future (see 1:7); rather, his emphasis shifts to the historical means by which God's people will make their way under the aegis of the Spirit from Pentecost to parousia. The narrative framework of the church's movement toward God's ordained future consists of two integral motifs: the church's Spirit-led mission from Jerusalem to Rome, the principal cities of two symbolic worlds that represent all people for all time, and an interpretive strategy that warrants each episode of this mission as fulfilling the promises of Israel's Scripture. The historic reality that confirms God's faithfulness is that a portion of Israel is restored (see 2:40; 3:19-23; cf. Rom 9:1-29). Despite the recurrent hostility of unrepentant Jews and Gentiles, this restored Israel, led first by the apostles and ultimately personified by the Paul of Acts, becomes "a light to the nations" from Jerusalem to Rome (see 3:25-26; 13:47; cf. 1:6-8).

The mode by which the Lord bids the covenant community to journey from Pentecost to parousia is to bear powerful witness to his resurrection (see 1:8). Scripture's promise of a restored Israel is not realized within "national" Israel—as many Jews anticipated—but within a remnant of repentant Jews (see 3:23) whom God calls out of Israel through the church's mission (see 2:37-41). Indeed, the church's mission to the whole household of Israel has already carried the Word of God to every group within the household of Israel (see 2:5-11): Hebrews and Hellenists (Acts 2–7), Samaritans and proselytes (Acts 8), those inside and those outside of the holy land. The conflict and mixed results that this mission has provoked fulfill Scripture's prophecies (see 28:25-27), and Paul personifies the prophesied vocation of repentant Israel in his mission as "light to the nations" (see 13:47; see also chaps. 9–28).

The church's hope in God's coming triumph is expressed through daily proclamation of God's faithfulness, in continuity with the risen Messiah and the prophetic community that succeeded him in this ministry of the Word. The ending of Acts (28:30-31), which summarizes Paul's mission in Rome, serves to facilitate the transition from the book's narrative world to the readers' real worlds. The book bids its audience to move ever forward to God's coming triumph by engaging in Spirit-enabled witness in the world.

ACTS AS CANON

Approaching Acts in search of the Word of God requires more than a rigorous analysis of the book's social world, literary artistry, and theological conception. For the most part, modern interpreters concentrate on reconstructing the book's point of origin, whether in historical, literary, or theological categories. From their perspective, Acts is typically read as the second volume of Luke's continuous narrative. This narrative is shaped by his pastoral intentions, composed with ancient literary, rhetorical, and historiographical conventions and informed by his theological convictions to serve in the Christian formation of his first readers and the church. This critical construction, however, is often based on scholarly conjecture and runs the risk of freezing *the* meaning of Acts in an ancient world far removed from that of its current readers.

Even on historical grounds, Acts followed a separate and more difficult course into the biblical canon from the one taken by the Third Gospel. Those who formed the church's Scriptures for future generations of believers evidently did not think it necessary or even profitable to read Luke and Acts together. More likely, the pre-canonical Acts circulated with different collections of letters, both catholic and Pauline. For this reason, by the time the canonical process had concluded a few centuries later, the canonical Acts had its own peculiar function within the biblical canon, different from that of the Third Gospel. The importance of its role *as Scripture* thereby underwrites a particular approach to the study of Acts and its distinctive deposit to the biblical witness.

Reading the Book of Acts as Scripture. A central critical question is, *What do Luke's reasons for writing Acts have to do with the church's reasons for reading Acts as Scripture?* Any interpreter must try to bridge these two hermeneutical horizons. However, they are in constant flux due both to new insights about Luke's world and his writing and to changes in the time and location of his various interpreters. In particular, this text's movement from personal "conversation" to the church's "canon" sharply resets the interpreter's angle of vision toward Acts.[43] Several implications of this shift should be briefly noted:

(1) Reading Acts as Scripture recognizes the importance of different literary relationships within the New Testament. The intracanonical relationships between Acts and the four Gospels and between Acts and the two collections of letters (especially Pauline) that follow it are elevated in importance within canonical context. The "canon logic" envisaged by the arrangement of the different parts within the New Testament whole, and sometimes even of individual writings within these canonical parts, stipulates important markers in guiding the reader's approach to the New Testament. According to this arrangement, then, the fourfold gospel (not just Luke's Gospel) is perceived as prerequisite reading for the study of Acts, and the study of Acts under the gospel's light is prerequisite reading for the study of the letters that follow.

(2) These new intracanonical relationships forged by the canonical process are also valuable when assessing the distinctive importance of the theology of Acts within the New Testament. No longer does the biblical theologian consider the thematic interests of Acts only in terms of their congruence with those found in Luke's Gospel. Rather, the theological contribution Acts makes to *biblical* theology is now measured as an indispensable part of an integral whole. Put in different words, upon consideration of the various theologies that make up the New Testament's entire theological conception, the interpreter is now pressed to imagine what a biblical witness to God might lack if it did not include Acts. What distorted idea of the church's faith, its religious or social identity, or of its vocation in the world might result from a conversation with a body of sacred writings that did not include this book? What thin reading of the Pauline letters would result if the interpreter failed to prepare by first reading the story of the canonical Paul of Acts? Simply put, reading Acts within its biblical setting reminds us that any theological understanding lacking the witness of Acts will distort Christian faith and life.

(3) The Paul of Acts is valued more keenly from this canonical perspective than when his role is reduced to a cameo appearance in the modern quest of the historical Paul. At stake in following the story of the Paul of Acts is not so much the historical accuracy of Luke's portrait—even though this is currently being reconsidered—or even the important questions about his credibility within earliest Christianity. The most important issues from a canonical angle of vision are theological ones: What does the Paul of Acts have to say about the future of the church? How does Paul's story in Acts orient its readers to the implied author of the Pauline letters that follow and the Pauline witness they enshrine (see the Overview to 15:13–28:28)?

(4) The church's conflict with the synagogue at the end of the canonical process was no doubt different from Luke's assessment when he wrote Acts (see "Acts as Conversation," above). What began as an intramural "Jewish problem" had become a "Judaism problem" by the end of the second century. Keen competition had developed between two "world religions," a problem made all the more prickly by their common history and theological conception. The scribal emendations to the Western version of Acts, with a more negative characterization of unrepentant Israel, may well reflect the canonizing community's heightened sensitivity to its relationship with Judaism and its sense of the canon's function to clearly delineate the church's identity. In a different sense, the portrait of Israel found in Acts clarifies the difference between Christianity and Judaism in christological rather than nationalistic or ethnocentric terms. Thus Acts subverts any "Christian" prejudice against Jews on ethnic grounds (= anti-Semitism) or on the mistaken presumption that God has either reneged on promises made to historic Israel according to the Scriptures or has replaced Jews with Christians in the economy of salvation (= supersessionism). God's faithfulness to Israel remains inviolate; therefore, today's church must become more—not less—Jewish in order to be fully Christian in its worship and witness.

(5) The "primitivism" of Acts simply reflects the ecclesial experience of the earliest church, which fashioned itself after the diaspora synagogues and other voluntary organizations of the Roman world. Worship consisted of prayer meetings and teaching, with Christian fellowship centered in the homes of believers. The sociology of the church dramatically changed during the canonical process; these loosely confederated house congregations became in time participants of an emerging church catholic. For

this reason, the ongoing interest in the images and ideas of "church" in Acts should focus on emulating its missionary vocation and prophetic message, its resurrection practices, and the nature of its spiritual leadership—important claims on any congregation in every age—rather than on replicating outward forms of governance and worship or other time-conditioned practices.

(6) In this regard, reading Acts as Scripture seeks to insinuate its narrative world into the changing "real" worlds of current readers. New layers of meaning hitherto hidden are discovered whenever sacred texts are allowed to penetrate and interpret the world of their interpreters. For example, contemporary readers will more easily discern the relevance of the Ethopian eunuch's story (8:26-40) for reflecting upon the relationship between the church and its homosexual membership or more readily recognize the example of Priscilla in chap. 18 (as well as other women in Acts) as a role model for prophetic ministry in congregations that once were reluctant to encourage women in ministry. The vivid snapshots of the community of goods or repeated episodes that depict Paul's relations with Rome may challenge today's congregations to a more prophetic understanding of church as counterculture. Read as Scripture, Acts provides an important element of a wider "canonical context" in which the faithful community gathers to reflect on those issues that either undermine or underscore God's presence in today's world.

(7) Finally, reading Acts as Scripture cultivates a fresh sense of sacred time and space. The church continues to live in "the last days," betwixt Pentecost and parousia, when the Spirit of God empowers Christ's disciples to bear witness to the resurrection throughout the world in anticipation of God's coming triumph and creation's final restoration (see 3:20-21). The book of Acts has continuing authority to form a church that proclaims God's word and embodies a witness to its truth, heralding that coming day.

Reading the Book of Acts Within Scripture. If Acts is approached as a narrative written for and relevant to only its first readers, then the book's current readers will find little of value for their own Christian formation. Perhaps it was precisely a concern for subsequent readers of sacred texts that guided the canonical process that produced the New Testament in its present form. For example, in its canonical setting the book of Acts is detached from Luke's Gospel, which is now read as one of a set of four. If Acts is read in its current canonical placement rather than as the second volume of Luke-Acts, then the reader will naturally reflect upon its narrative as continuing the story of Jesus presented by the four Gospels. The reader's understanding of "all that Jesus began to do and teach" will be greatly expanded and enriched by a fourfold presentation.

The book of Acts acquired two properties during the process of canonical development that continue to help readers envisage its distinctive role within the New Testament: (1) its title, "The Acts of the Apostles," and (2) its placement as a bridge between the Gospels, on one side, and the two collections of letters, Pauline and catholic, on the other. Most people begin reading a book by considering its title, for a book's subject matter is typically indicated by its title and/or its subtitle. Consider the curious title of this book, "The Acts of the Apostles." Commentators routinely adjure that Luke's story is inappropriately titled. The book is about the activity of the Holy Spirit, they claim, rather than that of the apostles. Or, if read as Luke-Acts, the "mighty acts" of Acts are best understood as the continuation of Luke's historical narrative about Jesus. Against this conjecture, the effect of recognizing the superscription of Acts as a canonical property is to call attention to a new set of orienting concerns for readers of Acts as Scripture.[44]

Canonically, the two halves of the title each function to signal a key concept about the role of the apostles in Acts. First, the literary genre of πράξεις *praxeis*, ("acts")[45] tells stories of people, real or imagined, who are divinely favored to act in powerful ways on behalf of their community or nation. Such an aretology, or "folk" story, also functions as social commentary, since supernatural powers are given to heroes as evidence of their special status (and by extension, the special status of those communities or nations they helped to found). Their mighty deeds are not of their own making but testify to divine favor, and anyone who links his or her destiny to these heroic characters is assured of divine favor.

In the case of the book of Acts, the canonical process recognized the importance of Jesus' successors, whose persuasive words and powerful deeds founded the church and formed its rule of faith.

The second half of the title—"of the apostles"—identifies those heroes of the faith whose special status and divinely ordained destiny ensures the salvation of all who submit to their spiritual authority (chaps. 4–5; 20:18-35). While it may seem theologically prudent to think of these characters as merely the means of the Holy Spirit's work, the effect of the canonical title is to shift the reader's interest from the Spirit's baptism to those prophetic successors of the Lord whom the Spirit fills for ministry. This concern to attach the church to its apostolic forebears reflects the sociology of the emergent "one holy catholic and apostolic church." This church's claims of special status in the economy of God's order were contested by rivals both within the church (Gnosticism, Montanism) and outside it (formative Judaism).[46] The book of Acts reminds its confessing readers that the church's sacred memories of the Lord's apostolic successors (including Paul) exemplify a vocation, character, message, and faith that all Christians must imitate in demonstrating their obedience to God.

The strategic placement of Acts between the Gospels and the letters suggests the transitional role it performs within the New Testament. The narrative of Acts continues and concludes the authorized biography of Jesus while introducing the Bible's readers to the apostolic writings that follow. Acts functions as a bridge connecting Gospels and letters in a logical relationship that mirrors the ultimate aim of the New Testament: to nurture Christian discipleship after the pattern of Jesus.

Acts can first of all be read as "commentary" on Jesus' story narrated in the four Gospels. Not only does the story Acts tells offer substantial proof of Jesus' resurrection as Lord and Messiah (cf. Acts 2:36), but it also issues Scripture's response to the theological crisis occasioned by his bodily absence from the Christian community (see John 13:31–14:31). Those disciples who follow after the exalted Lord are to continue in the power of the Holy Spirit to do and to say what Jesus began (see Acts 1:1-2). In this regard, the importance of retaining the final shape of the New Testament rather than combining Luke and Acts as a single narrative is indicated by the significant roles performed by Peter and the Holy Spirit in Acts where Jesus is absent—roles for which Luke's Gospel does not adequately prepare the reader of Acts. Peter's rehabilitation at the end of John (John 21:15-17) as well as the teaching about the Spirit's post-Easter role by John's Jesus (John 14–16) signify the important role that John's Gospel performs in preparing the reader for the story of Acts. Moreover, what it means to be a "witness" of the risen Jesus (Acts 1:8) is more fully understood by the biblical reader in the context of John's Gospel (John 15:26-27; cf. Luke 24:48).

The relationship between Acts and the following two collections of letters is more difficult for the interpreter to order. The conventions of epistolary literature are different from those of narrative literature and thus the differences between Acts and the letters are readily discernible. For example, Luke's portrait of Paul is sometimes at odds with Paul's self-understanding or missionary itinerary as given in his letters. Further, Luke does not quote any of Paul's letters. Reading Acts as Scripture, however, compels a dialogue between the Paul of Acts and the Pauline letters of the New Testament.[47] The potential gains of this perspective may be illustrated when considering the canonical "seam" that connects the final passage in Acts, which portrays a missionary Paul in Rome (see 28:17-31), to the opening text of the first Pauline letter, that to the Romans, which introduces biblical readers to a missionary-minded apostle who is eager "to proclaim the gospel to you also who are in Rome" (Rom 1:15).[48] The interplay between the ending of Acts and the beginning of Romans underscores the primary concern of Luke's Paul, who is not found in a secluded study writing dense Christian theology but on city streets or in living rooms of rented apartments relating the Christian gospel to life in practical and persuasive ways.

Perhaps the most important role Acts performs within the New Testament is to proffer biographical introductions to the implied authors of the letters that follow. In canonical context, such biographies serve a theological purpose by orienting readers to the religious and moral authority of apostolic authors as trustworthy carriers of the word of God. While the historical accuracy of Luke's narrative of Paul and other leaders of earliest Christianity may be challenged, the rhetorical and ethical power of these figures confirms and commends the importance of their letters. The salient issue is not whether Acts fails as a historical record but that it succeeds as a theological resource, contributing to the church's understanding of its vocation and identity in the world.

In this regard, Acts provides an angle of vision into the Pauline and catholic epistolary collections that follow.[49] For instance, the relations among Peter, John, James, and Paul and their respective missions, as depicted in Acts, suggest how the interpreter arranges the intracanonical dialogue between those New Testament writings attached to each leader. Similarities and dissimilarities in emphasis and theological conception found when comparing the catholic and Pauline letters may actually correspond to the manner by which Acts narrates the negotiations on theological convictions and social conventions between different missions (e.g., Acts 2:42-47; 9:15-16; 11:1-18; 12:17; 15:12-29; 21:17-26). The modern discussion has emphasized how a narrator committed to the practical requirements of an "early catholic" church softens the disagreements between the leaders of earliest Christianity. But what is often overlooked is that the church collected and eventually canonized a Pauline corpus whose principal letters are often polemical and potentially divisive. The question is never raised as to why these Pauline letters were included in the canon of an "early catholic" church if the aim was to shape theological uniformity. Might it not be the case that the church recognized the importance of Acts in introducing the apostolic writings not so much to smooth their disagreeable edges as to interpret them?

Indeed, perhaps the canonical role Acts best performs is to explain rather than to temper the diversity found in the two collections of biblical letters. According to Acts, the church that claims its continuity with the first apostles tolerates a rich pluralism even as the apostles did, not without controversy and confusion. What was achieved at the Jerusalem Council is a kind of theological understanding rather than a theological consensus. The divine revelation given to the apostles, according to Acts, forms a pluralizing monotheism that in turn informs two distinct missions and appropriate proclamations, Jewish and Gentile (see Gal 2:7-10). Thus, sharply put, Acts interprets the two collections of letters in a more sectarian fashion: The Pauline corpus reflects the gospel of a Gentile mission, while the catholic collection reflects the gospel(s) of a Jewish mission.

However, rather than causing division within the church, such a theological diversity is now perceived as normative and necessary for the work of the One who calls both Jews and Gentiles to be the people of God. As a context for theological reflection, Acts forces us to interpret the letters in the light of two guiding principles. First, we should expect to find kerygmatic diversity as we move from the Pauline to the catholic letters. Second, we should expect such a diversity to be useful in forming a single people of God. Against a critical hermeneutics that tends to select a "canon within the canon" from among the various possibilities, the Bible's own recommendation is for an interpretive strategy characterized by a mutually illuminating and self-correcting conversation among biblical theologies.

Finally, the dominant theological commitments of Acts guide theological reflection upon the letters. The point is not that a theology of Acts determines or even anticipates the various theologies found in the letters. Rather, Acts shapes a particular perspective, a practical concern, an abiding interest that influences the interpretation of the letters. For example, if according to Acts the church's vocation is to continue what Jesus began to do and to say, then a subsequent reading of the letters should bring to sharper focus the identity and praxis of a missionary people who respond to the Lord's demand to be his witness to the ends of the earth. This same perspective holds true of the catholic epistles, where believers constitute a community of "resident aliens" whose vocation is a costly faithfulness to God rather than that of the missionary witness to a needy world found in the Pauline letters. How does the catholicity of Acts deepen our understanding of God's people as a community of "resident aliens"? The canonical approach presumes that the connection is complementary rather than adversarial. In this case, the Pauline church, which may be inclined to accommodate itself to the mainstream of the world in order to more effectively spread the gospel (see 1 Cor 9:12*b*-23), is reminded by the catholic witness that it must take care not to be corrupted by the values and behaviors of that world (see Jas 1:27). That is, the synergism effected by the dominant theological commitments of Acts suggests that the diverse theologies ingredient in the biblical canon compose a dynamic, self-correcting system, preventing theological distortion.[50]

FOR FURTHER READING

Commentaries:

Barrett, C. K. *A Critical and Exegetical Commentary on the Acts of the Apostles.* 2 vols. ICC. Edinburgh: T & T Clark, 1994–98.

Bruce, F. F. *The Acts of the Apostles.* Rev. ed. NICNT. Grand Rapids: Eerdmans, 1988.

Dunn, J. D. G. *The Acts of the Apostles.* Valley Forge, Pa.: Trinity, 1996.

Fitzmyer, J. A. *The Acts of the Apostles.* AB 31. Garden City, N.Y.: Doubleday, 1998.

Haenchen, E. *The Acts of the Apostles.* Philadelphia: Westminster, 1971.

Jervell, J. *Die Apostelgeschichte.* KEK 3. Göttingen: Vandenhoeck & Ruprecht, 1998.

Johnson, L. T. *The Acts of the Apostles.* SP 5. Collegeville, Minn.: Liturgical, 1992.

Kee, H. C. *To Every Nation Under Heaven: The Acts of the Apostles.* NTC. Valley Forge, Pa.: Trinity, 1997.

Spencer, F. S. *Acts.* Readings: A New Biblical Commentary. Sheffield: Sheffield Academic, 1997.

Tannehill, R. C. *The Acts of the Apostles.* Vol. 2 of *The Narrative Unity of Luke-Acts: A Literary Interpretation.* Minneapolis: Fortress, 1990.

Witherington, B. *The Acts of the Apostles: A Socio-Rhetorical Commentary.* Grand Rapids: Eerdmans, 1998.

Other Studies:

Cassidy, R. J. *Society and Politics in the Acts of the Apostles.* Maryknoll, N.Y.: Orbis, 1987.

Evans, C. A., and J. A. Sanders. *Luke and Scripture: The Function of Sacred Tradition in Luke-Acts.* Minneapolis: Fortress, 1993.

Hill, C. C. *Hellenists and Hebrews: Reappraising Division within the Earliest Church.* Minneapolis: Fortress, 1992.

Jervell, J. *The Theology of the Acts of the Apostles.* NTT. Cambridge: Cambridge University Press, 1996.

Levine, Amy-Jill and Marianne Blickenstaff, eds. *A Feminist Companion to the Acts of the Apostles.* Feminist Companion to the New Testament and Early Christian Writings 9. New York: T & T Clark, 2004.

Marshall, I. H., and D. Peterson, eds. *Witness to the Gospel: The Theology of Acts.* Grand Rapids: Eerdmans, 1998.

Martin, C. J. "The Acts of the Apostles." In *Searching the Scriptures: A Feminist Commentary.* Vol. 2. Edited by E. Schüssler Fiorenza. London: SCM, 1995.

Nave, Guy D., Jr. *The Role and Function of Repentance in Luke-Acts.* Academia Biblica 4. Atlanta: Society of Biblical Literature, 2002.

Parsons, M., and R. Pervo. *Rethinking the Unity of Luke and Acts.* Minneapolis: Fortress, 1990.

Penner, Todd C., and Caroline Vander Stickele, eds. *Contextualizing Acts: Lukan Narrative and Greco-Roman Discourse.* SBLSym 20. Atlanta: Society of Biblical Literature, 2003.

Porter, S. E. *The Paul of Acts.* WUNT 115. Tübingen: Mohr Sebeck, 1999.

Powell, M. A. *What Are They Saying About Acts?* New York: Paulist, 1991.

Richter, Ivoni Reimer. *Women in the Acts of the Apostles: A Feminist Liberation Perspective.* Translated by Linda M. Maloney. Minneapolis, Minn.: Fortress, 1995.

Soards, M. L. *The Speeches in Acts: Their Content, Context, and Concerns.* Louisville: Westminster/John Knox, 1994.

Winter, B. W., and A. Clarke, eds. *The Book of Acts in Its First Century Setting.* 6 vols. Grand Rapids: Eerdmans, 1993–.

ENDNOTES

1. See J. Green, "Internal Repetition in Luke-Acts," in *History, Literature and Society in the Book of Acts*, ed. B. Witherington (Cambridge: Cambridge University Press, 1996) 283-99.

2. For this line of evidence, see A. Culpepper, "The Gospel of Luke," in *The New Interpreter's Bible*, 12 vols. (Nashville: Abingdon, 1994–2002) 9:4-10, and in this volume.

3. For a positive assessment of the relationship between the Paul of Acts and the historical Paul, see M. Hengel and A. Schwemer, *Paul Between Damascus and Antioch* (Louisville: Westminster John Knox, 1997) 1-23.

4. See R. Maddox, *The Purpose of Luke-Acts* (Edinburgh: T & T Clark, 1982) 6-9. D. Trobisch, *Paul's Letter Collection* (Minneapolis: Fortress, 1994), has argued that Paul (or a close associate) placed a collection of his letters into circulation at Ephesus, perhaps as early as the mid-60s. Whether Luke knew of a collection of Paul's letters in any case cannot be so easily dismissed if allusions to (rather than citations of) them are credible evidence. Luke may well be alluding to one or more Pauline letters (e.g., Romans; 1–2 Corinthians) and not simply to common Pauline traditions used in both Acts and certain (esp. later/deutero-) Pauline correspondence (e.g., Ephesians; 1–2 Timothy). See also W. Walker, "Acts and the Pauline Corpus

Reconsidered," *JSNT* 24 (1985) 3-23, who argues that Luke surely knew a collection of Paul's letters, was influenced by them, but had none open before him when writing Acts. This later conclusion is now revised in W. Walker, "Acts and the Pauline Corpus Revisited," in *Essays in Honor of Joseph B. Tyson*, ed. R. Thompson and T. Phillips (Macon: Mercer University Press, 1998) 77-86.

5. Any attempt to "update" religious conviction in the light of present contingencies is a kind of supersessionism—e.g., Judaism's efforts in rereading its Scriptures to take into account the destruction of the Temple/priesthood and its result in moving early Judaism toward its rabbinical expression is a kind of supersessionism. For this reason, R. Gordon, *Hebrews* (Sheffield: Sheffield Academic, 2000) 27-28, compares favorably the supersessionism evident in the Letter to the Hebrews with respect to the Scriptures with that taking place in contemporary Judaism.

6. Cf. J. Nolland, *Luke 1–9*, WBC (Dallas: Word, 1989) xxxii-xxxiii.

7. M. Powell, *What Are They Saying About Acts?* (New York: Paulist, 1991) 13-19.

8. This ambivalence is reflected in competing assessments of the church's relationship with Rome in Acts. P. Walaskay, *"And So We Came to Rome": The Political Perspective of Acts*, SNTSMS 49 (Cambridge: Cambridge University Press, 1983), argues that Acts defends Rome to the church, while R. Cassidy, *Society and Politics in the Acts of the Apostles* (Maryknoll, N.Y.: Orbis, 1987), argues that the church is a counterculture that brooks no political allegiance with Rome.

9. See B. Witherington, *The Acts of the Apostles: A Socio-Rhetorical Commentary* (Grand Rapids: Eerdmans, 1998) 77-97, for a full discussion of Acts' chronology.

10. H. Conzelmann, *The Acts of the Apostles*, trans. J. Limburg et al., ed. E. J. Epp and C. R. Matthews, Hermeneia (Philadelphia: Fortress, 1987) xlv-xlvii.

11. See R. Wall, "Israel and the Gentile Mission According to Acts and Paul: A Canonical Approach," in *Witness to the Gospel: The Theology of the Book of Acts*, ed. I. Howard Marshall and D. Peterson (Grand Rapids: Eerdmans, 1998) 437-58.

12. See C. Hill, "Romans," *Oxford Bible Commentary* (Oxford: Oxford University Press, 2001).

13. Cf. M. Parsons and R. Pervo, *Rethinking the Unity of Luke and Acts* (Minneapolis: Fortress, 1993). See also Witherington, *The Acts of the Apostles*, 2-39, for a careful review of Parsons and Pervo's work. The editorial tendency of many modern commentary series to assign both Luke and Acts to the same scholar reifies the assumption that common authorship presumes a common theological conception.

14. For a competent review of Luke's use of various sources when writing Acts, see J. A. Fitzmyer, *The Acts of the Apostles*, AB 31 (Garden City, N.Y.: Doubleday, 1998) 80-90. I will take up more specific problems with Luke's sources when apropos to the discussion of specific texts.

15. M. Dibelius, *Studies in the Acts of the Apostles*, ed. H. Greek (New York: Scribner's, 1956).

16. Cf. S. Porter, *The Paul of Acts*, WUNT 115 (Tübingen: Mohr Siebeck, 1999) 10-66, who argues that the use of "we" in Acts cues the reader to an independent and continuous Pauline source (which may be, but probably is not, Luke) whose favorable view of Paul was of special usefulness in advancing the narrator's apologetic interests.

17. For good examples of reading Acts as narrative, see R. Tannehill, *The Narrative Unity of Luke-Acts*, vol. 2 (Minneapolis: Fortress, 1990); F. S. Spencer, *Acts*, Readings: A New Biblical Commentary (Sheffield: Sheffield Academic, 1997).

18. See M. Soards, *The Speeches in Acts: Their Content, Context, and Concerns* (Louisville: Westminster/John Knox, 1994).

19. For a useful introduction to the speeches in Acts, this literary element, especially as they relate to ancient models of public speaking, see the relevant essays gathered together in *The Book of Acts in Its First Century Setting*, vol. 1, ed. B. Winter and A. Clarke (Grand Rapids: Eerdmans, 1993).

20. See R. Wall, "Intertextuality, Biblical," in *Dictionary of New Testament Background*, ed. C. Evans and S. Porter (Downers Grove: InterVarsity, 2000) 541-51.

21. S. Talmon, "Emendation of Biblical Texts on the Basis of Ugaritic Parallels," in *Studies in the Bible*, ed. S. Japhet (Jerusalem: Magnes, 1986) 279.

22. According to R. Hays, *Echoes of Scripture in the Letters of Paul* (New Haven: Yale University Press, 1989) 18-19, the critical task of finding echoing predecessors prevents a version of intertextuality that is purely literary and of the present moment.

23. For Luke's narrative style as midrash-like, see Evans and Sanders, *Luke and Scripture*, 1-13.

24. Cf. D. Boyarin, *Intertextuality and the Reading of Midrash* (Bloomington: Indiana University Press, 1990) 1-21; M. Fishbane, *The Garments of Torah* (Bloomington: Indiana University Press, 1989) 16-18.

25. See R. Pervo, *Profit with Delight* (Philadelphia: Fortress, 1987); D. Edwards, *Religion and Power* (New York: Oxford, 1996).

26. See J. Thomas, *The Devil, Disease and Deliverance*, JPTSS 5 (Sheffield: Sheffield Academic, 1998); H. Kee, *Medicine, Miracle and Magic in the New Testament Times*, SNTSMS 55 (Cambridge: Cambridge University Press, 1986).

27. See C. K. Barrett, *A Critical and Exegetical Commentary on the Acts of the Apostles*, 2 vols., ICC (Edinburgh: T & T Clark, 1994, 1998) 1:2-29.

28. R. Brown, *An Introduction to the New Testament* (New York: Doubleday, 1997) 327. For a full account of the history of this textual problem, see W. Strange, *The Problem of the Text of Acts*, SNTSMS 71 (Cambridge: Cambridge University Press, 1992).

29. See E. Epp, *The Theological Tendency of Codex Bezae Cantabrigiensis in Acts*, SNTSMS 3 (Cambridge: Cambridge University Press, 1966). The most balanced discussion of how this version of Acts compares with the other principal Greek text of Acts, the so-called Alexandrian text, is P. Head, "Acts and the Problem of Its Texts," in Winter and Clarke, *The Book of Acts in Its First Century Setting*, 1:415-44.

30. Cf. Epp, *The Theological Tendency of Codex Bezae Cantabrigiensis in Acts*, 166.

31. Cf. B. Childs, *Introduction to the Old Testament as Scripture* (Philadelphia: Fortress, 1979) 84-106.

32. In organizing the theological conception of Luke's Gospel, Culpepper, *Luke*, 13-30, considers a range of "christological emphases" before treating a "compendium" of the gospel's most important theological themes. The reader should keep in mind, that while various themes of Luke's Gospel do recur in Acts, the theological unity between them is much more dynamic. Luke's "confession of faith" in Acts adapts itself to a different historical setting and genre of literature; but his faith, reflected in the story he narrates, has also developed in consideration of new theological concerns facing his church. The theology of Acts is not redundant and makes its own distinctive contribution to a New Testament theology.

33. B. R. Gaventa, "Toward a Theology of Acts: Reading and Rereading," *Int.* 42 (1988) 150.

34. See R. Wall, "The 'Rule of Faith' in Theological Hermeneutics," in *Between Two Horizons*, ed. J. Green and M. Turner (Grand Rapids: Eerdmans, 2000) 88-107.

35. This summary follows the lead of J. Jervell, whose "theology of Acts" is found in several of his publications, especially *The Theology of the Acts of the Apostles* (Cambridge: Cambridge University Press, 1996). I disagree, however, with his description that repentant Gentiles *in every case* are found in the synagogue where their Jewish sensibilities have been cultivated prior to hearing the Christian gospel proclaimed. However, there are instances of pagans responding to the gospel in Acts (e.g., 14:8-9). Moreover, the point of Paul's proclamation to the pagans of Lystra (14:15-17) and Athens (16:22-33) is that God, the only God, is the God of every nation who desires to forgive everyone who calls upon the Lord for salvation.

36. Jervell, *The Theology of the Acts of the Apostles*, 61. Jervell contends that this "fundamentalism" extends from Luke's idea of Scripture's absolute authority and the validity of its teaching to his pervasive use of Scripture in support of his narrative's plotline.

37. See C. F. D. Moule, "The Christology of Acts," in *Studies in Luke-Acts*, ed. L. Keck and L. Martyn (Philadelphia: Fortress, 1980) 159-85, who argues that the developing christology the careful reader notes when moving from Luke's Gospel to Acts is integral to a realistic narrative that reflects changes in the church's confession of Christ in a post-Easter setting. Thus, e.g., the frequency of "Lordship" language in Acts (see 2:36) and the description of Jesus as the heavenly recipient of the church's petitions (see 7:59-60) is possible only *after* the events of the Gospel narrative are in "the past of Jesus."

38. Cf. R. O'Toole, *The Unity of Luke's Theology*, GNS 9 (Wilmington, Del.: Glazier, 1984) 38-61.

39. See R. Stronstad, *The Charismatic Theology of St. Luke* (Peabody, Mass.: Hendrickson, 1984), and *The Prophethood of All Believers*, JPTSS 16 (Sheffield: Sheffield Academic, 1999); cf. Jervell, *The Theology of the Acts of the Apostles*, 43-54.

40. Jervell, *The Theology of the Acts of the Apostles*, 51.

41. See M. Turner, *Power from on High: The Spirit in Israel's Restoration and Witness in Luke-Acts*, JPTSS 9 (Sheffield: Sheffield Academic, 1996).

42. Cf. L. T. Johnson, *The Acts of the Apostles*, SP 5 (Collegeville, Minn.: Liturgical, 1992) 12-14.

43. See R. Wall, "Canonical Context and Canonical Conversations," in *Between Two Horizons*, ed. J. Green and M. Turner, 165-82.

44. See R. Wall, "The Acts of the Apostles in the Context of the New Testament Canon," *BTB* 18 (1988) 15-23.

45. See J. A. Fitzmyer, *The Acts of the Apostles*, AB 31 (Garden City, N.Y.: Doubleday, 1998) 47-49.

46. Some scholars use the expression "early catholicism" when referring to an emergent Christianity whose principal concern was to delineate the theological boundaries of the faith—by means of a "rule of faith"—to regulate Christian preaching and preserve the core beliefs of the apostolic traditions from their internal and external religious rivals. See E. Käsemann, "Paul and Early Catholicism," in *New Testament Questions of Today* (Philadelphia: Fortress, 1969) 236-51.

47. For a comprehensive listing and analysis of the intertextual echoes of Pauline letters in Acts, see D. Wenham, "Acts and the Pauline Corpus," in *The Book of Acts in Its First Century Setting: Ancient Literary Setting*, ed. B. Winter and A. Clarke (Grand Rapids: Eerdmans, 1993) 215-58.

48. See R. Wall, "Romans 1:1-15: An Introduction to the Pauline Corpus of the New Testament," in *The New Testament as Canon*, ed. R. Wall and E. Lemcio, JSNTSup 76 (Sheffield: JSOT, 1992) 142-60.

49. See R. Wall, "Introduction to Epistolary Literature," in *The New Interpreter's Bible*, 12 vols. (Nashville: Abingdon, 1994–2002) 10:369-391, and in this volume.

50. For a defense of this interpretive strategy and illustrations of its usefulness for reading across the New Testament canon, see Wall and Lemcio, *The New Testament as Canon.*

PART TWO:
THE EPISTLES

Introduction to Epistolary Literature

ROBERT W. WALL

GENERAL INTRODUCTION

The New Testament canon includes twenty-one letters gathered in two collections, Pauline (Romans through Philemon) and non-Pauline (Hebrews through Jude), that are strategically sandwiched between the books of Acts and Revelation. Both collections are often divided and grouped according to certain judgments about their points of origin, content, or current influence–judgments that remain contested. For this reason the rubrics employed during the history of their interpretation enjoy only moderate success as explanatory constructs and sometimes even dampen the distinctive contribution each letter makes to the whole canon.

In particular, while the entire Pauline collection concerns the ministry and message of the apostle Paul, its letters are often divided into those that are "genuine" (written by Paul) and those that are "disputed" (thought to have been written after Paul's death but in the manner of his "genuine" letters). This division is intended to distinguish the theology of the "real" Paul from that of his followers. Some scholars think that an imprisoned Paul (when and where are disputed) wrote or transcribed the "prison letters" (Ephesians, Philippians, Colossians, 2 Timothy, Philemon). The themes of the "Pastoral Epistles" (1—2 Timothy and Titus, which are usually studied together and are listed among the "disputed" letters) concern the characteristics of Christian leaders as well as the organization of Christian congregations (even though 2 Timothy differs in significant ways in this regard from 1 Timothy and Titus). Still another group of Paul's letters, whose greater length and influence are deemed "major" (Romans through Galatians), is occasionally separated from the shorter letters (Ephesians through Philemon). The influence of the shorter letters is sometimes perceived as less significant in forming the church's theological understanding–a view that seems to persist among some Protestant communions.

Although scholars sometimes rearrange the thirteen Pauline letters to follow a chronological scheme, the final form of the modern NT follows the Latin Vulgate so that letters written to congregations (Romans through 2 Thessalonians) precede those written to individuals (1 Timothy through Philemon). Within each group, letters are arranged by decreasing length, even though Ephesians is slightly longer than Galatians (which may well account for its priority in early canon lists; e.g., Chester Beatty papyri from c. 200 CE and the Muratorian canon list from c. 190 CE). It should be noted, however, that the early church arranged the Pauline corpus in different sequences and often included Hebrews.[1] Sometimes these letters were arranged according to theological importance. For example, Marcion placed Galatians first among Paul's letters, since he thought its teaching best supported his own contention that the influence of the Old Testament(and its theology) ended with Christ. Typically, Romans is placed first in the Pauline corpus not only because of its length but also because it presumes to offer its readers the best theological introduction to the writings of Paul, a status surely justified by its history and use within the church.

Unlike the Pauline letters, which are named after those being addressed, all the letters that make up the second collection (except Hebrews) are named after their supposed authors. The placement of each within the NT once again follows their decreasing length. As with the Pauline corpus, however, other sequences are found in the early and medieval churches, perhaps indicating the estimation of their relative theological importance for the purpose of Christian formation. In the canon lists of the Roman church (e.g., those of Carthage, 397 CE) and Augustine, the Petrine correspondence is placed first, which may reflect the primacy of Peter's memory and his teaching. The present form, James—Peter—John, follows Paul's list in Gal 2:9.

The writings of this second collection are even more difficult to organize into groups of common denominators than are the Pauline letters because their literary diversity is more pronounced and their theological traditions more diverse. The rubric "non-Pauline" is used in reference to those letters that do not claim residence within the Pauline domain–no matter what others may claim for them. More important, "non-Pauline" intends to orient the reader to the presence of two discrete collections of letters and then to the reflexive relationship between them as integral epistolary parts within the biblical whole. In most cases, seven of these letters (James through Jude) are listed under the ancient rubric "catholic," or more recently "general," because it is thought they were originally encyclical epistles that circulated among geographically dispersed and ethnically mixed congregations. Missing from this and other catalogs is Hebrews, which is typically left orphaned without either a Pauline or a catholic home. Perhaps its placement within the letter canon between the Pauline and the catholic letters is strategic: Being neither and yet having elements of both, Hebrews is an effective bridge, reminding readers of the interdependent character of these two collections of letters.

A. Deissmann's well-known distinction between the "epistle," compositions of public art intended for a wide audience, and the "letter," occasional correspondence intended for private and confidential reading, supports the Pauline/ catholic distinction. That is, the catholic collection is composed of epistles written as artful homilies for a general readership, whereas the Pauline letters were written for and first read by particular congregations or individuals.[2] Upon closer analysis, however, this distinction does not seem appropriate for the catholic epistles, since nowhere do James, Jude, and 2 Peter (or Hebrews) claim to address a general audience; and 3 John addresses an individual. Moreover, 1 John and James (and Hebrews) only approximate literary epistles. Nor can it be said that all these epistles are known by their author, for those from "John" (and Hebrews) are anonymous.

Despite the difficulty of forming neat and convenient groups, these letters all share a common purpose: to combine theological instruction and moral exhortation toward particular practical and pastoral ends. Each addresses the spiritual struggles and theological controversies that face ordinary believers seeking a more mature witness to their faith in Jesus Christ, often within hostile social settings. Each reflects its own particular historical occasion and theological situation, where the gospel of God is adapted to the life of God's people. Each is deeply rooted in particular interpretive traditions judged acceptable by the early church as apostolic and divinely inspired. For this reason, "catholic" is sometimes also used to classify the subject matter of these letters as applicable to every Christian congregation; they were even called the *epistulae canonicae* (the canonical epistles) in the West because their divine inspiration (and so canonicity) was recognized by "all the churches."[3] However, this sense of universal significance is true of every biblical writing whose canonical status is due in part to its perceived usefulness in the spiritual formation of every generation and congregation of believers.

THE WORLD BEHIND THE LETTERS: CONVERSATIONS IN HISTORICAL CONTEXT

No letter began its life as a biblical writing, read by the whole church for theological understanding. Every letter was at first a pastor-teacher's written response to believers whose particular sociohistorical circumstances provoked a spiritual crisis that required theological explanation and practical resolution. The letters of the NT are occasional literature, then. That is, in every case writers adapted their core theological convictions to a particular audience's historical situation in ways that enabled their writing to be, in C. Beker's apt phrase, "a word on target."[4] Therefore, current interpreters, far removed from the social world that helped to shape the letter's subject matter, are obligated to narrow the gap by gathering and using as much historical, political, and socioeconomic information regarding the original setting as possible. The epistolary text becomes a "window" through which its ancient author and first readers/auditors (authorial audience) are viewed more clearly, their worlds and traditions more fully understood, and the events implied by the text better known.

The result is a "thickened" description of the letter's subject matter that can facilitate its present performance as the church's Scripture. Within the community of faith, rarely if ever does an interest in the "world behind the letters" marginalize the theological aspect of the text itself so that we view it merely as a historical resource. Rather, we use the tools of historical criticism to understand better the biblical text as a witness to God's revelation within history, within circumstances in which letters are heard or read as a "word on target." The interpreter approaches these ancient texts with historical sensitivity, then, to understand more precisely their meaning at the point of origin.

Since most NT letters deal with the concrete problems of specific communities, the letters themselves are the clearest line of sight into their social world. This methodological claim does not exclude non-biblical resources, literary or otherwise, whether from the early Roman Empire or from early Judaism. Rather, it insists only that we move outward from the epistolary literature itself to all other sources when reconstructing the world behind the letters.

THE PAULINE COLLECTION

The most important conversation partner in the Pauline correspondence is the author. To be sure, an interpreter's decisions regarding Pauline authorship depend on prior decisions about sources. Which of the letters that claim Pauline authorship were actually written by Paul? To what extent should we trust the historical veracity of Luke's portrait of Paul in Acts? And what of the apocryphal Paul of early Christian memory and legend, which many scholars think so idealizes Paul's memory and theological trajectory that both are badly distorted? Even the autobiographical portions of the authentic letters, which many suppose offer us the best window onto the historical Paul, serve primarily an apologetical (i.e., rhetorical) purpose. Other matters, such as those related to the authorial address and the date and place of origin of a particular letter, are all part of the historical matrix that help to settle the question of Pauline authorship. We leave these decisions and discussions to the commentators on the individual letters.

On balance, however, few figures from antiquity are better known than Paul. As N. Dahl has noted, "in his letters, Paul himself comes to life."[5] Current readers of his letters have sufficient raw material to sketch a basic chronology of Paul's life and mission. This historical project has a direct bearing upon the interpretation of the Pauline letters, especially when trying to date and place them in some historical sequence or social location. The construction of a Pauline chronology helps the interpreter to assess the development of Paul's theological conception; the subject matter of Paul's message is no longer presented as a static and systematic whole. Instead, on the basis of a chronology of his ministry and letters, the development of the most important theological themes of Pauline preaching (e.g., the promise and fulfillment of God's salvation, the results of Christ's death and resurrection, the life and witness of the church) and of the central theological controversies of his Gentile mission (e.g., election, law, theodicy, Israel) can be traced through the sequence of letters. Paul's theology was a work in process.[6]

The Book of Acts and the Chronology of the Pauline Collection. What is known about Paul comes to us from three sources: (1) the autobiographical portions of his letters, (2) his "authorized" biography found in the book of Acts, and (3) his "unauthorized" biography found in such apocryphal writings as The Acts of Paul and Thecla. These sources are not of equal value to Paul's chronologists. Accepting the historian's rule of favoring primary (or direct) over secondary (or mediated) evidence, preference is always granted to what Paul says about himself in his letters, even though the book of Acts contributes necessary information to fill out his epistolary portrait. Most scholars hold that Paul's portrait in Acts is the literary invention of the narrator, whose principal interests are theological and not historical. The apocryphal story of Paul is still farther removed from the historical Paul, deriving in part from the canonical Acts and in part from legend, and is thus deemed either redundant or useless as a historical resource.[7]

The most crucial task facing the chronologist is the correlation of datable events mentioned in Paul's letters or his story in Acts. Sharply stated, the primary problem is that the chronology of Paul's life according to Paul's letters differs at significant points from the chronology of Paul's life according to Acts. Further, the difficulty facing the chronologist is exacerbated by the lack of any clear reference to Paul's letters in the book of Acts. Acknowledging this disparity, a growing number of scholars now follow the lead of J. Knox and try to reconstruct Paul's life using only his writings, admitting into evidence information from Acts only when it is absolutely necessary for a coherent chronology and does not contradict Paul's testimony.[8]

Yet this position is not without problems. Paul surely colors his own story with rhetorical and theological intent; and there is a growing appreciation for the historical integrity of the second half of Acts, which narrates Paul's movements from the Jerusalem Council (Acts 15) to Rome (Acts 28; Paul tells us virtually nothing about the first stage of his missionary activity [Acts 9–14],[9] and none of his letters can be dated with any probability from this period in any case). Even if the pattern of Paul's mission according to Acts 15–28 serves the narrator's literary and theological interests, his story contains reliable information.[10] Therefore, most chronologists continue to work between Paul's letters and Acts to calculate the pivotal dates of his mission and letters.[11] The following provides a tentative chronology of Paul's life, with supporting textual evidence:

CE

33	Paul's conversion/call near Damascus (Gal 1:17; Acts 9:1-22 [22:6-21; 26:12-18])
35	First journey to Jerusalem (Gal 1:18-20; Acts 9:26-29)
47–48	Mission from Antioch to Asia (Phil 4:15; Acts 13–14)
48	Second journey to Jerusalem: the Jerusalem Council (Gal 2:1-10; Acts 15:1-12)
49	Macedonian mission from Galatia to Athens (1 Cor 16:1; 2 Cor 11:9; Gal 4:13; 1 Thess 2:2, 3:1; Phil 4:15-16; Acts 16:6–17:34)
49–52	Claudius's decree (Acts 18:2); Corinthian mission (2 Cor 1:19; 11:7-9; 1 Thess 3:6; Acts 18:1-11)
50	Paul writes 1–2 Thessalonians
53–56	Ephesian Mission (1 Cor 16:1-8; Acts 19)
53	Paul writes Galatians
54	Paul writes 1 Corinthians
55	Paul writes Philippians and Philemon
55–56	Paul writes 2 Corinthians
56	Paul's "painful" return to Corinth (2 Cor 13:2; cf. 10:11; 12:21; 2:13)
57	Third visit to Corinth (2 Cor 13:1; Acts 20:1-3)
57	Paul writes Romans
57	Third journey to Jerusalem (Rom 15:22-27; Acts 21:15–23:30)
57-59	Imprisonment and legal "trial" in Caesarea (Acts 23:31–26:21)
58	Paul writes Colossians (and Ephesians?)
60–62	Arrival and imprisonment in Rome (Acts 28:15-31)
62–?	Paul's Mission in Spain (Rom 15:22-4); Paul Writes to Timothy and Titus?

The NT says nothing about Paul's death. Acts concludes without mentioning the outcome of Paul's meeting with Caesar, but Paul does mention his intent to continue the mission in Illyricum (Rom 15:19) and then to Spain, following a visit to Rome (Rom 15:22-24, 28). Most scholars suppose that the narrator of Acts knew that Paul was executed in Rome (Acts 20:22-24) but realized that mentioning it would have undermined his literary purpose to portray Paul as the triumphant successor to Jesus and the Twelve. If, however, Paul was in fact released and allowed to continue his mission in Spain until his death, then we are provided a possible provenance for his final letters to his young colleagues in distant Asia, Timothy and Titus.

Paul and Judaism. Most reconstructions of Paul's life mention his youth in Tarsus of Cilicia, his Roman citizenship, his education in Jerusalem, and his career within Judaism. This biography is especially dependent upon Acts, where he is portrayed as a Pharisaic Jew and Roman citizen from Tarsus (22:3) who persecutes the first followers of Jesus for religious reasons (8:1-3), but who is forgiven (7:60) by them and then commissioned (9:15-16) by this same Jesus as a prophetic "teacher of Israel." Yet, Paul touches only briefly on these elements from his early life, and the references serve his writings' rhetorical design (Gal 1:11-15; Phil 3:2-11; cf. Rom 9:1-5). Nevertheless, these elements may well provide important clues in orienting us to his letters.

For example, we know that Tarsus, where Paul was apparently born and raised in diaspora Judaism, was an impressive center of Hellenistic culture and mystery religions. There, Paul could easily have picked up his understanding of moral philosophy and rhetoric as well as pagan religion, which then informs his letters and frames his message. Especially for those interpreters who explore the meaning of Paul's writings against the backdrop of Greco-Roman moral and religious culture, this feature of his early life is crucial.[12]

Paul himself points us in another direction: to his life within Judaism as "a Hebrew, born to Hebrews, and as to Torah, a Pharisee" (Phil 3:5). This identity marker reflects the formative influence of Judaism on both his religious understanding that Christianity is the fulfillment of Judaism and his missionary belief that God's elect people include Gentiles, who are also called out of the world as heirs of God's promised salvation.

Certainly Paul's background in diaspora Judaism may have contributed important symbols to his understanding of the gospel.[13] Two brief examples must suffice to illustrate this influence:

1. Paul's Bible was the Septuagint (LXX), the Greek translation of the Hebrew Scriptures used in diaspora Judaism. While true to the spirit of Jewish faith, the process of translating Scripture interprets its meaning for a new readership, infusing relevant tendencies of that readership's world into the text. The grand themes of the Jewish faith, then, were refined and even redrawn by the LXX in an effort to communicate to its Hellenistic audience. For instance, the resonances of **νομός** (*nomos*), the Greek word for "law" that translates the Hebrew **תורה** (*tôrâ*, "instruction"), broadens the concept's meaning within diaspora Judaism. Thus, while the Jews of the diaspora looked to the teaching of the nomos to settle issues of religious and moral identity (= torah), they also understood the law in a more abstract and philosophical way as constituting a cosmic rule, instituted by the Creator, by which all of creation is patterned. Paul's use of "law" in his letters is multiform and reflects the variegated uses of this word in Hellenistic literature.

2. Paul's willingness to cross cultural lines in preaching the gospel (1 Corinthians 9), and all the tensions he notes in doing so (Romans 12), may well have been shaped within diaspora Judaism. Many have noted that the Jews of the diaspora were caught between two very different worlds. The dominant world was non-Jewish and syncretistic, inviting compromise and assimilation. The Jews were a minority called by God to remain separate and distinctive as a witness to truth. Conflict was inevitable for those Jews trying to live in a non-Jewish world that rewarded conformity and punished deviance. The fact that Paul was a Roman citizen from birth suggests that his family was skilled in moving between both worlds–a skill, according to Acts and his letters, that Paul learned well.

In any case, the Jewishness of Paul's theological understanding is not really altered by his conversion to Christ. The deeper logic of Paul's theology is neither shaped by Greco-Roman religious culture nor created through some profound innovation on his part. He remains Israel-oriented, a committed monotheist; he utterly rejects the dualism of his pagan culture. Further, he retains a vital interest in the doctrine of divine election, even retaining its sociological importance as a primary marker for the community's public identity. Indeed, these very interests, which are the most important to his Jewish world, are at the center of the controversies provoked during his Gentile mission.

Why, then, did his message provoke so much confusion and commotion, especially within his Jewish audience? Primarily because Paul was a "christological monotheist."[14] That is, he reworked the core symbols of his Jewish world, including its "foundational story," which celebrated God's creation, God's promised salvation, and God's Israel and torah, in radically christological terms. Because of Christ, the confession of monotheistic faith had now been expanded to "one God, one Lord" (1 Cor 8:6); and the social marker of God's Israel was the public confession that Jesus is Lord (Rom 10:9). Those who belong to the Lord Jesus are the very same members of eschatological Israel whom God will vindicate on the future "Day of the Lord" (= resurrection from the dead).

Central to this symbolic world is Israel's Scripture, which both nurtures and justifies Paul's theological understanding. The critical issue in this regard is how Scripture functioned in the writing of Paul's letters. In his use of midrash and catenae (or connected series) of Scripture to interpret his message, Paul shared the exegetical strategies of other first-century Jewish interpreters. At an even deeper level, Paul's letters may be read as "intertexts," as texts written in intended (and reflexive) conversation with earlier Scripture. Images or words that link Christian letters with OT Scripture frame a theological setting that discloses additional layers of Paul's strategy: to confirm that Gentiles are also members of the elect community prefigured by Israel's Scriptures.[15]

Besides his penultimate commitment to God's election of Israel at the beginning of salvation's history and his ultimate concern for God's vindication of righteous Israel at the consummation of salvation's history, still other elements of Paul's teaching can be traced back to his own Pharisaic heritage. Perhaps because Pharisaism was a lay movement, engaged in all matters of the town square and marketplace, Paul's practical account of Christian faith extends God's rule and grace to every part of the community's life. Even though his rejection of the "laws of purity" seems anti-Pharisaic, his teaching about eating in 1 Corinthians 8–11 and Romans 14, especially as it relates to church order, is deeply rooted in the social world of Pharisaism. On the one hand, the pattern of Christian fellowship, as demonstrated by how and what believers eat together, is the social marker of their solidarity as a people belonging to Christ. On the other hand, the same social patterns that control the community's eating habits distinguish it from the other religious communities/options. As with Pharisaic Judaism, Pauline Christianity places a religious value on meals, eating habits, and foods–a value that when not observed can cause divisions within the community and that when observed can divide those inside the community from those outside.

Paul and Jesus. These two are the most prominent figures of the NT world; thus Paul's lack of contact with the historical Jesus remains an awkward feature of his resumé. Paul seemed aware of this omission (1 Cor 15:8-11; 9:1), even defensive about it (Gal 1:11-16). On this basis, Luke's defense of Paul's authority and mission in Acts tacitly admits that Paul lacked the credentials of the original apostolic successors to Jesus (see Acts 1:21-22).

The relationship between Jesus and Paul is the subject of an old debate.[16] There are still a few who appeal to the lack of contact as evidence for a fundamental discontinuity between the two, especially regarding the ongoing role of the law within the faith community. Some even speculate as to whether Jesus or Paul is the true founder of Christianity. To be sure, generic and thematic differences between the biblical Gospels and the letters contribute to this impression of discontinuity. On the surface, it seems that Paul lacked a vital interest in the details of Jesus' life. For example, although he paid heed to the dominical message, only twice does he actually cite sayings of Jesus (1 Cor 7:10-11; 9:14); on other occasions Paul alludes to his sayings (Rom 12:14, 17; 13:7; 14:12-4; 16:19; 1 Cor 11:23-25; 13:2; 1 Thess 4:2, 15; 5:2, 13, 15), often in support of his own instruction or apostolic authority. To be sure, the parables and proverbs of Jesus, so rooted in the agrarian life of rural Palestine, would have little relevance for those living in the cities of Paul's mission. However, even in those letters where Paul might have appealed to the memory of Jesus for support, he failed to do so. His teaching included a more "vertical christology," concentrated on the moment of Jesus' death and resurrection as the climax of salvation's history. As for the other great events of the Messiah's earthly ministry, there is a deafening silence.[17]

Paul's lack of personal contact with Jesus of Nazareth and the lack of crucial details from the "life of Jesus" in his letters prompt the critical issue raised by Paul in Galatians: To what extent is there continuity between the message of Jesus and his immediate successors and the message of Paul? According to Pauline autobiography, continuity exists by virtue of his personal revelation of Jesus (christophany), both "to" him on the Damascus road (Gal 1:12; cf. 2 Cor 4:6; 5:16) and "in" him by some religious experience (Gal 1:16). S. Kim takes this feature of Paul's autobiography to mean that his personal experience of Jesus on the Damascus road, along with subsequent charismatic episodes, was a primary source of Paul's christological understanding as well as of his central claim that God's saving activity results in human transformation.[18]

There is little explicit evidence from his letters that Paul was familiar with the Gospels or even with pre-Gospel stories of Jesus, the Lord's Supper (1 Cor 10:16-17 [cf. Matt 26:27]; 11:23-26 [cf. Luke 22:14-20]), and perhaps the synoptic apocalypse (1 Thess 2:16; 4:15; 2 Thess 2:2) being important exceptions. More likely, Paul was a beneficiary of early Christian traditions or memories of Jesus' ministry from "ear" and eyewitnesses, traditions that he received from believers throughout Palestine (Jerusalem, Antioch, Syria). He sometimes mentioned these sacred traditions to his readers (1 Cor 11:2, 23; 15:1, 3; cf. Rom 6:17; 1 Thess 2:13; 2 Thess 2:15; 3:6; 1 Tim 6:3). In still other passages (e.g., Rom 3:25), Jesus tradition from the Jewish church in particular was more implicit. More critically, Paul's message was informed by the thematics of messianic monotheism, grounded in the hope that God's promise to Abraham was now fulfilled and experienced for those who trusted in the redemptive results of Jesus' messianic death. Although he modified tradition about Jesus in order to recenter the significance of the Christ-event upon the cross, the grand themes of Paul's gospel are those of the Messiah. The biblical Gospels and Pauline letters are different parts of the same theological universe.

Paul and His Mission. Most of Paul's autobiographical statements defend his apostolic status and describe the costs of his missionary work (e.g., Rom 1:1-15; 1 Corinthians 9; 2 Cor 1:12–2:17; 7:5-16; 11–12; Phil 1:12-26; 3:1-14; 1 Thessalonians 1–3). Indeed, this self-understanding obligates the interpreter to understand Paul's letters as "missionary-minded," written for newly formed congregations of converts whose faith and witness he was committed to maintaining and nurturing. Given this understanding, in recent years much has been made of the social and cultural contexts of Paul's missionary work, located as it was in several important urban centers of the early Roman Empire. There Paul's message of God's grace found a ready audience among social groups constituted by the urban poor and powerless, who perhaps responded more out of psychological than spiritual need.[19]

In this light, scholars analyze the themes of the Pauline letters as intended for a readership formed from alienated and displaced city people. They were written to aid new converts in discriminating between the morality and life-style of a true Israel, and that belonging to "this evil age." Paul's letters to the Corinthians and the Thessalonians, in particular, can be read as primarily concerned with these sorts of issues. A sociohistorical approach makes the interpreter more sensitive to those themes that address moral or religious conflict with the surrounding pagan culture or with the social institutions of urban life. For example, D. Meeks contends that the typical member of an urban congregation founded by the Pauline mission was an artisan or trader, perhaps because Paul was an artisan.[20] R. Jewett suggests that the artisan membership of the Thessalonian congregation was primarily poor, in keeping with Paul's description of the Macedonian church in 2 Cor 8:2-4. It appears that these believers lived a hand-to-mouth existence, dependent on the sometimes fickle benefaction of their wealthy patrons. Against this social background, the modern reader of the Thessalonian correspondence can better understand Paul's admonition to "work" (1 Thess 4:9-12; 2 Thess 3:6-13) as the measure of a life pleasing to God and appreciate his concluding exhortation to depend on the steadfast benefaction of their Lord (1 Thess 5:24; 2 Thess 3:5, 16).[21]

The Apostle Paul and His Readers. A final element critical to Pauline autobiography defends his role and authority as a legitimate apostle (1 Cor 15:1-11; Galatians 1–2). Since this epistolary element conforms to the conventions of Greco-Roman rhetoric, we suppose Paul's intent was to posture himself and his correspondence before his reading/hearing audience: He and, therefore, what he says have religious authority for those being addressed. Yet, the subject matter of his letter and the spiritual crisis it addressed coheres as well to the definition of this relationship between the apostle and his audience.

In recent years, those interested in constructing a critical biography of Paul have turned to other questions, primarily concerning the internal life and organization of his congregations and their interaction with their surrounding social environment and with Paul, their apostle.[22] For this work, the letters provide primary information, whether to describe the characteristics of these interactions or to analyze them using the methods of social science. To be familiar with these social contingencies is to better understand the setting in which the Pauline voice was first heard as witness to the gospel of God.

THE NON-PAULINE COLLECTION

The eight "conversations" found in the second collection of letters (Hebrews through Jude) are sufficiently different from one another to preclude any general treatment of those historical features that may group these letters into a discrete and coherent collection. Nonetheless, these conversations were shaped by the same larger circumstances that fashioned the Pauline correspondence: the political and social institutions of the Roman Empire; the moral and philosophical thematics of Hellenistic culture; and the core theological convictions of Judaism, informed and interpreted by its Torah.

These letters, however, are grouped around a single feature of their social world that may well orient the interpreter to the distinctive subject matter of the non-Pauline letters *in toto*. While both collections can be read as different responses to the theological problem of theodicy, the non-Pauline letters locate the roots of this crisis in a sociological rather than a missiological setting. The primary marks of this readership were its poverty (James),[23] its social dislocation (Hebrews), and its alienation (1 Peter)[24] within a hostile environment. The readers of the general epistles suffered because they had been marginalized as a direct result of their faith (Hebrews, 2 Peter, Jude) or because the norms and values of their faith conflicted with those of the persons in charge of the present world order (James, 1 Peter). Although the conflict in the Johannine epistles is internal to the faith community, the dissidents who have left the congregation are sharply castigated as "antichrists" and "deceivers" (1 John 2:18-29; 4:1-4), "who have gone out into the world" (2 John 7). Rather than being received hospitably into one's home (3 John), they are to be shunned as evil (2 John 10-11). In turn, the spiritual test occasioned by suffering required the maintenance of community solidarity during seasons of suffering and social conflict. The marks of God's Israel, then, were not primarily their beliefs, as was true of the Pauline collection, but their behaviors in response to economic poverty and sociopolitical powerlessness.

The theological foundation of their response was, as with Paul, a particular understanding of divine election. However, in the case of the non-Pauline collection, election was redefined not in terms of being Gentile converts but in terms of being socially marginal: God has called out the "poor" (Jas 2:5), the "pilgrim" (Hebrews 11), the "alien and stranger" (1 Pet 1:2; 2:9), the religious sectarians (1 John) of this world, for salvation. The diverse audiences of this collection together formed a community of outcasts for whom the realization of God's promise of socioeconomic and political reversal lay still in the future, in a different world order where the last and the least will be first and fulfilled. The problem of theodicy was concentrated on the apparent contradiction of the community's dual citizenship, which forced it to ask: "Which reign is real, God's or Caesar's?" Surviving the present age in right relationship with God in order to get to the next was the religious project; the community's final, not initial, justification by God was its theological aim.

The distinctive theological accents of this collection interpret the Christian community's struggle to remain faithful to their sacred traditions on many fronts when faithlessness was the more natural response. The keenest stress, then, is on an exemplary (not crucified) Christ—a stress well suited for a collection more ethical than theological in tone. God's will is embodied in Christ's faithfulness (Heb 12:1-4; Jas 2:1; 1 Pet 2:21-25; 1 John 3:11-17; 4:7-21). Further, the terms of Christ's obedient life both legitimate and illustrate the paraenetic traditions used by these writers to give concrete direction to their audiences. The moral exhortations transform the ambiguity of the current crisis into order and tradition (2 Peter/Jude). The eschatological consequences of the community's defection from the truth are envisaged in the warnings and exhortations to view Jesus as the prophetic exemplar of piety. Thus to follow or imitate him during the trials and tribulations of spiritual testing will result in the future blessings of God's promised salvation (Heb 12:25-29; Jas 2:1-13; 1 Pet 3:13-19; 2 Pet 2:17-22; 1 John 3:19-24; Jude 19-20).

Finally, the writings of the non-Pauline collection fashion the social world of a pilgrim people. Suffering and oppression represent those hardships that all pilgrims must bear on their way to the "shrine." Especially in Hebrews, much of this articulates a code of conduct that prepares a people for a pilgrimage: to break from existing ties in the world outside of Christ, to launch out on a journey toward the heavenly shrine, so to enter into the full blessing promised there by God.[25] A pilgrim stands at a distance from the norms and values by which the non-believing world lives. There is an intense desire to obey God steadfastly as a condition of enduring the journey through human existence and entering into eternal life, the chief blessing awaiting the pilgrim people at their heavenly shrine. Every decision and every action prepares for and promotes that pilgrimage to the heavenly end (Heb 10:32–12:29; Jas 1:2-4, 12; 1 Pet 1:1, 6-9; 2:11-12; 2 Pet 1:4-11).

THE WORLD WITHIN THE LETTERS: COMPOSITIONS IN LITERARY CONTEXT

Any responsible interpretation of Scripture demands consideration of the diverse literary genres and rhetorical conventions that characterize its various writings. The full meaning of any letter is not determined solely by the reconstructed history behind the text but also by the literary structure of the composition itself. The discussion of this point will concentrate on two related elements: the literary genre and the rhetorical design of the NT letter. Biblical authors crafted and communicated meaning by using conventional or recognized patterns of speech.

Written correspondence and oral conversation are closely related activities, although their similaritycan be exaggerated.[26] Not only do letters convey what the writer might say in person, but also ancient letters were written to be read aloud to an audience (see Eph 3:2-4; Rev 1:3). The oral audience of antiquity was attuned to a speech that affects the ear. As a result, letter writers crafted literary compositions for auditors by using the same techniques of public orators, who steered their audiences and shaped their common histories for their own persuasive purposes. For example, oral communication tends to be sequential, with each new idea introduced and understood by what precedes it. The integral connection of each part of the literary whole is maintained by the repetition of catchwords (or digressions), which not only underscores the composition's unity but also draws the audience to its central point.

Today's audience, constituted by silent readers rather than auditors, is more familiar with other kinds of literary markers: computer fonts and typefaces, paragraph indentations, and creative punctuation, all of which organize our reading of a written text. However, an ancient audience heard a text read and organized its subject matter according to repeated words and phrases.

Literary critics usually classify NT letters according to types of oral discourse: sermons or homilies (Hebrews, 1 John), pastoral exhortation (James, 1 Peter), classroom instruction (Romans, Ephesians), and the like. Although the message is not its medium, it certainly is true that the author's message would be lost were not his or her ideas reconstituted in a language and presented in a literary form that connected with the intended readership. In this sense, then, biblical letters are sufficiently ambiguous or elastic in meaning that their current readers, who live in far different circumstances from those to whom they were written, can still appreciate them as resources for their own theological understanding. Yet, historical questions must still be addressed. The ancient world of literature treasured the act and art of letter writing. The genre and rhetorical artistry current in the literary culture of biblical writers would naturally have informed their decisions about the medium or mode of letter writing.

Two different methods were used in writing letters. One could either write a letter personally or have it written by a skilled scribe. Several of Paul's letters hint at the use of a secretary. The secretary would not be responsible for the subject matter but would do most of the writing. For instance, most epistolary addresses name more than Paul as sender; some scholars think that Sosthenes (1 Cor 1:1) and Silvanus (1 Thess 1:1; 2 Thess 1:1) served as Paul's secretaries. The benediction to 1 Peter mentions Silvanus as its scribe (1 Pet 5:12). References to a personal signature (Gal 6:11; 2 Thess 3:17; Col 4:18) or greeting (1 Cor 16:21) may well imply that the rest was dictated; Rom 16:22 actually names Tertius as "the writer of this letter" (although a few scholars still question whether Romans 16 belongs to the "authentic" Romans letter).[27] Shorter letters, such as Philemon, were probably written by Paul alone (Phlm 19); however, longer letters, such as Romans and the Corinthian correspondence, may have required secretarial assistance. Paul's employment of different scribes to help with his correspondence may well explain the literary and linguistic differences scholars have observed between his letters.

Letters were sometimes written as literary substitutes for personal (or even "official") visits.[28] They were often written as a practical matter, because authors could not visit their congregations, even though some communities needed apostolic attention. For example, Paul's stated preference was to address a spiritual crisis directly and in person (see Rom 1:9-12), but he was not always able to do so because of imprisonment or missionary obligations. To maintain his ministry and authority in the life of a particular congregation, Paul wrote and sent letters as vehicles of his theological instruction, pastoral care, and moral counsel. These same letters, which were subsequently preserved, collected, and canonized, continue to perform a similar role and to exercise a similar authority today. That is, the letters of the NT are the authorized substitutes for apostolic personae and powers. By reading these letters, the audience of contemporary believers continues to "hear" apostolic "voices" and benefit from their instruction. In this way, the community of faith develops under the aegis of the Spirit into the "one holy catholic and apostolic church."

This theological conviction cues a final literary point: The NT letters were written as if their authors were actually speaking to their audiences. There is nothing artificial or contrived about the epistolary literature of the NT; its expected purpose was to instruct and to persuade its readers, and its intended aim was to enable those readers to make decisions that conformed to the faith. The interpreter must approach these writings as literary art, crafted according to the conventions of the ancient world, whose aim was theological understanding.

THE LETTER GENRE: THE PAULINE COLLECTION

A literary genre is a conventional pattern of written speech that intends to facilitate communication from its author to an audience living in a particular social setting. The epistolary literature of the NT comprises several genres of ancient literature.[29] During the last two centuries, archaeologists have unearthed a treasure trove of Greco-Roman papyri (including Jewish) and clay tablets of the ancient Near East. Included in these finds are thousands of letters that exhibit many of the same literary structures, conventions, and functions as the letters of the NT. Although the NT letters resist formal classification, they exhibit no real literary innovation.[30] Their authors were not literati but pastors who employed the standard epistolary conventions of their day; these writers sought to communicate specific messages, not to create an innovative literary genre.

The modern interpreter approaches the letter genre in terms of its overall literary structure, the rhetorical role of its every part, and the anticipated effect each convention exacts upon the audience. For example, how should the interpreter approach the Pauline letters as a literary genre? The letters unfold according to the simple structure of the integral parts, each of which has a specific role to perform in the effective communication of his gospel:

(1) *Greeting.* In accordance with the conventions of his literary world, Paul begins his letters by introducing himself (and cosenders or secretaries) before greeting his audience with a salutation. The purpose of such prescripts was similar to that of modern business cards, a convention of today's professional world. Business cards make introductions and help to establish relationships with potential clients. Likewise, Paul greets his readers (or auditors) in order to establish a more intimate relationship with them, thereby providing a positive setting for reading (or listening to) his message and then responding accordingly.

In Paul's letters, however, variations of this opening formula carry important theological freight. Paul intends to frame a rhetorical relationship with his first audience through the phrases he uses to introduce himself, to describe his audience, and to fashion his salutation. This relationship is usually grounded in his apostolic charisma, so that his message is received as instructive if not also normative for life and faith. Sharply put, the Pauline writings of the NT are not personal letters; they are formal "apostolic" briefs, meant to be read to the entire congregation as a word to heed and to follow.

Paul's standard salutation combines χάρις (*charis*, "grace"), an innovation on the Hellenistic salutation χαίρε (*chaire*, "greetings"), and εἰρήνη (*eirēnē*, "peace"), the greeting found in most Jewish letters. The rhetorical effect of the salutation is twofold: It addresses the audience as beneficiaries of God's universal salvation and prefaces the subject matter of the letter by the essential promise of Paul's gospel—that salvation is entered into by "grace" and "peace" with God is the result (so Rom 5:1-2).

(2) *Thanksgiving.* The second part of a Pauline letter expresses thanksgiving for the spiritual formation of the audience. In giving thanks, Paul continues the convention of Hellenistic and Jewish letter writers who offered thanks for blessings received. There are notable exceptions to this convention, however, within the Pauline corpus. In Galatians, for instance, Paul substitutes stern rebuke for expected blessing with striking effect (Gal 1:6-9); and in 2 Corinthians, a letter to another difficult congregation, Paul offers a benediction for divine comfort where one would expect to find thanksgiving for his audience (2 Cor 1:3-7)! Since there is no specific addressee, the encyclical letter Ephesians (as with 1 Peter) offers thanksgiving to God in the form of a Jewish berakah, a liturgical prayer of thanksgiving. Personal letters to well-known colleagues (1 Timothy, Titus) need not include formal thanksgiving, which is implicit in the intimate relationship between author and reader and may not serve the hortatory character of the correspondence in any case.

In most Greco-Roman letters, divine blessings were perceived as deliverance from some physical calamity or economic ruin.[31] The phraseology of the Pauline thanksgivings is quite different, echoing rather the biblical psalms. For instance, the tone of Paul's thanksgiving is worshipful, often fashioned as a prayer that perhaps could serve as a call to worship for a public reading of his letter. Paul's thanksgiving is much like a pastor's invocation at the beginning of a worship service, exalted in language and full of important theological themes that will be taken up again in the following sermon. Long sentences are often used by Paul to evoke a sense of sustained conversation with God (e.g., 1 Cor 1:4-8; Col 1:3-8, 9-11). Only in this spiritual setting can Paul's letter be heard for edification.

Important theological themes supply the substance of Pauline thanksgiving, typically articulating God's saving action in Christ. Rhetorically, these themes bring the audience immediately to the core convictions of Paul's gospel and establish the foundation for the message that follows. Paul is careful to state the practical benefits of accepting these theological convictions. Here, in the most formal and worshipful section of his letter, Paul remains a pastor seeking to nurture his flock. He does not compose his letters from a scholar's study but from that of a pastor; the concerns of his flock press upon his heart and mind. Interpreters of Pauline writings must recognize them as missionary and pastoral in motivation.

The Pauline thanksgiving often includes a prayer for the audience's spiritual formation. Paul projects an intimate, caring attitude toward his auditors. Rhetorically, this prayer fosters a positive, constructive relationship between author and audience. The prayer is also intercessory and often hints at the crisis at hand–that is, at the vital theme of the letter. The words and phrases are not "devotional musings," detached from the main body of Paul's letter. Quite deliberately, they form the basis for what Paul will say to his readers. The prayers in Pauline thanksgivings petition God to resolve the audience's spiritual crisis that has occasioned the writing of the letter.

(3) *Main Body.* Paul next addresses the difficulties that have prompted the writing of the letter, often beginning with a transitional formula or even with a statement of a thesis (e.g., Rom 1:16-18). While the most important and longest part of his letters, the main body remains resistant to formal analysis. Generally, the style of the main body depends on the audience's social location and the circumstances that occasion the letter. Typically, Paul is interested in defending or clarifying his gospel and mission, and he uses those literary devices that help to make his case.

For example, much of the main body of Romans is fashioned as a diatribe, a Greco-Roman literary genre used by philosophers in teaching their students.[32] This kind of formal literature belongs to the classroom, where the teacher imagines himself in a debate with an opponent, who raises questions or makes objections that allow the teacher to argue (and win) his case. Paul addresses his Roman readers, then, as a teacher introducing his students to the grand themes of his gospel. Yet, Paul's self-understanding as a teacher is more deeply rooted in his Pharisaic culture. Recent scholars have made much of Paul's use of Scripture in his letters, in which midrashim, or interpretations of biblical texts (whether cited or "echoed"), are incorporated into Paul's arguments both to justify a point and to clarify his intended meaning.[33]

Many other literary genres are also used in the Pauline collection to advance the apostle's message and mission. These include autobiography (e.g., 1 Thess 1:2–3:13; Gal 1:10–2:21; 2 Cor 1:12–2:17; 7:5-16; 10:7–12:13; Col 1:23–2:3); vice and virtue lists (e.g., Rom 1:29-31; 1 Cor 6:9-10; Gal 5:19-23; Col 3:5-9, 12-13; Eph 4:2-3; 1 Tim 1:9-10); household codes (Col 3:18–4:1; Eph 5:21–6:9); and portions of early Christian or Jewish hymns and creeds (e.g., Phil 2:6-11; Col 1:15-20; 1 Tim 3:16).

Most interpreters note that the main body of a Pauline letter reflects the interplay of two integral parts of Pauline preaching: the indicatives of theological instruction (kerygma) and the imperatives of moral exhortation (paraenesis). Paul's use of common moral traditions found in both Scripture and Greco-Roman philosophy is not arbitrary; indeed, it is a remarkable innovation of his letter genre. While the subject matter of his moral instruction was well-known and widely accepted in his cultural world, he adapted it to the crisis at hand to fashion an exhortation that is "a word on target." More critically, the interplay between theology and ethics accords with the deeper logic of Paul's gospel. This deeper logic claims that the acceptance of right beliefs, or what he refers to as "the obedience of faith" (Rom 1:5; 16:26), yields right behaviors as the result of participating by faith in Christ's death and resurrection (Col 1:9-10). Believers become in life what they have already become in Christ (so Rom 6:1-12). The internal structure of the main body of the Pauline letter, then, envisages this deeper logic; moral exhortation is adapted not only to his audience's particular situation but also to his gospel.

(4) *Benediction.* Letter writers in the ancient world usually added various greetings, specific instructions, and general exhortations to their readers in the benediction. Paul is no different, although he baptizes these literary conventions by adding the distinctive phrases of his Christian ministry. The Pauline benediction includes personal news (e.g., Rom 15:14-23), general exhortation (e.g., 1 Thess 5:12-28), more specific advice or greetings to individuals (e.g., 1 Cor 16:1-24), a recap of the letter (e.g., Rom 16:17-20; Gal 6:15-16), and a signature like that of modern letters (e.g., Gal 6:11; 2 Thess 3:17), all concluding with a benediction (his "good-bye"), typically a doxology (e.g., 2 Cor 13:13) or prayer (e.g., Rom 16:25-27) that extends the benefaction of divine grace upon his audience.

Except for the occasional "recap," the benediction falls outside the letter's main body, where he addresses the audience's spiritual crisis in a more direct fashion. Paul's concern is for the general well-being of Christian congregations, regardless of the more particular problems of the moment. Benedictions also provide us with a window onto the complex and collaborative character of Paul's mission and early Christian congregational life.

THE RHETORICAL DESIGN OF THE NT LETTER

Not only were NT letters composed according to a variety of contemporary literary genres, but some were deliberately composed according to the ancient rules of rhetoric. Aristotle defined *rhetoric* as the public art of discovering the best possible means of persuasion on any subject matter of importance.[34] As so defined, rhetoric is hardly glib or idle conversation. Rather, antiquity understood rhetoric as the disciplined act of speaking about the pertinent issues of the public square, which combined compelling arguments with studied conclusions in a way that informed the audience and prompted its civil action. When a NT letter is approached in terms of its rhetorical art, then what is said can no longer be separated from how it is said, since both contribute to the fuller meaning of the text.

There is, of course, a rhetorical aspect to literary genre. Each part and every convention of a Pauline letter, for example, performs a persuasive role in the conversation between its author and his audience that intends to effect not only increased understanding of the theological crisis that occasioned the letter but also proper response to the writer's admonitions. Thus the rhetorical analysis of a NT letter seeks to combine an interest in how each part fits together in its overall literary design according to the rules of ancient rhetorical theory with the flow and aim of the author's argument. The anticipated result for exegesis is a keener sense of how the content and even language of the text helps to produce a particular response from a community of its readers (or auditors).

According to G. Kennedy's influential studies of ancient rhetoric, the design of a literary composition depends on the kind of response sought.[35] Rhetoricians term "epideictic" those compositions that intend to persuade readers to change their understanding of the world–somewhat comparable to what the gospel calls "repentance"—and "deliberative" those compositions that iterate and reinforce beliefs and values already embraced—akin to what the gospel calls "faith." These are judgments an audience makes about itself. In his letters, Paul sometimes calls for a verdict about his own ministry or apostolic charisma—that is, for a judicial decision by the audience regarding the author's credentials (e.g., 2 Corinthians 10–12; Galatians 1–2).

H. D. Betz's analysis of Galatians as a composition shaped by the rules of judicial rhetoric illustrates this approach to the literary structure of a letter.[36] According to the rules of this type of persuasive speech, Paul begins his correspondence with (1) a *superscriptio* or "prescript" (Gal 1:1-5), in which he first identifies the charges brought against him by laying out the contrast: "neither from human commission nor from human authorities, but through Jesus Christ and God the Father" (Gal 1:1; cf. Gal 1:11-12). The body of his letter begins with (2) a *stasis*, or sharp transitional statement of why the letter is necessary (1:6-10), immediately followed by the extended (3) *narratio* (Gal 1:11–2:14), an autobiography that supplies the audience with all the necessary information (the "facts" of the matter) to make an informed choice. The critical (4) *propositio* (Gal 2:15-21) suggests a common ground, but then sets forth the "proposition" to be proved (2:19-21). The (5) *probatio*, or "proof," follows (Gal 3:1–4:31), which justifies Paul's proposal. This proof consists of several different kinds of evidences: experiential (Gal 3:1-5; 4:12-20), biblical (Gal 3:6-14, 19-25; 4:21-31), legal (Gal 3:15-18), and historical (from Christian tradition, Gal 3:26–4:11).

Paul concludes the main body of his argument with (6) an *exhortatio*, in which the countervailing position of his opponents is refuted in a series of exhortations that both warn and encourage the Galatian believers (Gal 5:1–6:10). Recent literary critics, more concerned with praxis than with aesthetics, are especially drawn to this feature of Pauline (and non-Pauline) rhetoric, which draws the audience's attention to the consequences of their choices. That is, in refuting his opponents in the Galatian churches, Paul is less concerned about the internal logic of his case and more concerned about the success of his arguments in securing a particular kind of communal ethos among his readers.

A (7) *peroratio*, or "postscript," concludes the entire composition (Gal 6:11-18); here the main points of the debate are summarized and sharpened. This final statement, which contrasts his opponents (Gal 6:12-13) with Paul (6:14-15), suggests that the letter could also be read as a more deliberative discourse in which Paul is seeking to persuade his readers to make a right decision about their beliefs. In most of the Pauline letters, however, these two styles of rhetoric–judicial and deliberative–coexist: What one thinks about Paul and his mission is decisive in one's decision about the faith. Paul seems to recognize well the most important point of rhetorical discourse: The decisions made about the message and the messenger are inseparable.[37]

THE WORLD IN FRONT OF THE LETTERS: CONFESSIONS IN CANONICAL CONTEXT

The NT letters are more than the literary art of particular authors or mere artifacts of ancient history. These same writings belong to the Christian Bible, and their primary purpose in this biblical canon is to inform the theological understanding of believers who hear and read Scripture as "the word of the Lord." This final section, then, will consider the importance of the epistolary writings

of the NT from a third perspective, complementary to the other two. This perspective recognizes their canonical authority as part of the church's Scripture and their theological affirmation as part of the church's normative witness to God. Together, these writings form a "cloud of witnesses" that continues to supply their current readers (the "canonical audience") with authorized testimonies to the word of God, revealed in Jesus of Nazareth, and thereby help to define and maintain Christian life and faith "to the end of the age." From its composition by different authors and editors to its canonization as one discrete part of the Christian Bible, and throughout the history of its interpretation and application by the church catholic, the letter canon serves the theological aim of transmitting a normative and empowering interpretation of God's gospel to each generation of the canonical audience. A "text-centered" interpretation of Scripture is ultimately a theological approach by which the faithful seek to understand what it means to be God's people today.

This orienting concern for Scripture's theological (rather than historical or literary) referentiality and for its ecclesial (rather than authorial or rhetorical) intent supplies the final and most critical interpretive clues for readers of the NT letters. When reading a biblical writing as Scripture, the interpreter must determine meaning in terms of the church's intent to enrich our faith in God and to nurture our understanding of God's gospel. In this sense, the canon and creed of God's people give shape and structure to the world "in front of" Scripture. Faithful readers do not lie prostrate under Scripture in mindless devotion, nor do they stand above Scripture in intellectual arrogance; rather, they bow "in front of" Scripture in order to grasp what may be seen of God's mystery and what may be heard of God's Word. In a world centered by faith in the mercies of God, Scripture is trusted and treasured; its principal readers, members of the faith community, undertake interpretation as a sacred activity performed in obedience to the faith. These core convictions, imbued by experiences of Scripture's empowering effects upon life and faith, forge the faithful interpreter's approach to the meaning of the NT letters for life and faith.

READING THE LETTERS AS SCRIPTURE

The dramatic rise of scholarly interest in the NT canon in recent years has two focal points: the historical and the hermeneutical. Historians of the biblical canon are primarily interested in its formation within early Christianity, whether as a theological construct or as a literary collection. Although these historians sometimes recognize and consider substantial theological issues, they give most of their attention to the chronological development of the canon and to the ideological concerns that guided the canonizing process. For example, such scholars typically discuss the relationship between a book's authorship and its canonization in terms of how attribution of authorship influenced the reception of a particular book, both within the earliest church and later into the biblical canon.

The key interpretive issue for the church rests less upon these historical projects and more upon a theological idea: Scripture is the church's *canon* or "rule of faith." Scripture's role as the church's rule of faith presumes its trustworthy witness to him whose incarnation ultimately norms the community's faith. Only in this christological sense can one say that Scripture supplies both the subject matter for the church's theological reflection and the theological boundaries or context within which Christian theology and ethics take shape.

This conviction regarding the contributions of Scripture combines two integral beliefs: Scripture is both a "canonical collection" of sacred writings and a sacred collection of "canonical writings." In the first case, when Scripture's final literary form is privileged as a "canonical collection" (*norma normata*, or "that which becomes the rule")–the result of the canonical process that includes and arranges certain writings–the interpretive emphasis is on a specific and limited body of sacred writings. This emphasis not only values the Bible's subject matter for theological reflection and confession, but also discerns the very ordering of Scripture's subunits as the privileged, permanent expression of an intentioned, dynamic interaction between the faithful and their written rule of faith. Such an approach into the meaning of the biblical letters is less interested in the reconstructed history behind a particular letter or in the environs that gave that text its literary and rhetorical shape. These historical and literary interests are retained, but they are located in a later period of the letters' life when the Christian Bible took its final literary shape.[38]

While various historical constructions of the canonical process have been proposed, no one is entirely clear why the various writings eventually stabilized into the Christian Bible. Certainly, one possible reason is rhetorical or even aesthetic: Over time, different communions of believers came to recognize that particular arrangements of books were more persuasive articulations of the Word of God and performed in more useful ways within that community's life and worship. Indeed, diverse arrangements of books and collections (or "canon lists") may well suggest that different theological values were held among the numerous faith communions of the early church. Eventually, use and disuse narrowed this diversity of arrangements, and a specific form of biblical literature triumphed because it facilitated or better served its intended role as Scripture for the faith community. The theological principle suggested by the canonical process is this: The final shape of the Christian Scriptures best combines and relates its subject matter to serve the church as the literary location where theological understanding is well founded and soundly framed.

In the second case, emphasis is placed on its ongoing religious function (norma normans, or "that which is the rule") in the act of interpretation that enables biblical texts to function authoritatively in shaping the theology and guiding the praxis of the church.[39] The idea of a "canonical process" is not defined by a specific historical moment or literary product as before. Rather, it draws on the entire history of the Bible's interpretation, whenever the faith community draws upon its Scriptures to "norm" its faith and life. Beginning even before biblical texts were written and continuing today, faithful interpreters contemporize the meaning of their Scriptures so that the faith community might better understand what it means to be God's people.

This canonical function antedates and explains the canonical form, even as the final form facilitates those functions the faith community intended for its canon. In the ongoing act of interpretation, biblical texts "become" canonical when different interpreters pick up the same text again and again to "comfort the afflicted or afflict the comfortable." In the hands of faithful interpreters, past and present, Scripture acquires multiple meanings with the theological aim of forming a people who worship and bear witness to the one true God. In this sense the history of the Bible's formation and interpretation settled more than its final literary shape as the church's written rule of faith. The history also evinced a type of hermeneutics that contemporizes the theological quotient of biblical teaching to give it an authoritative voice for today's community whose worship and witness is again undermined by similar theological crises. What gets picked up again and again and reread over and over by God's people are these same writings that interpret the believer's spiritual testing and resolve it in a way that strengthens faith and transforms life.

The reconstructed meaning of epistolary conversations between ancient writers and their first readers, occasioned by particular sociohistorical circumstances, is now relativized and universalized within Scripture. The letters of the NT are read as biblical confessions that bear witness to God's ongoing relationship with current readers, rather than simply as ancient conversations between authors and first audiences. They are preserved and transmitted as Scripture precisely because they promise and demonstrate the practical authority to "norm" Christian faith and guide the life of every believer who struggles to remain faithful to God in ever-changing settings. Under the aegis of God's Spirit, these epistolary compositions, formed by the literary and rhetorical conventions of the ancient world (see above), continue to communicate the gospel and persuade a people to embrace it more fully.

What follows considers the practical importance of these observations: Two properties of the canonical process, evident in the final form and placement of the letters within the NT, are Scripture's own markers that orient the canonical audience to the epistolary literature of the NT as God's Word for today.

THE FINAL FORM OF SCRIPTURE'S MULTIPLE-LETTER CANON

The two collections of letters, pluriformed in literary shape and theological substance, raise problems and possibilities similar to those facing the interpreter of the fourfold gospel of the NT. While the multiplicity of gospels has long been a topic of scholarly investigation and comment, few have considered the relationship between the NT's two corpora of letters a matter of hermeneutical value. What possible relationship does the non-Pauline collection have with the Pauline? At the very least, the sum of all their various theologies constitutes Scripture's whole epistolary witness to God. Yet, different communions privilege different witnesses, each following a "canon within the canon" in turn. For example, the Pauline collection has served Protestant believers as the primary context for theological reflection and moral guidance. This preferential option for the Pauline witness has led some to a reductionism that either reinterprets the non-Pauline letters in Pauline terms or neglects them entirely. For example, Luther at first decanonized the book of James because it seemed to communicate a gospel contrary to the one found in Galatians and Romans. Many still read James through a Pauline filter as a way to preserve its authority. Theological coherence is maintained, then, but at a cost: James is read as a "Pauline" book, distorting or denying its distinctive message.

The witness of the full canon of letters, however, is that diverse theologies are gathered together to form a community of meaning that includes the Pauline and the non-Pauline. Moreover, there is a sense in which this epistolary whole is actually better focused by disagreement than by agreement. That is, the collection's witness to the truth is better forged by the mutual criticism of its contributors, making the whole greater than the sum of its parts. Through contrasting the theologies of Paul and James, the latter canon becomes more robust than if the contributions of James were simply added to what Paul has already brought to the table. The full effect is more like the vibrant sound produced by a complement of different and sometimes dissonant voices. The critical point is that the recognition of the complementary, reflexive relationship between these two collections is absolutely strategic in their interpretation; one cannot be read in isolation from the other lest the canonical purpose of both be diminished. More specifically, the theological substance of the second collection of letters actually extends and enhances the theological setting for reading the first. These epistolary writings, whose names and sequence recall the faith of the "pillars" of the Jewish mission (Gal 2:7-9), provide an authorized apparatus of various checks and balances that prevent the distortion and finally deepen the church's understanding of the Pauline letters–and so of the full gospel.

A common christological formula in the intracanonical conversation between Pauline and non-Pauline collections illustrates this point. According to the non-Pauline book of James, the faith community is exhorted to embrace "the faith of our Lord Jesus Christ" (Jas 2:1). This formulation is similar in phraseology to Paul's claim that the coming age of God's salvation has already been inaugurated because of Christ's own faithfulness to God's redemptive will, which is most significantly expressed in Gal 3:22 ("by the faith of Jesus Christ"), Rom 3:22 ("through the faith of Jesus Christ"), and Rom 3:26 ("the one who has the faith of Jesus"; but also in Gal 2:16; Eph 3:12; Phil 1:27; 3:9; Col 2:12; and 2 Thess 2:13).

These crucial phrases are variously translated, of course, depending on how one understands the genitive Ἰησοῦ Χριστοῦ (*Iēsou Christou*). In fact, most scholars, ancient and modern, have understood this genitive construction to be "objective": The genitive noun (*Iēsou Christou*) is the recipient or object of the action implied by the verbal noun to which it stands related (πίστις *pistis*, "faith"). Virtually every modern translation of Paul's claim, therefore, is rendered, "through/by faith in Jesus Christ." Especially since the publication of R. B. Hays's influential monograph on the Pauline formula in Gal 3:22,[40] however, an increasing number of scholars understand the Pauline phrase as a "subjective" genitive: The genitive noun is the subject of the action implied by the verbal noun. Thus this phrase gives expression to the personal faith of Jesus in God—"the faith of Jesus Christ"—because of which the salvation-creating grace of God now resides in the community of Jesus' disciples. In the light of this reading, the Pauline confession of the faithfulness of Jesus is taken to underscore the singular significance of his messianic death: God's salvation-creating power was publicly disclosed in the death of Jesus, whose "act of obedient self-giving on the cross became the means by which the 'promise' of God was fulfilled."[41] The object of Jesus' faith is the faithful God, who promises to bring forth life from death.

Likewise, it makes better sense of James to understand the relevant phrase's genitive construction as subjective: To "hold to the faith of the Lord Jesus Christ" (2:1) is to follow his example by not discriminating against the poor (Jas 2:2-4), who are the elect of God and heirs of God's coming kingdom (Jas 2:5). In both texts, then, the "faith of Jesus Christ" expresses his personal faith, which is embodied in his faithful actions, whether on the cross (Paul) or in his ministry among the poor (James). In each case, Jesus' faithfulness to God's will lays claim to his lordship and is exemplary for his eschatological community.

Yet, James uses the formula for a different reason and with a different meaning. Most significant, the nature of Christ's faithfulness serves a moral rather than a soteriological interest. According to James, God's will is summed up in the "royal law" that calls the community to love its (poor and powerless) neighbors (Jas 2:8). Jesus is the messianic exemplar of faithfulness to God's law (Jas 2:8-10), which prohibits playing favorites with the rich and promises life to those who care for the poor neighbor (Jas 2:12-13). There is no messianic death in James; rather, the life of Jesus bears witness to God's coming triumph and to the ultimate vindication of true and pure religion by caring for the needs of those in distress (Jas 1:27).

These two different ways of understanding the "faith of Jesus Christ" reflect different theologies, both normative for Christian faith. Given an interest in the complementary and reflexive character of their intracanonical relationship, the interpreter is obligated to consider these different conceptions of the "faith of Jesus Christ" together. At the very least, one is compelled by the witness of James to consider the significance of the exemplary life of Jesus, and particularly his treatment of the poor, as having messianic value. The resulting balance between Jesus' life and his passion brings the NT letters into greater congruity with the NT Gospels, whose narratives all make this same point. This emphasis on the utterly faithful life of Jesus corrects a tendency in Pauline hermeneutics to concentrate on Christ's death and resurrection as singularly important. Further, the profoundly ethical nature of Jesus' faithfulness helps to form an ethical Christianity that not only is more aware of social injustice but also is obligated to reject it.

On the other hand, the faith community that places emphasis exclusively on the ethical competence of Jesus' life denies the necessity of divine grace as that which both purifies the faith community and empowers its obedient and worshipful response to God. Again, what is lost is the essentially collaborative character of biblical faith, which joins God's response of grace to a needy humanity with humanity's response of obedience to a gracious God. In this case, the "faith alone" of the Pauline witness is replaced by the "works alone" of James. A christology that bears witness to both Paul and James as two discrete, yet complementary, parts of a whole looks to Christ as prototypical of the faith and faithfulness that characterize Christian faith.

THE PLACEMENT OF THE LETTERS WITHIN SCRIPTURE

Not only is it important for the interpreter to approach the two collections of letters as partners engaged in a complementary and reflexive conversation, but it is also important to consider the intracanonical relationships between the letters and the other parts of the canonical whole. Both the placement and the titles of NT writings are properties of the canonical process; each is suggestive of the writings' respective roles within the canon and, therefore, properly orient (or reorient) the interpreter to the NT's subject matter.[42]

Quite apart from authorial intentions or the rhetorical design of individual letters, then, the final literary design of the NT canon suggests that particular units of the NT canon (Gospel, Acts, letter, Apocalypse) have particular roles to perform within the whole. In particular, the sequence of these units within the NT envisages an intentional rhetorical pattern—or "canon-logic," to use A. Outler's[43] phrase—that more effectively orients the readership to the NT's pluriform witness to God and to God's Christ. By this internal logic, readers perceive that each part of the NT has a specific role to perform, which in turn explains the rich diversity of theology, literature, and language that presents Scripture's subject matter and facilitates the performance of Scripture in nurturing the faith community's theological understanding. For example, the Gospel is placed first within the NT because its narrative of the person and work of the Messiah, when taken as a fourfold whole, provides the canonical audience with a theological and moral foundation and focal point for all that follows. And the Apocalypse is placed last because it offers a visionary conclusion to Scripture's story of God.[44]

Along with the final placement of writings and collections within the biblical canon, sometimes the title provided for the various units by the canonizing community brings to clearer focus the particular contribution of that unit to a more robust understanding of God. For example, titles were provided for anonymous compositions to locate them within authoritative traditions (e.g., the four Gospels). In the case of 1 John (and Hebrews in some translations), the title included the word "epistle," even though it follows the homily rather than the letter in literary form and original function. The intent of the added superscription is not to classify its literary genre but to clarify its function within Scripture, which approximates that of a literary letter: to instruct and encourage its faithful readers who seek theological understanding.

The titles and arrangement of writings within the NT are the results of the canonizing stage of Scripture. They shed additional light on how these compositions and collections, written centuries earlier for congregations and religious crises long since settled, may continue to bear witness to God and to God's Christ for an unknown future readership. The importance of any one biblical voice for theological understanding or ethical praxis is focused or qualified by its relationship to the other voices that constitute the whole canonical chorus. Extending this metaphor, one may even suppose that these various voices, before heard only individually or in smaller groups, became more impressive, invigorating, and even "canonical" for faith only when combined with other voices to sing their counterpunctal harmonies as the full chorus.

The Gospels and the Letters. The interpreter's interest in the relationship between the Jesus of the Gospels and the Jesus of the letters within the world of Scripture differs from that in the relationship within either historical or literary contexts. On the one hand, the difficulties of reconstructing the relationship between the historical Paul and the pre-gospel Jesus traditions of earliest Christianity are well known (see above); equally so are the difficulties of relating narrative (Gospels) and epistolary literature. On the other hand, the canonical approach to the relationship between the Gospels and the letters is guided by theological convictions envisaged by the NT's own canon-logic. In particular, the two collections of letters, written to instruct and encourage faith communities, follow the Gospels, written as narrative interpretations of Jesus' earthly life and messianic ministry. That is, even as faith communities, constituted by the current disciples of Jesus, seek to "follow after" the teaching and example of their Lord, so, too, do the letters "follow after" the Gospels in the NT canon.[45] The very order of NT collections supplies the interpreter with a visual aid that sharpens this crucial concern: The theological aim of biblical letters is to inform and thereby fashion their readers into a people whose life and faith are patterned after the Jesus of the Gospels.

This approach suggests that there is a theology for the entire letter canon that coheres around an integrated set of beliefs, a set that is not propositional but narrative in shape. That is, the narrative of the biblical Jesus provides the readers of the letters with a narrative substructure that puts all the pieces back together again. If most interpreters agree that the letters seek to relate gospel to life, then the subject matter of that gospel, within the canonical context, is provided by the fourfold gospel tradition. In this case, this coherent center of the letters (and all NT literature) is not defined by the reconstructed life of the historical Jesus but by the kerygmatic story of God's actions through Jesus told by the Gospels. This latter story is the presupposition for all the practical advice given and theological claims made by the NT letters.

Acts and the Letters. By this same canon-logic, the final placement of Acts immediately prior to the letters alerts readers to the strategic importance of Acts in providing an introduction to the letters that follow.[46] The ancient church recognized the importance of this role; a version of Acts typically circulated with early collections of the Pauline and non-Pauline letters. The production and transmission of sacred texts in antiquity was limited by size and cost; thus smaller portions of the modern NT circulated independently, in service not only of the church's budget but also of its theological agenda. In the East, for example, Acts was combined with a collection of non-Pauline letters to form a smaller, more portable manuscript called the "Apostolos,"[47] apparently in memory of Jesus' apostolic successors whose stories are told in Acts and whose names are attached to the catholic epistles.[48] In the West, the Pauline corpus was added to the collection to prove Paul's apostolic character and to vindicate the right of his letters to share canonical status with the Gospels.[49] The authors of both collections of letters are introduced and authorized by Acts; and Acts' story of the church's mission to "the end of the earth" becomes a theological primer for its readers, making them more alert to the theological subject matter of the letters that follow. Three points will help to clarify these suggestions.

First, Acts offers biographical introductions to the authors of the letters. In the canonical context, such biographies serve a theological purpose by orienting readers to the authority (religious and moral) of apostolic authors as trustworthy carriers of the word of God. This is true even though the historical accuracy of Acts' portrait of Paul and the other leaders of earliest Christianity is still keenly debated (see above). Indeed, from Scripture's perspective Acts offers its readers a theological (rather than a chronological or historical) introduction to the letters that follow. The rhetorical and moral powers of these leaders of earliest Christianity confirm and commend the importance of the letters they wrote or that stand in their apostolic traditions.

The unstoppable expansion of Christianity into the pagan world through apostolic preaching, which Acts narrates with profound optimism, underscores the anticipated result of reading and embracing what these same agents of the divine word have written. Again, the issue is not that Acts fails as a historical resource; rather, its narrative succeeds as a resource that facilitates the theological aim of the epistolary literature. In Acts' case, the writer's intention to defend Paul and his Gentile mission, which especially shapes the second half of his narrative, serves well the overarching canonical intention to introduce Paul's letter collection as theologically normative, whether or not the author had read the letters in advance of writing Acts.

Second, Acts offers readers a narrative backdrop against which they can better understand the diverse theologies that make up both collections of letters, whether those linked with Paul and his Gentile mission or those linked with the "pillars" of the Jewish mission (so Gal 2:9). Acts retains, approves, and deepens the appreciation of the theological diversity found within this epistolary witness (see Acts 15:1-21).

Modern discussions have emphasized how the "catholicizing" narrator of Acts softens the disagreements between the leaders of earliest Christianity. What is often overlooked in making this point is that the church eventually collected and canonized a Pauline corpus whose principal letters were often polemical and potentially divisive. The question is never raised as to why these letters were included in the canon of a catholic church if the aim was to shape theological uniformity. Might it not be the case that the canonizing process looked to Acts not to smooth Paul's polemical edges but to interpret them?

According to Acts, the church that claims continuity with the first apostles tolerates a theological pluralism even as the apostles did, although not without controversy and confusion. The Jerusalem synod described in Acts 15 achieves a kind of theological understanding rather than a theological consensus (see Acts 15:19-21). According to Acts, the divine revelation given to the apostles forms a "pluralizing monotheism,"[50] which in turn informs two discrete missions and appropriate proclamations, Jewish and Gentile (so Gal 2:7-10). Sharply put, Acts interprets the two collections of letters in a more sectarian fashion: The Pauline corpus reflects the gospel of the Gentile mission, while the non-Pauline collection reflects the gospel(s) of the Jewish mission. However, rather than causing division within the church, such a theological diversity is now perceived as normative and necessary for the work of a God who calls both Jews and Gentiles to be the people of God.

As a context for theological reflection, Acts forces us to interpret the letters in the light of two guiding principles. First, we should expect to find theological diversity as we move from Pauline to non-Pauline letters. Second, we should expect such a diversity to be useful in forming a single people for God. Against a critical hermeneutics that tends to select a "canon within the canon" from among the various possibilities, the Bible's own recommendation is for an interpretive strategy characterized by a mutually informing and self-correcting conversation between biblical theologies.

Third, the core theological commitments of Acts guide theological reflection upon the letters. The point is not that a theology of Acts determines or even anticipates the theological subject matter of the letters but that Acts shapes a particular perspective, an abiding practical interest that influences the interpretation of the letters. For example, one may contend that the primary theological interest of Acts is the missionary advancement of the word of God to the "end of the earth" under the aegis of the Spirit. This missionary concern then functions in theological reflection as an implicit way of thinking about and organizing the subject matter of the letters that follow. That is, a reading of the letters under the light of Acts will bring to sharper focus the identity and praxis of a missionary people who respond to the Lord's demand to be God's witness to the end of the earth. Whether or not the authorial intent of the Pauline letters is missiological, their intent in canonical context becomes missiological because the Pauline letters are interpreted in the light of the missionary Paul of Acts.

The theological orientation to the letters provided by Acts holds even for the non-Pauline letters. The audiences of the non-Pauline letters are addressed in terms of their marginal social status rather than their missionary vocation. How does the missionary perspective of Acts, then, finally inform and deepen the understanding of God's people as a faith community, the outcasts from the cultural order? In part, the response is to read the non-Pauline and Pauline letters together for a fuller understanding of mission. On the one hand, the mission of the church requires accommodation in order to spread the gospel (1 Cor 9:12b-23); on the other hand, the mission of the church must take care not to be corrupted by the values and behaviors of the world outside of Christ (Jas 1:27). This more prophetic (and complete) definition of mission, which goes out into the world yet remains unconformed to it, is confirmed by Matthew's Jesus: "I am sending you out like sheep into the midst of wolves; so be wise as serpents and innocent as doves" (Matt 10:16).

The Letters and the Apocalypse. The strategic relationship between the letters and the book of Revelation within the NT is made evident to the interpreter by the similarity of their literary structure and theological function. While its literary conventions are mainly apocalyptic (Rev 1:1) and its message is prophetic (Rev 1:3), the Apocalypse is composed by its author as an encyclical epistle, similar in form to Ephesians or 1 Peter, and written for the theological instruction of "the seven congregations of Asia" (Rev 1:4), whose communicants are at very different places of their spiritual journey (Revelation 2–3). The placement of the Apocalypse at the end of the Christian Bible envisages its role as the conclusion to Scripture's story of God. God's final triumph over death has already begun through the messianic Lamb (Revelation 5; 19—21), by whom all creation will be purified and then restored to its original intent, which is to worship God and to rule with God forever (Rev 5:9-10; 21:22-27).

Of course, the congregation's response to this great confession of Christian faith depends on its spiritual maturity. If the communicants refuse to repent of their theological immaturity or moral impurity and become "overcomers" (Rev 2:7, 11, 17, 26; 3:5, 12, 21), then the message of God's coming triumph is heard with apocalyptic terror (Rev 3:14-22). However, this same message is heard by the mature and faithful, especially in a context of suffering and spiritual testing (Rev 2:8-11; 12–13), with profound hope for their eschatological vindication (Rev 14:1-5). And these same options do not change through space and time, for "the Lord God Almighty was and is and is to come" (Rev 4:8). No less than did its first auditors, contemporary congregations approach the book of Revelation as Scripture to read and reflect upon its message of God's coming triumph, either to repent or to hope because of their fidelity to the "eternal gospel" (Rev 14:6).

This orientation to the truth of the "eternal gospel," nurtured by the Apocalypse, infuses the interpretation of the NT letters with greater power and urgency, "for the time is near" (Rev 1:3; 22:10). This is the case not because the subject matter of the letters is more finely nuanced by the canonical interplay between epistle and Apocalypse but because the principal incentive and purpose of biblical interpretation are now understood more clearly than before. The church's interpretation of the NT letters aims at obedience to their inspired instruction–obedience now excited afresh by the Apocalypse's wondrous vision of the sovereign creator's sense of justice and the slain Lamb's conquering mercy.

FOR FURTHER READING

Childs, Brevard S. *The New Testament as Canon.* Philadelphia: Fortress, 1984.

Donelson, Lewis R. *From Hebrews to Revelation: A Theological Introduction.* Louisville: Westminster/John Knox, 2000.

Doty, William G. *Letters in Primitive Christianity.* GBS. Philadelphia: Fortress, 1973.

Dunn, James D. G. *The Theology of Paul the Apostle.* Grand Rapids: Eerdmans, 1998.

Fitzmyer, Joseph, S.J. *Paul and His Theology.* 2nd ed. Englewood Cliffs, N.J.: Prentice Hall, 1989.

Hengel, Martin. *Judaism and Hellenism: Studies in Their Encounter in Palestine During the Early Hellenistic Period.* 2nd ed. Minneapolis: Fortress, 1991.

Levine, Amy-Jill and Marianne Blickenstaff, eds. *A Feminist Companion to the Deutero-Pauline Epistles.* Feminist Companion to the New Testament and Early Christian Writings 7. New York: T & T Clark, 2003.

———. *A Feminist Companion to Paul.* Feminist Companion to the New Testament and Early Christian Writings 6. New York: T & T Clark, 2004.

Levine, Amy-Jill and Maria Mayo Robbins, eds. *A Feminist Companion to the Catholic Epistles and Hebrews.* Feminist Companion to the New Testament and Early Christian Writings 8. New York: T & T Clark, 2004.

McDonald, Lee M. *The Formation of the Christian Biblical Canon.* Rev. ed. Peabody, Mass.: Hendrickson, 1995.

McNamara, Martin. *Palestinian Judaism and the New Testament.* GNS 4. Wilmington, Del.: Glazier, 1983.

Meade, David G. *Pseudonymity and Canon: An Investigation into the Relationship of Authorship and Authority in Jewish and Earliest Christian Tradition.* Grand Rapids: Eerdmans, 1986.

Neyrey, Jerome. *Paul, In Other Words: A Cultural Reading of his Letters.* Louisville: Westminster, 1990.

Porter, Stanley E. *The Pauline Canon.* Pauline Studies 1. Boston: Brill, 2004.

Stambaugh, John E., and David L Balch. *The New Testament in Its Social Environment.* LEC. Philadelphia: Westminster, 1986.

Stowers, Stanley. *Letter Writing in Greco-Roman Antiquity.* LEC. Philadelphia: Westminster, 1986.

Wall, Robert. W. "Reading the New Testament in Canonical Context." In *Hearing the New Testament: Strategies for Interpretation.* Edited by Joel B. Green. Grand Rapids: Eerdmans, 1995.

Wall, Robert W. and Eugene E. Lemcio, *The New Testament as Canon.* JSNTSup 76. Sheffield: JSOT, 1992.

ENDNOTES

1. B. Metzger, *The Canon of the New Testament* (Oxford: Clarendon, 1987) 297-99.

2. A. Deissmann, *Light from the Ancient East,* trans. L. R. M Strachan, 2nd ed. (London: Hodder & Stoughton, 1928).

3. So J. Fitzmyer, "Introduction to the NT Epistles," *NJBC* (Englewood Cliffs, N.J.: Prentice Hall, 1990) 771.

4. Beker has argued that Paul is not a systematic theologian but an interpreter of the Christian gospel who adapts the unchanging convictions of his faith ("coherence") to the ever-changing "contingencies" of his audiences. According to him, then, Paul's interpretive activity seeks to make the "abiding Word of the gospel a word on target." See C. Beker, "Recasting Pauline Theology" in *Pauline Theology,* ed. J. Bassler (Minneapolis: Fortress, 1991) 1:15.

5. N. Dahl, *Studies in Paul* (Minneapolis: Augsburg, 1977) 6.

6. Trobisch has argued that Paul edited and published his own letter collection (consisting of Romans, 1–2 Corinthians, and Galatians) for his client-friends. See D. Trobisch, *Paul's Letter Collection: Tracing the Origins* (Minneapolis: Fortress, 1994). Paul's purpose was to supply them with a literary testament shortly before his death that would respond in a normative way to a variety of controversies generated by his Gentile mission. Trobisch's provocative thesis suggests that it was Paul (and not Marcion) who first devised a "Christian canon" by which his other writings were understood and that there is a literary and theological unity to these four letters, concentrated by a set of core themes, that fixes and stabilizes the meaning of the entire corpus.

7. See D. R. MacDonald, *The Legend and the Apostle* (Philadelphia: Westminster, 1983).

8. See J. Knox, *Chapters in a Life of Paul,* rev. ed. (Altanta: Mercer University Press, 1987); R. Jewett, *Chronology of Paul's Life* (Philadelphia: Fortress, 1979); G. Luedemann, *Paul, Apostle to the Gen-*

tiles: Studies in Chronology (Philadelphia: Fortress, 1984).

9. See M. Hengel and A. Schwemer, *Paul Between Damascus and Antioch* (London: SCM, 1997).

10. See F. F. Bruce, *Paul: Apostle of the Heart Set Free* (Grand Rapids: Eerdmans, 1977); W. W. Gasque, *A History of the Interpretation of the Acts of the Apostles* (Peabody, Mass.: Hendrickson, 1989); C. Hemer, *The Book of Acts in the Setting of Hellenistic History*, WUNT 49 (Tübingen: JCB Mohr, 1989).

11. A complicating factor in this historical project is the profound difficulty of dating the most pivotal of these events with precision. For instance, Luedemann accepts the Claudius decree, which expelled Jews from Rome and is mentioned in Acts 18:2, as a chronological marker for Paul's Corinthian mission (and so dates his letters written from Corinth accordingly). However, he dates this decree from 41 CE rather than from the commonly accepted date of 49 CE. As a result, he dates Paul's Macedonian mission, which antedates the Jerusalem Council, and the Thessalonian correspondence, which was written from Corinth, in the early 40s. Even those who accept Luedemann's reconstruction of Paul's Macedonian mission from its narrative in Acts 18 and references in 1–2 Thessalonians and yet reject Luedemann's dating of Claudius's decree will, therefore, locate the Thessalonian correspondence several years later.

12. On the influence of Paul's Jewish upbringing upon his life and thought, see J. Neyrey, *Paul, In Other Words* (Louisville: Westminster, 1990).

13. In elaboration of this point, see the interesting debate on Paul's relationship with first-century Judaism: E. P. Sanders, *Paul and Palestinian Judaism* (Philadelphia: Fortress, 1977); J. D. G. Dunn, *Jesus, Paul and the Law* (Louisville: Westminster, 1990); and N. T. Wright, *The Climax of the Covenant* (Edinburgh: T & T Clark, 1991).

14. So N. T. Wright, "Putting Paul Together Again," in *Pauline Theology*, ed. J. Bassler (Minneapolis: Fortress, 1991) 1:206.

15. See R. Hays, *The Echoes of Scripture in the Letters of Paul* (New Haven: Yale University Press, 1989).

16. For a fine historical survey of this debate, see J. Barclay, "Jesus and Paul," in *Dictionary of Paul and His Letters*, ed. G Hawthorne et al. (Downers Grove, Ill.: InterVarsity, 1993) 492-98.

17. Wenham contends that Paul knew a great deal about Jesus and had access to collections of his sayings and stories. See D. Wenham, *Paul: Follower of Jesus or Founder of Christianity?* (Grand Rapids: Eerdmans, 1995). Wenham concludes that Paul adapted the tradition implicitly and creatively in his letters in order to preserve it, not to alter or "remythologize" it. The historical-critical problem in this regard is hermeneutical–that is, a determination of how Paul represented Jesus tradition in his own voice and in a new idiom for a different audience.

18. S. Kim, *The Origin of Paul's Gospel* (Grand Rapids: Eerdmans, 1982). See also A. Segal, *Paul the Convert* (New Haven: Yale University Press, 1990).

19. For this point, see W. Meeks, *The First Urban Christians: The Social World of the Apostle Paul* (New Haven: Yale University Press, 1983); A. Malherbe, *Social Aspects of Early Christianity*, 2nd ed. (Philadelphia: Fortress, 1983) 1-28.

20. See Meeks, *The First Urban Christians.* See also R. Hock, *The Social Context of Paul's Ministry: Tentmaking and Apostleship* (Philadelphia: Fortress, 1980).

21. R. Jewett, *The Thessalonian Correspondence*, FFNT (Philadelphia: Fortress, 1986).

22. See G. Theissen, *The Social Setting of Pauline Christianity* (Philadelphia: Fortress, 1982); B. Holmberg, Paul and Power (Philadelphia: Fortress, 1980), both with special interest in the congregations at Corinth.

23. So P. Maynard-Reid, *Poverty and Wealth in James* (Maryknoll, N.Y.: Orbis, 1985).

24. So J. Elliott, *A Home for the Homeless* (Philadelphia: Fortress, 1981).

25. For the "pilgrim" motif in Hebrews, see W. Johnsson, *Hebrews*, KPG (Atlanta: John Knox, 1980).

26. D. E. Aune, *The New Testament in Its Literary Environment*, LEC (Philadelphia: Westminster, 1987) 159.

27. For a defense of the integrity of Romans, see H. Gamble, *The Textual History of the Letter to the Romans*, SD 42 (Grand Rapids: Eerdmans, 1977).

28. See R. Funk, "The Apostolic Parousia: Form and Significance," in *Christian History and Interpretation*, ed. W. Farmer, C. F. D. Moule, and R. R. Neibuhr (Cambridge: Cambridge University Press, 1967) 249-68.

29. For a survey, see Aune, *The New Testament in Its Literary Environment*, 158-82.

30. For details of this conclusion, see Aune, *The New Testament in Its Literary Environment*, 183-225.

31. The best discussion of Pauline thanksgivings is P. T. O'Brien, *Introductory Thanksgivings in the Letters of Paul*, NovTSup 49 (Leiden: Brill, 1977).

32. For this point, see S. Stowers, *Letter Writing in Greco-Roman Antiquity*, LEC (Philadelphia: Westminster, 1986); for the form and function of the "main body" in Pauline letters, see J. White, *The Form and Function of the Body of the Greek Letter*, SBLDS 2 (Missoula, Mont.: Scholars Press, 1972).

33. See, for example, Hays, *The Echoes of Scripture in the Letters of Paul.*

34. Aristotle, Rhetoric 1.1.

35. G. Kennedy, *New Testament Interpretation Through Rhetorical Criticism* (Chapel Hill: University of North Carolina Press, 1984). See also his important survey, *Classical Rhetoric and Its Christian and Secular Tradition from Ancient to Modern Times* (Chapel Hill: University of North Carolina Press, 1980).

36. Betz's work has been criticized by some for trying to "pour" Galatians into a preconceived cast of judicial rhetoric, esp. the nonautobiographical sections of the book (chaps. 3–6). Longenecker, for example, contends that Paul's composition evinces a more creative and synthetic literary art that combines rhetorical conventions with those of Jewish letters and personal innovation. See R. Longenecker, *Galatians*, WBC (Dallas: Word, 1990) cix-cxiii, for a summary of criticisms against Betz and his own suggestions on the rhetorical design of Galatians.

37. Significant studies emphasizing the interpretive importance of the rhetorical design of specific non-Pauline letters include H. Attridge, *Hebrews*, Hermeneia (Philadelphia: Fortress, 1989); T. Cargal, *Restoring the Diaspora: Discursive Structure and Purpose in the Epistle of James*, SBLDS 144 (Atlanta: Scholars Press, 1993); and D. Watson, *Invention, Arrangement and Style: Rhetorical Criticism of Jude and 2 Peter*, SBLDS 104 (Atlanta: Scholars Press, 1988.

38. The most influential studies of this approach to biblical studies come from B. Childs, *Introduction to the Old Testament as Scripture* (Phliadelphia: Fortress, 1979), and *The New Testament as Canon* (Philadelphia: Fortress, 1984).

39. Sanders understands the canonical process as orchestrated by the "hermeneutics of adaptation." See the important collection of his pioneering studies in J. A. Sanders, *From Sacred Story to Sacred Text* (Philadelphia: Fortress, 1987). For a synthesis of Childs and Sanders into another model of "canonical criticism," see R. Wall and E. Lemcio, *The New Testament as Canon*, JSNTSup 76 (Sheffield: JSOT, 1992).

40. R. B. Hays, *The Faith of Jesus Christ*, SBLDS 56 (Chico, Calif.: Scholars Press, 1983).

41. R. B. Hays, *The Faith of Jesus Christ*, 175.

42. See Wall and Lemcio, *The New Testament as Canon*, 161-207.

43. A. Outler, "The Logic of Canon-making and the Tasks of Canon-criticism," in *Texts and Testaments* (W. March, ed. San Antonio, TX: Trinity University Press, 1980) pp. 263-76.

44. For this point, see Wall and Lemcio, *The New Testament as Canon*, 274-98.

45. So P. Achtemeier, "Epilogue: The New Testament Becomes Normative," in H. C. Kee, *Understanding the New Testament*, 4th ed. (New York: Prentice-Hall, 1983) 367-86.

46. See R. W. Wall, "Acts," in *The New Interpreter's Bible*, 12 vols. (Nashville: Abingdon, 1994–2002),10:1-32, and in this volume.

47. K. Aland and B. Aland, *The Text of the New Testament* (Grand Rapids: Eerdmans, 1987) 49-50.

48. D. Trobisch, *Paul's Letter* Collection (Minneapolis: Fortress, 1994) 10.

49. See B. Metzger, *The Canon of the New Testament* (Oxford: Clarendon, 1987) 257-58. E. Goodspeed, now followed by others, hypothesized that an early canon of Paul's letters, mentioned in 2 Pet 3:15-16, was produced and in circulation by the end of the first century. Goodspeed speculated that the production of this proto-canon was prompted by the publication of the book of Acts, whose story of Paul rekindled interest in his literary work. There is no evidence to support Goodspeed's thesis; it rests on the perception that a literary relationship exists between the book of Acts and the letters of Paul. In my view, such a perception became possible only later during the canonical stage of the NT, when the book of Acts and the letters were bound together for the first time in the great uncials of the ancient church.

50. See J. A. Sanders, *Canon and Community* (Philadelphia: Fortress, 1984) 46-68.

The Letter to the Romans

N. T. WRIGHT

It has become customary to approach a biblical book by asking when, where, why, and by whom it was written and then, as a second stage, what it actually says. Some of these initial questions, fortunately, are not controversial in the case of Romans; nobody doubts that Paul wrote it in the middle to late 50s of the first century, from Corinth or somewhere nearby, while planning his final voyage to Jerusalem with the intention of going on thereafter to Rome and thence to Spain. But the remaining question, "Why?" has proved remarkably difficult. Romans stands as a reminder that "why" and "what" are more organically related than we have sometimes liked to think. Theories about why Paul wanted to write this letter to this church at this moment must remain in constant dialogue with the complex discussion of what the letter itself actually says. As in other disciplines, the greatest strengths of a hypothesis or theory are to make sense of the data, to do so within an appropriately simple overall design, and to shed light on other areas of cognate research. These large aims are in view in what follows.

THE SHAPE AND THEME OF ROMANS

It is no good picking out a few favorite lines from Romans and hoping from them to understand the whole book. One might as well try to get the feel of a Beethoven symphony by humming over half a dozen bars from different movements. Romans is, indeed, a symphonic composition: Themes are stated and developed (often in counterpoint with each other), recapitulated in different keys, anticipated in previous movements and echoed in subsequent ones. Although the demands of critical interpretation mean that the letter is often divided into different sections, we should not thereby be misled into supposing that each section is simply "about" one particular topic. That is not how Paul wrote, at least not here. He was far more likely, in individual sentences, paragraphs, and sections, to state a point in a condensed fashion and then steadily to unpack it, in the manner of someone unfolding a map stage by stage so that each new piece offers both a fresh vision and a sense of having been contained within what had gone before. At almost no point in this letter does he offer detached reflections on isolated "topics" (13:1-7 is perhaps an exception, which is one reason, though not the main one, why some have suggested that it may be an interpolation). Although Romans, written within the general Hellenistic culture of the Greco-Roman world, shares some rhetorical features with other letters of the time and place, it is impossible either to pigeonhole it within a particular genre or to use such possible parallels to infer what the letter is about independent of full-scale consideration of its argument. We must follow the sequence of thought, the inner logic, of the whole work.

The easiest thing to determine about Romans is its basic shape. Its four sections emerge clearly: chaps. 1-4, 5-8, 9-11, and 12-16. From time to time, impressed by the way in which chap. 5 draws out and in a way completes the thought of chaps. 1-4, some writers have suggested that the key break occurs between chaps. 5 and 6 rather than between 4 and 5;[1] but most are now content with the outline suggested, not least since it is clear that the opening of chap. 5 states in summary form the themes that are then developed through to the end of chap. 8. In any case, to note the divisions is not to say that Paul is doing more than rounding off one train of thought before proceeding to a closely cognate, and logically consecutive, idea. As we shall see, the most abrupt and decisive breaks—those at the ends of chaps. 8 and 11—by no means indicate that he is now going to write "about" something else altogether. Attempts to impose a formal structure on the letter are either trivial (e.g., pointing out that the opening of chap. 1 functions as the "Greeting" and 15:14-16:27 as the "Conclusion") or tendentious (e.g., suggesting that 1:18-11:36 is the "body of the letter," thereby implying that chaps. 12–16 are a mere exhortatory postscript).

In fact, to see how the different parts of the letter hang together and to understand why Paul wanted to say just this at just this moment to these people, the most important thing to do is to grasp the main theme of the letter and to see why it was important to first-century Jews in general, to Paul in particular, and to him in this setting most specifically.

"God's Righteousness." It is not difficult to discover the main theme of the letter. "God's gospel unveils God's righteousness": That, in effect, is Paul's own summary in 1:16-17, and the letter does, indeed, unpack this dense statement. Unfortunately, though, even this apparently simple sentence is controversial, and we must clarify what is meant and justify, at least preliminarily, the decision to treat the passage, and the letter, in this way. As often in Paul's writings, to understand one key phrase we need to draw on a range of evidence and pick our way through a minefield of arguments. Before we can even address the question of why Paul wrote this particular letter, we must examine the broader question of why a Jew like him would be concerned with this overarching issue.

"God's Righteousness" in Paul's Judaism: Covenant, Lawcourt, Apocalyptic. The phrase "the righteousness of God" δικαιοσύνη θεοῦ *dikaiosynē theou*) summed up sharply and conveniently, for a first-century Jew such as Paul, the expectation that the God of Israel, often referred to in the Hebrew Scriptures by the name YHWH, would be faithful to the promises made to the patriarchs. Many Jews of Paul's day saw Israel's story, including the biblical story but bringing it up to their own day, as a story still in search of a conclusion—a conclusion to be determined by the faithfulness of their God. As long as Israel remained under the rule of pagans, the great promises made by this God to the patriarchs, and through the prophets, had still not been fulfilled.

Thus, although the Babylonian exile had obviously come to a literal end some centuries before, the promises made at the time—promises of a glorious restoration of the nation, the Temple, and the whole Jewish way of life—were widely regarded as still awaiting complete fulfillment.[2] Loyal Jews living under the various post-Babylonian powers (Persia, Greece, Egypt, Syria, and finally Rome) continued to tell the whole story of Israel in terms of promises made to the patriarchs; of an early golden age under David and Solomon; of rebellion, decline, and exile; of a long period of waiting for restoration; and of the eventual new day of liberation that would dawn in God's good time. They believed that YHWH had entered into covenant with them to do all this; paradoxically, the exile was itself, as Jeremiah, Daniel, and others had insisted, part of the covenant, since it was the result of Israel's disobedience. But their God would remain loyal to the covenant, and this loyalty would result in the great day of liberation coming to birth at last.[3] The phrase that captures this whole train of thought, occurring in various forms in the Scriptures and post-biblical writings, is "God's righteousness," in the sense of God's loyalty to the covenant with Israel (see, e.g., Ps 33:4; Isaiah 40–55; Jer 32:41; Lam 3:23; Hos 2:20). The overtones of the phrase thus bring its semantic range very near to another great biblical theme, that of God's sure and steadfast covenant love for Israel—a point of considerable importance for understanding Romans, as we shall see.

Never leaving behind this covenantal meaning, the word "righteousness" is also shaped by the Second Temple Jewish setting of the lawcourt. In the lawcourt as envisaged in the Old Testament, all cases were considered "civil" rather than "criminal"; accuser and defendant pleaded their causes before a judge. "Righteousness" was the status of the successful party when the case had been decided; "acquitted" does not quite catch this, since that term applies only to the successful defendant, whereas if the accusation was upheld the accuser would be "righteous." "Vindicated" is thus more appropriate. The word is not basically to do with morality or behavior, but rather with status in the eyes of the court—even though, once someone had been vindicated, the word "righteous" would thus as it were work backward, coming to denote not only the legal status at the end of the trial but also the behavior that had occasioned this status.[4]

The word "righteousness" applied not only to the accuser or defendant; it also denoted the appropriate activity of the judge. His duty was clear: to be impartial, to uphold the law, to punish wrongdoing, and to defend those who, like the orphan and the widow, had nobody else to defend them. Thus the "righteousness" of the judge, on the one hand, and of the parties in the case, on the other hand, are very different things. Neither has anything directly to do with the general moral behavior or virtue of the persons concerned.

Covenant and lawcourt are far more closely linked than often imagined. Behind both categories there stands a fundamental Jewish self-perception, which, if we grasp it, will enable us to understand things Paul holds together in many passages in Romans, but which interpreters have consistently separated. Through many and various expressions of covenant theology in the biblical and post-biblical periods, a theme emerges that, though by no means central in all Second Temple Judaism, has a claim to represent a deep-rooted and biblical viewpoint. It can be stated thus: The covenant between God and Israel was established in the first place in order to deal with the problem of the world as a whole. Or, as one rabbi put it, God decided to make Adam first, knowing that if he went to the bad God would send Abraham to sort things out.[5] The covenant, in other words, was established so that the creator God could rescue the creation from evil, corruption, and disintegration and in particular could rescue humans from sin and death.

In biblical thought, sin and evil are seen in terms of injustice—that is, of a fracturing of the social and human fabric. What is required, therefore, is that justice be done, not so much in the punitive sense that phrase often carries (though punishment comes into it), but in the fuller sense of setting to rights that which is out of joint, restoring things as they should be. Insofar, then, as God's covenant with Israel was designed, at the large scale, to address the problem of human sin and the failure of creation as a whole to be what its creator had intended it to be, the covenant was the means of bringing God's justice to the whole world. Since "justice" and "righteousness" (δικαιοσύνη *dikaiosynē*) and their cognates, translate the same Hebrew and Greek originals, we discover that God's righteousness, seen in terms of covenant faithfulness and through the image of the lawcourt, was to be the instrument of putting the world to rights—of what we might call cosmic restorative justice.

The images of covenant and lawcourt thus draw together, within one complex range of imagery, a familiar Second Temple perception of the Jews' own story in relation to the rest of the world. Many Jewish writings of this period tell the story of Israel and the pagan nations in terms of a great cosmic lawsuit: When the psalmists beg God to vindicate them against their adversaries, they are expressing a characteristic standpoint (e.g., Psalm 143). The pagan nations are oppressing Israel; whether they are thought of as accusers and Israel as a defendant or whether Israel is accusing the pagans of wrong-doing is unimportant. YHWH is not simply Israel's God, but the creator of the whole world and its judge; as such, YHWH is under an obligation to set things right, not least to vindicate the oppressed. True, there are some biblical passages in which YHWH is Israel's adversary at law; but, although Paul recognizes this as a theoretical and problematic possibility, his argument sticks to the more usual conception. YHWH is the judge; the nations that make war upon Israel are to be tried and condemned; Israel is to be vindicated. This scene is classically portrayed in the seventh chapter of the book of Daniel.

It takes only a little reflection, and a little acquaintance with the Jewish history and literature of Paul's period, to see that a tension or conflict could arise between the covenantal and lawcourt meanings of "righteousness." YHWH was supposed to come to Israel's rescue because of the covenant obligations between them; but YHWH was also the judge in the cosmic court, committed to judging justly between Israel and the nations and to establishing an appropriately just rule over the whole world. Is Israel also guilty? What will YHWH do then?[6] That was a puzzle for many Jews in Paul's world, and we may suppose it had been so for Paul as well; as a zealous Pharisee (his own self-description; see Gal 1:13-14; Phil 3:6), he must have longed to see God's righteousness revealed against wicked pagans and renegade Jews alike, vindicating covenant-faithful Jews like him. Although recent scholars have emphasized that there is no evidence for the pre-Christian Paul suffering from a bad or troubled conscience in the post-Augustinian sense, we must insist that there is every reason to suppose that he agonized over the fate of Israel, longing for YHWH to act decisively in history, but uncomfortably aware that if this were to happen many Jews would face condemnation along with Gentiles.

All this brings into view a final dimension of the phrase "God's righteousness." Precisely because the term evoked covenant loyalty, on the one hand, and commitment to putting the whole world to rights, on the other, it was perhaps inevitable that Jews who longed for all this to happen would come to describe it in what we now call "apocalyptic" language. We need to be clear, however, what we mean by this. In common with many scholars, I use the term "apocalyptic" to denote not so much a state of mind or a set of beliefs about the future, but a way of writing that uses highly charged and coded metaphors to invest space-time reality with its cosmic or theological significance. "The stars will not give their light, and the sun and the moon will be darkened" (Isa 13:10); what Isaiah had in mind was the destruction of Babylon. "Four beasts will emerge from the sea"; what Daniel had in mind was the rise of great empires. "One like a son of man will come to the Ancient of Days"; what Daniel had in mind was "the saints of the most high" receiving the kingdom (Daniel 7). Even so, "God's righteousness will be revealed" was a coded way of saying that God would at last act within history to vindicate Israel. The word for "is revealed" in Rom 1:17 is ἀποκαλύπτεται (*apokalyptetai*), suggesting precisely, within the first-century Jewish world, the final unveiling within history of the secret plan that Israel's God had all along been hatching.

However, just because apocalyptic language was not designed to denote literal cosmic events (the collapse of the space-time universe, for instance), that does not mean that first-century Jews did not suppose that their God would act suddenly and swiftly to bring about these long-delayed purposes. On the contrary, as the night grew darker, as pagan power increased, and as disloyalty within Israel itself became more rife, Jews like Paul must have prayed and longed for actual space-time events that would demonstrate beyond any doubt that Israel's God was the creator and judge of all the world. Through God's actions on behalf of Israel, the world would see the truth for which it had longed, the justice for which it had striven. Since this expectation of a radically new event breaking into history is in any case what some mean by "apocalyptic," we can assert that "God's righteousness" is to be understood within a framework of thought in which "covenant," "lawcourt," and "apocalyptic" language and thought forms are joined together in mutual compatibility.

"God's Righteousness" as Paul's Christian Question. Paul's world of thought was a variation on the Second Temple Jewish worldview. However much his encounter with the risen Jesus on the road to Damascus challenged and changed him, and however much he saw himself as "the apostle to the Gentiles," he still thought like a Jew and, most important, regarded his own Jewishness as significant. He quickly came to regard the events of Jesus' death and resurrection as the apocalyptic moment for which he and others had longed, and he rethought his previous way of viewing the story of Israel and the world as a result.

This can be seen precisely in Paul's vocation to be "the apostle to the Gentiles," a theme of considerable significance for Romans. Paul did not take the message of Jesus the Messiah to the Gentiles out of mere frustration that his fellow Jews had refused it, as a kind of displacement activity, but rather out of the conviction that, if God's purposes for Israel had indeed now been fulfilled, it was time for the Gentiles to come in. As becomes increasingly clear, his Gentile mission was an eschatological activity—that is, a task to be undertaken once God had acted climactically and decisively within history. It was a key feature of the new age that had now dawned, part of Paul's sense that God's future had arrived in the present, in the person and achievement of Jesus and the power of the Spirit. Although Paul clearly believed that there was a further and final event still to come, which he describes variously at different points in his writings, the great promised "end" had already begun to happen (see particularly 1 Cor 15:20-28).

This, of course, forced him to reconsider what it was that Israel's God had promised. If this was how the promises had been fulfilled, had God suffered a change of mind? Or had Israel misunderstood God's intentions? Jesus' death and resurrection, seen as the messianic events through which Israel's God had brought the covenant story to its unexpected climax, functioned for Paul not unlike the way the fall of Jerusalem functioned for the author of 4 Ezra: as the catalyst for a serious rethinking of God's promises and intentions, God's covenant faithfulness. Paul's point, to which he stuck like a leech throughout his different debates, was that Israel's God had been true to the covenant and the promises. Paul resisted all tendencies to move toward what would later be called Marcionism.[7]

This notion emerges particularly in Paul's view of the Torah, the Jewish law. Paul's fundamental insights here, which have earned him much criticism from his fellow Jews from that day to this, are (1) to uncouple the Mosaic law from the Abrahamic covenant and thus (2) to regard the Abrahamic covenant as fulfilled "apart from the law" (3:21); (3) to see the Torah as applying to Jews and Jews only, and hence not being relevant to the eschatological period when the Gentiles were coming in to God's people; (4) to see the Torah as intensifying the problem of Adam's sin for those who were "under the Torah," and thus as something from which its adherents needed to be freed; and (5) to claim, nevertheless, that the Torah had been given by God, had performed the paradoxical tasks assigned to it, and was now strangely fulfilled in the creation of the new people of God in Christ and by the Spirit. Romans makes a substantial contribution to this complex but coherent picture.

Paul thus stuck to, and argued at length for, a view of what God had done in Jesus the Messiah according to which these events were to be seen as the fulfillment of what God had promised to the patriarchs. It was, of course, a sudden and surprising fulfillment, overturning cherished expectations, breaking in unexpectedly upon the worldview that Paul himself had cherished. Recent debates have highlighted the need to stress both the continuity, in Paul's mind, between his gospel and that which had gone before in Judaism and the discontinuity, the sense of radical newness, of a divine purpose suddenly and shockingly unveiled. To soft-pedal either of these strong points is to miss the inner tension and dynamic of Paul's thought. It is, in particular, to miss the peculiar force and glory of the letter to the Romans.

"God's Righteousness" as the Theme of Romans. Romans has suffered for centuries from being made to produce vital statements on questions it was not written to answer. All that has been said so far by way of historical and theological introduction will seem strange to those traditions of reading the letter that assume its central question to be that of Martin Luther: "How can I find a gracious God?" If we start there, as many commentaries will reveal, Paul's discussion of Israel and its Torah either takes second place or, worse, is relegated to a more abstract and generalized discussion of the sin and salvation of humans in general, in which the question of Israel's fate is essentially a side issue.[8] Within such a reading, it has been common to highlight the doctrine of "justification by faith," in which humans must realize their inability to make themselves "righteous" and must instead trust God's action in Christ, because of which they will be reckoned as "righteous" despite not having obeyed "the law"—that is, a general or universal moral code.

This "righteousness," the status now enjoyed by God's people in Christ, is described in Phil 3:9 as "a righteousness from God [ἡ ἐκ θεοῦ δικαιοσύνη *hē ek theou dikaiosynē*]," from which many have suggested that this status, too, is what is referred to in Rom 1:17 and elsewhere as the *dikaiosynē theou*, "the righteousness of God."[9] Although etymologically possible, this is historically very unlikely. When the latter phrase occurs in biblical and postbiblical Jewish texts, it always refers to God's own righteousness, not to the status people have from God; and Jewish discussions of "God's righteousness" in this sense show close parallels with Paul's arguments in Romans (obvious passages include Deut 33:21; Judg 5:11; 1 Sam 12:7; Neh 9:8; Pss 45:4; 72:1-4; 103:6; Isaiah 40—55 [e.g., 41:10; 45:13; 46:12-13]; Dan 9:7-9, 14, 16; Mic 6:5; Wis 5:18; *Ps Sol.* 1:10-15; 2 Bar 44:4; 78:5; 4 Ezra 7:17-25; 8:36; 10:16; 14:32; *TDan* 6:10; 1QS 10:25-6; 11:12; 1QM 4:6).

In particular, the flow of thought through the letter as a whole makes far more sense if we understand the statement of the theme in 1:17 as being about God and God's covenant faithfulness and justice, rather than simply about "justification."[10] It brings into focus chapters 9–11, not as an appendix to a more general treatment of sin and salvation, but as the intended major climax of the whole letter; and it allows for the significance of 15:1-13 as a final summing up of the subject. Within this larger theme, there is still all the room required for that which other readings have traditionally seen as the major subject—namely, the justification and salvation of individual human beings. But in this letter at least (remembering again that this is not, after all, a systematic theology but a letter addressed to a particular situation), these vital and highly important topics are held within a larger discussion. Paul's aim, it seems, is to explain to the Roman church what God has been up to and where they might belong on the map of these purposes.

Accustomed as we are to translating *dikaiosynē* as "righteousness," we should recognize from this account that the other obvious meaning of the word, "justice," is not far away. The sense of covenant faithfulness and the sense of things being put to rights, held apart within both the Reformation and the Enlightenment as "theology and ethics" or "salvation and politics," were not far removed in the mind of a Jew like Paul. Just as the Messiah was destined to be Lord of the world, so also, and for the same reasons, God's covenant with Israel had always been intended as the means of putting God's world to rights.[11] When, therefore, God's righteousness was unveiled, the effect would be precisely that the world would receive justice—that rich, restorative, much-to-be-longed-for justice of which the psalmists had spoken with such feeling (e.g., Pss 67:4; 82:8). Even a quick skim through Romans ought to reveal that this is indeed what Paul was talking about.

But we need to remind ourselves to whom Paul's great letter was sent. Looming up behind the various discussions of why Romans was written is an issue not usually noticed. Paul was coming to Rome with the gospel message of Jesus the Jewish Messiah, the Lord of the world, claiming that, through this message, God's justice was unveiled once and for all. Rome prided itself on being, as it were, the capital of justice, the source from which justice would flow throughout the world. The Roman goddess Iustitia, like the Caesar cult itself, was a comparative novelty in Paul's world; the temple to Iustitia was established on January 8, 13 CE, and Iustitia was among the virtues celebrated by Augustus's famous *clipeus virtutis*, the golden shield set up in the Senate house and inscribed with the emperor's virtues (27 BCE). So close is the link between the new imperial regime and the virtue Iustitia that this goddess sometimes acquires the title "Augusta."[12] So, without losing any of its deep-rooted Jewish meanings of the covenant faithfulness of the creator God, Paul's declaration that the gospel of King Jesus reveals God's *dikaiosynē* must also be read as a deliberate challenge to the imperial pretension. If it is justice you want, he implies, you will find it, but not in the εὐαγγέλιον (*euangelion*) that announces Caesar as Lord, but in the *euangelion* of Jesus.[13] The rest of Romans will show that this meaning is indeed in Paul's mind at point after point.

Nor is this meaning an indication that Paul is, as it were, shuttling to and fro between "Jewish" and "Gentile" contexts of meaning. Part of the whole point, for him, of the Jewish claim to be the covenant people of God was that the divine purpose for the whole creation would be revealed through Israel. In other words, when God at last fulfilled the covenant, the Gentile world would see, unveiled, what its own life was about. Applied to Rome, this meant that the very Jewish, very biblically based, revelation of the divine righteousness/justice was necessarily at the same time the revelation of the true Iustitia, that which really did accomplish what Caesar's Iustitia had claimed to do–namely, the putting to rights of the entire creation. We have only to think for a moment of Isaiah 40-55 to see how similar the train of thought is: Israel's God will reveal righteousness and salvation, confronting pagan empire as the sovereign creator and rescuing the covenant people in the process.

We may, therefore, offer the following highly compressed summary account of the flow of thought in the letter, which gradually unpacks the summary statement of the introduction (1:1-17).

Chapters 1–4: God's gospel unveils the fact that in the Messiah, Jesus of Nazareth, the God of Israel has been true to the covenant established with Abraham and has thereby brought saving order to the whole world. In the face of a world in rebellion and a chosen people unfaithful to their commission, God has, through the surrogate faithfulness of Jesus the Messiah, created a worldwide—that is, a Jewish and Gentile—family for Abraham, marked out by the covenant sign of faith.

Chapters 5–8: God has thereby done what the covenant was set up to do: to address and solve the problem expressed in biblical terms as the sin of Adam. In the Messiah, Jesus, God has done for this new people what was done for Israel of old in fulfillment of the promise to Abraham: Redeemed from the Egypt of enslavement to sin, they are led through the wilderness of the present life by the Spirit (not by the Torah), and they look forward to the inheritance, which will consist of the entire redeemed creation. This is how the creator will finally put the whole world to rights. All this is the result of God's astonishing, unchanging, self-giving covenant love expressed completely and finally in the death of Jesus.

Chapters 9–11: This section highlights the peculiar tragedy of the gospel's revelation of God's righteousness—namely, the ironic failure of Israel to believe in the Messiah. This, too, however, turns out to be held within the strange purposes of God, whereby Israel's fall, acting out on a grand scale the death of Jesus, is the means by which salvation can extend to the whole world. This cannot mean that Jews themselves are thereby forever debarred from participating in the covenant blessing; Paul himself is a counter-example, and God desires that even now, by recognizing that it is indeed their promised blessings that the Gentiles are enjoying, more of Paul's fellow Jews will come to share in new covenant membership. Gentile Christians, therefore, are warned severely against anti-Jewish arrogance. The section ends with a paean of praise for the strange but glorious purposes of God.

Chapters 12–16: The community that is created by this gospel must live as the true, renewed humanity, in its internal and external life. In particular, it must reflect God's intention that Jew and Gentile come together as one worshiping body in Christ. Paul's own plans are bent to this end, and his greetings to different groups in the Roman church may indicate his desire to bring together disparate groups in common worship and mission. How then may we understand the letter's situation, and how does the shape and detailed content of the letter address it?

THE HISTORICAL OCCASION FOR ROMANS

The letter appears to have two main "situational" aims that surface in the great climactic passages 11:11-32 and 15:7-13. Each has in view the relationship between Jews and Gentiles; the former, however, addresses Christian Gentiles who are faced with non-Christian Jews, and the latter addresses a community in which Christian Gentiles and Christian Jews find themselves in uneasy coexistence. Although the details remain unclear, it is certain that a large proportion of Rome's substantial Jewish population had to leave the city in the late 40s CE following rioting that may have resulted from early Christian preaching among the Jewish community in Rome.[14] The expulsion edict came from the Emperor Claudius, after whose death in 54 the new emperor, Nero, rescinded his decrees, making it possible for the expelled Jews to return. This historical sequence produces a situation into which Romans fits like a glove.

Consider, on the one hand, the position of Gentile Christians *vis-à-vis* non-Christian Jews. The Roman anti-Jewish sentiment, for which there is abundant evidence in late antiquity, would create a context in which many Romans would be glad to see the Jews gone and sorry to see them return.[15] How easy, then, would it be for the Gentile Christians who remained in Rome through the early 50s to imagine that God had somehow endorsed, at the theological level, what Caesar had enacted at the political level and that God had in fact written the hated Jews out of the covenant altogether. How easy, also, when the Jews returned to take up their property and positions in society, to suppose that, though the new faith would spread to include other Gentiles, there was no point in attempting to win over any more Jews.

But Paul was coming to Rome with a gospel that was "God's power for salvation to the Jew first and also to the Greek" (1:16). If the Roman church were to accept his gospel, and indeed to support him in his missionary intention to go on from Rome to Spain, it was vital for them to realize that, even as the apostle to the Gentiles, he remained under obligation to his fellow Jews as well. Paul's travel plans in chap. 15 are thus woven into the same picture: Having been undermined by the apparent failure of his earlier home base in Antioch to support him in his practice of incorporating believing Gentiles into the same social structure as believing Jews (see Gal 2:11-21), he was determined that in the western Mediterranean he was going to make things clear from the start.

Consider, on the other hand, the position of Christian Jews and Christian Gentiles in relation to them. Paul will have known of some Jewish Christians who had returned to Rome and who, alongside Gentile cobelievers, would now be facing the difficult question of how to live together as one family with those who cherished very different cultural traditions, not least food taboos. Paul knows that this will not be solved overnight and stresses instead a doctrine of *adiaphora:* There are some practical things over which Christians can legitimately disagree, and they should not impair common worship. Underneath it all is Paul's desire that the Scriptures should be fulfilled: "Rejoice, you Gentiles, with God's people!" (15:10, quoting Deut 32:43).

Romans 9–11 and 12–16 thus are explicable in terms of the double situation of the Roman church and Paul's agendas in addressing them. Why, then, does he write chaps. 1–8? Are they just an extended introduction, before Paul reaches his real point?

By no means. If he is to address the deep-rooted problems of the interrelationship between Jews and Gentiles within God's purposes, Paul must go down to those deep roots themselves, to the foundations of Jewish and Christian thinking: to creation and fall, covenant and Torah, to Israel's covenant failure and God's covenant faithfulness. He must show how the death and resurrection of Jesus, the basic announcement of "the gospel," are God's solution to the complex problems of Israel and the world and how these events have called into existence a people, composed of Jew and Gentile alike, led by God's Spirit and defined not by Torah but by faith, in whom all the promises of God have come true. Only so can his hearers sense the poignant tragedy of Israel's situation in Romans 9 and so move toward the main thrust of the letter. Only so can they appreciate the subtle logic of the argument that he then mounts. And only so can they be equipped for the larger questions that hover in the background—questions of the relation of Jesus' new empire with that of Caesar, of the justice of God facing the justice of Rome.

At the same time, the chapters in which he lays the foundation for his specific arguments can stand almost on their own as a statement of what God has done in the Messiah for the whole world. Here we must be careful. Romans is a tightly knit, coherent whole with an inner logic that affects every word and sentence. But the arguments of chaps. 1–4, on the one hand, and chaps. 5–8, on the other, have their own integrity. This is perhaps particularly true of chaps. 5–8, with their christological refrains tolling like a great bell at the end of almost every section. Here, if anywhere, Paul is clearly making Jesus the lens through which one may see the saving plan of God working its way out. At the same time, one must quickly add that it is precisely this section, for just this reason, that sets up the argument of chaps. 9–11. It is not simply that, having written chaps. 1–8, he finds he has to go on to 9–11; it is just as much that, because he wants to write chaps. 9–11, he finds he must write 1–8 in this way. Thus in key passages in Romans 1–8, Paul seems deliberately to set up problems and questions that he then leaves hanging in the air, only to resume them in chaps. 9–11.

FOR FURTHER READING

Commentaries:

Bryan, Christopher. *A Preface to Romans: Notes on the Epistle in Its Literary and Cultural Setting.* Oxford: Oxford University Press, 2000.

Byrne, Brendan. *Romans.* SP 6. Collegeville, Minn.: Liturgical, 1996.

Cranfield, C. E. B. *A Critical and Exegetical Commentary on the Epistle to the Romans.* ICC. 2 vols. Edinburgh: T & T Clark, 1975, 1979.

Dunn, James D. G. *Romans 1–8* and *Romans 9–16.* WBC 38A and 38B. Dallas: Word, 1988.

Fitzmyer, Joseph A. *Romans.* AB 33. Garden City, N.Y.: Doubleday, 1993.

Käsemann, Ernst. *Commentary on Romans.* Translated by Geoffrey W. Bromiley. London: SCM, 1980.

Moo, Douglas J. *The Epistle to the Romans.* NICNT. Grand Rapids: Eerdmans, 1996.

Talbert, Charles H. *Romans.* Smyth & Helwys Bible Commentary. Macon, Ga.: Smyth & Helwys, 2002.

Other Studies:

Berkley, Timothy W. *From a Broken Covenant to Circumcision of the Heart: Pauline Intertextual Exegesis in Romans 2:17-29.* SBLDS 175. Atlanta: Society of Biblical Literature, 2000.

Donfried, Karl P. *The Romans Debate.* Rev. ed. Peabody, Mass.: Hendrickson, 1991.

Dunn, James D. G. *The Theology of Paul the Apostle.* Grand Rapids: Eerdmans, 1998.

Esler, Philip Francis. *Conflict and Identity in Romans: The Social Setting of Paul's Letters.* Minneapolis, Minn.: Fortress, 2003.

Grieb, A. Katherine. *The Story of Romans: A Narrative Defense of God's Righteousness.* Louisville, KY: Westminster/John Knox, 2002.

Haacker, Klaus. *The Theology of Paul's Letters to the Romans.* Cambridge: Cambridge University Press, 2003.

Hay, David M., and E. Elizabeth Johnson, eds. *Pauline Theology.* Vol. III: *Romans.* Minneapolis: Fortress, 1991.

Hays, Richard B. *Echoes of Scripture in the Letters of Paul.* New Haven: Yale University Press, 1989.

Horsley, Richard A., ed. *Paul and Empire: Religion and Power in Roman Imperial Society.* Harrisburg, Pa.: Trinity Press International, 1997.

Sanders, E. P. *Paul, the Law, and the Jewish People.* Philadelphia: Fortress, 1983. *Paul and Palestinian Judaism.* Philadelphia: Fortress, 1977.

Wagner, J. Ross. *Heralds of the Good News: Isaiah and Paul "In Concert" in the Letter to the Romans.* NovTSup 101. Leiden: Brill, 2002.

Wright, N. T. *The Climax of the Covenant: Christ and the Law in Pauline Theology.* Edinburgh: T & T Clark; Minneapolis: Fortress, 1991.

______. *The New Testament and the People of God.* Vol. 1 of *Christian Origins and the Question of God.* London: SPCK; Minneapolis: Fortress, 1992.

ENDNOTES

1. See Ulrich Wilckens, *Der Brief an die Römer,* 3 vols., EKK 6 (Zurich: Benziger, 1978–82) 1:93.

2. This is still controversial, in my view needlessly. See N. T. Wright, *The New Testament and the People of God,* vol. 1 of *Christian Origins and the Question of God* (Minneapolis: Fortress, 1992) 268-71; and *Jesus and the Victory of God,* vol. 2 of *Christian Origins and the Question of God* (London: SPCK, 1996) xvii-xviii, with reference to the massive evidence in Second Temple Judaism. See also N. T. Wright, "In Grateful Dialogue: A Response," in *Jesus and the Restoration of Israel,* ed. C. C. Newman (Downers Grove, Ill.: InterVarsity, 1999) 253-61; and J. M. Scott, ed., *Exile: Old Testament, Jewish, and Christian Conceptions* (Leiden: Brill, 1997). Even if it is not accepted that most of his contemporaries would have agreed, I would still contend that this is demonstrably Paul's own point of view. Another Pauline passage that makes excellent sense on this reading is Gal 3:10-14, on which see N. T. Wright, *The Climax of the Covenant: Christ and the Law in Pauline Theology* (Minneapolis: Fortress, 1991) chap. 7; and S. J. Hafemann, "Paul and the Exile of Israel in Galatians 3–4", in Scott, *Exile,* 329-71.

3. This sequence of thought is clearly visible in passages like Ezra 9 and Daniel 9. See Wright, *The New Testament and the People of God,* chaps. 9–10.

4. A good example of this can be seen in Genesis 38:26, when Judah acknowledges that his daughter-in-law Tamar is in the right and he is in the wrong. This states a legal position; only secondarily, and by implication, does it comment on the morality of their respective behavior.

5. *Gen. Rab.* 14:6.

6. This question, and the question of "God's righteousness" that it raises, is a major theme of the book known as 4 Ezra, written after the destruction of the Temple in 70 CE. See B. W. Longenecker, *Eschatology and the Covenant: A Comparison of 4 Ezra and Romans 1–11* (Sheffield: JSOT, 1991).

7. Marcion was a 2nd cent. CE Roman heretic who taught that the God of the Jews was a different god from that revealed in Jesus.

8. See C. H. Dodd, *The Epistle of Paul to the Romans,* 2nd ed. (London: Fontana, 1959) esp. 161-63. For a recent commentary in the Reformation tradition, see P. Stuhlmacher, *Paul's Letter to the Romans: A Commentary,* trans. S. J. Hafemann (Louisville: Westminster John Knox, 1994).

9. For a classic statement of this, see C. E. B. Cranfield, *A Critical and Exegetical Commentary on the Epistle to the Romans,* ICC, 2 vols. (Edinburgh: T & T Clark, 1975) 91-99.

10. Statistically, the word "God" (θεός *theos*) occurs with far more frequency in Romans (once every 46 words) than any other Pauline work. See L. L. Morris, "The Theme of Romans," in *Apostolic History and the Gospel: Biblical and Historical Essays Presented to F. F. Bruce on his 60th Birthday,* ed. W. W. Gasque and R. P. Martin (Exeter: Paternoster, 1970) 249-63. Paul's other letters are also, of course, "about" God, but Romans makes God and God's justice, love, and reliability its major themes.

11. I have explored this theme in various places, e.g., N. T. Wright, *The Climax of the Covenant:*

Christ and the Law in Pauline Theology (Edinburgh: T & T Clark; Minneapolis: Fortress, 1991) 21-26; *The New Testament and the People of God*, vol. 1 of *Christian Origins and the Question of God*, chap. 9.

12. On *Iustitia*, the Roman equivalent of *dikē*, see, e.g., Ovid Letters from the Black Sea 3.6.25; the *Acts of Augustus*, chap. 34.

13. This point, though it was developed independently, has close analogies with the argument of Neil Elliott, *Liberating Paul: The Justice of God and the Politics of the Apostle* (Maryknoll, N.Y.: Orbis, 1994) 190-92. See also Dieter Georgi, *Theocracy in Paul's Praxis and Theology* (Minneapolis: Fortress, 1991) chap. 4, excerpted in Richard A. Horsely, ed., *Paul and Empire: Religion and Power in Roman Imperial Society* (Harrisburg, Pa.: Trinity, 1997) 148-57. See further Richard A. Horsely, ed., *Paul and Politics: Ekklesia, Israel, Imperium, Interpretation: Essays in Honor of Krister Stendahl* (Harrisburg, Pa.: Trinity, 2000) chaps. 1, 10.

14. See Wright, *The New Testament and the People of God*, 354-55; W. Wiefel, "The Jewish Community in Ancient Rome and the Origins of Roman Christianity," in *The Romans Debate*, rev. ed., ed. K. P. Donfried (Peabody, Mass.: Hendrikson, 1991) 85-101. Some scholars remain doubtful about whether the Jews were really expelled. See P. Achtemeier, "Unsearchable Judgments and Inscrutable Ways: Reflections of the Discussion of Romans," in *Pauline Theology*, vol. IV, ed. E. E. Johnson and D. M. Hay, SBLSS 4 (Atlanta: Scholars Press, 1997) 3-21; S. Mason, " 'For I Am Not Ashamed of the Gospel' (Romans 1:16): The Gospel and the First Readers of Romans," in *Gospel in Paul: Studies on Corinthians, Galatians, and Romans for Richard N. Longenecker*, ed. L. A. Jervis and P. Richardson, JSNTSup 108 (Sheffield: Sheffield Academic, 1994) 254-87.

15. See Menahem Stern, *Greek and Latin Authors on Jews and Judaism*, 3 vols. (Jerusalem: Israel Academy of Sciences and Humanities, 1974). On the Jewish community in Rome see H. J. Leon, *The Jews of Ancient Rome*, rev. ed. (Peabody, Mass.: Hendrikson, 1995).

The First Letter to the Corinthians

J. PAUL SAMPLEY

THE CITY OF CORINTH

Located about forty miles to the south-southwest of Athens on the shoulder of the isthmus linking the Peloponese to the rest of Greece, Corinth is, as important ancient cities needed to be, strategically defensible: It is set back from its two more vulnerable shore towns, Lechaeum on the Bay of Corinth a couple of miles to the north, and Cenchreae on the Saronic Bay about six miles to the east; it backs up against the 1,500-foot elevation of Acrocorinth; and its abundant springs assure an adequate water supply.

In Paul's time, Corinth was a hub commercially and religiously. Corinth was perhaps best known for its artisans' products, such as bronzes, but it also did a thriving business in pottery and earthenware. Religious diversity was ensured by Corinth's location. By portaging the couple of miles across the Corinthian isthmus, shippers of goods between the regions of the eastern Mediterranean basin and Rome could avoid the considerable hazards of storms in the exposed Mediterranean Sea (see Acts 27:2-44). Sailors and travelers brought with them their religions and planted them so successfully in Corinth that modern archaeologists find evidence for most of

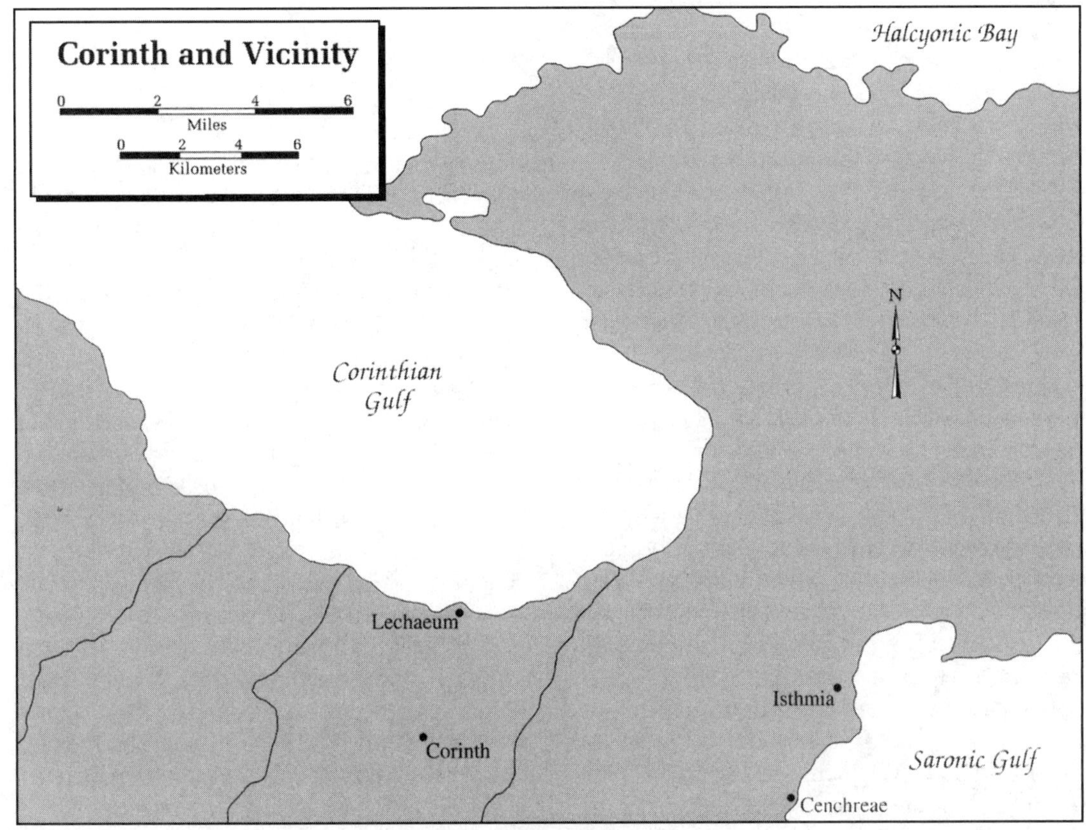

the more than two dozen temples, altars, and shrines that the mid-second-century Greek chronicler Pausanias described.[1] The archaeological evidence confirms that Greek and Egyptian religious shrines coexisted there along with the Roman imperial cult. In fact, Pausanias records that alongside the forum at Corinth there was even "a temple for all the gods."[2] Also Jews, some like Prisca and Aquila, no doubt expelled by emperors Tiberius (19 CE) and Claudius (49 CE), found Corinth attractive and settled there.

Politically, Corinth enjoyed colony status, the greatest civic honor that could be accorded cities in the empire.[3] Colony status assured a special relation with the Roman Empire in which Roman laws were operative, Latin was the official governmental language (even though the populace spoke Greek and Paul's letters to Corinth are written in Greek), and as noted, the imperial cult was established. Under the emperor Claudius (41-54 CE) the senate looked to Corinth even more than to Athens as the lead city of the Roman province of Achaia, and Corinth paid taxes directly to Rome well into the second century.[4] Roman proconsuls, in effect governors, went to the provinces as agents of imperial power; such a person was Gallio, who in 51 CE arrived in Corinth. Paul was brought before Gallio (Acts 18:12-17), and Sosthenes, who in Acts is described as the synagogue leader (ἀρχισυνάγωγος *archisynagogos*, Acts 18:17), was beaten in Gallio's presence for his association with Paul and the gospel (see 1 Cor 1:1).

Whether justifiably or not, cities sometimes get a reputation, coming to be thought of as having traits, one might even say as having a sort of ethos or personality of their own. So it was with Corinth. Apart from the renowned Isthmian games that were hosted in the area every two years, Corinth was said to have a "generally superficial cultural life,"[5] which may in part ultimately be traced to Julius Caesar's reestablishment of Corinth in 44 BCE and to his populating it, along with emigrants from other parts of the empire, with eager upwardly mobile freedpersons who were unloaded from Rome's burgeoning population.[6] Understandably, the transitory nature of ancient commerce, with sailors relishing life in a city and then moving along, contributed to Corinth's becoming known as "Sin City."

Corinth's reputation for wealth without culture and for the abuse of the poor by the wealthy was so well known that Alciphron, the second- or third-century CE composer of figmentary letters reflecting bygone times, could trade on Corinth's reputation in two of his fictional letters. In one he rejoiced that he was able to escape Corinth for Athens' more friendly setting, and he characterized Corinthians as persons "without grace [or charm] and not the least convivial."[7] In the other letter, he called Corinth "the gateway to the Peloponnesus" and described it as superficially lovely enough, with its great wealth and its location "between two seas," but he found it inhabited by persons whom he once again characterized as lacking charm and grace. In the same letter he calls wealthy people's behavior disgusting, coarse, and objectionable and details the grovelling of the abject, wretched poor for the smallest morsels of food.[8] Paul's letter confirms certain details of Corinth's ethos.

Not only does Corinth have a long-standing ethos, but so does the Corinthian church. *First Clement*, a document written from the church in Rome a full generation after Paul's time, notes that the Corinthian Christians continue to "engage in partisan strife" just as in Paul's time (*1 Clem.* 47.3). Paul's letter will give evidence that the Corinthian reputation, both as a city and as a church, is well deserved.

ESTABLISHMENT OF THE CORINTHIAN CHURCH

Paul probably arrived in Corinth for the first time in 50 CE, shortly after he had established churches in Philippi and Thessalonica, the major cities in the Roman province of Macedonia, to the north of the Aegean Sea. Our best efforts to arrive at such a date depend on a reading of Acts 18:11 and an establishment of when the Roman provincial proconsul Gallio (whose arrival in Corinth is mentioned in Acts 18:12) was appointed. By reasonable effort we can establish that Gallio was probably appointed in the summer of 51 CE[9] and that Paul appeared before him shortly thereafter (Acts 18:12). Then, if we measure backward from that time and credit the Acts 18:11 claim that Paul had already stayed in Corinth for a year and a half prior to the time he appeared before Gallio, we deduce sometime early in 50 CE for Paul's arrival and inaugural preaching in Corinth. Furthermore, the note that 1 Corinthians is written from Ephesus (1 Cor 16:8) corroborates Acts' picture in 18:18-19 that, when he left Corinth, Paul went to Ephesus later in the summer of 51 CE after he had been brought before Gallio.

PAUL'S EARLIEST LETTERS TO THE CORINTHIANS AND THE DATE OF 1 CORINTHIANS

Paul wrote the Corinthians a letter that we do not possess but that we learn about in what we call 1 Corinthians (1 Cor 5:9-12; often this lost document is referred to as the "previous letter"); so what the Bible refers to as 1 Corinthians is, in fact, Paul's second letter to them. Attempts have been made to identify 2 Cor 6:14-7:1 as a fragment of the "previous" letter, though that passage may not have been written by Paul and in any case argues that the believers should separate themselves from unbelievers, a notion contradicted in 1 Corinthians not only by the context of 1 Cor 5:9 but also by other places in which Paul clearly supposes that believers and unbelievers relate quite appropriately and openly to one another (1 Cor 7:12-16; 10:27-29; 14:24).

In the "previous" letter, Paul says that he wrote them not to associate with "immoral people," meaning by that not the immoral people of the world, because avoiding them would be an impossibility given their prevalence, but those immoral people who have become part of the believing fellowship (5:11). In part 1 Corinthians is occasioned by some ongoing Corinthian confusion regarding immorality as they had understood it in Paul's earlier—now lost—letter. The establishment of dates for the two letters must be coordinated, beginning with 1 Corinthians and then working backward to some suggestion regarding the lost "previous" letter.

Paul's travel plans mentioned at the end of 1 Corinthians (16:5-9) project a visit to Corinth (see also 1 Cor 4:21) but only after Paul stays in Ephesus until Pentecost (1 Cor 16:8), the Jewish-then-Christian festival that came fifty days after the second day of Passover. Appropriately, Paul's temporal reference has led us to assume that what we call 1 Corinthians was written in late fall or winter, leaving time for the pre-Pentecost, remaining work in Ephesus to which Paul alludes by the metaphor of the "wide door" opened to him there (1 Cor 16:9). But which fall or winter? Depending on the weight one gives Acts' portrait of Paul's work in Caesarea, Jerusalem, Antioch (Acts 18:22), Galatia, and Phrygia (Acts 18:23)—not to mention the time it would have taken to establish his mission in Ephesus to the point at which the "wide door" opened to him there—one may expect that 1 Corinthians was written in the fall or winter a couple of years after Paul left Corinth in late summer of 51. So the earliest reasonable estimate of the date for 1 Corinthians would be late fall or winter of 53-54 CE; at the very latest, one might stretch it to the next winter after that.

The dating of the lost letter mentioned in 1 Cor 5:9, then, would have to be enough prior to 1 Corinthians that Paul would have had occasion to discover that his effort at guidance on the issue of immorality had produced misunderstanding in the church at Corinth, though all we can say for certain is that the "previous" letter was written sometime between late summer of 51—that is, after Paul's departure from Corinth–and the fall or winter of 53 or 54.

THE MAKEUP OF THE CORINTHIAN CHURCH

The congregation at Corinth reflects the socioeconomic and religious makeup of the city. In keeping with the "steep social pyramid"[10] that was typical of that culture, very few believers were rich, and most were poor (1 Cor 1:26). Many persons are named in 1 Corinthians or are connected to Corinth in some other New Testament writing, and we know some things about these people. Some of those who have Latin names were probably of Roman descent: Fortunatus, Quartus, and even Gaius, whose wealth is clear from Paul's description of him in Rom 16:23 as host not only of Paul but also "of the whole church" in Corinth (1 Cor 1:14). Some have Greek names: Stephanas, Achaicus, and Erastus; the latter's status and quite likely his correlate wealth are probably indicated by Paul's identification of him as Corinth's town treasurer (Rom 16:23). Some few were Jews: Aquila and Prisca, mentioned by Paul as sending greetings from Ephesus (1 Cor 16:19), were known to the Corinthians, as may be supposed from Acts 18:2 and from Paul's sweeping claim that "all the churches of the gentiles" were indebted to these two (Rom 16:3); Sosthenes, who is credited by Paul as coauthor of 1 Corinthians and whom Acts says was the leader of the Corinthian synagogue (Acts 18:17); and Apollos, whom Acts identifies as an Alexandrian Jew "well versed in the scriptures" (Acts 8:24) and was an assistant to Paul in inculcating the gospel among the Corinthians (1 Cor 3:6). In 1 Corinthians, there is absolutely no evidence of any strife or even tension in the relation of Jewish believers and gentile believers.

Not surprisingly, when one takes Alciphron's characterization of Corinth into consideration, one finds an indication that wealth and its associated status played a part in some of the struggles between Corinthian believers. Only rich persons adjudicated matters in court (chap. 6); only wealthy persons had homes and staff large enough to host the church and provide for its celebration of the Lord's supper; and only the wealthy could arrive at the dinners early enough to eat the best food and get drunk before the other, less fortunate ones could arrive (1 Cor 11:17-34).

Clearly, most of the Corinthian believers were gentiles. Paul, whose treatment of spiritual gifts seems determined to embrace the entire congregation, describes the Corinthian believers as former idolaters who *as gentiles* were misled or carried away by devotion to idols (1 Cor 12:2). The Corinthians wrote to Paul about food offered to idols (1 Cor 8:1) because in their pre-faith lives they had been free to partake in the religious festivals as a matter of course. But they are gentiles who have been taught the Scripture and traditions of Israel—surely by Paul and perhaps also by the combined efforts of Prisca, Aquila, Apollos, and Sosthenes. That Paul's churches were strongly gentile cannot be a great surprise because Paul's understanding of his call is focused on the gentiles (Rom 11:13; Gal 2:7), and when he describes his churches to the Romans he calls them "the churches of the gentiles" (Rom 16:4).

Paul successfully resocialized the gentiles who make up most of the Corinthian church into thinking of themselves as a part of the ancient people of God, as members of what he elsewhere calls the Israel of God (Gal 6:16). In fact, Paul writes to the Corinthian gentiles about "gentiles" (τὰ ἔθνη *ta ethnē*) as if the recipients can no longer be counted among those persons (12:2; 5:1; 10:20; see also Eph 2:11; 3:1; 4:17). Paul's Jewish monotheism has become theirs (1 Cor 8:4, 6). Accordingly, they view representations of other supposed deities as "idols" and meat offered in sacrifice to those deities as εἰδωλόθυτος (*eidōlothytos*, "meat offered to an idol");[11] Christ is called "our Paschal lamb" in a context in which leaven is a primary motif, without need of any explanation (5:7); the scriptures of Israel have become theirs in an authoritative fashion (see 10:26; cf. Ps 24:1); the persons in the exodus out of Egypt are unabashedly called "our ancestors" (10:1). Paul expects his readers to understand the Jewish insiders' term ἀκροβυστία (*akrobystia*) as meaning "uncircumcised" (7:18-19); they have adopted Paul's Jewish terminology for at least one day of the week, the sabbath (16:2, μία σαββάτου *mia sabbatou*); and they know the Aramaic, pre-Pauline prayer of the earliest believers, μαράνα θά (*Marana tha*, "Our Lord, come," 16:22).

INTEGRITY AND STRUCTURE OF PAUL'S LETTER

In the past some scholars, seeing the variety of topics and failing to discern links and patterns between them, thought 1 Corinthians was made up of fragments of several letters, but now most scholars assume , the literary integrity of 1 Corinthians.[12] Even chapter 13, whose links to the material around it are not always explicit, functions as an encomium whose praise of love bears on what is written in the chapters on either side of it.

In one sense, the structure of 1 Corinthians is very much like other Pauline letters and, indeed, has much in common with other contemporary epistolography.[13] It opens with a salutation and thanksgiving and, after the body of the letter, closes with greetings and a blessing of the deity. On closer look, however, one sees that the letter is different from all other Pauline letters in some important particulars. Whereas Paul's letters often move toward a climactic appeal (Rom 12:1; Phil 4:2), here the *first* appeal follows directly on the thanksgiving (1:10) and is echoed in 4:16, encasing the opening chapters. Other Pauline letters seem to be dominated by one or two problems or issues that are treated by Paul's weaving them into the fabric of the letter (e.g., Philemon's concern about the runaway slave marks much of that letter; Philippians' concern with the two women's problems has recently been argued to be the main purpose in Paul's writing of that letter),[14] whereas 1 Corinthians has a string of issues or problems that Paul treats sequentially. Further, no other Pauline letter is even partially structured around answering questions that Paul's community has written to him. In 1 Corinthians, though, Paul has received a letter from the Corinthians (7:1) and needs to respond to matters they have raised in writing (see 8:1; 12:1; 16:1). Finally, the chapters that open the letter and only obliquely relate to specific Corinthian problems (chaps. 1–4) are relatively short and appear up front, setting a backdrop against which all the particular issues must be viewed.

PAUL'S RELATION WITH THE CORINTHIANS

Paul's relationship with the Corinthians needs to be addressed in three parts. First, prior to the writing of 1 Corinthians, Paul had known the Corinthian believers for at least three years, having first evangelized there and established the church in early 50 CE, and having lived and worked with them for a year and a half that first time (Acts 18:11). The "previous" lost letter (5:9) is our primary window into what may be known about Paul and the Corinthians before 1 Corinthians. From the reference to the previous letter we may deduce some important information. First, Paul's descriptions of his efforts in that letter indicate that some, perhaps all, of the Corinthians had some confusion about Paul's teaching regarding immoral people and the need to avoid them (1 Cor 5:9-11). From 1 Corinthians it is possible to see that some of the Corinthians, in response to that earlier letter, may have tried to dissociate themselves from "immoral people" (see the question of divorcing unbelievers, 7:12-16) and even from "immorality" in a more general way (see married persons' thinking that they might do well to abstain from sexual intercourse, 7:2-6). Second, Paul's reference to his earlier letter suggests that he and the Corinthians were on good terms, and he readily responds to their confusion.

An additional window onto Paul's relationship with the Corinthians prior to the writing of 1 Corinthians is the letter itself; it makes no specific reference to any preceding event, to any action of Paul, or to any development among the Corinthians that, since the previous letter, has marked a change in Paul's relationship to his Corinthian followers.

First Corinthians gives abundant evidence regarding Paul's relationship to the Corinthians at the time of its composition, but the evidence has been read in a variety of ways that one could readily range along a continuum from an interpretation of 1 Corinthians as depicting Paul and the Corinthians virtually at loggerheads with one another[15] to the other extreme where the letter is read as showing that Paul and the Corinthians are on good terms with one another.[16] In either extreme and all along the interpretive continuum, no one disputes that the Corinthians are a contentious, carping bunch among themselves. But what is Paul's standing with them at the time of his writing 1 Corinthians? The evidence most often featured to claim that Paul is under heavy attack by the Corinthians is as follows:[17] Chapter 4 is taken to indicate that the Corinthians are making judgments against Paul (4:3); the "puffiness" in 4:6 is construed as "for" Apollos and "against" Paul; and Timothy is sent to reinforce Paul's own ways (4:17) in the supposed struggle. Chapters 5 and 6 are read as Paul's effort to reestablish his authority "to direct their affairs."[18] Chapter 9 is taken as a "fierce defense" of Paul in which he tries to counter their opinion that it is beneath an apostle, a wise man, to work with his own hands. The last bit of evidence on the most extreme reading of Paul as being in strife with the Corinthians is 14:37, a verse in which Paul does, indeed, brandish his authority.

Toward the other end of the continuum, one finds a stress on the call for unity among the Corinthians.[19] Rather than Paul's being on the defensive, 1:10-4:21 is Paul's censure of the Corinthians for their divisiveness; his references to himself and judgment (4:1ff.), while no doubt enhancing his own ethos, his character, serve most directly to call the divisive Corinthians to task for their fractious and thoughtless behavior toward one another.[20] The comparisons (*synkrisis*) in 4:1ff. serve the standard function of showing someone who is behaving himself properly, as in the case of Paul and the other apostles, or doing it wrong, as in the case of the Corinthians;[21] and the sending of Timothy is Paul's effort to "strengthen the epistolary appeal by one who represents Paul" and is further support for his call to unity that the rest of the letter amplifies.[22] Finally, chapter 9 is not truly a "defense" but is Paul's setting up of himself as the exemplary person who forgoes the exercise of his rights in the gospel if someone might be harmed or hindered by his use of them.[23] Chapter 9 is Paul's exemplification of Christian freedom tempered by love.

Paul does relate to the Corinthians as their father in the faith (4:14) and feels responsible for them. Because he, as their father, sees problems with their conduct, he is at times harsh with them. Accordingly, he alternately warns them (4:14), shames them (6:5; 15:34), cajoles them (14:12), and encourages them (12:31; 14:20). Throughout the letter, however, his concern is to restore them to unity, to refurbish and reshape their concord, their genuine concern (his technical term for this is "love") for one another. We must be scrupulous not to tinge our reading of 1 Corinthians with the acrid atmosphere of 2 Corinthians, where matters on most fronts have deteriorated.

Between the time of 1 Corinthians and the writing of any fragment of 2 Corinthians, Paul's relationship with the Corinthians worsened. He had a "painful visit" with them when things did not go as he or they wanted (2 Cor 2:1-2). He had projected another visit and failed to show up, and some Corinthians were less than impressed (2 Cor 1:15-18). Paul's fiscal management becomes a significant problem in several ways: Some persons want to be Paul's patrons, but he refuses;[24] Paul accepts support from the Macedonians while still refusing support from the Corinthians (2 Cor 11:9); and the Corinthians' zeal for the collection destined for Jerusalem (cf. 1 Cor 16:1-4) waned considerably (2 Corinthians 8-9). But by far the most significant new development that distinguishes all of Paul's relations with the Corinthians subsequent to the time of 1 Corinthians is the arrival in Corinth of outsiders who challenge his authority (2 Cor 2:17; 3:1-3; 5:11; 10:12-18; 11:2-6, 12-15, 22-23). In 1 Corinthians the problems the Corinthians have are with one another, not with outsiders.

PRIMARY CULTURAL PATTERNS IMPORTANT FOR UNDERSTANDING 1 CORINTHIANS

The Corinthians and their apostle bring certain cultural, social, and literary suppositions to their engagement with one another. Some of these suppositions need to be mentioned as a context for interpretation.

Pater Familias. Paul and his readers share the knowledge that the father of the household is the one responsible for the well-being and comportment of the members of that social unit. It is the father's responsibility to inculcate values, to provide support, to enforce discipline, to train, and to protect all the members of the household. Most fundamental in carrying out these responsibilities is the father's modeling of proper behavior and comportment. The only feature of this social pattern lacking in Paul's letters is that the father trains the family members in a trade. This sweeping sense of responsibility is the proper context for Paul's epistolary efforts to have the Corinthians understand how they should properly behave (4:14-21). It also will help us to understand why it is natural for Paul—and for his readers—to set himself forward so regularly as the one who exemplifies proper life in Christ and who should, therefore, be emulated by his children in the faith.

Honor/Shame; Praise/Blame. The most important cultural norm in Paul's time was the attainment of honor and its equally powerful counterpart, the avoidance, or at least the minimization, of shame. Society was ordered vertically, with all persons concerned with identifying where they stood in the chain of descending power. To be sure, there were the sideward glances to see how others were doing by comparison, but decisions were made and actions were pursued with primary regard for how they would secure honor and avoid shame for oneself, how they would gain praise and limit blame. It was the understood obligation of the subordinate persons to praise and honor their benefactors, the ones on whom they found themselves dependent. The social indicators and patterns played to this structuring and to its attendant maintenance of honor. Seating assignments at social events were carefully arranged in accordance with varying degrees of status (Luke 14:7-11), and great shame was accorded anyone who breached propriety. The right to speak and, when granted, even the order in which persons were expected to speak were structured on the notions of the degree of honor.

Accordingly, when Paul writes that he does not seek to shame the Corinthians (1 Cor 4:14), when he writes something to their shame (1 Cor 6:5; 15:34), or when he mentions neither but in fact casts them in a shameworthy light (1 Cor 11:17-22), he will have hit on a hot-button item.

Patron/Client. In Paul's time everyone had a lord—that is, someone who could rightly be construed as being over someone else, to whom that someone else belonged or was indebted, and to whom that one was responsible. It was not just slaves who belonged to someone. Everyone right up the chain belonged to another person. Even Marcus Aurelius, the Roman emperor, mused that he was responsible to the gods. And one's comportment was understood as being keyed to pleasing one's lord, to whom one was responsible. Great effort was expended in nurturing, cultivating, and even increasing the number of one's patrons; equally prodigious care was given to one's clients to make sure that they remembered their indebtedness and to ensure that they took proper steps to show honor and praise. And so it was up and down the social ladder. One person's client was patron to many below. The power that one received from one's patron was used, by careful distribution of it to one's selected clients, and was subsequently passed on by them to clients who were then in turn indebted to them. Indebtedness and obligation were the fabric of this culture.

An abiding issue before the Corinthians in this letter is the identity of the one to whom they belong—that is Paul's way of tapping this cultural reservoir as a means of expressing the basic and defining relationship in all of life. Paul consistently reminds them that it is the Lord Jesus Christ to whom they are responsible and whom they must please. All are clients of a superior patron, and their actions are to yield honor, not shame, to their Lord. Some Corinthians seek to place themselves in the superior position with regard to other believers and thus to "lord" it over them. Status seeking will be an abiding problem with which Paul is confronted in 1 Corinthians. Paul's countercultural understanding of the gospel runs head-on into this social convention when, with its associated status seeking, it bears on how believers get along with each other.

Stoics. In Paul's time Stoics carried the day. One hardly needed to choose to be a Stoic or even to think of oneself as being a Stoic in certain ways; it was so much in the air that it was a part of the common coinage of life and its exchanges. Accordingly, Paul can and does use Stoic patterns and conceptions as a means of advancing his arguments and of explicating what it means to live the faith. For example, he frequently employs the Stoic conviction that certain matters are indifferent *adiaphora*, and he may even identify, as the Stoics surely did, things preferred and things not preferred from among those indifferent considerations (see 1 Corinthians 7). Another example could be Paul's conviction, expressed in different ways across the letter, that God has allocated or arranged matters as God has chosen (3:5; 7:17; 12:18, 24).

Rhetoric and 1 Corinthians. Rhetoric is the art of persuasion. In Paul's time, rhetoric was the basic form of education for those who could afford it. A growing body of scholarly studies of Paul show that he was indeed well tutored in rhetoric.[25] Even those not trained in rhetoric, as the majority of the Corinthians surely were not, were accustomed to it and knew its conventions by having lived in a rhetorical culture. All written and spoken words were rhetorical, so, in order to understand what was written or said, one always has to consider the rhetoric of what is there. To call something rhetorical is not to be confused with dismissing it as empty, as form prevailing over content. Everything in 1 Corinthians, therefore, is rhetorical, and we as interpreters of it must regularly inquire of its rhetorical force.

There were three types of rhetoric in those days. The first, *judicial rhetoric*, had its focus on the courtroom and generally inquired regarding what had happened in the past in order to make some judgment. The second, *deliberative rhetoric*, concerned itself with deliberations about what one should or should not do in the future, though that future could be quite imminent. The third type, *epideictic rhetoric*, concerned itself with praise and blame either of an individual or of a virtue or vice and had its primary focus on the present, the way things are, or, in the case of a virtue, as things should be. In a general and overall way, documents from that time tend to fall in one of those three categories, though the rhetorical handbooks clearly caution that no rhetorician of any worth sticks to one category, but freely mixes them according to the needs of the occasion.[26] First Corinthians falls primarily into the category of deliberative rhetoric, although there are features of the letter in which Paul employs, as we shall see, some judicial rhetoric and some epideictic rhetoric.[27]

The apostle and letter writer Paul, the Corinthians and some perceived problem or problems with them, and constraints consisting, for example, of shared beliefs and experiences—all three together form the rhetorical situation that must be the context for our evaluation of 1 Corinthians.[28] The dynamic among the three can never be out of sight. In this situation our primary data consists in the letter itself. In the letter we have most directly Paul's efforts to persuade the Corinthians; we can identify Paul's strategy, what he aims for, what he values or affirms, what he considers useless, and what he denies. We have less access and certainty to whether Paul understood his recipients and whether he reflects them and what is going on there accurately. In the letter we can see Paul's assessment of the Corinthians and of what they have been doing; even there, however, in the letter itself we can sense and will actually see evidence that Paul's estimate of the maturity of the Corinthian believers is at dissonance with what they probably thought about themselves (see 3:1ff.). As tempting as it might be, we cannot assume that we can penetrate the thoughts of the persons to whom the letter was written. So, positively put, what we do have greatest access to as we approach the letter are Paul's rhetorical moves and steps, and those will be of great interest in the study that follows.

According to Demetrius of Phalerum (c. 4th cent. BCE), and regardless of which of the three types of rhetoric one used, there were really only three options available to someone, like Paul, who wanted to call upon a person or a group to alter their behavior: flattery, adverse criticism, or figured speech ("indirect speech" or the "covert hint" as it may otherwise be called).[29] In 1 Corinthians we will see that Paul at different times uses each of the three, though in the culture and in the letter the last one, "figured, indirect speech" or the "covert hint," is the most common.[30] In each case we will have to take care to interpret whatever Paul writes within the conventions appropriate to the option he employs in that section.

Paul uses certain *topoi* or commonplaces to advance his case. For a first example, much note will be taken of exemplification. Like any good parent in that time, Paul, as the Corinthians' father in the faith, details positive and negative models of the faith and himself patterns the way his children in the faith should behave. In a second example, Paul several times employs *synecdoche*, a literary device in which reference is made to something by identifying one of its parts, where the part (e.g., wheels) represents and stands for the whole (e.g., car). Third, there will be several occasions to note that Paul uses a ring device called *inclusio* to tie together a literary unit or to finish a thought. Fourth, maxims, pithy distillations of generally accepted truths, are a feature of rhetoric in antiquity and in Paul's letters.

Paul displays a fundamental ambivalence to culture and the patterns in the world around the Corinthian believers. At times he embraces cultural conventions and patterns. At other times he distances himself and his believers from them. Perhaps such an ambivalence was unavoidable because Paul made the decision not to lead his believers to a Qumran-like isolation; perhaps it was inevitable because human transactions are always couched in culturally transmitted conventions and exchanges. Perhaps it was unavoidable because most persons have blind spots where their convictions have not fully penetrated every nook and cranny of their lives. In Paul's case, perhaps he did not carry his gospel-powered critique through consistently into every facet of his and his congregations' lives. However it happened, Paul's relation to the culture in which he and his followers lived is mixed. A few examples will illustrate the range of Paul's appropriation and critique of cultural patterns.

Beginning with an example of Paul's being critical of cultural patterns, he objects when the Corinthians use their worldly power and status to get their way in the community of believers. He severely chides the wealthy Corinthians for having taken poorer believers to court in order to have their own way (chap. 6) and for abusing their power as hosts of the Lord's supper (11:17-34). For an uncritical appropriation of cultural patterns, consider Paul's blithe assumption that men should have short hair and women should keep theirs long (11:6, 14-15). In between those extremes Paul seems to think that believers can live directly in the world, in the midst of the world's cultural patterns, without the culture's determining their stance or moral choices. We see that sort of reflection most clearly in 1 Corinthians when Paul writes about living ὡς μή (*hōs mē*), "as if not," which closely approximates John's expression of living "in the world" but not "of the world" (7:29-31; John 13:1; 15:19). In that passage and in its context, Paul encourages believers to live "as if not" because "the appointed time has grown short" (7:29 NRSV). Because God's purposes with the world (which include refurbishing it, Romans 8) are drawing to a close, Paul is convinced that the patterns of the world have lost their power, that believers experience a liberation from the definitional influence of social patterns and of participation in the world. Accordingly, Paul thinks that believers live their lives of faith while finding themselves within the world, whose present form is passing away (1 Cor 7:31).

ESPECIALLY PROMINENT CONVICTIONS SEEN IN 1 CORINTHIANS

In particular passages, Paul takes for granted that his readers understand him without saying as much in full detail. Whatever Paul may write to any of his churches, he has a common framework in which he thinks of the gospel. The frame runs from Paul's foundational conviction on the one horizon that Christ's death and resurrection inaugurate the new creation, the redemption of creation, to the other horizon—indeed, to the end of the age at Christ's parousia, when God's purposes, begun in Christ's death and resurrection, come to a conclusion.[31] This latter is a time of judgment when all will have to stand (or fall) before God and Christ and give an accounting for the life they have lived and for their actions.

For Paul, the Christian faith is lived in community. The individual is never simply and singly related to God. If "faith" is Paul's code word for right relation to God, then "love" is Paul's code word for right relation to others. Love, the proper caring for another, is the necessary expression of faith, the proper relating to God, because faith expresses itself in love (Gal 5:6). Caring for other believers, building them up, encouraging them, consoling and even warning them, are not options for believers; they are a requirement of faith. We can see this in 1 Corinthians because some of the believers there seem to have focused their attention on themselves and on God and ignored, neglected, or disregarded others; and Paul simply cannot abide it. In this sense, the whole of 1 Corinthians is a study in love.

Paul recognizes that the very constitution of community requires a sort of give-and-receive transaction between the individuals and the community. To be a believer apart from community is inconceivable for Paul. Therefore, believers must be ready to accommodate to the community. That accommodation always entails contributing to the enrichment of the fellowship by putting whatever gifts one has in service to the common good. Perhaps more problematic for modern readers, sometimes integration into the community will cause the individual to override selfishness or the rather natural desire to seek what seems so clearly in one's own self-interest. Paul's assumption is that all individuals in the association will share in the benefits of the affiliation (e.g., security, mutual care and protection, etc.). While Paul's reflections on this balance between individual and community appear at several points in 1 Corinthians, they are expressed most directly in chapter 9.

Paul is so committed to the community as the matrix of the life of faith that when he sees a conflict between the rights of the individual and the rights of the community, he will regularly recommend that the individual eschew the pursuit of individual rights and choose the community's well-being instead. First Corinthians shows this Pauline trait when Paul advises that the ones who speak in tongues withhold expression of them if no one is there to interpret (14:28) and that when one is speaking and another receives a revelation, the speaker should give way (14:30). Paul exemplifies this pattern when he expresses his willingness never to eat meat if it might cause another to stumble (8:13).

We must be careful, however, because in all of his concern for the health of the community, Paul never denigrates the importance of the believer's individuality. Variety and difference are not sacrificed for community. Rather, Paul strives to integrate the distinctiveness of individuals and relishes the importance of difference to the wholesomeness of the fellowship. Accordingly, he acknowledges that different people eat all sorts of different things while others have restrictive diets (8:7-13; 10:25-31); some have homes in which to host the church, and, probably in a rhetorical overstatement, some have nothing (11:18-22); some have a few χαρίσματα (*charismata*), gifts, and others have many (12:4-11; 14:1-5); some live with the law as the defining center of their lives while others do not (9:20-21); some plant, and others water (3:6-9); and every person experiences testing as if it belonged to that person alone (10:13). But each and every one of these quite distinctively individuated persons is welcome, is important, and is even necessary to the body of Christ.

Paul assumes that believers should be responsible moral agents, that their lives are not simply driven from the heart, and that their minds should be integrated with their spirits in all of their moral reasoning. His is the integrated life, at once moral, deliberative, and spiritual—and he models it for those who would follow him. All of life, in every moment and in every situation, must be lived as ready for God's final judgment, not in quaking boots betokening lack of confidence in God's grace active in one's life, but in thankfulness to God for great and abiding mercy, ever present in good and in tough times. Contemplated conduct, therefore, must be weighed with regard to several considerations: how it expresses God's love for us, how appropriate it is to the strength of our faith, and how it affects others.

Different believers are of differing maturity. Some are "babies" in the faith; others are more mature; none are completely mature. As surely as babies learn to crawl and later walk but can carry no additional load, and as more mature persons can not only walk but also carry burdens for themselves and for others, so also Paul thinks it is with believers. Though Paul comes nearest to discussing this problem directly in Gal 6:1-5, it is an issue in 1 Corinthians that Paul thinks at least some of the Corinthians are babies in the faith and surely are not as mature as they think they are (3:1-4). Elsewhere in the letter Paul takes their fractiousness as evidence of their immaturity in the faith.

Because of that dissonance between their self-estimation and Paul's, his letter urges them to take careful stock of their standing and of their maturity. Some of the believers at Corinth have (falsely, Paul declares) thought of themselves as having arrived at the fullness of what God can bestow; they have become "arrogant" or "puffed up" as he sometimes puts it. Their arrogance is having deleterious effects on their fellow believers, who seem altogether too ready to accept their compatriots' puffy self-estimate and, with it, too low a self-estimate of themselves. Out of that low self-esteem, the less puffy Corinthians live as if they have less to offer the community of believers. A considerable part of Paul's effort in 1 Corinthians is aimed at bringing all sorts of quite different people back into full and equal participation in the community.

First Corinthians is a case study of several features of the Christian life as it has been experienced through the centuries. First, it is a classic for the problems of unity because, after all, that is one of the major problems across the issues reflected in the letter. Churches, like other social groups, are subject to fractiousness from all sorts of sources, and Corinth certainly has its share. Whether it is wealthy persons treating the poorer with disdain, or especially religiously gifted persons becoming arrogant, prideful, and disdainful of those less gifted, or persons of whatever socioeconomic bracket who think first of themselves and little about the needs of others, or persons who overestimate how strong they are in faith, or persons who have low self-esteem and cower timidly before those they consider more advanced—the list could go on—the church at Corinth has them all.

Likewise, Paul's response to those challenges of the Corinthian believers' unity is a study in distinguishing genuine unity from uniformity. Paul labors to help the Corinthians see that they truly belong to one another in Christ despite the differences of gifts and graces they exhibit. In fact, Paul goes that one better: It is precisely in the differences they bring to the community that he sees the creative, stimulating work of the Holy Spirit. The community's health and growth depend on each person's contributing what the Spirit offers through him or her to the common good of all. Without the variety and distinctiveness that each one brings, the faithful community would be a pale imitation of what it ought to be.

1 CORINTHIANS AS A WINDOW ON EARLY CHRISTIANITY

Paul's letters provide a vista onto the earliest known Christian communities, on churches that existed perhaps as much as a generation ahead of the time the Gospels were written. Paul, the Jew who opposed the earliest Christian movement (2 Cor 11:22; Gal 1:14; Phil 3:3-11), took the gospel to gentiles (non-Jews), who largely populated his churches. In doing so, he did not require circumcision, the traditional mark of belonging to God's people. In its place, as a ritual of admission, Paul required baptism. Even though he did not himself baptize many Corinthians (1 Cor 1:14-17), they *were* baptized. Paul gladly reasons from his convictions about baptism and its significance (1 Cor

12:13; 7:17-24). Though the congregation at Corinth was predominantly gentile (1 Cor 12:2; 8:4-6; 10:6-14), Paul clearly considers them, along with himself, to be God's children (1 Cor 1:3).

Paul's churches, like their synagogue counterparts, regularly gathered in homes. Because the Corinthians' assemblies were so chaotic (1 Cor 14:26-33), and because the Corinthians abused the Lord's supper (1 Cor 11:17-34), we learn a great deal about their practices and about Paul's suggestions of how they ought to comport themselves.

We tend to think of the apocalyptic Paul as making sharp distinctions between his communities, their comportment, and their life-style and that of their neighbors, and from 1 Corinthians 5-6 we will see that, indeed, we should; but the separation is far from absolute. Paul thinks that believers can have dealings with unbelievers (1 Cor 10:27); indeed, some are married to unbelievers (1 Cor 7:12-16), and some unbelievers apparently freely wander into worship occasions. Paul considers none of these exchanges between believers and unbelievers as inappropriate.

PAUL'S LETTERS

Paul's letters—all of them—are situational documents in which he writes concerning the problems he thinks need attention in that particular community of believers. First Corinthians is through and through an argument for unity that honors distinctiveness and diversity; for the believers' proper care of one another, which at the same time is grounded in an accurate self-assessment; and for the formation and upbuilding of maturity of faith that leaves no one out. First Corinthians is a textbook on moral reasoning and on the relation of the individual with the community.

Because we are not privy to what Paul and the Corinthians knew about each other and what the latter knew about Paul's teaching, we are sometimes left with having to take what appears in the letter only as a clue, an allusion, and to figure out what is the larger picture that Paul and the Corinthians may know quite well. We can sometimes reconstruct that larger picture from what we find in the other letters; indeed, we must do so if we are to understand the allusions.

Thirteen New Testament letters name Paul as author, but scholars have long since wondered about the authenticity of that claim with regard to some of the letters. Concerning seven of them, 1 Corinthians included, almost no one doubts the Pauline authorship: Romans, 1 and 2 Corinthians, Galatians, Philippians, 1 Thessalonians, and Philemon.[32] After that group, though, scholarly consensus breaks down. Some scholars deem 2 Thessalonians, Colossians, and Ephesians authentic as well, but some find these letters to be what we would call Paulinist, indicating that they have come from someone in the Pauline school who writes in Paul's name and represents the Pauline tradition after the apostle has died. A smaller subset of scholars claim authenticity for the Pastoral Epistles, 1 and 2 Timothy, and Titus.[33]

FOR FURTHER READING

Aune, David E. *The New Testament in Its Literary Environment.* Philadelphia: Westminster, 1987.

Collins, Raymond F. *First Corinthians.* SP 7. Collegeville, Minn.: Liturgical Press, 1999.

Conzelmann, Hans. *A Commentary on the First Epistle to the Corinthians.* Translated by J. W. Leitch. Hermeneia. Philadelphia: Fortress, 1975.

Fee, Gordon D. *The First Epistle to the Corinthians.* Grand Rapids: Eerdmans, 1987.

Fitzgerald, John. *Cracks in an Earthern Vessel: An Examination of the Catalogues of Hardships in the Corinthian Correspondence.* SBLDS 99. Atlanta: Scholars Press, 1988.

Forbes, Christopher. "Comparison, Self Praise and Irony: Paul's Boasting and the Conventions of Hellenistic Rhetoric." *NTS* 32 (1986).

Krentz, Edgar M. "Military Language and Metaphors in Philippians." In *Origins and Method: Towards a New Understanding of Judaism and Christianity, Essays in Honour of John C. Hurd.* Edited by B. H. McLean. JSNTSup 88. Sheffield: Academic, 1993.

Lampe, Peter. "Theological Wisdom and the 'Word About the Cross': The Rhetorical Scheme in 1 Corinthians 1-4." *Int* 44 (1990).

Lyons, George. *Pauline Autobiography: Toward a New Understanding.* SBLDS 73. Atlanta: Scholars Press, 1985.

MacMullen, Ramsay. *Roman Social Relations 50 B.C. to A.D. 284.* New Haven: Yale University Press, 1974.

Malherbe, Abraham J. "Determinism and Free Will in Paul: The Argument of 1 Corinthians 8 and 9." In *Paul in His Hellenistic Context.* Edited by T. Engberg-Pedersen. Minneapolis: Fortress, 1995.

Marshall, Peter. *Enmity in Corinth: Social Conventions in Paul's Relations with the Corinthians.* WUNT 2/23. Tübingen: Mohr/Siebeck, 1987.

Meeks, Wayne A. *The First Urban Christians: The Social World of the Apostle Paul.* New Haven: Yale University Press, 1983.

Mitchell, Margaret M. *Paul and the Rhetoric of Reconciliation.* Louisville: Westminster/John Knox, 1991.

Murphy-O'Connor, Jerome. *St. Paul's Corinth: Texts and Archaeology.* Collegeville, Minn.: Liturgical, 1983.

Pogoloff, Stephen. *Logos and Sophia: The Rhetorical Situation of 1 Corinthians.* SBLDS 134. Atlanta: Scholars Press, 1992.

Ramsaran, Rollin A. *Liberating Words: Paul's Use of Rhetorical Maxims in 1 Corinthians 1–10.* Valley Forge, Pa.: Trinity, 1996.

Sampley, J. Paul. *Walking Between the Times: Paul's Moral Reasoning.* Minneapolis: Fortress, 1991.

Sigountos, J. G. "The Genre of 1 Corinthians 13." *NTS* 40 (1994).

Smit, J. "The Genre of 1 Corinthians 13 in the Light of Classical Rhetoric." *NovT* 33 (1991).

Theissen, Gerd. *The Social Setting of Pauline Christianity: Essays on Corinth.* Edited and translated by J. H. Schütz. Philadelphia: Fortress, 1982.

Tuckett, C. M. "The Corinthians Who Say 'There Is No Resurrection of the Dead' (1 Cor 15,12)." In *The Corinthian Correspondence.* Edited by R. Bieringer. Leuven: Leuven University Press, 1996.

Willis, W. L. *Idol Meat in Corinth: The Pauline Argument in 1 Corinthians 8* and 10. SBLDS 68. Chico, Calif.: Scholars Press, 1985.

Winter, B. W. "Civil Litigation in Secular Corinth and the Church. The Forensic Background to 1 Corinthians 6.1-8." *NTS* 37 (1991).

Wuellner, William. "Greek Rhetoric and Pauline Argumentation." In *Early Christian Literature and the Classical Intellectual Tradition: In honorem Robert M. Grant.* Edited by W. R. Schoedel and R. L. Wilken. Théologie Historique 54. Paris: Etudes Beauchesne, 1979.

Zaas, P. S. "Catalogues and Context: 1 Corinthians 5 and 6." *NTS* 34 (1988).

ENDNOTES

1. Jerome Murphy-O'Connor, *St. Paul's Corinth: Texts and Archaeology* (Collegeville, Minn.: Liturgical, 1983) 78-80.

2. Pausanias 2.6–3.1.

3. See Richard E. Oster, "When Men Wore Veils to Worship: the Historical Context of 1 Corinthians 11:4," *NTS* 34 (1988) 489-93, for an excellent weighing of the significance of colony status in Corinth.

4. Victor P. Furnish, *II Corinthians* (Garden City, N.Y.: Doubleday, 1984) 9.

5. Furnish, *II Corinthians*, 13.

6. Strabo 8.6.23.

7. Alciphron Letter 15.2.

8. Alciphron Letter 24.

9. See Murphy-O'Connor's excellent evaluation of the evidence and choice of this date, in *St. Paul's Corinth*, 154-58.

10. Ramsay MacMullen, *Roman Social Relations 50 B.C. to A.D. 284* (New Haven: Yale University Press, 1974) 89.

11. Gentiles not so resocialized would have used the term ἱερόθυτος (*hierothytos*), meaning "sacrificed to a divinity." See BAGD, 372.

12. Johannes Weiss opened the debate about the integrity of 1 Corinthians, *Der erste Korintherbrief* (Göttingen: Vandenhoeck & Ruprecht, 1910), xl-xliii. Some later scholars followed him. John C. Hurd, *The Origin of 1 Corinthians* (London: SPCK, 1965; repr. Macon, Ga.: Mercer University Press, 1983) 47, is the first modern scholar to review the evidence and make a consistent case for the literary unity of 1 Corinthians. Margaret M. Mitchell, *Paul and the Rhetoric of Reconciliation* (Louisville: Westminster/John Knox, 1991) 2-5, has a good review of literature on this topic and assumes the integrity of 1 Corinthians. Hers is the strongest argument yet because she demonstrates the literary integrity of 1 Corinthians as a rhetorical whole.

13. David E. Aune, *The New Testament in Its Literary Environment* (Philadelphia: Westminster, 1987) 158-82.

14. Nils A. Dahl, "Euodia and Syntyche and Paul's Letter to the Philippians," in *The Social*

World of the First Christians: Essays in Honor of Wayne A. Meeks, ed. L. M. White and O. L. Yarbrough (Minneapolis: Fortress, 1995) 3-15.

15. Gordon D. Fee, *The First Epistle to the Corinthians* (Grand Rapids: Eerdmans, 1987), describes the letter as "combative"; e.g., "Paul is taking them on at every turn" (6); "Paul's authority is eroded" (7).

16. Mitchell, *Paul and the Rhetoric of Reconciliation*, makes a strong case that at the time of writing 1 Corinthians Paul is on good terms with the Corinthians.

17. Following Fee, *The First Epistle to the Corinthians*, 8-10.

18. Fee, *The First Epistle to the Corinthians*, 9.

19. Mitchell, *Paul and the Rhetoric of Reconciliation*, 200, claims that the call to unity in 1:10 is the thesis statement of *"the entire letter"* (emphasis hers) and that everything subsequent serves that overriding purpose.

20. Mitchell, *Paul and the Rhetoric of Reconciliation*, 209-10.

21. Mitchell, *Paul and the Rhetoric of Reconciliation*, 219-22. See also Christopher Forbes, "Comparison, Self-Praise and Irony: Paul's Boasting and the Conventions of Hellenistic Rhetoric," *NTS* 32 (1986) 2-8.

22. Mitchell, *Paul and the Rhetoric of Reconciliation*, 224-25.

23. Mitchell, *Paul and the Rhetoric of Reconciliation*, 244. For the best analysis of the problems with treating chap. 9 as a defense, see Mitchell's careful treatment (245) and her conclusion: "all attempts to analyze 1 Cor 9 as a true defense against actual charges have failed" (244).

24. Peter Marshall, *Enmity in Corinth: Social Conventions in Paul's Relations with the Corinthians*, WUNT 2/23 (Tübingen: Mohr/Siebeck, 1987) 218-58.

25. Duane F. Watson, "The New Testament and Greco-Roman Rhetoric: A Bibliography," *JETS* 31 (1988) 465-72, and "The New Testament and Greco-Roman Rhetoric: A Bibliographical Update," *JETS* 33 (1990) 513-24.

26. Although epideictic rhetoric focuses on praise and blame, these topics are also appropriate to and are found in judicial and deliberative rhetoric. See *Ad Herennium* 3.8.15.

27. See Mitchell, *Paul and the Rhetoric of Reconciliation*, 165, where she recognizes that 1 Corinthians 13 is an encomium.

28. See Lloyd F. Bitzer, "The Rhetorical Situation," *Philosophy and Rhetoric* 1 (1968) 1-14, esp. 6-8.

29. Demetrius of Phalerum *On Style* 9.2.66.

30. Frederick Ahl, "The Art of Safe Criticism in Greece and Rome," *AJP* 105 (1984) 204: indirect speech was "the normal mode of discourse thoughout much of Greek and Roman antiquity."

31. See "The Two Horizons of Paul's Thought World," in J. Paul Sampley, *Walking Between the Times: Paul's Moral Reasoning* (Minneapolis: Fortress, 1991) 7-24.

32. L. E. Keck, *Paul and His Letters*, 2nd ed. (Philadelphia: Fortress, 1988) 5-6. This judgment also informed the decision of the Pauline Theology Group of the Society of Biblical Literature to focus on the seven mentioned letters. The papers from that seminar were subsequently published as *Pauline Theology*, 3 vols. (Minneapolis: Fortress, 1991–95).

33. See Luke T. Johnson, *The Writings of the New Testament* (Philadelphia: Fortress, 1986) 242-407, who argues for the authenticity of all the letters that bear Paul's name.

THE SECOND LETTER TO THE CORINTHIANS

J. PAUL SAMPLEY

Nowhere else in Paul's letters can we observe his enduring relationship with a particular church. In the documents called 1 and 2 Corinthians, Paul relates to the Corinthian believers across a number of years. In those two works scholars have found references to five—and text of at least three—letters Paul wrote to the believers at Corinth and one they wrote to him. When the letters or letter fragments are arranged in a sequence, they portray Paul's relations to the Corinthians as ranging from good times to times not so good. Though we know that Paul had enduring relations with other churches, such as the one at Philippi (Phil 1:5; 4:15-16), we have no such detailed evidence anywhere but with the Corinthians.

In the letters redacted into 2 Corinthians, personal relations, modest goals and purposes, and even what some might consider rather petty matters are the occasion for grand theological reflections. A near-fatal disaster elicits a rumination about the God of consolation and comfort (1:3-11). Paul's poor scheduling and failure to make a promised trip generate a profound reflection on the faithfulness of God (1:15-22). Paul's desire to re-cement relations with the Corinthians gives him the opportunity to reflect on his ministry to them in three original constructions, depicting himself as minister of the new covenant, as minister through affliction and comfort, and as minister of reconciliation (2:14–6:10). His commitment to the collection for the saints in Jerusalem generates powerful reflections on God's grace and the generosity it inspires (chaps. 8–9). Paul's strife with his opponents in chapters 10–13 provides striking ruminations regarding the Pauline paradox of (divine) strength in (human) weakness.

LITERARY INTEGRITY OF 2 CORINTHIANS

The literary integrity of 2 Corinthians has proved a problem for scholars. Though most agree that the text is made up of more than one letter fragment,[1] much disagreement remains over the number, scope, and even sequence of the fragments. Absolutely no textual variations or manuscript evidence supports any of the partition theories. The lack of such evidence, however, does not necessarily argue against partition; it could simply be that the editing together of available fragments was done before the oldest extant manuscripts were written.

Events and Circumstances Connecting the Fragments. Before he wrote what we now call 1 Corinthians, Paul had written the Corinthians what has come to be called the "previous" letter (1 Cor 5:9-11), his first to them (*Letter A*, lost). After some time he wrote his second letter to them—now labeled 1 Corinthians (*Letter B*)—in part because of apparent confusion regarding what he meant about holiness in the previous letter.

Sometime after Paul had written and sent 1 Corinthians, he went to Corinth, as 1 Cor 16:5-7 promised. During that visit, one of the Corinthian believers made a verbal attack on Paul, and, to his chagrin, no one came to his defense (2 Cor 2:3). Mortified, Paul left. Although he had promised another visit to the Corinthians, he rethought it (1:23) and instead sent a letter of rather harsh frank speech (*Letter C*, lost; see "Frank Speech," below), calling them to task for the "one who did the wrong," chastizing them for their abandonment of him, and calling them back into "obedience" to him (2 Cor 7:8-16).

The frank speech letter achieved considerable success, as reported by Titus, though it is probably fair to say not quite as much as Paul had wished (2 Cor 6:11-13; 7:2-3*a*). The majority of the Corinthians embraced Paul and disciplined the man who had attacked him (2:6-11; 7:8-16).

The Aegean Region
0
50
100
Miles
0
50
100
Kilometers
N
Black Sea
THRACE
MACEDONIA
Pella
Philippi
Neapolis
Thessalonica
Beroea
Thasos
Samothrace
Thermaic Gulf
Proportis
Troas
Assos
Pergamum
Aegean Sea
Lesbos
ASIA
Delphi
Euboea
Chios
Smyrna
Sardis
Patrae
Gulf of Corinth
ACHAIA
Corinth
Cenchreae
Athens
Ephesus
Laodicea
Miletus
Patmos
Myrtoan Sea
Cos
Rhodes
Crete
Mediterranean Sea

When Paul found Titus in Macedonia and got the report on the results of the frank speech letter, he also learned that Titus had been very successful among the Macedonians in gathering the collection for the saints at Jerusalem. The Macedonians had embraced the collection with considerable zeal (8:1-5; 9:2), thinking themselves emulating the Corinthians and the other Achaians. Paul thus found that his earlier plans for the collection (gather it in Macedonia, sweep through Achaia, go to Jerusalem; 2 Cor 1:16) were well under way in Macedonia and that a group was ready to leave for Corinth. Paul was in a bind: The Corinthians, in their recent hithers and fros with Paul, had lost their zeal for the collection. One group, ready and eager (the Macedonians), was about to encounter another group, reticent and unprepared (the Corinthians).

In this context, Paul writes his fourth letter to the Corinthians (*Letter D*, 2 Corinthians 1–9). Several tasks confront him: (1) He must try to build beyond his recently stressed relations with the Corinthians; in particular, he must account for his dependability, even though he broke his promise about a scheduled visit, and he must account for his having resorted to a harsh letter instead of the projected visit. (2) He needs to recognize, and sign off as satisfied by, the Corinthian punishment of the one who did the wrong. (3) He must consolidate his fresh gains with the Corinthians to the point that (4) he can appeal to them for full participation in the collection for the Jerusalem saints. Paul tries to accomplish these goals (1) by accounting for his relatively recent decisions and whereabouts (2 Cor 1:8–2:13; 7:5-16); (2) by an extended initial, *indirect* appeal for a fuller Corinthian embrace of him and his ministry as refracted through a series of powerful, thoughtful lenses (2:14–6:10), followed by a brief, *direct* request for what he has just indirectly sought—namely, more affection—and (3) by moving to an open discussion of his plans for the collection and for their participation in it.

So the letter fragment 2 Corinthians 1–9 reflects complex motives and goals on Paul's part. He has personal incentives: He wants more affection from the Corinthians and thinks that, as the one who was their father in the faith (2 Cor 6:13), he deserves it; and he wants to avoid the embarrassment of having bragged about the Corinthians' enthusiasm regarding the collection (9:2), only to have the Macedonians discover, on their projected arrival in Corinth, apathy and perhaps even dissension. He has public motivations as well: The collection is the crown jewel of his ministry because, more than anything else, it demonstrates the unity of believers in the midst of their social and ethnic diversities, and his desire to bring the Corinthians into a more affectionate relationship is not simply self-serving but also accords with his conviction that the Corinthians' destiny depends on their close adherence to his gospel.

A fragment of Paul's fifth letter to the Corinthians is found in 2 Corinthians 10–13 (*Letter E*). Several developments, none of them positive, have muddied the waters for Paul and the Corinthians since his writing of 2 Corinthians 1–9. The letter-commended intruders, whose presence was only a minor matter in 2 Cor 3:1-3, have become a major force because they aligned with some currents of resentment that have been building in Corinth for some time.

The exact dynamics between the outsiders and the Corinthians escape us, but they cannot be ignored because the lines of initiative could have come from disaffected believers or from the rival intruders—but more likely from some combination of the two. Whichever the source, some Corinthians have come to believe that Paul's fiduciary relations are problematic. First, by his refusal to receive support, he has openly shamed some Corinthian believers who bid to become his patrons (12:13). Among this group may be some who had long-standing resentment over his rebuke of their having taken poorer believers to court (1 Cor 6:1-8) and of their having been insensitive to the poor believers who came to the Lord's supper in their houses (1 Cor 11:21-22, 33-34). Second, some Corinthians think he is two-faced, preaching a gospel "free of cost" (1 Cor 9:18) and then drumming up a collection. Third, some Corinthians note Paul's inconsistencies in refusing to accept support from them while receiving help from the Macedonians and raise questions of his probity and motives.[2] Fourth, some Corinthians believe that Paul's insistence on working with his hands is inconsistent with his status as apostle—and they see in the rival intruders the pattern they wish was Paul's. Finally, Paul's letter of frank speech (*Letter C*, the third, lost one) probably also exacerbated some old irritations to which he likely added another when, in his next letter (*Letter D*, 2 Corinthians 1–9), he used frankness as a means of asking for more affection, a culturally problematic use of frank speech (2 Cor 6:13).

The ultimate blow comes when (comes when (some of) the Corinthians, sensitive about the differences between Paul and his rival intruders, want to "test" Paul, apparently with regard to his apostleship (2 Cor 13:3, 5-10). Paul can no longer avoid confrontation. He projects a third visit, a showdown encounter in which he and they can sort out their differences and he can reassert his authority. The letter fragment 2 Corinthians 10–13 (*Letter E*) announces this visit, warns the Corinthians of the stakes involved, and, by heavy use of irony and under the guise of the fool's weakness, rehearses some of his disputed credentials.

Deliberations Concerning Fragmentation and Sequence Within 2 Corinthians.

Possible Fragments Within 2 Corinthians 1–9. With regard to the literary unity of 2 Corinthians 1–9, interpreters have varied widely. Some hold that these chapters all belong to the same letter fragment, but different scholars have posited within those same chapters at least four distinct letter fragments, as listed below.[3]

*2 Corinthians 2:14–*7:4 *Within 2 Corinthians 1–7.* Although least convincing on its face, 2 Cor 2:14–7:4 is sometimes argued as a separate letter fragment by scholars who are struck by what they perceive as the lack of a link back to 2:13 and the preceding verses and forward to 7:5-16.[4] The supposed fragment 2:14–7:4 has been placed, on one construction, within a travel narrative, sometimes identified as yet another fragment—beginning in 1:8 (cf. 1:15-17), running through 2:12-13, and finding its completion in 7:5-16—whose travel plans have no clear connection, as these advocates see it, with what they consider the more theological reflections in 2:14–7:4. An alternative construction, but presuming the same intrusion of 2:14–7:4 into chapters 1–7, takes the framing material in 1:1–2:13 and 7:5-16 as a distinct "letter of reconciliation."[5]

*2 Corinthians 6:14–*7:1. Scholars are divided over whether 6:14–7:1 is a separate Pauline letter fragment that a later redactor has inserted into Paul's appeal for more affection, dividing the latter into two sections (6:11-13; 7:2-4).[6] Further, some declare that these verses are not even authentically Pauline.[7]

2 Corinthians 8:1 and 2 Corinthians 9:1. Chapters 8 and 9 both deal with Paul's collection for the saints in Jerusalem, but the opening words of 9:1 (περὶ μὲν γάρ *peri men gar*, "So concerning"; hidden in the NRSV and NIV translations) can be argued to introduce a new item and thereby to suggest that the two chapters once stood alone;[8] 9:2 features the Achaians as models for the Macedonians, while 8:1-5 runs the modeling in the opposite direction, and the accompanying "brothers" in 8:18-20 are a safeguard against accusations against Paul, whereas in 9:3-5 they are supposed to get the donation together before Paul arrives.[9]

2 Corinthians 10–13. Most scholars who admit to any fragmentation recognize that 2 Corinthians 10–13 is a literary unit distinct from what precedes it. If nothing else, its tone is so different, signaling a time of mutual distress between Paul and the Corinthians. Whether this letter fragment should be considered to have originated earlier or later than any other possible fragment is another matter and will receive its treatment below.

Sequence of the Letter Fragments. To compound matters, scholars who hold for the same partition theories do not always agree on the historical sequence of the fragments. Most of the permutations have their advocates. Chapter 9 was written before chapter 8;[10] chapter 8 preceded chapter 9.[11] Chapters 10–13 were written before chapters 1–9 or parts thereof;[12] and chapters 10–13 were written last.[13]

Possible Missing Letter. All of these reckonings are further complicated by Paul's unequivocal declarations (2 Cor 2:9; 7:8-12) that he has earlier written to the Corinthians a letter that has come subsequently to be denominated by scholars as "painful" (so described because of its effect on the Corinthians, 7:8-11) or "tearful" (so named because of Paul's description of his demeanor in writing it, 2:4). The question naturally arises as to whether any of the letter fragments that reputedly make up 2 Corinthians are part of that painful letter. The most obvious candidate is chapters 10–13 because it is the type of letter—indeed, the only extant candidate—that could aggrieve or bring pain to the recipients (7:8).[14] However, chapters 10–13 fail to qualify as the painful letter on every other count; most important, they make no mention of the one who "did the wrong" (2:3-11; 7:8-12); even though Paul sent the painful letter in place of a visit that he spares them (2 Cor 1:23–2:1), chapters 10–13 allude to no failed visit, but rather invite preparation for an impending visit. Finally, Paul's exuberant description of the Corinthians' change of heart (7:11) does not fit the problem of intruding rivals that pervades chapters 10–13. So we must conclude that the painful letter, though surely written before 2 Corinthians 1–9, is lost in its entirety. Because no fragments of it survive, its content can only be deduced from Paul's description of it in chapters 2 and 7.[15]

The Definition and Sequence of Fragments. This introduction assumes that 2 Corinthians 1–9 is the fragment of one letter, that 2 Corinthians 10–13 is a section of another, and that the sequence in which we find the fragments reflects their actual historical order. The change in tone and in the relation of Paul to the Corinthians in chapters 10–13 indicates that it is a distinct fragment and not a continuation of chapters 1–9. The reasons for adopting this sequence as historical will become clear in the detailed arguments.

The case for further fragmentation of 2 Corinthians 1–9 is not compelling. The purported break between 2 Cor 2:13 and 2:14 is an interpretive failure to see Paul's own connection between details of his travel plans—in particular his having decided not to come when he promised—and 2:14ff., where Paul depicts himself as a prisoner whom God leads around as *God*, not Paul, wills. Scholars' resistance to see 2 Corinthians 8–9 as a continuation of 2 Corinthians 1–7 rests in their failure to comprehend that Paul dare not make explicit mention of the collection, a matter for which they have lost their earlier zeal, until he has recemented his relations with the Corinthians, precisely the initial burden of his efforts in 2 Cor 2:14–7:16. Paul laid the groundwork in 2:1–7:16 for his treatment of the collection in 2 Corinthians 8–9. Paul's rhetorical purposes in 2 Corinthians 8–9 tie the two chapters together as a literary unit that caps off 2 Corinthians 1–9 as a single letter.

Methodological Caution. Although all five letters to the Corinthians were written by the same apostle to the same general group of believers in the same city, each letter has a singularly distinctive dynamic that must be honored and not read into or affected by the interpretation of any of the others. For that reason we must exercise great care not to import a conflict or problem from a later letter into an earlier one. The primary clues for determining the relation to Paul in any given letter or fragment must be generated from the document in question.

Taking the Temperature of Paul's Relations with the Corinthians in the Different Letters. The "previous" letter (*Letter A*, lost) leaves us in the dark except for the references to it in 1 Cor 5:9-10. The Corinthians have asked Paul for clarification about holiness and living in the world—a clear indication that they were interested to understand and follow his counsel.

First Corinthians (*Letter B*) manifests the Corinthians in good relations with Paul; they ask his counsel on a series of issues, and he openly seeks to guide and lead them even though their fractiousness with each other shows him that they are nearer being babies in the faith than adults—and are overly engaged in status seeking. Although the Corinthians are in disharmony with one another, they are in good relations with Paul, and no problems or persons impinge from outside the community of believers.

The painful letter (*Letter C*, lost), by the descriptions of it and references to it in 2 Corinthians 1–9, reveals that relations between Paul and the Corinthians have hit some problems. His response in that letter is to call the Corinthians to task; Titus's report reassures Paul that the letter has brought the Corinthians into fidelity to Paul again (2 Cor 7:6-16).

Second Corinthians 1–9 (*Letter D*) tries to build on the success of the painful letter and shows Paul striving to elaborate and to enhance his own ministry for and with them in ways that invite and increase Corinthian allegiance—with the ultimate goal of encouraging and assuring their full participation in the collection for the saints in Jerusalem. Outsiders are noted (2 Cor 3:1-3) but are not considered the threat that they will become by chapters 10–13; Paul's epistolary efforts are focused on the Corinthians and their relationship to him, and not on any intruders.

A ground shift of considerable proportions must be supposed as a context for 2 Corinthians 10–13 (*Letter E*). Paul and the Corinthians have never been in more contentious relations; some of them want to put Paul to the test regarding his apostolic standing and, therefore, authority. The intruders have been established among (at least some of) the Corinthians as rival authorities. Of course, Paul detracts from his rivals, but his attention is focused on the Corinthians and on a final effort to bring them into allegiance. The letter does two things: It addresses some of the differences from the rivals that Paul wants to claim as distinctive for himself, and it lays the groundwork for a personal visit in which the matters may be resolved.

The following table graphs Paul's relations with the Corinthians. The left vertical is a graduated scale depicting the quality of their relationship, ranging from excellent down to poor. Across the bottom is a time line depicting Paul and the Corinthians at the moment of each letter or letter fragment.

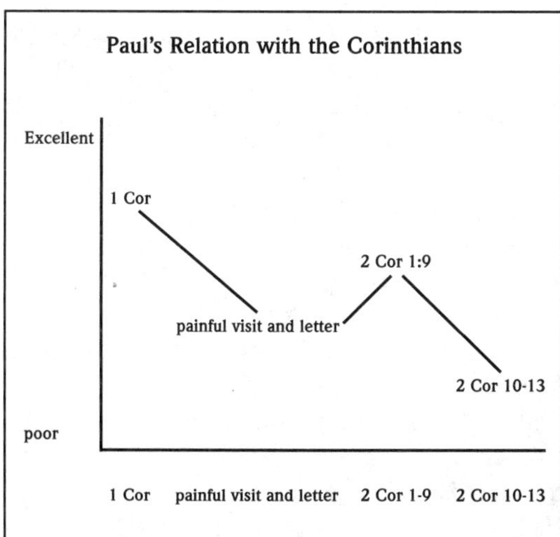

While honoring the methodological caution about keeping Paul's letters and letter fragments from affecting the interpretation of each other, we can observe certain continuities in the Corinthian community of believers. The same socioethnic makeup prevails from letter to letter fragment: A few rich people are part of the community, but most members are not wealthy (1 Cor 1:26); the affluent made a clear impact in taking cobelievers to court (1 Cor 6:1-8) and at the Lord's supper (1 Cor 11:17-34); in 2 Corinthians the wealthy seek to become Paul's patrons, but he refuses them (11:7-10, 20-21; 12:13); and most of the believers are Gentiles (1 Cor 8:1, 7; 12:2). Throughout the Corinthian correspondence, believers have been susceptible to status grasping, envy, fractiousness, and the lure of wisdom and fine speech (1 Cor 1:18-25; 2 Cor 10:10; 11:6).

DATES OF COMPOSITION OF THE LETTERS

The dates of the letters can only be estimated in general terms. The reckoning of dates must be interlaced with Paul's projected and actual visits. Starting from what we can know, Paul wrote 1 Corinthians from Ephesus (1 Cor 16:8) in the fall or winter (53 or 54 CE) and expected to stay there until Pentecost (spring). He promises a visit to Corinth, perhaps to stay for the winter, after he makes the land journey through Macedonia (1 Cor 16:5-6).

When he wrote 2 Corinthians 1–9 from Macedonia, he had only recently made the long-projected visit to Macedonia—but then only because he was desperate to find Titus and to know the Corinthian response to his letter of frank speech (lost to us). Timothy, as the co-author of the current letter fragment (2 Cor 1:1), has returned from Corinth (1 Cor 16:10-11) and accompanied Paul from Asia, where Paul (and Timothy, perhaps, since the plural is used) has recently been spared a threat to his life (2 Cor 1:8-11).

Between the writing of 1 Corinthians and 2 Corinthians 1–9, Paul has made a visit to Corinth that turned bad (with the one who "did the wrong," 2 Cor 2:1-3; 7:12), and, instead of the promised subsequent visit, he wrote them the (lost) letter of harsh frank speech (2 Cor 2:1-4; 7:8-16). What length of time transpired between the writing of 1 Corinthians, which can be dated to the fall or winter of 53 (or at the latest the same period in 54), and the composition of 2 Corinthians 1–9? We have a clue in Paul's description of the collection for the saints in Jerusalem. Twice he mentions that the Corinthians had begun the collection "a year ago" or "since last year" (πέρυσι *perysi*, 2 Cor 8:10; 9:2). First Corinthians 16:1-4 seems to have been a Pauline response to a Corinthian inquiry regarding the logistics of the collection, so we can presume that in fall 53 or fall 54 they were committed to the collection but not certain how they might best prepare. On this ground, it is possible to project that 2 Corinthians 1–9 was written by the fall of 54 CE (or fall of 55, allowing a year from the range of dates for 1 Corinthians). In the year that passed between the writing of 1 Corinthians and 2 Corinthians 1–9, Paul had time to make the unexpected, fateful return by sea to Corinth (spring or summer), to return to the Roman province of Asia (probably Ephesus), and to write and have Titus deliver his frank speech letter instead of a promised further visit.

Second Corinthians 10–13 requires sufficient time after chapters 1–9 for the following to have occurred: First, the logistics of the collection dictate a certain time lag. As Paul lays it out in 2 Cor 8:16-24, he sends ahead Titus and the two brothers, with the apparent expectation that they will oversee the Corinthians' preparedness before Paul's and some Macedonians' arrival (9:5). Paul's projected visit must have taken on different proportions when he heard for the first time the extent to which the intruders had captured the fancy of at least some of the Corinthians, subverting Paul's authority. The two-stage visit to Achaia would have required some time (during which Paul discovers the seriousness of the threat represented by the intruding rivals). Finally, the itinerary supposes that the sea passages must be opened after the winter and early spring for the projected trip to Judea.

Second, we do not know who informed Paul that matters in Corinth were much worse than he had suspected, but candidates aplenty suggest themselves: Titus, the two selected brothers (8:18, 22), and any of the Macedonians who may have accompanied them with the collection. Each of these people could be expected to be devoted to Paul and sensitively ready to report remonstrations against him. In any case, the writing of 2 Corinthians 10–13—one of whose major burdens is to announce and prepare for Paul's imminent showdown visit to Corinth—need not be more than a few months after the composition of 2 Corinthians 1–9. Accordingly, we can posit that 2 Corinthians 10–13 was also written from Macedonia, probably in the spring or early summer of 55 (or of 56, allowing for the same time range noted for 1 Corinthians).

PAUL'S OPPONENTS AT CORINTH

The identification of Paul's opponents has become a growth industry, often with more conjecture and speculation than certainty or substance emerging.[16] Truth be told, we know very little about Paul's opponents in 2 Corinthians. The Corinthians knew their identity; at some point Paul knew enough about them to be or become concerned about them, so he had no need to rehearse it for us as interlopers. Second, we must acknowledge that our primary source for knowing anything about the opponents is Paul, who is biased against them and who has no interest in being fair or what we might call objective in his representations of them. In any search for clues regarding the opponents' identity, we must expect that Paul depicts them in an unfavorable light—that was how opponents were treated in those days[17]—but we can suppose that he did not totally misrepresent them, if not because of his moral values, surely for fear that the Corinthians would dismiss him and all his argumentation if he were too out of line with reality. Exaggeration and distortion cannot be ruled out, however, because Paul's purpose is to overthrow them, to prevail—and to do that he must establish himself as the *sole* legitimate apostle for the Corinthians.

Third, and along the same line, Paul's knowledge about his opponents is always secondhand (only in 2 Cor 2:5 do we see Paul knowing firsthand a Corinthian opponent). His agents or his other supporters, themselves persons biased in favor of Paul, are the sources of what he knows about the opponents. That means that any knowledge we today have of Paul's opponents in Corinth is thirdhand. Fourth, mirror reading—that is, taking items in the text and assuming that in them Paul is responding to some criticism or to some claim of the opponents—has been overused in the study of Paul's letters.[18] Not every denial or distinction of him can be read as reflecting a charge.[19] Neither is every Pauline theological affirmation a response to something his opponents have said.

Finally, Paul's (indeed, the culture's) predisposition for indirect or figured speech has been underestimated. In such rhetoric one does not take issues head-on but chooses an alternate, less-heated matter, issue, or topic and, by treating it, leaves the hearers to make the application to the question at hand.[20] Paul's original hearers would bring enough information to the hearing of his letters so that they could readily distinguish what we can only surmise—namely, when Paul is speaking directly and when indirectly.

Two Stages of Opposition. For the purpose of identifying Paul's opposition, this introduction distinguishes between two distinct stages of Paul's struggle with the Corinthians as reflected in

2 Corinthians. The two stages correspond to the two letter fragments. The reckoning about Paul's opponents must be different regarding each letter fragment, because Paul's relation to the Corinthians is distinct at the two different times of writing. When he wrote 2 Corinthians 1–9, intruders were of little consequence. They had come to Corinth with their letters of commendation (3:1-3), but Paul does not treat them as a major problem. Paul is not unaccustomed to having other believers pass through his work sites (Gal 2:4, 11-12; cf. 1 Cor 9:5), so at first the appearance of these people might not have caused him great concern. At that point he has his own special issues with the Corinthians and has just recently heard that his letter of harsh frank speech (*Letter C*) has effected a rapprochement of the Corinthians to him. The lofty theological constructions that he struts before them in 2:14–6:10 are not a reflection of anything his opponents have said, but simply his own creative self-portrayal of his ministry as seen in three grand perspectives.

The exigence of 2 Corinthians 10–13 is starkly different. Now the outsiders, who were merely noted in 3:1-3, have become rivals who have bid with some success for Corinthian allegiance at the expense of Paul's status and authority. So here the central struggle is one of rivalry, of contested authority between Paul and his opponents—and, therefore, of fractured Corinthian allegiance. Much of past scholarship on Paul's Corinthian opponents has assumed, arguably anachronistically, that the central issues between Paul and his opponents were doctrinal—that is, disputes over theological ideas. In Paul's differences with the Corinthians, not ideas but practices, comportment, and standing are in contention.[21] Paul's theological assertions are not at dispute; Paul's authority is.[22] Paul's theological claims are adduced by him as a way of authenticating his authority.

Paul's standing and competence are at issue across all of 2 Corinthians; this fact has led interpreters to bleed what they see and know most clearly from 2 Corinthians 10–13, a distinct and subsequent letter, back onto 2 Corinthians 1–9. If we resist that simplification and importation, we can distinguish between the way Paul's standing and competence are treated in the two letter fragments.

When the focus is restricted to 2 Corinthians 1–9, then the questions of Paul's adequacy as an apostle, as *their* apostle, are best understood as a Pauline advocacy of himself as the very apostle who brought the gospel to them and who deserves their full adherence by dint of his work with and among them. Paul thus champions himself and his cause as the apostle, as their apostle, whom they should embrace more fully. Paul's rich self-portraits as minister of the new covenant (3:1–4:6), as minister sustained through affliction and mortality (4:7–5:10), and as minister of reconciliation (5:11-21) overlap and reinforce one another, identifying Paul as their apostle who is worthy of their full devotion. Why is Paul led to such a self-promotion? There are two prominent reasons, one directed toward the immediate past, the other targeted toward the immediate future. As to the past, Paul must overcome any residual reticence among the Corinthians not only because of his failure to visit them as he had promised, but also because he had upbraided them harshly with a letter of frank speech (*Letter C*). As to the future, he has to prepare the Corinthians for the Macedonians' imminent and enthusiastic arrival with the collection for the Jerusalem saints when he has learned that the Corinthians have lost their zeal for it. His success with healing the past wounds and with avoiding embarrassment regarding the collection both demand that his ethos, his character and his standing with the Corinthians, be strong—the ultimate goal of 2:14–6:10, the central portion of 2 Corinthians 1–9. Only when his ethos has been sufficiently refurbished can and does he turn explicitly to the touchy question of the collection (2 Corinthians 8:1–9).

In 2 Corinthians 10–13, Paul's adequacy and standing as an apostle are certainly directly under question and attack. Paul's response is different also—even though some self-commendation continues to be present. Here, in his defense, he is drawn onto the grounds of the opposition: He boasts and references visions and revelations, signs and wonders, but only as a fool. Then he rejects visions and revelations as a basis of authority and puts in their place the standard of day-in-day-out performance—that is, what he has done among them across the years (12:6). Whereas in chapters 1–9 Paul's ethos was burnished by three grand theological ruminations about ministry and how Paul enacted each of them, in chapters 10–13 we see Paul, God's warrior, ironically embracing weakness as his shield and engaging, in turn, in accusation, reproach, apology, and appeal. Finally, in chapters 10–13 we see him declare guidelines for how he and the Corinthians will resolve their differences when he arrives in Corinth.

In order to reconstruct what we can know about Paul's opponents at Corinth, we start from the text, the only evidence we really have, and distinguish three categories: more certain evidence; less certain, but plausible, evidence; and possible evidence.[23] Identification of certain clues regarding the opponents is the more difficult because it is not always easy to tell when Paul is speaking directly and when he is using indirect speech as an oblique way of relating to or describing his opponents.

More Certain Indices of Opponents. Nothing is clearer than this: By the time of 2 Corinthians 10–13, the intruders have become Paul's rivals for the leadership of the Corinthian believers. In significant ways they claim to be like Paul, but it is equally important that they distinguish themselves from him. *They* have made the comparison, and Paul finds it odious (10:12); he wants to remove any pretext they have for claiming that they are "just like us" (11:12). But they also move beyond parity, alleging to be superior to Paul (see Paul's mocking designation of them as "super apostles," 11:5; 12:11). This is at the heart of the rivalry.

Inherent in their comparative assessment of Paul is a critique of him at several points. It is impossible to tell just how much or how many of the following points the outsiders generated or how many they simply seized upon and focused sentiments already present among the Corinthians. Either way, however, the Corinthian soil was ready for the planting and harvest.

Paul's bearing and performance are not up to par for a person in such a position of authority, they claim (and appear to have convinced at least some Corinthians). Paul has provided them abundant evidence across the years; the Corinthians will remember that Paul did not come among them with "lofty words of wisdom" but simply preached the cross (1 Cor 2:1-2); that he likened himself, in an ironically self-deprecating way, to leftover dishwater (1 Cor 4:13); that his speech amounts to nothing (2 Cor 10:10); that he has a proclivity to find himself in humble, if not humiliating, circumstances (1 Cor 4:11-12; cf. 2 Cor 4:7-12; 6:1-10; 11:21*b*-29); that he made no credible defense when he was with them and that one of their own attacked him (2 Cor 2:1-11); and that he has steadfastly eschewed the perquisites appropriate to his status, insisting instead on supporting himself via demeaning hand work (1 Cor 4:12*a*; 9:4-14). Further, 2 Cor 10:10 suggests that Paul's opponents have derisively labeled him "weak" in bodily presence.

The intruders, on the other hand, at least by Paul's implications, share the status of being "apostles" in some sense (2 Cor 11:5, 13-15; 12:11), though they, in contrast to Paul, seem ready to relish the entitlements of status and honor (11:20; cf. 11:7-12; 12:17). Accordingly, they do not work to support themselves (11:20; cf., perhaps obliquely, 11:7-12; 12:13-16). Clearly the wealthier Corinthians who were eager to patronize Paul would have found ready recipients in his rivals.

Paul counters on several fronts. With regard to himself, his opening insistence is key: "Look at what is before your eyes" (2 Cor 10:7; 12:6*b*). The Corinthians' long (and mostly) good history with him should reassure them that he is dependable and faithful. He has never accepted support from them, so why should he start now? On the contrary, he has always worked for their benefit, never his own (12:19; 13:7-9). Absent or present, he has continually been the same Paul (10:11). He brought the gospel all the way to them (10:13-15), and he has stuck by them through thick and thin. Further, he embraces the charge of his weakness as a badge of ironic honor and portrays his weakness over and over as a positive sign of God's abundant power working through him for the gospel and *for them* (2 Cor 11:6*a*, 23–12:10).

Paul understands that God designated him to take the gospel to the Corinthians, that they are, therefore, part of his divinely appointed "sphere of influence/province" (κανών *kanōn*; see 10:13-16) and that he has paternal responsibilities with the Corinthians because God has given him responsibility for recruiting believers in that area. Others, such as Apollos, may be of assistance to him (1 Cor 3:5-9), but the Corinthians can have only one father (2 Cor 11:2; cf. 1 Cor 4:15). Paul's 2 Corinthians intruders have moved beyond being helpful; they bid to supplant Paul and have wrongly moved into Paul's *kanōn*.

More important, Paul does not directly counsel the Corinthians about what they should do toward the rivals (unless 2 Cor 6:14–7:1 is regarded as authentic and the "unfaithful" in 6:14-16 are dubiously deemed the opponents). Rather, his attention is focused on a call for the Corinthians to reassess their own standing in the faith, to return to their roots in his preaching and to his leadership, and to accord one another the proper attention that love demands.

Less Certain, but Plausible, Indices of Opponents. It is less sure that the opponents are Jewish, though Paul's question, "Are they Hebrews?" and his detailing of his high-caliber Jewish credentials surely point in that direction. Curiously, however, no problems between Paul and the Corinthians are traceable to Jewish issues such as one can see, by contrast, in Galatians, with its concern for circumcision and the place of the law. The two-covenant discussion in 2 Cor 3:1–4:6, which some scholars credit, at least in some measure, to Paul's opponents,[24] is hardly part of a dispute; rather, it is Paul's creative elaboration and enhancement—in a typical Pauline "not this, but that" form—of his own ministry as an appeal for increased Corinthian fidelity.[25] If Paul's adversaries are Jews, allowing for that reading of 11:22, then one can equally argue that Paul credits them with being "ministers of Christ" (διάκονοι Χριστοῦ *diakonoi Christou*, 11:23), though Paul is quick to claim superiority for himself.

We cannot be exactly certain what is behind the letters of recommendation mentioned in 2 Cor 3:1, though the practice is a commonplace in the Greco-Roman world, and it is plausible that the outsiders came to Corinth armed with supporting documents that credited them with a measure of ready-made authority (see 2 Cor 2:17). Whether those letters came from some of the original apostles and/or from some in leadership positions in Jerusalem we simply cannot know.[26] It is attractive to make such connections because the drama is enhanced and we can drift into the timeworn Peter-versus-Paul conundrum—for which there is no other evidence in 2 Corinthians.

Paul resorts to telling about his heavenly transit (12:2-5) as if forced. Did his rivals (or even worse for Paul, some of the Corinthians) credit visions and revelations as an indicator of status and authority? We know that the Corinthians have a long-standing attraction for silver-tongued speech (1 Cor 2:1), but Paul values "knowledge" over "speech" (2 Cor 11:6) as an assessment of apostolic credentials. Curiously, after telling of his extraordinary transport to paradise (12:2-5), Paul effectively rejects visions as an apostolic index, preferring instead what one sees and hears in him (2 Cor 12:6, an echoing refinement of 10:7*a*). Whether it was the intruders or the Corinthians,[27] visions and revelations bid to play too great a role in estimating status, for Paul's values.

Unclear Indices of Opponents. What are we to make of the reference in 11:4 to "another Jesus," "another spirit," and "another gospel"? Or should that be translated "another Spirit," indicating the Holy Spirit, as the expression could equally well be read? Have the outsiders offered these alternatives, or is this a dramatic rhetorical move on Paul's part? Nowhere in 2 Corinthians is there evidence of a dispute over Jesus or the Spirit (or spirit, for that matter). The Spirit is associated with the second covenant and with Paul's ministry (2 Cor 3:8, 17), as we would fully expect, because Paul sees the Spirit and its reception as the hallmark of the life of faith (see 1 Cor 12:13; Gal 3:2). But Paul does not treat his claims about the Spirit as if they are being defended or advocated over against competing claims about the Spirit.

Paul is given to stark antitheses, especially when he wants to distance an alternative from himself. Paul knows there is only one gospel (Gal 1:7*a*), but that gospel can be perverted (Gal 1:7*b*). Paul apparently has a commonplace saying to the effect that anyone who preaches a gospel different from his own is anathema (Gal 1:9: "As I said before, so now again I say"), and he may have recycled that saying here—with elaboration—as a way of setting himself antithetically over against his rivals. In his categories, Paul's rivals represent another gospel if they differ from him—whether the differences are in ideas or in practices. Finally, the Jesus whom Paul proclaims is "Christ Jesus as Lord, with ourselves as your slaves for Jesus' sake" (2 Cor 4:5). Paul's humble, weak demeanor is grounded in the Jesus he preaches, the Jesus who is Lord. So his comportment is, as always, fundamentally christologically based (e.g., 1 Cor 11:1).

Two passages in 2 Corinthians 1–9 have been mirror-read as references to Paul's opponents. Paul's disclaimer that "we are not, like many, hucksters of God's word" in 2:17 may be a reference to opponents. If it is, then we learn nothing in particular about them. Paul's differentiation may, however, be considered a patterned reference to others who preach the gospel out of different (and less noble) motives (see Phil 1:15-18). Interpreters have similarly read 4:2 to mirror Paul's opponents, but it may just as well be Paul's *via negativa* magnification of his own ethos and exemplary comportment (cf. 2:17). Without reinforcement from 2 Corinthians 10–13, a document from a later time and with different dynamics, the two references in 2:17 and 4:2 do not give any certain picture of opponents.

In sum, we can be sure that Paul's opponents include some intruders who have appeared in Corinth with letters of commendation from some unidentifiable, but putatively powerful, persons. Although the intruders have arrived in Corinth by the time of Paul's writing 2 Corinthians 1–9, their impact is not certain to be major until the time of his composition of chapters 10–13. By then, the intruders have surely found a hearing among some (but we cannot be certain how many) Corinthians and been accorded status and authority by them. When favorable to them, these outsiders claim to be like Paul; but in certain key matters they distinguish themselves from him: They do not act below their station; they do not stoop to menial labor to support themselves; they readily count on patronage from others as part of their apostolic perquisites.

Pauline opposition *among the Corinthians* may no longer be ignored, and sources of Corinthian discontent are signaled in the text of 2 Corinthians. At issue between Paul and his opponents (intruders and allied Corinthians alike) is Paul's status and authority with the Corinthians. All else in the contention takes its place around that central pillar. Whether the intruders are also Jews is plausible but is not necessary to determine for the interpretation of any part of 2 Corinthians.

Whatever else one may discern about Paul's opponents, it is clear that he wrote 2 Corinthians 10–13 with the major purpose of setting up the terms and conditions under which he expected to make an imminent, showdown visit to Corinth. He puts the Corinthians, supporters and opponents together, on notice that he expects to bring about Corinthian obedience. In doing so, he must be able to assume that the intruders will have been served a warning as well. In 2 Corinthians, Paul has no direct engagement or contention with his intruding rivals. Like silent third parties as Paul relates to the Corinthians, his rivals are an important part of what amounts to a triangle. And Paul's attention is devoted to regaining the affection and allegiance of the Corinthians; nowhere in 2 Corinthians does he engage the outsiders directly.

PAUL'S USE OF "WE" IN 2 CORINTHIANS

Paul employs the plural in self-reference more in 2 Corinthians than in any other letter. Before detailing Paul's goals in doing so, we must note that 2 Cor 1:1 does credit Timothy with co-authorship, so the plural may refer to Timothy as well. Other letters are jointly authored (Gal 1:2; Phil 1:1; 1 Thess 1:1; Phlm 1), however, without such heavy use of plural self-references. So the proliferation of the plural in 2 Corinthians demands an accounting.

By using plural pronouns so often in referring to himself, Paul accomplishes a variety of goals that are important for his rhetorical task of persuading the Corinthians to ally themselves (more fully) with him. First, with the plural self-references, Paul regularly invites the Corinthians to think of themselves as one with him—a major objective in all of 2 Corinthians.

Second, by using plural pronouns Paul encourages the Corinthians to think that Paul does not stand alone, that he has widespread support, and that he is part of a larger group—his rhetoric suggests the mainstream—who advocate the gospel as he does. Among those who can be associated in the plurals are Timothy, the co-author (1:1), the Achaians (i.e., the Corinthians' provincial neighbors, who are also named as addressees; 1:1), the Macedonians (9:2, 4; 11:9), Silvanus (1:19), Titus (2:13; 7:6, 13-14; 8:6, 16, 23; 12:18), and the "brother" praised by all the churches (8:18). All of these people, explicitly mentioned in 2 Corinthians, are allied with Paul.

Third, while some Corinthians might question that Paul was a minister of the gospel, Paul's regular description of his ministry in the plural "we" leaves them no room to deny that God has commissioned ministers such as he and must make it more difficult to deny that Paul is one of them. Fourth, the plural allows Paul to depict himself in rather grand fashion, with diminished risk of his being thought to be boasting inordinantly.[28]

Fifth, specifically in regard to the collection for the saints in Jerusalem, Paul's use of plural self-references suggests broad support for him and for the collection while also depicting him as the leader of such a larger movement (with which the Corinthians hopefully will want to ally themselves). Finally, his pervasive use of the plural as a way of referring to himself makes it all the more striking and powerful rhetorically when he explicitly invites the Corinthians into the picture that is otherwise described by the plurals (cf. 3:18; 5:10).

WHAT WE LEARN ABOUT PAUL IN 2 CORINTHIANS

Paul the Person. Paul was a passionate man, given to a wide range of emotions. We observe his anger and distress in 2 Corinthians 10–13 not only as Corinthian opposition hardens against him, but also as some of his beloved drift away under outside influences. Also visible, though, is his heartfelt affection, his sense that he loves the more and is loved less (12:15). Clear as well is his anxiety over whether his painful letter might have proved too painful for the Corinthians (7:6-16); equally clear and powerful are his expressions of relief and joy when he receives Titus's report of their return to filiation with him (7:6-7, 13-14). Professions of his love for them (11:11) fit well with other expressions of friendship, such as his preparedness to spend and be spent for them (12:15), his readiness to live and to die with them (7:3), and his willingness to speak frankly as a friend to them (6:11).

As reflected in 2 Corinthians, Paul's experiences range from the most sublime to the most precarious. What can surpass his being caught up into the third heaven, into paradise (12:2-6)? It is almost as difficult to imagine anyone having more hardships than Paul (4:8-12; 6:4-10; 11:23-27), including his thorn or stake in the flesh (12:7-9) and his Damascus escape (11:30-33). In fact, the letter fragment 2 Corinthians 1–9 opens with Paul's disclosure of a recent experience in Asia (roughly modern western Turkey), where he feared for his life; he refers to it as a virtual death sentence (1:8-11). Even if we allow for some inflation as part of a rhetorical appeal for pity, the experience must have been traumatic.

Paul's self-descriptions are illuminating because they show a Paul not always victorious, not always triumphant, but often vexed, put upon, and, at times, almost overwhelmed. His Asian affliction left him with no resource other than to trust in "God who raises the dead" (1:9). Regarding that situation, he describes himself, in evocative terms, as being utterly, beyond measure weighed down, as despairing of living (1:8). Elsewhere in the same letter he depicts himself as being pushed almost to the brink: afflicted, perplexed, persecuted, and struck down—to each of those powerful verbs he adds a codicil of grace-filled limitations: "but not crushed ... not driven to despair ... not forsaken ... not destroyed" (4:8-9). A similar self-portrait acknowledges a fundamental dissonance between the way he is treated or perceived and how he thinks he truly is: "treated as impostors, and yet are true; as unknown, and yet are well known; as dying, and see—we are alive; as punished, and not yet killed; as sorrowful, yet always rejoicing; as poor, yet making many rich; as having nothing, and yet possessing everything" (6:8*c*-10 NRSV). Another powerful self-description shows him with "conflicts on the outside, fears within" (7:5 NIV). Some important insights into Paul are available here. First, what one sees and experiences is, thanks be to God, not the whole picture. Second, as strong in faith as Paul was, he never expected his faith or his God to shelter him from the vicissitudes and vagaries of life. He did expect God to be present for him *in whatever circumstance*; indeed, that was Paul's experience.

Paul was a person of incredible theological imagination and resources. Second Corinthians 1–9 is a showcase of his reflections because in those chapters he projects three portraits of his ministry as a means of enhancing his ethos and Corinthian affiliation with him. Not only does he have his Scriptures as a potent resource and stimulus for his thoughts and for their expression, but he also has pre- and para-Pauline Christian formulations and the conventions of the Greco-Roman world to draw upon and to weave together with his own reflections. Throughout 2 Corinthians, and indeed across all his correspondence, he has no interest in theological notions for their own sake, but only as they engage life, as they bear on the way people comport themselves. His theologizing, therefore, is never abstract or abstruse; instead it is always engaged, always linked to life as real people—he and his hearers—are experiencing it.

Paul's Fiduciary Relations. Paul's flexible financial practices got him into difficulty with some Corinthians—perhaps not early on, but surely by the time 2 Corinthians was written. Although Paul clearly accepted support from the Philippians (Phil 1:5; 2:25; 4:10-16) and even had a Macedonian delivery of support to him while he was at Corinth (2 Cor 11:8-9), he resolutely and stubbornly persisted in his refusal to accept assistance from the Corinthians, even though some Corinthians apparently sought to become his patrons. It is not difficult to imagine, given the cultural suppositions of the time, that Paul refused to become client to some of the wealthy Corinthians because he could not allow himself either to be indebted to them or to be obligated to pay them honor in return for their favor.

Further, Paul regularly expects to be assisted on his journeys by local congregations as he pursues his itinerary (see Rom 15:24), and he does not count that aid as making him a client with its culturally assumed obligations. Even with the Corinthians he distinguishes between accepting their support and their helping him along in his travel (cf. 1 Cor 16:6; 2 Cor 1:16). We may suppose, therefore, that Paul distinguishes clientage from all forms of "hospitality" (see Rom 12:13; 15:24).

Finally, Paul's embrace of the collection for the poor at Jerusalem, an outgrowth of the Jerusalem conference (Gal 2:1-10), may not have created any early Corinthian confusion about his motives (1 Cor 16:1-4), but surely by the time of 2 Corinthians it had become a ground of contention. Witness Paul's extraordinary care to secure reputable representatives to accompany the delivery of the collection (2 Cor 8:18-23) in order to avoid any charges of fiscal abuse.

Unique Information from the Hardship Lists. For the most part, the hardship catalogs detail what we know about Paul from other texts and sources. He often was in danger and experienced great obstacles and problems in his efforts to advance the gospel. We might take special note of how frequently he experienced certain difficulties or the severity of them: "countless floggings, and often near death" (11:23 NRSV) or "afflicted...but not crushed...struck down" (4:8-9 NRSV).

Two details, however, shed unique light on Paul. First, five times he received the Jewish punishment of thirty-nine lashes (11:24). This discipline, founded on Deut 25:3, was enforced by the synagogues in Paul's time.[29] His submission to this penalty suggests that even after he became an apostle he continued to maintain his ties to Jewish synagogue worship and practice; otherwise, he would neither have been judged out of order or needed to allow himself to be thus chastened. Of course, we cannot tell at what points across his ministry he received the thirty-nine lashes, but five times suggests a longer rather than shorter period. That he kept contact with fellow Jews is also clear from passages like 1 Cor 9:20, but such a passage does not indicate as clearly that he submitted to synagogue authority.

Second, he reports that he was three times beaten with rods (11:25), a Roman punishment (see Acts 16:22-23, 37-39) that was not supposed to be administered to Roman citizens, as Acts 16:37 affirms. Josephus reports, however, that such propriety was not always honored everywhere.[30] Thus Paul's report of having been beaten with rods does not rule out his having been a Roman citizen, as Acts 16:37 declares he was.

PAUL'S THOUGHT WORLD

Although Paul spends much of his time in these letter fragments either commending or defending himself, his way of doing so yields a view of several basic convictions that structure his thought world.

The Cosmic Purposes of God. God is ultimately in control, and, with what has been begun in Christ, God's plan is nearing completion. Paul has been captured and put on display in God's triumphal victory procession as God's power sweeps across the world (2:14-16). The plan and the power belong solely to God. To be sure, Satan has plans (and agents), but he poses no real threat to believers if they stay alert and remember that they have been made privy to Satan's design (2:11). The conclusion of God's purposes is near, so all opposing power is doomed.

Across both letter fragments, Paul uses references to end-time considerations as leverage on the Corinthians. Believers are going to face Christ's judgment for the way they have comported themselves (5:10). The panoply of God's power is marshaled behind Paul as he promises to vanquish all foes and render their defenses useless (10:3-6). God's purpose, in Christ, is the reconciliation of the entire cosmos (5:19), with everyone included, to God; that is why Christ "died for all" (5:14-15). This grand portrait of purpose, sketched out across the letter fragments of 2 Corinthians, utterly transcends and renders foolishly impotent any opposition to God, and derivatively to Paul. Captured by and now the agent of this overwhelming divine power, Paul dismisses any rival claims to the Corinthians' fealty and announces himself ready, with God's power, to induce (2:9; 7:15; 10:6; 13:5-10), if not enforce, obedience (13:4).

The Life of Faith as Process, as Growth, as Being Transformed. Paul understands that believers, as a part of God's new creation (5:17), are works in process, that God is working in them to transform them from one degree of glory to another (3:18). The new creation starts when, by God's grace, a person dies with Christ and, in dying, is brought to newness of life (Rom 6:4). At the outset of faith, believers are called babies (1 Cor 3:1-2; Phlm 10) or "weak with respect to faith" (Rom 14:1). As believers progress in the faith, Paul thinks of them as more mature, more like adults (1 Cor 2:6; 14:20; Phil 3:15). Every believer is given a measure of faith by God (Rom 12:3), and they, like their paradigmatic father Abraham, are to grow strong in faith (Rom 4:20). The resurrection at the last day, featured so prominently in 1 Corinthians 15:1, is confidently expected by Paul to be the capstone, the zenith at which the life of faith is brought to its fulfillment.

Here in 2 Corinthians Paul several times makes clear his anthropological assumption that believers are being transformed, but nowhere clearer or more powerfully than in his declaration: "And all of us...are being transformed...from one degree of glory to another" (2 Cor 3:18 NRSV). In sharp contrast with "those who are perishing," Paul sees believers—those who are already justified and reconciled (Rom 5:9-10)—as "those who *are being saved*," who are going "from life to life" (2 Cor 2:15-16, italics added). In a passage where he uses three different terms for "house" as a means of referring to human life, he depicts believers as currently living in what he imaginatively describes as "this tent" and as longing for a transformed, heavenly dwelling (5:1-2). With a shift of metaphor, he again describes the anticipated permutation as an expectation of being "further clothed" (5:4). Believers have died with Christ; God, who "raised the Lord Jesus will raise us also with Jesus" (4:14). Believers have received the Holy Spirit, but that is only a down payment of all that is to come (1:22; 5:5; cf. Rom 8:11). Believers' outer selves are wasting away, but their inner selves are being renewed day by day (4:16). That which is transitory is being replaced by what is eternal (4:18). What is mortal will be swallowed up without remainder by life (5:4). Paul's explicit hope for the Corinthians is that their faith may grow (10:15; cf. 13:9).

Change, growth, and development are presupposed by Paul across the letters. Compare his own self-portrait in 1 Corinthians 13:1, where he looks back to his life as a child and forward to a time not yet here when he will "see face to face...and know fully" (1 Cor 13:11-12). He works with the Philippians for their "progress and joy in faith" (Phil 1:25). He labors with the Thessalonians "to complete what is lacking in your faith" (1 Thess 3:10).

Believers' Proper Care for One Another. Although Paul's overriding concern in 2 Corinthians is a return of the Corinthians to full, proper relationship to him, he does not lose sight of their need to be concerned about each other. Ever the model, Paul presents himself as the one who cares in an exemplary way about the Corinthians. In his most dramatic representation of his caring, reserved for the confrontational 2 Corinthians 10–13 fragment, he portrays himself as ready to fail personally if doing so will ensure their doing "what is right" (13:7). He is eager to spend and be spent for them in his effort to secure them in the faith (12:15; cf. similar sacrificial imagery in Phil 2:17). In another instance, he models compassion when he urges the Corinthians to restore to fellowship the one they have dismissed: "pardon and console him, lest he be overwhelmed by excessive grief...decide in favor of love for him" (2:7-8). Though the individual had aggrieved Paul and the community (2:5), the communal rebuke must not be so severe or so sustained that the person is permanently lost from the fellowship; even someone who has wronged the community must be cared for in love.

Paul's reflections about the collection provide other windows onto how he thinks believers are or should be related to one another. First, believers should pattern themselves after the best they see in other believers: The Macedonians were spurred to contribute by the reports of the Corinthians (9:2); now the Corinthians should renew their commitment when they see how readily and fully the Macedonians have embraced the collection (8:1-7). Second, one's bounty provides for the need of another, without anyone's being disadvantaged in the giving or lacking in the receiving (8:12-14). Instead, Paul sees that among believers generosity and need are so correlated that, when proper concern for one another is present, a fundamental equality should result among the believers (ἰσότης *isotēs*, "fairness/equality," 8:13-14; cf. another idealized portrait of believing community in Acts 2:43-47; 4:32–5:11).

Reassessment of Contemporary Values. Profoundly grounded in Paul's gospel and observable across 2 Corinthians are ideas that are at least contrary—and may even be properly deemed subversive—to the culture and to its impact on at least some of the Corinthians. Paul thinks that judgments made simply on what is seen, on what appears, on surface observations, are bound to be wrong. He employs various means to advocate that fundamental skepticism. He distinguishes walking by faith—that is, by trusting God—from walking by sight (5:7); he eschews reckoning from what can be seen in favor of "the things that cannot be seen" (4:18); and he distinguishes what appears on one's face from what is in one's heart (5:12). In embracing this perspective, Paul reaffirms to the Corinthians the same conviction expressed elsewhere in his letters: "Hope that is seen is not hope" (Rom 8:24); "Now we see in a mirror, enigmatically; then face to face; now we know partially; then we shall know completely just as we have been known" (1 Cor 13:12).

Paul acknowledges the same ambiguity in human estimations of other people. To consider another person "according to the flesh" (κατὰ σάρκα *kata sarka*)—that is, according to standard ways of reckoning, is certain to be misleading (5:16). Paul develops the thought christologically, saying that he no longer regards Christ *kata sarka*; to do so would be to view him wrongly, incompletely, without the resurrection that establishes his identity as Lord. Along these same lines, we must understand Paul's later self-description as not walking—that is, comporting himself—*kata sarka* (10:2), and his related assertion that the warfare he is prepared to prosecute against any opposition should not be confused with theoretically defeatable—that is, *kata sarka*—power (10:3).

The same undercutting of traditional cultural values is present in the hardship list of 2 Cor 6:4-10 but is packed especially into the verses at its end. As to the list, Paul's self-commendation comes not in the number of victories he can boast of or in his grand accomplishments or wealth, but is grounded instead in afflictions, hunger, and even disrepute (6:4ff.). The catalog concludes, however, with three couplets, each of which begins with cultural disvalues—"sorrowful," "poor," and "having nothing"—and turns each one of them radically, distinctly on its head—"rejoicing," "enriching many," and "possessing everything" (6:10). By doing this Paul depicts himself, and all those associated with him in the living of the gospel, as being shored up in joy even in the midst of sorrow, as showering riches where poverty seems to prevail, and as possessing everything while others might (wrongly) think the opposite is true. Believers possess everything because, as those who through Christ belong to God, believers share all that God possesses (1 Cor 3:21*b*-23).

Paul's fundamental critique of conventional values in 2 Corinthians should not have come as a surprise to the Corinthians. In an earlier letter to them, Paul had argued that, in the light of God's concluding purposes in reclaiming the cosmos, believers should comport themselves "as-if-not"; that is, they should live in the world so as to practice detachment from the values and entanglements it offers (1 Cor 7:30-31). As a predominantly Gentile congregation, the Corinthians will have been exposed to such Stoic reflection about "indifferent matters" (ἀδιάφορα *adiaphora*). Paul's inversion of values in 2 Cor 6:10 fits such a context and reinforces a certain distancing from cultural norms.

In a similar way, but focused on the cultural category of rich/poor, Paul's christological claim about Christ's having been rich and submitting himself to poverty for the believers so that by his poverty they might become rich offers a critique of riches and poverty and indirectly provides a model for Paul's relinquishing the accoutrements that some might think appropriate to apostleship (2 Cor 8:9). In this christological formulation, Paul does not offer an escape from poverty to riches as seen in the categories of the world; instead, Paul imparts a perspective that answers the question of what is truly valuable, of where real wealth resides.

Paul's basically contrary-to-culture outlook is also aimed, with great irony, at anyone among the Corinthians who is enamored of the intruders and their values. In focus is the way the intruders have inveigled the Corinthians into according to themselves grand status and support, both of which Paul has assiduously refused. Paul mocks the intruders, their Corinthian allies, and their values with an ironic parody: "You put up with it if someone enslaves you, if someone exploits you, if someone takes advantage of you, if someone is presumptuous, if someone slaps you in the face. With what shame I must say we were too weak to do that!" (11:20-21). Likewise, when acknowledging that, though he accepted support from other churches, he persisted in not burdening the Corinthians, he again feigns shame: "Forgive me this wrong" (12:13 NRSV).

All of Paul's subversion of cultural norms, every bit of his revaluation of values, is grounded in his christological conviction that Christ's resurrection overthrows not only death but also the structures of meaning by which people previously reckoned. If, in Christ, the fundamental antinomy of life and death has been cashiered from its governance of human encounters and significance, then indeed there is a "new creation" and truly "everything has become new" (5:17 NRSV). After Christ's death and resurrection, the norms of conduct have to be revised or newly invented, as the Corinthians have learned already from Paul in 1 Corinthians.

Because Paul's contention with the intruders and their Corinthian adherents comes to focus on his too humble status and demeanor, Paul moves his counter onto the weakness/power antinomy and grounds it in Christ, whom Paul claims "was crucified in weakness but lives by the power of God" (13:4 NRSV). So for Paul crucifixion/life and weakness/power are directly correlated.

By means of the weakness/power doublet, Paul at once defends himself and puts perspective on not only what is truly important, but also where the ultimate power resides. Paul's weakness/ power critique has long been known to the Corinthians (see 1 Cor 1:20-25; 15:43), but it probably emerges once again when some unidentified persons are reported to be claiming about Paul that "his letters are weighty and strong, but his bodily presence is weak" (2 Cor 10:10 NRSV). In 11:21, Paul, brimming with irony, embraces the description of himself as "too weak" to take advantage of the Corinthians as the intruders have. From that point in the letter, weakness becomes a major, positive theme of Paul's self-identification; having just recounted a list of hardships and sufferings (11:23-28), he pledges to boast of nothing but his weaknesses (11:30). And so he does, detailing how, in Damascus, he recently managed to escape with his life (11:31-33) and capping it off with a recounting of how he earnestly desired to have the stake or thorn in the flesh removed from him (12:7*b*-10). Paul depicts his weakness as a perfect avenue for God's power. Although he is not allowed to disclose the message that he received when he was in the third heaven (12:4), he readily recounts the word he received from the Lord in response to his failed petition for the removal of the thorn: "My grace is sufficient; my power is perfected in weakness" (12:9). It is in God's nature to display power in weakness, to place divine treasures in earthen vessels (4:7). God's power is perfectly suited to human weakness. So the culturally generated complaint against Paul, that he does not display the proper perquisites of power and status of a true apostle (12:12), is critiqued and rejected by Paul, who suggests indirectly that the complainers do not understand even the basics regarding the gospel and, by implication, about how God works.

Paul taps a widespread, popular contemporary notion of the inner and outer person and overlays it with a related contrast of temporary and permanent (4:16-18), as a part of his sustained argument that what one sees on the surface or outside is not predictably indicative of inner or permanent reality. In so doing he sets the stage for its amplification in the following, kindred antinomies between "face" and "heart" (5:12) and between knowing someone "according to the flesh" and as being related to the new creation (5:16-17).

The Importance of Works. With the classical emphasis on justification by faith we have sometimes lost Paul's perspective on works and their place in the life of faith. Much of 2 Corinthians is directed at the issue of how people behave, at what their conduct is. Paul's own comportment is a continuing topic, sometimes defined positively in terms of what he has done, sometimes delineated negatively as to how he has refrained from behaving (e.g., 2 Cor 1:12, 17; 2:17; 4:2; 11:7-9; 12:6, 14-18).

In 2 Corinthians, Paul is also attentive to the Corinthians' behavior, reminding them that they, like he, will have to face the judgment before Christ at the last day (5:10). Then and there, Paul holds, all believers will be accountable for what they have done (2 Cor 5:10), for their thoughts (Rom 2:16), and for their purposes of heart (1 Cor 4:5). The judgment will be based on "the things done while in the body" (2 Cor 5:10 NIV), whether for good or for bad. Satan's ministers also face an end (τὸ τέλος *to telos*) that will correspond to their works (2 Cor 11:15).

In Romans, Paul develops the final judgment motif more fully. There, using commercial terminology, Paul declares that God will "pay back to each person according to that one's works" (2:6): eternal life, glory, honor, and peace to those who patiently do good and seek immortality; wrath and fury to those who do evil (2:7-10). The repayment is reckoned in terms of the deeds one does (cf. 1 Cor 3:12-15), how one comports oneself in the body, and not whether one has faith, because faith is a gift (χάρισμα *charisma*) given by God to each believer (cf. 1 Cor 12:9-11) and, therefore, not the subject of judgment.

Judgment regarding works has sometimes not been given adequate attention in studies of Paul because interpreters rightly recognize that, for Paul, one does not come to faith by means of works, but by God's grace freely given. Faith—that is, right relation to God—does express itself in works, in deeds of love (Gal 5:6; 1 Thess 1:3). Paul consistently decries any attempt to attain right relation with God by performance of works, by dint of one's own efforts (cf. Rom 3:27-28; 9:30–10:3).

The topic of judgment according to works comes up in 2 Corinthians because Paul feels the need to defend his comportment, his works, among the Corinthians, and he is concerned about their works as expressed in relation to him. At several points in 2 Corinthians 1–9 Paul has reminded the Corinthians that he and they must live and behave in such a way as to be ready for the completion of God's purposes (2 Cor 3:18; 4:17-18; 5:4-5; 6:1-2). The eschatological, end-time references are designed to leverage the Corinthians into closer affiliation with Paul, who, in exemplary fashion, declares himself as aiming to please God in all that he does (5:9) precisely because he knows that "all of us" will have to appear before Christ's tribunal for judgment (5:10).

Continuity/Discontinuity Between Past and Present. On the one side, Paul is convinced that all of God's promises find their "yes," their fulfillment, in Christ (2 Cor 1:20; cf. Rom 1:3; 9:5). Christ is the confirmation of the promises granted the patriarchs (Rom 15:8). Likewise, the gospel was declared already to Abraham (Gal 3:8), and Abraham becomes the type of faithful person whose unconditional trust in God is the model for all believers who follow (Romans 4:1; Galatians 3:1). In 2 Corinthians as well, the first covenant shares with the second one, no matter how distinctive they may be in other respects, the fundamental characteristic of "glory," presumably a glory that is in both cases derived or reflected from God, who grants the covenants (2 Cor 3:7-11). So the new covenant is, like the first, still covenant, still made by God, and still manifests the glory from God so that some fundamental continuity between past and present is affirmed.

Driven by a desire to make absolutely clear to the Corinthians that their current relation to God stems from their relation to the gospel through Paul and his ministry, Paul ties his own ministry to a "new" covenant, which he affirms that he represents. To distinguish himself and his ministry from all others, he distances the new covenant from its predecessor in significant ways. He radicalizes the distinction between what he labels as two "ministries" and pictures these ministries as having distinctive covenants. In each instance his ministry and its covenant are distinguished by contrasts or described as surpassing the other one: written on stone/on hearts (3:3), with ink/with the Spirit of the living God (3:3), old/new (3:6, 14), death (stated)/life (implied; 3:7), letter/spirit (3:6), and fading away/permanent (3:11, 13). Indeed, Paul's eagerness to interpret his own ministry and its covenant as being of singular importance for the Corinthians leads him to an oxymoronic position: He knows that the old covenant had glory, but, being convinced that the new covenant's glory (and, therefore, his ministry) so exceeds the earlier glory, he says that the new glory is so dazzling as to make the earlier glory seem to be no glory at all (3:10).

Reconciliation. Reconciliation as a term presupposes a familial or friendship setting in which, after enmity has been overcome, relationships are restored to amicability. So it is also in Paul. All of creation was made by God for association with God's own self. Sin intervened and led creation, humans included, into alienation and even enmity with God (Rom 5:10). By a freely given gift—that is, grace in Christ—God overcame the enmity and established peace (Rom 5:1), another term for reconciliation.

Among the seven undisputed letters, Paul's most powerful delineation of reconciliation is found in 2 Cor 5:11-21, where the reconciliation is at once cosmic, communal, and personal. It is cosmic in that as surely as the world—that is, all of creation—has been subjected to futility and is in bondage to decay (Rom 8:20-21), in Christ God "was reconciling the world to himself" (2 Cor 5:19 NRSV). In Romans 8:1, Paul describes in more detail how he views God's ultimate rehabilitation of the entire created order: God's newly reclaimed children already experience the "freedom of the glory" for which the rest of creation still longs, much as a pregnant woman experiences her labor pains just prior to delivery (Rom 8:19-23). It is communal in that when Paul describes reconciliation it always has a plural object, "us" or the world in its collectivity (Rom 5:10-11; 2 Cor 5:18-19). Reconciliation is also personal because it takes place "in Christ," precisely the locus where individual believers become members of Christ's body and are given into one another's care (1 Cor 12:12-26). Further, in 2 Cor 5:11-21 Paul *explicitly* calls for reconciliation to God, but *the encoded message* is that he wants more filiation from the Corinthians and a heightened sense of reconciliation with them—*to him* as the one who brought the gospel of reconciliation to them in the first place. He is personally concerned that their already established reconciliation to God wash over onto him with new enthusiasm on their part (cf. 2 Cor 6:12-13; 7:2).

EXCURSUS: THE JERUSALEM CONFERENCE AND THE COLLECTION FOR THE POOR

Paul recounts to the Galatians his having gone, with Barnabas and the same Titus who figures so prominently in 2 Corinthians 1:1-9, to Jerusalem in response to a revelation (Gal 2:1-2). The conference had as its focus an issue generated at least in part, and perhaps completely, by Paul's mission to the Gentiles in which he did not insist on circumcision as a rite of entry into God's people. The issue can be put in the form of a question: Do Gentiles have to become Jews in order to be part of God's purpose? Paul's entire mission was a graphic no to that question. In a laconic accounting, Paul suggests that his whole mission might be "in vain" if the Gentile believers were not viewed as acceptable by their Jewish brothers and sisters in the faith (Gal 2:2). Paul reports a good outcome of the Jerusalem deliberation: Titus was not compelled to be circumcised, Paul was not subjugated to the Jerusalem leadership (James, Cephas [Paul's often-used name for Peter], and John); quite the contrary, these Jerusalem pillars "recognized the grace that had been given to" Paul (Gal 2:9 NRSV), gave Paul and Barnabas the "right hand of partnership," and collectively divided the mission among themselves in such a way that Paul and Barnabas should go to the Gentiles while the rest of them should take care of "the circumcised" (Gal 2:9). The pillars requested only that Paul (and Barnabas and Titus?) "remember the poor," which he reports himself eager to do (Gal 2:10). If we had no other Pauline texts we might be baffled about who these poor people were and what remembering them might mean.

By the "right hand of fellowship" (κοινωνία *koinōnia*) the Jerusalem pillars had symbolized that Paul's mission was on equal footing with theirs, an opinion *Paul* already had before he went to the conference. So the conference ratified that Paul's previous missionizing among the Gentiles had not been in vain; the Jewish believers in Jerusalem recognized that the Gentiles whom Paul had evangelized were one with them in Christ. To put the matter differently, Paul's successful efforts at the Jerusalem conference meant that there was indeed just one people of God, not two with one being Jewish and the other Gentile.

Paul variously denominates the recipients of this offering. They are "the poor" (πτωχός *ptōchos*, Gal 2:10),[31] "the poor who are among the saints in Jerusalem" (εἰς τοὺς πτωχοὺς τῶν αγίων *eis tous ptōchous tōn hagiōn*, Rom 15:26), and simply "the saints" (ἅγιος *hagios*, Paul's technical term for a person set apart for, claimed by God; Rom 15:25; 1 Cor 16:1; 2 Cor 8:4; 9:1, 12).

Similarly, Paul describes the offering using a range of terms. It is a "remembering" (μνημονεύω *mnēmoneuō*, "remember/keep in mind/think of," Gal 2:10), a "collection of money" (λογεία *logeia*, 1 Cor 16:1-2), a "ministry" (διακονέω *diakoneō*; also διακονία *diakōnia*, "aid/support/distribution," Rom 15:25; 2 Cor 8:4; 9:1, 12-13), and a "gift" (χάρις *charis*, 1 Cor 16:3; 2 Cor 8:6, 19).

We can develop a general picture of the way Paul's churches responded to the collection. The Macedonian churches at Thessalonica and Philippi, who seem to have had a good history with Paul, have vigorously embraced the offering and generated an astonishing collection (8:1-5). The Galatian churches are not listed in Romans, Paul's last letter, as among those who took part in the collection (Rom 15:26), so we may suppose that Paul's efforts with them (1 Cor 16:1) failed. The Corinthians started off with great enthusiasm for the collection (2 Cor 8:10); later they had some simply logistical questions and asked Paul for general guidelines about how to proceed (1 Cor 16:1-4), but there was no doubt of their readiness to take part at the time when 1 Corinthians was written.

By the time of the letter fragment 2 Corinthians 1:1-9, however, at least a year since the Corinthians had made a commitment to the collection (8:10), the Corinthians have lost their earlier enthusiasm for it; some (or all) may even be rebelling at taking part in it. Rom 15:26, written later than 2 Corinthians 8:1-9, shows that Achaia, the Roman province in which Corinth is located, *did* join with Macedonia in the collection. Whether Corinth was a part of that offering cannot be determined; perhaps Paul's inclusion of "all the saints in the whole of Achaia" among the letter recipients for 2 Corinthians 1:1-9 was also to increase the base from which he hoped to have participation in the collection even if the Corinthians were recalcitrant on the matter.

Paul's understanding of the collection can be pieced together from snippets of different letters. At its heart, the collection symbolizes for Paul a reciprocal partnership between Jewish and Gentile believers. Paul construes the Gentile believers as being "indebted" (ὀφείλω *opheilo*) to the Jerusalem believers who have preceded them in the faith (Rom 15:27), a picture that is in general supported by Paul's image of the olive tree in Rom 11:17-24. Paul's evangelization has been the occasion for Gentiles to be grafted onto the olive tree; now the roots of that tree nourish the engrafted Gentiles. So, shifting from botanical to business imagery, the Gentiles are indebted to their Jewish brothers and sisters in the faith who have shared spiritual matters. Paul's ready conclusion is thoroughly in line with the Greco-Roman expectations of reciprocity; therefore, the Gentile believers ought to reciprocate by being of service in physical matters (Rom 15:27). Indebtedness necessitates a response.

When the discussion is put in terms of need and abundance, then those who have more are obligated to help those who have less or who are in need. Proportionality and fairness come into play in Paul's reckoning. How much one puts aside is supposed to be commensurate with how well one has prospered during that week (1 Cor 16:2). Those with abundance must share with those with little so that there are reciprocity and equality (ἰσότης *isotes*, 8:13-14; 9:12). No one is to be "put upon" by this collection (8:13). At the same time, however, everyone "owes" love to others (Rom 13:8), and in this instance love calls for sharing the burden with those who have already shared what was theirs.

The "remembering of the poor"—in its being given and in its being received—becomes for Paul the supreme symbol of the unified people of God in Christ in whom truly there is "neither Jew nor Greek" (Gal 3:28 NIV). Paul construes the collection as a one-time, symbolic act in which the Gentile churches as donors and the Jerusalem believers as recipients each acknowledge that they belong to the other in Christ.[32] Paul sees in the collection a tangible confirmation that his work among the Gentiles is, indeed, recognized for what it is: an integral part of God's overall plan. Gentile believers' participation in the collection is a recognition of their indebtedness to their believing Jewish brothers and sisters (cf. Rom 1:16; 2:9-10).

SOCIAL AND RHETORICAL CONVENTIONS: EPISTOLARY STYLE

Thoroughly at home in the Greco-Roman world, Paul employs the practices and conventions of the time as a means of engaging with and relating to the Corinthians.

Frank Speech. Frank speech (παρρησία *parrēsia*)[33] was, along with indirect or figured speech and flattery, one of the three ways that a person in Paul's time could attempt to influence deliberation regarding proper behavior. Without ever mentioning it explicitly from 2 Cor 1:3

through 2 Cor 6:10, Paul *indirectly* bids for increased filiation from the Corinthians; in 6:11-13, however, he shifts to frankness and appeals *directly* for increased affection (see also 7:2). Indirect speech treats an issue or problem obliquely, in a roundabout fashion, never head-on, and often without even expressly mentioning the main concern; in 1:3–6:10, Paul strives in a variety of ways to cement his newly restored relations with the Corinthians, though, properly abiding by the canons of indirect speech, he never explicitly states in those verses his concern to do so.

Frankness has friendship as its locus. It is the highest "office of a friend" to call a friend to task, to encourage the friend to reach for the best and to perform at the optimum.[34] Frank speech ranges from "the gentlest sting," on the one extreme, where one pleasantly nudges the friend toward improvement, across a continuum of increasing degrees to the other, harshest extreme: a rebuke. The success of frank speech depends on many considerations, among which are the timing, the proportionality of the severity to the situation, the ethos or character of the frank speaker, and the care to mix in varying, appropriate degrees of praise. In some sense and degree, the friendship is always placed in hazard by the undertaking of frank speech, but true friendship, genuine caring for the other one, sometimes leaves no alternative but to take that risk.

Paul employs a range of frank speech in the correspondence reflected in 2 Corinthians. In the painful letter, he uses harsh frank speech and reports himself appropriately anxious about how the Corinthians have received it (2 Cor 7:5-7, 12-13). In 6:11-13 and 7:2, Paul uses a milder form of frank speech as he calls for the Corinthians to open their hearts to him.

Self-commendation. Modern readers often have great difficulty with Paul's persistent reminders to the Corinthians of his considerable efforts toward them. Similarly, his boasting seems extravagant; he even acknowledges as much in 2 Cor 11:16-17, 21*b*; 12:1. In that culture, friends commended each other, wrote letters of commendation for each other, and put in good words for each other at critical times.

Further, Paul's contemporaries were, as Paul shows himself to be also, not reticent to commend themselves as a part of the self-promotion that was so prevalent culturally. Encomiastic practices regularly expected that a speaker or writer detail, as Paul does here, his deeds that benefited others. Goodwill is earned when one details what one has done for others, when we "refer to our own acts and services without arrogance."[35] *Ad Herennium*, a contemporary rhetorical handbook, wrongly attributed to Cicero, concurs and urges the speaker to reveal "also our past conduct toward the republic, or toward our parents, friends, or the audience."[36] Paul has no interest in the republic; he is totally focused on his audience, the Corinthians, as he recites his good works and diligence in service of the gospel to the Corinthians[37] and hopes thereby to garner their increased goodwill.

Ideally, one should not be totally dependent on self-commendation. One's clients or dependents should rally. In one context where outsiders show up with letters of commendation, Paul assumes that he should not need any such letters of support from his followers (3:1). Later, when his relations with the Corinthians have deteriorated once again, Paul contends that the Corinthians should have met his opponents with commendations, with boasting about him and about what he has meant to them: "You forced me [to be a fool and commend myself], for I ought to have been commended by you" (12:11). When his Corinthian allies failed to commend him, he saw no option other than to commend himself. Therefore, he boasts, but he tempers his boasting with irony and by adopting a fool's pose (11:16, 21*b*, 23; 12:11). Had the Corinthians come to his defense, he would not have felt the need to engage in self-commendation.

Paul openly embraces a certain type of self-commendation: "In every way we commend ourselves as ministers of God" (6:4). The hardship list that follows shows that Paul's self-commendation is grounded in his difficulties and distress, an ironic testimony to the power of God working through and sustaining him in whatever circumstances he encounters. In 6:4-10 irony functions as did the fool's mantle and thus places Paul's self-commendation in perspective.

Epistolary expressions of self-confidence such as we see in 2 Corinthians (1:12-14; 5:11; 11:5; 13:6; cf. Heb 13:18) are an accepted part of persuasion and are necessary when the writer wants "to create or restore a good relationship between" the readers/hearers and himself.[38] In 2 Corinthians 1–9, Paul is especially eager to rehearse their grounds for mutual pride, so he mixes praise of them and self-commendation of himself (see 1:13*b*-14). The goal of self-commendation is to shape the way the audience thinks of the speaker. Paul's self-commendation lays out the picture he wants the Corinthians to have of him.[39]

Patron/Client, Honor/Shame. The culturally pervasive categories of patron and client, of honor and shame, continue to make their marks on Paul's communication with the Corinthians.

In the Greco-Roman world a gift or benefaction establishes or maintains a patron/client relationship and places the recipient under obligation. Seneca says it clearly: "The giving of a benefit is a social act, it wins the good will of someone, it lays someone under obligation."[40] For the one who receives a benefit, gratitude is merely the "first installment of his debt."[41] Epictetus deems the one who "repays a favor without interest" an ingrate.[42] In that world, patronage was the glue that bound every level of society to their benefactors. Not simply a political tool as we know it in modern times, patronage was omnipresent, in all relations, where one person's favor binds the recipient(s) to honor the donors and, in cases of money or possessions, allows the recipients to confer beneficence and, therefore, obligation, on persons beneath them in status.

In 2 Corinthians, patronage is a matter of great importance because some Corinthians seek to become Paul's patrons and thereby support his ministry. These Corinthians, who may reasonably be supposed to include some of the wealthy, are spurred to move in that direction by two forces that we can identify. First, they have seen the Macedonian believers arrive with support for Paul and him accept it (11:9). Given the prevalent cultural patterns, they have every superficial reason to view that transaction as a patron/client relationship between the Macedonians and Paul, exactly the association they seek with him. Second, they seem to have been encouraged by the intruders to think that real apostles did not do menial work (as Paul insisted on doing) as a means of self-support (11:7; 12:16). Paul, however, rejects their bid of patronage. In strong language he avers that his boast of self-support will not be silenced anywhere in the environs of Corinth (11:10). With an oath as to his truthfulness, he preempts any claim that his refusal of patronage is a sign that he does not love them (11:11). Further, he declares that he is not about to change his long-standing pattern of self-support with them. By refusing their offer of patronage, Paul has avoided being obligated to them, probably an important personal consideration, but, in the categories of the culture, he has rebuked and shamed them by his refusal. In that setting, as in many to this day around the world, patronage and its gifts cannot be refused without shame attaching itself to the would-be donors. Shame produces enmity.[43] No doubt a part of Paul's problems with the Corinthians is attributable to his contravention of the traditional cultural patterns of patronage.

The Types of Rhetoric in 2 Corinthians. In the Greco-Roman world, all rhetoric could be divided into three classes. *Judicial rhetoric*, the most common, addresses questions of culpability regarding the past. *Deliberative rhetoric* attends to questions of what a person or group will do in the (perhaps even imminent) future. *Epideictic rhetoric* focuses on praise and blame, usually of a person, though events may also be the subject. All of Paul's letters are deliberative, at least in part if not completely, because each of them at some point calls for the hearers to reflect on their comportment and to consider emending their current practices. Both letter fragments contained in 2 Corinthians do that, though 2 Corinthians 10–13, with its rehearsal of Paul's past behavior and its preparation for a confrontational showdown, may at times also be judicial. Both letter fragments, insofar as they shower praise or cast blame, engage in some epideictic rhetoric as well.

Epistolary Style. Much attention is properly placed on categorizing the Pauline letters as to type or literary style.[44] For 2 Corinthians, two determinations are necessary, one for chapters 1–9, another for chapters 10–13. Chapters 1–9 are "a letter of apologetic self-commendation."[45] As noted already, the primary burden of 2 Corinthians 1–9 is Paul's recovery of Corinthian filiation after he has subjected them to a frank rebuke.

Chapters 10–13 are an "excellent example of a mixed letter type."[46] Their legal overtones are prompted not only by Paul's eagerness to counter charges made against him, but also by his determination to put the Corinthians on warning of his imminent arrival when he expects to confront his accusers. But the letter is truly a hodgepodge as to style or type, containing as it does not only accusations, self-defense, and reproaches, but also self-commendation and apologies.

Frank speech, discussed above, is, along with indirect speech and flattery, a mode of the speaker's relating to the hearers and can be employed in any of the types of rhetoric noted above and in any epistolary style.

FOR FURTHER READING

Belleville, L. L. "A Letter of Apologetic Self-Commendation: 2 Cor 1:8–7:16." *NovT* 31 (1989).

Danker, F. W. "Paul's Debt to the *De Corona* of Demosthenes: A Study of Rhetorical Techniques in Second Corinthians." In *Persuasive Artistry: Studies in New Testament Rhetoric in Honor of G. A. Kennedy.* Edited by D. F. Watson, JSNTSup 50. Sheffield: Sheffield Academic, 1991.

DeSilva, D. A. "Measuring Penultimate Against Ultimate Reality: An Investigation of the Integrity and Argumentation of 2 Corinthians." *JSNT* 52 (1993).

Fitzgerald, J. T. *Cracks in an Earthen Vessel: An Examination of the Catalogues of Hardships in the Corinthian Correspondence.* Atlanta: Scholars Press, 1988.

Furnish, V. P. *II Corinthians.* AB 33. Garden City, N.Y.: Doubleday, 1984.

Georgi, D. *The Opponents of Paul in Second Corinthians.* Philadelphia: Fortress, 1986.

Lambrecht, Jan. *Second Corinthians.* SP 8. Collegeville, Minn.: Liturgical Press, 1998.

Marshall, Peter. *Enmity at Corinth: Social Conventions in Paul's Relations with the Corinthians.* WUNT44. Tübingen: J. C. B. Mohr, 1987.

Matera, Frank J. *II Corinthians: A Commentary.* Louisville, Ky.: Westminster/John Knox, 2003.

Savage, T. B. *Power Through Weakness: Paul's Understanding of the Christian Ministry in 2 Corinthians.* New York: Cambridge University Press, 1996.

Sumney, J. L. *Identifying Paul's Opponents: The Question of Method in 2 Corinthians.* JSNTSup 40. Sheffield: Sheffield Academic, 1990.

Thrall, Margaret E. *A Critical and Exegetical Commentary on the Second Epistle to the Corinthians.* 2 vols. ICC 34. Edinburgh: T & T Clark, 1994–2000.

ENDNOTES

1. For the interpretation that 2 Corinthians is one letter, see B. Witherington III, *Conflict and Community in Corinth: A Socio-Rhetorical Commentary on 1 and 2 Corinthians* (Grand Rapids: Eerdmans, 1995).

2. Though it may have looked to the Corinthians as if the Macedonian support of Paul was patronage, Paul's understanding of it seems quite different. See Sampley, *Pauline Partnership in Christ: Christian Community and Commitment in Light of Roman Law* (Philadelphia: Fortress, 1980) 55-77.

3. D. Georgi, *The Opponents of Paul in Second Corinthians* (Philadelphia: Fortress, 1986) 16-18, holds for five fragments. See M. E. Thrall, *The Second Epistle to the Corinthians* (Edinburgh: T & T Clark, 1994) 1:47-49, for a chart of various theories.

4. For the issues and an argument for the continuity of 2 Cor 2:12-13 to the section that opens with 2:14, see A. C. Perriman, "Between Troas and Macedonia: 2 Cor 2:13-14," *ExpTim* 101 (1989) 39-41. D. A. DeSilva, "Measuring Penultimate Against Ultimate Reality: An Investigation of the Integrity and Argumentation of 2 Corinthians," *JSNT* 52 (1993) 57, argues that the "latter section [2:14–7:3] develops themes which are introduced in the former [1:1–2:13]."

5. G. Bornkamm, "Die Vorgeschichte des sogennanten Zweiten Korintherbriefes," in *Gesammelte Aufsätze* IV, *BEvT* (München: Evangelischer) 53, 179-90, 192-94.

6. See J. C. Hurd, Jr., *The Origin of I Corinthians* (London: SPCK, 1965) 235-39.

7. See J. Fitzmyer, *Essays on the Semitic Background of the NT*, SBLSBS 5 (Missoula, Mont.: Scholars Press, 1974) 217.

8. So H. D. Betz, *2 Corinthians 8 and 9* (Philadelphia: Fortress, 1985) 90-91; countered decisively by S. K. Stowers, *"Peri men gar* and the Integrity of 2 Corinthians 8 and 9," *NovT* 32 (1990) 340-48.

9. For detailed examination of these and other arguments and their limitations, see V. P. Furnish,

II Corinthians, AB 33 (Garden City, N.Y.: Doubleday, 1984) 429-33.

10. R. K. Bultmann, *The Second Letter to the Corinthians*, trans. R. A. Harrisville (Minneapolis: Augsburg, 1985) 18.

11. H. Windisch, *Der zweite Korintherbrief* (Göttingen: Vandenhoeck & Ruprecht, 1924) 287.

12. F. Watson, "2 Cor X-XIII and Paul's Painful Letter to the Corinthians," *JTS* (1984) 346.

13. Furnish, *II Corinthians*, 38, 44-46.

14. So Watson, "2 Cor X-XIII and Paul's Painful Letter to the Corinthians," 345-46, and L. L. Welborn, "The Identification of 2 Corinthians 10–13 with the 'Letter of Tears,'" *NovT* 37 (1995) 153.

15. Furnish, *II Corinthians*, 37-38.

16. See J. L. Sumney's laudable methodological caution and circumspection in *Identifying Paul's Opponents: The Question of Method in 2 Corinthians*, JSNTSup 40 (Sheffield: Sheffield Academic, 1990) 15-67. He categorizes the traditional options for identifying Paul's opponents: Judaizers (led by Baur, followed by Barrett, Gunther, Lüdemann), Gnostics (Schmithals), divine men (Georgi and Friedrich), and pneumatics (Käsemann).

17. See J. Paul Sampley, "Paul, His Opponents in 2 Corinthians 10–13, and the Rhetorical Handbooks," in *The Social World of Formative Christianity and Judaism*, ed. J. Neusner, P. Borgen, E. S. Frerichs, R. Horsley (Philadelphia: Fortress, 1988) esp. 165-67.

18. So G. Lyons, *Pauline Autobiography: Toward a New Understanding* (Atlanta, Scholars Press, 1985).

19. Cf. A. J. Malherbe's compelling interpretation of 1 Thess 2:1-12 not as a denial of a charge against Paul but as Paul's distinguishing of himself from itinerant sages, in "Gentle as a Nurse," *NovT* 12 (1970) 216-17.

20. See Demetrius *On Style* 5.294-296. For a fuller discussion of indirect speech and its canons, see J. Paul Sampley, "The Weak and the Strong: Paul's Careful and Crafty Rhetorical Strategy in Romans 14–15:13," in *The Social World of the First Christians: Studies in Honor of Wayne A. Meeks*, ed. L. M. White and O. L. Yarbrough (Minneapolis: Fortress, 1994) 43-46.

21. Theirs was not an "intellectual confrontation." See A. J. Malherbe, "Antisthenes and Odysseus, and Paul at War," *HTR* (1983) 143-73, esp. 168, 172.

22. So C. J. A. Hickling, "Is the Second Epistle to the Corinthians a Source for Early Church History?" *ZNW* 66 (1975) 287, argued powerfully a quarter-century ago.

23. Sumney, *Identifying Paul's Opponents*, 118, distinguishes "five levels of *certainty of reference*," beginning with "explicit statements" and moving through two levels of "proposed allusions."

24. The most extreme example is D. Georgi, *Paul's Opponents in 2 Corinthians* (Philadelphia: Fortress, 1986) 229-83; cf. J. J. Gunther, *St. Paul's Opponents and Their Background*, NovTSup 35 (1973) 276.

25. Hickling, "Is the Second Epistle to the Corinthians a Source for Early Church History?" 286. L. L. Belleville, "Tradition or Creation? Paul's Use of the Exodus 34:1 Tradition in 2 Corinthians 3:7-18," in *Paul and the Scriptures of Israel*, ed. C. A. Evans and J. A. Sanders (Sheffield: JSOT, 1993) 185, shows that Paul's creativity comes not in his use of Exodus 34:1 and his portrait of Moses' fading glory, but in tying the fading glory to the "waning of the covenant."

26. So also J. L. Sumney, *Identifying Paul's Opponents. The Question of Method in 2 Corinthians*, JSNTSup 40 (Sheffield: Sheffield Academic, 1990) 177.

27. C. K. Barrett, "Paul's Opponents in II Corinthians," *NTS* 17 (1971) 244-45, holds it is the latter.

28. See Plutarch *On Praising Oneself Inoffensively* 542B-543F, where speakers can praise and, as in the case at hand, positively associate themselves with others "whose aims and acts are the same as...[one's] own and whose general character is similar."

29. See Josephus *Antiquities of the Jews* 4.238; *Mishnah Makkot* 3.

30. Josephus *The Jewish War* 2.308.

31. L. E. Keck, " The Poor Among the Saints in Jewish Christianity and Qumran" *ZNW* 57 (1966) 54-78.

32. Paul's collection is not to be identified with the famine relief of Acts 11:29 because Paul has taken at least one year to collect from the Corinthians 2 Cor 8:10; 9:2). Its symbolic significance for Paul can be seen clearly in the mutuality of Rom 15:27.

33. For the conventions and practice of frank

speech, see J. Paul Sampley, "Paul's Frank Speech with the Galatians and the Corinthians," in *Philodemus and the New Testament World*, ed. J. T. Fitzgerald, G. S. Holland, and D. Obbink, NovTSup (Leiden: E.J. Brill, 2001).

34. Philodemus *On Frank Criticism* col. XIXb.

35. Cicero *De inv.* 1.16.22.

36. Cicero *Ad Herennium* 1.5.8.

37. S. H. Travis, "Paul's Boasting in 2 Cor 10–12," *Studia Evangelica*, ed. F. L. Cross (Berlin: Akademie, 1973) 6:529-30; 554-55.

38. S. N. Olson, "Epistolary Uses of Expresssions of Self-Confidence," *JBL* 103 (1984) 588.

39. S. N. Olson, "Epistolary Uses of Expresssions of Self-Confidence," 593.

40. Seneca *Of Benefits* 5.11.5.

41. Seneca *Of Benefits* 2.22.1.

42. Epictetus *Epistles* 81.18; cf. 81.9-10.

43. Peter Marshall, *Enmity in Corinth: Social Conventions in Paul's Relations with the Corinthians*, WUNT44 (Tübingen: J. C. B. Mohr, 1987) 242-47.

44. See L. L. Belleville, "A Letter of Apologetic Self-recommendation: 2 Cor 1:8–7:16," *NovT* 31 (1989) 150.

45. Belleville establishes this identification quite clearly by comparing 2 Corinthians 1–9 with examples from Sophists. See Belleville, "A Letter of Apologetic Self-recommendation," 158-59.

46. J. T. Fitzgerald, "Paul, the Ancient Epistolary Theorists, and 2 Corinthians 10–13: The Purpose and Literary Genre of a Pauline Letter," in *Greeks, Romans, and Christians: Essays in Honor of Abraham J. Malherbe*, ed. D. L. Balch, E. Ferguson, W. A. Meeks (Minneapolis: Fortress, 1990) 200.

THE LETTER TO THE GALATIANS

RICHARD B. HAYS

Paul's angry, passionate letter to the churches of Galatia provides a glimpse of the controversy that surrounded the expansion of the Christian movement into Gentile communities in the ancient Mediterranean world. The identity of the newly established mission churches was up for grabs: Were they to be understood as branches on the tree of Judaism, or were they to be understood as belonging to a new and distinctive community, neither Jewish nor pagan? Were Gentile converts bound to accept Jewish practices and values? In what ways were they free to maintain their former ways of life? By the middle of the first century CE the struggle over such questions had burst into open conflict. Paul visualizes the struggle for identity formation of the Galatian churches in a vivid image: As the apostle whose preaching had brought these communities into being, he is like a mother in the throes of labor until they are fully formed according to the image of Christ (Gal 4:19).

The Letter to the Galatians is important not only as a primary source document for reconstructing formative Christianity but also for its theological message. Paul responded to the Galatian crisis with a trenchant theological analysis of the issues at stake. This analysis, and the proclamation of the gospel that follows from it, have exercised a powerful influence on subsequent Christian theology and preaching. Both Augustine and Martin Luther, for example, took their bearings from Paul's message of radical grace, apart from works of the Law. Thus the Letter to the Galatians is the fountainhead for all subsequent Christian theological reflection about justification by faith, the cross, the power of the Spirit, and the meaning of Christian freedom. The letter was preserved and cherished in the church because it offers a compelling model for how to think theologically about challenges faced in the community's life.

As we read this letter, we find that we have entered an argument already under way. Galatians is not a general theological treatise; it is an urgent pastoral letter written to a specific cluster of churches at a moment of crisis. Consequently, it is full of allusions to persons, events, and issues known well to the original readers and, therefore, not fully explained. To interpret the letter, then, we must do a certain amount of reconstructive guesswork about the circumstances Paul was addressing.

WHY DID PAUL WRITE THE LETTER?

Paul had founded the churches of Galatia during his missionary travels in Asia Minor, sometime after the Jerusalem meeting described in 2:1-10. Everything in this letter indicates that Paul's Galatian converts were formerly Gentile pagans (4:8-9). Paul came to them unexpectedly as a result of some sort of personal affliction (4:13-14) and preached to them the message of "Jesus Christ crucified" (3:1) as God's transformative deed to deliver humankind from "the present evil age" (1:4). The Galatians accepted the message joyfully (4:14-15), were baptized (3:26-28), and experienced dramatic manifestations of the Holy Spirit (3:2-5; 4:6). We do not know how long Paul spent in Galatia, but he left his fledgling churches there confident that they were "running well" (5:7).

At the time of the composition of the letter, however, Paul had received word that his apostolic work in Galatia was being undermined by Jewish-Christian missionaries who had arrived on the scene preaching "a different gospel" (1:6) and seeking to persuade the Gentile Galatians to be circumcised (5:2-4; 6:12-13). It is important to recognize that these missionaries were not non-Christian Jews trying to induce the Galatians to abandon their newfound Christian faith; rather, the conflict portrayed in Paul's letter is an *intra-Christian* dispute. The newly arrived missionaries in Galatia were arguing that Gentiles who had believed in Jesus should take the next step into full covenant membership by being circumcised. Apparently these Jewish-Christian preachers, telling the Galatians that Paul had failed to instruct them properly in God's Law, were finding a receptive audience among the Galatians (1:6; 3:1; 4:21; 5:4; 5:7), who were already adopting at least some aspects of Jewish Law observance (4:10-11). Outraged by this development, Paul fired off his letter to dissuade the Galatian churches from accepting this revision—Paul calls it a perversion (1:7)—of the gospel.

The identity of the rival missionaries is unknown. Paul does not identify them by name (this is perhaps a studied rhetorical tactic on his part), and we have no other sources of information about their activities or teachings. Thus we are forced to reconstruct their message from the evidence provided by Paul's polemical rebuttal. A few New Testament scholars have speculatively identified these Pauline opponents as Gnostics or as Gentile leaders indigenous to the Galatian churches, but such theories have not proved persuasive. The evidence indicates overwhelmingly that the rival missionaries were Jewish Christians, and all recent scholarly commentators have viewed them as such.

The term "Judaizers," once widely used to describe these missionaries, has recently fallen into disfavor for two reasons. First, it wrongly implies that the conflict in Galatia was between Jewish and anti-Jewish factions. In fact, Paul himself was a Jewish-Christian apostle, and the argument in this letter is between two different Jewish-Christian interpretations of the gospel. Second, the verb "to Judaize" (ἰουδαΐζω *ioudaizō*), which appears in 2:14, does not mean "to make someone else into a Jew"; rather, it means "to adopt Jewish practices." Thus the label "Judaizers" would aptly be applied to Gentiles who accepted the circumcision gospel, but it will not do to describe the rival missionaries themselves. Consequently, recent interpreters have sought other terms. The term "agitators," based on Paul's pejorative characterization of his opponents (1:7; 5:10, 12), has been widely adopted, but it, too, quickly skews our perception toward an unsympathetic interpretation of their motives. Certainly, they did not think of themselves as agitators, nor would they have defined themselves primarily as Paul's opponents. They saw themselves as preachers of the gospel and advocates of the Law. We will arrive at a deeper and more sympathetic reading of the situation if we choose a designation that does not prematurely dismiss them as troublemakers. J. Louis Martyn has dubbed them "the Teachers,"[1] and J. D. G. Dunn refers to them in his commentary as "missionaries."[2] The latter term seems most clearly to describe their activity, and it will be employed thoughout this commentary (capitalized to indicate that Paul is referring to a specific group of adversaries).

The basic elements of the Missionaries' message are reasonably clear: They believed Jesus to be the Messiah of Israel and saw themselves as summoning Gentiles in the name of Jesus to come under obedience to the Law revealed to Moses at Mount Sinai. They probably regarded Jesus as the authoritative interpreter of the Law. From the way that Paul constructs his counterargument against them (3–5:1), we may draw the following inferences with some confidence:

> (1) The Missionaries preached the necessity of circumcision as a means of entering covenant relationship with the God of Israel.
>
> (2) They called for observance of Jewish sabbaths and feast days (4:8-11) and presumably advocated obedience to everything written in the Law (3:10), promising that those who kept the commandments would find life (3:12).
>
> (3) They taught that the Law of Moses was divinely ordained to provide moral order and restrain human fleshly impulses (5:16, 24).
>
> (4) They claimed to represent more faithfully than Paul the teachings of the "mother" church in Jerusalem.
>
> (5) They based their message on Scripture, particularly on the story of Abraham and God's institution of the covenant of circumcision (Genesis 17:1). In accordance with Jewish tradition, they regarded Abraham as the father of proselytes, and they urged the Galatians to follow his example by being circumcised. We may infer that Deut 27:26 and Lev 18:5 also featured prominently in their preaching.

In short, they represented a form of traditional Jewish teaching that called for Law observance, and they sought, in the name of Jesus, to extend the good news about the Law of God to the Gentiles.

Why did Paul object so fiercely to this message? Why did he not view the Missionaries' preaching as a variant of the gospel that could be tolerated within a pluralistic early Christian movement?[3] The answer to this question must be provided through a careful reading of the letter, but we may summarize, by way of preview, some of the main lines of Paul's argument.

According to Paul's diagnosis, the Missionaries were preaching a false gospel despite their use of Christian language. We may identify four interlocking motifs in Paul's radical critique of their message.

(1) The Missionaries' emphasis on circumcision and Law observance as the *conditional* grounds for covenant membership negates the sufficiency of God's grace, which was shown through the death of Jesus for our sake (2:20-21). The cross, not the Law, is the basis of our relationship to God. In short, the Missionaries have a deficient christology.

(2) The Missionaries underestimate the power of the Spirit to animate and guide the life of the faithful community. Where God's Spirit has been poured out on the church, Paul claims, there is no more need for a written code of Law to direct and restrain the community. We need only to follow the life-giving Spirit to resist the desires of the flesh (5:16-26). In short, the Missionaries have a deficient pneumatology.

(3) The Missionaries deny "the truth of the gospel" (2:5, 14) by undermining the unity of Jews and Gentiles in Christ. The reconciling power of God is to be demonstrated not by forcing Gentiles to become Jews but by bringing circumcised and uncircumcised believers together at one common table. Thus the spread of the gospel requires a Law-free mission to the Gentiles. In short, the Missionaries have a deficient ecclesiology.

(4) The Missionaries act as though the death of God's Son on the cross had not changed the world irrevocably. They think that things can go on just as before, with the Law providing the fundamental structure for the identity of the people of God. But, in fact, the gospel is the revelation of God's apocalyptic action that has undone and transformed the world (6:14-15). In short, the Missionaries have a deficient eschatology.

Taken together, these four deficiencies constitute, in Paul's eyes, a fundamental betrayal of the gospel, a reversion to life under the Law before Christ came to set us free. That is why Paul so vehemently seeks to persuade the Galatians to reject the overtures of the Missionaries.

THEOLOGICAL THEMES

As the constructive alternative to the Missionaries' message, Paul reproclaims his gospel of grace. The central themes of that gospel may be summarized briefly.

1. Human beings are "rectified" (set in right relation to God) not through obeying the Law but through the faithfulness of Jesus Christ, who gave himself for us (2:20). Using a different metaphor, Paul proclaims that we are adopted as God's children solely as a result of Christ's redemptive death (4:4-7), not because of anything we have done or could do. As these examples show, Paul uses various images to describe God's saving action, but the message is consistent: We are included in God's covenant people ("the Israel of God," 6:16) solely by God's gracious action in Christ for our sake.

2. Paul's proclamation focuses on the cross as a liberating event (2:20-21; 3:1, 13-14; 6:14-15). In Galatians, the cross is interpreted not primarily as an atoning sacrifice for forgiveness of sins but as a cataclysmic event that has broken the power of forces that held humanity captive, brought the old world to an end, and inaugurated a new creation. Throughout the letter Paul is reflecting upon the story of Jesus' loving self-donation to rescue us from enslavement (1:3-4).

3. As a result of Christ's death on a cross, the Spirit is given to all who are in Christ (3:13-14). The Spirit gives us life (5:25), confirms our status as God's children (4:6-7), and transforms the character of our community life so that we produce fruit pleasing to God (5:22-25). Because of the transformative power of the Spirit, there can be no artificial division between the gospel and "ethics." God's redemptive work necessarily includes the reshaping of the community's life together.

4. In the new community created by the Spirit, the markers that once separated Jews from Gentiles have been invalidated—or, speaking more precisely, annihilated (3:28; 5:6; 6:15). God's purpose is to create a single new people who are "one in Christ Jesus," bound together in faith and love.

5. Those who recognize the saving work of God in Christ and live in the power of the Spirit experience *freedom*. They are no longer constrained, enslaved, or separated from one another. The climactic exhortation of the letter, therefore, urges the Galatians to stand firm in the freedom won for them by Christ (5:1).

EPISTOLARY, RHETORICAL, AND HOMILETICAL STRUCTURE

1. Galatians as a Letter. Galatians is a real letter, not a treatise or an essay composed in the fictive literary form of an epistle. Formally, the letter contains many features characteristic of Hellenistic letters of its time.[4] Most of these formal stylistic features have relatively little importance for our interpretation of the text. More significant is a comparison of the structure of Galatians to the structure of Paul's other letters. These usually contain the following components: opening salutation, thanksgiving or blessing, body, moral exhortation, closing (greetings, doxology, benediction). The letter to the Galatians noticeably lacks two of these characteristic elements: the thanksgiving and the closing greetings to individuals in the churches to whom the letter is addressed. These striking omissions are an indicator of the strained relationship between Paul and the Galatian churches.

The letter was composed to be read aloud to each of the assembled Galatian congregations. There is no indication in the letter itself of the identity of the person authorized to deliver and read it. The letter serves as a substitute for Paul's personal presence—a substitute recognized by Paul as frustratingly inadequate (4:20)—and seeks to reestablish his authority in the community.

2. Galatians as Deliberative Rhetoric. Because the letter was composed for public hearing, it has many structural and stylistic characteristics in common with the forms of rhetoric that were taught and practiced in the Hellenistic world. Any educated person in Hellenistic antiquity would have received training in how to structure a speech and influence an audience, and Paul's letter shows that he was well versed in such matters.

In 1979, Hans Dieter Betz made an important contribution to our understanding of Galatians by publishing a learned critical commentary arguing the thesis that Galatians was an "apologetic letter" structured in accordance with the conventions of ancient judicial rhetoric.[5] That is, Paul writes as though he were on trial before a jury, speaking in his own defense and in defense of the Spirit. Subsequent reviewers and commentators have observed that Galatians does not fit the apologetic letter genre as neatly as Betz argued;[6] nonetheless, Betz's work catalyzed numerous other studies of the rhetorical strategies embodied in Paul's letters.[7] Out of these studies, there is an emergent consensus that the rhetorical genre of Galatians is not primarily judicial but rather *deliberative*; it belongs to a category of rhetoric whose aim is to persuade the audience to follow a certain course of action.[8] In the case of Galatians, the persuasion is primarily negative in character: Paul is trying to persuade his Galatian readers not to be circumcised and not to become Law observers. (One can also discern in the letter positive statements of the action Paul urges; the Galatians should imitate him in abandoning Torah observance [4:12], drive out the Missionaries [4:30], and stand firm in their freedom [5:1].)

Paul was not slavishly following a rhetorical handbook on how to write a deliberative speech, but he was employing rhetorical strategies that were simply in the air in his culture. A knowledge of how such strategies worked may occasionally help us to see how the argument is put together. For example, the rhetoricians taught that a good persuasive speech should employ arguments appealing to *ethos* (the trustworthiness of the speaker), to *pathos* (emotive impact on the audience), and to *logos* (reasoned argumentation).[9] We see Paul deploying his argument in a way that honors this recommendation. For example, the account of his own apostolic credentials in chapters 1 and 2 functions as an *ethos* argument, the lengthy exegetical discussion in 3:6-29 is clearly a *logos* argument, and his otherwise puzzling shift to a relational appeal in 4:12-20 is a classic illustration of a *pathos* argument.[10]

Perhaps the most important function of rhetorical analysis is to remind us that Paul's original readers and hearers were shaped by a culture in which rhetorical performance was cultivated and prized. Their ways of listening and judging were shaped by the prevailing conventions of oratory—a fact that became a problem for Paul at Corinth, where his opponents and some of his own converts judged him deficient in the rhetorical arts (2 Cor 10:10; cf. 1 Cor 1:18–2:5).[11] Consequently, when we hear Paul pulling out all the rhetorical stops in Galatians, we should recognize that he is arguing in a manner conventional for his time and necessary if he was to persuade his hearers to hold fast to the gospel he had preached to them.

3. Galatians as a Sermon. Without excluding either the epistolary or the rhetorical mode of analysis, Martyn has highlighted one other important way of viewing the Letter to the Galatians: It is above all "an argumentative sermon" composed to be delivered "in the context of a service of worship—and thus in the acknowledged presence of God—not a speech made by a rhetorician in a courtroom."[12] As Martyn insists, the purpose of the letter is "reproclamation of the gospel," and for that reason it is not so much an argument as an *announcement.*[13] Paul is not merely trying to persuade the Galatians to agree with his opinions; rather, he is seeking to unleash the power of the gospel once again in their midst. The effectiveness of the letter will ultimately depend not on Paul's literary or rhetorical skill but on the activity of God's Spirit when the Galatians hear the letter read.

THE INTERPRETATION OF SCRIPTURE

As has been noted, the Missionaries based their preaching partly on scriptural texts, particularly the story of Abraham. An important part of Paul's strategy is to refute their interpretations and to reclaim the biblical story (i.e., the Old Testament) as a witness to the gospel. Paul's determination not to abandon the Bible into the hands of the Law-observant Missionaries was a crucial strategic decision that ultimately helped to preserve the Old Testament as part of the Scripture of the Christian church. According to his reading, anyone who really listens to the Law will find that it supports his proclamation, not that of his adversaries (e.g., 4:21).[14] Indeed, he claims that Scripture "preached the gospel beforehand" to Abraham by declaring that all nations (i.e., Gentiles) would be blessed in him (3:8). This shows, among other things, that Paul saw Scripture not just as a repository of proof texts about Jesus as the Messiah but as a *story*—a story focused on God's promise to bless and redeem all nations.[15]

Paul's portrayal of Scripture as a living, speaking agent plays a significant role in his argument, not only in 3:6-9 but also in his account of how Scripture "imprisoned all things under the power of sin" (3:22) and in his argument that Scripture commands the Galatians to expel the Missionaries (4:30). Because Paul believed that Scripture was a living voice through which God spoke to the church, he dared to propose startling new readings, such as his allegorical interpretation of the Sarah/Hagar story (4:21–5:1), claiming that the Gentile believers, not the Law-observant Jewish Christians, are the true children promised to Abraham. This bold revisionary reading stands at the climax of the central argumentative section of the letter.

While the Abraham stories are the most prominent scriptural texts in Galatians, Paul's language from start to finish is salted with scriptural imagery and allusions, such as his echoing of prophetic call narratives in the account of his own call (1:15); his citations of Deuteronomy, Leviticus, and Habakkuk in 3:10-14; his artful contrapuntal evocation of Isa 54:1 in Gal 4:27; his appeal to the love commandment of Lev 19:18 (Gal 5:14); and his echoing of Isaiah's "new creation" imagery (Gal 6:15). A careful reading of the letter, then, must attend to Paul's use of Scripture throughout the argument. He produces revisionary imaginative readings of the texts in service of his preaching of the gospel. Yet, at the same time, he claims with full seriousness that only the gospel truly discloses the meaning that remained latent in these texts prior to the coming of Christ.

EARLY CHRISTIAN CONFESSIONAL TRADITIONS

In addition to scriptural quotations and allusions, Paul weaves into his argument several early Christian confessional and liturgical traditions.[16] The most widely recognized of these traditions is the baptismal affirmation of the unity of the church in Christ (3:27-28). A number of other passages also appear to draw on early christological confessions (see, e.g., 1:3-4; 2:16, 20; 3:13-14; 4:4-5). These citations anchor Paul's arguments in a deep layer of early Christian tradition that would have been acknowledged not only by the Galatians but also by the rival Missionaries as authoritative. Paul's case will be made more persuasive if he can show how these confessional statements reinforce his gospel rather than the Law-observant anti-gospel he is combating. Here Paul stands on very solid ground, indeed, for these early confessions consistently narrate the initiative of God and/or Christ in bringing about the redemption of humankind; thus the narrative plot of the confessions supports Paul's insistence that it is Christ's grace—not the Law—that brings about rectification. Our reading of the letter will be enriched if we attend closely to Paul's deft use of these traditional materials.

Thus we see that Paul's Letter to the Galatians is a complex and rhetorically artful performance. He makes a formidable case for his gospel by linking the Galatians' experience of the Spirit with extended arguments based on Scripture and on early Christian tradition. Like a good orator, he also attempts to enlist their sympathies and to bolster their confidence in him as an authoritative interpreter of the gospel.

HISTORICAL PROBLEMS

Where were the Galatian churches located? This question is surprisingly difficult to answer. The Roman province of Galatia in Paul's time included a large area of central Asia Minor (modern Turkey). The province was named after the Galatian people, a tribe of Celtic origin that had migrated from Europe in the third century BCE and settled in the central highlands of Anatolia, the region around Ancyra (modern Ankara). In 25 BCE, Augustus created the *Provinicia Galatia*, which included not only the traditional territory of the Galatians but also a stretch of territory extending south to encompass the city of Iconium, as well as the towns of Lystra and Derbe; these places are mentioned in the Acts of the Apostles as sites of missionary activity by Paul and Barnabas (Acts 14:1-23).

Because Paul nowhere in the letter mentions any particular towns or cities, it is impossible to be sure whether "the churches of Galatia" (1:2) were located in the traditional territory of the ethnic Galatians ("North Galatia") or in the places mentioned in Acts 14:1, in Roman provincial Galatia ("South Galatia"). Likewise, we have no idea how many "churches of Galatia" there were.

As is so often the case in historical inquiry, scholarly argument has tended to focus on the problems for which we have the least evidence. Thus there is a massive quantity of secondary literature debating the North Galatian/South Galatian question. The debate remains inconclusive and almost entirely irrelevant for interpreting Paul's letter.

The issues that are primarily at stake in this debate are how to connect Paul's Letter to the Galatians with Luke's narrative in the Acts of the Apostles and how to date the composition of the letter. When Paul wrote to "the churches of Galatia," was he addressing churches in "South Galatia" founded during his "first missionary journey"

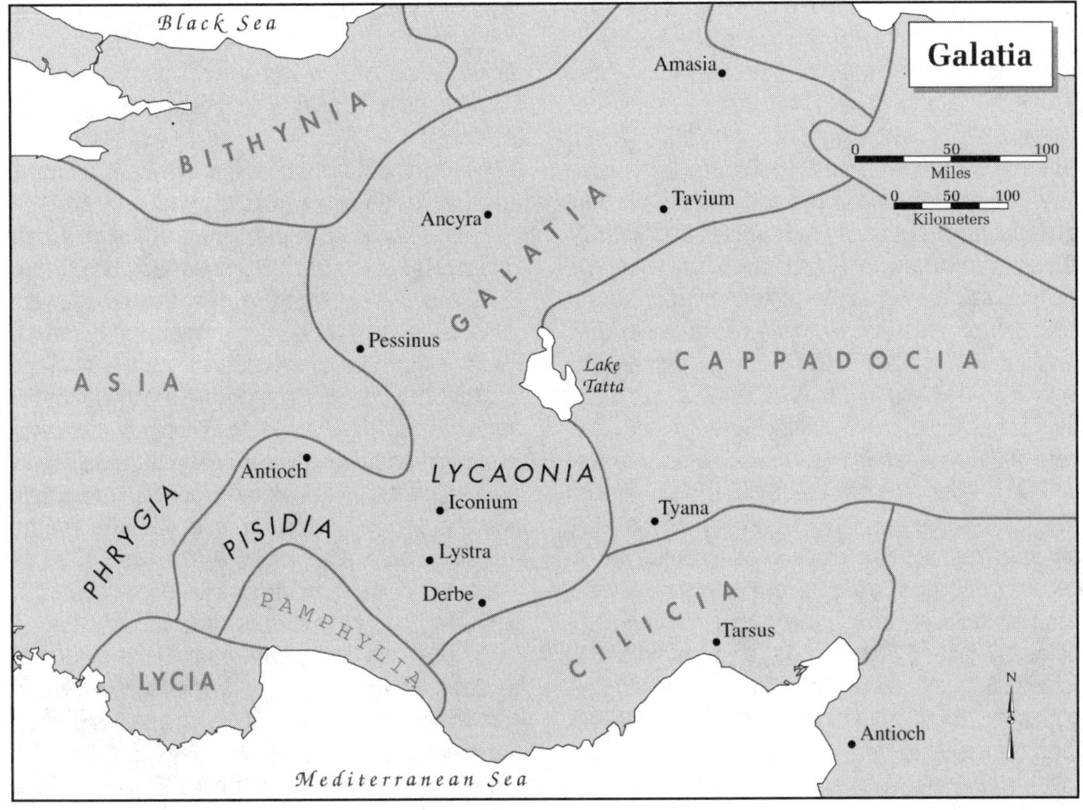

in the Lukan schema (Acts 13–14)? Or was he writing to churches he had founded in "North Galatia" during the "second missionary journey" (Acts 16:6) and later visited once again (Acts 18:23)? Since Luke's account is highly schematized and not a comprehensive account of Paul's activity (for example, Acts never mentions the fact that Paul wrote letters to his churches), the question remains unresolvable.

In favor of the North Galatian theory is the fact that Paul addresses his readers as "Galatians" (3:1), a designation more naturally applied to ethnic Galatians than to "South Galatian" dwellers in the Roman province, who might not have referred to themselves in this way. It should also be noted that Luke never uses the designation "Galatia" for the areas mentioned in Acts 13–14; he uses it only in Acts 16:6 and 18:23. Thus, in the history of the interpretation of the letter, from the patristic era up until modern times, it was almost unanimously held that Paul was writing to churches in central Asia Minor composed of the descendants of the Celtic tribe.[17]

In favor of the South Galatian theory is the fact that it enables a reconstruction of Paul's activity that minimizes contradictions between Galatians 2 and Acts 15 (see below on the date of composition). As already noted, however, the nature of Luke's epic narrative about the expansion of the early Christian mission is such that it should not be pressed for precision about matters of detail. (E.g., Acts 9:26-30 has Paul introduced by Barnabas to the church in Jerusalem shortly after his conversion experience and preaching publicly there; by contrast, in Gal 1:18-24 Paul emphatically insists that he was "unknown by sight to the churches of Judea" for at least fourteen years after his initial call.) Thus avoidance of contradiction between Acts and Galatians 2 should not be a decisive factor in determining the addressees and date of Paul's letter.

If Acts does not provide a precise chronology of Paul's life, and if even the location of the Galatian churches cannot be determined with confidence, it becomes difficult to ascertain a precise date for the composition of the letter. It must follow by some significant length of time Paul's meeting with the Jerusalem church leaders (2:1-10), which is probably to be dated about 48 or 49 CE. After the Jerusalem meeting, we have to allow time for the following events to occur: the confrontation at Antioch and Paul's falling-out with the Antioch church (2:11-21); Paul's preaching to the Galatians and their reception of the gospel; Paul's departure; the arrival in Galatia of the rival Missionaries; and the report to Paul of the changed situation. Some commentators date Galatians as early as 49 CE, while others place the letter as late as 56 CE, in close proximity to the writing of Romans. The thematic similarities between Galatians and Romans appear to favor the later date, but several recent commentators have argued for an earlier dating of 50–51 CE.[18] One advantage of this earlier dating is that it allows more time between Galatians and Romans for the refinement of Paul's position concerning the Law and the fate of Israel.

As Moises Silva has pointed out, although proponents of the South Galatian hypothesis tend to date the letter early, there is no necessary logical connection between this theory about the geographical destination of the letter and its dating. If one assumes the historical reliability of Acts, then the North Galatian hypothesis requires a date for the letter after the Jerusalem Council of Acts 15, since only afterward did Paul go to Galatia (Acts 16:6). But if one accepts the South Galatian hypothesis, the letter could have been written at any time after Paul's initial founding of the churches in Galatia.[19] In view of the paucity of hard evidence, the best we can do is to say that Galatians was written sometime in the period of 50–56 CE.[20]

One crucial question for interpretation concerns the relationship between Galatians 2 and Acts 15. Does Acts 15 describe the same meeting to which Paul refers in Galatians 2? The similarities between the accounts make it virtually certain that they are variant narratives of the same event. In both texts, Paul and Barnabas go to Jerusalem to meet with the leaders of the church and debate whether Gentile converts must be circumcised. There are, however, two significant discrepancies between the accounts: (1) Luke seems to describe the council as a public assembly, including all the apostles and elders of the church, whereas Paul insists that he met privately with a handful of Jerusalem leaders (Gal 2:2); (2) according to Luke's account, the council issued a statement approving admission of Gentiles but asking them "to abstain from what has been sacrificed to idols and from blood and from what is strangled and from fornication" (Acts 15:29). This latter account seems in tension with Paul's claim that the

Jerusalem leaders added nothing to his Law-free gospel for the uncircumcised, except a reminder to remember the poor (Gal 2:6-10). The first of these discrepancies does not present a major difficulty; Paul could be referring to a behind-the-scenes meeting with James and Cephas and John in the context of a larger public conference. The second discrepancy is more puzzling: If the "pillar" apostles had made a public decree that Gentile converts did not need to be circumcised, why did Paul not refer to it in support of his argument in Galatians? And why did Paul not instruct the Galatians that all the apostles had agreed that Gentiles need not observe the Law save for the restrictions of the apostolic decree (Acts 15:23-29)?[21] There are several possible explanations, but the likeliest one is that Paul knew of no such declaration of the apostolic council; his letters nowhere give evidence of the existence of such an agreement. It appears that Luke has telescoped events and read back into this meeting an agreement that emerged somewhat later in the development of early Christianity.[22] Here it will be assumed that Galatians 2 and Acts 15 refer to the same meeting in Jerusalem and that Paul's Letter to the Galatians, therefore, was written sometime after that meeting.

GALATIANS AS SCRIPTURE

Paul treated Scripture (by which he meant the collection of writings that Christians later came to call the Old Testament) as a living voice that had the power to speak to the church in his own time (Gal 4:30). By so doing, he set a precedent that has instructed Christians ever since about how to approach Scripture with an ear tuned expectantly to listen for the Word of God. What happens, then, when Galatians itself becomes incorporated into the canon of texts that the believing community confesses to be Scripture? Can we expect to hear in Galatians a living voice that will speak to our time, just as Genesis and Isaiah spoke to Paul's situation?

Martin Luther's reading of Galatians offers a classic illustration. He read Paul's polemic against the Torah-observant Missionaries as an attack on the abuses of the Roman church of his own day, for he believed Rome was teaching justification by works in a way just as destructive of the gospel as were the teachings of Paul's opponents. Luther knew, of course, that there was a difference between the ancient Jewish-Christian preachers of circumcision and the Christian sellers of indulgences in Europe 1,500 years later, but the analogy between the situations was so strong that the text of Galatians became a medium through which Luther heard God speaking directly to the struggles that he confronted.[23]

What would it mean for us to listen to Galatians for a similar word targeted to the church today? It may be useful to summarize some of the key themes that emerge again and again as we seek to listen to this text speaking to our time.

1. Rectification Through the Faithfulness of Jesus Christ. Much Christian preaching, particularly in some Protestant traditions, has fallen into the trap of celebrating the subjective faith experience of individuals as though religious experience were an end in itself, or as though we could somehow secure God's acceptance by the device of our believing. Indeed, Galatians has often been exploited for proof texts defending exactly such a message. Careful reading of the text, however, shows that Paul's Letter to the Galatians is a powerful attack on such self-referential accounts of salvation. From start to finish, Paul proclaims that *God* has acted to set the world right and to rescue us from slavery to human religious programs. God did this not merely through some mysterious change of feelings in the hearts of individuals, but through the faithfulness of Jesus Christ, whose love and fidelity culminated in his giving up his life on the cross for our sake. Our trust in him is a response to this saving deed. Reading Galatians in the light of this fundamental insight will require us to rethink the meaning of "faith" and "justification." It will also require us to examine critically the individualistic sentimentality that often surrounds talk in the church about "faith."

2. The Gospel and Judaism. Galatians is not an anti-Jewish text. It is, rather, a manifesto against distortions of the gospel introduced by *Christian* preachers who subordinate Christ to the Law. Reading Galatians after the Holocaust forces us to rethink how we have twisted Paul's good news into a pretext for violence. The Christian community, gathered as "the Israel of God" (6:16), as Abraham's children, must rediscover the ways in which Paul was a profoundly Jewish thinker, despite his ambiguous assessment of the Law. In order to think through this question fully, we will find ourselves moving beyond

Galatians into the issues that Paul was inexorably drawn to address in Romans 9–11. As a part of the canon of Christian Scripture, Galatians should never be read in isolation from Paul's further reflections on the ultimate salvation of Israel.

3. A Church United at One Table. Paul holds forth the vision of a community of faith in which all are one in Christ (2:11-21; 3:26-29). This is not merely a matter of an isolated slogan in Gal 3:28; it is a central theme of the letter as a whole. Jews and Gentiles are no longer to be divided, because Christ's death has brought us together. Therefore, all manifestations of racial and ethnic divisiveness are betrayals of "the truth of the gospel." Galatians is one of the canon's most powerful witnesses against a cultural imperialism that excludes anyone from fellowship on the basis of criteria not rooted in the gospel.

4. Freedom, Not Autonomy. We live in an age obsessed with personal freedom. In such a time, it is far too easy to hear Paul's proclamation of freedom (5:1) as a license for the indulgence of individual desires and interests. Galatians will teach us, to the contrary, that the freedom for which Christ has set us free is a freedom to serve one another in love (5:6, 13-14). The freedom of which Paul speaks is not autonomy. It is freedom for life together in community under God (6:1-10).

5. The Crucified World and the New Creation. Galatians proclaims an apocalyptic gospel. Christ came to defeat the oppressive powers that held us captive and to "rescue us from the present evil age" (1:4). As Paul develops the implications of this confession, he discloses to his readers that the entire world of orderly religious norms that he had once zealously defended has been "crucified" (6:14); it no longer has any claim upon him. The real world in which we now live is the "new creation" brought into being by Christ, in which we are given new life and are guided by the Spirit. As the church reads Galatians, then, we are constantly challenged to reject the wisdom of business as usual—including the business of religion—and to see reality as redefined by the cross. Those who live by this rule will no longer be manipulated by the popular culture's images of security and respectability. We will live, instead, manifesting the fruit of the Spirit, and our life together will be a sign of the world to come.

FOR FURTHER READING

Commentaries:

Betz, Hans Dieter. *Galatians: A Commentary on Paul's Letter to the Churches in Galatia.* Hermeneia. Philadelphia: Fortress, 1979.

Bruce, F. F. *The Epistle to the Galatians: A Commentary on the Greek Text.* NIGTC. Grand Rapids: Eerdmans, 1982.

Cousar, Charles B. *Galatians.* Interpretation. Atlanta: John Knox, 1982.

Dunn, James D. G. *The Epistle to the Galatians.* Black's New Testament Commentary. Peabody, Mass.: Hendrickson, 1993.

Edwards, Mark J., ed. *Galatians, Ephesians, Philippians.* Ancient Christian Commentary on Scripture. Volume 8. Downers Grove, Ill.: InterVarsity, 1999.

Longenecker, Richard N. *Galatians.* WBC 41. Dallas: Word, 1990.

Martyn, J. Louis. *Galatians.* AB 33A. New York: Doubleday, 1997.

Matera, Frank J. *Galatians.* Sacra Pagina 9. Collegeville, Minn.: Liturgical, 1992.

Williams, Sam K. *Galatians.* ANTC. Nashville: Abingdon, 1997.

Witherington, Ben III. *Grace in Galatia: A Commentary on St. Paul's Letter to the Galatians.* Grand Rapids: Eerdmans, 1998.

Other Studies:

Baker, Mark D. *Religious No More: Building Communities of Grace and Freedom.* Downers Grove, Ill.: InterVarsity, 1999.

Barclay, John M. G. *Obeying the Truth: A Study of Paul's Ethics in Galatians.* Studies of the New Testament and Its World. Edinburgh: T & T Clark, 1988.

Bassler, Jouette, ed. *Pauline Theology,* Vol. 1: *Thessalonians, Philippians, Galatians, Philemon.* Minneapolis: Fortress, 1991.

Beker, J. Christiaan. *Paul the Apostle: The Triumph of God in Life and Thought.* Philadelphia: Fortress, 1980.

Boyarin, Daniel. *A Radical Jew: Paul and the Politics of Identity.* Contraversions: Critical Studies in Jewish Literature, Culture, and Society 1. Berkeley: University of California Press, 1994.

Braxton, Brad Ronnell. *No Longer Slaves: Galatians and African American Experience.* Collegeville, Minn.: Liturgical Press, 2002.

Cousar, Charles B. *A Theology of the Cross: The Death of Jesus in the Pauline Letters.* OBT. Minneapolis: Fortress, 1990.

Dahl, Nils A. *Studies in Paul: Theology for the Early Christian Mission.* Minneapolis: Augsburg, 1977.

Donaldson, Terence L. *Paul and the Gentiles: Remapping the Apostle's Convictional World.* Minneapolis: Fortress, 1997.

Dunn, James D. G. *The Theology of Paul's Letter to the Galatians.* New Testament Theology. Cambridge: Cambridge University Press, 1993.

Hays, Richard B. *The Faith of Jesus Christ: An Investigation of the Narrative Substructure of* Galatians 3:1-4:11. SBLDS 56. Chico, Calif.: Scholars Press, 1983.

———. *Echoes of Scripture in the Letters of Paul.* New Haven: Yale University Press, 1989.

Hill, Craig C. *Hellenists and Hebrews: Reappraising Division Within the Earliest Church.* Minneapolis: Fortress, 1991.

Käsemann, Ernst. *New Testament Questions of Today.* Translated by W. J. Montague. Philadelphia: Fortress, 1969. Contains Käsemann's seminal essay "The Righteousness of God in Paul."

———. *Perspectives on Paul.* Translated by Margaret Kohl. Philadelphia: Westminster, 1971. Collected essays.

Martyn, J. Louis. *Theological Issues in the Letters of Paul.* Nashville: Abingdon, 1997.

Nanos, Mark D. *The Irony of Galatians: Paul's Letter in First-Century Context.* Minneapolis, MN: Fortress, 2002.

Perkins, Pheme. *Abraham's Divided Children: Galatians and the Politics of Faith.* Harrisburg, Pa.: Trinity, 2001.

Sanders, E. P. *Paul and Palestinian Judaism: A Comparison of Patterns of Religion.* Philadelphia: Fortress, 1977.

———. *Paul, the Law, and the Jewish People.* Philadelphia: Fortress, 1983.

Segal, Alan F. *Paul the Convert: The Apostolate and Apostasy of Saul the Pharisee.* New Haven: Yale University Press, 1990.

Silva, Moises. *Explorations in Exegetical Method: Galatians as a Test Case.* Grand Rapids: Baker, 1996.

Stendahl, Krister. *Paul Among Jews and Gentiles and Other Essays.* Philadelphia: Fortress, 1976.

Tamez, Elsa. *The Amnesty of Grace: Justification by Faith from a Latin American Perspective.* Nashville: Abingdon, 1993.

Wakefield, Andrew H. *Where to Live: The Hermeneutical Significance of Paul's Citations from Scripture in Galatians 3:1-14.* Academia Biblica 14. Atlanta: Society of Biblical Literature, 2003.

Westerholm, Stephen. *Israel's Law and the Church's Faith.* Grand Rapids: Eerdmans, 1988.

Witherington, Ben III. *Paul's Narrative Thought World: The Tapesty of Tragedy and Triumph.* Louisville: Westminster/John Knox, 1994.

Wright, N. T. *The Climax of the Covenant: Christ and the Law in Pauline Theology.* Edinburgh: T & T Clark, 1991.

———. *Paul for Everyone: Galatians and Thessalonians.* London: SPCK, 2002.

ENDNOTES

1. J. L. Martyn, *Galatians,* AB 33A (New York: Doubleday, 1997) 117-26. Martyn's reconstruction of their teachings provides the basis for the description given below.

2. J. D. G. Dunn, *The Epistle to the Galatians,* Black's New Testament Commentary (Peabody, Mass.: Hendrickson, 1993) 11.

3. Cf. his appeal for tolerance of differences in Rom 14–15:13.

4. For an extensive list of such elements, see Richard N. Longenecker, *Galatians,* WBC 41 (Dallas: Word, 1990) cv-cix.

5. H. D. Betz, *Galatians: A Commentary on Paul's Letter to the Churches in Galatia,* Hermeneia (Philadelphia: Fortress, 1979).

6. Particularly telling is the fact that 5–6:10, which Betz calls the *exhortatio,* has no parallel in actual apologetic speeches or in the instructions in rhetorical handbooks about how such speeches should be composed.

7. Among more recent Galatians commentaries, see especially Longenecker, *Galatians;* and Ben Witherington III, *Grace in Galatia: A Commentary on St. Paul's Letter to the Galatians* (Grand Rapids: Eerdmans, 1998).

8. G. A. Kennedy, *New Testament Interpretation Through Rhetorical Criticism* (Chapel Hill: University of North Carolina Press, 1984) 144-52; Witherington, *Grace in Galatia,* 25-36. Longenecker's analysis is more complicated; he sees

Galatians as a mixed type, showing both forensic and deliberative characteristics. Martyn dissents from the consensus; see below on "Galatians as a Sermon."

9. Aristotle *Rhetoric* 1.2.

10. For further discussion of these rhetorical modes, see Longenecker, *Galatians*, cxiv-cxix.

11. See D. A. Litfin, *St. Paul's Theology of Proclamation: 1 Corinthians 1–4 and Greco-Roman Rhetoric*, SNTSMS 79 (Cambridge: Cambridge University Press, 1994).

12. Martyn, *Galatians*, 21.

13. Martyn, *Galatians*, 22-23.

14. Paul is able to sustain this position by ignoring the narrative about Abraham's circumcision in Genesis 17. How might Paul have responded if pressed to deal with this text? His later treatment of Abraham in Romans 4 provides some clues; see esp. Rom 4:9-12.

15. On Paul's hermeneutical strategies, see Richard B. Hays, *Echoes of Scripture in the Letters of Paul* (New Haven: Yale University Press, 1989); "The Conversion of the Imagination: Scripture and Eschatology in 1 Corinthians," *NTS* 45 (1999) 391-412.

16. For a detailed list, see H. D. Betz, *Galatians: A Commentary on Paul's Letter to the Churches in Galatia*, Hermeneia (Philadelphia: Fortress, 1979) 26-28.

17. See Longenecker, *Galatians*, lxiii-lxiv. Longenecker nonetheless subscribes to the South Galatian hypothesis.

18. E.g., Dunn, *The Epistle to the Galatians*, 19, argues for 50–51 CE, and J. L. Martyn, *Galatians*, 19-20, for about 50 CE.

19. Moises Silva, *Explorations in Exegetical Method: Galatians as a Test Case* (Grand Rapids: Baker, 1996) 129-39. If one posits a longer interval between Paul's evangelization of the Galatians and the writing of the letter, some explanation is required for Paul's statement that the Galatians are "so quickly" deserting the gospel (1:6).

20. Betz, *Galatians*, 12, identifies the years between 50 and 55 CE as "a reasonable guess" for the date of composition.

21. These restrictions are based on the requirements imposed by the holiness code (Leviticus 18–20) not only on Israel but also on non-Israelites who are resident aliens in the land.

22. On the question of the relation between Acts 15 and Galatians 2, see esp. Craig C. Hill, *Hellenists and Hebrews: Reappraising Division in the Earliest Church* (Philadelphia: Fortress, 1991) 103-47.

23. Martin Luther, *Lectures on Galatians (1535)*, translated by Jaroslav Pelikan in *Luther's Works*, vols. 26-27 (Saint Louis: Concordia, 1963–64).

THE LETTER TO THE EPHESIANS

PHEME PERKINS

REMEMBERING THE APOSTLE: GENRE, CHARACTER, AND SOURCES

Although some still argue that Paul was the author of Ephesians,[1] most scholars agree that the letter is pseudonymous. For an audience accustomed to appropriating all written texts orally—that is, through hearing their contents read and perhaps even explicated by the person who actually conveyed the letter to its recipients—multiple voices in a text were a common experience. Consequently, when scholars speak of Paul as the "implied" or "fictive" author of Ephesians, they do not mean that the writer is making a fraudulent use of Pauline authority. The gap between this letter and Paul's personal correspondence is not hard to detect.[2] Ephesians lacks the personal greetings characteristic of Paul. No associates or fellow Christians are mentioned as co-senders. Those to whom Ephesians speaks do not know the apostle (1:15; 3:2). Yet, as Gentiles who have now been brought into the people of God (2:11-13), they owe a great debt to him. Paul's insight into the mystery (μυστήριον *mystērion*) of God's saving plan forms the basis of the gospel message (3:1-13). Their familiarity with the apostle has been mediated through writing rather than through his personal presence (3:2-4).

Paul's own letters contain specific details of the relationship between the apostle and those to whom he writes. Figuring out the prior history of the apostle's ministry in a particular church plays a crucial part in understanding those letters. Ephesians has no such clues. Sometimes interpreters supply reasons for a particular theme in Ephesians that have been taken from the context of another of Paul's letters. For example, the assumption that the growing numbers of Gentiles in the church have begun to denigrate the Jewish heritage of Christian faith (a concern of Romans 9–11) is proposed as the reason for writing Ephesians.[3]

Attempts to construct a setting for Ephesians run up against the literary genre of the work.[4] The author has adopted ancient rhetorical forms of celebratory and hortatory discourse.[5] The first half of the epistle (1:3–3:21) invites the audience to join in praising and thanking God for the plan of salvation that has united them with Christ. It concludes with a brief doxology (3:20-21). The second half encourages readers to persevere in the social and personal dimensions of their lives as new creations in Christ (4:1–6:20). It concludes in a dramatic peroration (6:10-20). Believers stand armed and ready to vanquish evil powers (6:10-17). They will also assist the imprisoned apostle in continuing his bold witness by remembering him in prayer (6:18-20).

Despite this clear understanding of the genre of the work, Andrew T. Lincoln cannot resist assuming that the rhetorical appeals to the audience built into the genres in question provide information about the epistle's readers. This methodological difficulty is masked by assuming that such mirror reading gives access to what literary critics mean by "implied readers." Not so, if the addressees recognize the rhetorical *topoi* involved. Lincoln comments, "It can be inferred from the implied author's prayers for them (3.14-19) and from his appeals which introduce and conclude the *parenesis* (cf. 4.1-16; 6.10-20) that their main problems are powerlessness, instability and a lack of resolve, and these are related to an insufficient sense of identity."[6] In fact, these passages tell us nothing about the problems of particular readers, actual or implied.[7] They do establish powerful images of Christian identity. The consolidation of communal identity can be understood as the basic function of celebratory rhetoric. A community that hears praises of its imperial—or, in this case, divine—benefactor, of the peace and well-being that a benefactor's gracious use of power has bestowed on it, that community also comes to know itself in relationship to the benefactor.

The lack of detail even appears in the opening greeting (1:1-2). The phrase "in Ephesus" (ἐν Ἐφέσω *en Ephesō*) does not occur in many of the earliest manuscripts. Nor would that locale be appropriate for an audience that does not know the apostle. Paul had worked extensively in Ephesus. He may even have been imprisoned there (1 Cor 15:32). Unlike either Colossians (Col 4:14; 5:6-7) or the Pastorals (1 Tim 1:18-20; 4:1-7), Ephesians never refers to false teachers whose doctrines must be avoided. Therefore, the epistle appears to be addressed to Christian churches in general, not to a particular situation. Some interpreters suggest that the author was concerned with the impact of the pagan religious environment in the Lycus Valley and wrote the epistle as a circular letter to churches in the environs of Laodicea and Hierapolis.[8] Nevertheless, the author does not appear to have any personal knowledge of the addressees. The discourse alternates between the second-person plural "you" and the first-person plural "we." Sometimes "we" designates Jewish Christians associated with the author, in contrast to "you" Gentile converts. Sometimes "we" refers to all Christians as a group. Ephesians never uses the common Christian designation "brothers" (ἀδελφοί *adelphoi*) in addressing the audience. The only use of the term occurs in the conclusion, where it is a third-person plural reference (*adelphoi*).

Ephesians encourages the audience to "imitate God" (Γίνεσθε οὖν μιμηταὶ τοῦ θεοῦ *Ginesthe oun mimētai tou theou*, 5:1) rather than the apostle, unlike the usual practice in Paul's letters. Even the Pastoral Epistles retain the motif of imitating Paul (2 Tim 1:8; 3:10-14). Since imitation of those who possess virtues is key to ancient paraenesis, the absence of the theme in Ephesians highlights the distance between its audience and the apostle.[9] With the exception of *topoi* in the household code, Ephesians has no significant parallels with the Pastoral Epistles.[10] Although the author has made extensive use of Colossians, he drops Timothy as co-sender from the opening greeting (1:1; cf. Col 1:1), even though this omission lives on in an odd first-person plural at the end (6:22; cf. Col 4:8). Perhaps this detail is more significant than it appears at first. The author and recipients of Ephesians do not belong to the circle of churches in which Timothy or Paul's other closest associates had been active.

Does Ephesians represent the first introduction these Christians have had to the apostle? Attempts to treat Ephesians as a summary designed to introduce an early collection of Pauline letters (assumed as the referent of 3:3-4) founder on the genre of the work. Ephesians does not read as an epitome of the apostle's teaching either in its formal rhetorical structure or its content. Further, the passage said to refer to other writings (3:3-4) does not indicate an established canon of Pauline letters. It could refer to the reading of Ephesians as a further explanation of what was said about the mystery in a previous letter. Ephesians may have taken its cue from Col 2:1-6. The apostle's trials are to benefit not only Christians known to him, but also others who have never seen him. Ephesians is claiming to express the mystery about which Paul was speaking.[11]

Verbal comparisons of Ephesians and Colossians make a strong case for the view that the author of Ephesians knew and used much of Colossians in his own epistle. But Ephesians has also recontextualized and changed the order of images and phrases taken from Colossians.[12] Even those sections that are substantially new contain some echoes of Colossians (1:3-14; 2:5-21; 4:8-16; 5:8-14, 22-33; 6:11-17).[13] Echoes of other Pauline letters are also evident.[14] Romans is more frequently evident in parallels to Ephesians than any other Pauline letter. Consequently, it does not seem likely that Ephesians relies simply on oral traditions circulating in Pauline churches. Knowledge of some Pauline letters themselves must be presupposed. But one can only make this argument with regard to the author of Ephesians. It is impossible to tell from the epistle whether the recipients were familiar with the passages that are cited here as parallels. The rhetorical strategies used in the letter presuppose that the audience recognizes what it hears as tradition, not new instruction. Lincoln has suggested using the phrase "actualization of an authoritative tradition" for the reuse of Pauline material in Ephesians.[15]

David Trobisch's study of letter collections has shed new light on the place of Ephesians in the Pauline corpus. Often the first collection of an author's letters was prepared by the author himself. Trobisch argues that Paul is responsible for creating a collection composed of Romans, 1–2 Corinthians, and Galatians. After an author's death other letters would be added at the end of the original group. Finally, someone might prepare a comprehensive collection from all available versions. Trobisch suggests that the first letter to break the principle that orders a collection indicates the point at which such expansion of an existing collection takes place. For the Pauline letters, the ordering principle appears to be length. However, on that criterion, Ephesians should come before Galatians. Therefore, it represents the first epistle added to the primitive collection produced by the apostle.[16] This research tells us nothing about the original addressees or how the Pauline letter canon came to be formed. It only indicates that Ephesians represented the first letter to be added to the originating collection of four major Pauline epistles.

If the more speculative side of Trobisch's argument holds—namely, that the apostle himself was responsible for Romans through Galatians—then the question of which letters other churches may have possessed looks slightly different. An early collection by the apostle himself may have been designed to be circulated. If Ephesians assumes that its audience has heard actual letters from the apostle, then this group of letters is most likely the group that was circulated. Ephesians may not presume that Colossians was read in the churches to which the apostle writes. Instead, Colossians provided the impetus for Ephesians to formulate Paul's own account of the mystery of salvation.

The basic picture of the apostle that Ephesians leaves with its readers contains few details. He is presented as the great apostle to the Gentiles whose Spirit-endowed insight (1:17; 3:2-3) has made the hidden plan of salvation accessible to all. This "mystery" made known through the apostle is also the tradition of the apostles and prophets who are the foundation of the church (2:20-22). Finally, the apostle's imprisonment is "for the sake of you Gentiles" (3:1 NRSV) and calls for courage to continue boldly proclaiming the gospel (6:19-20). Even these Christians who have no direct connection to the apostle's own churches are assured that the apostle suffers on their behalf. One cannot be sure whether the letter's audience knows that Paul has suffered martyrdom. Unlike the letters that Paul wrote from prison earlier, Ephesians never anticipates the possibility of his release. Unlike 2 Tim 4:6-18, Ephesians never hints that his death is near. But the conclusion of Acts indicates that an author and readers who know full well that the apostle has died may celebrate his heroic witness to the gospel without recounting his death.

WHERE EPHESIANS DIFFERS: THEOLOGY, LANGUAGE, AND STYLE

Ephesians was not composed as an epitome of Paul's teaching or as the celebration of an apostle hero. It focuses on God's foreordained plan of salvation, uniting Jew and Gentile in the body of the risen Christ. This theological insight develops a number of themes found in Paul's letters in a new direction. One no longer finds the event of salvation focused on the cross, though the traditional formulae concerning the redemptive effects of Christ's death do appear. Instead of speaking of the power of sin to hold humans in bondage, Ephesians refers to sins in the plural (ἁμαρτίαι *hamartiai*). Bondage is associated with evil powers whose effectiveness is linked to the earthly regions. Consequently, the dominant metaphor for redemption from their influence is exaltation "in the heavenly regions" with the risen Christ.[17]

1. Shifting Language. The language of Ephesians also departs markedly from Paul's style. The author constructs extensive, periodic sentences out of dependent clauses introduced by participles and infinitive phrases. In order to provide a readable text, translations break up these long sentences. However, the tables that compare the language of Ephesians with other Pauline letters will provide as literal a rendering as possible in order to indicate similarities of wording. Readers should consult commentaries based on the Greek text for detailed information about the elaborate Greek style in Ephesians. Such commentaries also provide lists of the unusual vocabulary used in Ephesians. Many words are either unique in the New Testament or appear in Ephesians and another New Testament writing, but not elsewhere in the Pauline letters. Some expressions appear to replace Pauline equivalents; for example, Ephesians uses "in the heavenly places" (ἐν τοῖς ἐπουρανίοις *en tois epouraniois*; 1:3, 20; 2:6; 3:10; 6:12) where Paul would speak of "in the heavens" (ἐν οὐρανοῖς *en ouranois*; 2 Cor 5:1; Phil 3:20; Col 1:5, 16, 20).[18] Instead of Paul's "Satan" (Σατανᾶς *Satanas*), one finds "devil" (διάβολος *diabolos*) in Ephesians. The formula used to introduce citations from Scripture, "therefore it says" (διὸ λέγει *dio legei*), is also not found in Pauline letters, and the expression "good works" (ἔργοις ἀγαθοῖς *ergois agathois*) in the plural (2:10) does not appear there, though it does occur in the Pastorals.[19]

Other features of Pauline letter form are missing, such as expressions of confidence, the formal opening to the body of a letter with a request or disclosure formula. The apostle typically uses a χάρις (*charis*, translated "thanks") formula as a contrast to a previously described negative situation (e.g., 2 Cor 2:12-15).[20] Ephesians does not use such contrastive formulae. Instead, *charis* (translated "grace") appears as the foundation of salvation and appears in expressions where one would expect "faith" if Paul had composed the letter (e.g., "by grace [*charis*] you have been saved through faith," 2:8). Or one would anticipate a discussion of righteousness in connection with the salvation of the Gentiles in 2:8-10. Instead, Ephesians refers to grace as the gift of God in opposition to works. The term "works" (ἔργα *erga*) also appears without Paul's normal qualifier "of the law" (νόμου *nomou*). In 2:10, the non-Pauline plural "good works" (*ergois agathois*) appears to refer to the moral conduct of those who are in Christ. The term "law" (νόμος *nomos*) only appears in 2:15, where the "law with its commandments and ordinances" has been canceled by the cross. There is no more distinction between Jew and Gentile. The whole complex of linguistic formulae that the apostle created to describe the inclusion of Gentiles in the promise of salvation has vanished with hardly a trace.[21]

This shift may be grounded in rhetoric as well as theology. Marc Schoeni's study of the "how much the more" formulae in Romans 5 discovered an important semantic distinction between using the topic "justification" and using "reconciliation." The language of justification is structured in such a way that it discriminates and divides. It acknowledges the singular differences between Jew and Gentile. Reconciliation "sublates and unites." By incorporating the differentiated singularities into a greater whole, reconciliation denies their significance.[22] Though Paul works with both reconciliation and justification, Ephesians has taken the reconciliation imagery of Rom 5:1-11 to be the Pauline understanding of salvation. Consequently, distinctions in Paul's terminology will be overridden by unity.

2. "Mystery" of Salvation. Several linguistic shifts are associated with the term "mystery" (μυστήριον *mystērion*). Ephesians often uses expressions that have their closest parallels in the Essene writings from Qumran, in which we find the "mystery" of the divine plan of salvation hidden in the prophets until the end time. Paul also uses this word for God's preordained eschatological plan of salvation.[23] "Mystery" designates different aspects of the overall plan of salvation: (a) 1 Cor 2:1, 7, the crucifixion; (b) 1 Cor 15:51, the end-time transformation of the righteous into resurrected bodies; and (c) Rom 11:25, the present hardening of Israel as a condition for salvation of the Gentiles, to be followed by salvation for "all Israel." In 1 Cor 4:1, Paul refers to the apostles, specifically himself and Apollos, as "stewards of God's mysteries" and uses the term in a general way for revealed knowledge in 1 Cor 13:2 (also 14:2, ironically?). Its use for the salvation of the Gentiles as hidden in the prophets until the present at Rom 16:25-27 may be an addition to the letter, but it maintains the overtones of apocalyptic revelation characteristic of Paul's usage.

When Paul applies the term "mystery" to his gospel in Rom 11:25, he is not only thinking of God's plan to summon all humanity to salvation, but he is also thinking of the story of Israel. God's promises to the covenant people and their apparent inability to recognize Christ as the fulfillment of the law issue in Paul's conviction that God must still bring salvation to Israel.[24] For Ephesians, only the first side of Paul's thought remains: God intends to bring all to salvation in Christ (3:8-9). This plan is grounded in the will of God from the beginning (1:9) and has been made known through the preaching of the apostle (6:19). It is also embodied in his writing (3:3-4). These examples are easily viewed as developments of Paul's own usage. After the apostle's death it would be natural to consider the written expression of his gospel as the way in which the mystery becomes known to others. However, a more significant shift becomes evident when Ephesians is compared with the immediate source for these expressions, Colossians (Col 1:27; 2:2; 4:3). In every one of the Colossians examples the shorthand that clarifies the term "mystery" is "Christ" and the fact that salvation comes to all people through faith in Christ.

Eph 3:1-13 and Col 1:23-28

Theme	Ephesians	Colossians
Introduce Apostle	**[3:1]**I Paul the prisoner	**[1:23*c*]** I Paul a servant for you (Eph 3:7) **[1:24*a*]**...for you
Sufferings of the Apostle	**[3:1]** prisoner **[3:13]** in my trials for you	**[1:24*b*]** the deficiency of the trials of Christ in my flesh for his body
Office of the Apostle	**[3:7]** of which I have become a servant **[3:2]** the administration of the grace of God given to me for you	**[1:25]** of which I have become a servant **[1:25]** according to the administration of God given to me for you
Revelation of the Mystery	**[3:4-5*a*]** the mystery of Christ that was not known to other generations **[3:9]** the mystery hidden from the aeons **[3:5]** has now been revealed to his holy apostles and prophets	**[1:26]** the mystery that was hidden from the aeons and the generations **[1:26]** but now has been manifested to his holy ones
Content of the Mystery	**[3:6]** that the Gentiles would be an inheritance with, body with, and sharers with the promise in Christ Jesus through the gospel	**[1:27]** the wealth of the glory... in the Gentiles, which is Christ in you, the hope of glory
Mystery Preached	**[3:8]** to preach to the Gentiles the incomprehensible wealth of Christ	**[1:27-28*a*]** to make known what the wealth of the glory of this mystery in the Gentiles, which is Christ in you ... whom we announce
God's Power	**[3:7*c*]** according to the activity of his power	**[1:29*b*]** according to apostle the activity that is working in me in power

Eph 4:17-19 and Rom 1:21, 24

Item	Ephesians	Romans
non-Jews lack effective knowledge of God: mind	**4:17*c*** in emptiness (ματαιότης *mataiotēs*) of their minds	**1:21** they have been given over to worthlessness (ἐματαιώθησαν *emataiōthēsan*) in their thoughts
non-Jews lack effective knowledge of God: darkened intelligence	**4:18*a*** being darkened in understanding	**1:21** their foolish heart was darkened
consequences of idolatry: impurity	**4:19** they handed themselves over to the practice of every impurity	**1:24** God handed them over to impurity

Ephesians uses a graphic description of the Gentile way of life to encourage readers to remain separated from their former conduct. Colossians provides images for both the old way of life and the new human beings that Christians have become:

Eph 4:17-24 and Col 3:5-10

Item	Ephesians	Colossians
not like the Gentiles	**4:17** you no longer walk as the Gentiles walk	**3:7** in which you also once walked
vices: impurity, greediness	**4:19** in practice of every impurity in greediness	**3:5** sexual immorality, impurity, passion, evil desire, and greediness (which is idolatry)

put off old human being	**4:22***a* put off from yourselves the old human being according to the former way of life	**3:8** now you put off... **3:9** having taken off the old human being
reject passions of old human being	**4:22***b* corrupted according to the passions of error	See vices in **3:5**
renew the intellect	**4:23** be renewed in the spirit of your mind	**3:10** renewed in knowledge
put on the new human being	**4:24** and put on the new human being	**3:10** and having put on the new
the new creation	**4:24** created according to God	**3:10** according to the image of the one who created him

Eph 5:3-8 and Col 3:5-8

Item	Ephesians	Colossians
vices not even named among Christians	**5:3** sexual immorality and all impurity or greed	**3:5** sexual immorality, impurity...and greed
vices of speech to be replaced with thanksgiving	**5:4** indecency and foolish talk or vulgar talk	**3:8** indecent speech
those who have no inheritance in the kingdom	**5:5** every evil or impure or greedy person who is an idolater	**3:5** and the greed (which is idolatry)
God's judgment falls on the wicked	**5:6** for because of these things the wrath of God comes	**3:6** through which the wrath of God comes
contrast past with present	**5:8** once...but now	**3:7-8** once...and now

Eph 5:15-20 and Col 3:16-17; 4:5

Item	Ephesians	Colossians
not like the unwise	**5:15** how you walk, not like the unwise but the wise	**4:5** walk in wisdom toward those outside
the times are evil	**5:16** employing the opportunity because the days are evil	**4:5** employing the opportunity
forms of worship	**5:19***a* speaking to one another in psalms and hymns and spiritual songs	**3:16***b* instructing one another in all wisdom, singing psalms, hymns, spiritual songs
sing to God from the heart	**5:19***b* singing and praising the Lord with your hearts	**3:16***c* singing with thanks in your hearts to God
giving thanks to God	**5:20** giving thanks always for all things in the name of our Lord Jesus Christ to God the Father	**3:17** and everything whatever you do...all things in the name of the Lord Jesus, giving thanks to God the Father through him

Eph 6:14-17 and the Armor of the Lord

Item	Ephesians	Isaiah and other parallels
belt ("having girded your loins")	**6:14** truth	**Isa 11:5** (LXX) righteousness
breastplate	**6:14** righteousness	**Isa 59:17** (LXX) righteousness (also **Wis 5:18**)
military sandals ("having shod your feet")	**6:15** equipment of the gospel of peace	[**Isa 52:7** (LXX) "the feet of those who preach the tidings of peace"]
shield	**6:16** faith	**Wis 5:19** holiness
helmet	**6:17** salvation	**Isa 59:17** (LXX) salvation
		Wis 5:18 impartial judgment
sword	**6:17** the Spirit, which is the word of God	[**Isa 49:2** (LXX) placed in the mouth of the servant "a sharp sword"]
		Wis 5:20 "wrath as a large sword"

Eph 6:21-24 and Col 4:7-9, 18

Item	Ephesians	Colossians
information about the sender	**6:21** and that you may know how I am and what I am doing,	**4:7** how I am doing,
person who brings the letter	**6:21** *b* Tychicus, the beloved brother, faithful minister in the Lord will make everything known to you	**4:7** *b* Tychicus, the beloved brother, faithful minister, and fellow servant in the Lord will make everything known to you
recommendation for the bearer	**6:22** whom I have sent to you for this purpose, that you may know how we are doing, and to be encouraged in your hearts	**4:8** whom I have sent to you for this purpose, that you may know how we are doing and be encouraged in your hearts
final blessing	**6:23-24** Peace to the brothers, and love with faith, from God the Father and the Lord Jesus Christ. Grace with all who love our Lord Jesus Christ in incorruptibility.	**4:18** I, Paul, write the greeting with my own hand. Remember my bonds. Grace be with you.

Ephesians shifts the playing field. The focus of the mystery is not the cosmic Christ of Colossians but the body of Christ, the church. The problem is not how Gentiles can participate in God's salvation while remaining free from the law. Instead, Ephesians conceives the problem as one of unity. The series of "with..." or "co-" terms in Eph 3:6 makes this point about the church: The Gentiles are "heirs with" (συγκληρόνομα *sygklēronoma*), "body with" (σύσσωμα *syssōma*), and "sharers [συμμέτοχα *symmetocha*] of the promise in Christ through the gospel." This perspective makes it quite natural for Ephesians to speak of the union of Christ, the head, with his body, the church, as a mystery (Eph 5:32).

3. Church as Body of Christ. This use of "body of Christ" (σῶμα τοῦ Χριστοῦ *soma tou Christou*) goes beyond Paul's own use of the expression. Paul employed a common image from the political philosophy of his day to appeal for order and harmony in the Corinthian church. Christians should understand that the Spirit has provided diverse gifts within the community so that the whole body can function together. Strife over gifts among Christians is as absurd as parts of the body claiming that they do not belong because they are not some other part (1 Cor 12:12-31). The image is repeated in the same sense in Rom 12:3-8. He can also extend the metaphor of Christians as members of the "body of Christ" to argue for appropriate separation from the two forms of immorality that Jews commonly associated with paganism—sexual immorality (1 Cor 6:15) and idolatrous cultic practices (1 Cor 10:17). Thus for the apostle the expression "body of Christ" (*sōma tou Christou*) involves a metaphor for how to order the concrete details of everyday Christian life. Like the term "church" (ἐκκλησία *ekklēsia*) in Paul's letters, the term "body of Christ" designates local communities of Christians.[25]

Ephesians does not address a local community. Its vision of the church is set in the largest possible framework, the cosmic body of all the faithful united with its head, the risen Christ (1:22-23; 2:6). When the image of the church as the "body of Christ" comes into the ethical exhortation, the picture is one of a "new human being" growing into the body of Christ, which serves under its head (4:13-16). Paul's reference to concrete gifts of ministry in the body are incorporated into this larger vision of the church as the agent through whom its growth takes place (4:11-12). The development toward a more cosmic image of "body of Christ" is anticipated in the hymnic tradition. Colossians 1:15-20 depicts Christ first as divine wisdom active in creation, then as redeemer. Christ the redeemer is head of the body that is the church by virtue of being "firstborn from the dead" (Col 1:18). Colossians 1:19 introduces another term that will figure in the cosmic vision of church found in Ephesians, "fullness" (πλήρωμα *plērōma*). For Colossians, "fullness" refers to divinity dwelling in Christ. For Ephesians, it will refer to the way in which Christ dwells in the cosmic body, the church (1:23; 3:19; 4:13).

Other metaphors used for the church are drawn into this picture of the church as "body of Christ." It can be described as a building or temple being built up into Christ (2:20-21). Christians are members of God's household as children of God, not as strangers or resident aliens (2:19). Because the "body of Christ" is depicted as a heavenly reality, some of the attributes that describe the church follow as natural consequences. The church must be a unity (2:14-16; 4:1-3, 10-13), holy (1:3-8; 4:17-22; 5:3-5, 25-27), universal (2:16; 3:1-6). It cannot be considered part of this world as though it were a sociopolitical institution (5:18-20).[26] If it were, the church would be subject to the powers and authorities that govern the lower regions. Because the body of Christ is the preordained vehicle by which God has chosen to unite all things with God and to subjugate the lower powers (3:10), the church has always belonged to the divine plan of salvation. The doxology of 3:21 insists that God is praised "in the church and in Christ Jesus."

Those who consider such a vision of the church as a dangerous precedent should attend to the metaphors used. None of them attach the reality of the cosmic body of Christ to a particular group of human authorities. No single community could embody the church. Rudolf Schnackenburg remarks:

> For the author all the congregations which lie within his field of vision do not yet, even taken together, constitute "the *ekklēsia*." This is rather an entity which has precedence over all, in which they participate and in accordance with which they should orient their lives.[27]

Similarly the "mystery" of the church united to Christ as bride thus transforms a common Jewish metaphor for Israel as the "bride of Yahweh" (Isa 65:5; Jer 2:2; Ezekiel 16:1; Hosea 1:1–3) by highlighting the realism of the unity between Christ and the church. Christ's self-offering on the cross is the foundation of its holiness (Eph 5:2, 25). Christ's loving concern for the welfare of the church extends to the realities of Christian life in this world. It is not merely a reference to the heavenly unity of the saints with their head (2:5-6). If Ephesians can use this concern to describe the conduct of husbands toward their wives in marriage, then it should also be reflected in the ways that Christian leaders go about their various ministries.

4. Ministries in the Church. The references to such ministries in Ephesians also create some difficulties. When Paul refers to himself as apostle (ἀπόστολος *apostolos,* 1:1) or servant (διάκονος *diakonos*) of the gospel chosen by God to make God's salvation known to the Gentiles (3:7-9), we are on familiar ground. The self-deprecating comment "although I am the very least of all the saints, this grace was given to me" (3:8 NRSV) sounds close to Paul's own account of his apostleship (1 Cor 15:8-10). But Ephesians appears to have slipped out of the apostolic perspective in Eph 3:5. What was unknown to previous generations has now been revealed to God's "holy apostles and prophets by the Spirit." Since "prophets" follows the reference to apostles, the speaker does not appear to mean the Old Testament prophets. The author appears to be looking back on a revelation transmitted by Christian apostles and prophets. When Paul refers to Christian prophets, they are not associated with the apostolic witness to the gospel. Their function involves speaking, prayer, and exhortation within the local assembly (1 Cor 11:2-16; 14:29, 32, 37). When he refers to other apostles positively, Paul highlights the unity of his message with theirs (see 1 Cor 15:11).[28]

Ephesians 2:20 puts "apostles and prophets" in the past. They are the foundation of the building, the church, which is growing into Christ. By contrast, Paul describes himself as the master builder (ἀρχιτέκτων *architektōn*) who builds on the foundation, Jesus Christ (1 Cor 3:10-14). The paraenetic section of the letter treats the term "apostles" (ἀπόστολοι *apostoloi*) as first in a list of gifts to the church: apostles, prophets, evangelists, pastors, and teachers (4:11). They are to equip Christians for service in building up the body of Christ until all attain maturity, the fullness of Christ (τοῦ πληρώματος τοῦ Χριστοῦ *tou plērōmatos tou Christou,* 4:12-13). Once again the relationship between such persons and local church communities remains undefined.[29] Only the last two, pastors (ποιμένας *poimenai*) and teachers (διδάσκαλοι *didaskaloi*), clearly designate resident leaders of the local church. The terms may not describe any particular church order. Ephesians merely wishes to indicate in a general way that God has charged certain persons with nurturing the church by aiding others to grow in unity and knowledge of God. This concern for harmony, internal unity, and growth might represent the concerns of a church facing the death of the apostolic generation.

5. Eschatological Shift. The cosmic picture of the church already united with the risen Christ shifts attention away from the end-time coming of the Lord (as in 1 Thess 4:13–5:11). For Paul, all things are not yet subjected to Christ. When they are, when every authority and power is destroyed, then Christ will bring all under God's rule (1 Cor 15:24-28). Ephesians refers to the subjection of all authorities and powers as a present reality. The risen and exalted Christ is far above all powers, whether in this age or in the age to come (Eph 1:19-23). Similarly, believers have been freed from the powers of darkness and raised up with Christ in the heavens. This exaltation also demonstrates God's extraordinary graciousness toward the faithful in the coming ages (Eph 2:5-7). Elements of future eschatology remain part of the author's conceptual world, but they do not serve as criteria to determine one's present position in the world. Nor is a culminating event in God's saving plan anticipated in the near future. Ephesians never uses the term "mystery" to designate a future act of redemption. The plan to bring all things together in Christ may not be completed, but it has already become a reality in the church (1:10).

This eschatological shift is evident in another formal difference between Ephesians and other Pauline letters. The apostle typically concludes major sections with references to elements of future judgment or salvation (e.g., Rom 11:31-36; 1 Cor 1:9-10; 15:54-58; Phil 1:10-11; 3:20–4:1; 1 Thess 1:9-10; 2:19-20; 3:11-13). Such references carry a hortatory message to the audience: Take care to persevere so that God may "strengthen your hearts in holiness that you may be blameless before our God and Father at the coming of our Lord Jesus with all his saints" (1 Thess 3:13 NRSV). Ephesians retains the liturgical character of Pauline transitions by using formulaic expressions (as in 1:20-23) or doxologies (as in 3:20-21). It uses "saints" (ἅγιοι *hagioi*) as its designation for believers (e.g., 1:1, 15; 2:19; 3:18; 5:3; 6:18). Concerns that the church be "holy and blameless" (ἁγίος καὶ ἄμωμος *hagios kai amōmos*) are reflected in the opening prayer (1:4) and the paraenesis (4:24; 5:27) but never appear with the reference to the Lord's coming in judgment. The conclusion to the whole letter (6:10-20) takes up the motif of divine armor, which occurs as part of the eschatological conclusion to 1 Thessalonians (1 Thess 5:8). Even here, where one would expect standing fast to be accompanied by an explicit indication that these are the "last days," there is no reference to a judgment day. All that remains are the linguistic tags "withstand on that evil day" (6:13) and "keep alert" (6:18). Ephesians never speaks of Christ's coming in judgment. Its ecclesiology short-circuits such language, since the church already exists in the unity of the saints with their exalted head.

SEARCHING FOR A SOCIORELIGIOUS CONTEXT

Scholars have mined various features of the letter to construct a background for its author or audience. Since the destination "Ephesus" was not original, those theories built on archaeological and religious descriptions of ancient Ephesus and its Artemis cult have no foundation in the text. Some advocates of an Ephesus argument claim that the pluralism of religious cults and magic practices evident there is representative of the environment of cities in Asia Minor. Since the emphasis on Christ's exaltation above the powers of the cosmos and the identification of believers with their exalted head forms the center of Ephesians, this imagery might be read as a response to pagan religion. The Artemis cult in Ephesus demonstrates the superiority of the goddess to all forces; she is queen of the cosmos, as the signs of the zodiac around her neck and the magic letters on her scepter demonstrate. Associated with her, one finds Hecate, goddess of the underworld.[30] Similar zodiac imagery is connected with other goddess figures, like Diana and Isis. Funerary reliefs at Philippi depict the deified male or female child being conducted into heavenly places.[31] Other authors compare the "seated in the heavenly places" of Ephesians with the heavenly ascent of Mithraism.[32] These parallels say little about the details of Ephesians, but they suggest religious images and prior convictions that its audience would bring with them to the letter.

Other interpreters follow the lead of classic commentaries[33] and look to ancient gnostic mythologies. The separation between the heavenly regions in which those with knowledge of God are linked with the redeemer and the lower world of darkness governed by hostile forces forms a central element in their speculation. The second- and third-century CE gnostic texts provide suggestive parallels to some of the images in Ephesians. Gnostic writers claim Ephesians as evidence that the apostle taught a gnostic doctrine of the soul fallen from heaven and trapped by hostile powers. Once awakened and enlighted by the heavenly revealer from heaven, the soul is superior to the powers. However, peculiarly gnostic terminology or *theologoumena* do not appear in Ephesians, so emerging gnostic sectarianism does not provide an explanation for the theological innovations found in the epistles.

Some interpreters have tried to combine all of these motifs. A gnostic dualism between the heavenly and earthly regions is said to cause the turn toward astrology and magic in order to gain security in a dangerous, hostile universe.[34] Or they assume that since Ephesians speaks of access to God through the knowledge that comes in Christ, it must be opposed to visionaries who claim to have ascended into heaven and to have been seated in God's presence.[35] Such visionary practices linked to Jewish speculation about heavenly realities have been more easily linked to the false teaching rejected in Col 2:8–3:4.[36] Though Ephesians adopts the image of believers seeking what belongs to the risen Christ (Col 3:1-4), none of the polemic details of the Colossians text are found in Ephesians. Further, as noted above, Ephesians erases the eschatological reservation found in earlier Pauline letters. Colossians does not. It limits the believers' identification with the exalted Christ to the future coming of Christ. For Ephesians, the saints are already one with their Lord. Once again, Ephesians shows no evidence of engaging a particular religious situation.

Since Ephesians highlights the incorporation of Gentiles with Israel in the new creation that God had planned from the beginning (2:11-18; 3:6), a natural context would appear to have been relationships between Jewish and Gentile Christians. Some interpreters lift the problematic of Gentile conversion from Pauline Epistles to explain the need for ethical instruction in Ephesians. But though the center of the apostle's gospel did require that both Jew and

Gentile be made righteous on the same basis, through faith (Gal 2:15-21), Ephesians never deals with those concrete details of the law that distinguish Jew and Gentile and make Paul's emphasis on righteousness through faith, not works of the law, essential. Ephesians can refer to "circumcision" and "uncircumcision" as markers of the two communities (2:11) without any indication that the distinction created a problem for relationships between Jewish and Gentile Christians in their unity. Contrast Colossians, where circumcision is spiritualized (Col 2:11) and Jewish sabbaths, holy days, and food laws are rejected (Col 2:16-17). Ephesians 2:15 refers without difficulty to the "law with its commandments and ordinances" abolished by the cross. Consequently, many scholars agree that the churches to which Ephesians was written cannot include an active Jewish Christian group.[37]

If the community envisaged by the letter consists solely of Gentiles being encouraged to remember themselves as brought into a common inheritance with Jewish believers, does the reminder provide any hints about the setting of the letter? Many of our best parallels to its religious language can be found among the Essene texts from Qumran. Such comparisons, along with the exegetical forms used by the author, suggest a person with a background in first-century CE Jewish sectarianism. At the same time, the ornate Greek rhetorical style suggests a Jew with a Hellenistic education. This combination is similar to that of Paul himself. In Paul's case, the sectarian piety through which he assimilated Judaism was Pharisaism. In this case, it was some form of sectarian piety closer to that of the Essenes. The author of Ephesians not only looks to the apostle Paul as the recipient of special understanding of God's plan, but he is also a student of Paul's letters. Given the Essene interest in texts, including preserving and continuing an exegetical tradition linked to its founder, one might infer that such a person had made an effort to obtain copies of Paul's letters.

Other interpreters suggest that Ephesians attempts to ward off a crisis similar to that addressed by Paul in Rom 11:17-36. Its repeated use of "with..." formulae, as well as the priority given "us" into which "you," Gentiles, have been incorporated, indicates a desire to hang on to the Jewish roots of Christianity.[38] But Ephesians has surrendered the careful distinction between the church and Israel so important to Paul. Its exhortations have nothing to do with Judaism. Rather, the Gentile audience must remain committed to the new Christian way of life, to worship, to mutual love and assistance among believers, and to the moral reform that marks them as "children of God."

On the one hand, it seems more accurate to think of the early Christian movement as an "internal migration" of a sectarian group within Judaism than as a "new religion."[39] On the other hand, Ephesians clearly perceives the Jew and Gentile believers who constitute the body of the risen Christ as a "new creation," not merely the righteous remnant of Israel with some Gentiles thrown in. For its readers, the existence of any actual relationships with the Jewish communities of Asia Minor remains in doubt.[40]

Ephesians presumes that preaching the gospel involves persuading others to turn away from paganism as cultic practice and from moral laxity in conduct to become part of the Christian community. But does this orientation reflect an attitude that the Gentile Christian mission assimilated from the Hellenistic synagogue? Martin Goodman has recently assembled considerable evidence against the view that either Jews or pagans thought it would be preferable if all humans worshiped the same God.[41] Scholars find the social boundaries of those Gentile sympathizers often referred to as "god-fearers" increasingly difficult to fix clearly. Without doubt, some outsiders found their way into Judaism as proselytes (see Tob 1:8).[42] When women of the Herodian family married, they required that their husbands be converted to Judaism.[43] In some areas, though by no means everywhere, one finds Jewish communities with a range of Gentile sympathizers or benefactors. Why would outsiders act as benefactors to the Jewish community? They must have been encouraged that such acts would have a reward (cf. Rom 2:12-16). Persons within the Jewish community may have encouraged such benefactors, whose assistance they required in order to maintain the political independence of their community.[44]

Would such Gentiles have been drawn to the early Christian movement as Acts suggests (see Acts 16:11-14; 17:1-5)? Some synagogue benefactors clearly retained their pagan ties and even priesthoods within pagan cult associations.[45] If that was a normal pattern of benefaction, then the language of Ephesians that highlights the radical break of conversion might be directed toward those who thought they could retain earlier associations while belonging to the Christian group (as in 1 Cor 10:1-22). What else these Gentiles from Asia Minor might have known about Jews can only be suggested by supplementing the few hints in the letter with general evidence for the region. Ephesians itself assumes that readers are familiar with "circumcision" as the decisive criterion for belonging to Israel, with Jewish monotheism and its critique of pagan gods, with Scripture, and in a general way with Jews as separated from non-Jews by "commandments and ordinances." None of these observations go beyond what ordinary Gentiles might know about Jews. Indeed, Ephesians does not refer to the other common items of information, sabbath observance and food laws, even though they appear in Colossians. This omission may indicate that Jewish or Jewish Christian practice was not an issue for the author or his audience.

Early Christian churches appear in those cities of Asia Minor that also had Jewish communities. Louis Feldman suggests that the lack of Pharisaic influence in the inland cities of Asia Minor indicates that Judaism there was less bound to the land of Israel. Jewish inscriptions lack the pious Jewish sentiments of longing for the Temple or artistic representations of the ark or the menorah so common elsewhere. Sardis appears to have been the exception to the rule of a lower degree of Jewish identity in inland Asia Minor. Its large, wealthy, and properous community evoked sharp anti-Jewish polemic from Melito, Bishop of Sardis in the second century. Even in the fourth century, the remodeled Jewish synagogue was a larger and more impressive building than the Christian church.[46] If the relative strength and social prestige of the two communities were as Feldman suggests, such that the Jewish community far outweighed that of the Christian offshoot, then the emphasis on Jewish origins evident in Ephesians might serve to intensify communal identity among the Christian minority.

After all, Ephesians makes the extraordinary claim that God's plan for humanity is represented by this community. Some have even compared that language to claims for the peace created by the Roman Empire.[47] Though there is no clear evidence that Ephesians is concerned with imperial ideology, the suggestion points to the spiritual importance of its message. The case for creating unity through imperial expansion was evident in the architecture of the great cities of Asia Minor. The Jewish community in many Asia Minor cities owed Roman power an important debt; appeals to Roman authorities secured Jewish rights to sabbath observance, protection of money collected for the Jerusalem Temple, and the like. Ephesians envisages a different basis for human unity, a religious one. As far as one can tell, this realization was unique to the Christian mission. Not even the Romans thought that all the citizens of their empire would worship Roman gods. Jews never undertook a systematic policy of proselytism to bring pagans to the worship of God. Ephesians has set Paul's own concern for a mission that would reach the ends of the Roman Empire (Rom 15:18-23) in a global perspective. God planned to unite all things in Christ even before creation.[48]

FOR FURTHER READING

Commentaries:

Barth, Markus. *Ephesians.* 2 vols. AB 34; 34A. New York: Doubleday, 1974.

Best, Ernest. *A Critical and Exegetical Commentary on Ephesians.* ICC. Edinburgh: T & T Clark, 1998.

Kitchen, Martin. *Ephesians.* London: Routledge, 1994.

Lincoln, Andrew. *Ephesians.* WBC 42. Dallas: Word, 1990.

MacDonald, Margaret Y. *Colossians and Ephisians.* SP 17. Collegeville, Minn.: Liturgical Press, 2000.

Martin, Ralph P. *Ephesians, Colossians, and Philemon.* Atlanta: John Knox, 1991.

Mitton, C. L. *The Epistle to the Ephesians.* Oxford: Clarendon, 1951.

O'Brien, Peter T. *The Letter to the Ephesians.* Pillar NT Commentary. Grand Rapids: Eerdmans, 1999.

Schnackenburg, Rudolf. *The Epistle to the Ephesians.* Translated by H. Heron. Edinburgh: T & T Clark, 1991 [Ger. 1982].

Other Studies:

Adams, Edward. *Constructing the World: A Study of Paul's Cosmological Language.* Edinburgh: T & T Clark, 2000.

Arnold, Clinton E. *Ephesians: Power and Magic. The Concept of Power in Ephesians in Light of Its Historical Setting.* SNTSMS 63. Cambridge: Cambridge University Press, 1989.

Best, Ernest. *Essays on Ephesians.* Edinburgh: T & T Clark, 1997.

Caragounis, Chrys C. *The Ephesian Mysterion: Meaning and Context.* ConB 8. Lund: Gleerup, 1977.

Dawes, Gregory W. *The Body in Question: Metaphor and Meaning in the Interpretation of Ephesians 5:21-33.* Biblical Interpretation Series 30. Leiden: Brill, 1998.

Harris, W. Hall, III. *The Descent of Christ: Ephesians 4:7-11* and Traditional Hebrew Imagery. AGAJU 32. Leiden: Brill, 1996.

Klauck, Hans-Josef. *The Religious Context of Early Christianity: A Guide to Graeco-Roman Religions.* Translated by Brian McNeil. Edinburgh: T & T Clark, 2000.

Lincoln, Andrew T., and A. J. M. Wedderburn. *The Theology of the Later Pauline Letters.* Cambridge: Cambridge University Press, 1993.

Meade, David G. *Pseudonymity and Canon: An Investigation into the Relationship of Authorship and Authority in the Jewish and Earliest Christian Tradition.* WUNT 39. Tübingen: J. C. B. Mohr (Paul Siebeck), 1986.

Neufeld, T. Y. *Put On the Armour of God: The Divine Warrior from Isaiah to Ephesians.* Sheffield: Sheffield Academic, 1997.

Usami, Koshi. *Somatic Comprehension of Unity: The Church in Ephesus.* AnBib 101. Rome: Pontifical Biblical Institute, 1983.

Wiles, G. P. *Paul's Intercessory Prayers: The Significance of the Intercessory Prayer Passages in the Letters of St. Paul.* SNTSMS 24. Cambridge: Cambridge University Press, 1974.

Wright, N. T. *Paul for Everyone: The Prison Letters: Ephisians, Philippians, Colossians and Philemon.* London: SPCK, 2002.

ENDNOTES

1. Markus Barth, *Ephesians,* 2 vols., AB 34-34A (Garden City, N.Y.: Doubleday, 1974); Peter T. O'Brien, *Letter to the Ephesians* (Grand Rapids: Eerdmans, 1999).

2. Ernest Best, "Recipients and Title of the Letter to the Ephesians: Why and When the Designation 'Ephesians'?" in *Aufstieg und Niedergang der römischen Welt* II 25/4, ed. Wolfgang Haase (Berlin: DeGruyter, 1987).

3. Ralph P. Martin, *Ephesians, Colossians and Philemon* (Atlanta: John Knox, 1991).

4. David G. Meade, *Pseudonymity and Canon: An Investigation into the Relationship of Authorship and Authority in the Jewish and Earliest Christian Tradition,* WUNT 39 (Tübingen: Mohr-Siebeck, 1986) 140-42.

5. See Andrew T. Lincoln, *Ephesians,* WBC 42 (Dallas: Word, 1990) xl-xlii; and "'Stand, therefore...': Ephesians 6:10-20 as *Peroratio,*" *Biblical Interpretation* 3 (1995) 99-114.

6. Andrew T. Lincoln and A. J. M. Wedderburn, *The Theology of the Later Pauline Letters* (Cambridge: Cambridge University Press, 1993) 82-83.

7. For a cautious treatment of the assumptions that Ephesians makes concerning its readers, see Ernest Best, *A Critical and Exegetical Commentary on Ephesians,* ICC (Edinburgh: T & T Clark, 1998) 1-6.

8. Larry J. Kreitzer, "'Crude Language' and 'Shameful Things Done in Secret' (Eph 5:1, 4, 12): Allusions to the Cult of Demeter/Cybele in Hierapolis?" *JSNT* 71 (1988) 51-77; and "The Plutonium of Hierapolis and the Descent of Christ into the 'Lowermost Parts of the Earth' (Ephesians 4:1, 9)," *Biblica* 79 (1998) 381-93.

9. Meade, *Pseudonymity and Canon,* 153.

10. Lincoln, *Ephesians,* lvi.

11. Meade, *Pseudonymity and Canon,* 150-51.

12. Best highlights the shifts in language between Colossians and Ephesians to argue for a more complex relationship between the two. Rather than conclude that Ephesians is directly dependent upon Cololossians, Best concludes that Colossians and Ephesians are independent representatives of a Pauline school tradition. See Best, *A Critical and Exegetical Commentary on Ephesians,* 20-25. Such a hypothesis has as many difficulties as the assumption that Ephesians is reworking Col. For a detailed analysis that argues that Ephesians is dependent upon Colossians and other written Pauline letters see Michael Gese, *Das Vermächtnis des Apostels, Die Rezeption der paulinischen Theologie im Epheserbrief,* WUNT 2 Reihe, 99 (Tübingen: J.C.B. Mohn [Paul Siebeck], 1997) 39-54.

13. So Rudolf Schnackenburg, *The Epistle to the Ephesians,* trans. H. Heron (Edinburgh: T & T Clark, 1991) 30-31.

14. Also see the chart of these relationships in Gese, *Das Vermächtnis des Apostels,* 76-78.

15. Lincoln, *Ephesians,* lviii.

16. David Trobisch, *Paul's Letter Collection: Tracing the Origins* (Minneapolis: Fortress, 1994) 50-52.

17. Arland J. Hultgren, *Christ and His Benefits: Christology and Redemption in the New Testament* (Philadelphia: Fortress, 1987) 92-93.

18. See the discussion of the phrase "in the heavenlies" in Best, *A Critical and Exegetical Commentary on Ephesians,* 115-18.

19. Schnackenburg, *The Epistle to the Ephesians,* 25-27.

20. Linda L. Belleville, *Reflections of Glory: Paul's Polemical Use of the Moses-Doxa Tradition in 2 Corinthians 3.1-18,* JSNTSup 52 (Sheffield: JSOT, 1991) 92-93.

21. Schnackenburg, *The Epistle to the Ephesians,* 26-27; Lincoln and Wedderburn, *The Theology of the Later Pauline Letters* 130-37.

22. Marc Schoeni, "The Hyperbolic Sublime as a Master Trope in Romans," in *Rhetoric and the New Testament: Essays from the 1992 Heidelberg Conference,* ed. Stanley E. Porter and Thomas H. Olbricht, JSNTSup 90 (Sheffield: JSOT, 1993) 181.

23. See the study of Markus Bockmuehl, *Revelation and Mystery in Ancient Judaism and Pauline Christianity* (Grand Rapids: Eerdmans, 1977).

24. See James D. G. Dunn, *The Theology of Paul the Apostle* (Grand Rapids: Eerdmans, 1998) 526-29.

25. L. O. R. Yorke, *The Church as the Body of Christ in the Pauline Corpus: A Re-examination* (Lanham: University Press of America, 1991); Dunn, *The Theology of Paul the Apostle,* 548-64.

26. Yorke, *The Church as the Body of Christ,* 101-3.

27. Schnackenburg, *The Epistle to the Ephesians,* 295. Others see the universalism in Ephesians as a loss for the theology of local church communities. Dunn remarks, "It is also true that Paul's own transforming vision was itself soon transformed, with many of its distinctive features lost to sight. His vision of the church of God as fully manifested in the local church was displaced by the thought of the Church universal (already in Ephesians)." Dunn, *The Theology of Paul the Apostle,* 563.

28. See Dunn, *The Theology of Paul the Apostle,* 579-82.

29. Lack of concern with the local community forms a striking contrast to Paul's understanding of the local character of all church ministry, including his own office as an apostle. See Dunn, *The Theology of Paul the Apostle,* 578-79.

30. Clinton E. Arnold, *Ephesians: Power and Magic: The Concept of Power in Ephesians in the Light of Its Historical Setting,* SNTSMS 63 (Cambridge: Cambridge University Press, 1989).

31. Valerie A. Abrahamsen, *Women and Worship at Philippi: Diana, Artemis, and Other Cults in the Early Christian Era* (Portland, Me.: Astarte Shell, 1995).

32. Timothy B. Cargal, "'Seated in the Heavenlies': Cosmic Mediators in the Mysteries of Mithras and the Letter to the Ephesians," SBLSP, ed. Eugene H. Lovering (Atlanta: Scholars Press, 1994) 804-21.

33. Esp. Heinrich Schlier, *Der Brief an die Epheser* (Dusseldorf: Patmos, 1957).

34. Ralph P. Martin, *Ephesians, Colossians and Philemon* (Atlanta: John Knox, 1991).

35. Michael Gouldner, "Vision and Knowledge," *JSNT* 56 (1994) 53-71.

36. James D. G. Dunn, "The Colossian Philosophy: A Confident Jewish Apologetic," *Bib* 76 (1995) 153-81.

37. A. Lindemann, "Bemerkungen zu den Adressaten und zum Anlass des Epheserbriefes," *ZNW* 67 (1976) 235-51, insists not only that there were no Jewish Christians in the audience of Ephesians, but also that the author was not a Jewish Christian either. He has adopted Paul's persona to bolster faith in a church threatened by persecution.

38. David G. Meade, *Pseudonymity and Canon: An Investigation into the Relationship of Authorship and Authority in the Jewish and Earliest Christian Tradition,* WUNT 39 (Tübingen: Mohr-Siebeck, 1986) 146.

39. So Dieter Georgi, "The Early Church: Internal Jewish Migration or New Religion?" *HTR* 88 (1995) 35-68, who does not deal with Ephesians.

40. On the paucity of evidence for Jewish life in Asia Minor during the first century CE, see John M. G. Barclay, *Jews in the Mediterranean Diaspora from Alexander to Trajan (323 BCE–117 CE)* (Berkeley: University of California Press, 1996) 259-81. Lack of involvement in the Jewish revolts of the period suggests that Jews in Asia Minor maintained friendly relations with non-Jewish neighbors.

41. Martin Goodman, *Mission and Conversion: Proselytizing in the Religious History of the Roman Empire* (Oxford: Clarendon, 1994).

42. Josephus *Against Apion* 2.210. However, Roman authors are aware of the difference

between persons who are Jewish sympathizers and actual proselytes. See Peter Schäfer, *Judeophobia: Attitudes Toward the Jews in the Ancient World* (Cambridge, Mass.: Harvard University Press, 1997) 80-115. Schäfer concludes that the pressure on collecting the *discus Judaicus* under Domitian was a response to increasing proselytism in Roman society.

43. Josephus *Antiquities of the Jews* 20.139, 145; Goodman, *Mission and Conversion*, 63-65.

44. Goodman, *Mission and Conversion*, 87-88.

45. Paul R. Trebilco, *Jewish Communities in Asia Minor*, SNTSMS 69 (Cambridge: Cambridge University Press, 1991) 58-59.

46. Louis H. Feldman, *Jew and Gentile in the Ancient World* (Princeton, N.J.: Princeton University Press, 1993) 73.

47. Franz Mussner, *Der Brief an die Epheser* (Gütersloh: Gerd Mohn, 1982).

48. Portions of this survey appeared originally in Pheme Perkins, *Ephesians*, ANTC (Nashville: Abingdon, 1997).

THE LETTER TO THE PHILIPPIANS

MORNA D. HOOKER

The characteristic note of Paul's letter to the Philippians is above all that of joy—a remarkable feature, in view of the fact that this letter was written in prison, where its author was held under a capital charge! Paul's faith triumphs over adversity and causes him to rejoice, whatever happens. The letter is written to a Christian community with whom Paul has had a long and happy relationship; though they are not yet perfect, they are nevertheless his joy and his crown, in whom he hopes to boast on the day of judgment (2:16; 4:1).

The founding of the Christian community at Philippi (probably in about 50 CE) had marked a significant development in Paul's ministry, opening up a new area for missionary work. According to Acts 16:1, Paul was prevented by the Holy Spirit from preaching in Asia or Bithynia, so he made his way to Troas, where he received a summons, in a dream, to go to Macedonia. This was considerably farther west than Paul had so far ventured. The Acts account is of particular interest, since it is at this precise point (Acts 16:10) that the "we" passages begin, suggesting that either Luke or his source had accompanied Paul on this mission.

Philippi was a fairly small city in the first century CE (approx. 10,000 inhabitants), situated on the Via Egnatia, which ran from east to west, taking travelers to the Adriatic coast and hence, by boat, to Italy. The port of Neapolis lay ten miles to the south and Thessalonica 100 miles to the southwest. Philippi

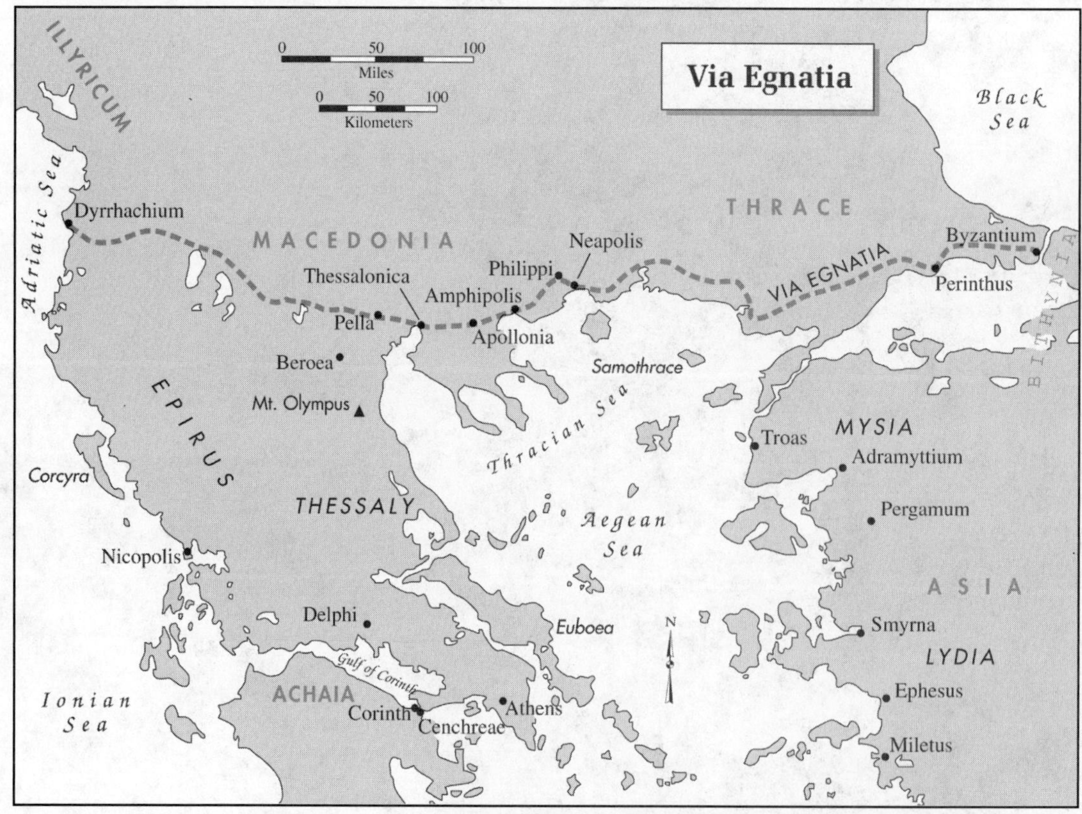

had originally flourished because of gold mines nearby, but these had been worked out long before the first century CE, and the city was important mainly as an agricultural center, being situated on the edge of a fertile plain where grain and wine were produced. The original inhabitants of the area had been Thracians, but in the fourth century BCE it had been taken by Philip II of Macedon, who founded a Greek city on the site of an earlier village and gave it his own name. The city had come under Roman rule in the second century BCE, and after Antony and Octavian defeated Brutus and Cassius at the battles of Philippi in 42 BCE it had been refounded as a Roman colony, and many Italians had been brought in and settled. It was not (contra Acts 16:12) "the leading city of the district of Macedonia." Macedonia was in fact divided into four districts, and Philippi was in the first of these. (Luke may have been confused, or it is possible that he wrote "a city of the first district of Macedonia," as the NRSV margin suggests.) The fact that the city was a Roman colony gave its citizens great privileges, for they enjoyed considerable property and legal rights and were exempt from the taxes imposed on those without this status. Citizens of the colony were also citizens of Rome, and the city's administration was modeled on that of Rome.

When Paul came to Philippi, therefore, he would have found a sizable nucleus of Roman citizens, many of whom were Italian by birth and who constituted the aristocracy of the city. He would have found Roman administration and discipline as well as Roman culture. The official language was Latin (public inscriptions in the city were written in Latin), and the city was loyal to Rome, which meant, among other things, that the cult of the emperor would have been much in evidence. The men who are described in Acts 16:16-21 as dragging Paul and Silas before the magistrates are clearly understood by Luke to have been Roman citizens, but the majority of the inhabitants of the city would have been Greeks who had flocked in after the earlier conquest by Philip of Macedon. In the rural areas around Philippi in particular Paul would have found some of the original inhabitants of the land, the Thracians. No archaeological evidence has been found for a Jewish presence in the city; perhaps it was not sufficiently important commercially to attract them. It is notable that Luke makes no reference to a synagogue in Philippi; to be sure, Paul discovers "a place of prayer," but apparently the only people gathered there are women, and the one with whom Paul speaks is not herself Jewish, but a God-fearing Gentile. This account supports the belief that any Jewish presence in Philippi was minimal. Paul's converts would have been entirely, or almost entirely, Gentile. As for their previous religious beliefs, the mixed population of the city meant that various religious cults would have been practiced in the city, alongside the official cult of the emperor.

In the letter itself, there are possible reflections of these circumstances. The term Paul uses to address the Philippians in 4:15 is a Latin form of their name, rather than Greek. The name "Clement" in 4:3 is also Latin, but the names "Syntyche" and "Euodia" (4:2) are Greek. The reference to bishops and deacons in 1:1 may indicate a more developed organization (under Roman influence) than elsewhere, while the references to "citizenship" would have had a special nuance for the inhabitants of Philippi. Finally, the declaration of Jesus Christ as Lord in 2:11 may well have been intended as a deliberate challenge to the loyalty they were expected to give to the Roman emperor as Lord.

AUTHORSHIP AND INTEGRITY

The authenticity of the epistle is not seriously in dispute, though doubts have been expressed from time to time. F. C. Baur's objections were entirely subjective—the letter did not conform to what he expected from a Pauline epistle—and more recent attempts to apply objective literary tests to the letter (with a negative result) have been treated with considerable skepticism.[1]

More serious questions, however, have been raised concerning the epistle's integrity. Many commentators believe that it consists of two—or even three—letters that have been joined together. The arguments in favor of this hypothesis are as follows:

(1) There are abrupt jumps in Paul's argument, most notably at 3:1. It is suggested that these are easier to understand if they are due to an editor's piecing various letters together. In fact, however, this "solution" merely creates another problem: Why did an *editor* make such unsuitable joins? The more it is argued that it is difficult to under-

stand why Paul should move abruptly from one topic to another, the more difficult it becomes to comprehend an editor's motives in doing so. Indeed, it is easier to attribute sudden changes in subject to Paul than to an editor!

(2) Paul had recently received a gift from the Philippian church, brought to him by Epaphroditus. Thus it is frequently assumed that one of the chief reasons why he had written to them was to thank them for that gift. This he does in 4:10-20, almost at the end of the letter, whereas courtesy and literary convention alike would surely have demanded that he begin his letter by expressing his thanks. It is suggested, therefore, that 4:10-20 is part of an earlier "thank-you" letter. Since the earlier part of the letter was clearly written some time after the receipt of the gift (news about Epaphroditus's illness having reached the Philippians and information about their reaction having come to Paul, 2:26), it is possible that Paul has indeed already expressed his thanks, either by letter or by a message of some kind. If that is the case, then his apparently belated and comparatively muted reference to the Philippians' gift in 4:10-20 is understandable. This would, of course, mean that any such earlier letter has been lost. If, on the other hand, we assume that this letter has been incorporated into the existing letter, then part of it (its opening paragraph at the very least) has been lost; it would seem, moreover, that the editor who placed it here did not feel that this (to us) strange position was inappropriate.

It has been pointed out, however, that there are in 4:10-20 "echoes" of the vocabulary used in 1:3-11 and that the two passages thus form an inclusio. If this is deliberate, then not only does it suggest that one of Paul's main purposes in writing to the Philippians was to express his thanks for their gift, but it means also that the letter must have been composed as a unity.[2]

(3) In a letter written to the Philippian church by Polycarp, a second-century bishop and martyr, there is a reference to letters written by Paul to the Philippian church.[3] Unfortunately there is great debate as to whether the plural should be taken seriously and whether Polycarp was perhaps confused about the destination of some of Paul's epistles. Even if we take Polycarp's words as evidence that more than one letter to the Philippians was in existence in his time, however, this does not prove that these letters were later amalgamated. There is no textual evidence to support the view that letters that were still separate in Polycarp's day were subsequently brought together. If there was, in fact, more than one letter, the others appear to have been lost.

In spite of the various problems this theory involves, the view that what we know as the letter to the Philippians represents an amalgamation of two or three letters is popular among many commentators. Although there is considerable disagreement about precisely how to distribute the material, 1:1–3:1 is usually allocated to one letter and 4:10-20 to another; there is much debate, however, as to where the fragment of letter beginning in 3:2 might end, and this uncertainty is an indication of the fragility of the arguments. Moreover, attempts to produce a coherent series of letters leave us with a huge problem: *Why* should an editor piece Paul's letters together in this way? Had the originals been damaged, so that one or two letters existed as fragments only? If so, why did the editor make such a bad job of joining them together? The problems arising from this theory are such that it seems much easier to accept the letter as a unity. The features in Philippians that puzzle us (such as the sudden change of subject in 3:2 and the position of 4:10-20) are probably due to factors in Paul's situation that we do not fully understand.[4]

PLACE AND DATE

The place and date of writing the letter have proved equally contentious. It is clear that Paul was writing from prison (1:7, 12-18); therefore, the question at issue is where this prison was situated. The traditional answer (dating from at least the second century) was Rome, and there are strong arguments to back this up. The chief of these is that the situation reflected in the letter suits the conditions of Paul's imprisonment in Rome, insofar as these can be reconstructed from Acts. Paul had appealed to Caesar and had been taken as a prisoner to Rome. There he waited for a long time in custody (at least two years, according to Acts 28:30). Acts tells us that Paul was under house arrest during this time, but Luke does not complete the story. The tradition that Paul was martyred in Rome means that we must allow that at some stage he found himself in prison under a capital charge, which is the situation reflected in Philippians 1. Support for Rome as the place where the letter was written is found in two incidental references in Philippians. The first is the mention of the praetorium in 1:13; unfortunately the meaning of the word is uncertain, since it can refer to a building as well as to the praetorian guard, and both building and guard could be situated in cities other than Rome. However, the context of 1:13 seems to indicate that Paul had the guard in mind, and they would have been more likely to have been stationed in Rome than elsewhere. The second is the reference to Caesar's household in 4:22, a term that included a large number of officials. Again, they could be found throughout the empire, but there would certainly have been a far greater number of them in Rome than elsewhere.

Three arguments have been brought against Rome as the place of origin. The first is that Philippians is much more "like" earlier letters, such as Romans, than it is like the other letter Paul may have written from Rome—Colossians (though the authorship, as well as the place, of that letter is strongly disputed). This, however, is a subjective judgment. Philippians is "like" Romans in some ways, and unlike it in others; similarly, it has interesting parallels as well as differences with Colossians. These similarities and differences are hardly surprising, since letters reflect the particular circumstances in which and the situations for which they were written. Moreover, Romans was probably the last of Paul's letters to have been written before his Roman imprisonment. A second argument has been given far more weight and relates to the distance between Rome and Philippi (approx. 800 miles), which would have made any journey between the two cities very long and tedious (approx. two months). Philippians implies several such journeys—news of Paul's imprisonment sent to Philippi, Epaphroditus sent by the Philippian church to Paul, news of Epaphroditus's illness sent to Philippi and news of their concern sent back to Paul, and now the letter itself sent to Philippi—far too many, it is suggested, to be possible if the distance was so great. The strength of this objection, too, seems to have been exaggerated. Communications in the ancient world were reasonably good, and Rome and Philippi were both strategically placed for such journeys. Travel was, of course, arduous and slow by modern standards—but this is reflected in the letter itself, in the reference to the anxiety of the Philippians as they await news of Epaphroditus. Moreover, since Paul spent at least two years in custody in Rome, there was plenty of time for numerous journeys.

The third objection to Rome as the place where this letter was written is that Paul says in 2:24 that he is hoping to visit the Philippians on his release, whereas in Rom 15:22-29 he had said that he planned to go on from Rome to Spain. If Paul is imprisoned east of Philippi, he could visit the city en route to Rome and Spain, but to visit it after Rome would be to head in the wrong direction. Romans 15:22-29 was written before his imprisonment, however, and several years in prison (both at Caesarea and at Rome) could well have caused Paul to change his mind. It would not have been the first time that Paul had altered his plans (see 2 Cor 1:15-23).

Two other suggestions as to the place of writing have been made. One is Caesarea, where Paul is said to have been imprisoned for two years (Acts 24:27) and where he was kept in a building called a praetorium (Acts 23:35). Caesarea was even farther from Philippi than was Rome, however, and the journey just as tedious. The serious objection to placing the letter's composition in Caesarea is that Paul was at no time in danger of execution while he was there, and it is difficult to relate his situation at Caesarea to what he says in Phil 1:19-26.

The other suggestion, which has gained wide support, is Ephesus, which is situated much closer to Macedonia so that the journey between the two cities would have been much shorter. There is, to be sure, nothing in Acts to indicate that Paul had been imprisoned there, but Paul says that he has been in prison many times (2 Cor 11:23). He also refers to an occasion when his life was in danger in Asia (2 Cor 1:8-10): Was this the occasion when he fought with wild beasts at Ephesus (1 Cor 15:32)? Unfortunately, we do not know what Paul was alluding to in that passage, but it can hardly have been meant literally, since he survived the experience. While it is possible that Paul was imprisoned in Ephesus, there is no evidence at all that he was incarcerated there for a considerable length of time under a capital charge. Moreover, Paul had many friends in Ephesus, whereas he appears to have been feeling extremely isolated when writing to Philippi.

If Paul wrote Philippians from Ephesus, then we would need to date it about 52–54 CE; if from Caesarea, then it would have been written about 60 CE. If, as seems most probable, we place it in Rome, then the date of composition would have been the early 60s.

PURPOSE FOR THE LETTER

Opinions differ widely as to the reason why Paul wrote the letter. Many commentators assume that his main purpose was to deal with some major problem in the Philippian church, which they deduce must have been that of disunity. Paul does not rebuke the church, however—apart from the implied mild rebuke directed to two leaders in 4:2. The gentleness with which Paul deals with that situation suggests that the problem is a minor one; when there were serious problems in a community Paul did not hesitate to deal with them vigorously.

Paul seems to have had two main reasons for writing. The first is to reassure his readers about his own situation. This he does—unusually—at the beginning of his letter (1:12-26), in order to allay their natural concern for him. The other reason is to commend Epaphroditus and to explain why he is returning to Philippi. Paul is probably anxious lest Epaphroditus be criticized for not staying with Paul.

A subsidiary reason for writing seems to have been to express his thanks (probably for a second time) for their gift to him. Although the section where he does so comes at the end of the letter (4:10-20), there are possible references earlier (1:5; 2:17, 25) that hint at his gratitude for what he regards as a response to the gospel rather than simply as a personal gift. The generosity of the church is witnessed to elsewhere (see 2 Cor 8:1-6).

It was probably Epaphroditus's return to Philippi that gave Paul the opportunity to send a letter. Paul took advantage of this journey to offer the Philippians encouragement and advice. How much of this was particularly related to the situation in Philippi we do not know, for what Paul wrote was appropriate to any Christian community. The references to suffering are particularly apt in the Philippian situation, however, since we know that the members of the church were being persecuted (1:28-29), and the stress on mutual forbearance was apposite in view of 4:2. The warning against Judaizers in 3:2 is fleeting, perhaps because Paul realized that there was no great danger from Judaizers in a city where there were almost no Jews.

These Judaizers are only one group among several who are often labeled "opponents." It is, perhaps, helpful to distinguish between them, since there appear to have been four distinct groups who are referred to in this letter: (1) Those who are personally opposed to Paul and whose motives in preaching the gospel are questionable (1:15-18). These people are nevertheless regarded as Christians, since they are acknowledged to preach the gospel. (2) The people who are described as opponents of the Philippians and who are persecuting them (1:28-29). This group consists of pagan outsiders. (3) Those attacked in 3:2 who are almost certainly Judaizers, whether Jewish or Gentile by birth. (4) The people described as "enemies of the cross of Christ" (3:18-19), who appear to be a group of libertines claiming to be Christians, but whom Paul clearly considers to be living in a manner totally at variance with the gospel.

IMPORTANCE OF PHILIPPIANS

Philippians has had a great influence on the thought of later theologians, largely because of the significant ideas expressed in the so-called hymn in 2:6-11. To a large extent, the passage was interpreted in a way never intended by Paul. Poetic language was analyzed as though it were the language of dogma, and the passage was taken as an authoritative statement about the divine and human natures of Christ. In the nineteenth century, the "kenotic" theory of the incarnation was based upon it. If we wish to attempt to understand the passage in its historical context, we need to remember that Paul wrote what he did here, not in order to deal with the issues of Christ's divinity and humanity that so exercised the Church Fathers in the fourth and fifth centuries, but to spell out the way in which those who are in Christ ought to live. The passage is, indeed, an important christological statement—but its importance lies not only in what it says about Christ, but also in its implications for the lives of those who acknowledge Christ as Lord. It is Paul's insight into the relevance of divinity (who and what God is and does) to true humanity (who and what men and women should be and do)—of what we term "theology" to "ethics"—that makes this letter of great and lasting theological significance.

FOR FURTHER READING

Commentaries:

Bockmuehl, Markus. *The Epistle to the Philippians.* Black's NT Commentary. Peabody, Mass.: Hendrickson, 1998. Orig. pub. London: A & C Black, 1997.

Caird, G. B. *Paul's Letters from Prison.* NCB. Oxford: Oxford University Press, 1976.

Fee, Gordon D. *Paul's Letter to the Philippians.* NICNT. Grand Rapids: Eerdmans, 1995.

Lightfoot, J. B. *Saint Paul's Epistle to the Philippians.* 7th ed. London: Macmillan, 1883.

O'Brien, Peter T. *The Epistle to the Philippians.* NIGTC. Grand Rapids: Eerdmans, 1991.

Thurston, Bonnie Bowman. *Philippians and Philemon.* SP 10. Collegeville, Minn.: Liturgical Press, 2004.

Other Studies:

Bloomquist, L. Gregory. *The Function of Suffering in Philippians.* JSNTSup 78. Sheffield: Sheffield Academic Press, 1993.

Martin, R. P. *Carmen Christi: Philippians 2:5-11 in Recent Interpretation and in the Setting of Christian Worship.* SNTSMS 4. Grand Rapids: Eerdmans, 1983.

Martin, Ralph P., and Brian J. Dodd, eds. *Where Christology Began: Essays on Philippians 2.* Lousiville: Westminster John Knox, 1998.

Peterman, G. W. *Paul's Gift from Philippi: Conventions of Gift Exchange and Christian Giving.* SNTSMS 92. Cambridge: Cambridge University Press, 1997.

Wright, N. T. *The Climax of the Covenant: Christ and the Law in Pauline Theology.* Edinburgh: T & T Clark, 1991.

———. *Paul for Everyone: The Prison Letters: Ephesians, Philippians, Colossians and Philemon.* London: SPCK, 2002.

ENDNOTES

1. See A. Q. Morton and James McLeman, *Paul, the Man and the Myth* (London: Hodder & Stoughton, 1966); their method was based on too many questionable assumptions to carry conviction.

2. G. W. Peterman, *Paul's Gift from Philippi,* SNTS Monograph 92 (Cambridge: Cambridge University Press, 1997) 90-120.

3. Polycarp *Epistle to the Philippians* 3.

4. Loveday Alexander has analyzed Philippians in the light of the structures of contemporary Hellenistic letters and argued that the latter are by no means inconsistent with the unity of the letter. See Alexander, "Hellenistic Letter-Forms and the Structure of Philippians," *JSNT* 37 (1989) 87-101.

The Letter to the Colossians

ANDREW T. LINCOLN

Colossians is a rich and yet enigmatic Pauline letter. It contains a magnificent hymnic passage about the cosmic scope of Christ's role, develops the notion of believers' union with Christ, and has extensive exhortations about the ethical implications of this relationship. There are also fascinating treatments of the theme of reconciliation, of the heavenly world with its cosmic powers and its relation to the earthly realm, and of the notions of growth, maturity, and fullness; and there is the first occurrence in early Christian literature of the use of the "household code," the set of instructions for various groups within the household. While claiming to have been written by Paul (and Timothy), however, Colossians has a style quite distinct from earlier Pauline letters and theological and conceptual emphases that differ somewhat from these letters. In addition, its thought is developed in opposition to a teaching or philosophy about which the letter itself gives only a few scattered clues.

Much is to be gained simply by focusing on the text, following its argument closely, and thereby appreciating the impact of its message. But other questions—about the force of particular terms in their first-century context, about the situation of the writer and the first readers, about the teaching that is being opposed—arise naturally from a close reading. Clearly, the more that can be discovered about the historical setting, the better our appreciation of the message and the writer's pastoral strategy in conveying it. This introduction looks at four key areas for the interpretation of Colossians: its form, structure, and persuasive strategy; the "philosophy" it opposes; the main themes that characterize its presentation of the Pauline gospel; and the identity of its author and those to whom it was addressed.

FORM, STRUCTURE, AND PERSUASIVE STRATEGY

The form of Colossians follows the Pauline letter's modification of the ancient letter form. The letter opening identifies the senders and the recipients and contains an initial greeting (1:1-2). There follows a statement of thanksgiving, with its opening formula found in 1:3 ("we thank God") and its intercessory prayer report.[1]

The thanksgiving section of Colossians introduces major themes of the letter, but there has been much debate about whether it ends at 1:12, 1:14, 1:20, or 1:23. The note of thanksgiving clearly continues through 1:12-14 with the participle, "giving thanks" (εὐχαριστουντες *eucharistountes*) and its relative clauses that take up traditional liturgical formulations. These in turn lead into the Christ hymn of 1:15-20, which is no longer a discrete independent composition. It now serves the function of the thanksgiving section to signal significant themes, this time specifically christological ones. The closing part of the Pauline thanksgiving typically consists of liturgical material that reflects or substitutes for the Jewish *bĕrākâ*, or "blessing," and has at its conclusion an "eschatological climax" in which the present time of thanksgiving is linked with the final days of the supreme rule of God.[2] Here both its introduction and the hymnic passage itself provide the liturgical material, and an eschatological climax may be seen in the brief application of the hymn in 1:21-23, where the readers' own reconciliation with God is with a view to their being presented as "holy and blameless and irreproachable before" God (1:22*b*). The appropriation of the hymn's language of reconciliation for the change that has taken place in the readers indicates that 1:21-23 retains a close connection with what precedes it. The talk of not "shifting from the hope of the gospel that you heard, which has been proclaimed to every creature under heaven" both makes explicit the paraenetical implications of the earlier material in the thanksgiving and provides an inclusio (a literary bracketing device) with 1:5, which had mentioned the hope the readers had heard of in the gospel that was growing in the whole world. In this way 1:3-23 can be seen as a coherent unit that forms an extended thanksgiving.

The letter body then begins with 1:24. The last clause of 1:23*c* had provided a transition in which the language of the writer shifts from first-person plural to singular and focuses on Paul: "of which I, Paul, became a servant." Paul's relation to the readers becomes the subject of the next section up to 2:5, which can be seen as the body-opening. Again an inclusio confirms this as a distinct unit, since it begins and ends with an expression of rejoicing: "I am now rejoicing in my suffering for your sake" (1:24*a* NRSV) and "rejoicing to see your good order and the firmness of your faith in Christ" (2:5*b*). A disclosure formula frequently serves as evidence of the body-opening;[3] this is found in 2:1, "For I want you to know..." (NRSV), alerting the readers to the importance of what follows—namely, Paul's desire for their unity in love and their assured understanding of Christ.

The phrase "as therefore" in 2:6 serves as a transition, introducing the major concern of the letter in the body-middle. Scholars disagree about whether the paraenesis, or ethical exhortation, should be treated as part of the body of the Pauline letter or as a separate section following it. In the case of Colossians, this issue is made more complicated by the fact that from 2:6 through 4:6 all the material is structured by imperatives and is hortatory. A division is apparent, however, within this material. The warning of 2:8 is about being taken captive by philosophy and empty deceit and has a particular teaching in view. It is followed by an extensive warrant in 2:9-15 based on the writer's view of Christ and of believers' relationship to Christ. The exhortations of 2:16–3:4 are all directly related to elements in the teaching being opposed. What is more, if an eschatological climax indicates an occurrence of transition in thought,[4] then such a transition can be seen in the assertion of 3:4, "When Christ who is our life is revealed, then you also will be revealed with him in glory."

Although there is still some relation to the alternative teaching in what follows from 3:5, the exhortations become more general from this point and employ traditional paraenetical forms, such as the listing of vices (3:5-11) and virtues (3:12-17) and the household code (3:18–4:1). The exhortations also become more frequent in this section. Although there are six imperatives in 2:6–3:4, there are eighteen instances of a verb in the imperative mood in 3:5–4:6. If it is the case that the body of the Pauline letter has as a generally distinctive characteristic two parts to its argumentation—a more tightly organized theological part and a less tightly constructed appeal for the concrete working out of the view of Christian existence advocated earlier—then the central part of Colossians can still be seen to approximate these two parts. The exhortations of 2:6–3:4, with their focus on the alternative teaching and their more extended theological warrants, correspond to the first part, and the more general exhortations of 3:5–4:6 correspond to the usual paraenesis of the second part. In this way, 2:6–4:6 as a whole can be seen to constitute the body-middle.

The twenty-four imperatives of this section clearly make its tone one of warning, admonition, and exhortation. Issues raised in the thanksgiving section and the body-opening are elaborated here. The writer's concern about the recipients' knowledge and understanding (1:9; 2:2) and his related interest in their continued faithfulness to the gospel (1:23) are amplified in the exhortations of 2:6–3:4. The implicit paraenesis about "every good work," patient endurance, and thankfulness in 1:9-12 becomes explicit in the exhortations of 3:5–4:6. Assertions from the Christ hymn of 1:15-20 are employed in the christological warrant for the warning against the philosophy in 2:9-10, 15, 19, and what is involved in the reconciliation accomplished by Christ's death (1:22) is developed in 2:10-15.

The following section, 4:7-9, relates the intention to send Tychicus and Onesimus as emissaries. The sending of emissaries was one means, along with a visit of the apostle or the sending of a letter, of bringing about the benefit of Paul's presence. This mention of what has been called "the apostolic parousia" indicates the body-closing.[5]

There then comes the closing of the letter as a whole. Among the concluding elements found in the Pauline letters are hortatory remarks, requests for prayer, a wish of peace, greetings, a command to the recipients to greet one another with a holy kiss, an autographic subscription (i.e., a reference to the writer's own handwriting), and a grace benediction. With the exception of the request for prayer, made earlier in the paraenesis in 4:3-4, the wish of peace, and the mention of the greeting with the holy kiss, all these elements are found in the closing section of Colossians. Personal greetings from his companions and from Paul himself are listed in 4:10-15. The hortatory remarks are contained in 4:16-17, which urge the recipients to exchange letters with the church at Laodicea and to pass on a message to Archippus. The placing of these remarks is slightly unusual, since the only other letter closing that has an exhortation after the final greeting is 1 Thessalonians (see 1 Thess 5:27). Paul's autograph is appended in 4:18. Its call to the readers to remember his "chains" is unique to a letter-closing. The final item is the brief grace benediction in 4:18*c* ("grace be with you"); and, as in other Pauline letters, the parallel with the opening greeting in terms of grace can be seen to provide an epistolary inclusio.

Epistolary analysis, therefore, yields the following outline:

I. Letter Opening—Address and Greeting (1:1-2)
II. Extended Thanksgiving Section (1:3-23)
III. Letter Body (1:24–4:9)
  A. Body-Opening (1:24–2:5)
  B. Body-Middle (2:6–4:6)
    1. Exhortation Related to the Philosophy (2:6–3:4)
    2. More General Exhortation (3:5–4:6)
  C. Body-Closing (4:7-9)
IV. Letter Closing—Greetings, Hortatory Remarks, Autographic Subscription, and Grace Benediction (4:10-18)

Since the letter was a substitute for speech and since Paul's letters were meant to be read aloud to their recipients, it is also appropriate to view their contents in the light of the conventions of ancient rhetoric. Although the categories from the ancient rhetorical handbooks should not be applied rigidly or mechanically, they may be employed, where they fit, to illuminate the letter writer's persuasive strategy.

The rhetorical situation or exigency of Colossians is produced by the writer's awareness of what he considers to be a false teaching that will have harmful consequences for the readers if they are taken in by it. To dissuade them from being enticed by the proponents of this teaching, he first encourages the letter's recipients by reminding them of the gospel and its hope, which he and they have in common, of the change of status it has effected, and of the fruits of Christian behavior it has produced among them. Assuring them of his special relationship to this gospel and of his desire for their increased knowledge and understanding of it, he underlines that they must remain committed to it. He spells out what this continuing commitment will mean by exhorting them both to resist the baneful influence of the teachers of the philosophy and to exemplify distinctively Christian patterns of behavior.

Of the three main rhetorical genres—forensic, deliberative, and epideictic—the first, with its aim of persuading an audience to make a judgment about events in the past, can be dismissed in regard to Colossians. If the deliberative genre involves the author's seeking to bring about some action in the future by persuading or dissuading the audience, and if the epideictic involves the author's seeking to persuade the audience to hold or to reaffirm some present point of view by assigning praise or blame, then it is not immediately obvious which more appropriately describes Colossians. Exhortation can function in both deliberative and epideictic genres, depending on whether it is calling for a change of behavior or reiterating common values.[6] Colossians could, in fact, be viewed as a case in which the genres of epideictic and deliberative rhetoric are mixed and overlap. After all, the actions that the recipients are being persuaded to take in the future are precisely to hold on to the values of the gospel that the writer believes they at present share with him. Only 2:20-21 suggests that some of the recipients may have succumbed to the philosophy. In the main the letter simply contains warnings against the teaching and against allowing its proponents to condemn or disqualify the Colossian believers. Nevertheless, the fact that the central section of the letter has as its focus the call for the specific future action of resisting the philosophy does suggest that the deliberative genre of rhetoric predominates. To be sure, such an action is a consequence of the reaffirmation of present values, but it goes beyond mere reaffirmation.

In an analysis of Colossians as a persuasive speech, 1:3-23 constitutes the *exordium.* The *exordium* functioned as the introduction, indicating the aim of the speech and attempting to secure the hearer's goodwill.[7] Since in Colossians the author claims to have no personal acquaintance with the people being addressed, it is necessary for him to establish an initial positive relationship with them if they are to be receptive to his message. So expressing his thankfulness for their faith and love, declaring his knowledge of the fruitfulness of the gospel in their lives, seeing them as part of the worldwide growth of the Christian movement, mentioning Epaphras as the go-between, assuring them of his constant prayers, citing the Christ hymn, and reminding them of their change of status and relationship in respect to God are all part of establishing a positive relationship that will make them conducive to accept what follows. In particular, the Christ hymn draws readers into its praise, and its application explicitly appeals to their own experience of Christ's reconciling work. The two elements combine effectively to create an initial sympathy for the writer's thoughts and concerns.

The rest of the analysis takes up and modifies the suggestions of the French commentator J.-N. Aletti. He points out that if the *propositio*, or thesis, of a discourse is not a simple one, then its component elements are set out in a *partitio*, a division of the thesis into separate headings. He sees the *exordium* as concluding with such a *partitio* in 1:21-23. It has three headings: the work of Christ to achieve the holiness of believers (1:21-22); the need for the recipients to continue in the faith of the gospel (1:23*a*); and the recognition of the role of Paul in proclaiming this gospel (1:23*c*).[8] As has been noted, the exordium anticipates either directly or indirectly the themes to be dealt with in the discourse. Here at the end of the *exordium* there is a clear move to apply the preceding material to the letter's recipients. It would be natural, therefore, for this initial application to contain the main points to be made in this primarily deliberative discourse.

The *propositio* is usually followed by a section of proof, or *probatio.* This confirmation of the thesis can be seen to run from 1:24 to 4:1 and takes up both the language and the conceptuality of each of the elements of the *partitio*, but in reverse order. It functions not so much as the proof of propositions but more as the confirmation and elaboration of themes. Paul's role in the proclamation of the gospel is treated in 1:24–2:5, the need for faithfulness to this gospel in 2:6–3:4, and the holiness of believers' lives in 3:5–4:1.

This leaves 4:2-6 as the *peroratio.* According to Aristotle, the *peroratio* aimed to recapitulate leading themes, to make the audience well disposed toward the speaker, and to produce the required kind of emotion in the hearers.[9] Here the summing up is carried out in a generalizing fashion. It picks up particularly the key motifs of thanksgiving and prayer (4:2), recalling for readers not only the mention of thanksgiving in 1:12; 2:7; and 3:15-17 but also the writer's own extended introductory thanksgiving and its intercessory prayer report in 1:3-23. Talk of declaring the mystery of Christ (4:3), and doing so in the requisite manner (4:4), takes up the earlier references to the mystery and may well have in view what the author has attempted in his own rehearsal of the gospel in the face of opposing teaching in this discourse in 2:6–3:4.

The writer had also expressed his concern for the readers' spiritual wisdom (1:9) and made clear that such wisdom is to be found in Christ (2:3). Now he calls on the Colossians to live wisely in relation to outsiders (4:5). This requirement of wise living sums up well the exhortations of 3:5–4:1; the interest in outsiders points appropriately to the motivation behind the use of the household code of 3:18–4:1 in particular. Knowing how to answer everyone (4:6) can be seen as a summary of what the writer wishes his communication to achieve for his readers and would include, therefore, their being in a position to respond adequately to the proponents of the philosophy. The *peroratio*'s function of making the audience well disposed to the speaker and arousing emotion would be achieved by its request for prayer (4:3*a*), by the reminder of Paul's imprisonment for Christ (4:3*b*), and by the sense of urgency conveyed through the exhortations to be watchful (4:2*b*) and to make the most of the time (4:5*b*).

Aristotle delineated three modes of persuasion: "The first kind depends on the personal character of the speaker (*ethos*); the second on putting the audience into a certain frame of mind (*pathos*);

the third on the proof, or apparent proof, provided by the words of the speech itself (*logos*)."[10] Ethos presents the speaker as having wisdom, excellent character, and goodwill. In Colossians the author's wisdom is displayed not only through the quality of the advice and instruction offered but also through the depiction of Paul's special role in his commission to make known God's Word, the previously hidden mystery (1:25-26; 4:3). Paul's character is conveyed through the unique role he has in respect to the sufferings of Christ (1:24) and by the references to Paul's imprisonment for the gospel (4:3, 18). His goodwill is manifested in his prayers for the Colossians (1:3-4, 9-12); in his relation to Epaphras as the link between him and the Colossians (1:7-8; 4:12-13); in conveying news and extending greetings (4:10-18); in the effort he expends to ensure that all believers, and especially the readers, will be mature, united in love, have assured understanding, and therefore not be deceived (1:28–2:4); and in assuring them of his spiritual presence with them and his rejoicing on their account (2:5).

A number of these features also function in the letter's pathos, putting the audience into a suitable frame of mind to receive the message by evoking their empathy and sympathy. The writer's rejoicing in the readers' faith, the mention of his prayers for them, and the references to his sufferings and imprisonment and to his struggles and efforts on their behalf are all intended to produce a positive emotional effect that will make them responsive to his exhortations. The use of the Christ hymn early in the letter evokes common feelings of praise and worship that also prepare the recipients for the message to follow.

If *logos* is the use of argument and appeal to reason to support the speaker's viewpoint and to convince the audience, then the assertions about Christ in the hymnic material can be seen as laying the groundwork for the arguments that follow and that take up its terminology in 2:9-15. The writer employs a form of deductive argument that involves a statement and a supporting reason. A number of his exhortations have warrants, and in these cases the exhortation constitutes the conclusion, and the supporting warrant constitutes the premise. Colossians, then, has all three modes of argumentation—*ethos, pathos*, and *logos*—in its rhetorical arsenal.

This rhetorical analysis has produced the following outline:

- I. Exordium (1:3-23)
  concluding with Partitio (1:21-23)
- II. Probatio (1:24–4:1)
  - A. Paul's Role in the Proclamation of the Gospel (1:24–2:5)
  - B. Exhortation to Faithfulness to the Gospel (2:6–3:4)
  - C. Exhortation to Holiness of Life (3:5–4:1)
- III. Peroratio (4:2-6)

Colossians is a letter that attempts to persuade its recipients to take certain actions in the future. Ancient letters could be classified on the basis of the purpose they were meant to achieve or the circumstances they were designed to meet. In terms of the listings found in Pseudo-Demetrius and Pseudo-Libanius, Colossians would in all probability be called by the former an "advisory type" in which "we exhort (someone to) something or dissuade (him) from something" and by the latter a "paraenetic style" in which "we exhort someone by urging him to pursue something or to avoid something."[11] As a paraenetic letter, Colossians shares numerous features with other letters of moral guidance produced in the Greco-Roman philosophical schools. Teachers in these schools would also frequently combine the three major functions of affirmation, correction of rival views, and exhortation in the attempt to shape their students' lives. Sometimes their letters would be composed in the name of a past philosopher and addressed to figures from the past while clearly having a contemporary audience in view.[12]

THE "PHILOSOPHY" OPPOSED IN THE LETTER

A Variety of Proposals. Despite, and probably because of, the somewhat meager evidence provided by the letter, the academic industry of publishing books and articles on the teaching that provoked the writer's response shows no signs of abating. In the past, scholars looked to a Jewish form of Gnosticism or to Jewish mysticism or to Hellenistic mystery cults or to neo-Pythagoreanism or to a syncretistic mix of some of these as the background that provides the identity of the philosophy. Recent monographs and commentaries have offered further variations. Sappington develops the view that some form of Jewish mysticism is the distinctive ingredient of the teaching, providing a full examination of the similar pattern of ascetic and mystical piety to be found in a number of Jewish apocalypses.[13] The distinctive contribution of DeMaris is to introduce Middle Platonism into the discussion as the context in which the letter's debate about achieving knowledge was conducted. He sees the teaching being opposed, therefore, as a mix of "popular Middle Platonic, Jewish and Christian elements that cohere around the pursuit of wisdom."[14] As the title of his monograph suggests, Arnold also finds a mix.[15] He provides the fullest investigation of local inscriptional and literary evidence, particularly that which deals with the practice of magic. For him the syncretistic teaching contained Jewish (cultic observances) and pagan (mystery cult initiation) elements that cohered within the general framework of magic and folk religion. Two further contributors to the debate refrain from a syncretistic solution. Dunn, in his commentary and in an article that preceded it, holds that the teaching was purely Jewish, a diaspora "synagogue apologetic promoting itself as a credible philosophy more than capable of dealing with whatever heavenly powers might be thought to control or threaten human existence."[16] Martin, on the other hand, views it as purely Hellenistic, claiming that Cynic teachers entered the Christian assembly to observe and then delivered a critical invective against Christian practices, to which the author of Colossians responds.[17]

The very number and variety of proposed solutions to the identity of the philosophy should caution against any overly confident claims to reconstruct it. Although the writer's prescription for curing the ailment he believed to be a threat to the well-being of his readers comes across reasonably clearly, the ailment itself defies any really accurate diagnosis. The writer had no reason for defining more exactly the teaching involved. He expects his readers to know perfectly well what he was talking about, and so he merely touches on some of its features, using some of its catchwords and slogans. Since the evidence the letter provides is piecemeal, it pushes the interpreter beyond the text to find an explanatory framework for the fragmented reflection of the teaching and its practices, found in the writer's response. Determining which does greatest justice to all the elements in the letter's polemic remains the criterion for evaluating the various proposals. Some of them fail to explain parts of the letter adequately, but in itself this criterion still allows for a number of competing hypotheses.

There are at least two further difficulties in any attempt to employ the letter to reconstruct the alternative teaching. How many of the writer's direct references to the philosophy in this polemical letter can be taken as straightforward description rather than negatively slanted caricature? And if reconstruction is based on the part of the letter that is in direct interaction with the opposing teaching, is it legitimate to see other parts of the letter as having the teaching more indirectly in view and to use their discussion to complete the reconstruction?

Despite the difficulties, and provided that one remains both self-conscious about how to proceed and tentative about one's conclusions, it is still worth the effort to take up the letter's clues, to point to similar concepts in the thought of that time, and thereby to endeavor to sketch the best picture available of the teaching in view. After all, this teaching caused the writer enough concern to provoke a response to it, and some historical reconstruction is necessary if we are to appreciate that response as fully as possible. This sketch will proceed in three stages. It will begin with the explicit terminology mentioned in 2:18, move to a more disputed issue involving 2:8, 20, and then suggest a general characterization of the teaching.

Visionary Experience and Asceticism. Two major features of the philosophy, as the writer depicts it, appear to be the claim to visions (and "the worship of angels" associated with such visions) and ascetic practices (including fasting as a preparation for visionary experiences). Even this feature involves questions of interpretation, however, since 2:18, in which it is mentioned, has a number of difficulties. In it the readers are urged not to let anyone who (literally) "takes pleasure in or insists on self-abasement and the worship of angels, which he has seen when entering" disqualify them. The term ταπεινοφροσύνη (*tapeinōphrosynē*), rendered here, as in the NRSV, as "self-abasement," as opposed to the NIV's "false humility," occurs three times in Colossians (2:18; 2:23; 3:12). In its third occurrence, it denotes the positive virtue of humility, but that does not appear to be in view in the first two instances where it is connected with the philosophy. Because of its close association with worship in both cases, it is likely that it stands for some cultic practice rather than a disposition of lowliness and was a quasi-technical term in the philosophy for fasting. This makes sense in a context in which practices connected with food and drink (2:16); regulations about not handling, not tasting, not touching (2:20-21); and an emphasis on severe treatment of the body (2:23) are mentioned.[18]

This interpretation gains further strong support from the use of *tapeinōphrosynē* as a technical term for fasting in Tertullian[19] and in *The Shepherd of Hermas*.[20] Cognate terms are also employed in the LXX for "fasting" in contexts where the practice is an expression of abasement before God (e.g., Lev 16:29, 31; 23:27, 29, 32; Isa 58:3, 5; Ps 34:13-14). Fasting was also frequently a preparation for visionary experience and the reception of divine revelations (Dan 10:2-9; 4 Ezra 5:13, 20; 9:23-25; 2 Bar 5:7-9; 12:5-7; 43:3). Sometimes it is the preparation specifically for entrance into the heavenly realm.[21] All this is highly relevant to Col 2:18, where the two elements associated with fasting are "the worship of angels" and visionary experience.

But what was this "worship of angels"? It was often assumed that the phrase referred straightforwardly to humans worshiping angels, either in place of or alongside Christ or God. But if that were the case, it is very strange that the writer is not more forthright in his condemnation of such a practice instead of simply mentioning it in passing. An attractive case has been made by F. O. Francis,[22] however, that the phrase should be taken as involving a subjective rather than an objective genitive construction and thus refers to the angels' worship—that is, the worship in which the angels are engaged. What has this to do with humans? Fasting would be the preparation that enabled human beings to share in heavenly worship with angels. The notion of participation in angelic worship was a common one in Second Temple Judaism. It is found in apocalypses[23] and in the Qumran literature where the community on earth is described as having liturgical fellowship with the inhabitants of heaven.[24] It is by no means foreign to the New Testament (cf. 1 Cor 11:10; Heb 12:22-23; Revelation 4:1; 5).

On the other hand, C. E. Arnold has mounted a strong case for taking the objective genitive not as actual worship of angels by humans but as the writer's way of describing the philosophy's practice of invoking angels in order to deal with the threat of hostile powers. He relies heavily on the evidence of the Greek magical papyri, believing that, although most date to the third and fourth centuries CE, they reflect ideas and practices that go back to the first century CE and earlier and that are corroborated by the lead curse tablets and magical amulets in use in this earlier period.[25] He shows convincingly that in both Jewish and pagan sources angels were invoked for protection, for revelations, for cursing other humans, for warding off evil, and for dealing with evil spirit powers. They were intermediaries who were also associated with the planets and stars and were viewed as being active in influencing the fate of humans. Moreover, the evidence for a syncretistic mixing of Jewish angelic and pagan divine names in magical practice is clear. Elements of Jewish belief about angels and actual Jewish names for angels could be combined with pagan deity cults. Frequently the setting for invoking angels is a visionary experience and the invocation is connected with stringent purity regulations.

Arnold bolsters his argument by isolating the evidence of this type of veneration of angels in popular Judaism and in paganism in Asia Minor, claiming that the invocation of angels in the context of magical practices was a major feature of Phrygian-Lydian folk belief.[26] Add to this his demonstration that the term θρησκεία (*thrēskeia*) in the sense of worship rather than religion was overwhelmingly employed with the genitive for the object of worship, and his case for treating the phrase "the worship of angels" as the writer's polemical depiction of the practice of invoking angelic help becomes a very strong one indeed.[27] He rightly distinguishes between calling on, invoking, and praying to angels and an "angel cult" in which these intermediaries were the objects of adoration and worship. Although there is evidence of the latter in some of the pagan material, he finds none in Jewish or Christian texts and inscriptions. He shows easily, however, that the author of Colossians was not the only one to dub the veneration entailed by invocation as "worship of angels."[28]

In deciding between these two interpretations, we should recall that the evidence for taking the key phrase as a subjective genitive is very weak. In the two examples of *thrēskeia* in a subjective genitive construction that are usually cited (4 Macc 5:7 and Josephus, *Antiquities of the Jews* 12.253), the reference is to the religion of the Jews, not to their act of worship; and there appear to be no texts where this term is employed for angelic activity. For this reason, and in the light of the case made by Arnold, it is more likely that "worship of angels" refers to the practice of invoking angels, a practice that the writer of Colossians, in line with his unfavorable evaluation of the philosophy as a whole, deems no better than worshiping angels. The practice may well have fulfilled the same functions that it did in popular magic—namely, coping with the threat of evil powers and providing special knowledge—but there is no need to follow the rest of Arnold's analysis and connect all of the philosophy's features with the magical tradition. It is one thing to see magic as being part of the religious milieu that helps to explain the appeal of the philosophy, but it is another to make magic the key that unlocks the door to the whole philosophy.

The next part of 2:18 fills out the reconstruction of the philosophy. What is insisted on by its proponents are fasting and veneration of angels "which he has seen when entering." The syntax could be construed as "entering into what he has seen," but it is more natural to take the neuter plural relative pronoun as modifying the whole of the preceding phrase, as in the previous verse, 2:17, and later in 3:6. The mention of "seeing" is a reference to what has been observed in visions. It may appear strange that fasting was part of what was seen in visions, but again such a feature was not uncommon in apocalyptic writings where instruction in fasting for the purpose of obtaining visions could itself be the subject of visions. The most likely reference of the participle translated "when entering" (ἐμβατεύων *embateuōn*) is to the visionary entering the heavenly realm. This, after all, is where a visionary is most likely to see and invoke angels; in apocalyptic writings, visionary experience was frequently conceived of in terms of the translation of the spirit and its entry into heavenly places (see, e.g., Rev 4:1-2).[29] The evidence of Col 2:18, then, indicates an insistence on fasting as preparation for visionary experience and invocation of angels in the heavenly realm.

The "Elemental Spirits of the Universe" and Dualistic Cosmology. Fasting, purity regulations, obtaining wisdom, visions, and even invocation of angels can all be found in various traditions within Judaism. Why not then simply conclude that the teaching being opposed was a particular strand of Judaism? This does not explain enough of the writer's emphases that appear to be directed against a strong dualistic strain in the philosophy. The stress in the hymnic material on Christ's agency in both creation and redemption and his reconciliation of heaven and earth, the insistence that God's presence and saving activity were in the physical body of Christ (1:22; 2:9), the discussion of "the body of flesh" in 2:11, and the treatment of the heavenly and earthly realms in 3:1-5 all suggest that the Jewish elements in the teaching had been assimilated into a framework that treated the earthly realm and the body as inferior and evil in contrast to the heavenly realm. In other words, the strands typical of Jewish apocalyptic writings and of popular Judaism now appear to be functioning within a Hellenistic dualistic cosmology. In addition, it is a reasonable inference from the letter's language about the principalities and powers (1:16, 20; 2:10, 15) that the philosophy held such heavenly powers to be threatening and hostile and in need of appeasement.[30] While belief in evil powers in heaven is, of course, found in Jewish apocalypses, their role as intermediaries who had to be placated is much more difficult to discover and far more closely akin to the function of similar powers in Hellenistic cosmology.

A key question in this regard is how to interpret the phrase τὰ στοιχεῖα τοῦ κόσμου (*ta stoicheia tou kosmou*) in 2:8, 20. A minority of scholars take the phrase to refer to elementary principles or rudimentary teachings of the world (NIV, "the basic principles of this world"). But since the genitive is "of the world" and not "of this world," "world" in this context is most naturally taken to denote the cosmos.

The term *stoicheia* itself means first of all the component parts of a series and came to be applied to the physical components of the cosmos—earth, fire, water, and air (see 2 Pet 3:10, 12).[31] In Hellenistic thought these parts were believed to be under the control of spirit powers. Together with the stars and heavenly bodies they could be conceived of as personal forces who controlled the fate of humans. For this reason the majority of interpreters opt for a translation such as "the elemental spirits of the universe" (NRSV). This also fits well the context of thought in the letter, for elsewhere the writer emphasizes Christ's supremacy and victory over just such spiritual agencies. It is significant also that, when the same phrase was employed by Paul in Gal 4:3, 9, it was to warn Gentile Christians that to turn to the law would be equivalent to returning to their previous enslavement to the *stoicheia*, who are linked with their pagan deities, designated by Paul as "beings that by nature are not gods" (Gal 4:8).

One difficulty for this interpretation is that explicit use of *stoicheia* to refer to personified cosmic forces outside the New Testament is first found later in the *Testament of Solomon* 8:1-4; 18:1-5, where they are described as the cosmic rulers of darkness (see also Col 1:13). Moreover, the date of Pseudo-Callisthenes, in which King Nectabenos of Egypt is said to control the cosmic elemental spirits by his magical arts, is uncertain.[32] Given other pointers in the direction of such a reference, there is no reason why the New Testament might not be the first extant source for this explicit usage. Arnold, however, claims that these references and those in the magical papyri[33] belong to traditions that predate the actual writing and originate in the first century CE or earlier.[34] In any case, the book of Wisdom could earlier speak of the elements, referring to earth, air, fire, and water (Wis 7:15), and then condemn Gentiles for treating these elements as gods: "They supposed that either fire or wind or swift air, or the circle of the stars, or turbulent water, or the luminaries of heaven were the gods that rule the world" (Wis 13:2 NRSV). Philo also speaks of the *stoicheia* as "powers"[35] and reports worship of them as named deities.[36] Jewish apocalyptic literature had also already paved the way for this development by associating angels closely with the elements and heavenly bodies.[37]

In all probability, in the philosophy against which the letter is directed these elemental spirits were classed with the angels and were seen as controlling the heavenly realm and as posing a threat both to human well-being and to access to the divine presence. It was thought that an effective means of placating such powers was the rigorous subduing of the body in order to gain visionary experience of the heavenly dimension and to invoke the assistance of good angels in dealing with the hostile spirits. Through such visions also special knowledge and access to the divine presence could be obtained. This program as a whole, claiming to be wisdom (see 2:8, 23) and incorporating elements of Jewish calendrical and dietary law observances (2:16), appears to have been offered to the readers to supplement the apostolic gospel they had heard, so that in the view of the writer it undermined the sufficiency of what God had done in Christ. It reduced Christ to just another intermediary between humans and God, to one among a number of links to the heavenly dimension, one among a number of means of dealing with the hostile powers.

One of the chief concerns of Hellenistic religious thought was how a person could escape from the lower earthly realm and reach the heavenly world and the divine. Usually the purified soul was believed to ascend after death and to remain above. It was possible, however, to experience this ascent of the soul during one's lifetime and to enter the heavenly sphere through various ecstatic experiences.[38] It was, of course, primarily the mystery cults that fostered this way of ascent. Often such cults demanded strict discipline, but their attraction was that by such means and through initiation into secret rites they promised freedom from the evil body, enlightenment, privileged knowledge, access to the heavenly realm, and union with the god or goddess. As people came to the view that, despite the apparent order of the heavenly regions, there were powers in them opposed to humanity, not only mystery religions but also magic flourished in order to influence the cosmic powers favorably. The philosophy being advocated in the Lycus Valley area, in which Colossae was located, would have spoken to these same needs, and, with certain features analogous to concerns of the mystery cults and magic traditions, would have seemed attractive for the same reason.

The "Philosophy" as Syncretistic. Despite the attempts of some scholars to avoid this conclusion, it seems clear from 2:18-19 that the one insisting on fasting and invocation of angels through visionary experience is viewed by the writer as a believer who is in some spiritual danger. This person is "puffed up without cause through a fleshly mind" (2:18) and is "not holding fast to the head, from whom the whole body...grows with a growth that is from God" (2:19 NRSV). The participle "holding" (κρατῶν *kratōn*) is singular in its Greek form and so does not refer to the readers but to the same person who was in view with the earlier singular form of the participle "insisting" (θέλων *thelōn*). It would make no sense for the writer to depict someone who made no claim to a relationship to Christ in the first place as not holding fast to Christ. This factor alone would appear to rule out viewing the philosophy simply as Judaism. Nor is there any evidence for use of the verb "to hold" meaning "to have an initial intellectual grasp," which would be required on the hypothesis that a Cynic critic of Christian worship is being described. Instead the proponent(s) of the teaching have taken a number of elements from Judaism and the Christian gospel and linked these with typical cosmological concerns from the Hellenistic world. It is quite plausible that a Hellenistic Jew who had left the synagogue to join a Pauline congregation or a Gentile convert who had had some previous contact with the synagogue would advocate such a philosophy, and the writer evidently was concerned that it might appeal to others among his preponderantly Gentile Christian readers. To label such teaching Hellenistic Jewish syncretism is not, therefore, simply an "easy both-and solution"[39] but an eminently plausible and fitting description of its components.

Obviously the Pauline gospel had a base in particular congregations in the Phrygian area, which included the Lycus Valley. It is equally clear that there was a strong Jewish presence in the area, because in 200 BCE Antiochus III had settled two thousand Jewish families in Lydia and Phrygia. It is not at all surprising, then, to find knowledge of specific features of Judaism in the syncretism that could have been picked up from the teaching of local synagogues. Jewish cultic regulations and calendrical observances have a role, but it remains significant that there is no mention of the law as such, as would surely be expected if the teaching were a straightforward variety of Judaism. It is also significant in this regard that the writer dismisses such elements as simply human tradition. This does not sound like the Paul of Galatians or Romans dealing with the law and having to account in his arguments for the claim that such observances were commanded by God, nor is it like the use of the charge of human tradition in Mark 7:1-13, where it is directed against the oral tradition. In addition, circumcision is mentioned in 2:11, but it functions in the writer's argument primarily as a metaphor for dealing with the physical body as a whole. The cultic and calendrical items and the interest in visionary experience also found in Judaism appear, then, to have been put to markedly different use in the philosophy.

The concepts of heaven and earth played an important part in Jewish thought, the apocalyptic writings included an increasing emphasis on the transcendent realm, and Hellenistic Judaism evidenced some similar cosmological concerns to those suggested for the philosophy. Yet in none of these strands was there the strong cosmological dualism that Colossians appears to combat. Such spatial concepts, however, readily lent themselves to a dualistic framework, which, as we have seen, was current in Greco-Roman cosmological speculation. Still, cosmological dualism and an emphasis on special knowledge do not mean that there should be an identification of the philosophy with Gnosticism. At most what is suggested are certain "gnosticizing" tendencies. It is not until the attested in the Nag Hammadi documents that some of the letter's terminology is found in a clearly identifiable gnostic schema.

THE LETTER'S MAIN THEOLOGICAL THEMES

The writer does his theological reflection in response to the specific dangers he sees in the rival teaching and employs traditional materials in the process. It would be a mistake to reduce the letter's theology simply to the writer's mode of theologizing. This mode has produced the letter as we now have it, and it is the assertions of that final form that have made their impact on the development of Pauline thought and on the thinking of later Christians, however much or little we think we can know about the details of the preceding interaction with the philosophy or the writer's modifications of the traditional materials he employs to make his points. The following brief depiction of some of the letter's dominant theological emphases will concentrate primarily on the product of the writer's theologizing in the conviction that it is with these claims that contemporary readers of the letter need to engage. Although, for the sake of convenience, the depiction is divided into separate topics, it should be clear that in the theology of the letter these are inextricably interwoven and that what connects them is the assessment of the person and work of Christ. In the theology of Colossians, christology is central and everything else flows from the belief that Christ is the key to the understanding of reality.

The Apostolic Gospel. The writer addresses the situation faced by his readers with a combination of confidence in the sufficiency of the Pauline gospel and a pastoral concern that the readers should not weaken in their allegiance to this gospel. The theology of the letter consists in reflections on the implications of this apostolic gospel. It does so because the writer is convinced that the gospel is the word of truth (1:5), conveying reliable insight into God's purposes for humanity and the world through what has taken place in Christ. As such, it is also the conveyor of hope and of God's grace (1:5-6) and can be spoken of in a personified and dynamic fashion as bearing fruit and growing both among the readers and in the whole world (1:6). It is depicted as universal in its scope and spread ("proclaimed to every creature under heaven," 1:23), and its dynamic quality is again in view when the readers are exhorted to petition God to open a door for "the word" (4:3), to provide opportunities for the gospel to continue its progress. As the "word of God" (1:25), the gospel has its source in God, and, as "the word of Christ" (3:16), it has Christ as its content.

Another synonym for "gospel" is the term "mystery," with its connotation of a previously hidden purpose of God that has now been disclosed. The content of the mystery is Christ among you—that is, among the Gentiles (1:26-27)—or simply Christ (2:2; 4:3). This exclusive focus on Christ as being at the heart of the gospel message is reinforced when the notion of proclaiming the gospel can be expressed simply as proclaiming him (1:28). The gospel not only has at its center a person but it also entails received teaching about this person. In two places this is the force of the phrase "the faith" (1:23; 2:7), and in the latter context the formulation "Christ Jesus the Lord" encapsulates the tradition that has been received by the readers (2:6).

The gospel is the apostolic or, to be more precise, the Pauline gospel. The letter makes clear the intimate connection between the apostle and the gospel. The opening words provide the credentials for Paul's exposition of the gospel in response to the rival teaching. As apostle, he is the authorized representative of the one at the center of the message (1:1). But it is 1:23*c*–2:5 that underlines that, as Paul played his unique role in its missionary proclamation, he became the suffering servant of the gospel who participated in the same pattern of suffering experienced by Christ. Service of the gospel was also stewardship of the mystery on the part of Paul; just as the gospel has a teaching content and is universal in its scope, so also Paul's stewardship of it involves a teaching role that is universal in its reach, "teaching every human being" (1:28). His commitment to this gospel ministry entailed the strenuous effort of the athlete in a contest (1:29) and is symbolized by the chains of his imprisonment for the mystery of Christ (4:3, 18). Paul's service of the gospel is carried on by the team of his associates and coworkers. Epaphras was the initial link between the gospel the readers received and Paul (1:7), and he continues this role (4:12-13), while Tychicus and Onesimus have a similar function as further links with the apostle (4:7-9).

Christology. In responding to the rival teaching, the writer did not limit himself to criticisms of it; his positive recommendation of the Pauline gospel sets out some of the most profound reflections on the person of Christ to be found in the New Testament. The focus on Christ is such that there is almost no mention of the Spirit (but see 1:8-9; 3:16). Christ as the center of God's purposes and, therefore, the key to reality is what, according to the hymn, holds the cosmos together; but this notion of Christ is also, appropriately, what holds the thought of the letter together.

The most distinctive feature of the christology of Colossians is its sustained treatment of Christ in relation to both the creation and the reconciliation of the cosmos. Christ is not simply to be seen as the firstborn of all creation (1:15); rather, all things were created in, through, and for him (1:16). God is the Creator, but Christ is both an agent of creation and, more than that, its goal. The climactic "for him" in 1:16 adds to the assertions of 1 Cor 8:6 about Christ's agency that he is also the one to whom all creation is directed, the very purpose of its existence. Not only so, but all things hold together in him (1:17); their integrity and coherence depend on his role. The claim is not that it is some rational principle or even personified Wisdom that holds the key to the created universe but that it is the person believers confess as Christ who does so. The hymnic material does not explain why, although Christ has always been the agent and sustainer of creation, it is in need of reconciliation. Presupposing that need, it underlines that the one who was firstborn, agent, and goal in creation is also appropriately firstborn, agent, and goal of reconciliation in the new creation.

One major implication of this belief in the cosmic Christ is that he is sovereign over the powers of evil seen as threatening human life. In 1:15-20 such cosmic powers are depicted as being created in and for Christ, as having fallen out of harmony, and as being reconciled through Christ's death. Christ is, therefore, head over every ruler and authority (2:10). Whereas the hymnic material speaks of the powers' reintegration through Christ's death as a way of making peace and a reconciliation, in 2:15 what took place through the cross is described as stripping them of their power and triumphing over them. It looks very much, then, as if the making of peace is to be interpreted in terms of pacification. In the language of worship of 1:20 the hostile powers are depicted as already reconciled, but 1:13 has also made clear that the power of darkness is still operative and opposed to Christ's rule. The letter's thought about Christ's relation to the cosmic powers appears, then, to share the Pauline eschatological perspective with its "already" and "not yet." Through Christ the powers have already been pacified and reintegrated into God's purposes, and believers can already appropriate this achievement, but the full recognition of their new situation by the powers themselves awaits the eschaton.

A formulation about Christ in cosmic terms, echoing the thought of 1:15-20, is employed in an ecclesiological context in 3:11: "Christ is all and in all." In the first part of the verse, there is an adaptation of the baptismal formulation, found also in Gal 3:28 and 1 Cor 12:13, which states that in the new humanity there are no longer ethnic, cultural, and social distinctions. Rather, adds the second part, Christ is all and in all. If he has this status in the cosmos, then he most certainly has it in the church that is the focus for and the medium of his pervasive presence in the cosmos. Since Christ is now absolutely everything, all that matters, the old human categories of evaluation are rendered insignificant.

Colossians also characteristically describes Christ's status in terms of lordship. In line with assertions in the undisputed Pauline letters, it assumes that, by virtue of his exaltation to the right hand of God (3:1), Christ is Lord. He is now the one to whom believers are accountable (1:10) and owe absolute allegiance (2:6; 3:17). Even everyday life in the household is to reflect this relationship (3:18–4:1). Indeed, in the motivation slaves are to have, "fearing the Lord," Christ substitutes for Yahweh in Jewish scriptural terminology (3:22).

There are also other formulations used of God that are functionally equivalent to those employed of Christ. Being nourished by Christ the head is the same as receiving growth from God (2:19), and the "kingdom of his beloved Son" (1:13) is equivalent to the "kingdom of God" (4:11). Whereas the undisputed Pauline letters talk of creation as "for him" with reference to God (Rom 11:36; 1 Cor 8:6), Colossians uses this phrase of Christ (1:16); and while the undisputed letters of Paul speak of God as all in all (1 Cor 15:28), Colossians employs the same language of Christ (3:11).

Colossians depicts Christ's relationship to God in terms of oneness yet distinction. The Lord Jesus Christ still has a Father (1:3) and is the beloved Son (1:13). He is not the Creator but the agent and goal of creation. At the same time, in 1:15-20, his agency is portrayed in terms of Wisdom with the implication that all the qualities of Wisdom as God immanent in creation are now to be found in Christ (see also 2:3). The expression "image of the invisible God" (1:15) sums up the relationship well. Christ is the one who uniquely makes God's presence visible and God's purposes effective. Colossians does not call Christ "God," but the striking formulations of 1:19 and 2:9 put the two in the closest possible relationship and provide an equivalent to the Johannine notion of incarnation: All the fullness of God dwells in Christ bodily.

The letter's combination of universalism and particularism is related to its christology. On the one hand, it sets out the universal horizons of Christ's work and claims as Lord. Yet, on the other hand, it presses the necessity of faith in this particular person in whom God is uniquely revealed for entry into the new humanity.

Soteriology. The actual terminology of "salvation" is not employed in Colossians, but the language of rescue and transference is found in 1:13. Here the divine rescue act is from one dominion to another, from the power of darkness to the kingdom of the beloved Son. Both deliverance and redemption (1:14) stand for God's act of liberating humanity. Through Christ, believers are freed from the hold of the cosmic powers and their regulations (2:15-16, 20). Their liberation is experienced at present in terms of the forgiveness of sins (1:14; 2:13; 3:13), an emphasis needed because the opposing philosophy engendered a sense of guilt about life in the body that served to reinforce the hold of the powers. The "once...now" contrast underlines the transference from plight to solution that God effects (1:21-22; 3:6-8). The depiction of the plight from which rescue is needed includes alienation and hostility (1:21), the old humanity and its vices (3:5-9), the wrath of God on this disobedient way of life (3:6), the flesh in its negative ethical sense (2:18, 23), and the death caused by sin (2:13). The depiction of the new situation and its benefits brought about through Christ includes reconciliation (1:22); the new humanity, both individual and corporate (3:10-11); and its virtues (3:12-14); the inheritance of God's people (1:12; 3:24); access to the heavenly realm (3:1-2); and being made alive (2:13). Among this variety of ways of portraying what God has achieved for humanity, reconciliation stands out. It appears in the hymnic material as the salvific image for God's accomplishment in Christ on a cosmic scale, where it is reinforced with the language of peacemaking (1:20), and it is this image that is then specifically applied to the readers (1:21-22). Later, too, they will be exhorted to appropriate the peace achieved by Christ in their corporate living (3:15).

The other major benefit highlighted in the letter can be termed wisdom (1:9, 28; 2:3, 23; 3:16; 4:5), knowledge (1:6, 9-10, 27; 2:2-3; 3:10), or understanding (1:9; 2:2). So God's rescue act in Christ also entails a revelation, a disclosure of God's previously hidden purposes in Christ, into which one can be given increasing insight. The mystery that was hidden has now been revealed to God's people (1:26-27), and the writer wants them to obtain "all the riches of assured understanding, the knowledge of God's mystery" (2:2).

Both the death and the resurrection of Christ play their part in the divine deliverance that produces the new humanity and the benefits it enjoys. Christ's death is spoken of as "the blood of his cross" (1:20), is seen as occurring in his body of flesh through death (1:22), and is described through the image of circumcision (2:11). Three further images describe how in Christ's death God overcame humanity's sense of condemnation: erasing the accusing record, setting it aside, and nailing it to the cross (2:14). It is not surprising that, when it comes to the reversal of death and the experience of new life, Christ's resurrection is at the fore as the means by which these are achieved for humanity. His resurrection makes him the firstborn from the dead, the first among brothers and sisters who will follow in his footsteps as they, too, are raised (1:18). Indeed, through union with Christ in his resurrection, they can already experience what it is to be made alive by God (2:12-13). Being raised with Christ also entails sharing his exaltation—thereby being given access to the heavenly realm—and participating in the future revelation in glory of Christ's life (3:1-4).

Eschatology. The letter's perspective on God's purposes for history and the cosmos provides the framework and presupposition for what it says about Christ and his agency in the rescuing of humanity. Colossians shares this basic eschatological framework with the undisputed Pauline letters in which Paul had in turn modified the Jewish eschatology he had inherited in the light of what he now believed to have taken place in Christ. Both these letters and Colossians see what God has done in Christ as having affected the whole cosmos with its two parts: heaven (in which there are also evil powers) and earth (the primary setting for humanity). They also see the time between Christ's death and resurrection and the eschaton as a period of tension between aspects of the blessings of the end times that can be experienced in the present and those that remain future. In Colossians, the stress is clearly on the present aspects. The decisive act that brings about the reintegration of the cosmos has already taken place, and believers can already appropriate its consequences so that they are no longer under the domination of the powers. Yet the powers continue to exist in their hostility to God's purposes and to pose a threat, so clearly the full realization of Christ's victory over them is not yet and is reserved for the eschaton.

Similarly, in response to the alternative teaching, Colossians emphasizes what has already taken place in believers' relationship of union with Christ. Romans 6 may well contain the notion of participation in Christ's resurrection, but it does not talk of this participation as having already taken place. Colossians does speak of believers as having been raised with Christ (2:12-13; 3:1). Indeed, it can go so far as to depict believers' lives as being linked with the life of the exalted Christ in heaven (3:2-3). Although the writer can appeal to a sense of urgency about the use of time (4:5), there is no imminent expectation of the end in this letter. Yet, as the writer moves away from thanksgiving and polemic to paraenesis or ethical exhortation, future references appear: negatively, to the coming wrath of God (3:6), and positively, to the reward of the inheritance (3:24).

Yet if Colossians can state that cosmic reconciliation has already been achieved and believers have already been raised with Christ, one might still want to ask whether anything substantial is left for the future. Crucial here is the assertion of 3:4 that Christ, who is believers' life, will be revealed, and believers will be revealed with him in glory. But will this be only the revelation of a present state of affairs, or will it involve some future change? Three considerations suggest that the latter option is in view. First, in 1:18 Christ has been described as the "firstborn from the dead" (πρωτότοκος ἐκ τῶν νεκρῶν *prōtotokos ek tōn nekrōn*). The clear implication is that, just as his resurrection was in bodily form, so also those who participate in the restored creation will experience a bodily resurrection from the dead. Second, the writer of Colossians stands in the Pauline school, and in Paul where life is found in an eschatological context it is equivalent to the resurrection or transformation of the body (Rom 8:11; 1 Cor 15:45; 2 Cor 5:4). Third, and similarly, if Colossians is interpreted as being in basic continuity with Paul, then, although it does not explicitly mention the resurrection of the body and the transformation of the cosmos, it is hard not to see these clear connotations of "glory" carrying over from Paul (Rom 8:17-23; 1 Cor 15:40-43; Phil 3:20-21).

The present and future aspects and the emphasis on eschatology in Colossians are summed up in its use of the term "hope" (ἐλπίς *elpis*). By definition hope entails some expectation about the future, and that temporal connotation is retained despite this letter's primary stress on its present content and heavenly dimension. Believers' hope is at present secured in heaven and so can be seen as foundational for their faith and love (1:4-5). Because Christ is the hope of glory (1:27), it is not surprising that this hope can be said to be located in heaven, where Christ now is until his revelation (3:1-4). Hope is closely identified with both Christ and the gospel (1:23). This is presumably because hope stands for confident assurance on the basis of what has already been achieved and is precisely what, in the writer's view, would be undermined by the philosophy.

Christian Existence in the Church and in the World. Believers' identity is dependent on their relationship with Christ. The primary way of viewing that relationship in Colossians is in terms of union with Christ, which is also the significance of the initiation rite of baptism (2:12). Believers can be said to be "in Christ" or "in the Lord" (1:2, 4, 28; 2:6-7), and the motif of incorporation into Christ is the thread running through 2:9-15. In union with Christ, readers have fullness (2:10). In him they were spiritually circumcised (2:11), and "with him" they died (2:20), were buried (2:12), were raised (2:12; 3:1), and were made alive (2:13). Since Christ is viewed as at present above, at the right hand of God, believers' union with him gives them a heavenly orientation that then is to be worked out on earth (3:1-2, 5). The relationship is such that believers' lives can be described as hidden with Christ in God (3:3); indeed, their life is Christ (3:4). Christian identity is inextricably bound up with the Christ who has died, been raised, is exalted in heaven, and is to be revealed.

Union with Christ is not a static relationship. It is seen in terms of growth (1:10; 2:19), leading to perfection or maturity (1:28; 3:14; 4:12). Those who are united to Christ have been filled (2:10), but the writer can also pray that they may be filled with the knowledge of God's will (1:9). Again there is an "already" and a "not yet" pattern to Christian existence. Believers have been given what is needed, but they must also appropriate this if they are to move toward their fullest potential. They have received Christ Jesus the Lord, but are exhorted to continue to live their lives in him (2:6-7) and are warned about the consequences of not continuing and holding fast (1:23; 2:19).

To live one's life in Christ the Lord (2:6) is to acknowledge his cosmic lordship as laying claim on all of life (3:17). The philosophy focused on specific rituals and on special days and abstinence from certain foods, but the sphere of Christ's lordship and, therefore, of obedient Christian response to that lordship is as broad as life itself. Everyday relationships in the most significant social and economic unit, the household, are singled out to illustrate what it means for the rule of the Christ who is Lord of the cosmos to be brought to bear within the structures of this world in which believers find themselves (3:18–4:1).

Believers have become new persons (3:10). This new humanity is not simply an individual but a corporate entity that transcends the divisions of the old humanity (3:11) and is an anticipation of the new creation as a whole. Reflecting its significant place in the writer's thought, in the Christ hymn the church is in fact mentioned before the reconciliation of the cosmos (1:18). Although Christ is the head over every ruler and authority, only the church, and not these powers or the cosmos as such, is designated his body (1:18, 24; 2:19; 3:15). Because of this special relationship to Christ, the church is the precursor of the reconciled cosmos. As Christ's body, it is distinctively related to its head, deriving its life and growth from him (2:19). Set in a cosmic context, Christ's body in Colossians is seen as a universal phenomenon. Similarly, Colossians employs the term ἐκκλησία (*ekklēsia*), for the assembly of the church with both a universal (1:18, 24) and a local (4:15-16) reference.

This church is a worshiping community. In implicit contrast to the veneration of angels and the ascetic regulations practiced by the philosophy, prominent in its worship are the word of Christ, the teaching of which inculcates wisdom, and thankful singing to God (3:16). The virtues that are to characterize the lives of its members are those that promote harmony and unity in the community (3:12-13). Peace, the reconciling activity of Christ that has been celebrated as affecting the cosmos (1:20), is to be appropriated particularly in the new community and allowed to rule (3:15). And what is necessary above all, if this community is to be what it is meant to be, is love (3:14; see also 1:4, 7).

A Theology of Wisdom and Grace. If setting out some of the themes of the letter reminds us that its theology transcends the setting that produced it, such a procedure may have its own dangers in obscuring this theology's essential characteristics. Perhaps what makes Colossians distinctive is its combination of a wisdom theology with a polemical theology of grace. Both elements are a result of the confrontation with the rival philosophy.

The philosophy's claims to wisdom (see 2:23) have provided the catalyst for a development of the Pauline gospel in terms of wisdom. This theme is explicit in each of the major sections of the letter's persuasive argument, occurring in the *exordium*, in each of the three sections of the *probatio*, and in the *peroratio*. In the first part of the letter, the intercessory prayer report reveals the concern that the recipients be "filled with the knowledge of God's will in all spiritual wisdom and understanding" (1:9), and the hymnic material in 1:15-20 is dominated by the application to Christ of the language and concepts associated with wisdom in the Hellenistic Jewish tradition.

In the body of the letter there is first a depiction of Paul and his gospel in terms of wisdom. Paul himself is humanity's great Christian wisdom teacher, "warning and teaching everyone in all wisdom" (1:28). The content of his gospel is "Christ himself, in whom are hidden all the treasures of wisdom and knowledge" (2:2-3). Next, in more direct interaction with the philosophy, the writer claims that its teachings may have a reputation for wisdom in its "worship of angels," fasting, and severity to the body. In fact, however, these are of no value in what he deems to be the real issue: dealing with the flesh in the negative sense of the sphere of humanity's opposition to God (2:23). Over against this otherworldly and ascetic wisdom, he then provides his own teaching on practical wisdom that is designed to deal with the sins of the old humanity. In the course of this, he makes clear that, because of their relationship to Christ, believers are to play their own role in such wise teaching of the community: "teach and admonish one another in all wisdom" (3:16). Finally, in the concluding exhortations, he can summarize the practical advice he has given, particularly in the household code, in terms of living wisely in regard to outsiders (4:5).

So wisdom features at all levels in the letter's theology. Christ embodies wisdom; Paul, supremely, but also all other believers are recipients and then teachers of wisdom; and Christian living is walking in wisdom. The wisdom christology of the hymn leads to the cosmic and universal dimensions of the letter's theology. These in turn color the depiction of believers' relation to the exalted Christ. United to this Christ, they have a genuine heavenly orientation that works itself out in their lives on earth. James 3:13-18 contrasts two sorts of wisdom: a wisdom that is from above, displaying itself in a life of goodness and gentleness on earth, and a wisdom that is earthly, unspiritual, and devilish, characterized by envy and selfish ambition. Colossians can be seen as presenting, in contrast to what it regards as earthly wisdom, a wisdom that has its source where Christ is—above—but that then becomes firmly earthed in the everyday. The letter constitutes its writer's own wise teaching. What is more, he provides this in the typical wisdom mode of paraenesis, as he affirms, corrects, and exhorts in the attempt to produce other mature practitioners of wisdom.

This wisdom theology is universal in scope; however, its conviction that God's activity in Christ is the wisdom that provides the key to the understanding of reality is an exclusive one. At this point the polemical setting leaves a lasting mark on the theology. This version of the Pauline gospel sees itself as antithetical to other types of claims. Those espoused by the philosophy, according to the theological perspective of Colossians, should not be set alongside its own in a "both/and" relationship.

Colossians is polemical, because, like the Paul of Galatians in a different set of circumstances, it will not allow God's gracious activity in Christ to be undermined. To add new practices and regulations to the gospel is to suggest not only that believers are disqualified unless they adhere to them but also, more fundamentally, that what God has already done in Christ is deficient. Colossians is essentially Pauline in having none of this. In its defense of the apostolic gospel, Colossians does not make grace a separate theme so much as an underlying presupposition that it reinforces through both the content and the mode of its theologizing. This presupposition is made explicit in the very first mention of the gospel, where to hear the gospel and to comprehend the grace of God are equated (1:5-6). From then on, the insistence on what God has already achieved in Christ for the cosmos and for the church and the "realized eschatology," with its stress on the present experience of the benefits of end-time salvation, are in the service of this gospel of grace. This is also the force of the repetition of the motif of thanksgiving at key places throughout the letter (1:3, 11-12; 2:7; 3:15-17; 4:2). Christian thanksgiving is nothing other than the grateful recognition of the grace of God in Christ at the center of life. The mode of argumentation of Colossians is also in line with this element of its theology. Only after an extended thanksgiving section do the exhortations follow, and these are punctuated by the reminders to give thanks. For Colossians the gospel is grace, and no response to it can depart from that foundation by adding human achievements as a requirement. Instead, authentic Christian living is motivated by a response to and empowered by an appropriation of the undeserved favor of God in Christ.

Colossians is frequently referred to as having a bridging role between the undisputed and the disputed letters in the Pauline corpus. If its wisdom content and mode signal a significant development in the articulation of the Pauline gospel, its polemical theology of grace makes clear its essential continuity with that same gospel.

AUTHOR AND ADDRESSEES

Whereas there is widespread scholarly agreement that Ephesians and the Pastoral Epistles are pseudonymous, more dispute surrounds Colossians and 2 Thessalonians. Colossians is closely related to Ephesians. Although a tiny minority of scholars hold that Colossians is in some way dependent on Ephesians, for the majority it is clear that the dependency is the other way and that the author of Ephesians has used Colossians as the model on which he builds.[40] On this view, the relationship between Colossians and Ephesians plays no role in the debate about the authorship of the former.

In this debate the argument revolves around judgments on style, vocabulary, indications of what looks like a later setting than Paul's lifetime, and changes in theological perspective. In the case of Colossians, as with the other disputed letters, no one argument is decisive, although many consider that the issue of style comes very close to being so. Instead, it is a matter of a cumulative argument involving all these factors; of course, judgment will differ about the weight of any individual factor.

Colossians, however, allows a possible mediating position. Since it names both Paul and Timothy as it authors, some have suggested that the actual author could have been Timothy, writing either just before or just after Paul's death.[41] Nonetheless, the very fact that scholars opt for this solution indicates that they have accepted that the style differs so much from the undisputed Pauline letters that it cannot be attributed directly to Paul.

The introduction of the question of Paul's use of amanuenses, or secretaries, whom he may also in some instances have named as co-authors, complicates the issue of authorship still further. If secretaries are given the maximum possible role in the writing of the letters, this could mean that the only writings we actually have from Paul himself are the few brief passages he claims to have written in his own hand. If it is simply urged that we take the naming of co-authors with full seriousness, then Timothy is the co-author of 2 Corinthians, Philippians, and Philemon and, along with Silvanus, of 1 and 2 Thessalonians. Yet, with the exception of 2 Thessalonians, these are all among the undisputed letters, the comparison with which has caused the authorship of Colossians to be questioned in the first place. Clearly modern notions of authorship should not simply be assumed in regard to Paul's letters; on the other hand, we have no evidence of how Paul actually used any secretaries or co-authors. It appears best, then, to proceed cautiously with the criteria listed above in order to build a cumulative case that would indicate whether or not it is likely that Colossians was written in Paul's lifetime and that he put his name to it.

In regard to style, W. Bujard has provided the most thorough analysis of the letter, concluding that its style is not Paul's.[42] What is most telling here is that the grammar and syntax of Colossians differ so much from the undisputed Pauline letters. Colossians lacks the adversative, causal, consecutive, recitative, copulative, and disjunctive conjunctions that are characteristic of Paul's style. Instead it is characterized by long sentences with relative clauses, nouns linked in genitive constructions, and the piling up of synonyms. There are some thirty cases of amassed synonyms in Colossians. It also lacks completely the articular infinitive, a construction frequently employed by Paul to represent a dependent clause. Whereas Paul uses repetition to develop his argument in a logical direction, the repetitions in Colossians mostly function to build rhetorical effect. Colossians employs "which is" (ὅ ἐστιν *ho estin*) as a special idiom five times (1:24, 27; 2:10, 17; 3:14), a feature absent in the undisputed letters. Such differences bear on a writer's personal style. It is one thing to say that in order to address a new situation writers are likely to adapt their ideas or take on new vocabulary, but it is quite another thing to assert that they would abandon their characteristic style of writing for some other. There is nothing about the setting of the Colossian letter that would demand such a major shift in style.

The argument about vocabulary is less decisive. There are thirty-four words that do not occur elsewhere in the New Testament (*hapax legomena*) and a further ten that would be found only in Colossians were it not for the fact that they occur in Ephesians, which is dependent on Colossians. Also significant is the absence of so many key Pauline terms, such as "sin" (in the singular), "to believe," "promise," "law," "freedom," "boasting," the "justification" and "salvation" word groups, and, despite the actual address, the absence of the vocative "brothers and sisters" that is employed liberally in the body of the undisputed letters. Quite striking is the uncharacteristic combination of characteristic Pauline terms, so that, whereas "blood" and "cross" and "body" and "flesh" appear separately in the undisputed letters, here we have the phrases "blood of the cross" (1:20) and "body of flesh" (1:22; 2:11).

The changes of theological emphasis in the letter do not appear to be as decisive for authorship as some scholars claim. A number of these different emphases could be reasonably attributed to Paul's addressing his message to a different pastoral setting. So, for instance, the notion of realized eschatology using spatial categories is far more to the fore than in the undisputed Pauline letters, with this letter spelling out explicitly that believers have already been raised with Christ (2:12; 3:1) and stressing that hope is already present in heaven (1:5). Yet, it can be argued that these notions are in basic continuity with Paul's eschatology and are developed here because of the concern of the philosophy with cosmological questions and the need to assure believers of the security of their salvation. Similarly, the focus on a cosmic christology and the depiction of Christ's work of salvation in relation to the cosmic powers and the cosmos as a whole can be explained as the apostle's development of earlier strands in his teaching in the face of the philosophy's particular interests.

On the other hand, while Colossians does mention the future revelation of Christ in glory, there is no mention of the imminence of the parousia or the eschaton at all, and the Spirit is mentioned explicitly only once (1:8). There is no reason why the interaction with the philosophy should have caused these characteristic emphases to disappear to this extent. Their almost complete absence gives a quite different dynamic to the relation between eschatology and ethics than that found in the undisputed letters of Paul. In those letters, end-time events frequently shape ethical appeals and the Spirit and the fruit and gifts of the Spirit are seen as the present manifestation of the salvation of the end times among believers. In addition, while Paul could use the term "mystery" in a number of different ways, there is no such variety in Colossians, where its personal content in reference to the one at the heart of the gospel message, Christ, is constant (see 1:26-27; 2:2; 4:3). The notions of Christ's body and of the church now become universal entities (1:18, 24), in contrast to Paul's characteristic employment of them with reference to local groups of believers (although Colossians can also retain the reference of "church" to a local group in 4:15-16); and for the first time in the Pauline corpus the idea of Christ as the head is brought into relation with that of the church as the body (1:18; 2:19). Despite this area of theological differences not being decisive in itself, since a number of the variations may well be explicable in terms of the circumstances of the letter, the question remains whether, when the differences are taken all together, Paul would have changed his perspective on so many significant matters.

Both the stress on "the faith" as a body of teaching (1:23; 2:7) and the inclusion of the household code (3:18–4:1) may well reflect a setting after the death of the apostle. In such a setting it would be necessary to maintain continuity with his teachings and to provide more help to churches of the Pauline mission on how to live in society over a longer period than Paul had anticipated. In particular, 1:24–2:5 reads very much like an admiring portrait of Paul from a follower. What stands out here in comparison with Paul's own reflections on his apostolic office are the exclusive focus on Paul and the stress on the universality of his mission. In Colossians, Paul alone is the apostle, while the undisputed letters mention other apostles, even if sometimes somewhat disparagingly. And here his ministry is for everyone without exception (1:28). There is no recognition that James, Peter, and John had a mission to Jews, while Paul and Barnabas were to go to Gentiles (see Gal 2:9). Indeed, Paul's gospel can be said to have been preached to every creature under heaven (1:23). Furthermore, while Paul can speak of his sufferings for the benefit of others (2 Cor 1:3-7), nowhere does he speak of these tribulations as making up a deficiency in Christ's sufferings or for the sake of the universal church (1:24).

The strongest arguments for the letter's authenticity are its close links with Philemon, whose Pauline authorship is undisputed, and the less than straightforward reading of 4:7-16, with its greetings to and mention of specific people, that is required if the letter is not authentic. Those who are persuaded on grounds of style and other factors that it is improbable that Paul wrote the bulk of the letter point out that there is a reasonable alternative explanation for the last section. Its features are typical of ancient pseudepigraphical letters that strive for verisimilitude as part of the device of pseudonymity.[43] Biographical reminiscences, personalia, and details of pseudo-recipients and their setting all further the appearance of genuineness. In Colossians not only does the author speak in Paul's name but, to add verisimilitude to his taking on the persona of Paul, he has also built on the list of greetings in Philemon and added one or two names known to the recipients from the Pauline mission. In the Pastoral Epistles, held by most scholars to be pseudepigraphical, the typical devices of verisimilitude are distributed throughout the letters, but also, as in Colossians, such details are grouped together at the end of 2 Timothy (see 2 Tim 4:9-22).

In the nature of the case, there can be no overwhelming proof for one's position on authorship; on balance, however, the cumulative argument that Paul was not the author and that Colossians was written by a follower after the apostle's death appears to have the greater probability. If this is indeed so, then there are implications for the identification of the addressees, since there are grave doubts about the existence of Colossae, let alone any church there, after 61 CE. Colossae was a small town in the Lycus Valley in the region of Phrygia. By the first century it was very much in the shadow of the neighboring cities of Laodicea and Hierapolis. But there are two ancient reports of an earthquake in the Lycus Valley. Tacitus says that Laodicea was destroyed by an earthquake in 60–61 CE,[44] and Eusebius talks of Laodicea, Hierapolis, and Colossae as all being destroyed by an earthquake in 63–64 CE.[45] It is usually suggested that these are references to the same earthquake and that the more important Hierapolis and Laodicea were rebuilt more quickly, while Colossae remained uninhabited for a considerable period. There are coins from the late second and the third century referring to Colossae but no mention of it in ancient evidence for the earlier period after 61 CE. So it is likely that it was not an inhabited site for quite a long time after Paul's death. Some have suggested, therefore, that the church at Colossae was chosen as the addressee as part of the letter's attempt at verisimilitude, precisely because there was a Pauline church there during the apostle's lifetime but not afterward. This also meant that the writer was able to make use of the greetings in Philemon, a letter that was sent to Colossae. If all this is true, then an address to the Colossians is a convenient one in a pseudepigraphical letter actually intended for the former neighboring church of Laodicea and perhaps also that of Hierapolis, as the letter itself hints despite its address to pseudo-recipients (see 2:1; 4:13, 15-16).[46]

To conclude that Colossians is pseudonymous is, of course, not to detract in any way from the validity of its message or from its authority as part of the New Testament canon. What was canonized by the church were not the complete thoughts of Paul but those texts in which it recognized apostolic tradition. Pseudonymity was, in fact, a literary device for passing on authoritative tradition. In the Jewish Scriptures writings are attributed to great personages like Moses, David, Solomon, and Isaiah, and apocalypses, testaments, prayers, and collections of sayings were written in the name of ideal or authoritative figures from the past.[47] The earliest Christian writers of pseudepigrapha remained under the influence of such Jewish notions of authorship and revelation, whereby pseudonymity involved the assertion of authoritative tradition. The Epistle of Jeremiah, the Epistle of Enoch (*1 Enoch* 92–105), the Epistle of Baruch (*2 Apoc. Bar.* 78-87), the letters contained in 1 and 2 Maccabees, and the correspondence between Solomon, Hiram, and Pharaoh in Eupolemos and Josephus[48] provide examples from Jewish literature. However, the pseudepigraphical letter form employed by early Christians was particularly a Greco-Roman literary device. The pseudonymous didactic letters of the philosophical schools, such as the Pythagorean, Cynic, and Neo-Platonist school productions, attempted to convey the presence of the sender to the readers and in doing so would invent personal references and extraneous mundane details for the sake of verisimilitude. The purpose was to provide the occasion for passing on philosophical teaching and portraying a particular philosopher as a model.[49]

In evaluating this phenomenon, it should be remembered that the notion of "intellectual property," so essential to discussion of legitimate claims to authorship and to plagiarism in a modern context, played little or no role in ancient literary production. We know little about the circumstances of the composition of Colossians. Given its direct address to a particular problem, it does not seem likely that it was slipped into a letter collection in the hope that some later general readers would take it for one of Paul's originals and find it edifying. If, instead, it was intended for a specific group of readers in Asia Minor after Paul's death and came from one of Paul's close followers, it is reasonable to believe that its readers would have known of such a significant event as the death of the apostle and, therefore, would have taken the letter as a product of a trusted Pauline teacher who was presenting his teaching not simply as his own but as in the Pauline apostolic tradition. Whether written by Paul or by a disciple of his, the letter was treated as faithfully conveying the apostolic message and has a foundational status in the canon as part of the Pauline corpus. If written by a disciple of Paul, then Colossians, in its attempt to be both faithful and creative in its interpretation of the Pauline tradition in a later situation, provides a canonical model for those engaged in the same task of reflecting on the apostolic gospel and reformulating it in the face of changed circumstances

Main Roadways of Asia Minor
0
50
100
Miles
0
50
100
Kilometers
N
Ancyra
GALATIA
LYDIA
Sardis
Smyrna
PHRYGIA
Philadelphia
Antioch
Iconium
Aegean Sea
Ephesus
Hierapolis
Laodicea
Colossae
PISIDIA
Lystra
ASIA
Derbe
LYCIA
Mediterranean Sea
N
Meander R.
Hierapolis
ROAD FROM EPHESUS TO THE EAST
MOSSYNA MTS.
Laodicea
Lycus
TO ANTIOCH
Colossae
SALBAKUS MTS.
CADMUS MTS.
0
10
20
Miles
0
10
20
Kilometers
Lycus Valley

and new challenges. Although the following commentary is written from the perspective that the letter is to be dated sometime after Paul's death and that the interpretation of 1:24–2:5 and 4:7-16 in particular is to be linked to the device of pseudonymity, this is a matter still under dispute. For those who disagree with such a stance on authorship, all that is necessary in most of what follows is, of course, to make the mental substitution of "Paul" or "Timothy" or both for "the writer."[50]

EXCURSUS: "THE HOUSEHOLD CODE": ITS ORIGIN AND ADAPTATION

Although some scholars had maintained that the household code was a Christian creation and others that it had been adapted from Stoic moral philosophy, the view that predominated for a considerable time was that the household code derived from the attempts of Philo and Josephus to show the links between the social duties of Judaism and Hellenistic moral philosophy. It was presumed that this type of Hellenistic Jewish ethical teaching was mediated to early Christianity via the Hellenistic synagogues.[51] More recently, however, it has been shown convincingly that such a hypothesis does not do sufficient justice to the more general discussion of household management in the ancient world and that the thought of Philo and Josephus needs to be situated within this broader stream of tradition.[52] This broader tradition, which also treats husband/wife, parent/ child, and master/slave relationships and focuses on authority and subordination within these relationships, connects the topic of the household to the larger topic of the state and derives from the classical Greek philosophers.[53] All the elements of their discussion are continued down into the later Roman period. Philo and Josephus also adapted Aristotle's outline of household subordination in their interpretation and recommendation of Mosaic law.[54] Typical of the content of all such discussions is the notion that the man is intended by nature to rule as husband, father, and master and that failure to adhere to this proper hierarchy is detrimental not only to the household but also to the life of the state.

Setting the household code within this tradition becomes significant for assessing its use within early Christianity. The tradition reveals that proper household management was regarded as a matter of crucial social and political concern. Any upsetting of the household's traditional hierarchical order could be considered a potential threat to the order of society. In Greco-Roman culture, wives, children, and slaves were expected to accept the religion of the *paterfamilias*, the male head of the household, and so religious groups that attracted women and slaves were particularly seen as likely to be subversive of societal stability. Stereotyped criticism about breeding immorality and sedition was leveled by Greco-Roman writers against the cults of Dionysus and Isis, which attracted female devotees, and also against Judaism, because Jewish slaves rejected the worship of their Roman masters' gods. Dionysius of Halicarnassus criticized foreign mystery cults and praised the virtues of Roman households with their insistence on the obedience of wives, children, and slaves.[55] And significantly, Josephus's stress on subordination within the three household relationships is a response to slander against the Jews in an attempt to show that Judaism was not subversive of the ethic demanded by Greco-Roman society.[56]

As women and slaves joined the new Christian movement in large numbers, it, too, became the object of suspicion and criticism. It may well, therefore, have been the need to respond to accusations from outsiders and to set standards in line with common notions of propriety as much as the need to respond to enthusiastic demands for freedom on the part of believers that led Christians to produce their own version of the household code. This was certainly a major factor by the time of the code's use in 1 Peter (see 1 Pet 2:12; 3:15-16).

In the first extant Christian household code here in Colossians, the reasons for its introduction are not made explicit. The primary reason for its adaptation appears to be that the writer found it appropriate in re-calling those who might have been attracted by the philosophy, with its stress on asceticism and visionary experiences, to the significance of earthly life with its domestic duties. It may well be, however, that his re-call takes this particular form precisely because of the social factors that have been noted. The philosophy had taken over some elements of Judaism in its observances, and they had become part of a package of teachings and practices that resembled those of mystery cults. What is more, by the second century CE, in popular thought asceticism, philosophy, and magic were all associated with signs of deviancy from social norms.[57] If "worship of angels" is the writer's description of the practice, frequently attested in magical traditions, of invoking angels in order to placate and ward off evil spirit powers, then the teaching being opposed in Colossians would bear all the marks of social deviance. It could be characterized as philosophy, was clearly ascetic, and advocated practices associated with popular magic. It would not be at all surprising that the writer would want to distance Pauline churches from outsiders' perception of this explosive combination. His instructions signal that, far from attempting to destabilize society, life in Christian households had its distinctive motivations but provided a model that those concerned with virtue in Greco-Roman society ought to be able to recognize not as subversive but as falling within the bounds of received wisdom about the household. The summarizing exhortation in 4:5 about living wisely in regard to outsiders lends support to this suggestion.

This first use of the code in Christian literature reflects a stage in which Christians were conscious of criticisms of subverting the social order and of the need to adjust to living as Christians in the Greco-Roman world without unnecessarily disrupting the status quo. The death of the apostle Paul and the delay of the parousia are also likely to have been secondary factors contributing to this need to take a more long-term perspective on assimilating to life in society while preserving a Christian identity. This use of the code can also be seen as part of the process of stabilizing communal relations in the Pauline churches while retaining continuity with their earlier ethos. As M. Y. MacDonald observes of the code:

> On the one hand, the rule-like statements reflect a more conservative attitude toward the role of subordinate members of the household; they leave much less room for ambiguity and, consequently, for exceptional activity on the part of certain members. On the other hand, the instructions are not incompatible with Paul's own teaching about women and slaves (cf. 1 Cor 11:2-16; 1 Cor 14:34-36; 1 Cor 7:20-24; Philem 10-20).[58]

What is distinctive about Colossians' and subsequent Christian adaptation of the code is the series of exhortations to different groups within the household, all of which are treated as moral agents in their own right. What is distinctive about the content of the code in Colossians is the way in which the warrants, with their motivation, link the exhortations to believers' relationship to Christ as Lord, so that each group, including by implication husbands and fathers, is seen as equally accountable to the church's one Lord.

In its context in Colossians, the household code now forms part of the paraenesis in the writer's version of apostolic wisdom. His prayer for his readers was that they be "filled with the knowledge of God's will in all spiritual wisdom and understanding, so that you may lead lives worthy of the Lord" (1:9-10). With their roots in the wisdom found in Christ (2:2-3), the recipients are to be wisdom teachers themselves (3:16) and to live wisely in regard to outsiders (4:5). The code is situated between these last two references to wisdom and represents the writer's perspective on wise living in the household. It is not surprising that household duties would have been seen as part of wise conduct, because the Jewish wisdom tradition contained practical advice for all three household groups. All three relationships are discussed in Sir 7:19-28. Elsewhere there are frequent mentions of what is considered wise behavior for husbands and wives (see, e.g., Prov 5:18-19; 12:4; 18:22; 19:13*b*; 31:10-31; Sir 9:1; 26:1-4, 13-18), for parents and children (see, e.g., Prov 1:8; 6:20; 10:1; 13:24; 15:20; 19:13*a*, 18, 26; 23:13-14; Sir 3:1-16; 30:1-13), and for masters and slaves (see, e.g., Prov 14:35; 17:2; 19:10; 27:27; 29:19, 21; Sir 33:25-33). Not only so, but the justice and equity demanded of masters in the code is explicitly said to be the product of wisdom in Prov 2:9, and, of course, the fear of the Lord, to which slaves are exhorted, is in this tradition deemed to be either the beginning of wisdom (Prov 9:9; Sir 1:14) or wisdom itself (Sir 1:27; 19:20). The wisdom tradition offered moral guidance based on the sages' experience of and observations on human affairs and life in the world and attempted to discern in this a divine pattern and purpose. Now the wisdom teaching of Colossians takes up an early Christian version of accumulated reflection on household management from the Aristotelian and Hellenistic Jewish traditions and by this means attempts to determine the shape of believers' conduct in the light of Christ's lordship.

FOR FURTHER READNG

Commentaries:

Barth, M., and H. Blanke. *Colossians.* Translated by A. B. Beck. AB 34B. New York: Doubleday, 1994.

Dunn, J. D. G. *The Epistles to the Colossians and to Philemon.* NIGTC. Grand Rapids: Eerdmans, 1996.

Harris, M. J. *Colossians and Philemon.* Grand Rapids: Eerdmans, 1991.

Lohse, E. *Colossians and Philemon.* Translated by W. R. Poehlmann and R. J. Karris. Hermeneia. Philadelphia: Fortress, 1971.

MacDonald, Margaret Y. *Colossians and Ephisians.* SP 17. Collegeville, Minn.: Liturgical Press, 2000.

Martin, R. P. *Colossians and Philemon.* NCB. Greenwood, S.C.: Attic, 1974.

———. *Ephesians, Colossians, and Philemon.* Interpretation. Atlanta: John Knox, 1991.

O'Brien, P. T. *Colossians, Philemon.* WBC 44. Waco, Tex.: Word, 1982.

Pokorny, P. *Colossians: A Commentary.* Translated by S. S. Schatzmann. Peabody, Mass.: Hendrickson, 1991.

Schweizer, E. *The Letter to the Colossians.* Translated by A. Chester. Minneapolis: Augsburg, 1982.

Other Studies:

Arnold, C. E. *The Colossian Syncretism.* WUNT 2/77. Tübingen: J. C. B. Mohr, 1995.

Barclay, J. M. G. *Colossians and Philemon.* Sheffield: Sheffield Academic, 1997.

Bevere, Allan R. *Sharing in the Inheritance: Identity and the Moral Life in Colossians.* JSNTSup 226. London: Sheffield Academic Press, 2003.

D'Angelo, M. R. "Colossians." In *Searching the Scriptures.* Volume 2: *A Feminist Commentary.* Edited by E. Schüssler Fiorenza. New York: Crossroad, 1994.

DeMaris, R. E. *The Colossian Controversy.* JSNTSS 96. Sheffield: JSOT, 1994.

Francis, F. O., and W. A. Meeks, eds. *Conflict at Colossae.* Missoula, Mont.: Scholars Press, 1973.

Kiley, M. *Colossians As Pseudepigraphy.* Sheffield: JSOT, 1986.

Levine, Amy-Jill, and Marianne Blickenstaff, eds. *A Feminist Companion to the Deutero-Pauline Epistles.* Feminist Companion to the NT and Early Christian Writings 7. New York: T & T Clark, 2003.

Lincoln, A. T., and A. J. M. Wedderburn. *The Theology of the Later Pauline Letters.* New York: Cambridge University Press, 1993.

Martin, T. W. *By Philosophy and Empty Deceit: Colossians as Response to a Cynic Critique.* JSNTSS 118. Sheffield: Sheffield Academic, 1996.

Sappington, T. J. *Revelation and Redemption at Colossae.* JSNTSS 53. Sheffield: JSOT, 1991.

Wilson, W. T. *The Hope of Glory: Education and Exhortation in the Epistle to the Colossians.* Leiden: E. J. Brill, 1997.

Wright, N. T. *Paul for Everyone: The Prison Letters: Ephisians, Philippians, Colossians and Philemon.* London: SPCK, 2002.

ENDNOTES

1. See P. T. O'Brien, *Introductory Thanksgivings in the Letters of Paul,* NovTSup 49 (Leiden: Brill, 1977) 100-104.

2. Cf. J. T. Sanders, "The Transition from Opening Epistolary Thanksgiving to Body in the Letters of the Pauline Corpus" *JBL* 81 (1962) 348-62.

3. J. T. Sanders, "Transition," 354; J. L. White, "The Introductory Formulae in the Body of the Pauline Letter" *JBL* 90 (1971) 91-97.

4. J. L. White, *The Form and Function of the Body of the Greek Letter* (Missoula, Mont.: Scholars Press, 1972) 112-13n. 13.

5. See R. W. Funk, "The Apostolic Parousia: Form and Function," in *Christian History and Interpretation,* ed. W. R. Farmer et al. (Cambridge: Cambridge University Press, 1966) 249-68.

6. See D. E. Aune, *The New Testament in Its Literary Environment* (Philadelphia: Westminster, 1987) 191, 208.

7. See Aristotle *Rhetoric* 3.13-14.

8. J.-N. Aletti, *St. Paul Épître aux Colossiens,* ÉB (Paris: Gabalda, 1993) 39.

9. Aristotle *Rhetoric* 3.19.

10. Aristotle *Rhetoric* 1.2.

11. See A. J. Malherbe, *Ancient Epistolary Theorists* (Atlanta: Scholars Press, 1988) 37, 69.

12. For an illuminating discussion of the similarities between Colossians and the moral exhortations of the Greco-Roman philosophical schools, see W. T. Wilson, *The Hope of Glory: Education and Exhortation in the Epistle to the Colossians* (Leiden: E. J. Brill, 1997) esp. 10-131, 219-29.

13. T. J. Sappington, *Revelation and Redemption at Colossae,* JSNTSup 53 (Sheffield: JSOT, 1991).

14. R. E. DeMaris, *The Colossian Controversy: Wisdom in Dispute at Colossae,* JSNTSup 96 (Sheffield: JSOT, 1994) 17.

15. C. Arnold, *The Colossian Syncretism,* WUNT 2/77 (Tübingen: J. C. B. Mohr, 1995).

16. J. D. G. Dunn, "The Colossian Philosophy: A Confident Jewish Apologia," *Biblica* 76 (1995) 153-81; *The Epistles to the Colossians and to Philemon,* NIGTC (Grand Rapids: Eerdmans, 1996) 35.

17. T. W. Martin, *By Philosophy and Empty Deceit. Colossians as Response to a Cynic Critique.* JSNTSup 118 (Sheffield: Sheffield Academic, 1996).

18. See F. O. Francis's influential essay "Humility and Angelic Worship in Colossae," in *Conflict at Colossae,* ed. F. O. Francis and W. A. Meeks (Missoula, Mont.: Scholars Press, 1973) 163-95.

19. Tertullian *On Fasting* 12.

20. *The Shepherd of Hermas* Vision 3.10.6; Similitude 5.3.7.

21. See *Apoc. Abr.* 9, 12; Philo *On the Life of Moses* 1:67-70; *On Dreams* 1:33-37.

22. F. O. Francis, "Humility and Angelic Worship in Col 2:18," in *Conflict at Colossae,* ed. F. O. Francis and W. A. Meeks (Missoula, Mont.: Scholars Press, 1973) 163-95. Francis has been followed by numerous recent scholars.

23. E.g., *2 Enoch* 20:3-4; *T. Job* 48-50; *Apoc. Abr.* 17; *Asc. Isa.* 7:37; 9:28, 31, 33.

24. Cf. 1QH 3:20-22; 11:10-12; 1QSb 4:25-26.

25. C. E. Arnold, *The Colossian Syncretism* WUNT 2/77 (Tübingen: J. C. B. Mohr, 1995) esp. 8-102.

26. C. E. Arnold, *The Colossian Syncretism,* 61-89.

27. C. E. Arnold, *The Colossian Syncretism,* 91-95.

28. C. E. Arnold, *The Colossian Syncretism,* 57-59.

29. See also *1 Enoch* 14:8; 71:1; *2 Enoch* 3:1; 36:1-2; *T. Abr.* 7-10; *Apoc. Abr.* 12, 15-16, 30; *T. Levi* 2:5-7, 10 ; 5:1, 3; 2 Bar 6:4.

30. J. D. G. Dunn, *The Epistles to the Colossians and to Philemon,* NIGTC (Grand Rapids: Eerdmans, 1996) 184 n. 35, admits that the weakest point of his hypothesis that the philosophy came from the Jewish synagogue is its failure to correlate such material satisfactorily and that this evidence provides the best support for the view that the philosophy was syncretistic.

31. See also Diogenes Laertius 7, 136-37; Philo *Who Is the Heir of Divine Things?* 134.

32. Pseudo-Callisthenes I.12.1.

33. See PGM IV.475-829; XXXIX.18-21.

34. Arnold, *The Colossian Syncretism,* 170-73.

35. Philo *On the Eternity of the World* 107-9.

36. Philo *On the Contemplative Life* 3-4.

37. See 4 Ezra 6:3; *Jub.* 2:2; *1 Enoch* 60:11-12; *2 Enoch* 4:1; *T. Abr.* 13:11.

38. See especially Plutarch *The Obsolescence of Oracles* 39-40; *Corpus Hermeticum* XI.20.

39. Dunn, *The Epistles to the Colossians and to Philemon,* 31.

40. For a detailed discussion of the relation between Colossians and Ephesians and its role in the debate about the authorship of Ephesians, see A. T. Lincoln, *Ephesians* WBC (Dallas: Word, 1990) xlvii-lxxiii.

41. See, e.g., E. Schweizer, *The Letter to the Colossians* (Minneapolis: Augsburg, 1982); Dunn, *The Epistles to the Colossians and to Philemon.*

42. W. Bujard, *Stilanalystische Untersuchungen zum Kolosserbrief als Beitrag zur Methodik von Sprachvergleichen* (Göttingen: Vandenhoeck & Ruprecht, 1973). This work is summarized briefly in English in M. Kiley, *Colossians as Pseudepigraphy* (Sheffield: JSOT, 1986) 51-59.

43. See L. R. Donelson, *Pseudepigraphy and Ethical Argument in the Pastoral Letters* (Tübingen: Mohr, 1986) 7-66.

44. Tacitus *Annals* 14.27.

45. Eusebius *Chronicle* 1.21-22.

46. So A. Lindemann, "Die Gemeinde von 'Kolossä.' Erwägungen zum 'Sitz im Leben' eines deuteropaulinischen Briefes," *WD* 16 (1981) 111-34; P. Pokorny, *Colossians* (Peabody, Mass.: Hendrickson, 1991) 21.

47. See D. G. Meade, *Pseudonymity and Canon* (Tübingen: Mohr, 1986).

48. Eupolemos, as preserved in Eusebius *Preparation for the Gospel* 9.31.1-34.5; Josephus *Antiquities of the Jews* 8.2.6-7.

49. See Donelson, *Pseudepigraphy and Ethical Argument in the Pastoral Epistles*, 7-66; Wilson, *The Hope of Glory*, esp. 49-50.

50. For a major commentary defending authorship of Colossians by Paul, see P. T. O'Brien, *Colossians, Philemon*, WBC 44 (Waco, Tex.: Word, 1982) esp. xli-xlix.

51. See J. E. Crouch, *The Origin and Intention of the Colossian Haustafel* (Göttingen: Vandenhoeck & Ruprecht, 1972) esp. 95-101, who provides the most detailed exposition of this view.

52. See D. L. Balch, *Let Wives Be Submissive: The Domestic Code in 1 Peter* (Chico, Calif.: Scholars Press, 1981), and also his review of the issues in "Household Codes," in *Greco-Roman Literature and the New Testament*, ed. D. E. Aune (Atlanta: Scholars Press, 1988) 25-50.

53. See Plato *Laws* 3.690A-D; 6.771E-7.824C; Aristotle *Politics* 1.1253b, 1259a.

54. See Philo *Hypothetica* 7.1-14; *On the Decalogue* 165-67; Josephus *Against Apion* 2.22-28.

55. Dionysius of Halicarnassus *Roman Antiquities* 2.24.3–2.27.4.

56. Josephus *Against Apion* 2.24, 27, 30.

57. See J. A. Francis, *Subversive Virtue: Asceticism and Authority in the Second Century Pagan World* (University Park: University of Pennsylvania Press, 1995) esp. 47, 49, 53.

58. M. Y. MacDonald, *The Pauline Churches: A Socio-historical Study of Institutionalization in the Pauline and Deutero-Pauline Writings* (Cambridge: Cambridge University Press, 1988) 102-3.

THE FIRST LETTER TO THE THESSALONIANS

ABRAHAM SMITH

Both 1 and 2 Thessalonians are powerful witnesses to the early church's struggles with the suffering of its members. The Thessalonian letters make it clear that separation from leaders, alienation from former friends, and perennial threats of persecution and even death were not solely the concerns of the fledgling communities behind the Synoptic Gospels, the virtually introverted Johannine believers, and the persecuted minority group addressed by John's apocalypse.

These struggles and the constraints through which the early churches were pressed to view them resound on every page of 1 and 2 Thessalonians. In consequence, the two letters offer remarkable challenges to contemporary churches. Understanding these challenges, however, does not come easily. Since all letters (past or present) are occasional documents, they imply more than they state explicitly. The circumstances that the first-century letter writers and their audiences took for granted must be reconstructed before we can even begin to interpret their letters as responses to those circumstances. Moreover, certain thought patterns shared by Paul and the church at Thessalonica (but not directly obvious to us) also must be reconstructed because the letters assume these patterns without directly drawing attention to them.

Reconstruction of the letters' circumstances and some of the writer's thought patterns is enhanced by examining the general nature and functions of most ancient letters—that is, the various formulae expected in a typical first-century letter and the basic strategies letter writers used to make their letters effective. Over the years of biblical scholarship, proven methods of careful analysis have developed that highlight these aspects of first-century letters to place 1 and 2 Thessalonians in the historical and literary milieu of the first century CE. It is important as well to place them more directly in the environs of early Christianity, particularly Pauline Christianity, to the extent that we can reconstruct it from the surviving literary and historical evidence. Accordingly, these chapters will begin with an examination of several general historical contexts related to Paul and the city of Thessalonica, and then move to a more specific reconstruction of the specific occasions and purposes of each letter. This chapter will focus on the literary character of the letters.

THE GENERAL HISTORICAL CONTEXTS OF 1 AND 2 THESSALONIANS

Three general historical contexts are essential for understanding 1 and 2 Thessalonians. Obviously, one critical historical context is Paul's work among the Gentiles. Equally important is the context of the city of Thessalonica itself, especially the city's ongoing dependence upon Roman patronage and the role that dependence likely played in the relations between Paul's church and the larger Thessalonian society. Yet another critical context is Paul's apocalyptic gospel—both the distinctive features of its thought pattern and its appeal to the church Paul founded in Thessalonica.

The Context of Paul's Work Among the Gentiles. Through the revelation of the risen Jesus to him (1 Cor 9:1; 15:8; 2 Cor 12:1-3; Acts 9:22, 26; Gal 1:12), Paul was called to preach the gospel among the Gentiles (Gal 1:16). He carried that gospel over considerable territory in the cities of the eastern Mediterranean. According to Wayne Meeks, the Pauline house-church movement took root in at least four provinces of the Roman Empire: Galatia (modern-day Turkey, e.g., the churches of Galatia), Asia (e.g., Colossae and Ephesus; see 1 Cor 16:19), Macedonia (e.g., the churches at Philippi and Thessalonica), and Achaia (the church at Corinth).[1]

In his Letter to the Romans (among whom he did not establish a church), Paul noted that his plan was to preach the gospel from Jerusalem to Illyricum (modern-day Dalmatia just to the east of the Adriatic Sea), to go on from there to Rome, and from there to Spain (Rom 15:19, 24). His goal, then, was a westward mission that would take him about ten thousand miles during the course of his career.[2] While it is possible to see Paul's travel to Thessalonica only as a reaction to difficulties he met at Philippi (1 Thess 2:1-2), the move was likely a strategic one, a part of the effort to move westward with his gospel to the Gentiles. Paul's letters and the book of Acts attest to his travel and to that of his coworkers, including Timothy, Titus, and Epaphroditus.

Just how Paul supported his house-church movement and extensive travel among the Gentiles is not altogether certain. On the basis of 1 Cor 4:12 (where Paul indicates that he "worked with his own hands") and Acts 18:3 (which identifies a trade for Paul), some scholars suggest that Paul's vocation involved some kind of leatherworking, whether that of making tents or other leather products.[3] If leatherworking was indeed Paul's vocation, we can imagine him traveling, like other artisans, with tools in hand, setting up a workshop wherever the local leather-workers' guild of a city met. Even if we cannot identify Paul's exact occupation, however, we can still imagine him plying some trade to support himself (1 Thess 2:9), though he certainly received help from others, and from some of them repeatedly (e.g., the Macedonians, who included at least the Philippians; 2 Cor 11:8-9; Phil 4:15-16). For his intended work in Spain, moreover, Paul even desired help from the Roman churches, though he had not established those churches (Rom 1:13; 15:28–16:2).

More certain than his vocation is the pastoral care Paul extended to his churches in the course of his career.[4] Not only did he establish churches, but also his letters witness to his profound love for and anxiety about these assemblies as he shaped them and nurtured their growth (2 Cor 11:28). His letters also testify to his use of the hortatory tradition—that is, the well-known tradition of exhortation. Examination of the letters of Plato, Epicurus, and Seneca, among others, reveals the evolution of a tradition in which philosophers placed "exhortations to the philosophical life into the form of letters."[5] Such letters were designed to help the recipients internalize the values of a particular philosophy, to help them "avoid feelings of isolation and the demoralizing effects they might have," and to affect their "habits and disposition."[6] Thus, in line with his call to take the gospel to the Gentiles, Paul seems to have planted house churches in strategic locations and to have sent them letters and emissaries in his absence in order to strengthen the solidarity of the assemblies and to correct any problems occurring in the wake of his departure. The church at Thessalonica was one of these assemblies that Paul established, molded, and nurtured.

The Context of the City of Thessalonica. In Paul's time Thessalonica was a part of the vast Roman Empire. When the city, named for Alexander's half-sister Thessaloniki, was founded in 316 BCE, one of Alexander's generals (Cassander) was its first benefactor. Due to the squabbles of Alexander's successors, however, Thessalonica eventually received Rome as its new patron in 167 BCE.[7]

The city was a commercial and cultic center. It did not stand toe to toe with Athens, the great intellectual capital. Nor did its size match that of Alexandria, the great international city of the day. Yet it was no mean place. With the construction of the Via Egnatia (Rome's gateway to its eastern colonies) in 130 BCE, Thessalonica benefited from the traffic of travelers and became a key trading center in the region.[8] Archaeological evidence suggests that the city enjoyed a rich cultic life—one that included indigenous Macedonian cults like those of Cabirus and Dionysus, foreign cults like those of Isis and Serapis, and the Roman imperial cult.[9]

The inhabitants of Thessalonica actively cultivated the beneficence of the Romans. The city's loyalty to the emperor Augustus (Octavian) and his successors favored it with the status of a free city (having an independent government) and with beneficence from both local and foreign Roman patrons. By the time Paul visited Thessalonica, sometime during the imperial reign of Claudius (41–54 CE), the Thessalonians had already erected a statue of Augustus as one of several honors to the Romans. Moreover, all of the Macedonians (in Thessalonica and beyond) had honored Augustus "by inaugurating an 'Augustan era.'"[10]

These data about the city in Paul's day are crucial to the interpretation of the Thessalonian epis-

Macedonia and Achaia
N
ILLYRICUM
Adriatic Sea
Dyrrhachium
MACEDONIA
THRACE
Philippi
Neapolis
VIA EGNATIA
Amphipolis
Pella
Thessalonica
Apollonia
Beroea
EPIRUS
Mt. Olympus
Thracian Sea
Corcyra
THESSALY
Aegean Sea
Nicopolis
Delphi
Euboea
ACHAIA
Gulf of Corinth
Corinth
Cenchreae
Athens
Ionian Sea
PELOPONNESIA
Sparta
0
50
100
Miles
0
50
100
Kilometers

tles because the letters presuppose conflict between those in the church and other Thessalonians. It is likely that the Christians' glorification of Christ precipitated the conflict with the communities favorably disposed to the Roman government. If so, terms found in 1 Thessalonians, such as παρουσία (*parousia*, "coming" or "presence," 1 Thess 2:19; 3:13; 4:15; 5:23); ἀπάντησις (*apantēsis*, "meeting," 1 Thess 4:17) and ἀσφάλεια (*asphaleia*, "security," 1 Thess 5:3) are not politically innocuous. Rather, as Helmut Koester asserts, these terms present Paul's view of Jesus' "coming" or "return" as that of a king being greeted by a delegation that has come out to meet him.[11] Koester notes, moreover, that Paul's view of "peace and security" "points to the coming of the Lord as an event that will shatter the false peace and security of the Roman establishment."[12] Other terms in 1 and 2 Thessalonians could also be reread in the light of this possible political conflict. The attribution of the appellation "Father" to God may have been used in opposition to the imperial establishment, for the term figured in the ideology of Augustus Caesar as he sought to construe his empire as one large family.[13] Even such terms as "gospel" (εὐαγγέλιον *euangelion*) and "savior" (σωτήρ *sōtēr*) in 1 and 2 Thessalonians or any of the other letters attributed to Paul could well have suggested "opposition to the imperial religion of the *pax Romana* [Roman peace]."[14]

If these terms carried the political weight that has been suggested, it is not difficult to understand why some Thessalonians (those not accepting Paul's teachings) would castigate Paul's salvific assembly, which viewed Jesus (not Augustus) as the benefactor and inaugurator of a new age.[15] In the eyes of these Thessalonians, support for Jesus weakened support for the Romans, who had brought tangible benefits to the city.

It is important to note, moreover, that criticism of the Pauline believers would have been severely hostile because most Gentiles vehemently opposed Christianity's exclusivistic claims on its adherents' lives. According to Segal, "Like the Jews and unlike the many clubs and associations that were a part of the civic life of the Hellenistic world, the Christians were exclusive in the sense that no *truly committed* gentile Christian could maintain cult membership. Thus, Christianity was subversive to the basic religious institutions of gentile society."[16] This shift in loyalty from various cult memberships to exclusive ties with the Christian assembly also meant that Christian believers lost the prestige they could have assumed through the commitments to their former networks.

Given this potential for conflict, why did any of the Thessalonians join this assembly? Why did they remain? What would they find valuable in Paul's gospel that could shape and nurture their lives? Answers to these questions are found in an exploration of Paul's apocalyptic gospel.

The Context of Paul's Apocalyptic Gospel. When Paul preached to the people of Thessalonica, some believed his gospel, even in the face of the hostile response of other Thessalonians (1 Thess 1:6; 2:13-16). But what exactly was Paul's gospel?

Beyond the hortatory tradition that seems to have shaped all of Paul's letters, both 1 and 2 Thessalonians are shaped by apocalyptic thought.[17] Proponents of this type of worldview hold that there is a fundamental distinction between the forces of good and the forces of evil. They envision an old age ruled by the forces of evil and a new one ruled by God, and they believe in an imminent judgment, at which time God will bring an end to the evil forces. Studies of Paul's letters reveal that all of Paul's churches and letter recipients struggled (healthily or unhealthily) with the delicate tension between the "already" and the "not-yet" aspects of his apocalyptic thought. The "already" refers to the things God accomplished through Jesus' death and resurrection; the "not yet" refers to those things yet to be accomplished at the parousia. Hence a reckoning of this tension—its distinctiveness and consequences—may give some insight into what Paul's hearers (and the followers of his tradition) took for granted about Paul's thought.

The *distinctiveness* of the delicate tension between the already and the not-yet lies in Paul's modification of Jewish apocalyptic thought. For many Jews, there were two sequential ages (or aeons)—one old and one new. For Paul, however, the power of the old age was already dealt a severe blow with the death and resurrection of Jesus (Gal 6:14-15), an event that also marked the dawning of the new age (Gal 1:4).[18] Moreover, for Paul, the manifestations of the old age—while doomed (1 Cor 2:6; 7:31)—are not yet at an end. They still affect believers, who await Jesus' parousia as the climactic event that will mark the consummation of the new age already begun (1 Cor 15:51-57). Therefore, believers live "between the times"—that is, between the already of what God has done through Jesus' death and resurrection and the not yet that awaits as the object of hope: resurrection (Phil 3:11), full adoption (and its consequence, heirship; Rom 8:15-17; Gal 4:4-7), and full conformity to Christ (Phil 3:21).[19]

Given the delicate tension of these aspects, what are the *consequences* of Paul's apocalyptic thought pattern? One consequence is that God's redemption or salvation of believers from sin's enslaving powers and death's corruption is a process that begins with God's free offering of grace (Rom 5:15), the creation of a new sphere of existence (2 Cor 5:17; Gal 6:15) not dependent on any previous entitlement (such as one's class status) or human performance (such as the keeping of the law), and the declaration of justification by God through the believer's faith (or reorientation, Rom 5:1). That process—lived between the times—is one of sanctification, in which the Spirit both dwells in believers as God's pledge (or down payment, 2 Cor 1:22; 5:5) of the final consummation and acts as God's agency of transformation, conforming their lives to the image of God found in Jesus Christ (2 Cor 3:18). A second consequence is that believers struggle to live according to the spirit of the new age even while they still are plagued by manifestations of the old age—sin, trials, and death.

A third consequence of this tension is that believers—who have already conformed to Christ's death—presently conform to Christ's suffering and live expectantly in the hope that they will conform to his resurrection and glorification (Rom 5:2; Phil 3:10-11). Thus throughout the tenure of their lives "in Christ," from baptism to the other side of the parousia, the life of Jesus is the theme of their existence.

Finally, a fourth consequence of this tension is that the new sphere of existence entails products of transformation. These fruits show God at work in the edification of God's people, in the strengthening of the individual believer against the old age's manifestations, and in the persuasion of others through the proclamation of the gospel and the believer's conformity to Christ. The fruits of the Spirit (Gal 5:22) stand in opposition to the works of the flesh (or of the natural [and self-seeking] person; Gal 5:16,17).

While we cannot be sure of the full content of Paul's preaching in Thessalonica, it is known that he spoke strongly about the relationship that believers have with God. Paul's repeated references to God as "Father" only make sense if he shared with the community their incorporation into the family of God, a family in which Jesus is God's special son (1 Thess 1:10), but one in which all believers can be the children of God as well (1 Thess 1:1, 3; 3:11). It is also known that he preached about the death and resurrection of Jesus and how these events were the basis for rescue from the coming wrath of God (1 Thess 1:10). Accordingly, he likely spoke to the assembly about one of the ultimate benefits of the new age: God's deliverance of believers from death.

Paul's repeated emphasis on the role of the Holy Spirit and sanctification suggests that his message also covered the more immediate and ongoing benefits of the new age. In the course of his description of the foundational events, Paul repeatedly mentions the Holy Spirit as proof of God's choosing of believers for salvation (1 Thess 1:4-5) and as a source of inspiration in the face of opposition (1:6). Even his later comments on the Holy Spirit as a gift from God (4:8) that helps believers to do God's bidding (4:3-8) and as a presence that should not be quenched (5:19) are offered in the context of what the Thessalonians are already doing and what they should continue doing (4:11; 5:11). It is in the course of reiterating some of his previous instructions that Paul describes sanctification, or the ongoing maturation of believers, as the will of God (4:3).

Because Paul writes of continuing opposition as something that he warned them of when he was with the church (1 Thess 3:3-5; cf. 2:1-2), he likely spoke to the Thessalonian believers about the continuing manifestations of the old age as well. The hostilities they were suffering, in fact, were a sign of the old age; and Paul could assume that they would understand him when he spoke of his inability to get back to the church as due to opposition from Satan (2:18).

It appears, then, that the Thessalonian church would have known at least the rudimentary form of Paul's mature gospel: the initiative of God in incorporating believers into God's family, the overlapping of the two ages, and some of the benefits and costs accruing to believers because of the tensions between these two ages. Exactly what had appealed to the Thessalonian believers about this gospel is not clear, and we should resist unfounded assumptions. In earlier studies of this church, some scholars too quickly suggested that the appeal was based on the relative deprivation of the Thessalonians in general (the belief that the Thessalonian Christians before their conversion were among the lower classes, even though they lived at a time when the economic life of Thessalonica in general was on the upswing). Other scholars presumed that the appeal was based on status inconsistency, the belief that the achieved status of the Thessalonian Christians before conversion was radically different from their inherited status and thus a source of tension for which they found some ease in early Christianity. However, we simply do not have enough material evidence to determine the status levels of the Thessalonian believers. And in the judgment of the most recent careful assessment of the little evidence we have available, these descriptions are examples of "ethnocentric anachronisms."[20]

If we look to Paul, a possible appeal may be that his gospel came with "power" (1 Thess 1:5). Indeed, much of 1 Thessalonians seems to be directed toward reminding the church of the power of this gospel both over the Thessalonians who believed it (1:6-10; 2:13-16) and over the apostles who proclaimed it (2:1-12). It is also likely that the gospel's power brought a level of prestige to this community for which they were even willing to accept hostility of and alienation from their former networks of support and honor. As we will see, the issue of the gospel's power and prestige will be crucial to both letters. Furthermore, we must not forget that both 1 and 2 Thessalonians, to the extent that they expose Paul's gospel, demonstrate the extraordinary hope of that gospel. Little wonder then that Jürgen Moltmann has advocated so forcefully that modern persons shun resignation and despair and embrace the hopefulness of Paul and other early Christians.[21] While many today might find difficulty in seeing the value of Paul's apocalyptic gospel, it was both an all-embracing statement about God's plan for the world and a "critique of this age and its values."[22] Many of those who heard Paul's preaching (including the Thessalonians) would have found in it a powerful challenge to the existing order. As we will see as well, both Thessalonian letters also imply this challenge.

SPECIFIC OCCASIONS AND PURPOSES OF 1 AND 2 THESSALONIANS

Paul's gospel not only brought the church at Thessalonica into being, but also became the basis upon which Paul molded its character and sustained its growth. Thus one could expect his apocalyptic gospel to be tightly woven into the hortatory tradition that he adopted—a tradition noted for shaping the distinctiveness of communities and for providing them with nurturing resources.[23] Because history has afforded us with two exhortative letters addressed to the Thessalonians, we have the opportunity to explore the distinctive appropriations of Paul's gospel in two related, but different, hortatory documents.[24] It is necessary, therefore, to clarify as much as possible the circumstances that gave rise to each letter. An appreciation of the similar yet distinct occasions and purposes of each letter will help us to see their respective appropriations of Paul's gospel in stark relief.

Specific Occasion and Purposes of 1 Thessalonians. Drawing exclusively on Paul's writings, we can say little with certainty about the specific occasion of his earliest extant letter. Paul formed the church that received this letter shortly after he left Philippi, where he and others were "shamefully mistreated" (1 Thess 2:2). His stay at Thessalonica must have been long enough for him to receive support from the church at Philippi on more than one occasion (Phil 4:16). Still, the tenure in Thessalonica also met with difficulty (2:2) and, most unfortunately for both parties, with a painful separation (2:17). When efforts to return to the Thessalonian church proved futile (2:18), Paul dispatched Timothy from Athens (3:1-2) with instructions to strengthen the community. As a set of follow-up instructions, in line with his desire to form, mold, and nurture communities, Paul wrote the letter we now know as 1 Thessalonians.

If we rely somewhat on the material from Acts, a few more details about the circumstances are evident. From Athens, Paul moved on presumably to Corinth (Acts 18:11-17), the place from which he likely wrote the first Thessalonian letter. Acts also suggests that Paul arrived in Corinth before Gallio became proconsul (Acts 18:11-17). If, indeed, Paul wrote to the Thessalonians from Corinth, we may deduce that the letter was likely written around 50 or 51 CE because the famous Delphi inscription dates Gallio's arrival in Corinth to sometime between January and August of 51 CE.

Some details about the specific historical circumstances, however, differ between Paul's letter and the Acts account. While both suggest that the trip to Philippi preceded the trip to Thessalonica (Acts 17:1; cf. 16:11-40; 1 Thess 2:2), which was about 90 miles southwest of Philippi on the Via Egnatia, Acts gives the impression that the Thessalonian converts included both Jews and Gentiles (Acts 17:4), while Paul implies that there were Gentile converts only (as can be inferred from 1 Thess 1:9, 10). If one accepts 1 Thess 2:14-16 to be from Paul's hand and not an interpolation, these verses also support an ethnic constituency of Gentiles.

Acts 17 also mentions Paul's going to a Jewish synagogue, which is not mentioned in 1 Thessalonians. To the extent of our archaeological data today, there is no evidence for a synagogue in Thessalonica at this early period. What must be remembered, however, is that Acts has a stereotyped pattern similar to ancient novelistic literature of the period. For example, in Chariton's *Chaereas and Callirhoe*, one of the ancient Greek novels, virtually everywhere the two protagonists, Chaereas and Callirhoe, go they find a shrine to Aphrodite, the goddess of love, where they offer her worship and thanks. Likewise, virtually everywhere Paul travels in Acts 13–28, he finds Jews and a Jewish synagogue. The function of the stereotyped narration of shrines in both cases is that the universal significance and power of an adherent's deity is highlighted if the writer can demonstrate that that the deity is worshiped all over the Mediterranean world.

If the Thessalonian Christians were a Gentile congregation, it is possible to posit some basic factors about the occasion of 1 Thessalonians. First, as has been noted, opposition from Gentile neighbors was likely a critical ingredient in the occasion of 1 Thessalonians. Their hostility was likely aroused by the Christian believers' countercultural glorification of Christ. A second factor in the letter's occasion was a concern for stability. Given the hostility from unbelievers, the congregation is encouraged to remain steady on its course. In 1 Thessalonians, Paul speaks of his leadership team (Paul, Silvanus, and Timothy) "living" if the community "stands firm" (3:8), and he implores God to "strengthen" the hearts of his congregation against external social alienation (3:13). Therefore, 1 Thessalonians seems written to encourage a beleaguered church to persist in its new way of life, in accordance with the apocalyptic gospel it has received, despite the fact that it might have been difficult for the members to see the power of God—and the prestige pertaining to that power—at work in their lives.

LITERARY CHARACTER OF 1 AND 2 THESSALONIANS

In determining the basic literary character of the two letters, Pauline scholarship profits from a variety of widely acknowledged perspectives and methods. An audience-oriented perspective, used here, in which contemporary readers seek to understand the audience that each author had in mind when composing the respective letters draws on two methods, epistolary analysis and rhetorical criticism, not to restrict Paul and other early Christians to the handbooks of their age, but to make contemporary readers aware of the basic textual markers by which the audiences for the two letters would have read or heard them. It is generally accepted that early Christian letters offered nuanced variations on Hellenistic epistolary formulae as well as on the rhetorical practices of that age. Thus early Christian letters exploited typical Hellenistic letter opening (prescript) and closing (postscript) formulae, variations of a typical health wish/thank you notice (to the gods or to the addressees) and prayer reports, and perhaps one or more parts of the conventional epistolary body (i.e., the main part of a letter).

As well, it is generally accepted that early Christian letters reflect rhetorical (or persuasive speech) conventions, as if the letters were all influenced by the rules that ancient Greeks and Romans applied to speeches. Accordingly, some scholars find in the letters the basic speech design indexed in handbooks on speech preparation—namely, an exordium (or opening of an argument), a *pistis* (or proof section, i.e., the central part of an argument) and the peroration (or closing of an argument). Others even characterize particular Christian letters in one of the three broad modal forms of argumentation: the deliberative mode (with the goal of persuading or dissuading), the epideictic mode (with the goal of praising and blaming), or the defensive mode (with the goal of accusing or defending).

Whether Paul learned the epistolary and rhetorical conventions in school or assimilated them from the larger culture is not known. What is generally believed, however, is that Paul (like anyone else of his time) was not straitjacketed by the rules and need not be held to exaction on the basis of either the set of practices in the handbooks of the period or those in the scholarly reckonings of our own age.

THEOLOGICAL CHALLENGES

Appreciating the signs of God's power already evident in a community lies at the heart of 1 Thessalonians (1:5; 2:13). Discovering that the effectiveness of the gospel extends beyond the limited parameters of one's own environs is a critical lesson as well (1 Thess 1:8; 2:14-16). Drawing on the past to discover models of perseverance in the face of present suffering is also a repeated challenge (1 Thess 1:6-7; 2:1-11; 3:1-11). Remaining firm in one's convictions without being beguiled by enticing words or false hopes is paramount for 2 Thessalonians (2:1-3). Knowing both how to wait on God and yet move toward practical pursuits is equally important (2 Thess 3:6-13). And discerning how to reach out in love to disorderly persons in the church without demonizing them is key to the spirit of 2 Thessalonians (3:14-15). These insights from 1 and 2 Thessalonians offer remarkable challenges for contemporary churches. But when fathomed sufficiently, 1 and 2 Thessalonians offer much deeper reservoirs of assistance to our world.

FOR FURTHER READING

Best, E. *A Commentary on the First and Second Epistles to the Thessalonians.* London: Black, 1972.

Collins, Raymond. *The Birth of the New Testament: The Origin and Development of the First Generation.* New York: Crossroad, 1993.

Gaventa, Beverly. *First and Second Thessalonians.* Interpretation. Louisville: John Knox, 1998.

Hughes, F. W. *Early Christian Rhetoric and 2 Thessalonians.* JSNT 30 Sheffield: JSOT, 1989.

Jewett, Robert. *The Thessalonian Correspondence: Pauline Rhetoric and Millenarian Piety.* Foundations and Facets. Philadelphia: Fortress, 1986.

Malherbe, Abraham J. *Paul and the Thessalonians: The Philosophic Tradition of Pastoral Care.* Philadelphia: Fortress, 1987.

———. *The Letters to the Thesalonians.* AB 32B. New York: Doubleday, 2000.

Marshall, I. H. *1 and 2 Thessalonians.* Grand Rapids: Eerdmans, 1983.

Menken, Maarten J. *2 Thessalonians.* London: Routledge, 1994.

Porter, Stanley E., and Jeffrey A. D. Weima. *An Annotated Bibliography of 1 and 2 Thessalonians.* NTTS 26. Leiden: Brill, 1998.

Richard, Earl J. *First and Second Thessalonians.* SP11 Collegeville, Minn.: Liturgical, 1995.

Smith, Abraham. *Comfort One Another: Reconstructing the Rhetoric and Audience of 1 Thessalonians.* Louisville: Westminster, 1995.

Thurston, Bonnie. *Reading Colossians, Ephesians and 2 Thessalonians: A Literary and Theological Commentary.* New York: Crossroad, 1995.

Walton, Steve. *Leadership and Lifestyle: The Portrait of Paul in the Miletus Speech and I Thessalonians.* Cambridge: SNTSMS 108. Cambridge University Press, 2000.

Wanamaker, Charles. *The Epistles to the Thessalonians: A Commentary on the Greek Text.* NIGTC. Grand Rapids: Eerdmans, 1990.

ENDNOTES

1. Wayne Meeks, *The First Urban Christians: The Social World of the Apostle Paul* (New Haven: Yale University Press, 1983) 41.

2. Ronald F. Hock, *The Social Context of Paul's Ministry: Tentmaking and Apostleship* (Philadelphia: Fortress, 1980) 27.

3. Hock, *The Social Context of Paul's Ministry,* 21.

4. Abraham J. Malherbe, *Paul and the Thessalonians: The Philosophic Tradition of Pastoral Care* (Philadelphia: Fortress, 1987).

5. Stanley Stowers, *Letter Writing in Greco-Roman Antiquity* (Philadelphia: Westminster, 1986) 37.

6. Walter T. Wilson, *The Hope of Glory: Education and Exhortation in the Epistle to the Colossians* (Leiden: Brill, 1997) 47, 48.

7. R. Malcolm Errington, *A History of Macedonia,* trans. Catherine Errington (Berkeley: University of California Press, 1990) 133.

8. Meeks, *The First Urban Christians,* 17-18.

9. Craig Steven de Vos, *Church and Community Conflicts: The Relationships of the Thessalonian, Corinthian, and Philippian Churches with Their Wider Civic Communities* (Atlanta: Scholars Press, 1997).

10. M. B. Sakellariou, *Macedonia: 4000 Years of Greek History and Civilization* (Athens: Ekdotike Athenon S.A., 1983) 196.

11. Helmut Koester, "From Paul's Eschatology to the Apocalyptic Schemata of 2 Thessalonians," in *The Thessalonian Correspondence*, ed. Raymond F. Collins (Leuven: University of Leuven Press, 1990) 446.

12. Koester, "From Paul's Eschatology," 447.

13. Mary Rose D'Angelo, "'Abba' and 'Father': Imperial Theology and the Jesus Traditions," *JBL* 111 (1992) 623.

14. Richard Horsley, "Innovation in Search of Reorientation: New Testament Studies Rediscovering Its Subject Matter," *JAAR* 62 (1994) 1157.

15. On Roman imperial propaganda and its celebration of Augustus as the inaugurator of the new age, see Helmut Koester, "Jesus the Victim," *JBL* 111 (1992) 13.

16. Alan Segal, *Paul the Convert: The Apostolate and the Apostasy of Saul the Pharisee* (New Haven: Yale University Press, 1990) 164. Wayne Meeks, "Social Function of Apocalyptic Language in Pauline Christianity," in *Apocalypticism in the Mediterranean World and the Near East: Proceedings of the International Colloquium on Apocalypticism*, ed. David Hellholm (Tübingen: Mohr, 1983) 691. Charles Wanamaker, *The Epistles to the Thessalonians*, NIGTC (Grand Rapids: Eerdmans, 1990) 276.

17. According to Wilson, *The Hope of Glory*, 49, "The history of the early church evidences a tradition, established, it seems, primarily by the apostle Paul, of letter-writing as an instrument of moral instruction."

18. J. Paul Sampley, *Walking Between the Times: Paul's Moral Reasoning* (Minneapolis: Fortress, 1991) 10.

19. On Paul's thought world and the lives of believers between the death and resurrection of Jesus and his parousia, see Sampley, *Walking Between the Times*, 10. See also W. Trilling, *Conversations with Paul* (New York: Crossroad, 1987).

20. De Vos, *Church and Community Conflicts*, 169.

21. Jürgen Moltmann, *Theology of Hope: On the Grounds and Implications of a Christian Eschatology* (New York: Harper & Row, 1967).

22. Sampley, *Walking Between the Times*, 108.

23. For more on the connections between apocalyptic language and the hortatory tradition, see Malherbe, *Paul and the Thessalonians*, 80.

24. This is the case even if Paul did not write both of the letters and even if we have no way of determining whether the same community actually received both letters. I assume that Paul wrote only 1 Thessalonians and that the dating of 2 Thessalonians and concrete details about its audience are difficult to determine. Still, it is justifiable to assume that the audience of 2 Thessalonians knew and respected 1 Thessalonians because 2 Thessalonians often adopts and adapts the language and style of 1 Thessalonians.

The Second Letter to the Thessalonians

ABRAHAM SMITH

Reflecting Paul's general concern for the church's stability in the face of mounting hostility from its neighbors and a more specific concern about an enthusiastic brand of apocalypticism, the writer of 2 Thessalonians crafts a letter to encourage the believers not to veer from his truth or traditions (2:15). That truth focuses on both the present and the future. Indeed, the present experiences of opposition are read in the light of traditions about the future, including the coming judgment at the parousia (1:5-10) and the apocalyptic events preceding the day of the Lord (2:1-12). Furthermore, the present works of the church are authorized when they stand in accordance with traditions that demand support for the image, care, and continuity of the whole church while it awaits its Lord's future revelation.

Like 1 Thessalonians, the letter falls within the hortatory tradition. It is a letter of exhortation not simply because it uses explicit hortatory appeals through imperatives, as in its requests for stability (2:15), prayer (3:1-2), and correct discipline (3:6-15). Like 1 Thessalonians and other letters of exhortation from the period, 2 Thessalonians uses other forms of exhortation: calls for imitation (3:7*a*, 9; cf. 1 Thess 1:6), reminders of a teacher's previous instruction (2:5, 15; 3:7*b*-10), and reminders of what recipients already know (2:6; 3:7; cf. 1 Thess 4:2; 5:2). Like 1 Thessalonians and unlike other letters of exhortation, however, 2 Thessalonians uses prayer forms with a hortatory intent as well (1:3-4; 2:13-14, 16-17; 3:5, 16; 1 Thess 1:2-5; 2:13; 3:9-13; 5:23).[1]

Specific Occasion and Purposes of 2 Thessalonians. Since some scholars are reticent to assign 2 Thessalonians to Pauline authorship, the determination of the specific occasion and purposes of the letter can only follow after a brief discussion of the evidence. Both 1 and 2 Thessalonians have simple letter openings (1 Thess 1:1; 2 Thess 1:2) and more than one thanksgiving notice (1 Thess 1:2; 2:13; 3:9; 2 Thess 1:3; 2:13). In addition, in both letters one of the thanksgiving notices (1 Thess 3:9; 2 Thess 2:13) is followed by a wish-prayer (1 Thess 3:11; 2 Thess 2:16) that itself is subsequently followed by the transitional marker "finally" (λοιπόν *loipon*, 1 Thess 4:1; 2 Thess 3:1). These similarities could suggest that Paul wrote both letters. However, many scholars think the similarities simply indicate that the author of 2 Thessalonians (not Paul) mimicked a copy of 1 Thessalonians to give his work authority at a time when other followers of Paul were also composing works in the apostle's name (2:1-2; cf. 3:17). Furthermore, because scholars respect Paul's creative abilities, they suggest that the similarities are signs pointing to the pseudonymous character of 2 Thessalonians. Bonnie Thurston's lament is typical: "The question this evidence [of literary similarity] raises is why Paul would so slavishly follow his own precedent. Why would Paul use his own work so unimaginatively?"[2]

Arguments for or against Pauline authorship of 2 Thessalonians usually have to reckon with stylistic differences (e.g., the relatively limited diction of 2 Thessalonians), the different tones of the letters (e.g., the apparently "cooler" tone of 2 Thessalonians), and different uses of eschatology (e.g., the use of futuristic eschatology to create a distinction between believers and outsiders in 1 Thessalonians and its use to critique an overrealized eschatology within the Christian community in 2 Thessalonians).

While judgments can vary on each of these points, perhaps the most salient argument against Paul's authorship is that the letter seeks to authenticate itself from other apparently spurious letters (cf. 3:17). But it is difficult to understand how anyone could write a forgery while an author was still alive.

Any individual piece of evidence against Pauline authorship of 2 Thessalonians is not sufficient; however, the cumulative effect of these pieces of evidence leans more against it. Whatever one's conclusions about the debate, the force of this commentary's examination suggests that the more crucial matters are the difference in what occasioned the two letters and their common testament to the continuing influence of Paul's apocalyptic gospel.

As for the occasion of 2 Thessalonians, two issues appear to be prominent. On the one hand, the writer (as with Paul in 1 Thessalonians) has a general concern for stability in the face of continuing hostility from the congregation's neighbors. The writer of 2 Thessalonians assumes that the earlier opposition and loss of prestige faced by the Thessalonians at its foundation and shortly thereafter have not abated. In 2 Thessalonians the congregation is enjoined to "stand firm and hold fast to the traditions" (2:15), and the writer implores God to strengthen "the hearts" of the congregation (2:17) because of the mounting afflictions they are suffering from unbelievers. In this respect 2 Thessalonians is generally similar to 1 Thessalonians, and it is not surprising that the second letter mimics the first in form and diction.

On the other hand, a new issue emerges in 2 Thessalonians—namely, the introduction of an enthusiastic brand of apocalypticism, a view that compensates for the letter recipients' loss of power through an overrealized eschatology. Koester persuasively argues that the origin of the enthusiastic message—even if its proponents justified it on the basis of 1 Thessalonians—actually lies in "the apocalyptic fervor of the second half of the first century."[3] It is not surprising that the writer uses several examples of apocalyptic material (assuming that the material will be convincing to his hearers) not to *support* the enthusiasm, but to *counter* it. Moreover, the writer's use of 1 Thessalonians is both plentiful (to show adequate acquaintance with it) and non-enthusiastic (to highlight the importance of not abandoning the everyday world as the enthusiasts would likely advocate).[4]

It is not necessary, then, to see 2 Thessalonians as Paul's correction of his own earlier writing, as some scholars purport. Nor need one postulate 2 Thessalonians as an argument advanced to dispute the claims of Colossians and Ephesians (though 2 Thessalonians does critique a realized eschatology on the order of the ones found in those letters). Rather, Earl Richard's hypothesis about 2 Thessalonians seems to be on target. The work was composed "to discredit the claims, made in Paul's name, of apocalyptic preachers which were causing alarm within the community (2:2) and social unrest within its ranks (3:6-12)."[5] It is critical to note, moreover, that Paul's apocalyptic thought (whether or not he wrote 2 Thessalonians) influenced the church that read 2 Thessalonians. Thus both 1 and 2 Thessalonians are apocalyptic documents, but the latter works against an enthusiastic brand of apocalypticism.

With these brief remarks about the letters' occasions and purposes, we are closer to understanding the circumstances and thought patterns of 1 and 2 Thessalonians. Another necessary step, however, is to consider some of the literary conventions of the day, to see how letters were read and heard in Paul's time in terms both of the various parts of ancient letters and of the special acoustical features that shaped the flow and argument of ancient letters.

FOR FURTHER READING

Commentaries

Malherbe, Abraham J. *The Letters to the Thessalonians.* AB 32B. New York: Doubleday, 2000.

Porter, Stanley E., and Jeffrey A. D. Weima. *An Annotated Bibliography of 1 and 2 Thessalonians.* NTTS 26. Leiden: Brill, 1998.

ENDNOTES

1. On the hortatory function of prayer forms, see Abraham J. Malherbe, *Paul and the Thessalonians* (Philadelphia: Fortress, 1987) 77.

2. Bonnie Thurston, *Reading Colossians, Ephesians, and 2 Thessalonians: A Literary and Theological Commentary* (New York: Crossroad, 1995) 160.

3. Koester, "From Paul's Eschatology to the Apocalyptic Schemata of 2 Thessalonians," 455.

4. Koester, "From Paul's Eschatology," 456.

5. Earl J. Richard, *First and Second Thessalonians* (Collegeville, Minn.: Liturgical, 1995) 299.

THE FIRST AND SECOND LETTERS TO TIMOTHY AND THE LETTER TO TITUS

JAMES D. G. DUNN

The Pastoral Epistles—1 and 2 Timothy and Titus—are among the most valued of New Testament writings. Yet the Pastorals are among the most discredited of New Testament writings. Why this paradox?

On the one hand, the Pastorals have been valued for a number of important reasons. They helped to establish the classic pattern of ministry and church structure (bishop, presybter, deacon), which was crucial in the triumph of the early Catholic Church over severe challenges from Marcionites and Gnosticism, and which has enabled the church to endure for nearly two millennia.[1] They helped to establish a pattern of "the truth," "the faith," and "sound teaching" as the yardstick and bulwark by which to judge and ward off false teaching and heresy.[2] And, less immediately obvious, they helped to secure the place of Paul within the New Testament canon; the more controversial aspects of his theology (e.g., seeming criticism of Peter in Galatians and a church order without bishops and elders in 1 Corinthians) were made more acceptable by the portrayal of Paul as founder of the tradition, ecclesiastical and dogmatic, by which the church lived and ordered its life. Recognition of this character of the letters lies behind their designation as "the Pastoral Epistles," common since the eighteenth century.[3]

On the other hand, the Pastorals have been widely disparaged for more than a century and a half. This is primarily because a majority consensus of scholarship has been convinced since then that the Pastorals were not written by Paul but by a later hand. Despite the same consensus that pseudonymity (false claim to authorship) was quite acceptable in those days, it has been difficult to escape the more negative modern judgment on pseudonymous writings: Can writings be so fully valued that misrepresent their hero so seriously? Bound up with this has been the particularly Protestant suspicion that the radicalism of the authentic Paul (the Paul of the undisputed Pauline letters)[4] has been compromised and blunted by the ecclesiastical orthodoxy of the Pastoral Epistles.

In the face of such a polarization of respected opinion, what is the modern reader of these letters to make of them? Before turning to the letters themselves, a number of issues need some clarification.

A SINGLE GROUP OR SEPARATE LETTERS?

The fashion has been to treat the three letters together, to talk of the theology or ecclesiology of the Pastorals, rather than of each letter separately. This can be misleading, since 2 Timothy has a significantly different scope. Most notably, the concerns for good order in church, household, and state that are such a feature of the other two letters are quite absent in 2 Timothy. Indeed, were it not for the other two, the personal character of 2 Timothy might have been sufficient within scholarly discussion to secure the authenticity of 2 Timothy on its own.[5] Tied in to this is the question of the order of the letters. In recent discussion, for example, Luke Johnson has placed 2 Timothy first.[6] On the other hand, Jerome Quinn tackled Titus first, its longer preface being treated as a preface to the whole three-letter corpus.[7] And both Gordon Fee and George Knight follow the order 1 Timothy, Titus, 2 Timothy.[8] The traditional order (1 Timothy, 2 Timothy, Titus), it should be remembered, was determined largely by length; the corpus of Pauline letters in the New Testament canon was laid out in decreasing length, and of the three 1 Timothy was the longest and Titus the shortest. Overall, however, it does seem sensible to treat the three letters together. They are certainly closer to one another than they are to any other New Testament writings, including the undisputed letters of Paul. They share the same broad characteristic: Paul's counsel to two of his most important aides and coworkers. Indeed, 1 Timothy and Titus stand closely together. We need only compare 1 Tim 3:1-13 with Titus 1:5-9 (church officers), 1 Tim 5:1–6:2 with Titus 2:1-15 (good household management), and 1 Tim 2:1-2 with Titus 3:1-2 (civic authorities). But if 1 and 2 Timothy were written to the same person or situation we would not expect them to cover the same ground. More to the point is the similarity between the two letters to Timothy in terms of personal recollection (cf. 1 Tim 1:12-16 with 2 Tim 1:8-15; 1 Tim 1:20 with 2 Tim 2:17-18), personal commission (cf. 1 Tim 1:18 and 6:13 with 2 Tim 4:1; 1 Tim 4:14 with 2 Tim 1:6), and warnings against false teaching (cf. 1 Tim 1:3-7 and 4:1-3 with 2 Tim 3:1-5 and 4:1-4; 1 Tim 6:4, 20 with 2 Tim 2:14, 16, 23). And overall we find in all three letters the same high regard, as indicated by vocabulary and attitude, for "the faith"[9] and for piety/godliness,[10] and the same dismissive disparagement of alternatives.[11]

In view of the degree of cohesion between the letters, it does continue to make sense to treat them as a loose unit, sufficiently distinct as such within the New Testament canon. It is simplest, therefore, to treat them in their historic and canonical order. By analyzing each one in turn, however, we should be able to gain a clear enough sense of the emphases of each as well as of the whole. Since few people will read the complete corpus of three letters at a sitting, it is more important that we focus attention on the internal coherence and thrust of each section within the letters.

AUTHORSHIP

Given, then, that the Pastoral Epistles form a relatively closely knit group, we may assume that they were written by the same person. But who? The obvious answer, of course, is Paul the apostle, the author of the other ten letters that bear his name. After all, each of the three letters explicitly claims to be from Paul. But for most of the last 150 years the majority of New Testament specialists have been more impressed by the differences between the Pastorals and the undisputed letters. So what is the answer?

For the last 150 years or so the debate on authorship of the Pastorals has been rehearsed over and over again. Here it will be sufficient to indicate the scope of the debate in broad terms, if only to alert readers to the features and factors that give the debate continued vitality. This seems to be the wiser course, since it is all too easy for this question to become the dominant one and for the value of the letters to be obscured by what in the end are questions of secondary importance.

The main features of the letters that continue to persuade the majority of specialists that they were not written by Paul are as follows:

(1) First is the distinctive vocabulary and style of the Pastorals. The most striking feature is the much higher proportion of *hapax legomena* (words occuring only once or only in the Pastorals) than in the other Paulines (between twice and four times as many as any other Pauline letter).[12] Style, of course, has an intangible quality, but it also leaves fingerprints in, for example, the choice of words, the use of conjunctions, and the structure of sentences; and in contrast to the typical liveliness of the earlier Pauline letters, the Pastorals seem consistently more prosaic.[13] These differences cannot be adequately explained by different subjects or different moods. The writer seems to be drawing from a different vocabulary pool, the writing to be of a different character. The perspective, in other words, seems to be at one remove from Paul, or one generation after Paul.

(2) The degree to which "faith" has been formalized into "the faith" (see endnote 9). The mood of the Pastorals is much less that of preaching faith than of preserving the faith, not so much of evangelism as of containment. In particular, it is notable that the most characteristic notes of Paul's gospel and theology appear in "faithful sayings" and formulae to be preserved (1 Tim 1:15; 2 Tim 1:9; 2:11-13; Titus 3:4-7). Clearly evident is the sense of a faith that was initially formulated by Paul and that has now to be passed on to future generations (esp. 2 Tim 1:12-14; 2:1-2).

(3) The threats to the gospel seem likewise to be different. Whereas the challenge from Christian Jews (usually designated "Judaizers") runs through the earlier Pauline correspondence (Romans 2:1–4; 2 Cor 2:14–4:6; 10–13; Galatians; Phil 3:2-11), all we hear in the Pastorals are at best echoes of that earlier dispute (1 Tim 1:7; Titus 1:10, 14). Notable again is the fact that the "faithful sayings" and formulae just mentioned lack the polemical thrust against Jewish Christians so characteristic of the

earlier Paul. So, too, the degree of precision with which Paul aimed his counterthrusts, whether in matters of theology or those of praxis, enables the reader to gain a quite clear picture of the positions to which Paul objected. But in the Pastorals there is no such precision, and the dismissive fulminations generate much more heat than light.

(4) The degree of church structure seems more developed than anything in the earlier Paul. A distinctive office of "overseer (bishop)" has emerged (1 Tim 3:1; Titus 1:7), as also that of "deacon (minister)" (1 Tim 3:8). These titles were already in use in Phil 1:1, but the concept of a formal office is more in evidence. Likewise, the office of "elder" appears in the Pauline corpus for the first time (1 Tim 5:17; Titus 1:5). It looks as though on this point the Pastorals share the hindsight perspective evident also in Luke's account of Paul's mission (Acts 14:23; 20:17), of which there is no trace in the earlier Pauline letters.[14] It may also be significant, then, that the only use of the term "charism," so central to Paul's concept of the body of Christ (Rom 12:6-8; 1 Corinthians 12:1), is limited to talk of Timothy's charism given through the laying on of hands in the past (1 Tim 4:14; 2 Tim 1:6).

(5) Finally, what might be described as a greater accommodation with the norms and structures of contemporary society should be mentioned. It is not simply the readiness to accept the political structures of the day (1 Tim 2:1-2; Titus 3:1); that was already true in Rom 13:1-7. It is, rather, the degree to which the contemporary ideal of good household order has become also a norm for the writer of 1 Timothy and Titus (1 Timothy 5; Titus 2) and, indeed, a norm for the good order of the church (1 Tim 2:11-15; 3:4-5, 12, 15; 5:14). This accommodation is evident also in the fact that virtues like "dignity, seriousness, respectfulness"[15] and "prudence, moderation"[16] are so strongly commended, not least because of the respect they commanded within the wider society.

These features have to be weighed alongside (or against) two others in particular. One has already been mentioned: the fact that all three letters explicitly claim to have been written by Paul (1 Tim 1:1; 2 Tim 1:1; Titus 1:1). Against the view that they were pseudonymous, and known to be so, is the universal acceptance of them from the earliest attributions as written by Paul himself (from at least 200 CE). The other is the strikingly personal character of several passages within the letters, particularly 2 Tim 4:6-21 and Titus 3:12-13. It is difficult to conceive of a later writer's having composed such passages except as an attempt to deceive his readers.

The issue of pseudonymity is a difficult one for us to grasp at this distance, especially when the importance of copyright and the wrongs of plagiarism have become such fundamental features of modern literary culture. Suffice it to say that the principles were not at all so clearly grasped or the conventions so firmly drawn in those days. Of particular importance here is the fact that, particularly within the Jewish literary tradition, there seem to have been other conventions that rather cut across the issue. One was the attribution of writings to heroes from the past (Gen 5:24).[17]

More to the point here is what we might call the concept of "living tradition." That is, within Israel's history we can readily discern several different streams of tradition, each originating with an authoritative earlier figure, but elaborated and extended within the immediate circle of that figure's disciples and retained under the name of the originator of the tradition. The Pentateuch is generally recognized to have reached its final form in this way, and the present book of Isaiah to be the work of two or three generations. Just as David was remembered as the originator of a still-growing collection of psalms,[18] so also to Solomon was attributed a sequence of wisdom writings (most notably Proverbs and Ecclesiastes). A close comparison of the Gospels, even of the Synoptic Gospels alone, indicates that there was a basically similar elaboration and extension of the Jesus tradition within the Gospel format. John 21:24 attests to the activity of a circle around the Fourth Evangelist, who had at least some hand in the final form of John's Gospel. The Pastorals can be readily seen in similar terms. The point is that this practice was familiar and that attribution of the extended literary form to the originator of the form would not have been regarded as unacceptable or deceptive.[19]

There is a corollary to this that is often neglected but should certainly be given some attention. If pseudonymous practice of this or some similar sort was accepted at the time of the writing of the Pastorals (so that the issue of pseudonymity loses its ethical dimension), then it follows that the pseudonymous writing would be attributed to the originator only if it was deemed to be an appropriate elaboration or extension of the original.[20] That is to say, the very factors of style and content that have moved modern scholars to deny Pauline authorship to the Pastorals would *not* have been deemed sufficient by the first readers to deny the letters to Paul. The Pastorals would have been deemed authentically Pauline; therefore, their attribution to Paul would have caused no problem. Already, in this early judgment, the canonical definition of what was and what was not "Pauline" was being determined.

If the problem of pseudonymity may thus be defused, what about the other feature that counts so strongly for Pauline authorship: the personal notes? There are probably only two choices here. Either they carry with them the whole sweep of the Pastorals, despite their differences from the earlier Paulines, in which case we have to envision Paul writing later in his career, his style changed by experiences later in a ministry extended beyond the limit suggested by Acts.[21] Or these personal notes were, in fact, brief notes, most of them dispatched or even smuggled from Paul's last imprisonment, treasured by the churches that received them, and used as a basis for the Pauline elaborations that are the Pastorals.[22]

Whatever the current answer, it is important not to let the issue of authorship weigh too heavily in one's appreciation of and response to the Pastorals.[23] On the one hand, if they were written by Paul himself, then we have to speak of a "late Paul" and of the earlier undisputed letters as bearing witness to the "early Paul." Recognition of Pauline authorship must not allow us either to blur the different and distinctive perspective we find in the Pastorals or to homogenize a thirteen-letter Paul. On the other hand, if they were written during some period subsequent to Paul's death, that should not allow us to justify their being devalued and treated as sub-Pauline.[24] They are *also* Pauline and show how the Pauline churches perceived and evaluated their great founding apostle and the heritage he left with them. Either way, they are invaluable evidence of how Christianity and Christian theology faced the challenges of the second generation and/or post-Pauline period.

DATE AND RECIPIENTS

These considerations permit a much briefer resolution of other introductory questions. If the Pastorals were written late in Paul's life (cf. 2 Tim 4:16-18), then we have to envisage that Paul had been freed from his (first) imprisonment in Rome (Acts 28:1), and that he had deemed it more important to return to the Aegean than to pursue his earlier plans to go to Spain (Rom 15:23-24, 28).[25] This would explain such references as 1 Tim 1:3 and Titus 1:5 and allow us to date the letters in the mid-60s. If, however, the letters are pseudonymous, then a date sometime between the deaths of Paul (early 60s) and of Ignatius (c. 110s) seems appropriate. This is principally because the more developed ecclesiology of the Pastorals seems to be in the process of formation and still some way from the monoepiscopacy that Ignatius promotes but also was able to assume.[26] Nor has the false teaching attacked in the Pastorals such clear shape as that attacked in the 110s by Ignatius. Some have argued for a still later date, but the later the exercise the less likely that a pseudonymous writing would have been accepted as still genuinely Pauline. Most elect for a date in the late 80s or 90s of the first century. The possible points of contact with Acts, which have suggested to some that Luke was the author,[27] also point to the latter years of the first century.

If the letters were written by Paul, then the recipients were those specified—Timothy and Titus—each serving as an apostolic delegate, Timothy in Ephesus (1 Tim 1:3) and Titus in Crete (Titus 1:5). If, on the other hand, the letters are post-Pauline, the naming of the recipients as Timothy and Titus may indicate either that they were indeed the recipients or that they were the inspiration behind the letters (What would Paul want to say to us were he still alive?),[28] or simply that the letters were from the close circle of Paul's coworkers or immediate successors. Either way, Timothy and Titus are clearly envisaged as Paul's representatives, functioning in a unique role between church founder and local leadership. At the same time, we should not confuse the letters' personal address with their function. Whatever their origin, they were not intended for the eyes and ears of Timothy and Titus alone. The plural form of the final "you" in each case indicates that these letters were intended to be read to the church as a whole and, therefore, to function as manuals of discipline for the benefit of whole congregations. As such, their value in effect bypasses the question of the historical status of Timothy and Titus, just as it outlasts the death of Paul.

The Eastern Mediterranean in Paul's Time

WHO WERE THE FALSE TEACHERS?

The other great debate concerns the opponents regularly castigated in the letters. It is difficult, however, to gain a firm handle on them, and the general assumption that they formed a single front should certainly be put under question. Most of the attack on false teaching is, as already indicated, vague and imprecise, often using conventional vilification of opponents, real or imagined.[29] There are only a few clear indications of concrete issues: 1 Tim 4:3, they forbid marriage and advocate abstinence from certain foods; 2 Tim 2:18, they claim that "the resurrection has already happened." These references, taken with the allusion to "knowledge [γνῶσις *gnōsis*] falsely so called" (1 Tim 6:20), could certainly be taken to imply an early form of Gnosticism, since all three features are present in the Gnostic systems of the later second century.

On the other hand, the references to those "desiring to be teachers of the law" (1 Tim 1:7) and to "those of the circumcision" (Titus 1:10) point to a Jewish dimension—that is, not just to Jewish elements in some syncretistic mix, but to people who prized a Jewish identity and valued the principal Jewish identity marker (the law). The repeated references to "myths" (1 Tim 1:4; 4:7; 2 Tim 4:4; Titus 1:14) and to "genealogies" (1 Tim 1:4; Titus 3:9) in themselves could point in several directions, but the reference to "Jewish myths" (Titus 1:14) and the association of "genealogies" with "fights over the law" (Titus 3:9) again indicate an opposition more likely to be rooted in the local synagogues than anywhere else. The attempt to combine both sets of features into something like "Judaizing Gnosticism" (as many suggest)[30] is not very helpful, since "Judaizing" means "living as a Jew," and no gnostic system that we know of taught the need to Judaize.

As with other letters (notably 1 Corinthians), the older assumption that the threats addressed could be categorized simply in terms of religious or theological systems has been heavily qualified in more recent discussions. Social and financial pressures were obviously also a factor, particularly in 1 Timothy (1 Tim 2:9; 3:3, 8; 5:8, 17-19; 6:5-10, 17-19),[31] and the role of women in certain aspects of community life obviously worried the writer (1 Tim 2:9-15; 5:3-16).[32] In reading such passages we should recall how little we know of the situations envisaged and how much more complex they no doubt were than we can now appreciate. Straightforward transposition to contemporary situations of advice given in the Pastorals will rarely be wise.

THE THEOLOGY OF THE PASTORALS

The value of the Pastorals is reflected on at each stage throughout the following pages. Here we need simply to draw attention to the principal features.

(1) One is the strongly re-emphasized Jewish heritage. It is particularly clear in the insistence on affirming one of Israel's principal foundation pillars: the oneness of God (1 Tim 1:17; 2:5; 6:15-16). Other important features include the use of Israel's own self-identity: "the household of God, which is the church of the living God" (1 Tim 3:15 NRSV); "a people of his own" (Titus 2:14).[33] This is all the more important given that some opposition seems to have come from the synagogue. Here, in other words, we see not only early Christianity continuing to affirm its continuity and identity with its Jewish heritage, but also the importance to Pauline Christianity of that continuity and identity as integral to Christianity's own self-definition. It will be no accident that part of the same theology is the affirmation that God desires to save everyone (1 Tim 2:4, 6).

(2) The centrality of the christology and of "salvation" as the preeminent goal[34] is also clear, as the faithful sayings and creedal or hymnic formulae confirm (1 Tim 1:15; 2:4-6, 15; 3:16; 2 Tim 1:9-10; 2:11-13; Titus 3:4-7). The fact that God and Christ can equally be described as "Savior" (see 1 Tim 1:1) is not an indication of confusion but of a recognition that Christ functions for God and that God has acted through Christ. The most careful formulations of the relationship between God and Christ are given in 1 Tim 2:4-6 and Titus 2:13-14, which should hardly be played off against each other. That salvation is a process working out between the two appearings of Christ[35] is a strong reaffirmation of a characteristically Pauline emphasis. Even if expressed primarily in traditional formulae, this gospel is still a matter of living faith[36] and may, indeed, have been freshly reformulated to present Christ as a more effective claimant to the title "Savior" than any emperor or other god.[37]

(3) The importance of faith clearly formulated and of the church well ordered has already been noted. Notable here is the affirmation of good household order as the model or criterion for good church order[38] and the concern for a proper respectability, or better, respect-worthiness as a measure of Christian conduct. One need not speculate about any influence of delay of parousia (of which there is no overt indication) to see in the Pastorals more helpful guidelines for churches confronted by a suspicious and dominant non-Christian society than in some of the earlier Paulines.

(4) Notable in this connection is the way in which theology and ethics are thoroughly integrated in the Pastorals—evident, not least, in the flow of argument in several passages (e.g., 1 Tim 2:1-6; 4:3-5; Titus 2:1-15; 3:1-7). Theology was not a mere clinging to old formulae; it issued directly in practical corollaries for daily living. Nor were ethics simply a nervous conformity to bourgeois ideals; their rationale was deeply rooted in the gospel.[39] The importance of this observation for churches of all time can hardly be overemphasized.

(5) Not least of value is the enriching of the church's memory of Paul. Whether the portrait is Paul's own or the beginning of a modest hagiography, the fuller portrayal of Paul is certainly to be cherished—from his conversion (1 Tim 1:12-16), through his ministry (2 Tim 1:11-12; 3:10), to his final testimony of trust (2 Tim 4:6-8). This portrayal serves not least to establish and keep open the line of continuity and tradition begun with Paul and so helps to ensure that the Christianity that Paul did so much to shape and to spread remains in living communication with Paul, apostle to the Gentiles, model for the gospel preacher, and teacher of the church.[40]

FOR FURTHER READING

Commentaries:

Barrett, C. K. *The Pastoral Epistles.* New Clarendon Bible. Oxford: Clarendon, 1963.

Bassler, J. M. *1 Timothy, 2 Timothy, Titus.* ANTC. Nashville: Abingdon, 1996.

Collins, Raymond F. *1 & 2 Timothy and Titus: A Commentary.* NTL. Louisville, Ky.: Westminster/John Knox, 2002.

Davies, M. *The Pastoral Epistles.* Epworth Commentaries. London: Epworth, 1996.

Dibelius, M., and H. Conzelmann. *The Pastoral Epistles.* Hermeneia. Philadelphia: Fortress, 1972.

Fee, G. D. *1 and 2 Timothy, Titus*. New International Biblical Commentary. Peabody, Mass.: Hendrickson, 1984; rev. ed. 1988.

Guthrie, D. *The Pastoral Epistles: An Introduction and Commentary*. Tyndale New Testament Commentary. Leicester: InterVarsity Press, 1957.

Hanson, A. T. *The Pastoral Epistles*. NCB. London: Marshall, Morgan & Scott, 1982.

Harrison, P. N. *The Problem of the Pastoral Epistles* London: Oxford University Press, 1921.

Houlden, J. L. *The Pastoral Epistles*. Pelican New Testament Commentaries. Harmondsworth: Penguin, 1976.

Johnson, L. T. *Letters to Paul's Delegates: 1 Timothy, 2 Timothy, Titus*. The New Testament in Context. Valley Forge: Trinity Press International, 1996.

———. *The First and Second Letters to Timothy: A New Translation with Introduction and Commentary*. AB 35A. New York: Doubleday, 2001.

Kelly, J. N. D. *The Pastoral Epistles*. Black's New Testament Commentaries. London: A. & C. Black, 1963.

Knight, G. W. *The Pastoral Epistles: A Commentary on the Greek Text*. NIGTC. Grand Rapids: Eerdmans, 1992.

Marshall, I. H. *The Pastoral Epistles*. ICC. Edinburgh: T & T Clark, 1999.

Quinn, J. D. *The Letter to Titus*. AB 35. New York: Doubleday, 1990.

Other Studies:

Davies, M. *The Pastoral Epistles*. New Testament Guides. Sheffield: Sheffield Academic, 1996.

Donelson, L. R. *Pseudepigraphy and Ethical Argument in the Pastoral Epistles*. Tübingen: J. C. B. Mohr (Siebeck), 1986.

Harrison, P. N. *The Problem of the Pastoral Epistles*. London: Oxford University Press, 1921.

Kidd, R. M. *Wealth and Beneficence in the Pastoral Epistles: A "Bourgeois" Form of Early Christianity?* SBLDS 122. Atlanta: Scholars Press, 1990.

MacDonald, D. T. *The Legend and the Apostle: The Battle for Paul in Story and Canon*. Philadelphia: Westminster, 1983.

Miller, J. D. *The Pastoral Letters as Composite Documents*. SNTSMS 93. Cambridge: Cambridge University Press, 1997.

Prior, M. *Paul the Letter-Writer and the Second Letter to Timothy*. JSNTSup 23. Sheffield: JSOT, 1989.

Towner, P. H. *The Goal of Our Instruction: The Structure of Theology and Ethics*. JSNTSup 34. Sheffield: Sheffield Academic, 1989.

Verner, D. C. *The Household of God: The Social World of the Pastoral Epistles*. SBLDS 71. Chico, Calif.: Scholars Press, 1983.

Wilson, S. G. *Luke and the Pastoral Epistles*. London: SPCK, 1979.

Young, F. *The Theology of the Pastoral Letters*. New Testament Theology. Cambridge: Cambridge University Press, 1994.

ENDNOTES

1. According to the Muratorian Fragment (traditionally dated to about 200 CE), the letters were held "in honor in the catholic church for the ordering of ecclesiastical discipline" (18-20).

2. As its preface indicates, with its explicit reference to 1 Tim 1:4, Irenaeus wrote his great work, *Against Heresies* (late 2nd cent. CE), in the spirit of the Pastorals.

3. See P. N. Harrison, *The Problem of the Pastoral Epistles* (London: Oxford University Press, 1921) 13-16.

4. The undisputed Pauline letters are generally reckoned to be Romans, 1–2 Corinthians, Galatians, Philippians, 1 Thessalonians, and Philemon. Many would also include 2 Thessalonians and Colossians. Not many would add Ephesians.

5. See particularly M. Prior, *Paul the Letter-Writer and the Second Letter to Timothy*, JSNTSup 23 (Sheffield: JSOT, 1989). J. Murphy-O'Connor, "2 Timothy Contrasted with 1 Timothy and Titus," *Revue Biblique* 98 (1991) 403-18, discusses over thirty points on which 1 Timothy and Titus agree against 2 Timothy and vice versa, but overstates the disagreements.

6. L. T. Johnson, *Letters to Paul's Delegates: 1 Timothy, 2 Timothy, Titus*, The New Testament in Context (Valley Forge: Trinity Press International, 1996).

7. J. D. Quinn, *The Letter to Titus*, AB 35 (New York: Doubleday, 1990) 190-200. Titus seems to have been placed first of the three in the Muratonian Fragment—"To Titus one and to Timothy two" (17).

8. G. D. Fee, *1 and 2 Timothy, Titus*, New International Bible Commentary (Peabody, Mass.: Hendrickson, 1984; rev. ed. 1988); G. W. Knight, *The*

Pastoral Epistles: A Commentary on the Greek Text, NIGTC (Grand Rapids: Eerdmans, 1992).

9. "The faith"—1 Tim 1:19; 3:9, 13; 4:1, 6; 5:8; 6:10-12, 21; 2 Tim 1:13; 3:8; 4:7; Titus 1:1, 4, 13; 3:15. "Sound teaching/words"—1 Tim 1:10; 6:3; 2 Tim 1:13; 4:3; Titus 1:9; 2:1-2, 8. "Faithful saying"—1 Tim 1:15; 3:1; 4:9; 2 Tim 2:11; Titus 3:8. "The truth"—1 Tim 3:15; 4:3; 2 Tim 2:15, 18; 3:8; 4:4; Titus 1:14. "Knowledge of truth"—1 Tim 2:4; 2 Tim 3:7; Titus 1:1.

10. "Piety/godliness"—1 Tim 2:2; 3:16; 4:7-8; 5:4 (verb); 6:3, 5-6, 11; 2 Tim 3:5, 12 (adverb); Titus 1:1; 2:12 (adverb). "Good works/deeds"—1 Tim 2:10; 3:1; 5:10 (twice), 25; 6:18; 2 Tim 2:21; 3:17; Titus 1:16; 2:7, 14; 3:1, 8, 14.

11. 1 Tim 1:3-6; 4:1-3, 7; 6:3-5, 20; 2 Tim 2:16-17, 23; 3:15; 4:3-4; Titus 1:10, 15-16; 3:3, 9. "Myths"—1 Tim 1:4; 4:7; 2 Tim 4:4; Titus 1:14. "Empty/vain talk"—1 Tim 1:6; 6:20; 2 Tim 2:16; Titus 1:10.

12. See Harrison, *The Problem of the Pastoral Epistles,* 20-38. Despite qualifications, the basic contrast stands; see, e.g., Kelly, *The Pastoral Epistles*, 22-24.

13. Quinn, *The Letter to Titus*, 6, states that the "PE read in a calm, slow, colorless, monotonous fashion. Their tone is sententious, stern, didactic, sober, stiff, domesticated." Quinn is in danger of overstatement, but not by much.

14. 1 Cor 16:15-18 and 1 Thess 5:12-13 seem to be calls to respect for those who have displayed leadership initiative rather than for those already appointed to recognized posts ("elders").

15. Six of the seven occurrences of σεμνός, σεμνότης (*semnos, semnotēs*) are in the Pastorals (1 Tim 2:2; 3:4, 8, 11; Titus 2:2, 7; otherwise only Phil 4:8).

16. Four of the six forms of the word σώφρων (*sōphrōn*) are found only in the Pastorals—1 Tim 2:9, 15; 3:2; 2 Tim 1:7; Titus 1:8; 2:2, 4-6, 12.

17. The document usually known as *1 Enoch* is itself a compilation of five books.

18. Several more psalms attributed to David are found in the Qumran Psalms Scroll.

19. A fuller discussion can be found in J. D. G. Dunn, "Pseudepigraphy," in *Dictionary of the Later New Testament and Its Developments*, ed. R. P. Martin and P. H. Davids (Downers Grove, Ill.: InterVarsity, 1997) 997-1084, which draws particularly on D. Meade, *Pseudonymity and Canon* (Tübingen: Mohr, 1986). For an alternative view see E. E. Ellis, "Pseudonymity and Canonicity of New Testament Documents," in M. J. Wilkins and T. Paige, eds., *Worship, Theology and Ministry in the Early Church*, ed. M. J. Wilkins and T. Paige, JSNTSup 87 (Sheffield: JSOT, 1992) 212-24.

20. Tertullian (*Concerning Baptism* 17) reports that the reason why the *Acts of Paul* were not accepted as Pauline is that they attributed to the woman Thecla, an authority (in teaching and baptizing) that ran counter to 1 Cor 14:34-35.

21. The differences cannot adequately be explained by the use of different secretaries; the differences of emphasis and ethos are so integral to the letters that they have to be attributed to the author of the letters.

22. See P. N. Harrison, *The Problem of the Pastoral Epistles* (London: Oxford University Press, 1921) 115-35. The newest variation is that of J. D. Miller, *The Pastoral Letters as Composite Documents*, SNTSMS 93 (Cambridge: Cambridge University Press, 1997). In contrast, L. R. Donelson, *Pseudepigraphy and Ethical Argument in the Pastoral Epistles* (Tübingen: J. C. B. Mohr [Siebeck], 1986) 54-65, sees the personal notes as evidence of current pseudepigraphical practice.

23. As is the case, e.g., with Kelly, *Pastoral Epistles*, and Johnson, *Letters*.

24. Isaiah 40–55 is usually classified as Deutero-Isaiah, but who would even begin to think of these chapters as sub-Isaiah?

25. According to Eusebius (*Church History* 2.22) "Tradition has it that after defending himself the apostle [Paul] was again sent on the misistry of preaching, and coming a second time to the same city, suffered martyrdom under Nero."

26. Particularly Ignatius *Smyrneans* 8.

27. See particularly S. G. Wilson, Luke and the *Pastoral Epistles* (London: SPCK, 1979).

28. See particularly R. Bauckham, "Pseudo-Apostolic Letters," *JBL* 107 (1988) 469-94.

29. Documentation is provided by R. J. Karris, "The Background and Significance of the Polemic in the Pastoral Epistles," *JBL* 92 (1973) 549-64; A. J. Malherbe, "Medical Imagery in the Pastoral Epistles," *Paul and the Popular Philosophers* (Minneapolis: Fortress, 1989) 121-36.

30. The most recent variation is M. Goulder, "The Pastor's Wolves: Jewish Christian Visionaries Behind the Pastoral Epistles," *NovT* 38 (1996) 242-56.

31. See R. M. Kidd, *Wealth and Beneficence in the Pastoral Epistles: A "Bourgeois" Form of Early Christianity?* SBLDS 122 (Atlanta: Scholars Press, 1990).

32. See, e.g., A. Padgett, "Wealthy Women at Ephesus: 1 Timothy 2:8-15 in Social Context," *Int.* 41 (1987) 19-31.

33. The degree to which the Pastorals draw on the OT is not usually appreciated, but see M. Davies, *The Pastoral Epistles*, Epworth Commentaries (London: Epworth, 1996) 15-16.

34. "Save"—1 Tim 1:15; 2:4, 15; 4:16; 2 Tim 1:9; 4:18; Titus 3:5; "salvation"—2 Tim 2:10; 3:15; "Savior"—1 Tim 1:1; 2:3; 4:10; 2 Tim 1:10; Titus 1:3-4; 2:10, 13; 3:4, 6; "saving"—Titus 2:11.

35. First "appearing"—2 Tim 1:10; Titus 2:11; 3:4. Second "appearing"—1 Tim 6:14; 2 Tim 4:1, 8; Titus 2:13.

36. Often missed is the fact that the Pastorals speak more of "faith" (1 Tim 1:2, 4-5, 14, 19; 2:7, 15; 3:13; 4:12; 6:11; 2 Tim 1:5, 13; 2:22; 3:15; Titus 1:1, 4; 2:10; 3:15) than of "the faith."

37. For more detail see M. Dibelius and H. Conzelmann, *The Pastoral Epistles*, Hermeneia (Philadelphia: Fortress, 1972) 100-103; F. Young, *The Theology of the Pastoral Letters*, New Testament Theology (Cambridge: Cambridge University Press, 1994) 63-65.

38. So particularly D. C. Verner, *The Household of God: The Social World of the Pastoral Epistles*, SBLDS 71 (Chico, Calif.: Scholars Press, 1983).

39. See particularly P. H. Towner, *The Goal of Our Instruction: The Structure of Theology and Ethics*, JSNTSup 34 (Sheffield: Sheffield Academic, 1989).

40. See further M. C. de Boer, "Images of Paul in the Post-Apostolic Period," *CBQ* 42 (1980) 359-80.

THE LETTER TO PHILEMON

CAIN HOPE FELDER

The Letter to Philemon is one of the seven letters that almost all biblical scholars hold were written by the apostle Paul. Having only twenty-five verses in its English rendering from the 335 words in the apostle's Greek original, Philemon is the shortest among the Pauline epistles. The textual integrity of the letter is complete (i.e., fully preserved) in twelve of the major uncial manuscripts, and there is a near-total word agreement among the Greek texts of the letter, with but few orthographical differences (in vv. 2, 6, 9, 12, 25).[1]

Most commentators agree that Philemon reflects Paul's spirit, theology, moral tone, language, and style, as do 1 Thessalonians, Galatians, 1 and 2 Corinthians, Romans, and Philippians, the six other undisputed letters. Ancient church tradition links the letter to Paul, and the major catalogs of the New Testament canon from the early centuries (e.g., the late second-century Muratorian Fragment and Bishop Athanasius's thirty-ninth Festal Letter to his clergy in 367 CE, among others) list it among Paul's writings.

DATE AND PLACE OF WRITING

The Letter to Philemon differs significantly from Paul's other writings in two ways. First, it is not addressed to a church but to specific persons. Second, it is a letter of mediation to foster reconciliation between two individuals to whom Paul bears common relation as their spiritual leader: Philemon, a slavemaster, and Onesimus, a slave who fled Philemon's household but who has returned, concerned to make things right. This letter was Paul's plea for a renewed relationship between the two, but one on better terms than before in the light of their mutual faith as Christians.

Three options are usually set forth regarding the place from which Paul wrote the letter: Caesarea, Ephesus, or Rome. These are the places where Paul was imprisoned for considerable periods of time (although there were other occasions when he was taken into custody, as 2 Cor 11:23ff. reports). The dating of this letter depends in large measure on the location of its composition. If Paul wrote to Philemon from Rome, as seems most likely, then the letter was composed about 61 CE. If written during his imprisonment at Caesarea, the letter should be dated about 58 CE. If written from Ephesus, a date of 55 CE would be required.

The argument for Rome as the place of composition has particular merit. Since Philemon was the overseer of the Lycus Valley house churches at Colossae, in Asia Minor, Onesimus, his slave, would most likely not have remained within a short distance from the household he had fled but would have found his way to Rome, where other runaway slaves from the provinces tended to seek refuge. Although Rome sought to protect slave owners' rights and even encouraged bounty for assistance in returning fugitive slaves to their owners, it is not certain that Onesimus was, in fact, a runaway at all or, if he was, that he had become one without just cause.

Those who suggest Ephesus as the place of origin for this letter cite Paul's request that Philemon prepare lodging for his visit (v. 22) as an indication that Paul must have been imprisoned nearby. In addition to this, Ephesus was a provincial capital whose proximity to Colossae made it a more convenient destination for a slave without resources. Against this argument, however, is the fact, based on Col 4:7-9, that Onesimus and Tychicus were commissioned by Paul to carry letters from him to Ephesus, Laodicea, and Colossae. As for Caesarea as the place of writing, it is the most improbable choice of the three because of the difficulty in aligning events surrounding Paul's imprisonment there (see Acts 23–25) and the contents of this letter to Philemon.

The circumstance occasioning the letter to Philemon has strong bearing on Col 4:7-9, which mentions Tychicus ("beloved brother, a faithful minister, and a fellow servant in the Lord," Col 4:7) as someone who will update the Colossian church members concerning Paul's situation. The same text refers to Onesimus as traveling with him; Paul there described Onesimus as "the faithful and beloved brother, who is one of you" (Col 4:9). It is also instructive, and doubtless indicative, that this mention of Onesimus occurs just after the segment in Colossians that details the subordination codes pertaining to slaves and masters (Col 3:22–4:1; it should be noted that the injunction in Col 4:1, advising those who owned slaves to "treat your slaves justly and fairly, for you know that you also have a Master in heaven" is a unique principle for such stock codes).

FOCUS

At first glance, the Letter to Philemon seems to focus almost entirely on the issue of slavery. Paul was imprisoned or under house arrest (vv. 9, 13, 23) as he wrote; nevertheless, he was able to provide refuge for the slave Onesimus, who for some reason had fled the household of his master, Philemon. Paul appeals to Philemon as a friend and fellow Christian to take Onesimus back and to receive him without penalty or prejudice, in view of the slave's conversion and new life in Christ, their common Lord. Thus the reference to Onesimus as a "beloved brother"; Onesimus had become a Christian in the interim between leaving Philemon's household and the time the letter was written. Paul's description of Onesimus as "my child, whose father I have become during my imprisonment" (v. 10) can be understood to mean that Paul was the primary human agent in helping Onesimus to become a Christian.

The view widely held across many centuries is that this is a fairly straightforward personal letter in which Paul petitions his friend Philemon to forgive and restore his runaway slave, who was both a fugitive and a thief. Now, various questions can be raised about why Onesimus left Philemon's household and why he sought out Paul. Had he been abused by Philemon? Had he, in leaving Philemon, caused him to undergo some financial loss? However, although Paul recognized Philemon's "claim" upon Onesimus, nothing in the letter provides warrant for the notion that Onesimus was a criminal fugitive who had stolen something from his master.

The central meaning and purpose of the Letter to Philemon concern the difference the transforming power of the gospel can make in the lives and relationships of believers, regardless of class or other distinctions. However, the way slavery has figured so prominently in modern history has obscured this deeper, more essential meaning and veiled the perennial significance of the letter. During the period of the European and American slave trade, many slave owners and other defenders of the system who laid claim to Christian leadership appealed to the Letter to Philemon to justify the racial stereotypes they held and the compliance they believed that Scripture requires from those under the slavery system. To be sure, the institution of slavery in the Roman Empire during the first century, the legal infrastructure that supported it, and the various moral judgments given in the New Testament regarding its legitimacy are issues that must be considered in reading the letter. However, close study of the text makes clear that Paul's primary focus is not on the institution of slavery but on the power of the gospel to transform human relationships and bring about reconciliation. There is no basis whatsoever for thinking of Onesimus as a progenitor of the African American slave, especially since the Roman Empire did not have a race-based policy for the institution of slavery, neither in the first century nor at any other time.[2] All things considered, the way Paul's letter to Philemon is viewed provides excellent opportunity for a case study about the ways in which a person's social location can serve as a tacit rationale for reading inappropriate values into the text, distorting the document's original intent.

Quite apart from the fact that it was the work of Paul, the inclusion of the letter to Philemon in the New Testament canon would be justified on the basis of its message about reconciliation. Lloyd Lewis draws attention to Paul's use of "family language" in the letter: "brother" (vv. 1, 7, 16, 20), "sister" (v. 2), "my child...whose father I have become" (v. 10), and the like. The frequency of use of the terms is so pronounced that the communal-family emphasis cannot be viewed as coincidental. Lewis highlights Paul's noble intent expressed in those terms of endearment; the apostle exposes "an unwillingness to canonize the social roles found in his environment."[3]

In addition to the many published studies that report traditional interpretations of the Letter to

Philemon, new studies have appeared seeking to buttress older views or to supply fresh perspective on how the letter should be viewed and explained. Sarah C. Winter has suggested that the Letter to Philemon was primarily written to a church and was only formally addressed to Philemon as the congregational overseer. The references to the situation between Philemon and Onesimus are explained as not so much dealing with personal matters as framing a paradigm for changing master/slave relationships into new opportunities for manumission and shared fellowship.[4]

Perhaps the most dramatic departure from the traditional understanding of the Letter to Philemon of late is found in the work of Allen D. Callahan.[5] Callahan seeks to dispel the idea that Onesimus was a slave at all, suggesting rather that he and Philemon were estranged biological brothers whom Paul sought to reconcile. Despite flashes of keen insight, Callahan's heavy reliance on "silences of the text" and his literal interpretation of Paul's words about Onesimus as "a beloved brother...in the flesh and in the Lord" (v. 16) as indicating a blood kinship between Onesimus and Philemon move the interpretive center of the letter too far from the more common and ancient understanding of Onesimus as a runaway slave.

Eduard Lohse calls attention to the interpretive center of the Letter to Philemon in his majesterial commentary, citing Martin Luther's influential evaluation of the Pauline writing:

> This epistle gives us a masterful and tender illustration of Christian love. For here we see how St. Paul takes the part of poor Onesimus and, to the best of his ability, advocates his cause with his master. He acts exactly as if he were himself Onesimus, who had done wrong. Yet, he does this not with force or compulsion, as lay within his rights; but empties himself of his rights in order to compel Philemon to waive his rights.[6]

Luther's observation conveys his view that Onesimus had done something wrong, yet exactly who in the letter is the injured party or real victim has remained open to debate. It is quite possible, for example, that Onesimus's only offense was leaving the household of a master—Philemon—who had abused him in some way. There is greater warrant for such a scenario than for viewing Onesimus as a lazy or dishonest servant—the view found in the folklore that circulated among the ruling classes of the modern Western world, especially those who championed and benefited from the institution of slavery.

While Paul's letter to Philemon does not focus on the issue of slavery, it certainly offers clues that help to clarify the apostle's moral stance on the issue. Paul was aware of the provisions in the Hebrew Bible that sanctioned some forms of slavery despite the abhorence of the Hebrews for the long period of their own bondage in Egypt. And, as a Roman citizen, he certainly knew the legal warrants for the system as practiced across the empire. He was astute enough to recognize that the role of a pronounced abolitionist would not only have been foolhardy for himself, despite his Roman citizenship, but it would also have been disastrous to the nascent Christian missionary movement. Such factors make all the more astonishing texts like Gal 5:1, "For freedom Christ has set us free. Stand firm, therefore, and do not submit again to a yoke of slavery"; or 1 Cor 7:21, which suggests that slaves should use every opportunity to gain manumission;[7] or 2 Cor 11:20-21, which castigates those who let others enslave them. These statements, rightly viewed, are hardly the words of someone who approves of the institution of slavery. On the contrary, they reflect an attitude consistent with the appeal made in the Letter to Philemon, making the words found there all the more poignant and significant, for Paul is also the one who brought Philemon into the faith.

FOR FURTHER READING

Commentaries:

Bruce, F. F. *The Epistles to the Colossians, to Philemon, and to the Ephesians.* NIGNT. Grand Rapids: Eerdmans, 1984.

Caird, George B. *Paul's Letters from Prison.* NCIB. Oxford: Oxford University Press, 1976.

Dunn, James D. G. *The Epistles to the Colossians and to Philemon: A Commentary on the Greek Text.* NIGNT. Grand Rapids: Eerdmans, 1996.

Fitzmyer, Joseph A. *The Letter to Philemon.* AB 34C. New York: Doubleday, 2000.

Knox, John. "The Epistle to Philemon: Introduction and Exegesis." *Interpreter's Bible.* Vol. 10. Nashville: Abingdon, 1955.

Lohse, Eduard. *Colossians and Philemon.* Hermeneia. Philadelphia: Fortress, 1971.

Metzger, Bruce M. *A Textual Commentary on the Greek New Testament.* New York: United Bible Societies, 1971.

O'Brien, Peter T. *Colossians, Philemon.* WBC. Waco, Tex.: Word, 1982.

Osiek, Carolyn. *Philippians, Philemon.* ANTC. Nashville: Abingdon, 2000.

Thurston, Bonnie Bowman. *Philippians and Philemon.* SP 10. Collegeville, Minn.: Liturgical Press, 2004.

Other Studies:

Bartchy, S. Scott. ΜΑΛΛΟΝ ΧΡΗΣΑΙ: *First Century Slavery and the Interpretation of 1 Corinthians 7:21.* SBLDS. Missoula, Mont.: Scholars Press, 1973.

Bruce, F. F. *Paul: Apostle of the Heart Set Free.* Grand Rapids: Eerdmans, 1997.

Callahan, Allen D. "Paul's Epistle to Philemon: Toward an Alternative Argumentum." *HTR* 86:4 (1993).

———. *Embassy of Onesimus: The Letter of Paul to Philemon.* Valley Forge, Pa.: Trinity Press International, 1997.

Lewis, Lloyd A. "An African American Appraisal of the Philemon-Paul-Onesimus Triangle." In *Stony the Road We Trod: African American Biblical Interpretation.* Edited by Cain Hope Felder. Minneapolis: Augsburg Fortress, 1991.

Martin, Ralph P. *Reconciliation: A Study of Paul's Theology.* Atlanta: John Knox, 1981.

Meeks, Wayne A. *The First Urban Christians: The Social World of the Apostle Paul.* New Haven: Yale University Press, 1983.

Sampley, J. Paul. *Pauline Partnership in Christ: Christian Community and Commitment in Light of Roman Law.* Philadelphia: Fortress, 1980.

Winter, S. C. "Methodical Observations of a New Interpretation of Paul's Letter to Philemon." *Union Seminary Quarterly Review* 39 (1984).

Wright, N. T. *Paul for Everyone: The Prison Letters: Ephisians, Philippians, Colossians and Philemon.* London: SPCK, 2002.

ENDNOTES

1. On the orthographical differences, see Bruce M. Metzger, *A Textual Commentary on the Greek New Testament* (London/New York: United Bible Societies, 1971) 657-58.

2. See, among other pertinent studies, Frank M. Snowden, Jr., *Before Color Prejudice: The Ancient View of Blacks* (Cambridge, Mass.: Harvard University Press, 1963) 63-64, 69-71; W.L. Westermann, *The Slave Systems of Greek and Roman Antiquity* (Philadelphia: American Philosophical Society, 1955) esp. 102-9. For a helpful study on how scorn and rivalry were expressed among the diversified peoples unified under Roman imperialism, see A. N. Sherwin-White, *Racial Prejudice in Imperial Rome* (Cambridge: Cambridge University Press, 1970).

3. Lloyd A. Lewis, "An African American Appraisal of the Philemon-Paul-Onesimus Triangle," in *Stony the Road We Trod: African American Biblical Interpretation*, ed. Cain Hope Felder (Minneapolis: Fortress, 1991) 246.

4. S. C. Winter, "Methodical Observations of a New Interpretation of Paul's Letter to Philemon," *Union Seminary Quarterly Review* 39 (1984) 203-12. See also her study, "Paul's Letter to Philemon," *NTS* 33 (1987) 1-15.

5. Allen D. Callahan, *Embassy of Onesimus: The Letter of Paul to Philemon* (Valley Forge: Trinity Press International, 1997). See also Callahan's earlier article, "Paul's Epistle to Philemon: Toward an Alternative Argumentum," *HTR* 86:4 (1993) 357-76.

6. Cited by Eduard Lohse, *Colossians and Philemon*, Hermeneia (Philadelphia: Fortress, 1971) 188.

7. See, however, on the history of interpretation of the Greek wording in 1 Cor 7:21, S. Scott Batchy, ΜΑΛΛΟΝ ΧΡΗΣΑΙ: *First-Century Slavery and the Interpretation of* 1 Corinthians 7:21, SBLDS 11 (Missoula, Mont.: Scholars Press, 1973).

The Letter to the Hebrews

FRED B. CRADDOCK

The Christian faith grows out of and is sustained by the conversation between the church and its Bible. From this engagement, generation after generation, come the beliefs, the ethics, the liturgy, the purposes, and the relationships that define the Christian faith. To be sure, other voices enter the conversation, invited and uninvited, affecting the language used and the conclusions reached; but the primary and most influential partners are the community and the book. Of course, not all persons in the community are equally engaged in the conversation; some prefer to be silent, and some are silenced. Neither do all the books of the Bible participate equally. The reasons for this unevenness usually lie in the contents of the writings themselves, but not always. Sometimes there is quite a distance between what a document has to say and the church's willingness or ability to hear it. The Letter to the Hebrews is a case in point.

Why has Hebrews not had a stronger and more influential voice in the conversation between the church and the Bible? This is not to imply that this letter has been silent or silenced. On the contrary, Hebrews has been called on to say a few words at quite a few assemblies of the church. Most commonly it is to offer the benediction:

> Now may the God of peace, who brought back from the dead our Lord Jesus, the great shepherd of the sheep, by the blood of the eternal covenant, make you complete in everything good so that you may do his will, working among us that which is pleasing in his sight, through Jesus Christ, to whom be the glory forever and ever. Amen.
>
> (13:20-21 NRSV)

However, there are other, and some would say more important, moments in the worship service at which Hebrews is invited to speak. Among churches that use the ecumenical lectionary, Hebrews provides the epistle reading every year on Good Friday as well as on Monday and Wednesday of Holy Week. Likewise, during the Christmas season, the prologue to Hebrews (Heb 1:1-4) always sings the praise of Christ in tandem voice with the prologue to the Gospel of John (John 1:1-14). Congregations that observe the Annunciation to Mary (March 25) and the Presentation of Jesus in the Temple (February 2) hear every year brief passages from Hebrews. For two brief periods between Pentecost and Advent semi-continuous readings from this epistle give preachers and listeners opportunities for a bit more extended engagement with Hebrews. Interestingly, this letter, which speaks every year on Good Friday, never says a word during the Easter season or on Pentecost. Does this seasonal silence reveal something about the message of the book or merely the preferences of the conversation partner, the church?

The ecumenical lectionary reflects what is broadly true of the conversation between the church and the Bible; namely, that while Hebrews is invited to speak on occasion, the church is not as attentive to this voice as it is to others, such as Romans or 1 Corinthians. Scholars have intervened on behalf of Hebrews: The author demonstrates greater skill in the use of the Greek language than does any other New Testament writer, including Luke; Hebrews is the finest example of homiletical rhetoric available to us from the first century CE; this letter offers the most elaborate Christian reading of the Old Testament to be found in the New Testament; as a theologian, the writer of Hebrews is not inferior to Paul or John. These witnesses have been heard with appreciation, but the distance between the church and Hebrews remains. Why?

Before the search for reasons takes us inside the letter itself, a partial explanation may lie in the location of Hebrews within the canon. In a New Testament of 251 pages, Hebrews begins on page 208. Justified or not, a position near the end is read as a value judgment. The reader of the New Testament moves through the Gospels, Acts, and Paul's writings as a traveler on a well-lighted street, not quite familiar but providing enough names and addresses so as to remove the sense of one's being a stranger. However, once past Paul, the traveler finds the road uncertain, the houses dimly lit, and no familiar landmarks. The temptation is to stop and turn back to the Gospels, Acts, and Paul. After all, for these areas there are excellent maps.

In addition to its location in the canon, this letter suffers from a title that has a distancing effect on the reader. Granted, the title is a later scribal addition (more later), but still it is the first word the reader sees—large bold print over the entrance to whatever may await the one who enters. Other titles temporarily distance us—after all, we are not Galatians, Corinthians, or Philippians—but these are geographical designations. All of us have traveled enough to know that initial strangeness soon dissolves, and, once inside, we find ourselves more alike than different. But "Hebrews" is not a geographical term; it is ethnic, and ethnic distances are more complex, more difficult to negotiate, requiring more energy than some people are willing to expend.

Once inside, the reader never relaxes, never quite feels at home. The paragraphs are not written in such a way that they can easily be extracted for devotional or sermonic use; rather, they are carefully linked in one long sustained argument. The furniture seems permanently in place. As for the message of the argument, it is offered in an idiom strange to most readers. The writer is certainly not estranged from the Christian tradition that we meet elsewhere in the New Testament, nor is there any attempt to contradict it. Rather, that tradition is recast in categories and images that make vivid and vital what other writers were content to handle by allusion and implication. As a framework for understanding the redemptive work of Christ, the writer takes us inside the cultus of the tabernacle of Israel's wilderness journey. Priest, altar, sacrifice, atoning blood, and cleansing rituals—these are not the ancient and remote trappings of a people past but the stuff of the writer's presentation of what Christ has done and is doing for us now.

Most other New Testament writers, in making christological affirmations, use Ps 110:1: "The LORD says to my lord,/ 'Sit at my right hand/ until I make your enemies your footstool'" (NRSV). Only Hebrews compels us to look at v. 4 of that psalm: "The LORD has sworn and will not change his mind,/ 'You are a priest forever according to the order of Melchizedek'" (NRSV). Suddenly a shadowy figure, hardly holding a place in the margin of our memories, moves center stage in the explication of christology. Most readers are not in familiar country. The author assumes an audience familiar enough with the Old Testament to make detailed exegesis of its texts convincing, word studies delightful, and swift allusions powerful. Most congregations will acknowledge, "We are not that audience." Then can one argue that the theological and practical yield from the extra work required of the reader will make the effort well worth it? Without qualification, yes.

In this brief survey of reasons for the church's relative inattention to Hebrews, one other matter needs to be mentioned: the very stern nature of its imperatives. Even though the writer does not think the readers have reached the point of no return (Heb 6:9), that grim possibility is held up before them in very sharp language. Those who receive all the blessings of salvation and then fall away are beyond restoration (Heb 6:4-6). Those who willfully continue in sin face the fearful prospect of certain judgment (Heb 10:26-29): "It is a fearful thing to fall into the hands of the living God" (Heb 10:31 NRSV). Be warned by Esau, says the writer, who sold his birthright, then later sought to regain it but "found no chance to repent, even though he sought the blessing with tears" (Heb 12:17 NRSV). A letter containing such sentences is usually attractive only to those groups who deal easily in judgments and ultimatums. Certainly those churches that not only do not believe they are anywhere near such dangerous spiritual brinks but also do not believe that such brinks even exist will look to other writings for words more gentle and gracious. Especially for those who have luxuriated in a world of grace without ethical demand, who regard all moral urgings as quaint echoes of a puritan past, Hebrews is not welcome reading. Investigation into the situation of the letter's recipients will not dull these sharp warnings, but will very likely increase empathy and understanding for both the writer and the readers.

Perhaps this is the moment to caution all who read Hebrews, especially those who read with a view to teaching or preaching to others, to be patient. Be in no hurry to collapse the distance between the church and the text. Restrain the appetite for immediacy, for a "lesson for today." Trust that that will come in due season. Recall the reminder of Clement of Alexandria that the Bible does not yield its hard-won truths to every casual passerby. It is in the service of that needed patience that the following considerations are offered.

HISTORICAL CONSIDERATIONS

Author. The King James Version answers the question of authorship quite clearly: "The Epistle of Paul the Apostle to the Hebrews." That heading does not simply reflect the opinion of English translators in 1611; that opinion has a long history. In a papyrus from the third century CE, designated P^{46} in the Chester Beatty collection, Hebrews follows Romans among the letters of Paul. Both Clement and Origen, leaders in the great Christian intellectual center of Alexandria, judged the content of Hebrews to be from Paul. However, the style of the letter was so different from the remainder of the Pauline corpus that they concluded the actual writing to have been done by another, perhaps Luke or Clement of Rome. This uncertainty, growing out of the language and style of the letter, is preserved in a note at the end of Hebrews in the KJV: "Written to the Hebrews from Italy by Timothy."

In the Western church, early writers and lists do not include Hebrews among the letters of Paul. Tertullian, for example, suggested Barnabas, a candidate supported by three arguments: his close association with Paul (Acts 9:27; 13:2–15:39); his name, which Luke interprets as "son of encouragement" (Acts 4:36); Hebrews is called a "word of exhortation" (Heb 13:22; "encouragement" and "exhortation" translate the same Greek word [παράκλησις *paraklēsis*]; and the fact that Barnabas was a Levite (Acts 4:36). Hebrews exhibits a detailed knowledge of the Levitical priesthood. However, by the fifth century CE, under the strong influence of Augustine and Jerome, the Western church had accepted Pauline authorship, a position dominant until the Reformation.

The debate would not die. Students of both Paul and Hebrews found difficulty attributing to Paul the language and literary style of this epistle (if, indeed, it is an epistle), the centrality of the cultus, a priestly christology, and the admitted second-generation position of the writer. Would Paul, who insisted his gospel was not from any human source but from a revelation of Jesus Christ (Gal 1:11-12), have written: "It was declared at first through the Lord, and it was attested to us by those who heard him" (Heb 2:3 NRSV)? There has been no lack of other candidates, Silas, Priscilla, and Apollos among them. Luther's choice was Apollos, the Jewish Christian from Alexandria, eloquent and well versed in the Scriptures (Acts 18:24). Among recent scholars who have been interested to pursue the question of authorship, the most extended arguments have been in support of Apollos as well.[1]

There was a time when establishing the authorship of a book was vital in arguing for its canonicity. Today, concerns about authorship are almost totally related to the larger issue of interpreting the text. Knowing the author would be of some help, but neither canonical authority nor theological merit depends on having that knowledge. In the case of Hebrews, although the name is lacking, the writer does have some visibility. The author was a Christian who lived and thought within the apostolic tradition (Heb 2:3). Timothy had been a companion in ministry and might be again (Heb 13:23). The writer was temporarily distanced from the readers but expects to return to them soon (Heb 13:19, 23). Their situation is known in great detail, either through their leaders (Heb 13:7, 17, 24) or by direct association. The writer joined strong pastoral concern with the authority of either person or office. Both the instructions and the exhortations of the letter reveal a person well educated in Greek rhetoric as well as in Judaism, especially Hellenistic Judaism formed in part by the Septuagint, a Greek translation of the Old Testament. The Greek translation and not the Hebrew text provides the major lines and the subtler nuances of the writer's argument and appeal.

Date. As with most documents of the New Testament, establishing the time of writing of Hebrews cannot be done with precision or certainty. However, with the external and internal evidence available, a chronological frame can be ascertained. The primary external evidence is the letter of Clement of Rome to the church in Corinth. In chapter 36 of that letter, Clement quotes and paraphrases key passages from Hebrews 1:1–3. Clement's letter is generally, though not unanimously, dated 95–96 CE. Thus Hebrews must be dated earlier, but how much earlier? For an answer, we look for internal evidence.

It must be pointed out that three arguments for dating based on internal evidence that once held favor among commentators are now considered seriously flawed. First, the high christology of Hebrews (the pre-existence, incarnation, and exaltation of the Son of God) demands as late a date as possible. This evolutionary view of christology cannot be supported by the New Testament. For example, high christology can be found in Paul's writing (1 Cor 8:6; 2 Cor 8:9; Phil 2:5-11), and he quite possibly quoted from earlier sources. Second, since Hebrews describes the priestly activity and culture of Israel using the present tense (e.g., Heb 7:27-28; 8:3-5; 9:7-8), then the letter must be dated prior to the fall of the Temple in the year 70 CE. However, it is not the temple cultus but that of the wilderness tabernacle that is presented for comparison and contrast with the sacrificial work of Christ. As for the use of the present tense, this literary device is commonly used in the service of persuasion, and as we shall see, the writer was a skilled rhetorician. And finally, if the Temple no longer existed at the time of writing, the writer would have used that fact as a strong argument against the validity of Judaism's claims. The fault of this argument is not only that it is based on silence but also that it fails to understand the author's perspective toward Judaism and the Old Testament. The writer appeals to the Old Testament as a living Word of God and presents his case for the Christian faith as being in continuity with that Word. To read Hebrews as an attack on Judaism is to misread Hebrews.

What, then, can we say about internal evidence for dating? Concerning his message, the writer says: "It was declared at first through the Lord, and it was attested to us by those who heard him" (Heb 2:3 NRSV). This statement seems to place the author in the generation following the apostles. In addition, we are told that Timothy was still active in ministry (Heb 13:23). If this is the same Timothy who was a young companion to Paul, a date between 60 and 90 CE would likely be appropriate. Since Clement knew the letter by the year 95, then we may consider the years 60–95 CE as the chronological frame for Hebrews. Obviously, we lack precision, but fortunately, precision in fixing the date of writing is not essential for understanding the message of the letter.

Intended Audience. For interpreters of this letter, more helpful than knowledge of author or date would be the identification of the intended readers. Who were they? Where were they? Quite early the addressees were identified as "Hebrews" in a scribal conjecture that gave to the document the heading "To Hebrews." It is with this "title" that the writing appears in the earliest manuscript evidence of its existence, a papyrus (P^{46}) from the beginning of the third century CE. But the heading raises more questions than it answers. Quite likely the scribe who made the designation did so on the basis of the content of the letter itself. Let us do the same: Allow the letter to characterize its recipients, and then determine if we can give them a name and an address.

It must be said at the outset that the intended readers are Christian (Heb 3:6, 14; 4:14; 10:23), lest the heading to the letter lead someone to think the writing was addressed to Jews in order to convert them. The work is not polemical but a strong pastoral exhortation to a church in crisis. The writer knew the readers, having been with them earlier and now hopeful of a return soon (Heb 13:19, 22-23). The relationship between the author and the addressees is not clear. Urging the church to obey their leaders (Heb 13:17) implies that the writer is one in a position of even greater authority, either by reason of office or long relationship. The entire letter carries a tone of authority, of one who has the right and the obligation to remind, to instruct, to warn, and to encourage.

The readers along with the writer were second-generation believers (Heb 2:3-4), having been baptized (Heb 6:4-5; 10:22) and fully instructed (Heb 6:1-2). In fact, they had been believers long enough to have become teachers (Heb 5:12), but had been stunted in their growth. In a vigorous pastoral move, the writer on the one hand chastises them for their infantile spiritual state (Heb 5:11-14) and on the other hand assumes that they are capable of following a lengthy and complex christological argument (6:9–10:39). Their earlier instruction not only focused on their "confession" (Heb 3:1; 4:14; 10:23), perhaps a digest of the faith (is Heb 1:1-4 that confession?), but also included extended engagement with the text of the Greek Old Testament. The author's freedom to argue from nuances of the Greek translation of the Hebrew text and to make allusions to persons and events in Israel's history certainly implies a familiarity with that material on the part of the addressees.

But the readers are a faith community in crisis. Some members have grown lax in attendance at their assemblies (Heb 10:25), and commitment is waning. If the writer's urgings are problem specific, then we have in the letter a painfully clear image of their condition. Listen:

> Let us hold fast to our confession.
>
> (Heb 4:14 NRSV)

> Therefore lift your drooping hands and strengthen your weak knees, and make straight paths for your feet, so that what is lame may not be put out of joint, but rather be healed.
>
> (Heb 12:12-13 NRSV)

> See that you do not refuse the one who is speaking; for if they did not escape when they refused the one who warned them on earth, how much less will we escape if we reject the one who warns from heaven!
>
> (Heb 12:25 NRSV)

> Anyone who has violated the law of Moses dies without mercy "on the testimony of two or three witnesses." How much worse punishment do you think will be deserved by those who have spurned the Son of God, profaned the blood of the covenant by which they were sanctified, and outraged the Spirit of grace?
>
> (Heb 10:28-29 NRSV)

The writer does not think the addressees have already fallen away (Heb 6:4-8) or are yet in the condition of Esau, who "found no chance to repent, even though he sought the blessing with tears" (Heb 12:17 NRSV). In fact, better things are expected of these believers in view of their past record of love and good works, a record that has not totally come to an end (Heb 6:9-10). The author recalls that past during which they were cheerful, generous, and caring under most difficult circumstances and asks them not to abandon what they possessed as dearer than life itself (Heb 10:32-29).

What is the root cause of this crisis in the church? The text of Hebrews reflects not one but a number of factors. The delay of the final return of Christ may have had a demoralizing effect in the community (10:25, 35-39). It has been speculated by some that all the attention on the cultus in this letter implies a felt need among the readers for a more adequate liturgical and ritual life. The long-held theory that Hebrews addresses the problem of Jewish Christians returning to Judaism has been argued in terms of a more attractive cultus or of the security of a long and established tradition or of government protection from persecution, a privilege enjoyed within Judaism at various times and places. There is no doubt that the addressees had been under extreme external pressure. Some members had been imprisoned, and others suffered the confiscation of their property (Heb 10:34). They had not yet shed blood for their faith (Heb 12:4), but the writer does use the words "persecution" (Heb 10:33), "hostility" (Heb 12:3), and "torture" (Heb 13:3 NRSV). By no means the least painful form of pressure was public abuse and ridicule (Heb 10:33). More recent cultural and sociological studies of the New Testament have opened our eyes to social, political, and economic values that governed life in the Mediterranean world. Chief among those values were honor and shame. It is difficult to imagine that the Christians addressed in Hebrews were not facing daily the problem of suffering dishonor as followers of one who endured the shame of the cross (Heb 12:2).[2]

Whatever may have been the external factors contributing to the crisis of the community of readers, the fact that the writer responds to them with a lengthy and carefully argued christological presentation strongly implies that at the heart of the crisis was a christology inadequate for their social context. Perhaps they had a christology that was long on divinity but short on humanity, providing no way to fit the flesh and blood, lower than angels, tempted, crying and praying, suffering and dying Jesus into the larger scheme of God's redemption. Or perhaps their christology ended with the exaltation and enthronement of the Son and offered no good news of his continuing ministry of intercession for the saints. At least in the writer's view, the crisis can best be met not with improved structures or social strategies but with a more complete christology.

Can we, from the text of Hebrews, name and locate the addressees? Not with any confidence. Focus on the cultus does not necessarily place the readers in Jerusalem, nor does an assumption of the readers' knowledge of the Greek Old Testament argue conclusively for a Jewish past. Paul made heavy use of the Old Testament in exhorting the Corinthians, who were presumably of Gentile background. Jewish and Hellenistic thought had been long blended as evident in such writings as the Wisdom of Solomon and the vast religious-philosophical works of Philo of Alexandria. The clues in the text have been too many and too few, prompting theories of identification ranging from Christian Zionists on their way to Jerusalem to Gnostic spiritualists, pilgrims moving through this alien world to the eternal realms from which they came.[3]

If we broadly identify the readers as Hellenistic Jewish Christians, perhaps the best guess for their location is Rome. When the writer says, "those from Italy send you greetings" (Heb 13:24 NRSV), it is not clear whether the expression locates the writer or the readers in Italy. Similarities to 1 Peter, a letter written from Rome (1 Pet 5:13), argue for a Roman origin. However, early knowledge of Hebrews by Clement of Rome indicates a Roman destination, and what we know of the house churches in Rome makes that city a likely candidate as the location of the addressees.[4]

THEOLOGICAL CONSIDERATIONS

Any overview of the theology of Hebrews must be prefaced with two observations: (1) The theology of the epistle is woven into a lengthy argument and can be extracted only at the risk of the loss of its vitality, and (2) the theology of the epistle is rhetorically presented in the service of urgent pastoral exhortations and can be extracted only at the risk of the loss of its purpose. With these cautions in mind, the reader of Hebrews might benefit from a brief sketch of its major theological tenets, most of which the writer and readers have in common, and some of which represents the writer's imaginative elaboration of elements within that common tradition of belief.

God. This is not a Christian writing so preoccupied with the person of Jesus or the work of the Holy Spirit that God is pushed into the background as a silent assumption. On the contrary, God is the subject of the opening sentence, the closing benediction, and the narrative of redemption in between. God created and maintains the world through the Son (Heb 1:2-3, 10; 2:10; 3:3-4; 11:3). The entire redemptive career of Jesus, from incarnation to exaltation, was according to God's will (Heb 10:7). It is God who offered the promise of rest to Israel (Heb 3:7-11) and continues to hold out that promise today (Heb 4:1-11). God enters into covenants with those who trust (Heb 8:8-12) and holds always before us not only the prospect of judgment (Heb 9:27; 10:30-31; 12:23) but also the promise of a better home, an abiding place, a heavenly city of God's own building (Heb 11:10, 13-16; 13:4). To describe God's work of love toward believers, the writer uses categories of cosmic proportions. The category of time stretches from creation to consummation; the category of space reaches from the real and abiding world above (Heb 8:4-6; 10:1) to this temporary world of shadows, not substance.

The single most recurring characteristic of God as portrayed in this letter is that God speaks. God spoke through the prophets (Heb 1:1), speaks through a Son (Heb 1:2), speaks through the Old Testament (Heb 1:5-12; 4:3, 7; 7:21; 8:8-12) and through the Holy Spirit (Heb 10:15-17). Important to notice is the frequent use of the present tense; God's voice is a living voice, whatever the medium through which it comes.

Jesus Christ. No New Testament writer presents a more human Jesus than does the author of Hebrews. In fact, among all the titles used to refer to the Christ, the writer's preference seems to be "Jesus." That Jesus was one of us (Heb 2:11), tempted as we are (Heb 4:15), that he submitted to God in tearful and prayerful obedience (Heb 5:7-8), and was subject to death (Heb 2:14) constituted for some within and without the church a flaw in the Christian faith, an offense to the human quest for honor and place. But the writer of Hebrews, rather than denying or subordinating such a portrayal of Jesus, accents it as essential in the larger scheme of redemption. As a priest, Jesus had to be chosen from among the people (Heb 5:1) in order to be able to sympathize with their weakness (Heb 4:15) and to "deal gently with the ignorant and wayward" (Heb 5:2 NRSV). As we shall see, establishing that Jesus was a priest, even though not a Levite, is the extraordinary theological achievement at the heart of the letter. Being one of us not only qualified Jesus to be a merciful priest, but also equipped him to be the model to whom believers look. He is the pioneer and perfecter of the faith pilgrimage, showing his followers how to bear suffering, endure hostility, and disregard shame (Heb 12:1-3). Believers could not be expected to walk in the steps of one who had not walked in theirs.

However, this is not the total picture; Hebrews rivals the Gospel of John in moving beyond the historical evidence to declare who Jesus really is in the grand sweep of God's saving purpose. Anyone who charges that the writer of Hebrews has reduced christology in order to portray Jesus as a model and guide to a church in crisis has not read the entire book.[5] Jesus was lower than the angels "for a little while" (Heb 2:9), incarnate (Heb 1:6; 2:14-18; 10:5-7) to make purification for sins (Heb 1:3), but is now seated at God's right hand (Heb 1:3), a high priest forever, making intercession for the saints (Heb 4:14–5:10; 7:23-25; 8:1-2). In a related but slightly different line of reasoning, the writer presents Jesus as the mediator of a new and better covenant (Heb 9:15–10:18). At the end of the age, Christ will return "to save those who are eagerly waiting for him" (Heb 9:28 NRSV; 10:37). These can be the achievements only of one who was not only of the people but also of God, and that he was of God the writer leaves no doubt. Jesus' divinity is anchored in his pre-existence as God's Son, heir of all things, agent of creation, sustainer of all things, the very mirror image of God's glory and character (Heb 1:2-3). In their assemblies the readers most likely recited as a confession this inclusive, embracing Christ's pre-existence, incarnation, and exaltation.

Holy Spirit. Hebrews does not contain any trinitarian formulas. God is the primary character in the narrative, and the person and work of Jesus Christ occupy the central place in the argument developed. However, the role of the Holy Spirit is of such significance as to merit our attention. The Holy Spirit is a revealer, with words of the Old Testament being attributed to the Spirit (Heb 3:7-11; 10:15-17), although some of the same words are also attributed to God (Heb 4:3). The Spirit is also an interpreter of the Scriptures (Heb 9:8). In relation to Christ, it was through the Spirit that he offered himself as a sacrifice without blemish to God (Heb 9:14). In relation to the church, the Holy Spirit comes as gifts to the members, distributed according to the will of God (Heb 2:4; 6:4). Because Christians share in the Holy Spirit, any willful persistence in sin constitutes a grave sin against the Spirit, called by the writer an "outrage" (Heb 10:29). It may also be said of the Spirit in Hebrews that along with God and Christ, the Holy Spirit provides continuity in revelation and in redemptive activity between Israel and the church.

Church. Even though the word usually translated "church" (ἐκκλησία *ekklēsia*) occurs only twice in Hebrews (Heb 2:12; 12:23), it is quite clear that the writer is addressing a congregation, a group identified by a confession of faith (Heb 4:14), having been called together as a fellowship of brothers and sisters, of each other and of Christ (Heb 2:11-17). They assemble regularly to offer the sacrifice of praise to God (Heb 13:13), to provoke one another to love and good deeds (Heb 10:24), and to identify through compassion and sharing with those members who are imprisoned and tortured (Heb 13:3). In addition to love for one another, they are obliged to love strangers, showing hospitality (Heb 13:1-2), and to make every effort to be at peace with everyone (Heb 12:4). In the two modes of the Christian life, tenacious faithfulness and continuous pilgrimage toward the city that is to come—that is, possessing both stability and flexibility—Christ is the model. He was unwavering in faithfulness to God and undeterred as the pioneer leading his people to glory.

Scripture. The Scripture for the writer of Hebrews is the Old Testament in Greek translation, hereafter referred to as the Septuagint (LXX), even though points at which the writer varies from the LXX as we have it will be noted. Even though the author holds in common with the readers a Christian tradition, no writings from that tradition known to us are quoted as Scripture. The only words of Jesus that appear in Hebrews are at 2:12-13 and 10:5-7, where words from Psalms and Isaiah are attributed not to the writers of those passages but to Christ. The Old Testament comes to the reader in direct quotations, paraphrases, and allusions. Sometimes the original historical context is preserved; sometimes a passage is set in a new context. Interestingly, the writer's appropriation of the life and faith of Israel is drawn from an earlier appropriation by the psalmist.

Why does the author draw so heavily on the retelling of Israel's narrative in the psalms? Is the reason hermeneutical? That is to say, is the writer's use of Scripture simply a continuation of what the psalmist had done, putting an old story in a new setting? Or is the reason liturgical, using Israel's worship materials to interpret and enrich the culture and liturgy of the church? Of course, the reason may be more practical: the psalms best provide the grounds for the author's own theological and christological construction. In any case, in this rich and imaginative engagement with Scripture, the Old Testament never ceases to be the living voice of God. In fact, the authority of the Old Testament is enhanced for the readers by the writer's practice of introducing quotations from it with the phrases "God says," "Christ says," and "the Holy Spirit says." As we shall see, the writer of the epistle does not, in an act of interpretive tyranny, simply make irresponsible raids on the Old Testament to construct his own theological house, leaving among his scriptural sources not one stone upon another. Hebrews is not only the most extended treatment of the Old Testament in the New, but is also, along with Luke, the most respectful of continuity. The Bible tells one story, not two, and it is the story of God's saving initiative toward humankind. This metanarrative is carried forward through many subnarratives.

LITERARY CONSIDERATIONS

Those who teach and preach the Bible are increasingly aware that literary factors no less than historical and theological ones demand attention in an honest and fruitful hearing of the texts. Every writer wants both to say something and to do something, and therefore employs available literary devices and rhetorical strategies in order to be clear and to be effective. The careful reader of Hebrews will, therefore, want to attend to the manner as well as the matter of this work. To alert us to the literary and rhetorical skills of this writer and to prepare us for a fuller experience of reading and hearing, we here attend briefly to three matters: integrity, genre, and structure.

Integrity. Keep in mind that the word *integrity* used in a literary discussion refers only to the unity of a writing and not to the merits of its content. In other words, is any part of the text from a different hand or from the same hand but not intended by the writer to be a part of this document? The question arises with Hebrews only with reference to chapter 13.

Doubts as to whether chapter 13 was originally a part of Hebrews have been prompted by two observations, one minor and one major. The minor observation is that there is a noticeable shift in both mood and content between chapters 12 and 13. Such a break, however, is not uncommon at that point where a writer concludes an argument and then moves to a list of practical admonitions, usually rather standard, along with words of a personal nature (note Gal 6:11; Rom 15:14; 16:1). There is no Greek manuscript of Hebrews that concludes at chapter 12. The major observation concerns the contrast between the epistolary ending (Heb 13:18-25) and the non-epistolary beginning. In its opening Hebrews is similar to 1 John alone among New Testament epistles, the others having the customary address, signature, and greeting. This seeming discrepancy has prompted, among other theories, speculation that chapter 13 was added by another person, perhaps a secretary or a disciple or someone imitating Pauline conclusions in an effort to get Hebrews accepted into the Pauline corpus. Analyses of vocabulary and themes in chapter 13 have not supported such theories. In fact, the unity between this chapter and the main body of the letter has been so convincingly argued that very few voices are raised to the contrary.[6]

Genre. Accepting chapter 13 as integral to the entire writing does, however, pose another question: What does one call a document that ends as a letter but begins as an oration? I have in these introductory comments continued to use the traditional designation "epistle," and there are some students of Hebrews who do not find sufficient reasons to abandon it. After all, in the ancient Mediterranean world, "epistle" (ἐπιστολή *epistolē*) could be used to refer to writings ranging from private correspondence to public statements sometimes posted on bulletin boards. As for the difference between the beginning and the ending, Hebrews is not alone in that feature. For example, James is like Hebrews, but in reverse: It begins as a letter but ends as an oration. Nor can one argue conclusively that the content of Hebrews is not epistolary. Writings indisputably epistolary contain expositions of Scripture with application (1 Cor 10:1-14), moral instruction (Gal 5:13–6:10), and even strong exhortations that seem to interrupt the context (2 Cor 6:14–7:1). Even so, there is no major gain or loss to the interpreter in proving Hebrews is or is not a letter in any formal sense.

However, when a writing bears a self-designation the author has provided a category that helps the reader to understand both the purpose of the communication and the literary strategies employed to achieve it. Hebrews is, says the writer, a "word of exhortation" (Heb 13:22 NRSV). This expression occurs at Acts 13:15 to refer to Paul's speech in Acts 13:16-41, a speech noticeably similar to Hebrews. Harold Attridge thinks "word of exhortation" is "probably a technical literary designation for a certain kind of oratorical performance."[7] Whether or not there is sufficient evidence to support such a claim, the term does alert the reader to what the writer is doing. For example, every reader of Hebrews observes the alternation between exposition and application throughout the work. But to the question of whether applications are simply postscripts to a major expository argument or exposition of Scripture serves the application, the writer gives an answer: This is not a word of exposition but a word of exhortation. Even the most elaborate expository sections serve as fuel to keep alive a fire that seems to be flickering out. The writer rushes forward after each phase of the argument, eager to press home the lessons from every Old Testament text cited.

In the expression "word of exhortation" a host of literary devices and rhetorical strategies find their reason. Notice the force of an argument expressed in double negatives (Heb 4:15; 6:10; 7:20); the energy of words joined without the homogenizing effect of conjunctions (Heb 7:3, 26; 11:32-34, 37; 12:25); the sharp edges of vivid contrasts (Heb 7:18-20, 23-24, 28; 10:11-12); the cumulative effect of repeated phrases, such as "by faith" in chapter 11; and the pleasant attention-getting sounds of alliteration (Heb 1:1; 2:1-4; 4:16; 10:11). Metaphors abound, drawn from athletics, agriculture, education, architecture, seafaring, courts of law, and more. Verbs are noticeably in the present tense, and the language of speaking prevails over that of writing (Heb 2:5; 5:11; 6:9). Greek and Latin rhetoricians had long urged these and other strategies in the service of persuasion. There is no question that the writer is preaching.

However, simply to call Hebrews a homily seems not sufficiently to acknowledge its magnitude and complexity. After all, a homily, at least in the early days of the church, was an informal discussion or conversation about a topic (Luke uses the word in his Gospel at 24:14-15), and Hebrews exhibits the formal qualities of a carefully constructed piece of rhetoric. And a homily lacks the complexity of Hebrews, which is not solely a sermon but a sermon containing sermons (e.g., Heb 1:5–2:4; 2:5–3:1; 8:1–10:25). In this respect, Hebrews resembles Deuteronomy, which is Moses' final sermon to Israel but also is a collection of sermons within the sermon. If Hebrews is sometimes called a letter and sometimes a sermon, the reader will understand why both are true but neither is fully true.

Structure. While there is broad agreement about the rhetorical skills of the writer of Hebrews, there is no consensus about the structure of this sermon. Some analyses fail because they try to fit Hebrews into one of the three major types of ancient rhetoric: Is it forensic, persuasion concerning the truth of a past event; or deliberative, persuasion concerning a future decision or course of action; or epideictic (ceremonial), persuasion concerning the virtues of one whose life is worthy of emulation? The fact is that Hebrews contains some of all three. Other analyses prove inadequate because they locate focal points in the expositions or doctrinal portions and merely attach the exhortations as subordinate to the argumentation. The location and extent of hortatory materials make it clear that for the writer these sections are of equal if not greater importance for the purpose of the sermon. At the risk of making oversimplified divisions, the following broad outline may give some perspective:

Exposition 1:1-14
Exhortation 2:1-4
Exposition 2:5–3:6
Exhortation 3:7–4:16
Exposition 5:1-10
Exhortation 5:11–6:20
Exposition 7:1–10:18
Exhortation 10:19–13:25

Such a flat list does not register the cumulative effect of sections tumbling one upon the other. No analysis focusing on exposition alone can be fair to the whole. Perhaps all structural displays fail to the extent that they lose sight of the extremely urgent pastoral situation that prompted Hebrews. A concerned leader seeks to persuade a church from its path of decline in faith and communal love before it is too late. Every communication skill must be called into service because the end is to save a church, not to please an instructor in a rhetoric class. Perhaps this accounts for there being too many rather than too few clues to the structure of Hebrews within the composition; the writer speaks to a crisis.

All recent attempts to discern the structure of Hebrews have had to respond to the lifelong studies of A. Vanhoye.[8] He was impressed by the remarkable symmetry of the work and came to the conclusion that it was structured concentrically, moving toward and away from the central argument. This literary form is called a chiasmus, fairly common in briefer units in the New Testament. In this case, the chiasmus consisted of five parts: 1:1–2:18; 3:1–5:10; 5:11–10:39; 11:1–12:13; 12:14–13:25, on the pattern of ABCB´A´. This means that parts one and five are parallel, parts two and four are parallel, and part three is the centerpiece. Support for Vanhoye's analysis has been only partial; but reading Hebrews in this pattern has been stimulating, and modifications of his conclusions have found their way into much of the literature on Hebrews.[9]

A major problem with Vanhoye's and other similar analyses, however, is a practical one. Granted, Heb 7:1–10:18 is a major and complex section for which the writer gradually prepares the reader, but is it the climax? If so, one would expect that after Heb 10:18 the arguments and exhortations would draw heavily from the theological achievement of that central section; otherwise, why have the climax in the center of the composition? But such is not the case. Chapters 11–13 make only minimal use of the lengthy argument about Christ's priesthood. The final three chapters move the reader to a climax of intellectual, emotional, and volitional energy at the point where homiletically it belongs: at the end.

FOR FURTHER READING

Commentaries:

Attridge, H. W. *A Commentary on the Epistle to the Hebrews.* Hermeneia. Philadelphia: Fortress, 1989.

Bruce, F. F. *The Epistle to the Hebrews.* NICNT. Rev. ed. Grand Rapids: Eerdmans, 1990.

Buchanan, G. W. *Hebrews.* AB 36. Garden City, N.Y.: Doubleday, 1972.

Ellingworth, P. *The Epistle to the Hebrews: A Commentary on the Greek Text.* NIGTC. Grand Rapids: Eerdmans, 1993.

Gordon, Robert P. *Hebrews.* Readings: A New Biblical Commentary. Sheffield: Sheffield Academic Press, 2000.

Isaacs, Marie E. *Reading Hebrews and James: A Literary and Theological Commentary.* Reading the New Testament. Macon, Ga.: Smyth & Helwys, 2002.

Jewett, R. *Letter to Pilgrims.* New York: Pilgrim, 1981.

Koester, Craig R. *Hebrews.* AB 36. New York: Doubleday, 2001.

Lane, W. L. *Hebrews 1–8; Hebrews 9–13.* WBC 47A and 47B. Dallas: Word, 1991.

Montefiore, H. W. *A Commentary on the Epistle to the Hebrews.* Harper's NT Commentary. New York: Harpers, 1964.

Williamson, R. *The Epistle to the Hebrews.* London: Epworth, 1965.

Wilson, R. M. *Hebrews.* NCBC. Grand Rapids: Eerdmans, 1987.

Other Studies:

Hay, David M. *Glory at the Right Hand: Psalm 110:1 in Early Christianity.* SBLMS. Nashville: Abingdon, 1973.

Hughes, Graham. *Hebrews and Hermeneutics.* SNTSMS. Cambridge: Cambridge University Press, 1979.

Hurst, L. D. *The Epistle to the Hebrews: Its Background of Thought.* SNTSMS. Cambridge: Cambridge University Press, 1990.

Käsemann, E. *The Wandering People of God.* Translated by R. Harresville and I. Sandberg. Minneapolis: Augsburg, 1984.

Levine, Amy-Jill and Maria Mayo Robbins, eds. *A Feminist Companion to the Catholic Epistles and Hebrews.* Feminist Companion to the New Testament and Early Christian Writings 8. New York: T & T Clark, 2004.

Lindars, Barnabas. *The Theology of the Letter to the Hebrews.* Cambridge: Cambridge University Press, 1991.

Schenck, Kenneth. *Understanding the Book of the Hebrews: The Story Behind the Sermon.* Louisville, Ky.: Westminster/John Knox, 2003.

ENDNOTES

1. Anyone wishing to follow this matter further will be well informed by H. W. Montefiore, *A Commentary on the Epistle to the Hebrews* (London: A and C. Black, 1964) 9-16; and Luke T. Johnson, *The Writings of the New Testament* (Philadelphia: Fortress, 1986) 215-16.

2. A strong case has been made for understanding Hebrews in these categories by David DeSilva, *Despising Shame: A Cultural-Anthropological Investigation of the Epistle to the Hebrews,* SBLDS 152 (Atlanta: Scholars Press, 1995).

3. W. L. Lane, *Hebrews 1–8,* WBC 47A (Waco, Tex.: Word, 1991) li-lx, provides a brief but clear discussion along with a thorough bibliography.

4. Lane, *Hebrews 1–8,* lviii-lx.

5. E. Käsemann almost makes such a charge against Hebrews in *Jesus Means Freedom* (Philadelphia: Fortress, 1970) 101-16.

6. See Floyd V. Filson, *"Yesterday": A Study of Hebrews in the Light of Chapter 13* (Naperville, Ill.: Alec R. Allenson, 1967).

7. Harold Attridge, "Paraenesis in a Homily," *Semeia* 50 (1990) 217.

8. Vanhoye's literary analyses of Hebrews began in the early 1960s, and his publications have been in French. However, the fruit of his work is available in English in A. Vanhoye, *Structure and Message of the Epistle to the Hebrews* (Rome: Pontifical Biblical Institute, 1989).

9. For a review of various structural analyses and their justifications, see Lane, *Hebrews 1–8,* WBC lxxv-ciii.

The Letter of James

LUKE TIMOTHY JOHNSON

Traditionally included as the first of the "general" or "catholic" epistles, the Letter of James is as clear and forceful in its moral exhortations as it is difficult to place within the development of earliest Christianity. Although its formal canonization was relatively late, there are signs that James was used by some writings (e.g., *1 Clement* and the *Shepherd of Hermas*) before the middle of the second century CE. Largely through the enthusiastic endorsement of Origen, it became part of the church's collection, first in the East and, by the end of the fourth century, in the West. Martin Luther's distaste for James is well known, but was not widely shared by other reformers. Luther considered that Jas 2:24 ("You see that a person is justified by works and not by faith alone" [NRSV]) contradicted Paul's teaching on righteousness in Gal 2:16 ("a person is justified not by the works of the law but through faith in Jesus Christ" [NRSV]). Luther's view dominated much of the scholarly approach to the letter until very recently.

Most readers through the ages, however, reached a position like that of patristic interpreters, and the opposite of Luther's: (1) James and Paul do not contradict each other, because they are not addressing the same point; (2) when read on its own terms, James is a powerful witness to both the diversity in early Christianity and the moral imperative of Christian identity in every age.

CHARACTER OF THE COMPOSITION

Before considering the circumstances of composition, which are a matter of considerable debate, the distinctive voice of the composition itself should be appreciated. James is written in a clear and even somewhat elegant *koine* Greek that shows the influence of the Septuagint (LXX) not only in its explicit citations and allusions but also in its diction. The style does not lack adornment or rhetorical force. Its short sentences adhere to the ancient ideal of brevity, and although to some readers they appear disconnected, closer analysis reveals careful construction and vigorous argument.

James presents itself as a letter, although after the greeting (1:1) it lacks specifically epistolary elements (for instance, there is no prayer for grace and peace, no declaration of thanksgiving or pronouncement of a blessing on God). The determination of whether it was a "real" letter depends to a considerable extent on the decision concerning authenticity. In any case, the readership is a general one, and the situations portrayed in the letter are better thought of as general and typical rather than actual and local. It is widely agreed that James is a form of moral exhortation, but refining that definition has proved more difficult. James has appropriately been compared to the Greco-Roman diatribe because of its lively, dialogical style, especially in the essays of 2:1–5:20 (see, e.g., 2:14-26). Because it conveys traditional moral instruction, it has also been thought of as paraenesis. It is, however, best understood as a form of protreptic discourse in the form of a letter: James seeks to persuade the readers to live up to the profession to which they have committed themselves—namely, the faith "in our glorious Lord Jesus Christ" (2:1 NRSV).[1]

The structure of James's moral discourse is also difficult to determine with precision. One influential position argues that James has no real compositional structure, but is a collection of separate traditions only loosely joined together. The exegetical implication of this position is that each verse must be interpreted separately without reference to its immediate context. At the opposite extreme, a variety of complex—and not easily visible—structures have been suggested. Most scholars have preferred a less radical position. They recognize that James contains a number of easily identifiable and coherent "essays," although the precise delimitation of these is debated (e.g., 2:1-11 on the incompatibility of faith and discrimination; 2:14-26 on the inadequacy of faith without deeds; 3:1-12 on the misuse of speech; 3:13–4:10 on the contrast between friendship with the world and friendship with God; see also 4:13–5:6; 5:7-11, 13-18). Analysis from the perspective of ancient rhetoric demonstrates that these essays follow the conventions of argumentation in the Hellenistic world. The biggest problem is the relationship of chapter 1, which is far less obviously coherent and far more aphoristic in character, with these later and longer essays. It is clear that themes that are touched on in chapter 1 by way of aphorism are also found developed in the essays: The prayer of faith in 1:5-7 is advocated more elaborately in 5:13-18; the reversal of fortunes of the rich and poor in 1:9-10 is developed by 2:1-6 and 4:13–5:6; the theme of enduring testing in 1:2-4, 12 is found further in 5:7-11; the contrast between wicked desire and God's gift in 1:12-18 is argued more extensively in 3:13–4:10; the use of the tongue in 1:19-20 is picked up by the essay in 3:1-12; the necessity of acting out religious convictions in 1:22-27 is elaborated by the essay in 2:14-26. In effect, then, 1:2-27 serves as an *epitome* of the entire composition, setting out in concentrated form the themes to be developed by the essays. As for the final statement in 5:19-20, it serves as an excellent conclusion, recommending that the reader do for others what the author has tried to do for the readers.

JAMES AS WISDOM WRITING

As moral exhortation (there are some 59 imperatives in its 108 verses), James can be compared to other ancient writings whose concern is the practical wisdom of right behavior. James resembles the popular moral philosophy of the Greco-Roman world in its insistence on control of the passions and of speech and on the demonstration of verbal profession in practice, as well as in its perception of envy and arrogance as destructive vices.[2] The specific symbolic world of James, however, is that of Torah. James appropriates the multiple dimensions of Torah in a way distinctive among New Testament writings. First, James has a positive view of the *law*, not as a set of ritual obligations but as moral commandment expressed most perfectly by what it calls "the law of the kingdom" or "royal law"—namely, the law of love of neighbor from Lev 19:18 (Jas 2:8-13). Second, James appropriates the voice of the *prophets* in its understanding of human life as fundamentally covenantal and relational and in its harsh condemnation of those whose desire for self-aggrandizement leads them to oppress and defraud others (4:13–5:6). Third, James represents the *wisdom* tradition of Torah, not only in its liberal use of proverb and maxim, but also by understanding human freedom in terms of an allegiance either to a "wisdom from above" or to a "wisdom from below" (1:5; 3:13-18).

As a kind of wisdom literature, James naturally bears a certain resemblance to the wide range of wisdom writings that were produced in the ancient Near East. Wisdom has an international character, not only because human behavior does show some constants across cultures, but also because wisdom literature was produced by scribes in ancient bureaucracies who borrowed freely from other cultures in shaping wisdom for their own. James most resembles certain Jewish writings that shared its commitment to the world of Torah within the wider cultural setting of Hellenism, such as the *Sentences of Pseudo-Phocylides* and the *Testaments of the Twelve Patriarchs.*[3] When a thorough comparison is made between James and all these other wisdom writings, however, the distinctiveness of James emerges more clearly.

There are four ways in which James stands out among all ancient moral literature. First, James's concern is with morals rather than manners. Much of the moral exhortation of antiquity dealt with finding and keeping one's place in the world as a means to success and honor. James has none of those concerns, but deals exclusively with moral attitudes and behavior. Second, James addresses an intentional community rather than a household. It has nothing about obligations within the household or the state, nothing about duties owed by parents to children or slaves to masters. It says nothing about sexual morality. Its attention is exclusively devoted to an *ekklēsia* gathered by common values and convictions, summarized by faith in Jesus Christ (2:1). Third, James is egalitarian rather than hierarchical. Much of ancient wisdom assumes and reinforces the differences in status, especially between parents and children. In James, the only kinship language is that of "brother" and "sister," with even the author presenting himself as a "slave" rather than as an authority. God is the only "father" in this community (1:17-18, 27). The egalitarian outlook of James is shown as well in its condemnation of favoritism in judging (2:1, 9) and every form of boasting (3:14-15) and arrogance (4:6), slander and judging (4:11-12). Fourth, James is communitarian rather than individualistic. Against every form of self-assertion that seeks advantage at the expense of another, James calls for attitudes of solidarity, mercy, and compassion. In contrast to the logic of envy that leads to oppression and "killing the righteous one" (5:6), James calls for a community that rallies around the sick and sinful in order to heal/save them (5:14-16).

JAMES AS A CHRISTIAN WRITING

Despite such noteworthy points of connection to the broader world of ancient wisdom literature, James is unmistakably a Christian writing.[4] Recent scholarship has properly abandoned the once popular view that James originated as a Jewish composition that was subsequently lightly baptized. It is true that the name of Jesus is mentioned only twice (1:1; 2:1) and that the composition lacks the characteristic themes associated explicitly with Jesus. It makes no mention of his earthly life or miracles, does not explicitly speak of his death and resurrection, and never adverts to baptism, the Holy Spirit, or the Lord's supper. Yet the language and perceptions of the composition are without question those of the nascent messianic movement, with its sense of an inheritance according to promise, of belonging to a kingdom proclaimed by Jesus, and of a life normed by faith and love.

Of all the compositions from the first-century Mediterranean world, in fact, James most resembles the letters of Paul in its style and outlook. The resemblance is not restricted to the disputed lines in 2:14-26, nor is it due to the dependence of one writer on the other. Rather, despite the obvious differences between the extant literature of each author, James and Paul share a range of convictions and perceptions that is best explained by the hypothesis that both are first-century Jewish members of the messianic movement with significant roots in the world of Palestinian Judaism. James has its own distinctive christology, based less in the deeds of Jesus than in Jesus' words. In James 1:5-6, 12; 2:5, 13; 4:8, 11-12; 5:9, 12, we find language that appears to be derived from the tradition of Jesus' sayings at a stage prior to their incorporation into the synoptic Gospels.[5] For James, then, "the faith of Jesus" means living before God in a manner shaped by the words of Jesus, and above all by his declaration that loving the neighbor as oneself is the "royal law" (2:8 NRSV).

Nevertheless, James is clearly less christocentric than theocentric. It would be difficult to find a New Testament writing with as rich a collection of statements concerning the nature and activity of God. James begins with the confession that God is one (2:19), but scarcely stops there. God is the living God, who makes "even the demons believe—and shudder" (2:19 NRSV) and is the "Lord of hosts" (5:4 NRSV). God is constant and without change (1:17) and has nothing to do with evil (1:13) or human anger (1:20). God is the creator of all (1:17), who, by a "word of truth," has "given birth" to humans as a first fruits of all creatures (1:18) and has created them in God's own likeness (3:9). God has revealed the "perfect law of liberty" (see 2:8-12) and will judge humans on the basis of that revelation (2:12; 4:12). God is fit to judge because God alone is able "to save and to destroy" (4:12 NRSV). God has implanted a word within humans that is able to save them (1:21) and has made a spirit to dwell in them (4:5). God directs human affairs (4:15) and declares righteous those who have faith (2:23). Above all, God is defined by the giving of gifts (1:5, 17; 4:6), especially those of mercy and compassion (5:11). God has promised the crown of life to those who love God (1:12; 2:5), has chosen the world's poor to be rich in faith and heirs of the kingdom (2:5), considers true religion to include the visiting of orphans and widows (1:27), hears the cries of the oppressed (5:4), raises up the sick (5:15), listens to the prayers made in faith (1:5-6; 5:17-18) rather than wickedly (4:3), and forgives the sins of those who confess them (5:15). This is a God who approaches those who approach (4:10) and enters into friendship with humans (2:23; 4:4), even while resisting the arrogance and pride of those who oppress others (4:6; 5:6).

JAMES'S THEOLOGICAL ETHICS

Such characterizations are not random but fit within a coherent understanding of God as the source of all reality ("the giver of every good and perfect gift") who calls humans into a life shaped according to the gifts given them and a community of mutual gift-giving and support rather than of rivalry and competition. In a word, James's theological statements serve as warrants for his moral exhortations.

James's ethical dualism is consistent and based on a contrast between the measure of reality offered by "the world," on the one hand, and "God," on the other. The "wisdom from below" is the wisdom of the world, which is based in desire and envy and leads to every form of competition, violence, and eventually murder and war (3:13–4:3). In contrast, the "wisdom from above" is that given by God through the "implanted word," a wisdom that measures reality according to God's gifts rather than according to human possessions, and that leads to a life lived in cooperation and peace (3:13-18). James expresses this dualism in terms of friendship, which in the ancient world was regarded as a particularly profound form of sharing all things: Friends share not only their material things but above all their view of the world. Friends were of "one mind." In 4:4, James reminds his readers (and thus assumes their previous grasp of the point) that they cannot be "friends of the world" and also "friends of God," because God and "the world" represent entirely different and opposed measures of reality. Thus one who is a "friend of the world" seeks to kill a righteous person in order to gain more possessions, convinced that life must be seized. But Abraham is called a "friend of God," because he is willing to offer his son Isaac on the altar, recognizing that God is the constant giver of gifts (2:21-23).

James's particular targets, however, are those of his readers, who may understand these things theoretically, but whose practice does not match their profession. They want to be friends of God, yes, but also friends of the world. James calls them "double-minded" (1:8; 4:8), because they want to live by two measures simultaneously. Much of James's instruction is intended to show the moral illogic and self-deception involved in such vacillation. The heart of the composition is 3:13–4:10, a call to conversion from double-mindedness to that "purity of heart" which is to will one thing.

CIRCUMSTANCES OF COMPOSITION

The circumstances of James's composition are the most difficult to determine and have been the cause of considerable debate within critical scholarship. The letter does not offer many clues to the circumstances of the readers (but see, e.g., 2:2, 6-7; 5:4). If taken literally, "the twelve tribes in the dispersion" in the greeting would refer to Jewish Christians outside Palestine; if taken metaphorically, the original readers could be regarded as those who are spiritual heirs to Israel and sojourning away from their heavenly homeland. In either case, we learn nothing about the specific circumstances of the first readers. The situations portrayed by the composition are also, as noted above, typical in character. It is probably safe to assert, however, that the readers either are, or perceive themselves to be, among "the poor" who are called into God's kingdom and are persecuted and oppressed by the rich (see esp. 2:1-6; 5:1-6).

As for the inscribed author, the best candidate is "James the brother of the Lord," who figured prominently in the first generation of the Christian movement as one of the leaders of the church in Jerusalem (see Mark 6:3; Acts 12:17; 15:23-29; 21:20-25; 1 Cor 15:7; Gal 1:19; 2:9, 11-14). If this James actually wrote the letter, then the composition would be important evidence for Jewish Christianity within Palestine before the year 62.[6] The traditional attribution to James has vigorously been challenged on two basic counts. The first is that Jas 2:14-26 appears to presuppose the Pauline teaching in Galatians and Romans, and thus must come from a time after the first generation. The second is that the Greek style is too fine for a Palestinian Jew to have written. Many scholars, therefore, consider James to be a pseudonymous composition. Once the tie to James is broken, even less can be said about the time and place of writing, and it has been dated variously between the beginning and the middle of the second century.

Many other scholars—even a majority until recent years—consider the traditional attribution reasonable. Some have dealt with the critical problems by proposing that Paul was responding to James, rather than the reverse, and that the Greek style of the letter might be accounted for by a translation of an Aramaic original. These expedients, however, are not necessary in order to hold that James the brother of the Lord may well have been the author of this letter. In the first place, as was recognized already by patristic interpreters, James in 2:14-26 is simply not addressing the same topic as Paul does in Galatians and Romans. When James declares that faith co-works the works of Abraham and that faith is perfected by those works (2:22), he simply addresses the necessity of convictions to be translated into action, a position also held by Paul (see Gal 5:6). As for the Greek style, research over the past thirty years has decisively demonstrated that Palestine was as thoroughly Hellenized with regard to language as was the diaspora, and there is no reason why a Christian of the first generation who grew up in Galilee and wrote from Jerusalem should not have a style as good as that revealed in this composition.

The position that James is a first-generation writing has much to recommend it. First, it lacks any of the signs usually associated with pseudonymous authorship, such as the fictional elaboration of the author's identity, and shows none of the characteristics of institutional development. Second, James reveals the social situations and perspectives appropriate to a sect in the early stages of its life, with no attention to generational changes, and an active anticipation of an imminent judgment. Third, James makes use of Jesus traditions at a stage earlier than their incorporation into the synoptic Gospels.[7] Fourth, James closely resembles in its language and outlook our earliest datable Christian writer, the apostle Paul. The best way to account for the similarity is to view both as first-generation Christians deeply affected by Greco-Roman moral traditions, yet fundamentally defined by an allegiance to the symbols and story of Torah. Even if the writing is from the first generation, it need not necessarily have been written by James, the brother of the Lord, but that hypothesis remains as convincing as any other that has been offered in the history of scholarship. The value of James's witness, in any case, is not determined by a decision concerning its authorship or date or circumstances of composition.

There are at least three ways in which James speaks to every generation of Christianity with unparalleled clarity and conviction. First, it is uncompromising in its demand for a clear rejection of "the world," together with a consistent commitment to an understanding of reality as measured by God. Second, because its teaching is rooted less in christology than in theology, it is among the most ecumenical writings in the New Testament, able to speak also to those who do not confess Jesus as Lord but who share the faith of Abraham. Third, it is the New Testament writing that most clearly yields a social ethics grounded in the perception of the world as created and gifted by God.

FOR FURTHER READING

Adamson, J. B. *The Epistle of James.* NICNT. Grand Rapids: Eerdmans, 1976.

———. *James: The Man and the Message.* Grand Rapids: Eerdmans, 1989.

Baker, W. R. *Personal Speech-Ethics in the Epistle of James.* WUZNT 2.68. Tübingen: J. C. B. Mohr (Siebeck), 1995.

Cargal, T. B. *Restoring the Diaspora: Discursive Structure and Purpose in the Epistle of James.* SBLDS 144. Atlanta: Scholars Press, 1993.

Davids, P. H. *Commentary on James.* NIGTC. Grand Rapids: Eerdmans, 1982.

Dibelius, M. *James: A Commentary on the Epistle of James.* Edited by H. Greeven. Translated by M. A. Williams. Hermeneia. Philadelphia: Fortress, 1975.

Hartin, Patrick J. *James.* SP 14. Collegeville: Liturgical Press, 2003.

———. *James and the Sayings of Jesus. JSNT* 47. Sheffield: JSOT, 1991.

Isaacs, Marie E. *Reading Hebrews and James: A Literary and Theological Commentary.* Reading the New Testament. Macon, Ga.: Smyth & Helwys, 2002.

Johnson, L. T. "Friendship with the World/Friendship with God: A Study of Discipleship in James." In *Discipleship in the New Testament.* Edited by F. Segovia. Philadelphia: Fortress, 1985.

———. *The Letter of James.* AB 37A. New York: Doubleday, 1995.

Laws, S. *A Commentary on the Epistle of James.* HNTC. San Francisco: Harper & Row, 1980.

Lodge, J. C. "James and Paul at Cross-Purposes? James 2:22." *Biblica* 62 (1981) 195-213.

Martin, R. P. *James.* WBC 48. Waco, Tex.: Word, 1988.

Via, D. O. "The Right Strawy Epistle Reconsidered: A Study in Biblical Ethics and Hermeneutics." *Journal of Religion* 49 (1969) 253-67.

Wall, R. W. *Community of the Wise: The Letter of James.* The New Testament in Context. Valley Forge, Pa.: Trinity Press International, 1997.

Ward, R. B. "The Communal Concern of the Epistle of James." Ph.D. diss., Harvard University, 1966.

ENDNOTES

1. See Robert W. Wall, "Introduction to Epistolary Literature," in this volume.

2. See Abraham J. Malherbe, "The Cultural Context of the New Testament: The Greco-Roman World," in *The New Interpreter's Bible*, 12 vols. (Nashville: Abingdon, 1995) 8:12-26.

3. These can be found in J. H. Charlesworth, ed., *The Old Testament Pseudepigrapha*, 2 vols. (New York: Doubleday, 1983; 1985).

4. For a full discussion, see L. T. Johnson, *The Letter of James*, AB 37A (New York: Doubleday, 1995) 48-64.

5. For treatment of the Jesus tradition assumed in James, see P. J. Hartin, *James and the Q Sayings of Jesus*, JSNTSup 47 (Sheffield: JSOT, 1991).

6. When, according to Josephus's *Antiquities of the Jews* 20:200, James was martyred.

7. See Johnson, *The Letter of James*, 55-57.

THE FIRST LETTER OF PETER

DAVID L. BARTLETT

First Peter is one of the general or catholic epistles, along with Hebrews; James; 1, 2, 3 John; 2 Peter; and Jude. The general epistles are distinguished from other letters in the New Testament in two ways. First, they are not attributed to Paul. Second, they are (for the most part) addressed not to a particular church but to a group of churches—they are general and, in that sense, catholic.[1] First Peter is also "catholic" in a larger sense: It speaks to the condition of the churches across the traditional lines of time and place. A letter written for churches that are alienated from the surrounding society and for Christians who are slandered for their faith, it has provided comfort for believers in troubled times from the end of the first century to the beginning of the third millennium. Using the imagery of baptism, it provides a reminder for the baptized of what it means to live out of the sacrament and to live out the sacrament in their lives as individuals and as a community. As early as Polycarp's *Letter to the Philippians,* there is evidence that Christian writers found in 1 Peter words of encouragement that were worth cherishing, repeating, and interpreting. Polycarp alludes to 1 Pet 1:8 as he recalls the suffering and resurrection of Christ, "in whom, though you did not see him, you believed in unspeakable and glorified joy."[2] This brings to mind also 1 Peter's, "Although you have not seen him, you love him; and even though you do not see him now, you believe in him and rejoice with an indescribable and glorious joy" (NRSV).[3] So, too, Polycarp's *Letter to the Philippians* 8:1 reflects 1 Pet 2:22, 24, while both texts also interpret Isaiah 53:1.[4]

From 1 Peter churches in Europe and America may find clues to faithful living as Christendom fades and Christians again feel like sojourners and aliens. Churches in developing countries will find reminders of like-minded Christians, bearing witness to a faith that is still professed by a small minority, but that history shows will hold fast, grow, and flourish.

AUTHOR, DATE, AND AUDIENCE

First Peter begins straightforwardly enough: "Peter, an apostle of Jesus Christ." An early Christian audience would think what we might: that this was a letter written by Simon Peter, one of the first disciples called by Jesus (Mark 1:16-20 par.), designated by Acts as one of the apostles. Peter was recognized by Paul both as a fellow apostle with special responsibility for the mission to the Jews and as an antagonist on issues relating to the obligation of Gentile Christians in regard to observing the Jewish Law (see 1 Cor 9:4; Gal 2:7-14). Yet in more recent years scholars have raised a number of questions to challenge Simon Peter's authorship of the first letter that bears his name.[5]

First there is the question of style. The Greek prose of 1 Peter is fairly sophisticated and the syntax fairly complicated. Is it likely that Simon, the Galilean fisherman, would be capable of writing Greek of this sophistication (see Acts 4:13)?[6]

Related to this issue is the fairly clear indication that when the writer of 1 Peter quotes Scripture (the Old Testament), it is the Greek version of the Old Testament that he uses. Usually the citations are very close to the Septuagint. Again, recognizing Peter's background as one who almost certainly would have known Scripture either in Hebrew or in Aramaic, is this familiarity with the Greek text plausible? Furthermore "Peter" uses the Greek form of his own name, whereas even in writing to Gentiles Paul always refers to Peter by the Aramaic name "Cephas."[7]

Further, there is the issue of theological development. All our guesses about the way that doctrine developed in the first century and a half of the church's existence are in large measure conjectural, but on one fairly plausible reading of doctrinal development, 1 Peter already presupposes conditions that might seem to be later than the time of the apostle. In theology the Jewish/Gentile controversies so central to Paul seem to have faded to the background, and motifs seem closer to those in letters by Paul's disciples (Colossians, Ephesians, and the Pastorals).[8]

Indeed, while there is no clear evidence that the author of 1 Peter knew or used Paul's letters, there are themes and motifs within it that suggest this epistle was written after the ministry of Paul. Parallels most often cited are between 1 Peter and Romans, on the one hand, and between 1 Peter and Ephesians, on the other hand. For instance, 1 Pet 3:8-9 uses language reminiscent of Rom 12:16-17:

Finally, all of you, have unity of spirit, sympathy, love for one another, a tender heart, and a humble mind. Do not repay evil for evil or abuse for abuse; but, on the contrary, repay with a blessing. It is for this that you were called—that you might inherit a blessing. (1 Pet 3:8-9 NRSV)	Live in harmony with one another; do not be haughty, but associate with the lowly; do not claim to be wiser than you are. Do not repay anyone evil for evil, but take thought for what is noble in the sight of all. If it is possible, so far as it depends on you, live peaceably with all. (Rom 12:16-18 NRSV)

It is certainly possible that 1 Peter depends on a recollection of Romans here, but it is also possible that each reflects a growing Christian tradition about non-retaliation, a tradition also reflected in other early Christian literature, such as Matt 6:39.

So, too, the close correspondence to some material in Ephesians may reflect the widespread development of particular themes and motifs rather than any direct dependence of 1 Peter on this (deutero-)Pauline letter:

Blessed be the God and Father of our Lord Jesus Christ! By his great mercy he has given us a new birth into a living hope through the resurrection of Jesus Christ from the dead. (Eph 1:3 NRSV)	Blessed be the God and Father of our Lord Jesus Christ, who has blessed us in Christ with every spiritual blessing in the heavenly places. (1 Pet 1:3 NRSV)

The strong similiarity between the two doxologies results in part from the fact that both are doxologies and share similar, perhaps liturgical, language to declare the thanksgiving that frequently follows the salutation in early Christian letters.

Paul Achtemeier judiciously sums up the evidence for the relationship of 1 Peter to the Pauline letters:

> While the relationship of 1 Peter to the Pauline way of theological reflection cannot be denied, how much of the "Pauline" flavor of 1 Peter is the result of a common use of early liturgical or confessional material is difficult to say with precision. Similarly, whether the author of 1 Peter was aware of the Pauline letters, or had read them, or whether the "Pauline" material in 1 Peter had already passed into common tradition by the time 1 Peter was written is equally difficult to demonstrate.[9]

In either case, the probable trajectory of influence suggests that 1 Peter was written later than the Pauline letters, and perhaps even later than a probable deutero-Pauline book like Ephesians. If this is true, then it is all the more clear that this epistle is pseudonymous.

In terms of the social strictures of the letter, the concern for the fixed orders of house or church seem more likely contemporary to letters thought of as deutero-pauline than to Paul himself. The closest analogies are found in Colossians, Ephesians, and the Pastoral Epistles.[10]

In terms of the spread of Christianity, one has to assume a quite rapid expansion to the churches of Asia Minor so that before Peter's death (traditionally held to be in the 60s of the common era) there were already churches established in a number of towns in Asia Minor, with their own leaders and nascent structures.

On the other hand, none of these doubts provides indisputable evidence that Peter could not have written the letter. They raise a complex of issues that have caused a number of students of the epistle to say that the probability rests with the claim that the letter was written after Peter's death but in Peter's name.

There are mediating positions that try to find a place between the claim that Peter wrote or dictated this epistle word for word and the claim that a later Christian penned the whole thing, using Peter's name to give weight to its affirmations and prescriptions. One position interprets the epistle in the light of 1 Pet 5:12: "Through Silvanus our faithful brother, as I reckon, I have written to you briefly, exhorting (you) and bearing witness to the true grace of God" (author's trans.). While it is logically possible that "I have written you through Silvanus" could mean, "I have written this letter and am sending it through Silvanus," the fact that "Peter" says, "I have written briefly through Silvanus" makes it more likely that the impression the reader is to gain is that Silvanus was the scribe who took down Peter's dictation.[11]

There is ample precedent in the New Testament for letters whose author acknowledges a helper. In 1 Cor 1:3, the address is from Paul and Sosthenes, and in 1 Cor 15:21 Paul insists that the final greeting is in his own hand, indicating that the letter up until that point had been dictated. Second Corinthians 1:1 addresses the Corinthian church from Paul and Timothy. Galatians ends with the indication that Paul is (now) writing with his own hand (Gal 5:11) (cf. Col 4:18). Philippians is from Paul and Timothy (Phil 1:1). First Thessalonians is from Paul, Silvanus, and Timothy (1 Thess 1:1) and also ends with Paul's handwritten greeting (1 Thess 3:17), emphasized perhaps to contrast it with pseudonymous letters written in Paul's name.

Some have thought that the Silvanus mentioned in this epistle is more redactor than scribe, taking Peter's general themes or fragmentary exhortations and shaping them into a fuller and more coherent letter. If this Silvanus is the Silvanus of 1 Thessalonians and Acts, he was Paul's companion and might well have been versed in Greek and in the Greek version of the Old Testament; and he would have used that knowledge to present Peter's themes in a form accessible to the Gentile, Greek-speaking Christians of Asia Minor.[12] Still another position suggests that 1 Peter is a letter from the church at Rome to the churches in Asia Minor. The church at Rome honored Peter and remembered much of his teaching, and, therefore, it was bold to write in his name to the other churches in the East without making any direct claim that Peter penned or dictated the letter himself.[13] Each of these mediating positions represents an attempt to maintain the integrity of the claim that Peter was responsible for the epistle while acknowledging the doubts that its every word was written or dictated by the fisherman apostle.

Obviously, no one has solved the problem of authorship to the satisfaction of every other interpreter. Not surprisingly, there is a congruence between the interpreter's understanding of scriptural authority and the claims about authorship. Interpreters for whom scriptural authenticity depends in large measure on its factual accuracy are inclined to support authenticity, either outright or in one of the mediating positions. Interpreters who are more skeptical about the factual accuracy of other parts of the New Testament (the authorship of the Pastorals, for example, or the possibility of harmonizing the events of the Gospels into a single synopsis) are more skeptical of Peter's authorship.

In terms of the theological claims of the epistle, the answer one gives to the question of authorship may make surprisingly little difference. Whether it was written by Peter or by a later Christian in his name, the epistle helps to strengthen Christians in times of distress; sets their lives within the history of God's activity, which moves from creation to consummation; holds up the atoning death of Jesus Christ; and encourages mutual love among Christian people and forbearance of enemies. Nothing in this list would be impossible for the historical Peter to enjoin; nothing loses its power to shape faith if the words were written by some later Christian in his name.

The one difficult interpretive issue, however, is the question of the relationship between authorial integrity and doctrinal authority. There are benign and less benign theories of pseudonymity. On the benign theory, the disciple of an apostle writes a letter in the apostle's name to say what the disciples believe the apostle would want to have said in a particular situation. Whether or not readers were deceived into believing the letter to be authentic, deception was not the point.[14] On the more suspicious theory of pseudonymity, the whole purpose of writing a pseudonymous letter was to mislead readers into believing that the words of some anonymous Christian carry the authority of the apostle. So, for instance, the author(s) of the Pastoral Epistles tries to correct what he thinks is a wrong interpretation of Pauline doctrine by forging a letter, or letters, purporting to be from Paul and throwing in some false memorabilia about fellow Christians, cloaks, and books, deliberately to throw suspicious readers off the scent.[15]

The question of the authorship of 1 Peter is probably unanswerable. The question of its usefulness to the church is not. We have every scriptural treasure in earthen vessels, and the historical question about the intention of the original author may be less important than the question of what the letter enjoined of its first readers and how it might have brought comfort to them and, by extension, to their successors in every generation, including our own.[16]

One's guess about the date for 1 Peter, of course, is closely related to one's guess about its authorship. If Peter wrote the epistle, and if the tradition that places his death in the 60s is accurate, then the epistle was probably written toward the close of his life. If the letter is pseudonymous, the range of possibilities grows accordingly, and one's hypothesis is based largely on one's reading of the historical circumstances of the epistle.

From the perspective of the pseudonymous theory, this letter was written long enough after the deaths of Peter and Paul for Christianity to have spread and received some institutional shape in Asia Minor, and long enough for Pauline motifs to have entered into the broader stream of Christian tradition. On this hypothesis, it is appropriate to suggest that the epistle be dated toward the end of the first century.

The other clue that might help with dating the epistle is its references to suffering and trouble for the Christians of Asia Minor. Nero's persecution of the Christians would have been confined largely to Rome and would have been too early for this letter if it was written in the generation after the death of Simon Peter. The emperor worship that seems to have been instituted under Domitian and carried on by his successors is not mentioned in 1 Peter. On the contrary, the emperor is worthy of honor (1 Pet 2:13). Nor is 1 Peter driven by the intense hatred of empire that drives Revelation, written probably around the turn of the first century. Furthermore, the troubles that seem to be bothering the recipients of the letter may be more aptly described as local harassments than as systematic persecution. The people are being slandered and perhaps even accused, but there is no sense that the government has turned against them.

All this suggests a date toward the end of the first century, when a growing Christian movement had already stirred up trouble among its neighbors but had not yet attracted the attention of the emperor or been forced to choose between allegiance to him and allegiance to Christ. About 110 CE, Pliny the Younger, writing from Asia Minor, asked the emperor Trajan for advice about how to deal with people accused of being Christians. The correspondence between Pliny and Trajan reflects developments somewhat later than the situation in 1 Peter; emperor worship was now prescribed, and the Christian movement was growing so fast that Pliny thought it needed to be checked.

However, the atmosphere of accusation, charge, and slander that 1 Peter reflects was still present in this somewhat later period. Trajan's response to Pliny shows something of the circumstances of the growing Christian movement in Asia Minor:

> You have followed the right course of procedure, my dear Pliny, in your examination of the cases of persons charged with being Christians, for it is impossible to lay down a general rule to a fixed formula. These people must not be hunted out; if they are brought before you and the charge against them is proved, they must be punished, but in the case of anyone who denies that he is a Christian, and makes it clear that he is not by offering prayers to our gods, he is to be pardoned as a result of his repentance however suspect his past conduct may be. But pamphlets circulating anonymously must play no part in any accusation. They create the worst sort of precedent and are quite out of keeping with the spirit of our age.[17]

Already in 1 Peter, the label "Christian" was making life difficult if not dangerous (see 4:14, 16), and already in 1 Peter there are hints of anonymous accusations and slanderous insults (see 2:12; 3:9, 16).

The evidence seems to point to a letter written between Paul's letters to the Gentile churches and Pliny's and Trajan's letters to each other. Given the evidence of emperor worship as a problem for John of Patmos and not for the writer of 1 Peter, we can also put this letter before Revelation. One might guess that the letter was written sometime around 90 CE, knowing that one speaks at best of probabilities.

The evidence that helps to date the letter also helps us to understand the situation of the audience. First Peter 1:1 gives us much of the crucial information. The letter is written to churches of Asia Minor, and they are probably listed in the order in which the letter might be circulated from one church to the next. The recipients are "exiles," as later they are both "resident aliens" and "exiles." The author is also presumably an exile, since his word for Rome, from which he writes, is "Babylon," not only a cipher for an enemy of God's people (as in Revelation), but also the reminder that Rome itself is a place of exile. Recent work in sociological theory has debated whether these Christians can also be described according to their socioeconomic setting—that is, members of a class of resident aliens, living as guest workers in communities where they had no citizenship and no power.[18] More traditional interpretations have seen the language of exile as a metaphorical reminder to these Christians that on this earth they have no lasting home; their citizenship is in heaven.[19] Careful study of the letter suggests a third possibility, one that does not necessarily contradict the other two (anymore than they necessarily contradict each other). Language of exile and alienation is language that distinguishes the Christians who received this letter from the larger culture around them. It is that culture from which they emerged, but now they are a slandered minority, exiled as Israel was exiled in Babylon, strangers in a strange land (all the more strange because it used to be home).

It is also quite clear that the recipients of the letter were Gentiles who formerly shared the paganism of the neighbors who now reject them (see 4:3-4). As is so often the case with early Christians, these former pagans, who were ethnically Gentiles, took on the identity of Israel, no people become a people (2:10). "Gentiles" in the epistle refers to those friends and neighbors who had not left their old ways in order to join this Israel in exile, this community of faith.

If we can judge the social setting of the recipients of the letter from the rhetoric of its specific advice (2:18–3:7), we can also guess that there were more slaves than masters among these Christians, and more believing wives with pagan husbands than vice versa. No advice is given to masters, but much to slaves. Women are told how to get along with their unbelieving husbands, but husbands (who presumably set the religious rules for the household) receive shorter instructions, all of which presume that their wives are believers, too.

THE USE OF THE OLD TESTAMENT IN 1 PETER

This epistle is steeped in Old Testament themes, quotations, and allusions. Although the recipients of the letter are mostly Gentiles, the epistle assumes that the Old Testament had become their Scripture. Several features of the use of the Old Testament are noteworthy.

(1) As Paul Achtemeier points out, the letter is permeated by a governing metaphor: the image of the church as Israel. "In a way virtually unique among Christian canonical writings, 1 Peter has appropriated the language of Israel for the church in such a way that Israel as a totality has become for this letter the controlling metaphor in terms of which its theology is expressed."[20] Unlike such New Testament writings as Romans and the Gospel of Matthew, 1 Peter does not attend to the relationship between Christians and Jews as possible heirs to Israel. The epistle simply takes over images and phrases that the Old Testament applies to Israel and applies them to the church. Christians are now the people who were once no people; the church is the community of those who were without mercy but have now received mercy (1 Pet 2:10, quoting Hos 2:23).

One image in particular from Israel's story is crucial to 1 Peter's claims about the Christians of Asia Minor. Just as God's people were once exiled in Babylon, so also the recipients of this letter are exiles in Asia Minor (1:1). Just as Abraham was a stranger among the Hittites, so also Christians are strangers within the dominant pagan culture (Gen 23:4; 1 Pet 2:11).[21] Non-Christians are referred to as "Gentiles," implying that the Christians are "Israel," though ethnically most of those who would hear this letter were Gentiles, too (2:12). The author hints that he, too, knows what it means to live in exile, since his code name for the city from which he writes is "Babylon" (5:13).

The story of Jesus, too, is foretold by Israel's story. In particular the Servant Songs of Isaiah provide the explicit and implicit background for 1 Pet 2:22-25 (see Isa 53:4-9). First Peter 2:21 introduces this passage on suffering, in a word to Christian slaves: "For to this you have been called, because Christ also suffered for you, leaving you an example, so that you should follow in his steps" (NRSV). The epistle thus presents a threefold typology. The suffering servant foreshadows the suffering of Christ; Christ foreshadows the suffering of Christian slaves; and slaves model appropriate behavior for all Christians in the face of suffering.

(2) Also pervasive in 1 Peter is the use of passages bound together by key words or images, images that link the passages to each other and also to the situation of the first-century Christians (for other instances in the New Testament see, e.g., Rom 9:14-21; Heb 1:5-13). In this epistle, the most striking examples are found in chap. 2. In 2:4-8, "stone" is the central image, with allusions or quotations from Ps 118:22; Isa 28:16; and Exod 19:6 with Isa 61:6. Christ is the stone, and Christians are the stone; the stones together build a house or temple. Christ is the cornerstone, the stone the builders rejected, the stumbling block.

Similarly, in 1 Pet 2:9-11 a host of Old Testament images and phrases related to being a people are built one on top of the other, leading up to the climactic quotation from Hos 2:23 (in these three verses there are allusions to Exod 19:6; Deut 4:20; 7:6; 14:2; Isa 43:20-21 LXX; 61:6—all woven together).

(3) First Peter provides a rationale for its own use of Scripture:

> Concerning this salvation, the prophets, who spoke of the grace that was to come to you, searched intently and with the greatest care, trying to find out the time and circumstances to which the Spirit of Christ in them was pointing when he predicted the sufferings of Christ and the glories that would follow. It was revealed to them that they were not serving themselves but you, when they spoke of the things that have now been told you by those who have preached the gospel to you by the Holy Spirit sent from heaven.
>
> (1 Pet 1:10-12 NIV)

For 1 Peter, the Old Testament was not written to point to Israel but to point to Christ and through Christ to point ahead to the life of the church. The Holy Spirit, who inspired the prophets (and was instrumental in Christ's resurrection, 3:18), also speaks among contemporary Christian preachers. Indeed, the Old Testament was written for the sake of those preachers and the Christian congregations to whom they speak.

(4) At some points, at least, the context of the passage 1 Peter quotes adds further light on the significance of that passage in the argument of the letter. For example, 1 Pet 1:24-25 quotes Isa 40:6-8. These verses are immediately pertinent to the epistle's claim that God's Word lives and endures. More than that, the larger context in Isaiah reinforces themes found elsewhere in 1 Peter. Isaiah 40:5 declares the revelation of God's glory, a theme evident in 1 Pet 1:7; 2:12; 4:11; 5:1, 10. Isaiah 40:9 calls for a herald of "good news" to speak to Zion. The verb in the Septuagint of Isa 40:9 is εὐαγγελίζω (*euangelizō*), the same as in 1 Pet 1:12, 25. The larger context of the quotation echoes other themes in the epistle.

(5) The "scriptural" resources on which 1 Peter draws may be larger than our own version of the Old Testament canon. At least in the complicated claim about Christ's proclamation to the spirits after his resurrection, 1 Peter seems to draw on traditions from *1 Enoch*.[22] While the epistle never explicitly says that this extra-biblical material counts as Scripture, the author relies on those traditions in much the same way that he elsewhere draws on canonical Old Testament themes.

(6) Finally, 1 Peter implies that the life of Scripture—and its power—lives on in the community of faith. In 1 Pet 1:12, the very purpose of Old Testament Scripture is to provide the good news for Christian preachers. In 1 Pet 4:11, the author is writing about mutual service in the community of faith: "Whoever speaks must do so as one speaking the very words of God" (NRSV). This may imply a reliance on Scripture as the basis for preaching.[23] More likely, it claims for preaching a representation of that authority found in Scripture; like the prophets of old, Christian preachers speak of Christ for the sake of Christ's people.

SOCIAL SETTING AND THE LIFE OF FAITH

Social context shapes faith, and faith reshapes the social context. The clearest evidence for the nature of the communities for which this letter was written is 1 Peter itself. Yet on the basis of this epistle one can present reasonable hypotheses about the Christians of Asia Minor, and then, of course, use the hypotheses to help interpret the letter. Study of 1 Peter suggests that the Christians for whom it was written had an ambivalent relationship to the larger society around them.

The references to being sojourners, aliens, strangers indicate the distance of these Christians from the society around them. They were not rescued *from* exile; they were rescued *into* exile. Their alienation is a mark of their faithfulness: "Live in reverent fear during the time of your exile. You know that you were ransomed from the futile ways inherited from your ancestors" (1:17-18 NRSV).

On the other hand, it is clear that the approval of the larger society is crucial not only to the Christians' safety but also to their self-esteem: "Beloved, I urge you as aliens and exiles to abstain from the desires of the flesh that wage war against the soul" (2:11 NRSV). Here we might expect an exhortation to shun those pagans whose standards are unworthy of the faithful, but the exhortation continues: "Conduct yourselves honorably among the Gentiles, so that, though they malign you as evildoers, they may see your honorable deeds and glorify God when he comes to judge" (2:12 NRSV).

There is intense concern for the internal life of the Christian community, but the "world" is not roundly condemned (as in the Johannine epistles) except as it represents a set of practices that the Christians have left behind (1:18; 4:3-4). Indeed, the hope of 2:12 that the "Gentiles" might in the end glorify God implies a hope for redemption that extends beyond the community of faith. There is an absolute devotion to God as the only God; honoring the emperor is not only allowed but is commended as well (2:13, 17). It is probably the case that the emperor did not yet make the idolatrous demands that lie behind the book of Revelation, but it is also the case that the reverence for authority in 1 Peter lies very far from the suspicion of authority in the later book. Yet 1 Peter 2 is also quite different from Romans 13; the emperor is merely a human figure, one more authority within the created order. There is no sense that the authority is itself divine (unlike Rom 13:1-2). The behavior enjoined in 1 Peter 2 and Romans 13 is very similar, but there are important distinctions between the warrants given for that behavior.

First Peter is, therefore, sectarian without being countercultural.[24] It raises problems for contemporary Christian obedience. In a time when Christian social action seems to many an essential element in discipleship, is 1 Peter too sectarian and passive to be a guide for Christians in society? On the other hand, does the epistle's too easy acceptance of the larger society prevent the author from seeing how profoundly Christians must stand against culture? Does the epistle fail to recognize that Christians, who are resident aliens, must be alien, indeed?

Study of 1 Peter further suggests that the Christians for whom it was written lived or were enjoined to live uncomplainingly in social structures that were both hierarchical and patriarchal. Pauline churches never fully worked out the implications of Paul's gospel in Gal 3:28 that "there is no longer Jew or Greek, there is no longer slave or free, there is no longer male and female; for all of you are one in Christ Jesus" (NRSV). For the churches of 1 Peter, such a radical claim barely appeared on the horizon.

The strong attention to right behavior on the part of slaves and wives (with no attention to masters and slight attention to husbands) probably reflects churches still dominated by slaves and non-slave owners and marked by the Christian wives of pagan husbands. Nonetheless, the demand that slaves and wives be properly subject to masters and husbands enforces a picture of Christianity as meekly submissive—and stands over against quite different visions, such as Mary's magnificat in Luke 1:46-55.

The strongest christological warrants are brought forth to remind slaves to "accept the authority of your masters with all deference, not only those who are kind and gentle but also those who are harsh" (2:18 NRSV). Christ's suffering becomes a model for the suffering of slaves, and the suffering of slaves becomes a model for all Christians who suffer unjustly for their faith or for doing good. Therefore, the appeal to submissive behavior colors the christology. Not only does Christ become a model for slaves, but also slavery becomes the lens through which the epistle views christology and enjoins discipleship.

Furthermore, wives are urged to be quiet about their faith in order to entice their husbands toward believing, not by explicit profession of faith, but by modest and gentle demeanor. The letter—almost—unquestioningly takes up the androcentric assumptions of the larger society. There is one notable exception. There is no claim that Christian wives should give up their faith in order to conform to their husbands' religion; in this way, 1 Peter stands against the norms of its larger society.

Nonetheless, in our time, when the gospel is rightly seen as including a profound concern for liberation, 1 Peter can be seen as profoundly unliberating. And for churches that urgently need to hear women's voices, the injunctions to quiet demeanor can be seen as profoundly unfaithful.

EXCURSUS: THE HOUSEHOLD TABLES

The material in 1Pet 2:18–3:7 is formally very like the sets of exhortations on household order in Col 3:18–4:1 and Eph 5:21–6:9, and it is quite similar to material found more dispersed through the Pastoral Epistles (1 Tim 2:8-15; 5:1-2; 6:1-2; Titus 2:1-10; see also *Did.* 4:10-11; Ignatius to Polycarp, 4:3–5:2). The concern for proper order within Christian community and family appears again in 1Pet 5:1-5. Further, the concern for proper submission within the household is closely related in 1 Peter to proper submission to governmental authorities (as also in 1 Tim 2:1-2; Titus 3:1). David Balch argues persuasively that the antecedents for these household codes are to be found as early as Plato and Aristotle and are continued among Stoics and the Hellenistic Jews Philo and Josephus.[25] In these non-Christian writings there was great concern for the proper management of the household, with some sense that the security and unity of the state depended on the security and unity of the families within that state.[26] So, too, in 1 Peter the overall injunction to orderly behavior begins with the appeal to obey human authorities, starting with the emperor. Governors, masters, and husbands are all examples of the general category of those people who have special authority.

Balch argues that the social context for the code in 1 Peter is to be found in 3:15: "Always be ready to make your defense" (NRSV). Part of what Christians have to defend is the accusation that their religion overturns the approved social order. Following the household code is a way of making sure that there is no substance to these pagan accusations.[27]

The following interpretation will acknowledge much truth to Balch's claims, but the close parallels to Colossians and Ephesians (where there is not the same concern with confounding pagan opponents) suggest that—whatever its origins—the household code now seemed an appropriate way of encouraging social order within the Christian community. Indeed, in the case of slavery, for 1 Peter the right domestic order is an enfolding of right christology. Slaves suffer unjustly, as did their Lord (2:20-25).

THEOLOGICAL THEMES

The motifs of the epistle are best understood in their context, as one reads through its argument and allusions. Several motifs, however, can be extracted as guides to a more thorough reading.

God. Only in 1 Peter in the New Testament is God explicitly designated by the noun "Creator" (κτίστης *ktistēs*; 4:19). The whole epistle presupposes that history is in God's hands, from beginning to end. From the beginning God has created the earth and called Christians to be God's own people. At the end, God will provide the imperishable award granted to those who have proved faithful. In between times, God provides the Spirit to encourage believers and to inspire appropriate—and joyful—worship.

Christ. Christ is the one who brings believers to God (3:18). He does this especially through his crucifixion and resurrection. His suffering is both the example and the ground for the faithfulness of Christians who also face suffering. His resurrection is the vindication that makes faith possible and prefigures the final victory, when God, having judged the living and the dead, will be glorified forever (4:11).

Suffering. In 5:12, the author says that he has written a letter of encouragement, and certainly a major purpose of the epistle is to strengthen the Christians of Asia Minor in their time of distress. Whatever the nature of that distress, it serves to strengthen their faith for the last days and to bring them into communion with Christ, whose suffering prefigures and validates their own.[28]

EXCURSUS: SUFFERING IN 1 PETER

There are four key sets of references to unjust suffering in this epistle. First is the passage about "unjust trials" (vv. 6-7). Second is the long section on slaves who have to suffer unjustly (2:18-25). Third is the encouragement for those who apparently suffer for their open confession of their Christian faith (3:17-18). Fourth is the reference to the "fiery ordeal" in 4:12-19.

The material in chaps. 1, 3, and 4 may deal with the suffering that comes to Christians for maintaining their faith in the face of opposition. The reminder to slaves is explicitly encouragement to suffer courageously unjust treatment at the hands of their masters, though implicitly this too may include mistreatment precisely because of their Christian faith. Because slaves suffer unjustly, as Christ suffered, they become a paradigm and example for all Christians, slave and free, who suffer unjustly at the hands of their masters or at the hands of society.

We cannot be sure whether the suffering that Christians undergo includes actual judicial proceedings, but certainly it includes slander, innuendo, and abuse (see 2:12; 3:17; 4:14). We also cannot be sure whether the "fiery ordeal" of 4:12 is a new and more threatening example of opposition that calls forth the strong response to be brave and to rejoice or whether, as the letter draws to a close, the rhetoric takes on even greater passion.

What is clear is that in this epistle the issue is not why bad things happen to good people. Rather, the issue is how to interpret the suffering Christians undergo as a result of their conviction and confession. First Peter interprets the suffering of Christians in at least these ways:

(1) Suffering can provide for the refining of faith. As Achtemeier suggests, in 1 Peter 1:6-7 there is a comparison between the lesser and the greater: If fire can purify gold, then how much more can the fire of suffering purify the faith of those who are steadfast?[29] There is the implication that the suffering may be sent from God and the promise that the value of faith tested by hardship will be revealed at the end (see also Matt 5:11-12).

(2) The one who suffers imitates Christ, who also suffered unjustly, not only as Christians' redeemer but also as their example (2:21-25; 3:17-18; 4:13; 5:13).

(3) Suffering is not only the result of human bad will but also is a consequence of the power of the devil (5:8).

(4) Nonetheless, part of the power of Christ's resurrection was his power to proclaim victory over the forces of evil (3:18-20). Therefore, by implication, Christians know that those who cause their suffering will also finally be judged and defeated.

(5) Suffering for being a Christian is itself a sign that the end of history is at hand (4:12-16).

(6) When Christ does return, those who have suffered for their faith will receive the reward of eternal glory, and the Spirit, which is the firstfruits of that glory, already is given to the faithful who suffer (1:7; 2:11; 4:13; 5:4, 10-11).

Baptism. The only explicit reference to baptism is in 1 Pet 3:18-21, where Christian baptism is an antitype to Noah's escape in the flood and a laying hold of the assurance made possible through Christ's resurrection. Yet much of the epistle plays on themes that are appropriate to new Christians, whether explicitly growing out of baptismal traditions or otherwise.

First Peter deals with two contrasts appropriate to baptismal reflection. There are the temporal contrasts between then and now. In some cases, "then" is what the Christians used to be when they were among the Gentiles. "Now" is what they are as resident aliens in a Gentile world (see 4:1-4). In some cases, now is the era in which Christians live by faith even in the midst of suffering, and then is what will happen in the future, when their opponents will be surprised by God's judgment and Christians will be given their everlasting inheritance (see 1:4-8; 4:7, 12). Now is the time when Christians live by faith; then is the time when that faith will issue in salvation (see 1:5, 9).

There is also the contrast between "us" and "them." They are the Gentiles who represent the life that Christians have left behind. But within the theology of 1 Peter, there is hope even for them, who may be shamed or astonished into the final redemption (see 3:12).

Furthermore, appropriate to the life of new Christians is the assumption, also evident elsewhere in the New Testament, that the gifts of the faithful life will be shown in faithful conduct—in traditional terms, the combination of indicative and imperative (see 1:14-15; 2:1-3, which is explicit in its reference to rebirth and implicit in its allusion to baptism).

The new life is life in community, with emphasis on shared responsibility, shared worship, and shared identity as a "chosen race, a royal priesthood, a holy nation, God's own people" (2:9 NRSV). Those who seem to outsiders to be barely legal immigrants, sneaked over the border to stir up trouble, are really citizens in the only country that counts and members of the family that nurtures and endures.

Life in Exile. Finally, Christians are exhorted to be exemplary aliens in the land that does not welcome them. This means that they are to be as upright as the most upright of their neighbors. More than that, they are to forge for themselves an identity that sets them apart without necessarily setting them in conflict with the pagans around them. They are to return good for evil, blessing for slander—hoping, perhaps against hope, that in the judgment their very fidelity may shame their slanderers into believing.

LITERARY FORM

It seems obvious that 1 Peter is a letter, with the style of address and final salutation, the thanksgiving or blessing, and the exhortation that are typical of Hellenistic letters of the first centuries CE and quite analogous to other letters in the New Testament. It has also been noticed for many years that there seems to be a kind of break between 1 Peter 4:11 and 4:12, representing either a new subject or a new intensity of interest in subjects already raised. Early in the twentieth century it was proposed that the letter really consisted of two separate pieces joined together. First Peter 1:3–4:11 was a baptismal homily full of the joy of the new life in Christ, and 4:12–5:14 was a word of encouragement in a time where persecution had moved from possibility to reality.[30] While this is a possible explanation for the text as we have it, like all such literary constructions, it remains unprovable. There is clear evidence of themes appropriate to baptism in the first part of the letter, but the last part (beginning with 4:12) is an appropriate expansion and application of themes already introduced, brought to deeper intensity because 4:12 begins the closing exhortation. Whatever the truth about the sources of 1 Peter, the letter as we have it makes its own literary and theological sense, and we shall read it as one document read or heard by its intended audience from 1:1 through 5:14.

Beyond the obvious fact that the epistle moves from salutation to thanksgiving to body to closing salutation, the analysis of the structure of the letter depends in part on one's interpretation of how the argument or exhortation of the epistle moves. One can detect a continuing alternation between claim and exegetical grounding (cf., e.g., 1:22-23 with 1:24-25; 2:4-5 with 2:6-8). And one can find an alternation between indicative claims and imperative applications (1:1-12 leads to 1:13-16; 2:9-10 grounds 1:24-25 [which validates 1:22-23] and also grounds 2:1-30).

David Balch has found helpful internal clues for dividing the body of the letter (1:13–5:11). First Peter 1:13–2:10 works out the themes of the introductory blessing (1:3-12); therefore, these verses form a unit. First Peter 2:11–4:11 is marked by the recurrence of a number of themes—slander, suffering, the contrast between doing good and doing evil, judgment and justice.[31] There is also a repetition of themes in the beginning and end of this section, in the stress on God's coming judgment on believers and unbelievers alike (2:12; 4:5) and the stress on glorifying God (2:12; 4:11). First Peter 4:12, with its renewed address ("Beloved") and its renewed urgency, begins the final section of the main body of the epistle.

FOR FURTHER READING

Commentaries:

Achtemeier, Paul. *1 Peter.* Hermeneia. Minneapolis: Fortress, 1996.

Boring, M. Eugene. *First Peter.* ANTC. Nashville, Tn.: Abingdon, 1999.

Craddock, Fred B. *First and Second Peter and Jude.* Westminster Bible Companion. Louisville: Westminster John Knox, 1995.

Elliot, John Hall. *1 Peter.* AB 37B

Goppelt, Leonhard. *A Commentary on 1 Peter.* Edited by Ferdinand Hahn. Translated and augmented by John E. Alsup. Grand Rapids: Eerdmans, 1993.

Michaels, J. Ramsey. *1 Peter.* WBC. Waco, Tex.: Word, 1988.

Perkins, Pheme. *First and Second Peter, James, and Jude.* Interpretation. Louisville: Westminster John Knox, 1995.

Senior, Donald. *1 Peter.* SP 15. Collegeville, Minn.: Liturgical Press, 2003.

Other studies:

Balch, David L. *Let Wives Be Submissive: The Domestic Code in 1 Peter.* SBLMS. Chico, Calif.: Scholars Press, 1981.

Dalton, William Joseph. *Christ's Proclamation to the Spirits: A Study of* 1 Peter 3:18–4:6. 2nd ed. Rome: Pontifical Biblical Institute, 1989.

Elliott, John H. *A Home for the Homeless: A Sociological Exegesis of 1 Peter, Its Situation and Strategy.* Philadelphia: Fortress, 1981.

ENDNOTES

1. The designation of 1 Peter as a catholic epistle is found as early as Eusebius (c. 300 CE). See Pheme Perkins, *First and Second Peter, James, and Jude*, Interpretation (Louisville: Westminster John Knox, 1995) 1.

2. Polycarp *Letter to the Philippians* 1:3. See Kirsopp Lake, trans. *The Apostolic Fathers*, LCL (Cambridge, Mass.: Harvard University Press, 1969) 1:283-85.

3. The word for "glorified" or "glorious" (δοξάζω *doxazō*) in the two quotations is the same.

4. See Paul J. Achtemeier, *I Peter*, Hermeneia (Minneapolis: Fortress, 1996) 44. Polycarp was martyred in 155 CE.

5. A clear summary of many of these points is found in Norbert Brox, *Der erste Petrusbrief, Evangelisch-Katholischer Kommentary zum Neuen Testament* (Zurich: Benziger Verlag and Neukirchener Verlag, 1979) 44-46.

6. See A clear summary of many of these points is found in Norbert Brox, *Der erste Petrusbrief,* 44.

7. See Perkins, *First and Second Peter, James, and Jude*, 10.

8. So Brox, *Der erste Petrusbrief*, 51.

9. Achtemeier, *1 Peter*, 18-19.

10. It is obvious that if one takes Colossians, Ephesians, and the Pastoral Epistles to be Pauline, then the kind of social development 1 Peter reflects may have been taking place in Peter's lifetime.

11. Leonhard Goppelt thinks that Silvanus helped with the writing. See L. Goppelt, *A Commentary on I Peter*, ed. Ferdinand Hahn, trans. John E. Alsup (Grand Rapids: Eerdmans, 1993) 369. Achtemeier cites the use of similar formulas for the one who carries the letter and argues that this is Silvanus's role. See Achtemeier, *1 Peter*, 350n. 56.

12. This is the position of E. G. Selwyn, *The First Epistle of Peter* (London: Macmillan, 1958) 9-17.

13. This seems to be Goppelt's position. See Goppelt, *A Commentary on I Peter*, 51-52. J. Ramsey Michaels finds a mediating position between this one and the claim of Petrine authorship. See Michaels, *1 Peter*, WBC (Waco, Tex.: Word, 1988) lxvi.

14. I take this position to be close to the consensus of the contributors to *Peter in the New Testament*, ed. Raymond E. Brown, Karl P. Donfried, John Reumann (Minneapolis and Paramus: Augsburg and Paulist) 149-50.

15. This is a simplification, but not an unfair one, of Lewis Donelson's reading of pseudonymity in the Pastorals. See Donelson, *Pseudepigraphy and Ethical Argument in the Pastoral Epistles* (Tübingen: J.C.B. Mohr [Paul Siebeck], 1986) esp. 54-66.

16. Goppelt puts this argument more elegantly. See Goppelt, *A Commentary on I Peter*, 52.

17. Pliny *Letters* 10, 97, from *Pliny, Letters and Panegyricus*, trans. Betty Radice (Cambridge, Mass.: Harvard University Press, 1969) 291-93.

18. See John H. Elliot, *A Home for the Homeless* (Philadelphia: Fortress, 1981), and the essays by Elliot and David Balch in Charles H. Talbert, ed., *Perspectives on First Peter* (Macon, Ga.: Mercer University Press, 1986).

19. See C. Spicq, *Les Épitres de Saint Pierre* (Paris: Librarie Lecoffre, 1966) 40.

20. Achtemeier, *1 Peter*, 69; the whole discussion is found on 69-72.

21. Achtemeier, *1 Peter*, 69, 71.

22. See William Joseph Dalton, *Christ's Proclamation to the Spirits: A Study of I Peter 3:18–4:6*, 2nd ed., AnBib (Rome: Pontifical Biblical Institute, 1989) 166-71. See also Commentary on 1 Pet 3:18-22.

23. Achtemeier acknowledges this possibility. See Achtemeier, *1 Peter*, 298-99.

24. A phrase suggested by Marion Soards in editorial correspondence.

25. Balch, *Let Wives Be Submissive* SBLMS (Chico, Calif.: Scholars Press, 1981) 14-15, 25-56.

26. Balch, *Let Wives Be Submissive*, citing Friedrich Wilhelm, 14.

27. See Balch, *Let Wives Be Submissive*, 90.

28. Brox thinks that 1 Pet 5:12 is the key to the whole epistle, and he uses that as a criticism of a too great emphasis on baptismal themes. See Norbert Brox, *Der erste Petrusbrief, Evangelisch-Katholischer Kommentary zum Neuen Testament* (Zurich: Benziger Verlag and Neukirchener Verlag, 1979) 18-19.

29. See Paul J. Achtemeier, *1 Peter*, 100. Cf. Rom 5:3-4; Jas 1:2-4, as cited in Goppelt, *A Commentary on I Peter*, 91.

30. See the discussions in Goppelt, *A Commentary on I Peter*, 15-17; and Achtemeier, *1 Peter*, 58-59.

31. David L. Balch, *Let Wives Be Submissive*, 123-29.

The Second Letter of Peter

DUANE F. WATSON

AUTHORSHIP, ORIGIN, AND DATE

Although 2 Peter is presented as the work of "Simeon Peter, a servant and apostle of Jesus Christ" (NRSV), most scholars ascribe the book to an unknown author writing under the name of the apostle Peter.[1] Scholars consider 2 Peter to be pseudonymous for several important reasons:

(1) Second Peter is a farewell address, a literary genre in Jewish literature that was predominantly pseudonymous.

(2) Regardless of opinion reached about the authorship of 1 Peter, there are no indications that 1 Peter and 2 Peter were written by the same author. The books differ significantly in style and do not share a distinctive vocabulary or theological terminology. For example, in 1 Peter the Second Coming is a "revelation" (ἀποκάλυψις *apokalypsis*; 1 Pet 1:7, 13; 4:13), and in 2 Peter it is a "coming" or "advent" (παρουσία *parousia*; 2 Pet 1:16; 3:4).

(3) The picture of the author derived from the letter does not conform to what we know of the apostle Peter, a rural fisherman from Galilee whose native language was Aramaic. The author of 2 Peter was highly educated, perhaps of a scribal background. He was highly literate, exhibiting a rich Greek vocabulary complete with Hellenistic terminology. He was skilled in the art of Greco-Roman rhetoric, especially Asiatic rhetoric, a flowery, verbose, and excessive rhetoric popular in the late first-century CE. Greek, Jewish, and Christian traditions were familiar to him. These characteristics indicate a man (education was typically the prerogative of males in ancient society) raised in an urban setting where formal education was available. The writer's extensive knowledge of the Old Testament, Jewish tradition, and Hellenistic terminology suggests that he was a strongly Hellenized Jewish Christian.[2]

(4) The author was conscious of the fact that he was living in the post-apostolic era. The scoffers whom the apostles had predicted would appear in the end times had now appeared (2:1-3*a*; 3:3-4). All the apostles are considered to have taught the same message, and apostolic tradition is the norm to be defended (1:12, 16-18; 3:1-2, 15-16).

Being a letter to churches once addressed by the writer of 1 Peter from Rome (3:1; 1 Pet 1:1; 5:13), and being similar to early Christian literature from Rome, 2 Peter also may have originated from that city. The author may have been a member of the Roman "Petrine circle," composed of close associates and disciples of Peter. Perhaps one of these associates felt that he knew enough of the teaching of the apostle Peter to write an epistle in Peter's name after Peter's death, in essence giving Peter a new voice in the next generation. He would have been writing as a representative of the Roman church under the name of its most prominent leader. In fact, however, the letter was accepted into the canon as a product of the apostle Peter, but that conclusion was based in part on the assessment that it contained apostolic doctrine.[3]

Dating 2 Peter cannot be done with any certainty. Dates given range from the 60s (if written by the apostle Peter) to the mid-second century (if pseudonymous). Often the documents that have been used in the construction of 2 Peter (e.g., Jude) or those citing the letter (e.g., *Apocalypse of Peter*) are dated, and then a probable date for 2 Peter is surmised. However, those documents themselves cannot be dated with any certainty. Bauckham offers a helpful hypothetical approach.[4] He notes that the death of the first Christian generation was the impetus for the eschatological skepticism of the false teachers (3:4). The early church expected the parousia within the lifetime of the first generation of Christians, and the death of this generation created a crisis of belief. Bauckham calculates that this generation would have been born no later than 10 CE and would have lived about seventy years, thus arriving at a date of 80–90 CE as the earliest probable time for the writing of 2 Peter.

THE RECIPIENTS, THEIR OPPONENTS, AND THE HISTORICAL SITUATION

The recipients of 2 Peter were undesignated churches once addressed by 1 Peter (2 Pet 3:1) and by some of the Pauline Epistles (2 Pet 3:15-16). That would include, in Asia Minor, churches in Pontus, Galatia, Cappadocia, Asia, and Bithynia (1 Pet 1:1). The historical situation that prompted the author to write is the presence in the church of false teachers (2:1) who apparently were backslidden Christians (2:15, 20-22). These false teachers had convinced some, particularly spiritually weak or new Christians, to accept their doctrine and practice (2:1-3*a*, 14, 18). They even posed a danger to those mature in faith who as yet had remained unconvinced by them (1:12; 3:17).

The doctrine of the false teachers was based on eschatological skepticism (2:3*b*; 3:4, 9). They, as well as many other early Christians, anticipated that the parousia of Christ would transpire during the lifetime of the first generation of Christians. But that generation died without the parousia's materializing. As a result, they claimed that the apostolic proclamation of the parousia was a myth (1:16). Old Testament prophecies thought to support the apostolic proclamation were not inspired, they claimed, but were the result of the prophets' misguided personal interpretations of their own prophetic visions (1:20-21).[5]

Naturally the false teachers also denied the judgment that will accompany the parousia (2:3*b*; 3:5-7). Disregarding the constraint of judgment, they justified a moral libertinism that the author of 2 Peter details in a striking denunciation (2:10*b*-22). The false teachers denied the true freedom that lies in obedience to the moral commands of God and knowing Christ, and they returned to the bondage of sin (2:2, 15, 19-22). This antinomianism was attractive because Christian morality excluded the early Christians from many aspects of business and social life. Businesses and social clubs often held meetings in temples associated with the worship of pagan gods. The idolatry and sexual immorality associated with this kind of worship precluded Christians from participating in such meetings. Any teaching justifying a Christian's renewed participation in these activities would have been tempting to new converts who were accustomed to the benefits of these social events.

Since Paul's letters were known in these churches, this antinomianism might also have arisen from a misinterpretation of the Pauline doctrine of freedom in Christ (3:15-16; cf. 2:19). However, it seems to be rooted more in eschatological skepticism, which denied judgment, than in a perversion of the understanding of grace. Also, the false teachers were not gnostics, for the antinomianism is not based in a cosmic dualism that denigrated the flesh; rather, it was based on the delay of the parousia.

The situation was serious, because the doctrine and practice of the false teachers were contrary to those taught by the apostles. Apostolic doctrine defined the Christian life as one of living a "holy" life while awaiting the parousia (1:3-11; 3:11, 14-15*a*, 18). Believing and acting as they did, the false teachers and their followers would not be spiritually prepared when the parousia arrives, and they will suffer judgment (2:1, 3*b*, 4-10*a*, 12; 3:7, 16; cf. 2:17). The author's urgency stems from the conviction that the parousia would occur in the lifetime of the Christians addressed (3:11-18). Since the appearance of false teachers and their scoffing is a precursor or sign of the parousia of Christ and the judgment of the world (3:3-4), the author believed that the parousia was near.

Neyrey suggests that the false teachers' doctrine is similar to that usually associated with Epicureans.[6] The Epicureans affirmed the complete transcendence of God. God was not troubled by the goings-on of humanity. As a corollary, they also denied the providence of God, the prevailing understanding of God at the time. According to them, God is not provident. God does not work in the world according to a divine plan. The world was made by chance; humanity has freedom of choice; there is a delay of justice upon the wicked; and prophecy goes unfulfilled. A denial of the providence of God led likewise to a denial of the afterlife and its rewards and punishments. Epicurean thought filtered down into Jewish and Greek thinking in more popular forms and certainly could have influenced the audience of 2 Peter.

Noting the delay of divine judgment, the false teachers deny the intervention of God in the world and deny judgment altogether (2:3*b*; 3:4, 9). They consider important prophecies to be "cleverly devised myths" (1:16 NRSV) and "one's own interpretation" (1:20 NRSV), and they scoff at apostolic prophecy (3:3-4). They promise their followers freedom (2:19). The author of 2 Peter employs topics typically used in polemics against Epicureanism. He affirms the providence of God in judgment, both past and future (2:3*b*-10*a*; 3:5-13), and the truth of the prophecies that undergird it (1:16-21).

THE STANCE AND RHETORICAL APPROACH OF THE LETTER

Many interpreters have classified 2 Peter as an "early catholic" document. This designation refers to a now-questionable reconstruction of early Christianity that postulates that beginning with the second generation of Christians there was a movement toward institutionalization of offices in the church and toward "faith" denoting a body of doctrine and practice rather than a personal commitment. This movement was fostered by delay of the parousia and an encounter with heresy, which necessitated the creation of church offices to centralize authority and the clear articulation of doctrine.[7]

Yet 2 Peter should not be classified as early catholic. Although the delay of the parousia underlies the eschatological skepticism of the false teachers (2:3*b*; 3:4, 9), the author expects both the churches and the false teachers to be alive when the parousia does arrive (1:19; 2:12; 3:14). The judgment of the false teachers at the parousia will not forever be delayed, and when it comes it will be swift (2:1-3*a*). The author does not address any church officers (unless the false teachers of 2:1 hold an office), but assumes that the churches will understand the situation and respond as desired. Also, faith is not understood as a set body of orthodox doctrine. The author is defending apostolic tradition against perversion of its eschatological and ethical teachings, but there is no indication that these are encapsulated in creedal formulae and governed by church authorities.[8]

Second Peter is predominantly deliberative rhetoric that, by proofs and advice, tries to persuade an audience to do what is advantageous, necessary, and expedient and to dissuade it from what is the opposite. The letter is explicit that its aim is to remind the audience of the apostolic tradition on eschatology and ethics (1:12-15; 3:1-2). Its aim, therefore, is not to heed the false teachers' doctrine and practice, and thus come under like judgment at the encroaching parousia. However, 2 Peter also contains sections of judicial and epideictic rhetoric. Judicial rhetoric, rhetoric of accusation and defense, comprises portions in which the author refutes and counteraccuses the false teachers (1:16–2:10*a*; 3:1-13). Epideictic rhetoric, the rhetoric of praise and blame for the purpose of uplifting what is honorable and casting down what is dishonorable, is found in 2:10*b*-22. Here the author denounces and negatively characterizes the false teachers and their doctrine and practice by comparing them with great sinners and sins of the past. He does so in order to increase the churches' assent to the received faith and preserve them from impending judgment.[9]

To minimize the influence of the false teachers, the author urges the faithful to strive for Christian maturity and godliness in accordance with apostolic doctrine (1:3-11; 3:11-18). He refutes the false teachers' denial of Christ's parousia and prophecies that support its proclamation (1:16-21; 3:1-13) and their denial of judgment (2:3*b*-10*a*; 3:1-13). He exposes their doctrine and practice for the evil they really are (2:1-22). He brings to bear the authority of the Old Testament and Jewish tradition (2:3*b*-10, 15-16, 22; 3:5-6), the Old Testament prophets (1:19-21; 3:2), the New Testament apostles (1:3-11, 16-19; 3:1-4), the Epistle of 1 Peter (3:1), Paul (3:15-16), the Letter of Jude (2:1-18; 3:1-3), and Jesus (3:2).

LITERARY GENRE, COMPOSITION, AND CONTENT

Second Peter is a blend of two literary genres. As indicated by its opening (1:1-2), one genre is that of the letter. The other genre is the farewell speech or testament. The testament was popular in Judaism and was used to relate the last words of dying men of renown, both within and beyond the Old Testament (Genesis 49; Deuteronomy 33), and was borrowed by early Christian writers (John 13–17; Acts 20:17-34; 2 Timothy). In a testament, the dying leader announces his death and rehearses ethical teachings and traditions central to the community that he wants them to continue to observe after his death. Thinking that a dying individual was given prophetic powers just prior to death, people understood the testament to provide revelation about the future of the community, and this future provided a basis for the particular emphasis of the ethical instruction.

In 2 Peter, "Peter" gives ethical instruction to remind the churches of their heritage (1:3-11), announcing his death and wishing that his instructions be remembered (1:12-15; 3:1-2). He reveals that after his death there will be a rise of false teachers in the last days who will deny eschatological expectation and will corrupt ethical practice (2:1-3*a*; 3:1-4). The remainder of the letter defends the apostolic teaching on eschatology and ethics. The testament is not usually in the form of a letter, but when it was to be sent to a specific congregation, the letter genre was a natural adaptation.[10]

When comparing the prophecies of "Peter" with the current situation of the churches, the author shifts from the perspective of a testament, often in future or past tense (2:1-3*a*; 3:1-4), to the perspective of the churches, addressed in the present tense (2:3*b*-22; 3:5-10, 16*b*). These tense shifts are not the result of forgetting that he was presenting a testament that prophesies events in the future; nor is it the futuristic use of the present tense, which substitutes the present tense for the future when there is great confidence about future events. This juxtaposition of past prophecies of false teachers and their teaching with their present manifestation in the churches is a teaching tool that helps the churches to understand that what has been prophesied about false teachers in the past is being fulfilled in their present.

The author of 2 Peter is familiar with a variety of literature. He quotes the Old Testament (LXX) three times (2 Pet 2:22 = Prov 26:11; 2 Pet 3:8 = Ps 89:4[90:4 MT]; 2 Pet 3:13 = Isa 65:17; 66:2) and alludes to it many other times (e.g., 2 Pet 1:17-18 = Ps 2:6-7). He uses extra-biblical Jewish haggadic traditions (2:4-5, 7-8, 15-16) and a Jewish apocalypse (3:4-13). His letter exhibits many similarities with Hellenistic Jewish literature (like the works of Philo and Josephus). Gospel tradition that is independent of the canonical Gospels is also present (1:14, John 21:18; 1:16-18, Transfiguration; 3:10, Matt 24:43-44, Luke 12:39-40). He knows a partial or complete collection of Pauline letters, which he regards as inspired and authoritative (3:15-16), but does not seem to be influenced by them. He also knows of 1 Peter, but does not use it (3:1). This independence of 1 Peter is unusual because pseudonymous authors usually tried to emulate known works by the person in whose name they were writing. Parallels in language and tradition with *1 Clement, 2 Clement,* and the *Shepherd of Hermas* are present, and their presence can be explained only if 2 Peter derives from the same Christian community in Rome.

Second Peter is most noted for dependence upon the Letter of Jude (2 Pet 2:1-18 = Jude 4-13; 2 Pet 3:1-3 = Jude 16:1-18). The verbal resemblances are not as close as those between Matthew and Mark, for example, but redaction criticism indicates that the author of 2 Peter used Jude in his composition. Jude is a carefully crafted letter, and the corresponding portions of 2 Peter are scattered throughout a denunciation of the false teachers. It is easier to see the author of 2 Peter mining the Epistle of Jude for images and examples helpful in building a denunciation than it is to see the writer of Jude using scattered portions of 2 Peter to write a carefully constructed letter aimed at the problems of a specific community. In his use of Jude, the writer of 2 Peter omits allusions and quotations to *1 Enoch* (Jude 14:1-15) and the *Testament of Moses* (Jude 9). This may be because these works were not well-known outside Palestinian Judaism, the community in which Jude was written, and not because the author of 2 Peter was working with a growing sense of canon, as claimed by those classifying it as an early catholic epistle.

The letter begins with a typical prescript (1:1-2), followed by a miniature homily that outlines apostolic teaching on the nature of the Christian life and provides the basis for the argumentation to follow (1:3-11). The homily is followed by a statement of the purpose of the letter as being a reminder of apostolic teaching, an element central to the testament genre (1:12-15). The body of the letter is composed of 1:16–3:13. It refutes the proposition of the false teachers that the apostolic preaching of the parousia is a myth supported by Old Testament prophecies that are not inspired (1:16-21). In turn, the author counteraccuses the false teachers of standing in the tradition of the false prophets (2:1-3*a*) and refutes their denial of the parousia judgment based on its delay (2:3*b*-10*a*). Breaking up the refutation is a strong denunciation of the false teachers, aimed at destroying their credibility (2:10*b*-22). The body of the letter closes with an apology for the delay of the parousia, refuting the false teachers' denial of the parousia and the belief that God has not acted in judgment in history on a cosmic scale (3:1-13). The letter closes with moral exhortation and a doxology (3:14-18).

THE THEOLOGY OF 2 PETER

The false teachers charged that the apostolic teaching about the parousia and its accompanying judgment was a "cleverly devised myth" based on uninspired prophecies in the Old Testament (1:16-21). Their eschatological skepticism was fueled by the delay of the parousia, which they expected in the first Christian generation (3:3-4), and their denial that God had or ever would intervene in history with judgment (2:3*b*, 9-10*a*; 3:3-4). The author's theological approach is conditioned by the needs of refuting this eschatological skepticism. He emphasizes apostolic tradition, which affirms the parousia and its judgment. This tradition is founded on the teachings of Peter (1:12-18), Paul (3:15*b*-16), the other apostles (1:16-18; 3:1-2), and the Old Testament prophetic witness (1:20-21; 3:2).[11]

The Nature of Scripture. In his appeal to apostolic tradition, the author of 2 Peter makes several comments about the nature of Scripture. Old Testament prophecies are the prophets' inspired interpretations of the signs, dreams, and visions they received from God. These prophecies provide preliminary revelation into the future purposes of God (1:19-21; 3:2). The author regards a collection of Paul's letters (the letters involved are unknown) as inspired Scripture, a designation that includes the Old Testament and perhaps other writings in the New Testament. Paul is said to have written with the wisdom given him, just as the Old Testament prophets were moved by the Holy Spirit to give their prophecies (3:15*b*-16; cf. 1:20-21).

The Parousia and Judgment. In contrast to the false teachers' denial of the parousia and its accompanying judgment, the author affirms both. God's perspective of time is different from our own, and what seems to us to be a delay is not so for God (3:8). The parousia and judgment have been delayed because God is allowing time for the ungodly to repent; but Christ will eventually return at an unexpected time, and all the works of humanity will be exposed and subjected to judgment (3:9-10). The ungodly will be destroyed at the judgment (2:1, 3*b*, 9-10*a*, 12; 3:7, 16), whereas the godly will share the incorruptibility and immortality that characterizes God's nature (1:4; 2:19-20); they will be given entrance into the eternal kingdom (1:11) and provided a place in the new heaven and new earth (3:13).

The false teachers' denial of God's intervention in judgment is countered by the author's stressing the interrelated roles of God as Creator and Judge. As is understood from Genesis 1, God created the heavens and earth by God's Word, or divine fiat. God's Word separated the waters of the cosmic sea both above and below to form land (3:5). It was by God's same Word that the waters above and below the earth were released to produce the judgment of the flood (3:6). It will also be by God's Word that the heavens and the earth will be judged with destruction by fire (3:7). It is presumed that this same Word will create the new heavens and the new earth, where only righteousness can dwell (3:11-13). Examples of God's judgment from the past are used to prove that God intervenes in history for judgment and thus will do so again (2:3*b*-10*a*; 3:3-7).

The Christian Life Under Christ's Lordship. The denial of the parousia and judgment led the false teachers to disregard the moral implications of the gospel. Thus the author of 2 Peter emphasizes the Lordship of Christ. Jesus is both Lord and Savior (1:11; 2:20; 3:2, 18). The title "Lord" (κύριος *kyrios*) indicates Jesus' authority at God's right hand to rule both people and the cosmos. The title "Savior" (σωτήρ *sōtēr*) is used in conjunction with "Lord," indicating that by his redemptive work as Savior, Jesus is now Lord, particularly of those he has redeemed. He is the Master who bought them from slavery to sin (2:1), and knowledge of him enables release from slavery to corruption, decay, and mortality (1:4; 2:19-20).

Christ's gift of salvation and everything needed for the moral life is grounded in the knowledge of him (1:3-4). Christians must make every effort to grow in righteousness in order to confirm Christ's call and election (1:3, 11; 3:18). Such moral effort rooted in the knowledge of Jesus Christ is needed in order to escape corruption and mortality (1:4; 2:19-20) and to be able to enter the eternal kingdom (1:11). This moral effort includes nurturing virtues (1:5-7) and following the way of righteousness established by Christ through the holy commandment to love God with all our being and to love other people as we love ourselves (2:21). Christians are to live with vital eschatological expectation that the parousia will come "like a thief" (3:10 NRSV).

They are to be morally blameless in the interim in order to be ready to become citizens of the new heavens and the new earth, which are characterized by righteousness (3:11-14). The righteous will be rescued from the world and its corruption only if they remain righteous (2:5, 8-9).

Immoral behavior is an affront to Christ's status as Lord and Savior. It amounts to denying his authority and maligning the way of truth (2:1-2), departing from the way of righteousness and the holy commandment (2:15, 20-21), and returning to slavery to corruption under the pretense of freedom from moral constraint and judgment (2:19-20). It is to be unfruitful in the knowledge of Christ and not confirm Christ's call and election (1:8-9), to stumble in the moral walk and forfeit salvation (1:10-11).

FOR FURTHER READING

Bauckham, R. J. *Jude, 2 Peter.* WBC 50. Waco, Tex.: Word, 1983.

———. *Jude, 2 Peter.* WBT. Waco, Tex.: Word, 1990.

Chester, A., and R. Martin. *The Theology of the Letters of James, Peter, and Jude.* New Testament Theology. Cambridge: Cambridge University Press, 1994.

Gilmore, Michael J. *The Significance of Parallels Between Second Peter and Other Early Christian Literature.* Academia Biblica 10. Atlanta: Society of Biblical Literature, 2002.

Kraftchick, Steven J. *Jude, 2 Peter.* ANTC. Nashville, Tn.: Abingdon, 2002.

Neyrey, J. H. *2 Peter, Jude.* AB 37C. New York: Doubleday, 1993.

Perkins, Pheme. *Peter: Apostle for the Whole Church.* Studies on Personalities of the New Testament. Columbia: University of South Carolina Press, 1994.

Watson, Duane F. *Invention, Arrangement, and Style: Rhetorical Criticism of Jude and 2 Peter.* SBLDS 104. Atlanta: Scholars Press, 1988.

ENDNOTES

1. For a discussion of the introductory issues, see R. J. Bauckham, "2 Peter: An Account of Research," in *Aufstieg und Niedergang der remischen Welt*, ed. W. Haase and H. Temporini (Berlin: Walter de Gruyter, 1988) II.25.5, 3713-52; T. Fornberg, *An Early Church in a Pluralistic Society: A Study of 2 Peter*, ConBNT (Lund: CWK Gleerup, 1980).

2. For the social location of the author, see J. H. Neyrey, *2 Peter, Jude*, AB 37C (New York: Doubleday, 1993) 128-42.

3. See R. J. Bauckham, *Jude, 2 Peter*, WBC 50 (Waco, Tex.: Word, 1983) 158-62; T. V. Smith, *Petrine Controversies in Early Christianity: Attitudes Towards Peter in Christian Writings of the First Two Centuries*, WUNT 15 (Tübingen: J. C. B. Mohr [Paul Siebeck], 1985) 65-101; M. L. Soards, "1 Peter, 2 Peter, and Jude as Evidence for a Petrine School," in *Aufstieg und Niedergang der remischen Welt* (with addenda by V. O. Ward), ed. W. Haase and H. Temporini (Berlin: Walter de Gruyter, 1988) II.25.5, 3827-49.

4. Bauckham, *Jude, 2 Peter*, WBC, 157-58.

5. See C. H. Talbert, "II Peter and the Delay of the Parousia," *VC* 20 (1966) 137-45.

6. Neyrey, *2 Peter, Jude*, 122-28; "The Form and Background of the Polemic in 2 Peter," *JBL* 99 (1980) 407-31.

7. E. Käsemann, "An Apologia for Primitive Christian Eschatology," in *Essays on New Testament Themes*, trans. W. J. Montague, SBT 41 (London: SCM, 1964) 169-95.

8. Bauckham, *Jude, 2 Peter*, WBC, 151-54.

9. See D. F. Watson, *Invention, Arrangement, and Style: Rhetorical Criticism of Jude and 2 Peter*, SBLDS 104 (Atlanta: Scholars Press, 1988) 81-146.

10. E.g., *2 Apoc. Bar.* 78-86.

11. For the theology of 2 Peter, see R. J. Bauckham, *Jude, 2 Peter*, WBT (Waco, Tex.: Word, 1990) 39-107; A. Chester and R. P. Martin, *The Theology of the Letters of James, Peter, and Jude*, New Testament Theology (Cambridge: Cambridge University Press, 1994) 134-63.

The First, Second and Third Letters of John

C. CLIFTON BLACK

"How plain, how full, and how deep a compendium of genuine Christianity!"[1] Thus did John Wesley (1703–91) estimate the First Epistle of John. As three of the canon's catholic or general epistles (along with James, 1 and 2 Peter, and Jude), the Johannine letters have justly enjoyed esteem disproportionate to their size. As well as rewards, these texts offer their interpreters some mysteries.

THE AUTHORSHIP OF 1, 2, AND 3 JOHN AND THEIR ATTRIBUTION IN THE EARLY CHURCH

Very little can be said with confidence about the author of these documents. Like the Fourth Gospel, the First Epistle of John is anonymous. The sender of 2 John (v. 1) and 3 John (v. 1) identifies himself, not as "John," but as ὁ πρεσβύτερος (*ho presbyteros*, "the elder"), a designation patient of alternative interpretations. While the matter is beyond knockdown proof, the Second and Third Epistles are sufficiently similar to 1 John, stylistically and substantively, to suggest that "the elder" authored all three letters (cf. 1 John 2:7; 3:11/2 John 5-6; 1 John 3:6/3 John 11). This chapter will proceed from the assumption that the Johannine letters were composed by the same author, who, for the sake of convenience, will be referred to as "the elder."

For its first seven centuries the church's reception of the Johannine epistles was fitful and heavily dependent on assumptions about their authorship. First John is the earliest and consistently best attested of the three; its wording is echoed as early as 135 CE in Polycarp's *Letters to the Philippians* (cf. 7.1 with 1 John 2:24; 3:8; 4:2-3). Along with 2 John, 1 John is indisputably quoted around the year 180 in Irenaeus's *Against Heresies* (cf. 1.16.3 with 2 John 11; 3.16.5 with 1 John 2:18-19, 21-22; 3.16.8 with 2 John 7-8 and 1 John 4:1-2; 5:1). From the third century onward, acceptance of the First Epistle was secure and widespread, owing mainly to its ascription to John the son of Zebedee, whom the early church came to identify as the "disciple whom Jesus loved" (John 13:23; 19:26-27; 20:1-10; 21:7, 20-24) and the author of the Fourth Gospel. Furthermore, 1 John's content was found congenial with several religious and theological interests of the patristic church, such as refinements in the doctrine of sin and the refutation of heresy.[2] Doubtful apostolic authorship and sparseness of content probably account for the slight use, neglect, or rejection of the Second and Third Epistles during the same period.[3] Third John is unattested until the mid–third century.[4] It appears to have been carried into scriptural recognition on the coattails of 2 John, just as the popularity of the Second Epistle derived from the church's recognition of the First. By the late fourth century, in some regions, the three epistles were regarded to be a unit and were circulated as such. As confirmed by the Venerable Bede (672/73–735), their collective acceptance into the canon was ultimately based on the medieval church's consensus that the apostle John had authored all three epistles.[5]

Nevertheless, there is no hard evidence to support the composition of 1, 2, or 3 John by John the apostle and son of Zebedee, an inference challenged as early as 130 CE by Papias of Hierapolis.[6] Likewise, Dionysius of Alexandria (d. c. 264) expressed doubt that John of Patmos, the author of Revelation (Rev 1:9; cf. Rev 1:1, 4; 22:8), had written either John's epistles or the Gospel of John.[7] The authorship of the Johannine letters remains a mystery. Unlike many patristic interpreters, however, we may safely regard these letters' continuing benefit for the church as both logically and theologically independent of their authorship. If "the elder" did not consider the verification of his identity crucial for his message's validity, then neither need we.

THE RELATION OF THE EPISTLES TO THE GOSPEL OF JOHN

Most interpreters, ancient and modern, have recognized an appreciable resemblance in the ideas and phraseology of the Fourth Gospel and the Johannine letters: among others, "to know [or walk in] the truth" (see John 8:32; 1 John 2:21; 2 John 1, 4; 3 John 3); "a commandment" to "love one another" (John 13:34; 15:12, 17; 1 John 3:23; 2 John 5); the completion of joy among believers (John 15:11; 16:24; 17:13, 1 John 1:4; 2 John 12). The likenesses between the Gospel of John and 1 John are especially abundant; for instance, the address to believers as little children (John 13:33; 21:5; 1 John 2:1, 12, 14, 18, 24); the presentation of Jesus as advocate, or "Paraclete" (John 14:16; 1 John 2:1); the world as the realm of disbelief or hostility (John 7:7; 8:23; 15:18, 19; 17:16, 25; 1 John 2:16; 3:1, 13; 4:5); the importance of "abiding" in God or in Christ (John 6:56; 15:4, 5, 6, 7; 1 John 2:6, 27, 28; 3:6, 24; 4:13, 15, 16). Such resemblances as these would seem to support the composition of 1, 2, and 3 John by the Fourth Evangelist, a position held by some scholars.[8] Their equally impressive differences, some of which will be detailed below, lead most interpreters (including me) to think that the Gospel and the epistles were probably composed by different authors within a circle of communities that shared a common Johannine tradition.[9]

Heavier debate swirls around the letters' dating. Which came first: one or all of the epistles or John's Gospel? The question of chronology usually turns on the interpretation of perceived divergences, between the letters and the Gospel, in their social situation and theological point of view. Commentators' assessments of the evidence split into roughly four groups: (1) those who believe that one or more of the letters antedated the Gospel; (2) those who think that John was written before 1, 2, or 3 John; (3) those who hypothesize a more fluid, mutually contemporary process of composition, in which the characteristics of one or more of the epistles are in some way presupposed by parts of the Gospel; and (4) those who find the evidence too ambiguous to invest confidence in any proposed sequence for the creation of these writings.[10] The complexity implied by alternative (3) is plausible, though by its nature impossible to reconstruct without considerable speculation. Option (4) is laudable for its candor and (1) for its inclination to treat the letters on their own terms; still, it is difficult to interpret the vagaries of 2, 3, and especially 1 John apart from the Fourth Gospel.[11]

Less problematic is a modified version of possibility (2): if the letters do not rely on John in its finished form, they manifestly draw from a Johannine tradition whose most extensive extant deposit is that Gospel. Such an assessment comports with a date for the epistles' composition around the turn of the first century CE, as most commentators suggest and the evidence of Polycarp supports.[12] We cannot be sure that these letters were composed in the order that they were canonized. Working from the assumption that all three were written at about the same time, in practice most interpreters have found 2 and 3 John more intelligible in the light of 1 John. Since Smyrna's Bishop Polycarp knew 1 John, Asia Minor (modern-day Turkey) is a possible provenance for the letters; of late, however, scholars have tended to locate the Johannine literature closer to Palestine, perhaps in Syria. It is impossible, in any case, to confirm the epistles' original locale. Also beyond verification is their composition after the Fourth Gospel. Nevertheless, 1 John appears to know at least the tradition on which that Gospel was based.

THE SETTING OF THE JOHANNINE LETTERS IN RELIGIOUS ANTIQUITY

Introducing his exegesis of the Johannine epistles in *The Interpreter's Bible*, Amos N. Wilder observed that, in contrast to John's Gospel, 1 John "lacks evidence of Semitic style. It reflects more directly than John a Hellenistic milieu...not Greek, properly speaking, but Oriental-Gnostic."[13] Wilder's appraisal conformed with Rudolf Bultmann's analysis of the First Epistle, which hypothesized a source with oriental, non-Christian gnostic tendencies, used but corrected by the author of 1 John.[14] Especially in Germany there is continuing support for the view that John's Gospel and letters are at home within gnosticism (a syncretistic movement, characterized by a radically dualistic worldview, which proposed salvation by revealed, esoteric knowledge). Such a theory is by no means impossible; nevertheless, it runs up against substantial problems. The correspondence between gnostic and Johannine conceptuality is not as precise as sometimes alleged, and the literature of gnosticism, though indebted to older traditions, is considerably later than any of the New Testament documents. At present many scholars speak with less certitude than Bultmann or Wilder of a gnostic background for the Johannine letters. They are more inclined to regard Johannine Christianity as a part of the background for gnosticism as it evolved in the second century and beyond.

An important reassessment of Johannine literature has occurred with the discovery of the Dead Sea Scrolls, which can be confidently dated to the century before the New Testament. Understandably, Wilder's treatment of 1 John's background does not engage the Qumran texts, the first of which had been found less than ten years before he penned his introduction. The parallels between the scrolls and John's epistles should not be exaggerated. To take but one example, Qumran's radically pious devotion to the law of Moses[15] is obviously different from 1 John's radical obedience to the commandments of Jesus Christ (2:3; 3:23). Yet the affinities between Johannine and Qumran language are equally hard to deny; among others, "doing the truth" (1 John 1:6 [also John 3:21]/1QS 1:5; 5:3; 8:2) and "walking in light" or "in darkness" (1 John 1:6-7; 2:9-11 [also John 12:35-36]/1QS 3:20-25). Although the nature of the relationship between John and Qumran remains a debated question, the discovery of the scrolls has indisputably enhanced scholars' appreciation of Jewish influence, beyond the Old Testament, on the Johannine writings.[16] As a result, John's vocabulary and ideas, which at one time seemed closely akin to Greco-Roman mysticism or "higher paganism,"[17] have been largely reconceived within the contexts of Palestinian and Hellenistic Judaism.

More conspicuous in the religious background of John's letters, especially 1 John, are basic confessions within early Christianity about God, Christ, and Christian responsibility.[18] The claim that God sent the Son into the world (1 John 4:9) to accomplish, by his sacrificial death, atonement for sin (2:2; 4:10), salvation (4:14), and familial fellowship with God (1:3) lies at, or very near, the core of the proclamation of other New Testament witnesses (cf. Matt 11:25-27/ Luke 10:21-22; Acts 3:19; Rom 3:25; 8:15-17; Gal 4:4; Eph 2:1-10; Heb 4:15–5:10; 9:11–10:18). While nuanced in a distinctively Johannine idiom (cf. John 7:17; 13:34; 16:8, 10), the importance of doing God's will (1 John 2:17), the performance of righteousness (1 John 3:7, 17), and the commandment to love God and neighbor (1 John 4:21) are closely paralleled in the synoptic Gospels (Matt 7:21; Mark 3:35 par.; 12:28-34 par.; Luke 6:46; 13:25-27), in Paul (Rom 12:2; 13:9-10; Gal 5:14), and in James (Jas 2:15-16). Like Paul (1 Cor 15:3-11), the author of 1 John (1:1-4; 2:7; 3:11) underscores the indebtedness of his preaching to Christian tradition shared with his readers.

Close verbal and conceptual similarities that obtain between the Gospel and epistles of John were noted earlier in this introduction. The letters of John apparently drew from, and exemplify, a discrete Johannine tradition within primitive Christianity. Whether this tradition manifested itself sociologically as a "sect" or a "school" has been much discussed in the past twenty-five years; predictably, judgments in that matter depend greatly on how those terms are defined.[19] One need only observe that 1 John implies, and 2 John (v. 1) and 3 John (v. 1) expressly indicate, the existence of different Christian congregations within a Johannine network, for which those letters' author assumes an advisory and perhaps supervisory responsibility. The situation seems similar to that in Revelation 1–3, where John of Patmos issues encouragement and warning to a nearby circle of seven churches in Asia Minor. At the time of the composition of the Johannine epistles, the communities addressed by the elder showed signs of disintegrating.

THE GENRE OF 1, 2, AND 3 JOHN

On at least one feature of the Johannine epistles there is practically universal agreement: Second and Third John are real letters, adhering as closely to the epistolary conventions of antiquity as any such literature in the New Testament. Second John contains petitions addressed to a community. Third John is a more private communication (v. 1), adopting the form of a letter of recommendation (v. 12).

Identifying the genre of the First Epistle, however, has proved vexing, both for what it contains and for what it lacks. In comparison with ancient letters, 1 John has neither a formal salutation nor a formal conclusion. While epistolary material may stand without the former (Hebrews) or the latter (James), it is unusual for an epistle to omit both. Most commentators concur that the form of 1 John does not clearly register as that of an epistle, but there is no consensus on how this document should be classified—whether as an essay, or a treatise, a sermon or a manifesto, an encyclical or a circular letter, to name but a few proposals. Functionally at least, some of these alternatives (sermon or essay) are more closely analogous to documents contemporaneous with 1 John than are others (encyclical). Furthermore, many scholars judge 1 John to be a commentary on, or in some sense an application of, the Johannine tradition, perhaps even to the extent of being modeled after the Fourth Gospel's general framework.[20]

If these questions cannot be resolved, they can be clarified. Whatever its genre, 1 John is a written communication (1:4; 2:1, 7- 8, 12-14, 21, 26; 5:13), which does not preclude its having been experienced orally or aurally by its first readers. It is unwise to force 1 John into a single generic pigeonhole. In antiquity literary categories—letters, in particular—were often conflated with other genres (as we can witness throughout the canon). In the New Testament, form typically follows function; it is more important that we understand what 1 John does, less crucial that we agree on the right tag with which to label it.

On the face of the evidence, 1 John is concerned with proclamation (1:1-3), exhortation (2:7-11), and encouragement (2:12-14). Frequently, all three activities are tightly entwined (e.g., 1:5–2:6). Like Hebrews, 1 John functions as a "word of exhortation" (λόγος τῆς παρακλήσεως *logos tēs paraklēseōs*; Heb 13:22; cf. Acts 13:15), though that term appears in none of the Johannine writings and should not be pressed as a hard-and-fast classification of 1 John. Provided that we bear in mind the limits of the traditional characterization, there is no harm in our calling 1 John a "letter" or an "epistle," as a matter of convenience and responsible alignment of that document with 2 and 3 John. Finally, while the Johannine letters manifest an appropriation of the Johannine tradition, it is less clear that 1 John is so closely patterned after the Gospel of John that the First Epistle was intended to serve as an extended commentary on the Fourth Gospel. That is to say, the elder engages his community's tradition, drawing out some of its theological implications for the life of the church in a new day.

THE STRUCTURE AND STYLE OF THE JOHANNINE LETTERS

Exhortations to communal life in Christian love and truth lie at the heart of the more general Second Epistle of John and the more pointed Third. Combined with the letters' brevity, this hortatory core has made it rather easy for interpreters to articulate the structure of 2 and 3 John. Again, however, the First Epistle is more difficult to analyze. Thoughtful interpreters have long disagreed on this document's organization. Some perceive in 1 John an intricately woven structure; others a pattern no more discernible than "the waves of the sea."[21]

Describing the argument of the First Epistle, John Calvin (1509–64) noted that "it contains teaching mixed with exhortations." Many modern interpreters concur that proclamation and paraenesis (moral exhortation) distinguish the framework of 1 John.[22] Most commentators agree, further, that its thought does not adhere to a single, tightly reasoned line of argument. In musical terms, 1 John is not a *Brandenburg Concerto* that chugs relentlessly along a straight line from start to finish. The First Epistle is more like Ravel's vertiginous *Bolero*, which repeats a few themes with increasingly complex orchestration. "The writer 'thinks around' a succession of related topics," as C. H. Dodd observed. "The development of a theme brings us back almost to the starting-point; almost, but not quite, for there is a slight shift which provides a transition to a fresh theme; or it may be to a theme which had apparently been dismissed at an earlier point, and now comes up for consideration from a slightly different angle.[23]

The movements of thought within 1 John are held together by at least two devices. The author uses particular words or phrases to link clusters of thought—e.g., "sin" or "walks in darkness" (1:5–2:11/2:12-17); "born of God" and "children of God" (2:18-29/3:1-24); to "know the spirit of truth" and to "know God" (4:1-6/4:7–5:5). The elder also employs "hinge verses" whose themes pivot between the letter's parts—e.g., 2:28-29 ("abide in him"/"born of him") and 5:12-13 ("the Son of God"/"have [eternal] life"). Many commentators are less inclined than some of their early twentieth-century predecessors to regard conceptual tensions within 1 John as vestiges of a complex redaction of traditions or sources. While not inconceivable, such a process is largely if not entirely untraceable.[24]

In pointing up its convoluted structure, an important and pervasive aspect of 1 John's style comes into focus. The technical term for its circular redundancy is "amplification": a rhetorical technique, based on patterns of parallelism, that suggested to ancient listeners a grandeur appropriate for the consideration of lofty, even divine, matters. Even to modern ears 1 John's famous disquisition on love (4:7-21) registers with extraordinary gravity because of what the elder says and the sonority with which he says it. Yet the elder is not merely an accomplished stylist. His manner has a theological point, for the discourse in 1 John is unmistakably redolent of Jesus in the Fourth Gospel (cf. John 17:20-26). The rhetoric of 1 John "abides" in the speech of the Johannine Jesus, enacting the elder's assurance, "This is the message we have heard from him and proclaim to you" (1 John 1:5*a* NRSV; cf. John 17:7-8).[25]

THE ADVERSARIAL CHARACTER OF 1, 2, AND 3 JOHN

> Who is the liar but the one who denies that Jesus is the Christ?
>
> (1 John 2:22*a* NRSV)

> Many deceivers have gone out into world...any such person is the deceiver and the antichrist!
>
> (2 John 7 NRSV)

> Whoever does good is of God; whoever does evil has not seen God. (3 John 11*b* NRSV)

Since the Middle Ages most commentators have detected a polemical edge in John's epistles. There has been considerably less agreement on the nature of the opposition challenged by the elder. Such a question is still worth pondering, for if we grossly misunderstand the elder's points of resistance, we may vastly misconstrue the letters' implications in our own day.

The Third Epistle patently revolves around the offer and refusal of hospitality among communities within the Johannine circle (see 3 John 3, 5-8, 10*b*, 12). Larger issues of authority may underlie this controversy (3 John 4, 9). The elder's brush across theologically charged topics within Johannine tradition ("love," 3 John 1, 6; "truth," 3 John 1, 3-4, 8, 12) has prompted many interpreters to imagine a doctrinal component in this letter's dispute over jurisdiction. The elder, however, neither makes that connection explicit nor elaborates any theological terms in 3 John. The issue of hospitality, particularly the basis for its denial, recurs in 2 John (vv. 10-11), though here the topic is eclipsed by a more obviously theological concern: the teaching of many deceivers that Jesus Christ has not come in the flesh (2 John 7-9).

Similar worries apparently motivate some comments in the First Epistle. The nub of the dispute alluded to in 2 John 7 is echoed in 1 John 4:2*b*-3. The elder insists, in addition, that Jesus is the Christ (1 John 2:22), belief in which assures that one is born of God (1 John 5:1). Those who confess Jesus as the Son of God abide in God (1 John 4:15) and conquer the world (1 John 5:5). Jesus Christ came, not with the water only, but with the water and the blood (1 John 5:6). The denial of such claims is associated with "many antichrists," "false prophets," and "liars" (1 John 2:18-19, 22; 4:1, 3*b*, 5; 5:10). Also considered a "liar" is one who claims sinlessness but disobeys the commandments (1 John 1:10; 2:4), who professes love for God but hates other Christians (1 John 4:20). First John indicates, furthermore, that certain dissidents have broken off relations with the elder and his audience (1 John 2:18-19; 4:1-3). On its face the evidence suggests that 1 John, like 2 and 3 John, has arisen from an adversial situation.

Beyond this point any assessment of the elder's opponents becomes deeply conjectural and impossible to verify with confidence. The position challenged by the elder appears to have an affinity with docetism (δοκεῖν *dokein*, "to seem"), a second-century theological trend that, according to Ignatius (d. c. 110 CE), disavowed Jesus Christ as "flesh-bearing,"[26] claimed that Christ "merely seemed to suffer,"[27] and rejected the saving significance of Christ's death.[28] In spite of ingenious attempts by some commentators to fill the gap,[29] the elder himself does not clarify the connection, if any, between his adversaries' docetic leanings and their dubious conduct.

While the Johannine letters bear real marks of contentious literature, we should beware of over-interpreting the evidence. Of the elder's opponents we have no direct knowledge independent of his imputations, which are scant, vague, and partial. Moreover, some of 1 John's refutations probably reflect their author's dialectical style; he is not always rebutting adversaries, but sometimes provoking friends to self-examination (see 1 John 1:6-7; 2:9-11; 4:7-8, 19-21; 5:12).[30] One's perception of these epistles' whispered quarrels should be balanced, therefore, by confessing one's ignorance of their depth, coherence, and precise profile. "The work of reconstruction is always fascinating," A. E. Brooke mused. "But we have to remember how few of the necessary bricks are supplied to us, and how large a proportion of the building material we have to fashion for ourselves."[31]

MAJOR THEMES OF THE JOHANNINE EPISTLES

The primary subjects to which the elder returns are tightly interwoven, though no more systematically coordinated than those of any New Testament author. It is vital that we take our bearings on these letters' theology with attention to its development beyond the Gospel of John.

1. "God is Light and in Him There is no Darkness At All": The Nature of God. C. K. Barrett's assessment of the Fourth Evangelist may also be pertinent to the author of the Johannine epistles: "There could hardly be a more Christocentric writer than John, yet his very Christocentricity is theocentric."[32] If anything, this "theocentric Christocentricity" is clearer in the letters. For the elder, God is the standard of fidelity, of righteousness (1 John 1:9; 3:7), and of goodness (3 John 11), the agent of forgiveness (1 John 1:9; 2:12) whose essential character is light (1 John 1:5, 7), purity (1 John 3:3), truth (1 John 5:20), and, most especially, prevenient love (1 John 4:7-12, 16, 19). From this central understanding of God radiate most of the letters' other themes. Jesus, God's Son, has been sent by the Father as the Savior of the world (1 John 4:14). Through the Son (1 John 2:23; 5:20), who enables obedience to his commandments (1 John 2:3-5), all believers "have" or "know" God (1 John 2:23; 4:7-8; 2 John 9). They abide in or experience a fully reciprocal relationship with God (1 John 1:3; 2:24; 3:24; 4:13-16). Throughout the Johannine epistles (1 John 1:2-3; 2:1, 15-16, 22-24; 3:1; 4:14; 2 John 3-4, 9), the image of God as father is adopted by the elder to convey God's personal and caring nature, not God's gender. Much like John Wesley centuries later, the elder favors a model of God as provider and loving parent.[33]

2. "What we have seen and heard we proclaim to you": The Traditional Context for Theological Understanding. If God is the magnetic north of the elder's theological compass, then the Johannine *kerygma* ("proclamation") shared with his readers is one pole of that magnetic field. Incisive interpretations of this tradition are not the elder's forte, and its innovative reformulation is not his aim (cf. 2 John 9). Instead, the believing community is repeatedly driven back to "that which was heard from the beginning," a primordial declaration of faith that still impinges forcefully on the church's present experience (1 John 1:1-5; 2:7, 24; 3:11; 2 John 5-6). Although less overtly engaged with Scripture than is the Fourth Gospel (John 5:39, 45-47; 7:23), "the message we have heard and declare" remains wedded in 1 John with Old Testament precept and example (1 John 2:2/Lev 16:16, 30; 1 John 3:12/Gen 4:1-6). The community's faith is crystallized in remembered commandments of Christ (1 John 2:7-8; 2 John 5-6), the example of Jesus (1 John 2:6; 3:16-17), and Christian creedal affirmations (1 John 4:2, 5:6). For proper interpretations of that tradition, the elder recognizes the church's experience of being anointed as "children of God" (1 John 2:20, 27; 3:1-2) and the necessity of "test[ing] the spirits" for their authenticity (1 John 4:1-6).

3. "Children, it is the last hour!" The Eschatological Context for Theological Understanding. The elder's retrospection should not mislead us to think that he and his readers are stuck in the past. To the contrary, the Johannine epistles are attracted to an apocalyptically charged expectation. In this view—played down in the Fourth Gospel (cf. John 3:36; 5:24-29; 6:39-40; 11:23-26) though prevalent in New Testament documents early (1 Thess 4:13–5:11) and late (2 Peter 3:1-18)—history is hurtling toward its divinely appointed end. Confirmation of this belief lies, for the elder, in the coming of "antichrist" (1 John 2:18, 22; 4:3; 2 John 7). This expression, unique to the Johannine letters, personifies a cataclysmic evil that some expected to flare up before God's final victory (cf. Dan 11:36–12:13; 2 Thess 2:3-9). Not fear, but confidence (παρρησία *parrēsia*), encouragement, and hope for the church flow from the prospect of Christ's coming (παρουσία *parousia*; 1 John 2:28; 3:2-3; 4:17-18; 2 John 8). This apocalyptic view of the future provides a lens through which the community's present experience is viewed; the elder regards both confession and schism within the church, not as theologically neutral, but as indicators of a cosmic drama, played out under the direction of a provident God.

4. "Jesus Christ has come in the flesh": Who Jesus Is. Since the christology of the Johannine epistles is not systematically presented, one can safely speak only of emphases in the elder's portrayal of Jesus. Undeniably, Jesus is the Christ, "the anointed one" (1 John 2:22; 5:1). That identification of Jesus is exceeded by another: the Son of God (2:22-23; 4:15; 5:5, 10, 20), which, though apparently interchangeable with Christ (5:1, 5), accents his intimate relation with God the Father (1:3; 2:23-24; 4:13). This conjunction is so close that at many points in 1 John it is impossible to tell whether the pronouns "he" or "him" refer to Jesus or to God (see 1 John 1:9-10; 2:3-6, 27-28; 3:23-24; 4:17). This ambiguity may suggest a high christology, effectively equating Jesus with God; or it may simply betoken a lack of precision in the elder's wording. "Jesus Christ has come in the flesh" (1 John 4:2 NRSV) is a confession that, for the elder, appears to have acquired the status of proper doctrine (διδαχή *didachē*; 2 John 7-10). That a claim so unobjectionable on its face requires such emphasis, and elicits such sharp repudiation of those who deny it, suggests that Christ's incarnation had become a disputed point within Johannine Christianity at the time of these letters.[34]

5. "He is the expiation for our sins": What Jesus Does. In general, Jesus in 1 John deals with sin and its consequences. By his blood, believers are cleansed from all unrighteousness (1 John 1:7*b*, 9), their sins forgiven for his sake (1 John 1:9; 2:12). Indeed, Jesus expunges the sins of the whole world (1 John 2:2; 3:5; cf. John 1:29). These claims are related to the depiction of Jesus as a ἱλασμός (*hilasmos*), an "atoning sacrifice" for sins (1 John 2:2; 4:10). This term is unique to 1 John in the New Testament, although Romans (Rom 3:25) and Hebrews (Heb 2:17; 9:5) contain cognates. Antecedents for the concept of vicarious expiation by one who is pure or without sin can be found in Old Testament descriptions of cultic sacrifice (cf. Lev 4:1-35; 16:1-34 with 1 John 3:3, 5; 1 Pet 1:18-19), which later were broadened in reference to pious martyrs for the Jewish nation (4 Macc 6:28-29; 17:21-22). For any believer who sins, Jesus Christ the righteous is an advocate (παράκλητος *paraklētos*) before the Father (1 John 2:1; cf. John 14:16, 26; 15:26; 16:7, where intercession is performed by the Holy Spirit). "Anointing" by "the Holy One," which instructs the church and verifies its knowledge, is yet another expression of Christ's (or the Spirit's) benefits (1 John 2:20, 27). An interesting feature of all these models of salvation is that they are confined neither to Jesus' past death nor to his future coming, but are considered perpetually effective in the church's present experience.

6. "Beloved, let us love one another": The Shape of Christian Existence. God's activity in Christ establishes the context for Christian life and self-critical discernment. First John insists on the inseparability of religious experience from moral conduct, with reciprocal testing of the one's soundness by the other's vitality (1 John 1:6-7; 2:3-6, 9-11; 3:6-18, 24; 4:7-12, 20-21). Thus, being "born" of God (1 John 2:29; 3:9; 4:7; 5:1, 4, 18) or a "child" of God (1 John 3:1, 2, 10; 5:2), "knowing" God (1 John 2:3; 3:6) or "abid[ing] in him" (1 John 2:6, 10, 17; 3:6-10, 24; 4:16), do not describe an inward, mystical state but are concretely manifested by "doing what is right," "keeping his commandments," or "walk[ing] just as he walked" (1 John 2:3, 6; 3:10, 14*a*, 22; 5:3). By contrast, "the children of the devil," who "abide in death" and falsehood, are recognizable by their unrighteousness, disobedience, and lack of love (1 John 2:4; 3:10, 14*b*; cf. 3 John 11). Pulsing throughout the First Epistle is a tension, if not contradiction, between candid acknowledgment of persistent sin within the church (1 John 1:8–2:1; 5:16-17) and categorical denial that one begotten of God can sin (1 John 3:6, 9; 5:18). If 1 John does not resolve this theological dilemma, it effectively crystallizes it as a pressing question for subsequent Christian theology.

The observation of Augustine (354–430) that 1 John commends nothing else but love is only slightly exaggerated.[35] More than any other concept, love (ἀγάπη *agapē*) expresses the abiding nature of the unseen God (1 John 4:7*b*, 8*b*, 12, 16), whose initiative in sending his Son reveals that love (1 John 3:16; 4:9-10), evokes love as a possibility among us (1 John 4:11, 19), and specifies the practical pattern to which our responsive love should conform (1 John 3:17-18; 5:3; 2 John 6). God's love for us (1 John 2:5; 3:1; 4:16-17) and our love for God (1 John 4:20-21; 5:1) are perfected in our sibling love for one another (1 John 2:10; 3:10-11, 14, 23; 4:7, 11-12, 20-21; 5:2; 2 John 5; see also John 13:34; 15:12, 17). While the world's hatred belongs to the sphere of darkness and is not to be reciprocated (1 John 2:9-11; 3:13-15), the elder's attention to love does appear intramurally preoccupied, the universal potential of the Johannine love command recognized (1 John 2:2; 4:14), yet left undeveloped.

THE LETTERS OF JOHN IN THE LIFE OF THE CHURCH

Just as for the rest of the New Testament, the church is the native habitat for 1, 2, and 3 John. These documents offer us, as it were, blurred snapshots of primitive Christian communities—congregations that grappled with some implications of their own religious tradition, appealing to doctrine, policy, and authority that were all at an embryonic stage. These epistles adapted the legacy of John for a new day, much as 1 and 2 Timothy and Titus appropriated the Pauline tradition. To characterize 1, 2, and 3 John as "Johannine Pastorals" thus captures something essentially true to their aims and theological temperament.[36]

In our own era John's epistles have not wanted for scholarly commentary. The depth of their appropriation within the church is harder to gauge. The *Revised Common Lectionary* (1992) assigns six excerpts from 1 John (1:1–2:2; 3:1-7; 3:16-24; 4:7-21; 5:1-6; 5:9-13) as the epistle readings for the second through seventh Sundays of Easter (Year B), as well as 1 John 3:1-3 for All Saints (Year A). Neither 2 John nor 3 John appears in the *Common Lectionary*, which is not surprising; also missing are other New Testament passages that blaze with controversy, such as John 8:12-59; 1 Cor 4:6–5:5; Gal 2:1-14; 1 John 2:18-27; 4:1-6; and Jude. Regrettably, pitched conflict is as much a part of our past as it is of our present, no less in Christianity than in other religions. However we assess the responses of early Johannine Christians, the issues that these letters raise—among others, the maintenance of confessional integrity and the potential for congregational self-destruction—must be faced by Christians in every age.

Finally, the Johannine letters assure Christians of their calling, grounded not in their own ability under stress but in God's enduring, self-sacrificial love for them. First John's confidence was abundantly clear to Martin Luther (1483–1546): "This is an outstanding epistle. It can buoy up afflicted hearts. Furthermore, it has John's style and manner of expression, so beautifully and gently does it picture Christ to us."[37] What Luther implies, Wesley states outright in a comment that for many readers of these epistles still rings true: "And in [addressing his contemporaries, the elder] speaks to the whole Christian church in all succeeding ages."[38]

FOR FURTHER READING

Commentaries:

Brown, Raymond E. *The Epistles of John.* AB 30. Garden City, N.Y.: Doubleday, 1982.

Bultmann, Rudolf. *The Johannine Epistles: A Commentary on the Johannine Epistles.* Edited by Robert W. Funk. Hermeneia. Philadelphia: Fortress, 1973.

Dodd, C. H. *The Johannine Epistles.* MNTC. New York: Harper and Bros, 1946.

Kysar, Robert. *I, II, III John.* Augsburg Commentary on the New Testament. Minneapolis: Augsburg, 1986.

Painter, John. *1, 2, and 3 John.* SP 18. Collegeville, Minn.: Liturgical Press, 2002.

Schnackenburg, Rudolf. *The Johannine Epistles: Introduction and Commentary.* New York: Crossroad, 1992.

Smalley, Stephen S. *1, 2, 3 John.* WBC 51. Waco, Tex.: Word, 1984.

Smith, D. Moody. *First, Second, and Third John.* Interpretation. Louisville: John Knox, 1991.

Strecker, Georg. *The Johannine Letters: A Commentary on 1, 2, and 3 John.* Edited by Harold Attridge. Hermeneia. Minneapolis: Fortress, 1996; German original, 1989.

Other Studies:

Brown, Raymond E. *The Community of the Beloved Disciple.* New York: Paulist, 1979.

Calvin, John. *The Gospel According to John 11–21 and The First Epistle of John.* Edited by David W. Torrance and Thomas F. Torrance. Grand Rapids: Eerdmans, 1961.

Lieu, Judith. *The Second and Third Epistles of John: History and Background.* Studies of the New Testament and Its World. Edinburgh: T & T Clark, 1986.

———. *The Theology of the Johannine Epistles.* New Testament Theology. Cambridge: Cambridge University Press, 1991.

ENDNOTES

1. John Wesley, *The Works of John Wesley*, vol. 21: *Journal and Diaries IV (1755–65)*, ed. W. Reginald Ward and Richard P. Heitzenrater (Nashville: Abingdon, 1992) 427 (journal entry for Thursday, September 1, 1763).

2. Cf. Tertullian *On Modesty* (c. 220) 19.10, 26-28 with 1 John 4:2; 5:16-17.

3. See Eusebius *Ecclesiastical History* 3.24.17-18; 3.25.2-3.

4. See Eusebius *Ecclesiastical History* 6.25.10, citing Origen (c. 185–254).

5. Bede, *Commentary on 2 John* 1, in *The Commentary on the Seven Catholic Epistles of Bede the Venerable*, Cistercian Studies Series 82 (Kalamazoo, Mich.: Cistercian Publications, 1985) 231.

6. See Eusebius *Ecclesiastical History* 3.39-3-4.

7. See Eusebius *Ecclesiastical History* 7.25.18-23. See R. Alan Culpepper, *John, the Son of Zebedee: The Life of a Legend*, Studies on Personalities of the New Testament (Columbia: University of South Carolina Press, 1994). This work is a definitive study of the figure of John in Christian antiquity. On traditions related to the Johannine letters, see 89-95.

8. See, for instance, A. E. Brooke, *A Critical and Exegetical Commentary on the Johannine Epistles*, ICC (Edinburgh: T & T Clark, 1912) i-xix; Werner Georg Kümmel, *Introduction to the New Testament*, rev. ed. (Nashville: Abingdon, 1975) 442-45, 449-51.

9. Among others, C. H. Dodd, "The First Epistle of John and the Fourth Gospel," *BJRL* 21 (1937) 129-56, which is presupposed by the same author's *The Johannine Epistles*, MNTC (New York: Harper and Bros., 1946); Judith Lieu, *The Second and Third Epistles of John: History and Background*, Studies of the New Testament and Its World (Edinburgh: T & T Clark, 1986) 205-22; Hans-Josef Klauck, *Der erste Johannesbrief*, EKKNT 23 (Z∞rich: Benziger/Neukirchener, 1991) 42-47; Rudolf Schnackenburg, *The Johannine Epistles: Introduction and Commentary* (New York: Crossroad, 1992) 34-39.

10. Each of these alternatives is exemplified, respectively, by Georg Strecker, *The Johannine Letters: A Commentary on 1, 2, and 3 John*, Hermeneia (Minneapolis: Fortress, 1995) xxxv-xliii; Stephen S. Smalley, *1, 2, 3 John*, WBC (Waco, Tex.: Word, 1984) xxxv-xliii; Charles H. Talbert, *Reading John: A Literary and Theological Commentary on the Fourth Gospel and the Johannine Epistles*, Reading the New Testament (New York: Crossroad, 1992); and Judith M. Lieu, *The Theology of the Johannine Epistles*, New Testament Theology (Cambridge: Cambridge University Press, 1992).

11. Similarly, see D. Moody Smith, *First, Second, and Third John*, Interpretation (Louisville.: John Knox, 1991) esp. 14, 28, 32, 36.

12. Polycarp *Letter to the Philippians* 7.1.

13. Amos N. Wilder, "The First, Second, and Third Epistles of John," in *IB*, ed. George Buttrick et al., 12 vols. (Nashville: Abingdon, 1957) 12:213.

14. Rudolf Bultmann, "Analyse des ersten Johannesbriefes," *Festgabe für Adolf Jülicher zum 70. Geburtstag* (Tübingen: Mohr [Siebeck], 1927) 138-58. Bultmann's theory, refined to posit an "ecclesiastical redaction" of the First Epistle, was presupposed for his commentary *The Johannine Epistles: A Commentary on the Johannine Epistles*, Hermeneia (Philadelphia: Fortress, 1973).

15. See 1QS 5:8, 21; 6:6; 8:15; 1QpHab 7:10-11.

16. See Marie-Émile Boismard, "The First Epistle of John and the Writings of Qumran," in *John and the Dead Sea Scrolls*, ed. J. H. Charlesworth (New York: Crossroad, 1991) 156-65. The influence on 1 John of Old Testament narratives (like that of Cain and Abel, 1 John 3:12; cf. Gen 4:1-16) and ideas (notably sin and its atonement, 1 John 2:2, cf. Lev 16:1-34) is real, though apparently minimal. The question of Scripture's bearing on the Johannine letters has been usefully reopened by Judith M. Lieu, "What Was from the Beginning: Scripture and Tradition in the Johannine Epistles," *NTS* 39 (1993) 458-77.

17. Notably, Dodd, *The Johannine Epistles*, xvi-xxi, which anticipated his more extensive account in *The Interpretation of the Fourth Gospel* (Cambridge: Cambridge University Press, 1953) 3-130.

18. On this subject Otto A. Piper, "I John and the Didache of the Primitive Church," *JBL* 66 (1947) 437-51, remains well worth consulting.

19. Noteworthy are the studies by Wayne A. Meeks, "The Man from Heaven in Johannine Sectarianism," *JBL* 91 (1972) 44-72; R. Alan Culpepper, *The Johannine School: An Evaluation of the Johannine-School Hypothesis Based on an Investigation of the Nature of Ancient Schools*, SBLDS 26 (Missoula, Mont.: Scholars Press, 1975); and D. Moody Smith, "Johannine Christianity: Some Reflections on Its Character and Delineation," *NTS* 21 (1976) 222-48.

20. For two very different hypotheses in this vein, see Raymond E. Brown, *The Epistles of John: Translated with Introduction, Notes, and Commentary*, AB 30 (Garden City, N.Y.: Doubleday, 1982) 116-29, and Kenneth Grayston, *The Johannine Epistles*, NCB (Grand Rapids: Eerdmans, 1984) 3-4.

21. Friedrich Hauck, *Die Briefe des Jakobus, Petrus, Judas und Johannes: Kirchenbriefe*, 5th ed., NTD (Güttingen: Vandenhoeck & Ruprecht, 1949) 115. Brown tabulates over four dozen discrepant divisions of 1 John, proposed by as many commentators. See Brown, *Epistles of John*, 117n. 269, 764.

22. Along this line, Theodor Häring, "Gedankengang und Grundgedanke des ersten Johannesbriefes," in *Theologisches Abhandlungen*, ed. Carl von Weizsäcker (Freiburg im Breisgau: Mohr, 1892) 171-200, has proved influential. Cf. John Calvin, *The Gospel According to St John 11–21 and the First Epistle of John*, ed. David W. Torrance and Thomas F. Torrance (Grand Rapids: Eerdmans, 1961) 231.

23. C. H. Dodd, *The Johannine Epistles*, MNTC (New York: Harper and Bros., 1946).

24. Nevertheless, Kysar considers 1 John "a hurried union of disparate pieces...a kind of anthology of bits of sermons patched together and rendered into a written form for circulation." See Robert Kysar, *I, II, III John*, Augsburg Commentary on the New Testament (Minneapolis: Augsburg, 1986) 16.

25. See C. Clifton Black, "'The Words That You Gave to Me I Have Given to Them': The Grandeur of Johannine Rhetoric," in *Exploring the Gospel of John in Honor of D. Moody Smith*, ed. R. Alan Culpepper and C. Clifton Black (Louisville: Westminster John Knox, 1996) 220-39.

26. Ignatius *Smyrn.* 5.2.

27. Ignatius *Trall.* 9.1; 10.

28. Ignatius *Smyrn.* 7.1; *Magn.* 11.

29. See, e.g., John Painter, "The 'Opponents' in 1 John," *NTS* 32 (1986) 48-71. Brown's magisterial commentary (Raymond E. Brown, *The Epistles of John,* esp. 69-115) is predicated on his subtle reconstruction of contesting interpretations of Johannine thought and practice: Raymond E. Brown, *The Community of the Beloved Disciple* (New York: Paulist, 1979) esp. 93-167.

30. See Pheme Perkins, *The Johannine Letters*, New Testament Message 21 (Wilmington, Del.: Michael Glazier, 1979) xvi-xxiii; Judith M. Lieu, "'Authority to Become Children of God': A Study of 1 John," *NovT* 23 (1981) 210-28.

31. A. E. Brooke, *A Critical and Exegetical Commentary on the Johannine Epistles*, ICC (Edinburgh: T & T Clark, 1912) xxxix-xl.

32. "'The Father Is Greater Than I' John 14:28: Subordinationist Christology in the New Testament," in C. K. Barrett, *Essays on John* (Philadelphia: Westminster, 1982) 32. See also the finely nuanced treatment by Paul W. Meyer, "'The Father': The Presentation of God in the Fourth Gospel," in *Exploring the Gospel of John*, ed. Culpepper and Black, 255-73.

33. On the language of God's fatherhood in the Johannine tradition, see B. F. Westcott, *The Epistles of St John: The Greek Text with Notes and Essays* (London: Macmillan, 1909) 27-34; on the appropriation of that language in our day, see Gail R. O'Day, "John," in *The Women's Bible Commentary,* ed. Carol A. Newsom and Sharon H. Ringe (Louisville: Westminster/John Knox, 1992) 303-4. On Wesley's characterizations of God, consult Randy L. Maddox, *Responsible Grace: John Wesley's Practical Theology* (Nashville: Kingswood, 1994) 48-64.

34. See M. de Jonge, "The Use of the Word ΧΡΙΣΤΟΣ in the Johannine Epistles," in *Studies in John Presented to Professor Dr. J. N. Sevenster*, NovTSup 24 (Leiden: Brill, 1970) 66-74.

35. Augustine, "Ten Homilies on the First Epistle of St. John," in *Augustine: Later Works*, selected and trans. John Burnaby, The Library of Christian Classics (Philadelphia: Westminster, 1955) 259-348, esp. 329.

36. The landmark statement of this idea is Hans Conzelmann, "'Was von Anfang War,'" in *Neutestamentliche Studien für Rudolf Bultmann zu seinem 70. Geburtstag*, ed. Walther Eltester, BZNW 21 (Berlin: Töpelmann, 1954) 194-201. The polychromatic picture of the church emerging from these documents is examined in C. Clifton Black, "The Johannine Epistles and the Question of Early Catholicism," *NovT* 28 (1986) 131-58.

37. Martin Luther, "Lectures on the First Epistle of St. John," *Luther's Works*, vol. 10. *The Catholic Epistles*, ed. Jaroslav Pelikan and Walter A. Hansen (St. Louis: Concordia, 1967) 219.

38. John Wesley, "Spiritual Worship" (sermon 77), in *The Works of John Wesley*, vol. 3: *Sermons 71-114*, ed. Albert C. Outler (Nashville: Abingdon, 1986) 89.

THE LETTER OF JUDE

D.F. WATSON

AUTHORSHIP, ORIGIN, AND DATE

Nothing definite can be said about the author, origin, or date of the Epistle of Jude.[1] The author calls himself Jude (Judas), brother of James. For the author to have identified himself through his brother James indicates that both Jude and James were well-known to the letter's addressees. The only brothers with the names Jude and James mentioned in the New Testament are the brothers of Jesus (Matt 13:55; Mark 6:3). Although several other men from the first century named Jude have been suggested as the author of this letter, the most likely reference is to the brother of James and Jesus, the leader of the church in Jerusalem (Acts 12:17; 15:13-21; 1 Cor 15:7; Gal 1:19; 2:9).[2] Jude did not believe that Jesus was the Messiah during Jesus' lifetime (Mark 3:21, 31; John 7:1-5). However, he came to faith after Jesus' resurrection and ascension (Acts 1:14), and probably became a missionary for the gospel (1 Cor 9:5).

The question is whether "Jude" is Jesus' brother's self-reference or a pseudonym used by someone within Jewish Christian circles, in which the memory of Jude and his brother James was prominent. On the one hand, the letter writer's familiarity with Jewish literature and traditions, as well as the Jewish Christian apocalyptic stance of the argumentation, supports Jude, Jesus' brother, as author. On the other hand, a pseudonymous author may have wished to use the name and authority of Jude to counter the false teachers in the post-apostolic era. It is often argued that a pseudonymous author would have claimed to be the brother of Jesus rather than the brother of James, but claiming membership within the holy family offered considerable status to the writer. Eusebius mentions that many persons traced their ancestry to the holy family.[3]

Several prominent arguments in support of the author's pseudonymity can be readily countered. (1) The content of the letter requires a late date because it either reflects early Catholicism or combats gnosticism of the post-apostolic era. However, these assumptions are unlikely (see "The Stance and Rhetorical Approach of the Letter," below). (2) The author excludes himself from the apostles, whom he presents as belonging to a previous generation (v. 17). However, he is only excluding himself from the apostles who founded the church(es) he addresses, and not from the apostolic era. (3) The brother of Jesus, a Galilean peasant whose native language would have been Aramaic, could not have produced this letter. The author appears to have had a scribal background, because he is able to write a letter, he uses literary Greek in which to write it, he possesses knowledge of Jewish tradition and writings and has access to those writings (e.g., *Testament of Moses, 1 Enoch*), and he is skilled in the use of rhetoric.[4] However, having an elementary education (which included some rhetorical training), hearing weekly exposition of the Old Testament in the synagogue, living in Galilee (an area dotted with Greek-speaking cities), and needing to increase proficiency in Greek to effectively preach to Greek audiences would have gone a long way toward explaining how Jesus' brother could come to possess competency in these skills. Thus there is really no strong reason to argue that the author could be anyone other than Jude, the brother of Jesus and James.

Decisions about the date of the writing of the letter depend on those for authorship and the nature of the false teachers involved. Dates offered range from the early apostolic age (50s CE) to the mid-second century CE. If the letter was written by the brother of Jesus, then a date in the mid-first century is warranted. If it is pseudonymous, a date in the latter part of the century of the post-apostolic era is logical. The letter's implication that the original converts of the church were still living (vv. 17-18), its use of a Jewish-Christian apocalyptic argumentative stance, and the use of the Epistle of Jude as an authoritative document by the author of 2 Peter (around 80–90 CE) indicate a date closer to the mid-first century. This places the letter's writing during the lifetime of Jude, Jesus' brother. A late first- or early second-century date loses still more appeal once it is recognized that the letter takes neither an early catholic nor an anti-gnostic stance of that period, nor does it necessarily look upon the apostolic era as being past (see "The Stance and Rhetorical Approach of the Letter").

RECIPIENTS, OPPONENTS, AND HISTORICAL SITUATION

The letter is not a tract against heresy or a "catholic" letter addressed to all Christians, but a letter addressed to an unspecified church or group of churches. Jude did not found the church that he addresses, for it had learned the gospel from the apostles (v. 17). The church is probably Jewish Christian, for Jude quotes and alludes to Jewish documents and traditions without explanation, assuming the people's familiarity with them.

The geographical location of the church is unknown. The antinomian character of the false teachers' doctrine and their ability to influence the church indicate a predominantly Gentile context lacking the presence of strong Jewish moral teaching. Scholars have proposed Palestine, Syria, Egypt, or Asia Minor as the location of the recipient church(es). If the letter was written by Jesus' brother, then Palestine is the most likely candidate for the recipients' location, since Jude himself can be located there. If it is pseudonymous, then Asia Minor is a good candidate, for it boasted large Jewish populations within a Gentile environment, or Egypt, where the letter was popular with Clement of Alexandria and Origen. Syria is not likely because the letter was not accepted as canonical in churches there until the sixth century.[5]

The occasion of the letter is the infiltration of the church by a group whose doctrines and practices are at variance with the apostolic tradition the church had received (vv. 4, 17-19). The group is sectarian, having divided the church by rejecting its leadership (v. 8) and gathered a following of its own (vv. 19, 22-23). Their motivation is partially financial gain (vv. 11-12, 16). The description of them in v. 4, "certain intruders have stolen in among you" (NRSV), indicates that they may be itinerant prophets or teachers, who were common in early Christianity. Itinerant prophets and teachers could rely on the hospitality of their host church (1 Cor 9:4; *Did.* 13:1-3) and thus were in a position to misuse this privilege for financial gain (Rom 16:18; *Did.* 11:3-6, 12). The contorted doctrines of some of these itinerants, coupled with their desire for gain, often posed problems for the churches they visited (Matt 7:15; 2 Cor 10:1-11; 1 John 4:1; 2 John 10; *Did.* 11-12; Ign. *Eph.* 9:1).

The doctrine of these false teachers is antinomian—that is, they understand the gospel of freedom in Christ to relieve a Christian of ethical responsibilities, an understanding that "perverts grace" (v. 4). They deny the authority of the law of Moses (vv. 8-10) and of Christ himself (vv. 4, 8). This denial may be based on a claim of prophetic revelation (v. 8; cf. v. 19), a problem in early Christianity (Col 2:18), or it may be an overly realized eschatology that stressed that judgment was past rather than future for those in the Spirit. As a corollary of this rejection of authority, they are immoral, especially in sexual behavior (vv. 4, 6-8, 10, 16). They corrupt the church (vv. 22-24), even tainting the love feast, which is at the core of the fellowship (v. 12).

Such antinomianism is akin to that faced by Paul (Rom 3:8; 6:1, 15; 1 Cor 5:1-8; 6:12-20; 10:23; Gal 5:13), but there is no firm support for thinking that the false teachers were of the ilk encountered by Paul. Neither do the false teachers seem to be the gnostics of later times. Their reviling of angels who guard the law of Moses (vv. 8-10) is not part of a cosmic dualism in which angels are demigods of the material universe. Their indulgence in sin does not originate in the emphasis on spirit and knowledge to the disparagement of anything material (like the body). If gnosticism were involved, Jude would best have attacked the doctrine of the false teachers, not emphasized their immorality.[6]

Jude believes the situation may be spiritually fatal and, therefore, seeks immediate, drastic action. The presence of the false teachers, their teaching, and their behavior are precursors of the parousia, and they and their following will be destroyed with its coming (vv. 14-15, 17-18, 23). To save members of the church from destruction, Jude wants to convince them that the false teachers are the ungodly of prophecy (vv. 14-19) and that they are headed for destruction (vv. 5-16). The church is to cling to traditional doctrine (vv. 3, 5, 17, 20), bolster its spiritual life (vv. 20-21), and actively convince those persuaded by the false teachers to abandon them and their ways (vv. 22-23).

THE STANCE AND RHETORICAL APPROACH OF THE LETTER

Many interpreters have classified the Letter of Jude as an "early catholic" document. This designation refers to a reconstruction of early Christianity (needing serious rethinking) that postulates that beginning with the second generation of Christians there was a movement away from a hope in the imminent return of Christ and toward institutionalization of church offices and the understanding of faith as a body of doctrine rather than a personal commitment. This movement was fostered by the delay of the parousia and the encounter with heresy, which necessitated the creation of a central authority and clearly articulated doctrine.

Yet Jude should *not* be classified as early catholic. The parousia hope in the letter is strong. Jude tried to persuade the church to see that the false teachers of their day are those prophesied to appear in the last days. They are precursors of the parousia and designated recipients of its approaching judgment (vv. 4, 14-19). Their followers must be snatched quickly from the impending fire of judgment (v. 23). Jude does not address any church officers, but assumes that the church as a whole will respond as suggested. Jude also affirms that faith is not a set body of orthodox teachings but the gospel itself, which demands faith and which the church members received at the time of their conversion and instruction by the apostles (vv. 3, 17-18).[7]

As the use of Jewish sources, apocalyptic texts, and tradition (e.g., *1 Enoch, Testament of Moses*) indicates, Jude was working within the confines of Jewish Christianity, which had a vibrant apocalyptic outlook,[8] and this outlook underlies his rhetorical approach.[9] The letter is predominantly deliberative rhetoric, which, by proofs and advice, tries to persuade an audience to embrace what is advantageous, necessary, and expedient and dissuade it from the opposite. The letter specifies that it aims to persuade the church "to contend for the faith" (v. 3)—that is, not to heed the false teachers' message and practice and thus come under like judgment at the encroaching parousia. In its effort to persuade the church, the letter also relies upon epideictic rhetoric, which both praises and blames. The aim of such rhetoric is to uplift what is honorable and to cast down what is dishonorable, especially with a view to increasing audience assent to honorable values. Verse 4 refers to the letter as a "condemnation" (τὸ κρίμα *to krima*). The false teachers are denounced as being (a) comparable to great sinners of the past and (b) the subject of prophecies of judgment. The denunciation of the false teachers is meant to strengthen the church in the faith received from the apostles and to preserve its members from impending judgment.

LITERARY GENRE, COMPOSITION, AND CONTENT

Jude is a genuine letter of the mixed variety. Its deliberative rhetorical style classifies it as a paraenetic letter meant to advise and dissuade.[10] The petition in vv. 3-4 classifies it as a letter of request or petition.[11] Jude's stated purpose is to persuade the church to "contend for the faith" (v. 3). The letter occupies a middle ground between documentary letters (e.g., personal, business) and literary letters written according to rhetorical conventions and meant for public consumption. Thus it contains both epistolary and rhetorical conventions, and its structure is best described by discussing both genres.[12]

The letter begins with a typical Jewish-Christian letter prescript, introducing the sender and the recipients, followed by a blessing (vv. 1-2). Verses 3-4 are the body opening of the letter, which establishes common ground between the sender and the recipients and informs the recipients of the main reason why the sender wrote the letter. In v. 3, the reason for writing is stated as a petition that the recipients "contend for the faith that was once for all entrusted to the saints." The background of, or reason for, the petition follows in v. 4: Ungodly false teachers have appeared in the church, as was foretold in prophecy. Verse 3 corresponds to the rhetorical convention of *exordium* and v. 4 to *narratio.* The *exordium* works to obtain the audience's goodwill and introduces the reason for an address. The *narratio* gives the facts to explain the need for that address and to outline the main point(s) the remainder of the address will develop.

Verses 5-16 are the body (middle of the letter), which develops the material of the body opening. It begins with a typical disclosure formula, expressing the sender's desire that the recipients know something: "Now I desire to remind you..." (NRSV). The body middle corresponds to the rhetorical *probatio,* which presents proofs to verify the claims and propositions of the *narratio.* In Jude, the body middle proves that the false teachers in the church are ungodly and that they are the very ones foretold in prophecy. To make this assertion, the body middle uses proofs from example (vv. 5-10) and from prophecy (vv. 11-16) respectively.

Verses 17-23 are the body closing of the letter, which underscores the main reason for writing by reiterating and amplifying what has already been stated in the body of the letter. The body closing often urges that responsibility be taken for the matters discussed. Like the body middle, the closing begins with a disclosure formula: "But you, beloved, must remember..." (NRSV). It corresponds to the rhetorical device called *peroratio,* which reiterates the main points of the *probatio* and appeals to the emotion of the audience to persuade it to respond as desired. The repetition occurs in vv. 17-19, and the emotional appeal by exhortation is repeated in vv. 20-23. The letter ends in vv. 24-25 with a doxology for a postscript.

In proving that the false teachers are ungodly and that they are the ungodly of prophecy (v. 4), Jude uses Jewish types and prophecies sacred to the church as well as Christian instruction previously delivered to the church by apostolic missionaries (vv. 3, 5, 17-18). This material includes three OT narrative types (vv. 5-7), an OT prophecy (v. 11), a prophecy from *1 Enoch* (vv. 14-15), and a prophecy from the apostles (vv. 17-18). Each prophecy or narrative type is applied to the false teachers in order to identify them as ungodly and subject to judgment, those who were prophesied would appear in the end times (vv. 8-10, 12-13, 16, 19). The alternation of types and prophecy with interpretation is carefully constructed to underscore that the types and prophecies find counterparts and fulfillment in the false teachers. This alternation is accentuated by alternating verb tenses. The past tenses (vv. 5-6, 9), prophetic aorists (vv. 11, 14), and a future tense (v. 18) in the types and prophecies are juxtaposed with present tenses in the interpretations. Also, the interpretations are preceded with the Greek word "these" (οὗτοι *houtoi*) or "these are" (οὗτοί εἰσιν *houtoi eisin*), which clearly distinguishes them (vv. 8, 10, 12, 16, 19).

The entire letter is linked with the repetition of topics (sometimes called catchwords) in rhetorically strategic places. Take, for example, the topic of "keeping" (τηρέω *tēreō*; φυλάσσω *phylassō*). In the letter's prescript, the addresses are said to be kept for Jesus Christ (v. 1), and in the closing doxology God is the one said to be doing the keeping (v. 24). The saints are to keep themselves in God's favor (v. 21). In contrast, the angels and false teachers who have not been able to keep their place will be kept in deepest darkness (vv. 6, 13).

The letter is characterized by a rich vocabulary and many rhetorical figures of speech and thought. One particularly noteworthy feature is the appearance of triplets that amplify the message (vv. 1, 2, 5-7, 8, 11, 19, 20-21, 22-23, 25). For example, three types of ungodly persons are described, who find counterparts in the false teachers (vv. 5-7); and the application of these descriptions to the false teachers is a triplet (v. 8). In addition, words are carefully chosen for their associated imagery. Noteworthy are the images of the prophecy and the interpretation of vv. 11-13, which provide a strong negative characterization of the false teachers.

THE THEOLOGY OF JUDE

Jude is not concerned solely with doctrinal issues. Rather, the author is concerned with the moral implications of errant doctrine. This false teaching denies the parousia and judgment, thus removing moral constraints and, in effect, licensing immorality. In the light of this challenge, Jude's theological approach is to stress the need for adherence to the proclamation of the gospel as received from the apostles (vv. 3, 5, 17). This doctrine and the behavior it espouses are normative and can be used as the measure of new teaching that may be proposed in the church.[13]

Jude works with a vital eschatological expectation. He believes that the parousia and judgment will occur within the lifetime of the letter's recipients, and he points to the presence of the false teachers as an indication that they are, indeed, living in the end times (vv. 17-18). He affirms the reality of the divine judgment that will accompany the parousia. As surely as God acted in history to judge sinners, God will so judge sinners at the consummation of history (vv. 5-13). However, faithful Christians will be extended mercy and eternal life (vv. 2, 21, 24). The faithful themselves are to try to save sinners from the fire of judgment by pulling them away from the false teachers (v. 23).

Jude strongly affirms the lordship of Christ (vv. 4, 14, 17, 21, 25), a lordship based on his work of salvation, his current position of sitting at God's right hand, and his future role as Savior and Judge. Christians owe obedience to Christ as Lord for his work for their salvation, a salvation whose completion is based on a lifetime of obedience (v. 21). By contrast, immorality perverts the moral order of creation, which Christ enforces, and denies his lordship, leaving the person who sins vulnerable to judgment (vv. 4, 8-16). In the light of eschatological expectation and the lordship of Christ, Jude provides ethical instruction for Christian living. Christians are to make a concerted effort to advance their individual and corporate spiritual lives (v. 3). The Christian life is sustained on two interdependent fronts. One is remaining in the love of God through one's own moral effort and obedience (v. 21), and the other is God's working for us to keep our salvation safe until it is complete (vv. 1, 24). Christians are to work for the spiritual good of all, to pray with the inspiration of the Holy Spirit, to obey God in order to remain in God's love, and to live in the expectation of the impending parousia (vv. 20-21). The faithful are to extend mercy to the errant, while remaining cognizant of the real danger of possibly being influenced by their doctrine and practice (vv. 22-23).

FOR FURTHER READING

Bauckham, Richard J. *Jude, 2 Peter.* WBC 50. Waco, Tex.: Word, 1983.

———. *Jude, 2 Peter.* WBT. Waco, Tex.: Word, 1990.

———. *Jude and the Relatives of Jesus in the Early Church.* Edinburgh: T & T Clark, 1990.

Charles, J. D. *Literary Strategy in the Epistle of Jude.* Scranton: University of Scranton Press, 1993.

Chester, Andrew, and Ralph Martin. *The Theology of the Letters of James, Peter, and Jude.* New Testament Theology. Cambridge: Cambridge University Press, 1994.

Kraftchick, Steven J. *Jude, 2 Peter.* ANTC. Nashville, Tn.: Abingdon, 2002.

Neyrey, Jerome H. *2 Peter, Jude.* AB 37C. New York: Doubleday, 1993.

Watson, Duane F. *Invention, Arrangement, and Style: Rhetorical Criticism of Jude and 2 Peter.* SBLDS 104. Atlanta: Scholars Press, 1988.

ENDNOTES

1. For a discussion of the introductory issues of Jude, see R. J. Bauckham, *Jude, 2 Peter*, WBC 50 (Waco, Tex.: Word, 1983) 3-17, and *Jude and the Relatives of Jesus in the Early Church* (Edinburgh: T & T Clark, 1990) 134-78.

2. For a list of other identifications of Jude, see Bauckham, *Jude, 2 Peter*, 21-23.

3. Eusebius *Ecclesiastical History* 1.7.14. See J. H. Neyrey, *2 Peter, Jude*, AB 37C (New York: Doubleday, 1993) 45. For more on the holy family and Jude, see Bauckham, *Jude and the Relatives of Jesus in the Early Church*, 5-133.

4. See Neyrey, *2 Peter, Jude*, 29, 35.

5. Bauckham, *Jude, 2 Peter*, 16-17.

6. Bauckham, *Jude, 2 Peter*, 11-13.

7. Bauckham, *Jude, 2 Peter*, 8-9, 32-33; J. D. G. Dunn, *Unity and Diversity in the New Testament* (Philadelphia: Westminster, 1977) 341-66.

8. For a thorough study of Jude's use of Jewish traditions and source materials, see J. D. Charles, *Literary Strategy in the Epistle of Jude* (Scranton: University of Scranton Press, 1993); Bauckham, *Jude and the Relatives of Jesus in the Early Church*, 179-280.

9. For a rhetorical analysis of Jude, see D. F. Watson, *Invention, Arrangement, and Style: Rhetorical Criticism of Jude and 2 Peter*, SBLDS 104 (Atlanta: Scholars Press, 1988) 29-79.

10. Cf. Neyrey, *2 Peter, Jude*, 44.

11. Bauckham, *Jude, 2 Peter*, WBC, 28.

12. For a concise discussion of the ancient Greek letter genre, see John L. White, "Ancient Greek Letters," in *Greco-Roman Literature and the New Testament*, ed. David E. Aune, SBLSBS 21 (Atlanta: Scholars Press, 1988) 85-105.

13. For discussion of the theology of Jude, see Bauckham, *Jude, 2 Peter*, 11-37; A. Chester and R. P. Martin, *The Theology of the Letters of James, Peter, and Jude*, New Testament Theology (Cambridge: Cambridge University Press, 1994) 65-86.

PART THREE:
THE BOOK OF REVELATION

The Book of Revelation

C.C. ROWLAND

THE APOCALYPSE OF JESUS CHRIST

Apocalypse, revelation, promises comprehensibility and freedom from opacity, with no need for an intermediary to interpret what is immediately available to disclosure. Yet in the Apocalypse of Jesus Christ "a host of perceptions suddenly come together to form a dazzling impression (to dazzle is ultimately to prevent sight, to prevent speech),"[1] provoking instead fear, awe, and even distaste, leading to avoidance and incomprehension rather than to understanding. John's book demands attention, but its arresting manner cannot mask the fact that it, too, is only indirectly related to that awesome apocalyptic experience that took place on Patmos. We would not have John's vision unless he had been obedient to the command to write down what he had seen. It may momentarily seem to beckon us into the visionary's unconscious, but, whatever the sophistication of our psychoanalytic tools, that path into the mind of the prophet is barred to us. All that we have are traces of history and biography woven into the fabric of vision and transformed by it, no longer readily available as a means of explaining what now lies before us.

In its emphasis on revelation, apocalyptic can seem to offer easy solutions whereby divine intervention, by offering insight to unfathomable human problems, can cut the knot of those intractable problems. It can be an antidote to a radical pessimism whose exponents despair of ever being able to make sense of the contradictions of human existence except by means of the revelation of God. The kinds of answers offered by the apocalypses are by no means uniform, however. There are apocalypses (or at least parts of them) that use the concept of revelation to offer a definitive solution to human problems. For instance, in the book of *Jubilees*, an angelic revelation to Moses on Sinai, there is a retelling of biblical history following the sequence of what is found in Scripture. But there are also significant divergences, especially when halakhic questions emerge. The fact that the book is a revelation to Moses functions to vindicate one side in contentious moral matters in Second Temple Judaism and to anathematize opponents. In this situation the text's meaning is transparent and is promulgated as the final, authoritative pronouncement.

Not all apocalypses offer unambiguous and exclusive answers that seem to brook no dispute, however. They certainly offer revelation, much of which is, in effect, what was traditionally believed already. The horizon of hope is reaffirmed by revelation and the historical perspective of salvation supported. But sometimes the form of the revelation is such that it can produce as much mystification as enlightenment. There is frequently a need for angelic interpretation of enigmatic dreams and visions (e.g., Rev 7:14; 17:15). Even these angelic interpretations are not without problems. It proved necessary for revelations coined in one era to be the basis of "updating" and application in the different political circumstances of another. Thus the symbolism of the fourth beast of Daniel 7 was given new meaning in the Roman period when it ceased to refer to Greece and began to refer to Rome (a process that continued, as the history of the interpretation of Daniel 7 shows). Examples of this interpretive change may be found in both Revelation 13 and 4 Ezra 12. So some apocalypses do not provide answers through revelation and offer nothing more than the refusal of a complete answer as being beyond the human mind to grasp. Instead there is a plethora of imagery or enigmatic pronouncements that leaves the reader with either no possibility of ever knowing the mind of God or tantalizing glimpses into the enigmatic symbols of dreams and visions. In 4 Ezra, the seer wishes to know why Israel has been allowed to suffer and why God seems content to allow the bulk of humanity to perish. The role of revelation, akin to God's answer in the final chapters of the book of Job, is to stress the puny nature of human understanding in the face of the transcendence of God, to stress the ultimate victory of God's righteousness and to urge the need for those committed to the ways of God to continue in the narrow way that leads to salvation. No solution to the problem is posed by the human seer. The only enlightenment offered is the need to struggle, a theme paralleled in Revelation's demand for "the endurance of the saints" (14:12 NRSV).

The book of Revelation—paradoxically the most veiled text of all in the Bible—makes great demands on those who read or hear it in pursuit of the blessing it offers. Always there is the temptation to move too quickly to interpret or translate its imagery into a more accessible mode of discourse. But then it ceases to be apocalypse, whose distinctive blend of strange symbols and oscillating narrative confronts and engages the reader, and it becomes explanatory, more prosaic discourse, dependent on the enlightened interpreter to distill (and thereby reduce) the welter of images to the prosaic and accessible. That is what we find contained within Daniel, the other apocalyptic text in the Bible. There the perplexity of the apocalyptic seer is relieved by an enlightened, angelic, rather than human, interpreter, who explains the mysterious visions Daniel has seen. The images of statue, beasts, clouds, and thrones are reduced to historical prediction, less suggestive and more tied to specific events in the past. Daniel's images, however, and not historical prediction, are included in Revelation and become part of a new disclosure, here transformed as a catalyst of new visionary wisdom. But this time no key is offered to unlock their meaning.

There have been several ways of interpreting Revelation. First, the book has been treated as a relatively straightforward account of the end of the world. In such an interpretation it is usually linked with other prophetic and eschatological texts, like Daniel, Ezekiel, and 1 Thess 4:16ff. to produce a coherent eschatological chronology. Second, the visions are related to their ancient first-century context (the so-called preterist method of interpretation). Here questions are concerned with the meaning for the original author and readers and with the need to decode the complex symbolism and its relationship to (ancient) contemporary historical realities. Third, the images are regarded as an account of the struggles facing the journey of the soul to God. Fourth, the book has been used as an interpretative lens through which to view history. With this approach, one reads a text like Revelation as a gateway to a greater understanding of reality, both divine and human, spiritual and political, that not only includes, but also transcends the understanding offered by the human senses. "What must happen soon" refers to the apocalyptic disclosure, a way of illuminating the nature of politics and religion in every age. Some interpreters of Revelation relate the text to a single set of events, whether historical or eschatological, while other interpreters allow the possibility of a multiplicity of reference. There is also a distinction between those who regard prophecy as prediction and those who regard it as pronouncement. For the former, the apocalyptic imagery is a code that can be translated into another (usually historical) discourse and in which an alternative account can be offered of the various ciphers contained in the apocalyptic texts. We assume that we are in a less fortunate position than were the original readers. There may be some force in the suggestion that, like the modern political cartoon, related as it is to a very particular context, Revelation's imagery may have struck home in ways that are difficult, if not impossible, now that the original situation that provoked the images is no longer the case. But there is no evidence that the ancient readers found it any easier to understand than we do. The only difference is that they were probably less resistant to using, and being challenged by, this kind of literature than we are.

To decode Revelation, as if it were like Morse code—a language whose only function is to conceal and is a means to an end, namely, the communication of something that has to be kept secret—fails to take seriously the apocalyptic medium. John, as the recipient of a revelation from Jesus Christ, has bequeathed to us an apocalypse, a prophecy, not a narrative or an epistle, a text requiring of its readers different interpretative skills—imagination and emotion, for example. Like a metaphor, it startles, questions, even disorients before pointing to a fresh view of reality by its extraordinary imagery and impertinent verbal juxtapositions.[2] However difficult it may be for us, we must learn to exercise those faculties that are needed to engage such a medium.

Throughout the history of interpretation it has proved impossible to resist the temptation to decode, whether in the imaginative reconstruction of Revelation's past situation or in the distillation of its symbols into a historical program, past, present, or future. As soon as the interpreter does this, the images are left behind and the peculiar ethos of the apocalyptic narrative, the story, with all its abrupt transitions and allusive quality, is lost. To put it another way, the literal gives way to the allegorical as the other story, the "translation" of those images becomes the meaning of apocalypse rather than the interweaving of image and movement of the text itself, interacting with the reader's own social location and the mysterious action of the Spirit. Succumbing to the temptation to offer what the text *really* means, in another genre, can in fact mean intellectual and spiritual laziness, demonstrating a failure of nerve and a refusal to allow the imagination to be engaged by the letter of the text. It is impossible in interpreting to avoid some kind of decoding (Rev 17:9ff. pushes us in this direction); yet the force of Revelation depends on the ability of the reader to allow its images to inform by means of a subtle interplay of text, context, and imagination.

The words of Revelation do not offer a view of things in any kind of literal way. A word used frequently in the book is ὡς (*hōs*), "as" or "like," suggesting the world of metaphor, the juxtaposition of words and ideas that connote a mind groping for adequate expression, rather than precise, uncomplicated depiction. Apocalyptic imagery beckons us to suspend our pragmatism and to enter into its imaginative world. That means being prepared to see things from another, unusual, point of view and being open to the possibility that difference of perspective will enrich our view and lead to difference of insight. The Apocalypse, not itself biblical interpretation but Scripture commissioned by Christ, presents the symbols and myths of what was Scripture in a new visionary form, much as Blake was to do in his mythic writings.

The visions of Revelation do not provide the currency of our everyday exchange of ideas and patterns of existence. Yet in the ancient world (and today in non-Western cultures) visions and dreams are regarded as important. The world of dreams is akin to that less ordered imaginative part of us that becomes active only when our dominant intellectual equipment itself lies dormant. When it comes to the imagination, we are like people who, having had little exercise, find themselves severely taxed by strenuous physical effort. Our imaginations are out of condition; we lack the skills to exercise our imaginations. So we are in no fit state to read Revelation with real insight. Like those who fail to see the point of the mysterious in the material, we need to cultivate imaginations that can grasp profound truths:

> "What," it will be Question'd, "When the Sun rises, do you not see a round disk of fire somewhat like a Guinea? O no, [responds William Blake] no, I see an Innumerable company of the Heavenly host crying, 'Holy, Holy, Holy is the Lord God Almighty.' I question not my Corporeal or Vegetative Eye any more than I would Question a Window concerning a Sight. I look thro' it & not with it.[3]

Apocalyptic offers us no excuse for resorting to a life based solely on fantasy; however, an understanding of what apocalypse is can lead to a more informed and obedient life. As Revelation itself indicates, to live in this way may be controversial, costly to ourselves and to our public esteem, because to live such a life is to refuse to conform to the expectations of the world unless those demands are compatible with Christ's teaching. We cannot underestimate the extent of resistance required of us. And we must be wary of hermeneutical strategies that would prevent us from making full use of a resource that would enable us to understand what to resist.

For example, the whole scope of demythologizing is really linked with the decoding mentality that has a long history in Revelation's interpretation. Demythologization was intended to enable strange texts to keep their value by getting at their "spirit" or "essence"—a typical strategy of Christian hermeneutics down the centuries. The letter of the text seems to kill, and this seems to be particularly true in the case of Revelation. The spirit, the essential message of the myth, however, can live on. But the cost of such a reading is that the literal, the medium of the message, is lost and with it the message, too. Is it a coincidence that the demythologization project got off the ground in 1942, at the height of Nazi tyranny and the most diabolical perversion of the millennial hope in the Third Reich and the unspeakable horror of the Holocaust? Bultmann's seminal essay was published then, offering a modern explanation of the gospel.[4] In one respect, such a project marked a challenge to the way mythology had been appropriated for such demonic ends.

What passed as rationality needed a critique that could interpret the horror and effects of evil, a perverted millennial dream destructive in its scope.[5] But demythologizing, which at its heart sought to explain the words and images of myth in other terms, also reduced its power by its individual focus. The church's suspicion of the Apocalypse did not help, epitomized by Bultmann's description of the book as "weakly christianized Judaism," an assessment, echoing Luther's negative opinion of 1522, that Revelation is "neither apostolic nor prophetic."

Dietrich Bonhoeffer, on the other hand, exhorted fellow church men and women to be "a community which hears the Apocalypse...to testify to its alien nature and to resist the false principle of inner-worldliness" and so to be at the service of "those who suffer violence and injustice." In his view "the Church takes to itself all the sufferers, [all] the forsaken of every party and status. 'Open your mouth for the dumb'(Proverbs 31:8)."[6] That witness and countercultural character of the church, so well exemplified by the dualistic contrasts of the Apocalypse, challenged church people to raise their voices in protest at the treatment of Jews. It is one thing to admit the importance of apocalyptic and Revelation for the understanding of the New Testament and to see it as the "mother of Christian theology";[7] it is rather different to allege that such ideas have a continuing resonance in contemporary life.

Contemporary interpreters of the book of Revelation are in a treble bind. First of all, they are confronted with an authoritative text that claims to reveal and turns out to be, at best, enigmatic and, at worst, off-putting. Second, a century and a half of historical exegesis has only served to underline the strangeness of the text and its distance from the sophisticated discourse of the First World. Third, Revelation has a reputation for fomenting an apocalyptic, irrational attitude of a catastrophic end for humanity or of fantasies about escaping from the problems and contradictions of life. In contrast to the situation of our ancestors, and many readers of this text in developing nations, Revelation has ceased to be a significant part of our linguistic currency. We are relieved that secularism and historicism have enabled us to tame the Apocalypse and subordinate its angularity to a liberal, apparently less threatening and more inclusive spirit by decoding its message and situating its significance in a previous, more credulous age. This text, which, despite its ambiguity and transgression of boundaries, is in large part about chaos, the loosening of the bands of historical order. It bears witness to aspects of our world that we fear. Ordering, and taming, the text enables us to avoid engaging our emotions and imaginations and, eventually, our wills and thereby evacuates the text of its power to change us.

If there is a text that required a reading "against the grain"[8] of what is accepted as normal in our current situation, it is Revelation. Read "against the grain," it may put us in touch with "utopian hopes and critical energies" as "a necessary corrective to the repetition of the ever-the-same in the guise of the new, the return of the seemingly repressed even amidst apparent enlightenment."[9] It can put us in touch with a subversive, apocalyptic memory "that seems so out of place against the more frequent hopes of bleak despair" that can characterize everyday life. The "unmasking of Babylon" and the truth about empire can enable us to see, perhaps to our discomfort and sadness, that "the cultural monuments celebrated by official, establishment history could not be understood outside the context of their origins, a context of oppression and exploitation." Apocalypse offers a fleeting glimpse of an alternative, the "involuntary memory of a redeemed humanity which contrasts with convention and false tradition."[10] It beckons us to rescue tradition from convention and to wrest it away from a conformity that is about to overpower it. Walter Benjamin's words, written at the end of his life, as he contemplated persecution and death, offer an eloquent description of the hermeneutics of the book of Revelation.

Revelation, and the apocalyptic tradition generally, has often been linked to the projects of agents of social change; yet it can be found buttressing the projects of those whose quest for utopia is firmly rooted in conventional values and the nostalgic yearning for a golden age of moral perfection based on hierarchy and subservience. In this nostalgic quest, apocalyptic symbolism serves to undergird a view of the world that supports the conviction of a comfortable elect that they will ultimately be saved. This outlook, with its alternative horizon beckoning toward a different future, enables a group to maintain clearly defined lines between the godly and the godless. On the other hand, apocalyptic symbolism can serve to enable the oppressed to find and maintain a critical distance from an unjust world, to claim the hope of a reign of justice. There is little new in this struggle over the language of apocalypse; apocalyptic symbolism has never been the sole preserve of the oppressed and the poor. Even in post-exilic Israel, in the very years when eschatological hope was being formed, there was a common stock of images that both sides in a struggle for power used to achieve preeminence for their own positions.[11] In our time, the rhetoric of the "evil empire" is as likely to be found in the corridors of economic and political power as in the grassroots Bible study groups of developing nations.

In the last century, we have labored to reconstruct an original historical context with care and precision, thinking it would enable us to hear the message as it was heard originally. But we cannot achieve that aim, in spite of the sophistication of our endeavors and the extent of our knowledge. Few of us are either a frightened minority or a people saturated with the images and outlook of apocalypse (some may say, though, that those of us in the West or in the "North" are "Laodiceans" or "Ephesians," who are lukewarm or have lost our first love), desperately and unwittingly compromised in our allegiance to the beast and Babylon. We are resistant to a text that confronts our particular interests and the power structures in which we are so deeply implicated. So we either avoid it or simply cannot hear "what the Spirit says to the churches." We fulfill the pessimistic prophecy of Isaiah and become more deaf rather than more receptive. Our deafness is increased as we treat the text as marginal to most churches or simply ignore it.

It is a telling fact that few people may, in fact, hear this text in the normal course of Christian worship. *The Revised Common Lectionary* prescribes ten readings from Revelation over the three-year cycle. Of these ten readings, five are from Revelation 21–22, four from two passages (1:4-8; 7:9-17), and one from chapter 5. That what we read in the church is a matter of ecclesiastical politics is evident from the fact that for centuries the Church of England allowed only small parts of the book of Revelation to be read at morning and evening prayer.[12] In churches that assert in their formularies that the Scriptures contain everything necessary for salvation, this is a remarkable phenomenon. To paraphrase Bonhoeffer's words, we have ceased to be a community that hears the Apocalypse, for the simple reason that we do not allow ourselves the opportunity of hearing, let alone keeping, its words.

A necessary check in our quest for understanding is to pay attention to the way the text has been interpreted in different theological and socioeconomic settings. Such a diachronic perspective ensures that the contemporary commentator's line is placed firmly in the broader context of the experience of a cloud of witnesses, whose insight is an essential context of any contemporary crystallization of meaning. Short of writing a commentary that included all strands of interpretation of this text in a vast compendium, there is the need to be selective, and so to constrict.

So determining the meaning of the text is always a contextual enterprise that cannot avoid an individual and social dimension. That will require of us discipline and self-critical awareness of what we bring to our reading. If we are going to seek to understand God's Word, we need honesty about ourselves, whether individually or socially. Like the biblical writers, we have a story to tell that we would do well not to avoid lest it reappear as a kind of unseen and, perhaps, unwelcome guest at our interpretative feast. We cannot put our experience to one side. Too often, unfortunately, the welter of concerns and opinions about matters religious, political, and psychological is unseen, but all too pervasive. We bring to our interpretation who we are, our personal and psychological history, and where we are, whether we approach the text from an inner-city community or a wealthy suburb, from a prosperous Western nation or from a poor shanty town of a developing nation.[13] It is helpful when we read any biblical book, but particularly one like Revelation, where the opportunity for variety of interpretation and application is much greater, to read with heightened awareness of ourselves and our own concerns. Feminist and liberationist perspectives in particular have pointed out how much we can miss in our reading. Recognizing what we most have to lose by taking the challenge of the text seriously or what it is we might need to learn to support or justify by reference to Scripture will help us to have ears to hear what the Spirit says in the text.

Although there are some peculiarities about the exegesis of Revelation, as with any biblical book, it is necessary to acknowledge the importance of the interaction of three dimensions in the hermeneutical process: text, context, and reader. The interaction constantly demands the highest level of awareness of self and of circumstance on the part of the interpreter. Space is created to reflect, so that the interpreter can explore the extent to which self-interest is projected onto the text or whether one is resistant to it. It is necessary for interpreters to distance themselves from the text in order not to make facile assumptions or to be controlled by unstated commitments to a particular tradition's reading of the text. Strategies of distancing can also call attention to the reasons for resistance to or too-ready acceptance of a text. We shall want to ask ourselves why we allow ourselves to be carried along by a text or a particular way of reading and what the resistance to a text says about us. Also, and most important, we must avoid treating texts as a problem that we as enlightened, modern interpreters can solve. Part of the process of reading is that critical self-awareness and attentiveness that may mean a reversal of roles in which interpreters in humility recognize that they need to become the ones who in some sense are being interpreted by the text.

A commentator on Revelation struggles to find ways to enable interaction with the text as we have it, thereby engaging the imagination, so that the book, with its peculiar network of imagery, may begin to pervade the reader's consciousness so that prejudice can be challenged. It is *this* text, *these* images that we need to read, not an explanation, however politically or theologically acceptable it may be. Revelation summons us into an apocalyptic world to be confronted by, infused with, and, perhaps, overpowered by (for good or ill) its images. Like John, we are called to "come up here, and I will show you what must take place"—not as interpreters or calculators of a precise eschatological program so much as co-participants in mental agony that wrenches us from our prejudice. The door of perception lies open, and we can experience apocalypse, just as John found himself reading or recalling, meditating upon, seeing again, writing, and being formed by the images of Ezekiel, Daniel, Isaiah, and the prophets. John sees the vision as Ezekiel would have seen it had the exilic prophet been inspired in John's circumstances. John repeats Ezekiel's experience in seeing the heavens opened (4:1; cf. Ezek 1:1) and seeing the awesome divine throne and the eating of the scroll (10:9; cf. Ezek 3:1ff.); like Daniel, John sees a divine figure who is the author of the revelations of what is to come (1:13ff.; cf. Dan 10:5-6).[14]

The way Revelation engages us and transforms us is as much a story of how apocalypse takes place with every reading, every "digesting" of this text.[15] A new moment of unveiling occurs through the images and the configuration of visions that John has bequeathed to us, and not in spite of them. We may be curious about the meaning of symbols or perhaps distracted by the odd historical reference, but we need to remember that our fundamental task is to read, to hear, and to appropriate, in whatever way our faculties allow us, the contents of this book, having thereby our perspective transformed and our imagination engaged. What we have in Revelation is the opening of an interpretative space for readers or hearers to be provoked, to have their imaginations broadened, and to be challenged to think and behave differently. The words of the book resist neat encapsulation and the precision of definition. It is a classic example of art that *stimulates* rather than *prescribes*. Readers do not require explanation so much as the encouragement to explore its words and images, so that they may be able to see and behave differently. The point is put very succinctly by William Blake in response to a request for the elucidation of his images:

> You say that I want somebody to Elucidate my Ideas. But you ought to know that What is Grand is necessarily obscure to Weak men. That which can be made Explicit to the Idiot is not worth my care. The wisest of the Ancients consider'd what is not too Explicit as the fittest for Instruction, because it rouzes the faculties to act.[16]

Blake was a visionary and thought of himself as a prophet. In this respect, he differs from most of us who are exegetes, who, whatever our desire to exercise a prophetic ministry, cannot pretend to have the kind of call that Blake had and that he shared with John, whose words were such a fundamental part of his life and writing.

Apocalypse is not a manual of eschatology, ethics, or theology, and yet it enables all of these. By refusing the predictable and by demanding that suspension of what counts for normality, we may perceive where the beast and Babylon are to be found. Whether as a result of reading and hearing the words of this prophecy we will see, understand, and repent of our allegiance to Babylon and to the beast—whose power over our minds and our social and economic structures is revealed to John in Revelation—and so choose to stand with the Lamb. What Revelation offers is the hope of a time when "the war of swords departed now" and "the dark Religions are departed & sweet Science reigns."[17]

JOHN, THE GOSPEL OF JOHN, AND THE REVELATION TO JOHN

External evidence concerning the apostle John and his relationship to Revelation comes relatively early in the Christian tradition. In commenting on Rev 20:4, Justin talks of John as one of the apostles of Christ who prophesied of the apocalypse that came to him.[18] Papias is reputed to have attested to the worth of Revelation,[19] though earlier Eusebius had a low opinion of Papias because of his millenarian views, as also did Melito of Sardis.[20] According to Tertullian, Marcion rejected Revelation as being a Jewish text,[21] and in the aftermath of the Montanist movement, Dionysius of Alexandria denied that Revelation was written by John the apostle.[22]

Traditionally the date of the book's writing has been set toward the end of the reign of Roman Emperor Domitian (the mid-90s), who took action against some members of the imperial household for their atheism; that may be a reference to Christianity, but equally could have been Judaism.[23] That may have been part of a much wider attempt to impose a tax on Jews and Jewish sympathizers (Christians would have fallen into that category). In that situation, there may have been a wave of sporadic persecution or harassment, but it is uncertain whether it was empire-wide in scope.

Evidence from Revelation itself suggests that an earlier date is equally likely. This derives from the most obvious reading of Rev 17:9-10. After Nero's death in 68 CE, there were four claimants to the throne in one year. So it may have been during the period of great upheaval in the empire while the power struggle was going on that John saw his vision. But the events of the 60s could easily have dominated the visionary horizon if he had his vision thirty years later.[24]

We know little other than what the book tells us about how John received this revelation. We will never know whether, like a poet, he exercised that mixture of imagination and attention to form that is characteristic of poetry, or whether he offers in the book the account of a true visionary experience. Many commentators suppose that Revelation is a conscious attempt to write an apocalypse, much as Paul would have written an epistle. Such an assessment is unsatisfactory, however. There are signs in the book of that dream-like quality in which the visionary not only sees but also is involved (e.g., 1:12, 17; 5:4; 7:13; 11:1; 17:3; cf. 1:10; 21:10). We should pay John the compliment of accepting his claim—unless we find strong reasons for denying it. There is in it a semblance of order, that, whatever the reservations of commentators, does yield a coherent pattern and deserves to be made sense of unless the juxtapositions seem totally contradictory. In some respects, Revelation differs markedly from a Jewish apocalypse like *1 Enoch*, which is a collection of heterogeneous material. The ordering in Revelation, however, need not exclude the possibility that it contains the visions that John saw, either on one single occasion or over a long period of time.

It has become something of a commonplace in New Testament scholarship to suppose that the Gospel of John represents the antithesis to the apocalyptic spirit of the Apocalypse. The Gospel of John at first sight seems a strange companion to Revelation, not least because its form and content are so markedly different. It has been so linked with Revelation because Christian tradition almost entirely asserts common authorship for the two works.[25]

The tradition that John the son of Zebedee ended his life in Ephesus offers an important connection with Revelation's setting in Asia Minor.[26] Obviously the narrative form of the Gospel places it at a significant distance from the Apocalypse. The Gospel contains few of the elements of an apocalypse, with the word ἀποκάλυψις (*apokalypsis*, "revelation") being used.

The Gospel of John is apparently the least apocalyptic document in the New Testament. It has frequently been regarded as an example of that type of Christianity that firmly rejected apocalyptic. By that is often meant that there is no imminent expectation of the end but rather the necessity of preparing for an unexpected and uncertain future for the church devoid of an apocalyptic horizon. Yet the main thrust of the message of the Gospel of John appears to have a remarkable affinity with apocalyptic. John Ashton rightly calls the Gospel of John "an apocalypse in reverse,"[27] for the heavenly mysteries are not to be sought in heaven but in Jesus, "the one who has seen the Father" (5:37) and makes the Father known. Admittedly, the mode of revelation stressed in the Gospel differs from that outlined in the apocalypses. The goal of apocalyptic is the attainment of knowledge of the divine mysteries, in particular the mysteries of God. Much of what the Fourth Gospel says relates to this theme. Jesus proclaims himself as the revelation of the hidden God (1:18; 14:8). The vision of God, the heart of the call experiences of Isaiah and Ezekiel and the goal of the heavenly ascents of the apocalyptic seers, is in the Fourth Gospel related to the revelation of God in Jesus. All claims to have seen God in the past are repudiated; the Jews are told: "You have never heard his voice or seen his form" (John 5:37 NRSV; cf. Deut 4:12). Even when, as in Isaiah's case, Scripture teaches that a prophet glimpsed God enthroned in glory, this vision is interpreted in the Gospel of John as a vision of the pre-existent Christ (John 12:41). No one has seen God except the one who is from God; he has seen the Father (John 6:46). So the vision of God reserved in the book of Revelation for the fortunate seer (4:1) and for the inhabitants of the new Jerusalem, who will see God face to face (22:4), is found, according to the Fourth Evangelist, in the person of Jesus of Nazareth. Possibly in the Fourth Gospel an attempt is made to repudiate the claims of those apocalyptists who claimed to have gained divine knowledge by means of heavenly ascents to God's throne when Jesus says to Nicodemus: "No one has ever gone into heaven except the one who came from heaven—the Son of Man" (John 3:13 NIV). In the Gospel of John, the quest for the highest wisdom of all, the knowledge of God, comes not through the information disclosed in visions and revelations but through the Word become flesh, Jesus of Nazareth. Thus, even if there is a rejection of any claim to revelation except through Christ, there is presupposed a claim to revelation with many affinities to Revelation.

John's narrative seems, on the face of it, totally devoid of the apocalyptic symbolism of the cosmic struggle. There is nothing of Jesus' struggles with the powers of darkness, familiar to us from the synoptic exorcisms, or the eschatological discourse of Mark 13 and parallel texts; John's Gospel seems to be devoid of the prophetic message of institutional judgment and cosmic upheaval. It is striking how apparently matter-of-fact the account of the passion of Jesus appears to be in the Fourth Gospel. There are no portents like the rending of the veil or the darkness that attends Jesus' death.

Yet telling the merely human story is insufficient to give an adequate impression of its significance, perhaps hinted at in Jesus' words to Pilate in John 19:11. The confrontation between darkness and light, between truth and the lie, between God and Caesar is all bound together and acted out in the discussion with Pilate. These machinations of the political powers cannot be understood apart from the apocalyptic struggle—a moment of eschatological judgment is going on behind the scenes (e.g., John 3:19), which is not confined to individual members of humanity (as 12:31; 14:30; and 16:11 make clear). The advent of Christ effects a cosmic judgment in which the dominance of the rule of the present is both called into question and brought to an end.

In John 12:27ff. there is a rare appearance of apocalyptic discourse epitomized by the heavenly voice, for which the crowds, faced with the characteristic ambiguity of the heavenly revelation, offer differing interpretations. Jesus then asserts: "*Now* is the time for judgment on this world; now the prince of this world will be driven out" (John 12:31 NIV, italics added). There is a link with the cross (e.g., John 12:33; cf. 13:1; 17:1). But the emphatic "now" in John 12:31 suggests that the triumph is not solely focused on the cross. Indeed, according to John 3:19 the eschatological judgment has already been brought into effect by the coming of the Son into the world. The life of Jesus, therefore, is a struggle that reaches a decisive moment in John 12:31.

In Rev 12:7, the battle in heaven leads to Satan's ejection from heaven to earth with the consequent threat to its inhabitants and their corruption by the evil empire. It is then followed in Revelation 13 by the specific embodiment of the diabolical threat in the beasts of political power. In John 12, the moment of the judgment of the world comes shortly after the declaration of the ruler of the world's ejection and just before the reference to the devil's/Satan's entering Judas (John 13:2, 27; note the eschatological role of humans in 1 John 2:19-20; 3:12ff.) and the beginning of the political maneuverings that lead to Jesus' death. The apocalyptic struggle is acted out on the plane of human history and reaches its climax in the cross. We can go further and note that in Revelation 12 there is the juxtaposition of Satan's ejection and the snatching up of the messianic child to heaven, similar to the juxtaposition of Satan's ejection and the lifting up of the Son of Man in John 12.

As in Rev 11:5 and 12:7, there is a decisive moment at the end of John 12, suggesting that a moment of decision has come and passed. There is now division between those who follow Jesus and those who, like Judas, find themselves permeated by darkness, and follow the ruler of the world. Yet the diabolical initiative that leads to the crucifixion is in reality the moment of the lifting of the Son of Man to heaven. To put it in the language of the Apocalypse, it is the moment when the Lamb opens the heavenly book of judgment and takes a place in the throne of glory. In the "ordinary" world of narrative (with only the barest hints of the apocalyptic scenario acted out, as it were, behind the scenes), the crisis in John 12 reverberates throughout the universe. However much the Gospel seems to offer hope only to that small remnant of perceptive people (John 17:24), that wider vision of the decisive shift in the fundamental nature of things, symbolized by the fracture of the power of all that is opposed to God, is not lost completely. Those who identify with Jesus bear witness to that shift in power, which demands of them public and costly witness, much as is required of those who refuse to conform to the demands of the beast in Revelation. In this they are accompanied by the cosmic role of the Spirit, whose function is not merely ecclesial but social and cosmic also (John 16:9ff.).

According to Revelation 14:7, the hour of judgment will have come when God's just and true judgments are revealed (cf. 16:7; 18:10). That true judgment is stressed by the Johannine Jesus in John 8:16. The judgment is focused on the fact that "the light has come into the world, and people loved darkness rather than light because their deeds were evil" (John 3:19; cf. Rev 9:20; 16:9). Judgment comes through believing the Son (3:18) who is not sent as judge (3:17; 8:15; 12:47; cf. 8:50); the one who does not believe is judged already (3:18). Yet elsewhere it is for judgment that Christ came into the world (9:39) and exercises judgment as the Son of Man (5:27; cf. 12:10; Dan 7:13-14). Father and Son are linked together like the Lamb and the one seated on the throne in 7:17. In Revelation, the judgment belongs to God but is exercised, too, by the rider on the white horse (19:11). John 5:24 echoes the blessings of Revelation on those who hear and keep the words of the prophecy (Rev 1:3; 22:7, 14). Judgment is in the past tense for the one who "hears my word and believes him who sent me" (John 5:24 NRSV), just as in Revelation the martyr who participates in the millennium does not come to judgment and the second death that is linked with it (20:6; that judgment is described in John 5:28 in terms remarkably similar to Rev 20:13).

These similarities of theme cannot mask the difference of perspective that an apocalypse gives. Here the veil is removed, and the reader glimpses what goes on behind the scenes. This is only hinted at in the Gospel of John. Readers' attention is focused not on the "beyond" but on the Word become flesh: "Whoever has seen me has seen the Father" (John 14:9 NRSV). We shall never know whether the Gospel and the Apocalypse were written by the same author. Yet the ancient tradition that links the two has, on closer inspection, something to commend it and suggests that more than merely superficial similarity that may offer by connection and contrast fruitful interpretative avenues for the exegete.

THE WORLD OF THE APOCALYPSE

There are other works that offer revelations of divine secrets similar in form and content to the New Testament apocalypse; indeed, they derive their generic description "apocalypse" from Rev 1:1. It is not the way in which the writers of these works, which are formally so similar to Revelation, describe their writings, however. The use of the words "revelation" (ἀποκάλυψις *apokalypsis*) and "reveal" (ἀποκαλύπτω *apokalypto*) to describe a vision from God or a revealing of divine secrets is relatively rare in literature written around about the time of Revelation.[28] They include a work heavily interpolated by a Christian editor, the *Testaments of the Twelve Patriarchs*[29] and *Joseph and Aseneth*, a work written probably in Egypt around about the beginning of the Christian era (16:7; 22:9).

The words are more common in the New Testament. In the Gospels, *apokalypsis* is found at Luke 2:32 in Simeon's song in a context in which already the revelation of a mystery, which angels desire to look upon, had been celebrated (Luke 2:13; cf. 1 Pet 1:11-12). The salvation is described by Simeon as light and glory, suggesting a mystery revealed "for the Gentiles" (cf. Eph 1:17; Col 1:26). Elsewhere, *apokalypsis* appears in contexts dealing with the eschatological revelation of secrets (Matt 11:25 // Luke 10:21; Matt 11:27; 16:17; in the quotation of Isa 53:1 in John 12:38 [see also John 1:31; 2:11; 7:4; 9:3; 17:6; 21:1, where *phanerō* is used]; and of the day of the Son of Man in Luke 17:30).

Apokalypsis is central to Paul's self-understanding (Gal 1:12). It is both something past and a future hope as well (1 Cor 1:7; cf. 2 Thess 1:7; 1 Pet 1:7; Rev 1:13; 4:13). Such revelations could be experienced both by him and by members of the church (1 Cor 14:26; 2 Cor 12:2ff.; Gal 2:2; Eph 1:17; Phil 3:15). The enigmatic passage in 2 Cor 12:2ff. is closest to what we find in Revelation. There Paul writes of an ascent to heaven and "visions and revelations" (ἀποκαλύψεις *apokalypseis*). The former (*optasia*) is used of angelic appearances in Luke 1:22 and of Paul's conversion experience in Acts 26:19. It is the word used for the translation of the Hebrew word מראה (*marēh*), the chief term for the visions in Daniel 10:1 (in Theodotion's Greek translation of the Old Testament, *apokalyptō* is introduced in passages where the earlier Greek versions used other words, e.g., Dan 2:19, 47; 10:1; 11:35). *Apokalyptō* is used of the present manifestation of God's wrath (Rom 1:17-18) and the divine mystery (1 Cor 2:10). Paul writes of the gospel as that which is made manifest (Rom 3:21), echoing the way he speaks of Christ's impact on him (Gal 1:16). The mystery of hidden things made manifest is found in Col 1:26 (*phanerō*; cf. 3:4; Eph 3:3, 5) and in the doxology that concludes Romans (Rom 16:25). The terminology is used of eschatological unveiling as well. The coming of Antichrist has still to be revealed (2 Thess 2:3), as do the judgment of human works (1 Cor 3:13) and the demonstration of the identity of the children of God (Rom 8:18-19; a usage evident also in 1 Pet 1:5; 5:1).

"Apocalyptic" has passed into common parlance as a way of speaking of a doom-laden outlook on life or a pattern of thought replete with the symbols and imagery of Revelation, and it can often be found in discussions of contemporary economic, social, and political affairs.[30] There has been much confusion in the discussion of apocalyptic, in particular regarding its relationship to eschatology. Indeed, the two are often closely related and used virtually interchangeably.

A distinction is usually made in contemporary scholarly discussion between apocalyptic (or apocalypticism) and the apocalypse. Indeed, it is important to note that apocalyptic is used by modern interpreters as an interpretative device to explain certain features of Second Temple Jewish prophetic texts.[31] Apocalypse is used to describe a particular literary type found in the literature of ancient Judaism, characterized by claims to offer visions or other disclosures of divine mysteries concerning a variety of subjects. Usually in Jewish and early Christian texts, such information is given to a biblical hero like Enoch, Abraham, Isaiah, or Ezra, so pseudonymity is characteristic of these writings. The apocalypse is to be distinguished from apocalyptic, a cluster of mainly eschatological ideas having to do with the secrets of heaven and God's plan for the cosmos. Apocalyptic ideas may also be found in a variety of texts that are not revelatory in form or intent. In the New Testament, the book of Revelation is an obvious example of an apocalypse. But passages like Mark 13, where Jesus speaks of the future, and 1 Thess 4:16 have been regarded as examples of apocalyptic, with their descriptions of the irruption of the Redeemer into history and (in the case of Mark 13) the cosmic catastrophes that must precede the coming of the heavenly Son of Man (indeed, Mark 13 is often misleadingly called "the little apocalypse").

We may best understand the enormous variety of material in the apocalypses if we consider them not merely as eschatological tracts satisfying the curiosity of those who wanted to know what would happen in the future but as revelations of divine secrets whose unveiling will enable readers to view their present situation from a completely different perspective. So, in the case of Revelation, the letters to the churches offer an assessment of the churches' worth from a heavenly perspective: The vision of the divine throne room in Revelation 4 enables the churches to recognize the dominion of their God; in Revelation 5, the death and exaltation of Christ are shown to mark the inauguration of the new age; and in chapters 13 and 17 the true identities of the beast and Babylon are divulged.

The origins of the apocalyptic genre are much disputed. In their concerns with the mysteries of God and the fulfillment of the divine purposes, these works have a close affinity to the prophetic literature of the Old Testament. That only one apocalypse is included in the canon of the Old Testament, the book of Daniel, should not be taken as an indication that the compilers of the canon did not have much interest in the apocalyptic tradition, as there seems to have been a lively apocalyptic oral tradition in Judaism that had a long history. The discovery of fragments of the Enoch apocalypse at Qumran have pushed the date of this particular text back well before the second century BCE—back, in other words, into that obscure period when the prophetic voice began to die out in Israel. Apocalyptic continued to play a vital part within Jewish religion throughout the period of the Second Temple, and even in rabbinic circles it persisted as an esoteric tradition that manifested itself in written form in the much later *Hekaloth* tracts and later on in the Kabbalah.[32] There is a paucity of references to apocalyptic matters in early rabbinic literature,[33] and apocalypses like the books of Enoch are not quoted or thought of as authoritative.

During the period of the Second Temple and immediately after its destruction in 70 CE, there existed a mystical tradition among several prominent rabbis that was based on the startling description of the throne-chariot in the first chapter of Ezekiel and the account in Genesis 1. While there was considerable suspicion of this tradition among the rabbis, there is also evidence that many treasured apocalyptic ideas. It is likely that some of the rabbis who occupied themselves in the study of texts like Ezekiel 1 actually experienced ecstatic ascents to heaven to behold the divine throne-chariot, similar to that described by John in Revelation 4. The resort to apocalypticism by visionaries and writers took place in a variety of circumstances. While many of the apocalypses written during the Second Temple period in their present form are products of careful editing, it is possible that actual experiences may lie behind them, and this possibility should not be ruled out in the case of the New Testament apocalypse. The discovery of apocalypses in the Gnostic library at Nag Hammadi may indicate some relationship between apocalyptic and gnosticism, particularly in the light of their common concern with knowledge. As far as one can see, apocalyptic did not reach a stage where its revelation was of itself salvific, but at times it comes very close to being so.[34]

In the study of the antecedents of apocalyptic literature and its ideas, there have been significant differences of opinion about those origins. On the one hand are those who consider apocalyptic to be the successor to the prophetic texts of the Old Testament, and particularly to the future hope of the prophets.[35] The concern with human history and the vindication of Israel's hopes in Revelation all echo themes from the prophets, several of whom have contributed widely to Revelation's language, particularly Ezekiel, Daniel, and Zechariah. Some, on the other hand, see a subtle change taking place in the form of that hope in the apocalyptic literature as compared with most of the prophetic texts in the Bible. It is suggested that the future hope has been placed on another plane, the supernatural and otherworldly (e.g., Isaiah 65:1–66; cf. Revelation 21:1; 4 Ezra 7:50). But evidence for such a change from the earthly to the supramundane is not, in fact, widespread. More important is the subtle change of prophetic genre in the later chapters of Ezekiel, with its visions of a new Jerusalem; the highly symbolic visions of Zechariah's early chapters and the cataclysmic upheavals of its last chapters; and the probably late eschatological chapters of Isaiah 24:1–27; 55–66. Also important is the emergence of the apocalyptic heavenly ascent, evident in texts like *1 Enoch* 14. The glimpse into heaven, which is such a key part of John's vision from chapter 4 onward, has its antecedents in the call visions of Ezekiel (Ezekiel 1:1; 10) and Isaiah (Isaiah 6:1) as well as the parallel glimpses of the heavenly court of 1 Kings 22:1 and Job 1–2.

Antecedents of apocalyptic literature have been found in the wisdom tradition of the Old Testament as well, with its interest in understanding the cosmos and the ways of the world. Apocalyptic is concerned with knowledge, not only of the age to come but also of things in heaven (e.g., *1 Enoch* 72ff.) and the mysteries of human existence, akin to features of the wisdom literature. While it is the case that the concern with the destiny of Israel, so evident in parts of some apocalypses, is hardly to be found in works like Ecclesiastes and Sirach, both of which seem to discourage the kind of speculation found in the apocalypses (see Sir 3:21ff.), the activities of certain wise men in antiquity were not at all dissimilar from the concerns of the writers of the apocalypses. This includes interpretation of dreams, oracles, astrology, and divine mysteries concerning future events. There is some trace of the role of such figures in the Old Testament, for instance, in the Joseph stories in Genesis and in the book of Daniel. But the most obvious apocalyptic moment in the wisdom corpus is the opening and dramatic climax of the book of Job. The latter enables Job's entirely reasonable stance to be transcended and for Job to move from an understanding based on hearsay to one based on apocalyptic insight (Job 42:5).

A comparison of Revelation with Daniel reveals differences as well as similarities. In certain visions, Revelation is clearly indebted to Daniel (e.g., Daniel 10 in Rev 1:13ff.; Daniel 7 in Revelation 13; 17). Both books are eschatologically oriented. Unlike Revelation, however, Daniel is pseudonymous (probably written in the second century BCE at the height of the crisis in Jerusalem under the Seleucid king Antiochus IV). John's authority resides primarily in his prophetic call (1:9ff.) rather than in any claim to antiquity or apostolicity. The form of the visions differs also. Daniel's dream vision followed by interpretation is almost completely lacking in Revelation (chap. 17 is a solitary exception in which contemporary historical connections are most explicitly made).

A significant part of the book of Daniel has to do with the royal court in Babylon, and Daniel 2 offers an interpretation of Nebuchadnezzar's dream. Here are men who are comfortable, cosmopolitan Jews who have a good reputation in the land of their exile, though they are nostaligic for Zion (Dan 6:10) and there are limits on what they will compromise. As in Revelation, idolatry is a problem for the Jews (Dan 3). The fiery furnace and the lions' den are the terrible consequences for those who refuse to conform to Babylonian worship. Yet Nebuchadnezzar (unlike Belshazzar) is depicted sympathetically; there is evidence of admiration on the part of the king for the young Jewish men (cf. the signs of that in Rev 11:13) and of his reluctance to see these significant courtiers die.

And these men who resist the imperial system, and are thus prepared to face suffering, miraculously escape. This story contrasts with Revelation, where religious persecution is expected to include suffering and death (2:11; 6:9; 7:14; 11:7; 13:10; 12:11). In Revelation, there is the promise of vindication (11:7-8), but at the same time a clear recognition that there can be no escape from the great tribulation (7:14).

There is in Revelation a more distanced and antagonistic attitude toward empire. Although Revelation 18 briefly reflects on Babylon's fall from the perspective of the kings, the mighty, and the merchants, the position of the writer is that of vigorous rejection of the power and purposes of empire and satisfaction at the ultimate triumph of God's righteousness (14:11; 19:3). Whereas Daniel presents persons who are immersed in the life of the pagan court, Revelation countenances no such accommodation. The only acceptable stances are resistance and withdrawal (18:4). Accommodation may be a sign of apostasy (2:20ff.). Pagans react with awe (6:15), with fear (11:10), and with anger toward God (6:10; 9:20).

In the New Testament, Mark 13 and 1 Thess 4:16–5:11 have affinities with eschatological sections of Revelation, but particular attention should also be given to the many New Testament passages that refer to the importance of visions and revelations. Mark 1:10 records at the outset of Jesus' ministry a private vision, reminiscent of the apocalypses and the call visions of the prophets; the reference to the open heaven is a typical feature of visionary accounts (cf. Isa 49:1; Jer 1:5; Gal 1:12, 16). Matthew's Gospel gives an often missed but significant role to dreams and revelations (Matt 1:20; 2:12-13, 19; 27:19; 11:25-26; 16:17; 17:9). But it is Luke's account of the origins of the church that has most of the references to visions. Even allowing for Luke's special interest in the divine guidance of the church and its mission, the vision of the tongues of fire at Pentecost (Acts 2), the martyr Stephen's vision of the heavenly Son of Man (Acts 7:56-57), the twice-told decisive vision of the sheet descending from heaven, which preceded Peter's preaching to Cornelius (Acts 10:11), and the thrice-told account of Paul's conversion (Acts 9; 22; 26) all indicate the importance Luke attached to visions and revelations. The polemic of Paul against false teachers at Colossae (e.g., Col 2:18) indicates that they may have had an interest in visions of the activity of the angels in heaven and needed to be pointed to the centrality of Christ. Outside the New Testament, figures like Elchesai,[36] Cerinthus,[37] and the *Shepherd of Hermas*,[38] as well as the Montanist movement[39] may be mentioned.

Spatial categories form an important part of apocalyptic thought.[40] Such categories are presupposed by several New Testament writers; indeed, they form part of the argument of one or two documents. In Ephesians, for example, the author speaks of a heavenly dimension to the church's existence; by his use of the phrase "in the heavenly places," he links the church with the exalted Christ (Eph 2:6). An important part of the argument of the Letter to the Hebrews concerns the belief that the superiority of Christ's sacrifice is that his offering of himself enabled him to enter not the earthly shrine, but heaven itself, into the very presence of God (Heb 9:11, 24). This framework of contrast between the world below and the world above facilitates the writer's presentation of the saving work of Christ. Christ the heavenly pioneer has entered into the inner shrine, behind the veil (Heb 6:19-21). He has entered into not a sanctuary made with hands, a mere copy of the true one, but into heaven itself to appear in the divine presence on behalf of God's people.[41]

The book of Revelation fails to satisfy the desire for an unambiguous, final utterance on faith and morals. Revelation never allows the reader complete certainty. There is no simple division between the church and the world. There are no grounds for complacency—only watchfulness (3:3) and the constant endeavoring to keep one's robes clean (22:14). The practice of the church is confused and compromised. Despite the authoritative status it claims for itself, the book of Revelation hardly offers a definitive prescription of the religious life. There is in it an implied intense suspicion of the values of the surrounding culture and institutions, but nowhere does it set down precise rules of how one should exemplify the divine wisdom. We are not offered a detailed and immediately applicable code of laws but the revelation of divine mysteries that bemuse and perplex and seem to veil as much as they reveal. And unlike the interpretations of the visions in Daniel (see Dan 2:7), rarely is there an angelic interpreter on hand to tell readers what the imagery means.

To discern the true nature of a culture in thrall to war and virtue "calls for wisdom" (13:18 NRSV; see also 17:9). This means more than astute observation of the world. What is required is a recovery of imagination as a necessary complement to all-conquering reason. In *1 Enoch* 2–5, the wisdom deriving from observation of the world is juxtaposed with apocalyptic, revelatory, wisdom. Apocalyptic wisdom does not offer unambiguous and unequivocal answers. The appeal to revelation may seem to promise solutions to intractable human problems through divinely bestowed insight. Apocalypses produce as much mystification as enlightenment, however, revealing the extent of the problem of human perception and the complex strategies needed to compel an uncomprehending humanity to begin to see things differently. That is how apocalyptic visions function. We should not ask of apocalypses, What do they mean? Rather, we should ask, How do the images and designs work? How do they affect us and change our lives? The intellectual asceticism of 4 Ezra, the opacity of Revelation's symbolism, and the tantalizing parables of God's reign in the Gospels all indicate that until "sweet Science reigns" those whose minds are darkened will need a variety of ways to open their intellects to glimpse the mystery of apocalyptic wisdom.

EXCURSUS: GOD'S THRONE, THE HEAVENLY MERKABAH, AND THE HUMAN FIGURE

Interest in God's throne and the one seated upon it, as well as the cosmos and its origins, formed key aspects of Jewish mysticism. This interest almost certainly antedates the fall of Jerusalem in 70 CE and had a long history from the very earliest times after the return from exile in Babylon down to the hasidic movements nearer our own day.[42] Interest in

Ezekiel 1 is attested mainly in apocalyptic writings that in part antedate the Christian era. The material from Qumran Caves 4 and 11 known as the *Songs of the Sabbath Sacrifice* has given considerable support to the view that the origin of the idea that the speculative, visionary interest in the heavenly temple, liturgy, and the existence of a complex angelology linked with attempts to pierce the veil surrounding the profound secrets of God's dwelling lies early in the Second Temple period.[43] According to the Mishnah, two biblical passages provide the foundation for this speculative interest: Genesis 1 and Ezekiel 1.[44] Jewish mysticism is divided into two main branches: one concerned with cosmogony and cosmology, based on Genesis 1 (מעשה בראשית *ma'ăśeh bĕrē'šît*), and the other based on Ezekiel 1 and the throne-chariot of God (מעשה מרכבה *ma'ăśeh merkābâ*). The latter is much more theologically oriented insofar as it deals specifically with God's nature and immediate environment in heaven. Reading Ezekiel 1 was severely restricted by ancient Jewish teachers because of its use by visionaries and the dangers to faith and life that such visionary activity posed.[45]

The reconstruction of the content of the *merkabâ* tradition in the late first century is not easy. The focus of the tradition was the throne-chariot of God and the glorious figure enthroned upon it. Meditation on passages like Ezekiel 1, set as it is in exile and in the aftermath of a previous destruction of the Temple, would have been particularly apposite as the rabbis sought to come to terms with the devastation of Jerusalem in 70 CE.

We know that Paul was influenced by apocalyptic ascent ideas (2 Cor 12:2ff.)[46] and that he emphasizes the importance of this visionary element as the basis of his practice (Gal 1:12, 16; cf. Acts 22:17). His apocalyptic outlook enabled him to act on his eschatological convictions, so that the apocalypse of Jesus Christ became the basis for his practice of admitting Gentiles into the messianic age without the Law of Moses. The threat posed by apocalyptic may be discerned elsewhere, particularly in its possibilities for christology.[47] There may have been a "seeing again" of that awesome vision of Ezekiel, or perhaps that vision becomes itself the object of analysis and speculation.[48]

Texts that resemble Revelation 4:1's vision of God and the throne and can be dated to the same period are now quoted.

1 Enoch 14:8–25 (At Least 3rd Century BCE and Probably Much Older)

And behold I saw the clouds: And they were calling me in a vision; and the fogs were calling me; and the course of the stars and the lightnings were rushing me and causing me to desire; and in the vision, the winds were causing me to fly and rushing me high up into heaven. And I kept coming (into heaven) until I approached a wall which was built of white marble and surrounded by tongues of fire; and it began to frighten me. And I came into the tongues of the fire and drew near to a great house which was built of white marble, and the inner wall(s) were like mosaics of white marble, the floor of crystal, the ceiling like the path of the stars and lightnings between which (stood) fiery cherubim and their heaven of water; and flaming fire surrounded the wall(s), and its gates were burning with fire. And I entered into the house, which was hot like fire and cold like ice, and there was nothing inside it; fear covered me and trembling seized me. And as I shook and trembled, I fell upon my face and saw a vision. And behold there was an opening before me (and) a second house which is greater than the former and everything was built with tongues of fire. And in every respect it excelled (the other)—in glory and great honor—to the extent that it is impossible for me to recount to you concerning its glory and greatness. As for its floor, it was of fire and above it was lightning and the path of the stars; and as for the ceiling, it was flaming fire. And I observed and saw inside it a lofty throne—its appearance was like crystal and its wheels like the shining sun; and (I heard?) the voice of the cherubim; and from beneath the throne were issuing streams of flaming fire. It was difficult to look at it. And the Great Glory was sitting upon it—as for his gown, which was shining more brightly than the sun, it was whiter than any snow. None of the angels was able to come in and see the face of the Excellent and the Glorious One; and no one of the flesh can see him—the flaming fire was round about him, and a great fire stood before him. No one could come near unto him from among those that surrounded the tens of millions (that stood) before him. He needed no council, but the most holy ones who are near to him neither go far away at night nor move away from him. Until then I was prostrate on my face covered and trembling. And the Lord called me with his own mouth and said to me, "Come near to me, Enoch, and to my holy Word." And he lifted me up and brought me near to the gate, but I (continued) to look down with my face.[49]

4Q405 20.II.21-22 (Probably 1st Century BCE)

The cherubim prostrate themselves before him and bless. As they rise, a whispered divine voice [is heard], and there is a roar of praise. When they drop their wings, there is a [whispered] divine voice. The cherubim bless the image of the throne-chariot above the firmament, [and] they praise [the majest]y of the luminous firmament beneath his seat of glory. When the wheels advance, angels of holiness come and go. From between his glorious wheels there is as it were a fiery vision of most holy spirits. About them, the appearance of rivulets of fire in the likeness of gleaming brass, and a work of...radiance in many-coloured glory, marvellous pigments, clearly mingled. The spirits of the living gods move perpetually with the glory of the marvellous chariots. The whispered voice of blessing accompanies the roar of their advance, and they praise the Holy One on their way of return. When they ascend, they ascend marvellously, and when they settle, they stand still. The sound of joyful praise is silenced and there is a whispered blessing of the gods in all the camps of God. And the sound of praise...from among all their divisions...and all their numbered ones praise, each in his turn.[50]

Apocalypse of Abraham 18:1-14 (Probably from the End of the 1st Century CE and Contemporary with Revelation)

And as I was still reciting the song, the mouth of the fire which was on the firmament was rising up on high. And I heard a voice like the roaring of the sea, and it did not cease from the plenitude of the fire. And as the fire rose up, soaring to the highest point, I saw under the fire a throne of fire and the many-eyed ones round about, reciting the song, under the throne four fiery living creatures, singing. And the appearance of each of them was the same, each having four faces. And this (was) the aspect of their faces: of a lion, of a man, of an ox, and of an eagle. Each one had four heads on its body so that the four living creatures had sixteen faces. And each one had six wings: two on the shoulders, two halfway down, and two at the loins. With the wings which were on their shoulders they covered their faces, with the wings at their loins they clothed their feet, and they would stretch the two middle wings out and fly, erect. And when they finished singing, they would look at one another and threaten one another. And it came to pass when the angel who was with me saw that they were threatening each other, he left me and went running to them. And he turned the face of each living creature from the face which was opposite it so that they could not see each other's faces threatening each other. And he taught them the song of peace which the Eternal One has in himself. And while I was still standing and watching, I saw behind the living creatures a chariot with fiery wheels. Each wheel was full of eyes round about. And above the wheels was the throne which I had seen. And it was covered with fire and the fire encircled it round about, and an indescribable light surrounded the fiery crowd. And I heard the voice of their sanctification like the voice of a single man. [51]

Parallels to John's Vision of the Human Figure

The opening of the book describes a christophany with few parallels in the NT (the transfiguration being a notable exception).[52] There are some similarities with various christophanies and angelophanies from both Jewish and Christian texts. The elements of Revelation 4 are inspired by several OT passages, one of which is the first chapter of Ezekiel, particularly the climax of his call-vision, in which the prophet catches a glimpse of the form of God on the throne of glory in the dazzling gleam of bronze. It is also similar to Dan 10:5-6, where we find a vision of a heavenly being, broadly based on Ezekiel 1. There are hints of a tradition of interpretation of Ezekiel 1, particularly in visionary contexts, in which the glorious figure on the throne acts in a quasi-angelic role.

> At that time I, Daniel, had been mourning for three weeks. I had eaten no rich food, no meat or wine had entered my mouth, and I had not anointed myself at all, for the full three weeks. On the twenty-fourth day of the first month, as I was standing on the bank of the great river (that is, the Tigris), I looked up and saw a man clothed in linen, with a belt of gold from Uphaz around his waist. His body was like beryl, his face like lightning, his eyes like flaming torches, his arms and legs like the gleam of burnished bronze, and the sound of his words like the roar of a multitude. I, Daniel, alone saw the vision; the people who were with me did not see the vision, though a great trembling fell upon them, and they fled and hid themselves. So I was left alone to see this great vision. My strength left me, and my complexion grew deathly pale, and I retained no strength. Then I heard the sound of his words; and when I heard the sound of his words, I fell into a trance, face to the ground. But then a hand touched me and roused me to my hands and knees. He said to me: "Daniel, greatly beloved, pay attention to the words that I am going to speak to you. Stand on your feet, for I have been sent to you....Do not fear, Daniel, for from the first day that you set your mind to gain understanding and to humble yourself before your God, your words have been heard. (Dan 10:2-12 NRSV)

> And I stood up and saw him who had taken my right hand and set me on my feet. The appearance of his body was like sapphire, and the aspect of his face was like chrysolite, and the hair of his head like snow. And a kidaris (was) on his head, its look that of a rainbow, and the clothing of his garments (was) purple; and a golden staff (was) in his right hand. And he said to me, "Abraham." And I said, "Here is your servant!" And he said, "Let my appearance not frighten you, nor my speech trouble your soul. Come with me! . . . and I got up and looked at him who had taken my right hand and set me up on my feet; and his body was like sapphire, and his face like chrysolite, and the hair of his head like snow, and there was a linen band about his head and it was like a rainbow and the robes he was wearing were purple, and he had a golden staff in his right hand.[53]

> And a man came to her from heaven and stood by Asenath's head. And he called her and said..."I am the chief of the house of the Lord and commander of the whole host of the Most High. Rise and stand on your feet, and I will tell you what I have to say." And Asenath raised her head and saw, and behold, (there was) a man in every respect similar to Joseph, by the robe and the crown and the royal staff, except that his face was like lightning, and his eyes like sunshine, and the hairs of his head like a flame of fire of a burning torch, and hands and feet like iron shining forth from a fire, and sparks shot forth from his hands and feet. And Asaneth saw (it) and fell on her face at his feet on the ground. And Asenath was filled with great fear, and all of her limbs trembled. And the man said to her, "Courage, and do not be afraid, but rise and stand on your feet, and I will tell you what I have to say."[54]

With the book of Revelation we are in the midst of the world of apocalyptic mystery. Despite attempts over the years to play down the importance of this book, the indications suggest that its thought forms and outlook were more typical of early Christianity than is often allowed. The fact that there is no visionary material elsewhere in the NT accounts for some of the differences, but they are only superficial. Beneath the surface, we have here convictions about God, about Christ, and about the world that are not far removed from the so-called mainstream Christianity of the rest of the NT. The synoptic eschatological discourses are an obvious example of a similar outlook, but they are by no means alone. Revelation, with its indebtedness to a shadowy, perhaps embryonic mysticism of the Second Temple period, prompts us to look closer at other NT texts to see whether they, too, exhibit some of the telltale marks of mysticism. This unique early Christian example of the apocalyptic genre is profoundly indebted to Jewish apocalyptic ideas. In Revelation, the first chapter of Ezekiel, the *merkabâ* chapter, has not only contributed to the visionary vocabulary of John, but also the initiatory visions (Rev 1:13ff.; 4:1ff.) are dominated by it. When taken alongside those other descriptions of the divinity that are now extant from the Second Temple period, we may suppose that we have in Revelation a glimpse of the tip of a mystical iceberg now largely lost from view. What is visible points to a distinctive use of prophecy parallel to, but in significant respects different from, other apocalyptic texts.

CONTEMPORARY APOCALYPTIC: 4 EZRA AND REVELATION

Revelation's imagery and its hope in the messianic vindication and defeat of Rome parallels in many ways the roughly contemporary 4 Ezra (2 Esdras 3–14).[55] This work has for centuries been an important resource for understanding the milieu of the New Testament. It has a place in the Vulgate, and some Christian traditions have placed it among the books of the Old Testament. Its similarity of outlook in regard to human sinfulness with the Paul of Romans and Galatians sets it apart from other Jewish texts. Its messianic vision in chap. 13, dependent as it is on Daniel 7, has often been used as a resource for the discussion of the Son of Man in the canonical Gospels. The book of 4 Ezra is an apocalypse that emerged in the dark days of despair after the fall of the Second Temple in 70 CE. It offers "a fountain of wisdom" (4 Ezra 14:47) in its secret books.

In the dialogues between Ezra and the angel, which occupy the first part of the book, the contrast between human and divine wisdom and the inability of even the most righteous humans to understand the divine purposes are repeated themes (echoes here of Isaiah 40:21ff.). Ezra's words embody an enlightened, commonsense position with regard to the lot of humanity, the injustices of the world, and the perplexity at the fate of the chosen people in the wake of the destruction of the Temple. He is concerned for the majority of humanity whose unrighteousness seems to be about to consign them to perdition (4 Ezra 7:62ff.). The divine perspective is uncompromising, however, and only partially understandable. The dialogue between Ezra and the angel indicates the contrast between human and divine wisdom. At times it appears that Ezra's concerns are more merciful than the divine reply. Despair is dealt with by urging the righteous to concentrate on the glory that awaits those who are obedient to God (4 Ezra 8:52; 9:13). God's patience is not for the sake of humanity, but because of divine faithfulness to the eternal plan, which was laid down before creation (4 Ezra 7:74). Throughout the book, the ways of God, the Most High, are vindicated (parallels here with Paul's agony in Romans 9–11). God is the one who orders the times and the seasons, and God alone will bring about the new age (4 Ezra 6:5). Just as in the book of Job,[56] where the divine answer stresses the inadequacy of human wisdom, so here, too, the impossibility of understanding the divine purposes in the midst of the old order is stressed (4 Ezra 4:1ff., 21; 5:36). Ezra cannot presume to be a better judge than God or wiser than the Most High (4 Ezra 7:19). Humanity's problem is that despite being given a mind to understand, they have sinned. So torment awaits them (4 Ezra 7:72; cf. 4 Ezra 9:20), sentiments reminiscent of Paul's description of a benighted humanity in Romans 1. All speculation and argument are irrelevant compared to the eschatological concerns that should occupy the attention of the righteous (4 Ezra 9:13).

In 4 Ezra 6:11ff., Ezra is shown the signs of the end of the present order. These visions involve a dreadful period of disease and deprivation (4 Ezra 6:20ff. In 4 Ezra 7, there is a much longer and more explicit description of the future purposes of God. The hidden city and land will appear (presumably a reference to the fulfillment of the hidden purposes of God, vouchsafed to the seer and soon to be made manifest on earth). The Messiah also will be revealed, and those who are left on earth will reign with him for four hundred years. This will come to an end with the death of the Messiah and all humanity, with the world returning to primeval silence for seven days. Only after that will the world, which is not awake, be roused; whatever is corruptible will perish (4 Ezra 7:32), and the resurrection will take place as a prelude to the judgment of all humanity, confronted by the furnace of hell and the paradise of delight.

What emerges in the work is a perceptive insight into the pervasiveness of evil, which makes difficult the attempts of men and women to fulfill the divine command. There is free will (4 Ezra 3:8; 8:50-51), but Adam's sin has had devastating effects on human life and understanding (4 Ezra 3:20; 4:30; 7:118). A blessed place is reserved for those who persevere to the end. The message is uncompromising. There is little of the arresting symbolism that permeates virtually the whole of the book of Revelation (though 4 Ezra 9ff. marks a change of mood). The effect of reading the early chapters of 4 Ezra is to disinfect the mind of any presumption of being able to fathom the wisdom of God and to warn against flights of metaphysical fancy. What the righteous need do is view all things in the light of the end rather than concentrate on the apparent injustices of the present time (4 Ezra 7:16). Eschatology offers the hope of final resolution. Those who, like Ezra, continue in obedience, a way of life that seems so pointless to the majority of humanity, receive reassurance that faithful endurance ultimately will pay off. If there can be any answer to human questioning in 4 Ezra, that is the only one on offer. The stark message is that the righteous need to view all things in the light of eschatological salvation and to persist in obedience to God rather than allow themselves to become depressed or allow their reason full rein to seek explanations to the apparent injustices of the present (4 Ezra 7:16).[57] The mystery that offers salvation is perseverance in the righteous way of life, whatever the apparent contrary indications (cf. Mark 13:13).

Revelation has several parallels with 4 Ezra and with Daniel. The beasts from the sea and land in Revelation 13 are dependent on the opening verses of Daniel 7 and, like 4 Ezra 11, focus on one beast only, which is an epitome of the awfulness and oppression of tyranny. Like the messiah in 4 Ezra 13, the Lamb can stand on Mount Zion (Rev 14:1); and at the dramatic parousia in Rev 19:11, the rider on the white horse is described in language reminiscent of Dan 10:6, with the same capacity as the messiah in 4 Ezra 13 to take effective action in judgment (here there is a sharp sword rather than a stream of fire, 19:15). Both 4 Ezra and Revelation agree in separating the political critique (the opening verses of Daniel 7, dealing with the beasts emerging from the sea) from the "messianic solution" focused on in Dan 7:13. So Revelation 13 focuses on the critique of empire, whereas Revelation 14 and 19 (though the latter is not formally dependent on Dan 7:13-14) present us with a contrasting scene in which the dominion of the Lamb under God is outlined. In 4 Ezra 11–12 the eagle vision is a critique of and prediction of the destruction of the last empire, while 4 Ezra 13 is a messianic vision. Both Revelation and 4 Ezra concentrate on the fourth beast of Daniel, a preoccupation that was to feature in a wide range of apocalyptic scenarios down the centuries.[58]

The vision in 4 Ezra 11–12 is a complicated account of an eagle with twelve wings and three heads that rises out of the sea. The complexity of this vision has often prompted the suggestion that it is an artificial construction reflecting recent Roman history. That assessment is entirely understandable, but needs to be set alongside the difficulties commentators have had in offering a historical explanation of the various details. The wings of the eagle spread over the whole earth. The eagle reigns over the earth with all things subjected to it. Out of the wings, eight rival small wings emerge. The first twelve wings rise and fall, and of these none rule as long as does the second (v. 16). Eventually the twelve large wings and two of the eight little wings disappear. Nothing remains except three heads, which are at rest, and six of the little wings. Two little wings separate from the six and remain under the head on the right side, while four little wings plan to rule. Two set up their kingdom and then disappear, leaving the two who plan to reign together. In v. 29 the head in the middle awakens and with the two remaining heads devours the little wings that are planning to reign. The head gains control over the world and oppresses its inhabitants. Eventually the head in the middle disappears, and the two remaining heads rule until the head on the right side devours that on the left.

Then the focus of interest changes. In v. 37 a lion is roused from the forest; it speaks to the eagle, the last of four beasts that were made to reign in the world and the sign that the end of time has come. This fourth beast conquers all that have gone before and holds sway in an oppressive manner. It is condemned in 4 Ezra 11:41-42: "You have judged the earth but not with truth, for you have oppressed the meek and injured the peaceable; you have hated those who tell the truth, and have loved liars; you have destroyed the homes of those who brought forth fruit, and have laid low the walls of those who did you no harm." Its destruction is "so that the whole earth may be freed from violence." The remaining head disappears, leaving two wings to set themselves up to reign, after which follows a period of tumult until they vanish; the body of the eagle is burned, and the whole earth is left terrified.

This vision, with its far-fetched multiplications of the wings of the eagle, demands an explanation. As we might expect from an apocalypse, the seer is offered an interpretation of this complicated vision by an angel. In 4 Ezra 12:11, we are told that the eagle from the sea is the fourth kingdom that appeared in Daniel's vision. This is more terrifying than all the kingdoms that came before it. This fourth kingdom will be ruled by a series of twelve kings, the second reigning the longest. After the second king's death there will be great conflicts. and the empire will be on the verge of collapse. Of the eight kings whose times will be short, two will perish; four will be kept for the time when the end approaches, but two will be kept until the end. According to 4 Ezra 12:22, the culmination of its dominion will come when three kings represented by the three heads raised up by the Most High in the last days will rule the earth more oppressively. They will sum up the wickedness of the regime. One of the kings dies in his bed; one will fall victim to the sword of another; and the last one will fall by the sword as well. The lion who appears is the Messiah, the offspring of David, kept for the end of days to execute judgment and bring about the liberation of the "remnant of my people" and to "make them joyful until the end comes."

Whereas in 4 Ezra the eagle is Daniel's fourth beast, in Revelation the beast that arises from the sea incorporates characteristics of the previous empires. The imagery of 4 Ezra 11–12 is more complicated than anything in Revelation, though something approaching that complexity is to be found in Revelation 17, where the seven heads of the beast upon which the woman is seated are both kings and hills (Rev 17:9). The Messiah in both texts is symbolized by a lion (Rev 5:5; 4 Ezra 12, probably dependent on Gen 49:9). Revelation lacks the pessimistic tone of 4 Ezra, though it, too, contemplates a world that is seduced by the power and brilliance of the Beast. The interpretation of the eagle vision suggests that the reign of the Messiah precedes the end and so is part of a two-stage eschatology. This twofold scheme of a messianic reign followed by a new age, possibly used for the first time in such an explicit form, is evidence in a Jewish apocalypse of the hope for a new age that is transcendent. It appears, however, alongside the conventional hope for a this-worldly reign of God (4 Ezra 7:28-29; cf. 4 Ezra 6:18ff.). In this it parallels Revelation, where the vision of the new heaven and new earth is preceded by the millennial messianic reign. This particular pattern represents a significant development of late first-century eschatology, when political despair may have contributed to the emergence of a transcendent eschatology alongside the hope for a messianic kingdom on earth.

For all their differences, a scheme of woes, messianic kingdom, resurrection, judgment, and new age is clearly discerned in both works. Revelation uses much more vivid imagery as compared with the prosaic prediction found in 4 Ezra (and the contemporary Syriac *Apocalypse of Baruch*). The role of the redeemer figure is much more obvious in Revelation. There is little sign in any of these works of the warrior role found in the *Psalms of Solomon* (and in 4 Ezra 13). Indeed, the Messiah's reign on earth in 4 Ezra 7:28-29 lasts only four hundred years, at the end of which he dies.

Eschatological concerns in 4 Ezra are to some extent eclipsed by another concern: the evil of humanity, the wrestling with the apparently merciless character of the divine purposes and human frailty in the face of God's inscrutable purposes. The issues raised are what we would have expected Jews to have struggled with after the traumatic experience of 70 CE. There was an inevitable reappraisal of attitudes with the need for more precise definitions of what was required of the people of God and an emphasis on the centrality of the law. The burning question in 4 Ezra is not so much, When will the end be? but, How can one make sense of the present and ensure participation in the kingdom of God? Apocalyptic insight is part of the way in which the impoverished character of existence and the injustices of the world are given a different perspective.

A HISTORY OF THE INTERPRETATION OF THE APOCALYPSE

The Early Christian Context: Apocalyptic Tradition in the New Testament. We cannot regard other New Testament texts as interpretations of Revelation, because most were contemporary with Revelation. Yet there are connections between them that should be noted.[59]

Eschatological passages in the Gospels (esp. Matthew 24–25; Mark 13; Luke 21:1) all have connections with passages from Revelation.[60] Luke's Gospel in particular, perhaps surprising given its reputation as the one least in touch with apocalyptic ideas, shows several points of contact. Thus whereas Mark's Gospel talks of the sea as the destination of the demons (Mark 5:13) in the struggle with Legion, Luke's version of the story uses the same Greek word as does Revelation (Luke 8:33; cf. Rev 19:20; 20:14).[61] Contacts between Luke's Gospel and Revelation deserve particular attention. Verbal connections between the two texts are quite striking (e.g., cf. Luke 16:19 with Rev 18:12 and 17:4; Luke 10:19 with Rev 9:3; Luke 4:5-7 with Rev 13:7-8; Luke 21:27 with Rev 14:14; and, most striking of all, Luke 12:8 with Rev 3:5). Several of these connections are apparent in Luke's version of the eschatological discourse (Luke 21). The features are distinctive and suggest that Luke has a broader horizon to the prophecy more in keeping with that found in Revelation. Thus in Luke 21:28 the reference to liberation suggests that more could have been said, but there has instead been concentration on the time of distress preceding it (Luke 21:23; cf. 1 Cor 7:26, 28). What Luke predicts are days of vengeance (picking up on Isa 61:2, but omitted from the quotation of these verses in Luke 4:19). The tribulation in Luke 21:25 reminds us of the chaos in Rev 6:8-9, as also does the reaction of humanity in Luke 21:26 (cf. Rev 6:15ff.) in the face of the time of wrath (cf. Luke 23:30). The allusive reference to the trampling of Jerusalem by Gentiles (Luke 21:24) recalls John's vision in Rev 11:1ff. Elsewhere in the story of Jesus, it is Luke who reports the absence of Satan from the life of Jesus (Luke 4:21; cf. Luke 22:3 with Rev 7:22 and 13:16; see also Rev 20:2ff., where Satan is bound and removed from the earth). It is the Gospel of Luke that portrays Jesus as offering an interpretation of the mission of the seventy and their triumph over the powers of darkness, which is linked with the vision of Satan's fall from heaven (cf. Luke 10:18 with Rev 12:7ff.). The critical moment of Jesus' death is marked by an eclipse (there is an explicit reference in Luke 23:45; cf. Rev 8:12; 16:10).[62]

Paul's doctrine of the parousia, the allusive eschatological description in Rom 8:18ff., with the tribulations of the messianic age, and, of course, the manifestation of God's wrath (Rom 1:17-18) and the gospel (Rom 3:21) all connect with the apocalyptic way Paul speaks of Christ's impact on him (Gal 1:16). Paul includes in the gospel message the revelation of God's justice and of God's wrath (Rom 1:16-17). It is a juxtaposition that is very much akin to the revelation of God's salvation and judgment (as is the case in Deuteronomy 28ff:1.) as interlocking manifestations of the divine purpose in Revelation.[63] As in Revelation, in Romans 1:1 the wrath mentioned is God's eschatological wrath against impiety and injustice, particularly evident in idolatry. In Rom 1:17ff. there is a repeated stress on revelation. The refusal to acknowledge God leads to a determined response from God. There is a threefold assertion that "God gave them up" (Rom 1:24, 26, 28 NRSV), a more direct assertion of divine judgment than the string of passives in Revelation suggesting the same thing (e.g., Rev 6:2, 4).

Humanity did not give God the glory (Rom 1:21). It is the proclamation of the eternal gospel in Rev 14:6 that humanity should fear God (cf. the quotation of Ps 35:2 in Rom 3:18) and give God the glory and worship God the Creator (cf. Rom 1:25). Idolatrous behavior leads to a perverted outlook on the world (Rom 1:21) and a failure to recognize the ways and acts of God (cf. Rev 9:20). Idolatry is the problem in Revelation, both generally in 9:20 and specifically in the context of worship of the Beast in 13:8, 12. "Uncleanness" (Rom 1:24; cf. Rom 6:19) is the mark of the dragon (Rev 16:9) and of Babylon (Rev 17:4; 18:2). The sexual immorality of Rom 1:25 parallels the warning to be ready and not to be found naked and "exposed to shame" in Rev 16:15. The concern with the natural and the unnatural in sexual activity in Rom 1:26 corresponds to that frame of mind seen so often in Revelation, where the clarity of boundaries is sharply defined and transgression of those boundaries that result in one's becoming "lukewarm" (Rev 3:14-16) is resisted. This state of mind is one of deceit, the heart of the activity of Satan and the beast (e.g., Rev 12:9; 13:14); in Revelation, it is focused on idolatrous practices (Rev 2:20).

The "lie" (Rom 1:25; cf. Rev 2:2; 21:8; 22:15) and false service (Rom 1:25) need to be replaced with the true service of those who are priests in the new world (Rev 7:15; cf. Rom 12:1). That threefold "giving up" by God covers three areas:

the desires of the heart, shameful passions (Rom 1:26), and the undiscerning mind, which does that which is unbecoming; then follows a list of vices that result in disrupted and inharmonious living. We may compare Paul's focus on sexual misdemeanors in Romans 1 with the characterization of the offense of "fornication" throughout Revelation (e.g., Rev 2:20).

This also includes behavior that contributes to society's malfunctioning, all of which is a consequence of idolatry. In Romans, it is God who consigns the impious to particularly distorted patterns of behavior, just as in Revelation the source of the crisis for a disordered cosmos is in the divine book with seven seals, preserved in God's presence. The cataclysmic effects may not be immediately apparent in the list of consequences in Romans 1. What we are offered in Romans is a prose description of a world marked by deceit and human selfishness. Stripped of the apocalyptic symbolism, its message is much the same as that of Revelation 6 and 8–9, however. In Rev 6:4, the second horseman removes peace from the earth, so that people slay one another; here is the consequence of the strife, envy, and covetousness that Paul had spoken of in Rom 1:28.

While Paul's extant writings include no apocalypse, the opening chapters of 1 Corinthians reflect an apocalyptic perspective, access to which comes through revelation through the Spirit. The divine mystery precedes and is then backed up by Scripture (e.g., Rom 11:25-26). Paul describes himself and his companions as apocalyptic seers who are entrusted the privilege of administering the divine secrets (1 Cor 4:1). In 1 Cor 2:6-7, Paul talks of the content of the gospel itself as a mystery hidden from the rulers of the present age. The success of the saving act of God results from the inability of those who are dominated by the present age and its gods to see the significance of what they were doing in crucifying the Lord of glory (1 Cor 2:9). The cross, the sign of failure in human estimation, turns out to be the very heart of the divine mystery for the salvation of the world. It points to an apocalyptic mystery hidden before all ages and revealed only in the last days (cf. Luke 10:23-24; 1 Pet 1:11-12). The divine wisdom to which the true apostle has access is a mystery taught by the Spirit, and it can be understood only by those who have the Spirit (1 Cor 2:10). The divine wisdom is something revealed rather than something immediately clear and compelling to those whose minds are darkened and cannot understand its significance. It remains hidden until the veil is removed (2 Cor 3:14-15). The cross is a sign that transcends the plethora of apocalyptic imagery. Like every sign, it is ambiguous. To some it remains foolishness (1 Cor 1:18). Like the Lamb, which forms the centerpiece of the apocalypse, the cross stands at the fulcrum of history and is the determinant of a true understanding of reality. In continuity with the Jewish apocalyptic tradition, Paul thinks of another dimension of human existence, normally hidden from sight but revealed to those with eyes to see. His apocalypse of Jesus Christ is the basis for his practice, not the least that of admitting Gentiles into the messianic age without the law of Moses. His relegation of the Sinai covenant to a subordinate position to the new covenant in the Messiah contrasts with the firm subordination of the disclosures of the apocalyptic spirit to the Sinai theophany in the rabbinic traditions.

The contrasts in Hebrews between the sacrifice of Christ and the sacrifices of the levitical system have been taken as indications of Greek platonic influence. But the likelihood is that the apocalyptic tradition, with its contrasts between the heavenly world above and the earthly world below, may explain the distinctive soteriology of Hebrews.[64] The author seeks to understand the work of Christ as the important moment in the piercing of that barrier between heaven and earth that is so familiar to us from the apocalyptic literature. The climax of history has now occurred in Jesus, and he is the first to enter the heavenly sanctuary, which is at the same time the sign of the new age. Jesus, the pioneer, has gone into the innermost part of heaven and has sat down with God. He is behind the veil. Calvary becomes the moment when the unmediated access to God becomes a possibility. Paradoxically, the death outside the camp (Heb 13:12) becomes the place where heaven and earth coincide in that the sacrifice of Jesus opens up the way into the heavenly shrine. The cross has become a meeting point between heaven and earth. The place of reproach and rejection turns out to be the very gate of heaven.

In Hebrews (and in the Letter to the Ephesians also), apocalyptic categories are taken up and utilized in the expression of convictions about

Christ's exaltation and its consequences. The cosmology of apocalyptic and the notion of revelation found in the apocalypses and the mystical literature was a convenient starting place for reflection on the understanding of revelation, which Christian writers believed had been inaugurated by the exaltation of Christ. The glory of the world above, which was to be manifested in the future, had now become a present possession for those who acknowledged that the Messiah had come and had already made available the heavenly gifts of the messianic age.

EXCURSUS: THE PAROUSIA IN THE NEW TESTAMENT[65]

There is ample evidence of the belief in the Second Coming of Christ, most apparent in Rev 1:7; 19:11ff.; and 22:20 (the word παρουσία [*parousia*] is not used in Revelation, though it is a technical term elsewhere in the NT; e.g., Matt 24:3; 1 Cor 15:23; 1 Thess 5:23; 2 Thess 2:1; 2 Pet 1:16; 1 John 2:28; cf. Jas 5:7). In eschatological Jewish texts contemporary to Revelation, reference may be made occasionally to a messianic agent,[66] though even these texts are less concerned with the identity of the Messiah than with the conviction of some future reign of God on earth.

In Rev 19:11-21, there are explicit links with the vision of the Son of Man in Rev 1:14, which inaugurates John's vision. Revelation 19:11-21 forms part of a much longer symbolic account of the culmination of the manifestation of the divine wrath within human history, stemming from the exaltation of the Lamb and its claiming the right to open the sealed scroll.

After the diversion in Rev 17:1–19:10, which considers the character of Babylon and speaks of its destruction and the reaction in heaven to it, John's vision resumes with the heaven opened and the appearance of a rider on a white horse, which leads to a holy war. Like the descendant of David, described in Isaiah 11:1, it is with the sword proceeding from his mouth that this rider will rule the nations. He comes as "King of kings and Lord of lords" (Rev 19:16 NRSV); his victory, therefore, in the struggle that is to take place has already been assured (exactly what we would expect in the light of Rev 11:17). There gather together the beast, the false prophet, and the kings of the earth to make war against the rider on the white horse (19:19). The beast and the false prophet are thrown into the lake of fire, and their allies are slain with the sword that proceeds from the mouth of the rider on the white horse.

This triumph immediately precedes the establishment of the messianic kingdom on earth (Rev 20:4). But this is not the end of the struggle against the forces opposed to the divine righteousness, because the messianic reign is temporary and depends on the binding of Satan in the abyss (Rev 20:2). Satan's release, however, leads to another terrible conflict. But whereas the rider on the white horse had conquered the beast and the kings of the earth, in the next battle, Satan, released from prison, gathers the armies of Gog and Magog to wage war against the camp of the saints and against the holy city—only to be destroyed by fire from heaven. The devil will join the beast and the false prophet in the lake of fire for eternal torment. This is then followed by the last assize, which paves the way for the new heaven and new earth and the establishment of God's dwelling with humankind.

The closest parallel in the New Testament to Rev 19:11–21 is the short eschatological account in 1 Corinthians 15:1. In a discussion focusing on the belief in the resurrection and the character of the resurrection body, Paul alludes to the future consummation in two passages. In the first passage (1 Cor 15:20-34), Paul outlines the order in which the resurrection from the dead will take place: Christ, "the first fruits" (which has already taken place), then those who belong to Christ at his coming (cf. 1 Thess 4:16). Then comes the end, when Christ hands over the kingship to God, "after he has destroyed every ruler and every authority and power" (1 Cor 15:24 NRSV). Paul then interpolates the comment that Christ must exercise the sovereignty until he has put all his enemies under his feet (an allusion to Ps 110:1); the last enemy to be destroyed is death itself. It is only when all things are subjected to the Messiah that the Son will himself be subject to the Father and God will be all in all (1 Cor 15:28).

Later in the chapter, in a discussion of the character of the resurrection body (1 Cor 15:35-58), Paul stresses that flesh and blood cannot inherit the kingdom of God and tells his readers of the mystery of the resurrection of the elect: Not all will die, but all will be "changed, in a moment, in the twinkling of an eye, at the last trumpet" (1 Cor 15:52 NRSV; cf. Matt 24:31; 1 Thess 4:17). When the heavenly trumpet sounds, the righteous dead will be raised, incorruptible. It is when what was corruptible has put on immortality in the form of the resurrection body that death will be swallowed up in victory. It is not clear whether this passage contradicts the earlier hint of a period of a messianic kingdom on earth at some point during the lordship of the Messiah, during which he puts under subjection the enemies of God. But it is possible to read 1 Cor 15:25-28 as indicating that Paul's eschatology follows the general outline of that found in Revelation 19:1–21 and presupposes a messianic reign on earth.

Also related to Revelation 19 is the account of the parousia in 2 Thessalonians 2. This eschatological passage is to be found in a context dealing with a particular pastoral problem. As such, like 1 Corinthians 15, it offers only a fragment of an eschatological scheme, sufficient to deal with the particular issue confronting the writer: the threat of disturbance to the community because of an outburst of eschatological enthusiasm, prompted by the belief that the day of the Lord had already arrived (1 Thess 2:2). In order to counteract such enthusiasm, Paul reminds his readers that a rebellion must first take place, and the "lawless one," who opposes God and sits in the Temple of God, "declaring himself to be God" (1 Thess 2:4 NRSV), must be revealed. This sign of the coming of Christ has not yet occurred, because it is being restrained until the proper time (1 Thess 2:6). It is unclear as to what the restraint Paul asks his readers to remember might be. Is it Paul himself? Is it the evangelization of the Gentiles? Is it the Roman Empire? Is it some divine/angelic restraint, such as that found in Rev 7:1? Meanwhile the mystery of lawlessness is already at work. In other words, the present is, in some sense, an eschatological time. The coming of the lawless one will be accompanied by signs and wonders that will deceive those who are on the way to destruction, just as the activity of the beast and the false prophet deceive the nations of the earth in Rev 13:7, 12-18. Finally, the Lord Jesus will slay the man of lawlessness with the breath of his mouth (2 Thess 2:8). So there is some similarity between this passage and Revelation, where the exaltation of the Lamb provokes the initiation of the whole eschatological drama, which moves forward according to its own apocalyptic logic. Until the restraint is removed, there can be no manifestation of the Antichrist figure (cf. the reason for delay given in Mark 13:10).

As it does for Rev 19:15, Isa 11:4 has contributed to this passage from 2 Thessalonians, particularly in the description of the destruction of the lawless one. A similar description turns up in *Ps. Sol.* 17:24 as well: "With a rod of iron he shall break in pieces all their substance; he shall destroy the godless nations with the word of his mouth. At his rebuke shall the nations flee before him." Likewise, in the vision of the man from the sea in 4 Ezra 13, we find a similar description of the destruction of his enemies (4 Ezra 13:8ff.). In the interpretation of the vision, we are told that, after a period of unrest when nation will rise up against nation (4 Ezra 13:30ff.), the one whom the Most High has been keeping for many generations will appear to reprove the assembled nations for their ungodliness (4 Ezra 13:37-38) and destroy them by the law. After this, the tribes of Israel will gather at Mount Zion, where they will live in peace. In all of these passages from 4 Ezra it is made quite clear that those forces opposed to God will be destroyed. Thus the appearance of the Messiah will be more than just a prelude to a better order, made quite explicit in passages like 4 Ezra 13 and Revelation 19, for he will act as the agent of destruction of the evil that stands opposed to the righteousness of God.

When viewed in the light of Rev 19:11-21, the eschatological discourses in the synoptic Gospels (Matthew 24–25; Mark 13:1; Luke 21) show some remarkable omissions. There are the messianic woes that are so characteristic of eschatological writings of this period of Judaism. While there may well be some kind of connection between the sort of focus on evil that is cryptically outlined in Mark 13:14 and the hubris of the man of lawlessness mentioned in 2 Thessalonians 2, nothing is said about the effects on the forces of evil of the coming of the Son of Man. Indeed, the description of the coming of the Son of Man in all three synoptic Gospels is linked primarily with the vindication of the elect, thus focusing on the final aspect of the messianic drama in the vision of the man from the sea in 4 Ezra 13:12. The certainty of vindication is there, but the lot of the elect when they have been gathered from the four corners of the earth is not touched on at all in Mark.

The element of judgment at the parousia of the Son of Man is not entirely absent from the synoptic discourses. The climax of the Matthean version is the account of the final assize, with the Son of Man sitting on God's throne, separating the sheep from the goats (Matt 25:31-46). Here, too, the focus of attention is on the present response of the elect. It is those who recognize the heavenly Son of Man in the brethren who are hungry, thirsty, strangers, naked, weak, and imprisoned in the present age who will inherit the kingdom prepared by God from the foundation of the world. There is a possible link here with the much disputed *1 Enoch* 3–71, where the Son of Man sits on the throne of the lord of the spirits and exercises judgment (*1 Enoch* 69:2).

The primary concern of the Markan discourse on the parousia is not satisfaction of curiosity about the details of the times and seasons so much as dire warnings of the threat of being led astray, of failing at the last, and of the need to be ready and watchful to avoid the worst of the coming disasters. In the bleak moments of the last days there is little attempt to dwell on the delights awaiting disciples in the messianic kingdom (though an eschatological promise is made a little later in Luke's Gospel in the context of the supper discourse; Luke 22:29-30). The reader's thoughts are made to dwell on responsibilities in the short and medium term as the essential prerequisite of achieving eschatological bliss. These sentiments are very much at the fore in 4 Ezra, where the emphasis is on the need to follow the precepts of the Most High in order to achieve eternal life.

In comparison with the more extended accounts of the coming of the new age to be found in other material, both Christian and Jewish, the synoptic discourses concentrate on the period of strife and tribulation leading up to the coming of the Son of Man, itself an expectation only hinted at in the *Similitudes of Enoch.* In the Gospels what happens after the coming of the Son of Man is not mentioned, though in the Lukan version there is the expectation that the arrival of the Son of Man will be the beginning of the process of liberation, for which the tribulations and destruction had been the prelude (Luke 21:26ff.). The implication is that the kingdom does not arrive with the coming of the Son of Man; that is only part of the eschatological drama, whose climax is still to come—exactly what we find in Revelation. The arrival of the rider on the white horse in Revelation is the prelude to the struggle that must precede the establishment of the messianic kingdom, an event still to come, when there will be a reversal of Jerusalem's fortunes (Luke 21:24).

In the Pauline letters, the word παρουσια (*parousia*) is used in the context of Christ's coming (e.g., 1 Thess 3:13; 2 Thess 2:8; cf. his revealing at 1 Cor 1:7), and also that of the apostle (2 Cor 10:10; Phil 1:26; 2:12) or his agent (1 Cor 16:17; 2 Cor 7:6-7). The present experience of the Christ who is to come can be discerned also in aspects of Paul's understanding of apostleship.[67] There is a close relationship between the parousia of Christ and the apostolic parousia, so that through the presence of the apostle, whether in person, through a co-worker, or through letter, the presence of Christ was confronting his congregations (Rom 15:14ff.; 1 Cor 4:14ff.; 1 Cor 5:3ff.; Phil 2:12). Paul's presence brings eschatological power, despite his human weakness and humility (2 Cor 10:10; cf. 1 Cor 4:9-10). According to 1 Corinthians 4–5, Paul is a father in Christ Jesus to the Corinthians (4:15); Paul's person is to be imitated (4:16) as he is the embodiment of Christ (11:1). Paul's coming will be with power (1 Cor 4:19). His emissary Timothy will remind the church of the way of Christ (1 Cor 4:17), and even Paul's absence will not diminish the force of the apostolic will (1 Cor 5:3). When he comes, it is either with discipline (1 Cor 4:21; cf. 1 Cor 2:27; 3:19) or with gentleness (cf. the gentler tone of the letter to the Philadelphian angel in Rev 3:7-13). And he promises the Roman church that when he finally reaches Rome his coming will bring blessing to them (Rom 15:29). Like the risen Christ, who stands in the midst of his churches as judge and sustainer (Rev 1:13), the apostle of Christ comes as a threat and a promise—a threat to those who have lost their first love or exclude the Messiah and his apostle; a promise of blessing for those who conquer.

The Fourth Gospel's account of the coming of Jesus has been seen as a development of the early parousia hope that moves away from the public cosmic scenes we find in the other Gospels. Jesus will come to his disciples (John 14:21, 23). The dwellings that Jesus goes to prepare for the disciples can be enjoyed by the one who loves Jesus and is devoted to his words (John 14:2; cf. John 14:23). Likewise, the manifestation of the divine glory is reserved not for the world, but for the disciple (John 14:19). Whereas all flesh will see the salvation of our God in Isa 52:7-10 and those who pierced the victorious Son of Man will look upon him in glory (Rev 1:9; cf. Mark 14:62), the world cannot see the returning Jesus. Indeed, the goal of the new age in Revelation, where those who bear the name of God on their foreheads (Rev 22:3-4) and will see God face to face, is part of the bliss reserved for the disciples in heaven to be with God and to see God's glory (Rev 17:24). Just as Jesus comes again to the disciples, so too does the Paraclete (NRSV, "Advocate"). The world cannot receive Christ, and it is the Paraclete that enables the disciples to maintain their connection with the basic revelation of God, the Logos who makes the Father known (Rev 14:17ff.; 15:26). The Paraclete thus points back to Jesus, the Word made flesh, and is in some sense a successor to Jesus, a compensation by his presence for the absence of Jesus, who has returned to the Father.

An issue that always arises when the parousia is discussed is the problem caused for Christians by the non-fulfillment of the expectation of Christ's return. Explicit evidence that the delay of the parousia was a problem within early Christianity is not as vast as is often suggested; 2 Peter 3 is, in fact, a rather exceptional piece of evidence. Other passages that are often mentioned, for instance, in Matthew (the parables at the end of Matthew 24) and Acts 1:7 need to be seen as indirect rather than direct evidence of the supposed problem.

Within the eschatological tradition there was an attempt to come to terms with the delay of the coming of God's reign.[68] The apocalypses are an important resource for dealing with the non-appearance of God's reign on earth, since they reflect interest in the world above, where God's reign is acknowledged by the heavenly host and where the apocalyptic seer can have access to the repository of those purposes of God for the future world. Thus the visionary can either glimpse in the heavenly books about the mysteries of eschatology or be offered a "preview" of what will happen in the future of human history. The privilege of having the heavenly mysteries revealed could be extended to a wider group. The *Hodayoth* from the Dead Sea Scrolls (1QH) and the *Odes of Solomon* offer the elect group a present participation in the lot of heaven and a foretaste of the coming glory.

The Patristic Period.[69] There is a close link between the closing invocation in Rev 22:20 and the "maranatha" of *Didache* 10:6 (cf. 1 Cor 16:22):

> Let grace come, and let this world pass away. Hosanna to the Son of David. Whoever is holy, let them come; whoever is not, let them repent. maranatha. Amen.

The priority given to the prophetic in *Didache* 11–13 echoes what we find in Revelation (e.g., Rev 1:3; 2:20; 10:11; 11:2, 10; 16:6; 18:20, 24; 19:10; 22:2, 6-7, 9-10, 18-19), suggesting that distinguishing true from false prophecy is an issue in both writings.

In the struggle with gnosticism, insistence on the materiality of the doctrine of the resurrection and on this-worldly eschatology played their part in the writings of both Justin[70] and Irenaeus,[71] though Justin recognized that not all share his hope for a messianic reign on earth. Elsewhere in the earlier books of *Against Heresies*, however, Irenaeus regards Revelation as primarily about the first coming of Christ and the witness of the church. Thus the enmity between humanity and the devil is related to the advent of Christ viewed through the lens of Rev 20:2.[72] What is also evident in *Against Heresies* V is an integration of eschatology and creation. What began with creation, Adam, and the fall ends with the new creation, the new Adam, and the final temptation and overthrow of Satan. Irenaeus periodizes history into seven ages.[73] The parousia inaugurates the seventh millennium, when the sabbath rest comes (cf. Gen 2:2). The events of Genesis 1–3 are seen as archetypes of the last days. When Irenaues comes to discuss the Beast and its number in Rev 13:18,[74] he thinks that *Lateinos* or *Teitan* or *Evanthus* may be intended and so affirms an anti-imperial reference.

Hippolytus, in his treatise on Antichrist, reads Revelation 12 as being of the church and the struggle to bring the gospel to a hostile world.[75] Revelation is seen as the completion of the journey of God's people, of which the exodus is a type, and there is a link between the Christ of Rev 1:13ff. and the prophets of old.[76] Rome and the kingdom of Antichrist merge;[77] and there is a Jewish dimension to the Antichrist figure, because he will come from the tribe of Daniel (see Daniel 14–15) and will rebuild the Temple. The two witnesses of Revelation 11 are identified with Enoch and Elijah. Hippolytus uses the cosmic week to show that only five and a half of the six periods have elapsed before the millennium (note the emphasis on the penultimate here, though he does not dwell on the delights of that age as Irenaeus had done.

Origen's reading of Revelation (he wrote no commentary on it) is decidedly anti-chiliastic—that is, he rejects the belief in a messianic reign on earth. His interpretation is christological. He sees Rev 19:13, for example, as an image of the victorious Logos (Word) marked by the signs of crucifixion. The prophecies of chaps. 12–22 are linked with the life of Christ and the church, and the millennium is seen as past.[78] The defeat and binding of Satan (Rev 20:3) has already occurred.[79] The heavenly Jerusalem is a spiritual reality, made possible by the resurrection; the new heaven and new earth began with Christ's resurrection.[80]

The earliest extant commentary on Revelation, used by Jerome, is by Victorinus of Pettau (c. beginning of the 4th cent.). His work is thoroughly contextual and relates the text to the circumstances of his day. The seven churches represent the universal church and are not intended for John's area alone. Although Victorinus was a chiliast, his method included a typological reading, which presented Revelation as a series of events recurring in sacred history. So the trumpet blasts of Revelation 8ff. relate not only to the period after the coming of Christ but also to both the Babylonian exile and the period of Antichrist, whose malevolence can be seen in the actions of Roman emperors as well as in the figure of the last days. His interpretive approach blends the christocentric and ecclesiological with the eschatological. He uses an exegesis that blends present relevance and eschatological prediction. Thus the two witnesses (Rev 11:3) represent the deaths of prophets, both those of the past and the ones to come under Antichrist,[81] and the sixth king is Nero, past and future persecutors of the saints.

The book of seven seals is the Old Testament, a legal document sealed until the death of its testator, Jesus Christ. The unsealing of the seals reveals that the Old Testament has been fulfilled in the person of Christ. In the Son of Man vision in Rev 1:13ff., the two-edged sword indicates that Christ uttered both the law and the gospel. Victorinus explains the images of Revelation 4–5 as symbols of the old and the new economies.[82] Just as Revelation 4 is seen as a résumé, of salvation history, so also the seals fulfill the old and reveal the totality of the new. The repetition of the sequence of seven is the means whereby the Spirit provides the opportunity for fuller appreciation of the mystery of God. In Revelation 6 the white horse and its rider are the Holy Spirit and the gospel message: "after the Lord ascended to heaven...he sent the Holy Spirit, whose words the preachers sent forth as arrows reaching to the human heart...and the crown on the head is the promised Holy Spirit."[83] Whereas the white horse signifies the Christian revelation from Christ to eschaton, the other horses are primarily eschatological. In Revelation 11, Elijah is both the witness and the precursor of Antichrist. He is the angel of Rev 7:2[84] and the eagle of Rev 8:13. The woman in chap. 12 is both an Old and a New Covenant figure. The devil's attempt to devour the child is a reference to the temptation and passion of Christ. The flood of water from the dragon's mouth is the persecution of the church. The war in heaven in Rev 12:7 is the beginning of the eschaton, which then becomes the focus for the rest of the commentary. Antichrist is Nero redevivus.[85] Victorinus follows earlier commentators in seeing in the number 666 the Greek word *Teitan* or the Latin *Diclux*. The seven heads of the dragon refer to the seven emperors who reigned near the beginning of the Christian era, from Galba to Nerva.[86] Antichrist is associated with civil and religious corruption. Rome is Babylon, but the false prophet is associated with Judaism. He will cause an image of Antichrist to be set up in the Jerusalem Temple.[87] Antichrist sums up all evil in himself so that the condemnations of Babylon refer to one final embodiment of evil already partially glimpsed in earlier history. Victorinus stresses the concrete character of the new Jerusalem and the life enjoyed by the saints,[88] in a way similar to earlier evocations of the earthly eschatological delights in Papias and Irenaeus. Victorinus picks up on the element of inclusivism in the final vision and suggests that the gates are always left open because saving grace is always available.

Tyconius's (c. 400) reading of the book of Revelation, now no longer extant,[89] has been reconstructed from various sources. Its importance is great, because it had a profound influence on the mature Augustine and thence on later Christendom.[90] In his exegesis of Revelation, he uses the book to interpret contemporary reality. His work epitomizes those trends in exegesis that did not consign its message solely to the eschatological future. Tyconius encapsulates trends that had been in force at least since the time of Origen and of which there had been hints earlier in parts of Irenaeus' writings. The text becomes a tool to facilitate the discernment of the moral and spiritual rather than to search out the eschatological in the text. So the millennium becomes a medium for understanding the present rather than merely the eschatological future.

The mature Augustine continued in that tradition. He had originally believed that there would be a sabbath rest for the people of God that would last a thousand years, but, influenced by Tyconius, he accepted an approach to Scripture that enables Revelation to be a source of insight both eschatologically and for the contemporary church. Thus in his discussion of the millennium in *The City of God*[91] he argues that with the first coming of Christ and the establishment of the church the devil has been bound "in the innumerable multitude of the impious, in whose hearts there is a great depth of malignity against the church of God."[92] Eschatological elements, like Antichrist, Gog, and Magog, are stripped of their eschatological significance and relate to the experience of the church in this age.

Augustine's approach to empire is in certain key respects at one with the dualistic and suspicious attitude evident in earlier Christian apocalyptic interpretation. This contrasts with a different tone in the writing of Eusebius of Caesarea, a militant opponent of millenarian hope and an apologist for a Christian empire. For him the fulfillment of eschatological promise had come with the conversion of Constantine, which had enabled the divine peace to envelop the world.[93]

The Joachite School.[94] The Augustinian exegesis held sway for much of the next five hundred years. The later Middle Ages saw the emergence of the next influential reading by Joachim of Fiore (c. 1132–1202), which was to use Revelation as a way of understanding salvation history and thereby embolden people to see themselves as being part of the imminent apocalypse. In a highly complex interpretative method formulated by allowing one part of Scripture to offer the model for interpreting the whole (what he calls concordia), Joachim related closely the Old and the New Testaments. He divided the book of Revelation into eight parts: (1) 1–3:22, letters to seven churches; (2) 4–8:1, the opening of the seals; (3) 8–11:18, the trumpet blasts; (4) 11:19–14:20, the two beasts; (5) 15–16:7, the seven bowls; (6) 18:16–19:21, destruction of Babylon; (7) 20-10, the millennium; and (8) 20:11–22:21, the new Jerusalem. The parts of the book correspond to the seven periods of the church, which are then followed by eternity. Each of the series of seven is then related to the seven ages (tempora) of the church. The seven seals relate to the seven ages of both Israel and the church. In the sequence of seven, the sixth assumes great importance as the penultimate period, anticipating the consummation of history. Thus the sixth letter is a prophecy of the sixth period, which is imminent in Joachim's day. In Israel's history and in the beginnings of the church, the Babylonian exile and the birth of Jesus, respectively, herald the renewal of the church in the sixth period of history. The preoccupation with the penultimate period, the sixth, is typical of exegesis in the Joachite tradition; it is the period of Antichrist and leads to the fulfillment of Joachim's final age of the Spirit.

So Joachim finds a parallel between the experience of Israel and that of the church, but he broke decisively from the Augustinian tradition in being willing to find significance in history. Joachim used a trinitarian reading of history in which a coming third age, that of the Spirit, would be characterized by an outburst of spiritual activity in the form of monastic renewal. That time, for him, was imminent. The opening of the sixth seal would be a time of persecution and exile, parallel to that of the Jews in Babylon, that would purify the church. The coming of the seventh era, the opening of the seventh seal, would herald the era of the Holy Spirit, and the seeds of that new age, sowed long before, would come to fruition. Revelation, therefore, offered the key to the reading of the Bible as a whole and to the interpretation of history.

Most daring of the commentators in this tradition is Peter Olivi (1248–98), who used Joachim extensively in his *Postilla in apocalypsim.*[95] Olivi's commentary on the book of Revelation was investigated and condemned in 1326. For him, the sixth period is the beginning of the time of renewal. Olivi places himself in the sixth period and identifies Francis of Assisi, whom he identifies with the angel of the sixth seal in Rev 7:2, as the inaugurator of that period.

What is remarkable about Olivi's exegesis are his predictions of the corruption of the church and the conflict over the issue of poverty in the Franciscan order, which dominated the early history of the order, which are to be seen as an eschatological tribulation. Olivi predicts that the pope and Franciscan leaders would reject the "true" Franciscan view of poverty. Like Joachim, he divided salvation history into three periods, corresponding to Father, Son, and Spirit. In the seven ages of the church, the sixth age is that of evangelical men, from Francis to the death of Antichrist; the final age will last from Antichrist until the end of the world. Olivi matched the seven heads of the dragon with seven persecutions of the church and the seven periods of the church to the seven ages of world history: Adam to Noah, Noah to Abraham, Abraham to Moses, Moses to David, David to Christ, Christ to Antichrist, Antichrist to the end of the world. He spoke of three advents of Christ: first in the flesh, then in the spirit of evangelical reform, and third in judgment. Just as Christ came in the sixth age to replace Judaism, so also in the sixth age of the church, it will be renewed, something initiated by the appearance of Francis of Assisi.

What is new in Olivi's interpretation is that he saw the forces of evil as being concentrated in a worldly church, a present, or at least imminent, reality, that is identified with the whore of Babylon. A mystic antichrist appears, possibly a false pope, though this is unclear from his writing. On the basis of the second half of Revelation 13, Olivi sees this mystic antichrist as one who excludes those who contradict ecclesiastical authority. During the time of Antichrist, the doctors of the church will take the side of Antichrist, and they will attack the life and spirit of Christ in the lives of those engaged in the renewal of the church. Like Augustine, Olivi declared that the millennium began with the church's reign, starting in the time of Constantine and lasting until the last judgment, which would take place at some point in the fourteenth century. In the light of views like this, it comes as no surprise that the later Middle Ages were a period of such intense upheaval fired by apocalyptic revivals.[96]

The Reformation.[97] Bullinger was the only magisterial Reformer to write a commentary on Revelation arising from lections and sermons, and the importance of that commentary to sixteenth-century theological study should not be underestimated. In the first edition of the German Bible, however, which was richly illustrated (in the 1522 edition Babylon is depicted wearing a papal crown), Luther outlined his reasons for relegating the book to a subordinate place within the canon of the New Testament, in words that echo much earlier (and later) assessments in the Christian tradition:

> About this book of the Revelation of John, I leave everyone free to hold his own ideas, and would bind no man to my opinion and judgment: I say what I feel. I miss more than one thing in this book, and this makes me hold it to be neither apostolic or prophetic. First and foremost, the Apostles do not deal with visions, but prophecy in clear, plain words, as do Peter and Paul and Christ in the gospel. For it befits the apostolic office to speak of Christ and his deeds without figures and visions but there is no prophet in the Old Testament, to say nothing of the New, who deals so out and out with visions and figures. And so I think of it almost as I do of the Fourth Book of Esdras, and I can in nothing detect that it was provided by the Holy Spirit.
>
> Moreover, he seems to be going much too far when he commends his own book so highly—more than any other of the sacred books do, though they are much more important, and threaten that if any one takes away anything from it, God will deal likewise with him. Again, they are to be blessed who keep what is written therein; and yet no one knows what that is, to say nothing of keeping it. It is just the same as if we had it not, and there are many far better books for us to keep. Many of the fathers rejected, too, this book of old, though St. Jerome, to be sure, praises it highly and says that it is above all praise and that there are as many mysteries in it as words; though he cannot prove this at all, and his praise is at many points, too mild.
>
> Finally, let every one think of it as his own spirit gives him to think. My spirit cannot fit itself into this book. There is one sufficient reason for me

> not to think highly of it—Christ is not taught or known in it; but to teach Christ is the thing which an apostle above all else is bound to do, as He says in Acts 1 "Ye shall be my witnesses." Therefore I stick to the books which give me Christ clearly and purely.[98]

Revelation's theological shortcomings and the dangers it posed for the faithful meant that it was to be considered as little better than an apocryphal book. Luther subtly modified his view of Revelation in the later editions of his New Testament from 1530 onward, offering the advice: "The first and surest step toward finding its interpretation is to take from history the events and disasters that have come upon Christendom until now, and hold them up alongside these images and so compare them very carefully. If then the two perfectly coincided and squared with one another, we could build on that as a sure, or at least unobjectionable interpretation."[99] "In this book," wrote Luther in his Preface to Revelation of 1545, "we see that, through and above all plagues and beasts and bad angels, Christ is with his saints, and wins the victory at last."

Luther came to the view that the pope was Antichrist, a view held also by Calvin, who believed that "all the marks by which the Spirit of God has pointed out antichrist appear clearly in the Pope,"[100] a view worked out in detail by many Protestant commentators. This notion was repudiated by Roman Catholic expositors like Bellarmine, who argued that the advent of Enoch and Elijah (Revelation 11), the emergence of Antichrist from the tribe of Dan, and the universal proclamation of the gospel had to precede Antichrist, and so the Roman Catholic pontiff could not be that figure. [101]

A fascinating witness to the interpretation of Revelation in the early Calvinist tradition is provided by the Geneva Bible, which offers a historicizing interpretation typical of the day.[102] It enables us to see how Revelation was used as part of the ecclesiastical struggle of the time. Its Protestant leanings are everywhere apparent. On Rev 15:2, the promise is that the afflictions of the world are all overcome by the saints of God. According to 14:1, Christ is ever-present with his church: "there can be no vicare; for where there is a vicare, there is no church." The mark on the forehead of the elect is "the mark of their election, their faith." The throne of Satan (2:13) is "all townes and countries whence God's words and good living is banished...and also the places where the word is not preched syncerly, nor manners right reformed." As may be expected, there is an identification of Rome with the antichrist (the papacy is the inheritor of the power of the Roman Empire, in the interpretation of the two beasts of Revelation 13). The beast from the sea has two horns, "which signifies the priesthode and the kingdoms, and therefore he giveth in his armes two keys, and hath two swordes caryed before him." The Roman Catholic character of Antichrist is supported by the interpretation of 666 as *lateinus* (an early patristic exegesis as well). The locusts of Rev 9:3 are "worldlie suttil Prelates, with Monkes, freres, cardinals, Patriarkes, Archbishops, Doctors, Bachelors and masters which forsake Christ to maintain false doctrine." There is explicit rejection of the Anabaptists (the Nicolaitans of Rev 2:6 are said to be "the heretics which helde that wives shulde be commune") and of their doctrine of the State in the comment on Rev 21:24: "here we see as in infinite other places that Kings and Princes (contrarie to what wicked opinion of the Anabaptists) are partakers of the heavenlie glorie, if they rule in the feare of the Lord."

The opening of the first seal in Rev 6:1 is the declaration of God's will, and the white horse signifies "innocence, victorie and felicitie which shilde come by the preaching of the gospel" (an echo of the exegesis of Victorinus). The plagues that come through the sequence of seals, trumpets, and bowls refer to the corruption of the church from within and the persecutions from without. The only remedy is to appear before God "by the meanes of Jesus Christ" (on 8:2). True ministry should resemble that of the two witnesses, who are types of "all the preachers that shulde buylde up God's church" (11:3).[103] The ministers "ought to receive the worde into their hearts and to have grace and deep judgment and diligently to studie it with zeale to utter it" (on 10:9). So zeal is required, for "nothing more displeaseth God than indifference and coldness in religion" (on 3:19).

The marginal note urges readers to recognize the contemporary relevance of the book: "this is not then as the other Prophecies which were commanded to be hid till the time appointed...because that these things shulde be quickly accomplished and did now begin" (on 22:10). Urgency and watchfulness are essential: "Seeing the Lord is at hand, we ought to be constant and rejoyce, but we must beware we esteme not the length or shortness of the Lord's coming by our own imagination." What is needed is to "read diligently: judge soberly, and call earnestly to God for the true understanding thereof" (the conclusion of The Argument, The Revelation of John the Divine). The interpretation of Revelation's imagery includes recognition of the historical background of the original work, evident also in the approach to passages like Dan 9:24ff. These passages have often been a subject of eschatological speculation, but in the Geneva Bible they are interpreted entirely in terms of Jewish history before Christ. So while Christopher Hill writes that "the main offence of the Geneva Bible lay in its notes,"[104] it cannot be said that they fomented eschatological enthusiasm, for "the time shall be long of Christ's second coming, and yet the children of God ought not to be discouraged" (on Dan 12:11). Rather, they are a testimony to a use of Revelation as a crucial tool for "the true kings and priests in Christ" whereby may be disclosed "the wicked deceit" in their midst (on 16:12) and acting in a way appropriate to their election and continued perseverance. Given that this historicizing and hortatory reading of Revelation rejects both Anabaptist and chiliastic enthusiasm, it is strange that Revelation should have a less favored position in the lectionary of the *Book of Common Prayer* than do apocryphal books (read in October and November).[105]

Joachite influence continued in differing forms. On the one hand, in his widely influential book *The Image of Both Churches*, John Bale combined the historical interpretation of the Joachite tradition with the Augustinian apocalyptic dualism of an eternal struggle between two classes of people: those of Christ and those of Antichrist. Revelation, therefore, offers an important insight into the nature of this eternal struggle, which has gone on through the ages.[106] In the spirit of Joachim, Bale suggested that the sixth trumpet and seal introduced his own period: The sixth age is the age of reformation. Another interpreter who was influenced by the Joachite tradition, yet in an overtly revolutionary direction, was Thomas Muentzer (d. 1525). Despite his reputation as the epitome of apocalyptic radicalism, Muentzer's use of the book of Revelation itself is quite sparse. His political radicalism is rooted in the mystical tradition influenced by the writings of Tauler rather than in the Apocalypse,[107] which may have influenced early Anabaptism. Hans Hut, for example (who may have been part of Muentzer's army, which was routed at Frankenhausen in 1525 and who himself died in prison the following year), wrote of the situation at the time of the Peasants Revolt that "the final and most terrible times of the world are upon us."[108]

The evidence of an extensive use of Revelation is apparent, however, in the writings of Muentzer's contemporary Melchior Hoffman (d. c. 1534).[109] He saw Revelation as the key to the understanding of history, the meaning of the secrets of which had been revealed to him. There were three revelations of divine glory in the time of the apostles, the second at the time of Jan Hus, and the third at the time of the Reformation. Following each was a period of decline. He saw his own time as the coincidence of the last kingdom of Antichrist and the last outpouring of the Holy Spirit. He shared an Augustinian view of the millennium: There had been a Christian Jerusalem in which the elect, together with Christ, ruled the faithful for a thousand years. After Hus, God had given the church time to repent, but the papacy was antichrist and still prevailed. Hoffman, like Muentzer, identified his own mission with Elijah to come, one of the two witnesses of Revelation 11. Their defeat was a certain sign of the Second Coming, after which there would be a persecution of the true church, at the end of which a company of 144,000, inspired by the Spirit, would proclaim God's grace throughout the world (echoes here of Joachim's "spiritual men").

Although his own vision had no place for the exercise of violent retribution by the elect, Hoffman's views were an ingredient in the establishment of the millennialist commonwealth in the city of Münster. He appears to have given tacit support to the Münster commonwealth, as when he described one of the leaders, Jan Matthijs, as one of the divine witnesses of Revelation 11. His successor as prophet was Jan of Leyden, who believed himself to be the eschatological Davidide. A reign of terror in Münster in 1534 fueled by antinomianism ensued. The influx of people into the city was seen as the fulfillment of the gathering of 144,000 into the new Jerusalem in Revelation 14. The Melchiorite interpretation of Revelation is an unusual example of the use of Revelation in the practice of a millenarian politics that, like the revolutionary actions of Thomas Muentzer a decade earlier (and like the Branch Davidian compound at Waco, Texas), did not remain at the level of utopian idealism but resulted in violent attempts to establish an eschatological theocracy.[110]

The use of the sword by the elect was not accepted by all Anabaptists of this period, however. The catastrophic effects of Münster as well as the career of Thomas Muentzer led to reaction against notions of eschatological theocracy.[111] It was viewed as a diabolical exercise whose enthusiasm was to be repudiated by all Christian people. Menno Simons, for example, the key figure in the revival of the Anabaptist movement after the Münster debacle, attacked the Munster prophets as false. He talked of the kingdom of Christ as not being of this visible world. The church is the visible form of the kingdom. It is visible in this world to the extent that Christians are obedient to the teachings of Christ. Despite the sense of an expectation of imminent fulfillment, what one finds in the post-Münster Anabaptism is the sense of being in the penultimate period rather than in the eschatological commonwealth on earth.[112]

Alongside the place of Revelation in radical religion in the sixteenth and early seventeenth centuries is a rich stream of interpretation in which the careful exposition of the book was carried out in a more measured and less heated atmosphere, encouraging a long tradition of apocalyptic speculation. Chief among such interpreters was Joseph Mede (1586–1638), whose work had enormous influence on subsequent generations (and whose interpretation of Revelation was taken up and used by more politically active groups during the Commonwealth period in England after the execution of Charles I).[113] By an interpretive method that viewed the book as a series of "synchronisms," or recapitulations in which several passages are said to relate to the same period of history, he calculated a period of 1,260 years from the rise of the papacy (dated to 365 CE) to its overthrow sometime in the seventeenth century. He considered his hermeneutical method to be based on a careful exegesis of the text:

> The Apocalypse considered only according to the naked Letter...hath marks and signs sufficient by the Holy Spirit, whereby the Order, Synchonism and Sequele of all the Visions therein contained, may be found out...without supposall of any Interpretation whatsoever.[114]

In a diagram in the 1833 edition of *Clavis Apocalyptica*, the last in each of the three series of sevens is viewed together as a moment of climax. That synchronic approach to the visions has been typical of many commentators on Revelation down to the present day, and his work has been frequently quoted in subsequent centuries. Similar in approach (explicitly indebted to Mede's work) and dictated by a concern to manifest evidence of divine providence in history are Isaac Newton's commentaries on Revelation, written a century and a half later. These are detailed and exhaustive attempts to demonstrate the marvelous orderliness of the pattern of the history of church and world, condensed in the books of Daniel and Revelation and parallel to what may be observed in the physical world.[115]

A link between revelation and radical politics is particularly evident in English Civil War writing,[116] best exemplified in the brief radical career of Gerrard Winstanley, who, with others, laid claim to the common land of the basis of a belief that the earth was a common treasury. The rule of the beast is not merely eschatological but is seen in the political arrangements of the day. Professional ministry, royal power, the judiciary, and the buying and selling of the earth correspond to the four beasts in the book of Daniel. The struggle between the dragon and Christ is exemplified in the advocacy of communism over against the rival claims to private property. The new heaven and earth can be seen here and now. Royal power is the old heaven and earth that must pass away. The new Jerusalem is not "to be seen only hereafter." Winstanley asserts, "I know that the glory of the Lord shall be seen and known within creation, and the blessing shall spread within all nations." God is not far above the heavens; God is to be found in the lives and experiences of ordinary men and women. God's kingdom comes when God arises in the saints. The perfect society will come when there takes place "the rising up of Christ in sons and daughters, which is his second coming." Winstanley used apocalyptic imagery to speak of the present as a critical moment in the life of the nation. He was convinced that Christ would reign and judge the world in and through his saints.[117] This millenarian vision was to permeate English religion through the individualized reading of the apocalyptic narrative in Bunyan's *Pilgrim's Progress*, itself a product of a period when the revolutionary politics of the mid-seventeenth century were on the wane.[118]

William Blake and His Contemporaries. The German commentator Albrecht Bengel had an enormous influence on contemporary readers, not least John Wesley, who quotes from Bengel's *Gnomon* in his introduction to Revelation. Bengel speaks for many eighteenth-century commentators in appreciating this quality in the prophetic literature in writing thus about Revelation:

> The whole structure of it breathes the art of God, comprising in the most finished compendium, things to come, many, various; near, intermediate, remote; the greatest, the least; terrible, comfortable; old, new; long, short; and these interwoven together, opposite, composite; relative to each other at a small, at a great distance; and therefore sometimes as it were disappearing, broken off, suspended, and afterwards unexpectedly and most seasonably appearing again. In all its parts it has an admirable variety, with the most exact harmony, beautifully illustrated by those digressions which seem to interrupt it. In this manner does it display the manifold wisdom of God shining in the economy of the church through so many ages.[119]

While the existential, individualistic appropriation of the book in early Methodism suggests a move from the world of politics to that of the human soul,[120] the approach to Revelation that saw in it an account of universal history in which contemporary events could be found had a new lease of life at the time of the French Revolution.[121] Throughout his life, Samuel Taylor Coleridge retained a fascination for Apocalypse, the visionary manifestation evident in the fragmentary "Kubla Khan."[122] In the context of the French Revolution, Coleridge, like his contemporary Joseph Priestley, saw the prophecy of Revelation being fulfilled, as is evident from his explicit use of Revelation in his "Religious Musing," published in 1796. As he became more conservative in his political views, however, he stressed the need for interpretation and set store by the emerging historical study of the text (e.g., in the work of Eichorn).

Arguably, the person who has understood most about Revelation without ever explicitly commenting on it was William Blake. He inhabited and was suffused with the world of the Bible in a way without parallel. Blake wrote no commentary on Revelation, but wrote his own prophecy, weaving images of Revelation into the fabric of his own visionary mythology. He read Revelation not as an end in itself but as a means to an end: the permeating of consciousness with the apocalyptic outlook. Blake recognized the prophets of the Old Testament as kindred spirits, and he wrote in their style and used their images, but for his own time and in his own way.

Blake's mythological writings challenge the God of the Bible, who had become a key figure in the creation of the ideology of the state.[123] Blake manifests the prophetic impulse that is in opposition to the kind of conformity to church and monarch typical of his day. Throughout the 1790s Blake's writing and designs returned to the themes of prophetic struggle and the need to be aware of the dangers of the prophetic spirit's degenerating into the apostasy of state religion.[124] For Blake, Revelation offered a supreme example of the prophetic impulse. And yet its authoritarianism, asceticism, and emphasis on divine transcendence are often implicitly criticized by him in the light of divine immanence and a spirit of forgiveness and mercy, which, according to Blake, characterized the religion of Jesus.

The Eschatological Synthesis of Modern Fundamentalism. The use of Revelation as a repository of prophecies concerning the future has been evidenced from the start and reached an influential climax in the work of Joseph Mede. In the last two hundred years, it has become very much a part of a growing trend toward eschatological interpretation. It was given an impetus from an unlikely source when an Anglican clergyman, John Nelson Darby, founder of the Plymouth Brethren, interpreted the book as unfulfilled prophecy. In his interpretation of the rapture, which is not in Revelation but is described in 1 Thess 4:17 (though Darby thought he could find it alluded to in Rev 3:10), this event was to occur before the resurrection, thereby opening the way for a period of great tribulation.

This kind of reading is supported by the widely influential Scofield Reference Bible, first published in 1909. Here the letters in Revelation 2–3 have a prophetic as well as a local application, disclosing seven phases of the spiritual history of the church. Thus Thyatira is the papacy: "as Jezebel brought idolatry into Israel, so Romanism weds Christian doctrine to pagan ceremonies." There is a close link between Revelation and Daniel: Revelation 4:–19 synchronize with Daniel's seventieth week (Dan 9:24), with the great tribulation of Rev 7:14 coming in the middle of the "week." This is brought to an end by the parousia and the battle of Armageddon. The day of the Lord is preceded by seven signs: the sending of Elijah; cosmic disturbances; the insensibility of the professing church; the apostasy of the church; the rapture of the true church (1 Thessalonians 4:1); the manifestation of the man of sin (2 Thessalonians); and the apocalyptic judgments of Revelation 11–18 ("the great tribulation"), which involve the people of God who have returned to Palestine. The beasts of Revelation 13:1 are the last civil and ecclesiastical heads respectively. The "ten horns" of Dan 7:24 and Rev 17:12 refer to the last form of Gentile power, "a confederated ten-kingdom empire covering the sphere of authority of ancient Rome." The return of Christ in glory, which will bring to an end Gentile dominion, is followed by the destruction of the beast, the millennium, the satanic revolt, the second resurrection and final judgment, and the coming of the day of God.

Although thoroughly influenced by the peculiar fears of the late twentieth century, most influential in this tradition has been Hal Lindsey's *Late, Great Planet Earth.*[125] For Lindsey, the seals predict war in the Middle East. The sixth seal concerns the beginning of nuclear war, and the trumpet heralds the terrible disasters of such a war. The 200 million cavalry are the army of China, which will do battle with the armies of the West at Armageddon. The beast from the sea is Antichrist, which will emerge from the European Union, whose member nations are symbolized by ten horns. The beast from the land is religious and seeks to unite all religions in a spurious faith. The decline in religious and moral life, castigated in the Laodicean letter, is addressed to the twentieth century's generations. It is a sign that the end is near. The book of Revelation encourages the elect to dream of a miraculous rescue by the rapture and is a license for escape from political struggle to change the present world order, doomed as it is to destruction. There is no role for humans in saving it. All that matters is to be found as part of the elect, who will enjoy the escape of the rapture. The panorama of destruction in Revelation offers no human solution but ensures flight from the world.[126]

The nature of Revelation's polyvalent imagery means that there is at the end of the day no refuting of readings like this. One can only appeal to consistency with the wider demand of the gospel and its application by generations of men and women in lives of service and involvement with the suffering and the marginalized to counter such world-denying and dehumanizing appropriations of Revelation and other biblical books.

Historical Criticism and Modern Exegesis. The rise of historical scholarship led to a different perspective on the book, which focused more on past meaning than on present use. Earlier critics, like Hugo Grotius (1583–1645) in his *Annotations on the New Testament*, had argued that the book's meaning was almost entirely related to the circumstances of John's own day (the so-called preterist method of interpretation). He considered that John's visions related to the fall of Jerusalem and the end of Rome and that the millennium had started with the accession of Constantine, though he did not exclude some eschatological fulfillment. Typical of the method that has dominated study not only of Revelation but of all biblical texts since is evident in the work of J. J. Wettstein (1693–1754). In his *Novum Testamentum*, he dated the work at the outbreak of the Jewish war against Rome (66–73 CE) and saw it in part as a prophecy about the collapse of Jerusalem and then of Rome, and a prediction about the fate of Domitian. The form of his study is significant, and it exemplifies the subtle change that the rise of the historical method brought with it. Attention is paid entirely to the book in its ancient context. As well as detailed text-critical analysis, there are lengthy quotations from ancient sources, including rabbinic parallels that illuminate particular passages of Revelation. Ferdinand Christian Baur's (1792–1860) theory of texts as mirrors of church conflict (given a new impetus in recent years in the writing of Michael Goulder)[127] considered the Apocalypse as an example of a Jewish-Christian anti-Pauline text. Attacks on Balaam, Jezebel, and the Nicolaitans are thinly veiled attacks on Paul. Thus Rev 2:14, 20 contrasts with advice that Paul offers on the issue of food offered to idols in 1 Corinthians 8; 10:23ff. The early dating of Revelation by members of the Tübingen school of biblical exegesis led Friedrich Engels to regard Revelation as the prime witness to the character of primitive Christian religion.[128]

Perhaps the most distinctive contribution of historical study of the book has been the application of source-critical study to it. The recognition of inconsistencies led Grotius to think that the book was written at different times in John's life, a view that has had many variations. So, for example, Revelation 11, with its reference to Jerusalem under siege, may have been written in the 60s and later incorporated into a book written in the 90s. R. H. Charles, the doyen of source critics of apocalyptic texts, considered that the author was responsible for compiling much of the first twenty chapters, but a later redactor wrote most of chapters 20–22 and made additions to the rest of the book, bringing about severe dislocations to the original.

Questions about the authorship of the book are not confined to the modern period but go back to the early centuries of the church, when anti-Montanist polemic led writers like Dionysius of Alexandria to question its apostolic origin and to suggest that it may have come from the hand of the heretic Cerinthus because of its espousal of a messianic, this-worldly eschatology. Luther and Zwingli also questioned its apostolic origin. Doubts about a common author for it and the Johannine Gospel are now widespread, with the consensus being that it was written by an unknown John in Asia. In the light of source criticism, the view that the book contains non-Christian elements recurs from time to time.[129] Such a theory reflects the kind of source-critical ingenuity applied to other apocalyptic texts in which there is some evidence of Christian revision (e.g., the *Testaments of the Twelve Patriarchs*, the *Apocalypse of Abraham*, and the *Ascension of Isaiah*), but enough evidence remains of a Jewish work untouched by the Christian gospel (though what counts as Christian in this context is never really discussed).

A distinctive voice in modern interpretation of the book, particularly in British circles, has been Austin Farrer. His careful and ingenious treatment of Revelation's number symbolism as well as an eye for the visionary character of the book have given him a peculiar position in the interpretation of the book.[130]

The recognition of the importance of apocalyptic for the understanding of Christianity, particularly the New Testament, has meant that Christian theologians have had to wrestle with the visionary and the eschatological as central features of their interpretive agenda.[131] At one and the same time the strange world of the apocalypse, far removed from the demythologized world of the Enlightenment, has contributed a golden thread that runs through modern scholarship on early Christianity and, in part, on ancient Judaism also. The reasons for the rediscovery in the second half of the nineteenth century of eschatological beliefs as a significant aspect of earliest Christianity are complex. The books of Daniel and Revelation, and for some traditions 2 Esdras, were for centuries part of the Christian canon of scriptures. The exploration of Abyssinia led to the discovery of Jewish apocalyptic works like *1 Enoch*, which for centuries had been part of the Old Testament canon of the Ethiopic church. The *Apocalypse of Enoch*,[132] for example, now extant in full only in Ethiopic (though fragments have been found among the Dead Sea Scrolls), contains ideas similar to Daniel and Revelation and the Gospels; it confirmed that the world of Jesus and the first Christians was very much that of the Jewish apocalypses.

Such ideas made perhaps their most dramatic impact on the study of the New Testament in the work of Albert Schweitzer. After reviewing the various attempts, over the previous hundred years, to go behind the pages of the New Testament to get at the historical Jesus,[133] he proposed that Jesus' mission could be understood only if one took seriously the eschatological convictions found in Jewish apocalypses. In Schweitzer's view, the early church had to deal with an initial and dramatic disappointed hope; the result is found in what Schweitzer calls Paul's Christ mysticism, the identification of the messianic age in the lives of believers and the church. Much of what has been written since Schweitzer's work has been an attempt to come to terms with the impact of the eschatological ideas brought to the fore in such a dramatic way by exegetical pioneers like him and Johannes Weiss. Yet despite its problematic character, eschatology paradoxically was the means whereby Jesus' apocalyptic message could continue to speak to every generation—precisely because its strangeness meant that it could never be transformed into the compromises of history.

A feature of modern discussion has been the extent to which Revelation corresponds to contemporary Jewish apocalypses. The flowering of scholarship on Second Temple Judaism after the Second World War (coinciding with the discovery of the Dead Sea Scrolls) has led to a renewed interest in and sophisticated analysis of apocalypses.[134] Revelation's apparent lack of pseudonymity, its tightness of structure, and its author's assertion that the book is prophecy have led some to question how well it fits into the genre of apocalypse, despite its title in 1:1 and the inclusion of some typical features of the apocalypses of Second Temple Judaism (e.g., symbolic visions and heavenly journeys).

Social sciences have made less of an impact on the study of Revelation than one might have expected, given that a significant part of the emerging study of the sociology of religion has been concerned with the rise and character of sectarianism and its ideology.[135] A sectarian origin for apocalyptic has been canvassed.[136] The influential theory of cognitive dissonance pioneered by L. Festinger, with its origins in the study of the millenarian movements in Melanesia, has been applied to early Christian eschatology.[137] The result is to suggest that the failure of the materialization of the millennial hope might prompt a community to engage in various forms of activism (e.g., proselytizing) to cope with their disappointment. Revelation, then, is viewed as a myth for an oppressed community that found itself confronted with the dissonance between its beliefs and the sociopolitical realities of a militant Roman Empire, by which the reader can overcome the contradiction between the present, with its threat of persecution and the hoped-for life of bliss. The link with millenarian movements has been explored historically by Norman Cohn, who has continued to explore the social psychology of a dualistic mind-set.[138] Perhaps the most relevant (though not specifically related either to Revelation or to the New Testament) work is Stuart Hall's study of the rise and character of the Rastafarian movement (which is itself indebted in various ways to passages from the book of Revelation).[139] The social-psychological perspective is evident also in Adela Yarbro Collins's exploration of the extent to which reading can be a way of dealing with aggression. The process of engaging with the book can bring about catharsis and displacement of difficult emotion.[140] This follows in the footsteps of C. G. Jung, who juxtaposed the gospel and the Apocalypse as examples of different and unresolved aspects of human personality—the gospel a testimony to love, and the Apocalypse a cry of vengeance. The perfectionist teaching of the First Epistle of John has its dark side in Revelation, replete with its primal myths. The shadow side of the gospel of love is fear and vengeance, which are split off and removed from the character of God.

There is much evidence of the power and influence of the book of Revelation among the grassroots groups influenced by late twentieth-century liberation theology. Two commentaries written from that perspective reflect these concerns, though, strictly speaking, their interpretative approach differs little in most respects from the mainstream of historical exegesis. Allan Boesak, for example, favors what he calls "a contemporary historical understanding" of the book of Revelation.[141] By this he means that John's book cannot be understood outside his own political context, but as prophecy does not receive its "full and final fulfillment in one given historical moment only but will be fulfilled at different times and in different ways in the history of the world." That enables him to relate the images of beast and Babylon, for example, to the struggle against the apartheid regime in South Africa. Similarly, Pablo Richard[142] sees the bulk of Revelation until 19:10 to be about the present, the challenge to the community and its role in the world (through his examination of the structure of the book, chap. 14 becomes the center of the message) and its own struggles, only the final chapters being concerned with the eschatological judgment of the world.

In the liberationist perspective, the book of Revelation both offers hope and stimulates resistance. It is a way of looking at the world that refuses to accept that the dominant powers are the ultimate point of reference. Apocalyptic discourse, consisting of picture and symbol, asks the reader to participate in another way of speaking about God and the world that makes it more readily understood by all. It taps the well of human response in those whose experience of struggle, persecution, and death has taught them what it means to wash their robes and to make them white in the blood of the Lamb. Two other interpreters ought to be mentioned in this context: Jacques Ellul[143] and William Stringfellow.[144] Both are marginal to the mainstream of modern biblical exegesis, but each reflects the way in which the Bible, and particularly the book of Revelation, challenges ideology by unmasking the principalities and powers. Perhaps few have understood the meaning of an apocalyptic witness in Babylon better than these two.

The liberationist perspective is apparent in the marginal notes of *Biblia Sagrada*, published in Brazil.[145] The introduction declares that the work is explicitly geared to promote the relationship between text and life and thereby initiate a dialogue between the word of God and "our reality," albeit one qualified by the communal context of reading.[146] In the notes to the first verses of Revelation it is stated that "the Apocalypse is a book read and expounded in meetings of Christian communities." The final verses in 22:6ff. are seen as a dialogue between Christ and the churches, where the book should be read in a liturgical context in which it can be explained and meditated upon and its message applied (thereby asserting a degree of control over individualistic and idiosyncratic readings). Revelation urges that John's mission is that of all Christians: to be prophets, announcing the word of God and continuing the testimony of Jesus Christ. Main themes include warnings against syncretistic religion (particularly applicable in Brazil, where the Afro-Brazilian religions are prominent) and the domination of imperial religion. The sketch of the age in which Revelation was written, particularly the references to the decadence and the prevalence of autocratic regimes, echoes the recent experience of Latin American nations. John's aim, according to the marginal notes, is to recall Christians to their original option and involvement in liberating action, which has to be informed by an understanding of the oppressive situation in which the communities found themselves and the maintenance of a horizon of hope for a new society. John, in his visions, is said to analyze the nature of the victory over evil (on 12:1). Throughout the work are several resonances with the favorite terms within the theology of liberation: option for the poor, oppression, liberation, new society, and the "see, judge, act" of popular pastoral practice. Salvation is said to consist, not in reform, but in radical transformation, "bringing to birth a new world of justice and fraternity."

Revelation offers the opportunity to discern "God's project in history," the title of a pamphlet about the life and history of the people of God down the ages, written by Carlos Mesters, and widely used by the basic ecclesial communities. The interpretation of chap. 13 in this edition as compared with the Spanish translation *La Nueva Biblia Latinoamerica* indicates the more overtly modern political reading of the Brazilian version. In the former the interpretative notes concentrate mainly on the original context of Revelation, whereas in the latter the beast is stated without qualification to be "absolute political power," which takes the place of God and enslaves humans, "totalitarianism, dictatorships and oppressive regimes." The crime of Babylon is to persecute those who reject absolute political power and who are not taken in by the ideological propaganda that ensnares those not vigilant enough to see through it. Although the (ancient) Roman context is not ignored, a general message is found in which the second beast represents manipulative power on the ideological and political levels. When Babylon's fate is lamented in chap. 19, the notes speak of the laments coming from wielders of political, economic, and commercial power. In addition to the eschatological dimension of the book there is the assertion that the coming of Jesus is something that is in process and is evident in the testimony of those who maintain the faith: "to manifest truth, reveal the love of the Father, and promote conversion. Whenever Jesus comes there is the destruction of an unjust world and the construction of a new one." The contextual character of the notes parallel, in their contemporary concern, the approach of those in the sixteenth-century Geneva Bible, whose marginal glosses occasionally suggest politically subversive readings.[147] The narrowly religious interpretations that are standard fare in most modern commentaries are replaced in the Latin American texts by an interpretative lens through which the world can be perceived afresh.

There are examples in abundance of the work's appealing to the oppressed, whether whether in our time or in the ancient world, and of its being the ideology of what Leonard Thompson calls a "cognitive minority." Nevertheless, it has appealed also to those well established in society, albeit through different reading strategies (Newton's interpretation contrasts sharply with the roughly contemporary Winstanley's in this respect). People can think in the manner of the Apocalypse without themselves being part of a minority or even discontented with their personal life circumstances. The neat correspondence between literature and life, in which an apocalyptic text reflects a persecuted or threatened minority, does not do justice to the wide dissemination of such ideas in the ancient or modern world. The appeal of Revelation to the oppressed in Latin America as they practice their liberation theology lends plausibility to the hypothesis that apocalyptic is peculiarly applicable to the situation of an oppressed minority. But when the images of the Apocalypse can contribute to the mind-set of a significant group within the mainstream of North American society, we should beware of supposing that we have a book that appeals only to persons on the fringes of society.

Liberal Christianity's distaste for Revelation's vindictiveness and lack of concern with love, viewed as prime among all Christian characteristics, has led to attempts to domesticate or tone down its barbarous tone.[148] Recent feminist scholarship has a different objection. Tina Pippin has examined the references to women in the book and found it impossible to regard them as anything other than negative; the transformation of the world is only partial, as gender relations remain untouched.[149] The disparagement of women's activism and encouragement of a passive, dependent attitude is so firmly rooted in the domain of patriarchy that women everywhere remain subject to male dominion.

The Apocalypse and Art.[150] Exegetical commentary on a biblical text like Revelation needs to be complemented by the artistic exposition of the text. Indeed, a commentary cannot do justice to the character of apocalyptic discourse in the way that a picture or a poem can. An explanation, however suggestive and allusive, reduces and diminishes the hermeneutical power of symbol and myth. Thus art may be better able to stimulate our aesthetic faculties. A commentator on Revelation struggles to find ways to enable interaction with the text as we have it, so that the book, with its peculiar network of imagery, may begin to pervade the reader's consciousness. Whereas exegesis renders texts in ways that systematize and explain, art defies explanation. Art assists in the new moments of unveiling that can occur through the repristination of the apocalyptic images in artistic work. If what we have in Revelation is the opening of an interpretative space for readers or hearers to be provoked, to have their imaginations broadened and the incentive to think and behave differently, then that process requires new methods to ensure that the original impact of a metaphorical text is maintained in different circumstances. Readers of Revelation require a variety of explanatory mediums to explore its words and images, so that they may be able to see, and behave, differently.

Different artistic uses of Revelation may be found over the centuries, ranging from the iconography of ecclesiastical architecture to designs that accompany the text itself. Revelation also lent itself to the catena of illustrations evident in texts like the *Trier Apocalypse* and the long series of "Beatus" manuscripts, which go back to Beatus of Liebana. Apart from manuscripts, there are cycles from the Apocalypse in church murals, the Angers tapestry (late 14th cent.), and stained glass (e.g., the east window in York Minster, England, from the early 15th cent.). Artistic representation of the apocalypse continued in the Renaissance art form of the woodcut, the most famous being Albrecht Dürer's depictions (1497–98). The prominent place given to illuminations of the apocalypse in Luther's Bible of 1534 is an indication of the continuing role of artistic imagination in the exegesis of what continued to be a controversial text. In the eighteenth and nineteenth centuries the contrasting images of Revelation evident in J. M. W. Turner's (1775–1851) work *Death on a Pale Horse* (c. 1825) can be compared with William Blake's less abstract painting of the same title (c. 1800). In our more secular world, the dependence on the inspiration of Revelation is less direct and more subtle. Yet the evocation of cataclysm in art, often distasteful and even banal in the written word, affects a generation saturated with images, not least of human and cosmic disaster, and is a profound influence on the artistic work of a century that has witnessed humanity's worst evils.

The different exegetical approaches to Revelation are manifest in art. Revelation has had from the start of New Testament interpretation a preeminent place as the primary eschatological text of the Bible. Last judgment scenes are common in European ecclesiastical buildings. In addition to the eschatological, Van Eycks's *Mystical Lamb* (1432) indicates another way of appropriating the book, following a tradition of interpretation that goes back to Tyconius and Augustine. The division between heaven and earth is transcended in the eucharistic feast as the Lamb, in the midst of the throne, is found on an altar on earth. Contextual readings, in which visions are related to their ancient historical or contemporary contexts, and thus used as an interpretative lens through which to view contemporary history, are seen in severe medieval cycles of apocalypse illustrations and the later woodcuts (e.g., in the depiction of Babylon as papal Rome in the Luther Bible).

William Blake (1757–1827) offers a significant example of the artistic appropriation of the book of Revelation and the creative exploitation of its exegetical potential. He is a unique example of a visionary who was an accomplished artist and poet and whose visionary imagination was combined with creative productive techniques, very much in the tradition of the medieval combination of text and design, to give him a unique place among cultural critics.[151] Blake explicitly traced a continuity not only between his own mythology and the vision seen by John,[152] but also between his own vocation to prophesy and that of John of Patmos. While John's apocalyptic vision is a central component of many aspects of Blake's visionary world and informs Blake's understanding of his own political situation, Blake uses the Apocalypse as inspiration rather than a prescription of his own apocalyptic visions. He is not a conventional commentator on it, unlike the emerging German historical critics in his day. Blake's relationship with the text represents that of the visionary who stands in continuity not by visualizing again Revelation's images but by using Revelation as a means of true insight into vision, who sees more clearly by means of the ancient apocalyptic text. Unlike his medieval forebears, he does not illuminate the text of Revelation, for his work stands alongside Revelation, not as exegesis but as a further exemplification of the prophetic tradition.

For Blake, the visionary and imaginative is all important, and the Bible has an apocalyptic role in encouraging this. Allowing reason to triumph over imagination denies a wisdom "Permanent in the Imagination," through which one could be "open [to] the Eternal Worlds." This would "open the immortal Eyes/Of Man inwards into the Worlds of Thought, into Eternity/Ever expanding in the Bosom of God, the Human Imagination."[153] A way in which he achieves this is to juxtapose text and design in his illuminated books. Readings of the text must be set in the context of the illuminations. He achieves hermeneutical creativity by this juxtaposition. Often text and illumination seem to have little contact. The indeterminate relationship between writing and illustration demands that readers engage with the text, and their own imagination contributes to making sense of the two. Language and portrait function in an apocalyptic way, a hermeneutical device that opens up the imagination. Blake demands of the reader imaginative participation to explore the tensions and problems that the text poses. Nature itself can function in this way, for "to the Eyes of the Man of Imagination, Nature [can be] Imagination itself."[154] Blake expects "to see a World in a Grain of Sand and a Heaven in a Wild Flower."[155] "The Old & New Testaments are the Great Code of Art"[156] are just the best examples of art that can, with proper use, open up the way to the eternal: The Bible is "more Entertaining & Instructive than any other book," because it is "addressed as to the Imagination, which is Spiritual Sensation, & but mediately to the Understanding or Reason."[157] For Blake, the exegetical task involved reading, hearing, and appropriating in order to break what he called the "mind forg'd manacles" that prevent imagination and human community from flourishing. Essays in apocalyptic exegesis of the Bible must involve a variety of ways, in which the artistic is paramount, of rousing the faculties to new moments of understanding.

An Apocalyptic Tone in Recent Theology and Philosophy.[158] There are alternative modern perspectives outside the Christian tradition. One is that of D. H. Lawrence.[159] Lawrence saw Revelation as representing the vengeful Christianity of self-glorification, contrasting with the tender religion of Jesus. At its heart is a vital pagan original that has been overlaid by subsequent editors who in each succeeding edition made the book more mean-spirited. And yet there is sufficient evidence of the link with the pagan religion of nature that it can be appropriated by those who will put aside the historical perspective of the final versions and relish the cyclical world of nature that lies dormant in the text.

Jacques Derrida[160] looks at the antimonies sketched by Kant between poetry and mysticism, on the one hand, and philosophy on the other hand (echoes of Blake). Just as the Enlightenment claimed to bring new awareness, so also do apocalypses. When viewed more closely, apocalypse turns out to be an unveiling that reveals only another enigma. Far from offering answers, "the apocalyptic tone" leads to indeterminancy. What apocalyptic unveiling achieves is the revelation of the metaphorical character of all languages, which thereby challenges the fantasy of "answers" by demonstrating in the starkest way possible the indeterminancy of all reality.

The influence of the apocalyptic dimension was not felt within biblical scholarship alone, for the eschatological emphasis found in the work of Weiss and Schweitzer was to spill over in dramatic form into the theology of the immediate post-war scene in Barth's commentary on the Epistle to the Romans.[161] Eschatology offered a stark alternative to the world of destruction and devastation of 1919 and the compromises that contributed to it. It was a situation that provoked acute pessimism about humanity's resources to build a better world. Barth asserted that knowledge of God could come only through God's own revelation, which humanity could only accept or reject. Like the apocalypses of old, which seemed to offer some explanation of human existence and God's purposes through a revelation, Barth stressed the subordination of the human intellect to the revelation of God. He repudiated human attempts to comprehend God (what is referred to as natural theology). Instead, he stressed the centrality of revelation as the only basis for understanding anything about God; that is an "unveiling" or apocalypse.[162]

Contemporary with Barth and equally committed to the eschatological inheritance of the Jewish tradition, but with a very different assessment of it, is Ernst Bloch. He rehabilitated the perspectives of Joachim of Fiore and Gerrard Winstanley and recognized the significance of utopian elements in a variety of cultures. He was committed to the rehabilitation of that millenarian, apocalyptic inheritance on the fringes of orthodox Christianity. His mammoth book, *The Principle of Hope*,[163] explores the ways in which that longing for a future age of perfection has colored the whole range of culture in both East and West. Bloch called attention to the power of the utopian inheritance and its contribution to Marxism as well as the Judeo-Christian tradition (though his views are tangential to the mainstream Marxist tradition and have been received with considerable skepticism by other Marxists). He promoted the eschatological traditions that mainstream Christianity has preferred to forget. It is as the philosopher of "utopia" that Bloch will be remembered. Bloch considers that utopia is not something far off in the future, but is at the heart of human experience; it is already at hand in an anticipatory and fragmentary way. These fragments are themselves an encouragement to human action in the present, even if the hoped-for utopia is not fully possible without changing the present order of things.

Despite its kaleidoscopic quality, Bloch's work often provides suggestive insights into the character of Christian doctrine and its mutation into an ideology.[164] He does not see the Bible as an elaboration of a social utopia, but it "does point most vehemently to exodus and kingdom.[165] Apocalypse is the breaking in of the "novum" (Rev 21:5 is a favorite text of Bloch's). The Apocalypse is the vehicle of an unparalleled phenomenon in the history of religion: "the apocalyptic transformation of the world into something as yet completely nonexistent."[166] Not surprisingly, Bloch pays great attention to the chiliastic tradition: "Utiopian unconditionality comes from the Bible."[167]

Bloch's own work, echoed in a more attentuated form in the later writing of Walter Benjamin[168] and even Theodor Adorno,[169] all of whom were close friends of Gershom Scholem, the great pioneer of the modern study of Jewish apocalypticism and mysticism,[170] reminds us of neglected aspects of the eschatological tradition and its political potential. In the light of Bloch's work it is not surprising that Christians and some Marxists influenced by this utopian tradition have been united in a common quest for change and a new social order based on peace and justice in this world. Modern political theology owes a great debt to Bloch's appropriation of the Christian chiliastic tradition. The German theologian Jürgen Moltmann is particularly indebted to him.[171] Political theology in Europe in the post-war period has echoes in turn in the influential political theology of Latin America: liberation theology, in which the language of utopianism has sometimes been used as a way of speaking of the relationship between the future kingdom and present movements for social change in church and state, particularly among the downtrodden at the base of Latin American society.[172] In their refusal to divide history and eschatology, the present from the future, liberation theologians have inherited the mantle of that alternative political eschatology championed by Bloch.

Conclusion. The shifting fortunes of the Apocalypse can be traced in the history of interpretation. That ambivalence manifest in the work of the earliest commentators, where an ecclesiological and eschatological hermeneutic are woven together without comment, has characterized the two poles of interpretation. Despite their theological and political differences, Augustine, Winstanley, and Melchior Hoffman all seem to agree that key images relate to contemporary realities. Those who interpret the book wholly eschatologically effectively diminish its contemporary significance, as do those who see the book as applying totally to the past. But the differences of the contemporizing approach suggest that the impact of the images has as much to do with the complex preferences and interests of the readers as it does with what the text demands. We can say that Augustine's interpretation of Revelation 20 as a reference to the rule of bishops in the church conveniently ignores the fact that the text itself places the rule firmly with the martyrs, only a few of whom could be expected to be bishops (particularly in the post-Constantinian age). Equally the realized eschatology that dominates the theocratic applications of Revelation, such as those of Melchior Hoffman, ignore the fact that although what is described may be coming soon there is still an unfulfilled dimension to its apocalyptic evocation.

The demand for understanding has gone hand in hand with attempts to find precise equivalence between history and every image in the book and has resulted in a long tradition of interpretation based on the decoding principle. An image has a particular meaning, and if the code is understood in its entirety the whole apocalypse can be rendered in another form when the code is cracked and the inner meaning laid bare. It is only the occasional reader who refuses to settle for simple meanings, who insists on leaving open the possibility of polyvalence. Instead we typically find meaning confined as the details of images and actions are fixed on some historical personage or event. That applies also to encapsulations of Revelation's theology, for the problem posed by this book is the difficulty imagination places on that desire for the ordered systematic presentation that lies at the heart of theology. A book that requires interpretation and seems to demand order in the face of the apparent chaos of its imagery in the end confounds such attempts, not least those that are furthest from its own prophetic impulse. Schüssler Fiorenza aptly summarizes the peculiar importance of the text and of the context in which it is read:

> Revelation will elicit a fitting...response...only in those socio-political situations that cry out for justice. When Christian groups are excluded from political power, Revelation's language of divine kingship and royal reward, as well as its ethical dualism, stands against unjust authority and champions the oppressed and disenfranchised. Whenever Christians join the power structures of their society and seek to stabilise them, the same rhetorical world of vision serves to sacralise dominant authorities and preach against their enemies.[173]

In situations where its imagery is allowed to work, however, it can disturb the convention maintained by the commonsensical. Like metaphors, whose function is to lay bare the realities of experience by the abrupt and jarring impact of their linguistic juxtapositions, apocalypse seeks to stop us in our tracks and get us to view things differently. For many, however, metaphors are "dead," themselves having become part of mere convention or habit without the effect they once had; they are salt that has lost its savor. Revelation requires the recovery of that ability to hear or read and to be stirred or shocked and scandalized into repentance and action rather than indifference or rejection: "Let any one who has an ear listen."[174]

FOR FURTHER READING

Aune, D. E. *Revelation 1–5.* WBC. Nashville: Word, 1997.

———. *Revelation 6–16.* WBC. Nashville: Word, 1997.

———. *Revelation 17–22.* WBC. Nashville: Word, 1997.

Barr, David L., ed. *Reading the Book of Revelation: A Resource for Students.* SBLRBS 44. Atlanta, Ga.: Society of Biblical Literature, 2003.

Bauckham, R. *The Theology of the Book of Revelation.* Cambridge: Cambridge University Press, 1993.

Beale, G. K. *The Book of Revelation: A Commentary on the Greek Text.* Grand Rapids: Eerdmans, 1998.

Bindman, D., ed. *William Blake's Illuminated Books.* 6 vols. London: Tate Gallery Publications/ William Blake Trust, 1991–95.

Boring, M. Eugene. *Revelation.* Interpretation. Louisville: John Knox, 1989.

Burdon, C. *The Apocalypse in England 1700–1834: Revelation Unravelling.* London: Macmillan, 1997.

Cohn, N. *The Pursuit of the Millennium.* London: Paladin, 1957.

Collins, J. J. *The Apocalyptic Imagination: An Introduction to the Jewish Matrix of Christianity.* New York: Crossroad, 1987.

Daley, B. *The Hope of the Early Church.* Cambridge: Cambridge University Press, 1991.

Emmerson, R., and B. McGinn. *The Apocalypse in the Middle Ages.* Ithaca, N.Y.: Cornell University Press, 1992.

Hill, C. *The English Bible and the Seventeenth Century Revolution.* London: Penguin, 1993.

Maier, Harry O. *Apocalypse Recalled: The Book of Revelation After Christendom.* Minneapolis, Minn.: Fortress, 2002.

Malina, Bruce J., and John J. Pilch. *Social Science Commentary on the Book of Revelation.* Minneapolis: Fortress, 2000.

Mathewson, David. *A New Heaven and a New Earth: The Meaning and Function of the Old Testament in Revelation 21.1-22.5.* JSNTSup 238. New York: Sheffield Academic Press, 2003.

Rowland, C. *The Open Heaven: A Study of Apocalyptic in Judaism and Early Christianity.* London: SPCK, 1982.

———. *Radical Christianity: A Reading of Recovery.* Oxford: Polity, 1988.

Schüssler Fiorenza, E. *Revelation: Vision of a Just World.* Edinburgh: T & T Clark, 1993.

Wainwright, A. *Mysterious Apocalypse.* Nashville: Abingdon, 1993.

Wengst, K. *Pax Romana and the Peace of Jesus Christ.* London: SCM, 1988.

ENDNOTES

1. Roland Barthes, *A Lover's Discourse: Fragments* (Harmondsworth: Penguin, 1990) 18.

2. See D. Cooper, *Metaphor* (Oxford: Blackwell, 1986); J. M. Soskice, *Metaphor and Religious Language* (Oxford: Oxford University Press, 1985); P. Ricoeur, *The Rule of Metaphor* (London: Routledge, 1978); N. Wolterstorff, *Divine Discourse* (Cambridge: Cambridge University Press, 1994) 193-99.

3. William Blake, *A Vision of the Last Judgment*, in *Blake: Complete Writings*, ed. G. Keynes (London: Oxford University Press, 1966) 617.

4. R. Bultmann, "The New Testament and Mythology," reprinted in *Kerygma and Myth*, ed. H. W. Bartsch (London: SPCK, 1964).

5. N. Cohn, *The Pursuit of the Millennium* (London: Paladin, 1984).

6. Dietrich Bonhoeffer, *No Rusty Swords* (London: Collins, 1965) 324-25.

7. E. Käsemann, *New Testament Questions of Today* (London: SCM, 1969).

8. W. Benjamin, "Theses on the Philosophy of History," in *Illuminations*, ed. H. Arendt (London: Collins Fontana, 1978).

9. Benjamin, "Theses on the Philosophy of History," 255ff.

10. On the importance of the church as a place of alternative and healing memories see W. Benjamin, *Memory and Salvation* (London: Darton, Longman and Todd, 1995).

11. P. Hanson, *The Dawn of Apocalyptic* (Philadelphia: Fortress, 1974); cf. O. Plöger, *Theocracy and Eschatology* (Oxford: Blackwell, 1968).

12. F. E. Brightman, *The English Rite* (London: Rivingtons, 1915) 1:51. In 1661, lessons from Revelation were to be read only on certain feasts. The situation changed later when Revelation (except chaps. 9; 13; and 17) was prescribed to be read in the month of December.

13. See the general articles on reading the Bible from particular social locations in *The New Interpreter's Bible*, 12 vols. (Nashville: Abingdon, 1994) 1:150-87.

14. D. Halperin, *Faces of the Chariot* (Tubingen: Mohr, 1988) 71.

15. See G. Loughlin, *Telling God's Story: Bible, Church and Narrative Theology* (Cambridge: Cambridge University Press, 1996).

16. William Blake, Letter to Dr. Trusler, 23 August 1799, in *Blake: Complete Writings*, ed. G. Keynes (London: Oxford University Press, 1966) 793

17. William Blake, *The Four Zoas*, in *Blake: Complete Writings*, 855.

18. Justin *Dialogue* 81:4.

19. See W. G. Kümmel, *Introduction to the New Testament* (London: SCM, 1975) 470.

20. A commentary on Revelation is listed among the works of Melito. See Eusebius *Ecclesiastical History* 4.26.2.

21. Tertullian *Against Marcion* IV.4.

22. Eusebius *Ecclesiastical History* vii.25.1ff.

23. Dio Cassius *Histories* 67-68.

24. See the discussion in Leonard L. Thompson, *The Book of Revelation: Apocalypse and Empire* (New York: Oxford University Press, 1990); and C. Rowland, *The Open Heaven: A Study of Apocalyptic in Judaism and Early Christianity* (London: SPCK, 1982) 403-13.

25. See M. Hengel, *The Johannine Question* (London: SCM, 1989).

26. Irenaeus *Against Heresies* iii.1.2. Cf. Eusebius *Ecclesiastical History* v.20.4.

27. J. Ashton, *Interpreting the Fourth Gospel* (Oxford: Oxford University Press, 1991) 381-406.

28. The evidence is set out in M. Smith, "On the History of ἀποκαλύπτω/ἀποκάλυψς," in *Apocalypticism in the Mediterranean World and Near East*, ed. D. Hellholm, 2nd ed. (Tübingen: Mohr, 1989) 9ff. See also F. Mazzaferri, *The Genre of the Book of Revelation from a Source Critical Perspective* (Berlin: De Gruyter, 1989); M. Bockmuehl, *Revelation and Mystery* (Tübingen: Mohr, 1990); M. Freschkowski, *Offenbarung und Epiphanie* (Tübingen: Mohr, 1995–97); D. Aune, *Prophecy in Early Christianity and the Ancient Mediterranean World* (Grand Rapids: Eerdmans, 1983); J. C. VanderKam and W. Adler, *The Jewish Apocalyptic Heritage in Early Christianity* (Assen: Van Gorcum, 1996).

29. See *Reuben* 3:15; *Judah* 16:4; *Joseph* 6:6; *Levi* 1:2; 18:2; *Benjamin* 10:5.

30. See Rowland, *The Open Heaven*; J. J. Collins, *The Apocalyptic Imagination* (New York: Crossroad, 1985).

31. J. Barton, *The Oracles of God: Perceptions of Ancient Prophecy in Israel After the Exile* (London: Darton, Longman & Todd, 1986).

32. G. Scholem, *Major Trends in Jewish Mysticism* (New York: Schocken, 1955); D. Halperin, *The Faces of the Chariot.*

33. In the Mishnah, *Hagigah* 2.1 is a solitary example.

34. I. Gruenwald, *Apocalyptic and Merkavah Mysticism* (Leiden: E. J. Brill, 1978); and *From Apocalyptic to Gnosticism: Studies in Apocalypticism, Merkavah Mysticism, and Gnosticism* (Frankfurt: Lang, 1988).

35. E.g., P. D. Hanson, *The Dawn of Apocalyptic* (Philadelphia: Fortress, 1974), though note the critical comments of R. Carroll, "Twilight of Prophecy or Dawn of Apocalyptic," *JSOT* 14 (1979) 3ff.

36. Hippolytus *Refutation of All Heresies* IX. 13.1ff.

37. Eusebius *Ecclesiastical History* III. 281-82.

38. E.g., *Shepherd of Hermas* Visions III.1.6ff.

39. Eusebius *Ecclesiastical History* V.16.6.

40. L. Thompson, *The Book of Revelation: Apocalypse and Empire* (New York: Oxford University Press, 1990); P. Minear, "The Cosmology of the Apocalypse," in Klassen and Snyder, *Current Issues in New Testament Interpretation* (London: SCM, 1962) 23-27; Andrew T. Lincoln, *Paradise Now and Not Yet: Studies in the Role of the Heavenly Dimension in Paul's Thought* (Cambridge: Cambridge University Press, 1981) 198.

41. See further C. Rowland, "Apocalyptic, Mysticism, and the New Testament," in *Geschichte Tradition Reflexion: Festschrift für Martin Hengel*, ed. P. Schäfer (Tubingen: Mohr, 1996) 405ff.

42. G. Scholem, *Major Trends in Jewish Mysticism* (New York: Schocken, 1955); I. Gruenwald, *Apocalyptic and Merkavah Mysticism* (Leiden: E. J. Brill, 1978); D. Halperin, *The Faces of the Chariot* (Tübingen: Mohr, 1988); Rowland, *The Open Heaven* (London: SPCK, 1982) 1; P. Schäfer, *The Hidden and Manifest God* (New York: State University of New York Press, 1992).

43. On the expositions of the chapter in the apocalyptic tradition see C. Rowland, "The Visions of God in Apocalyptic Literature," *JSL* 10 (1979) 138ff.

44. *m. Hagigah* 2:1.

45. *m. Megillah* 4:10; *Tosefta Megillah* 4:3.11ff.; *b. Megillah* 24.6.

46. See M. Dean-Otting, *Heavenly Journeys: A Study of the Motif in Hellenistic Jewish Literature* (Frankfurt: 1984); M. Himmelfarb, *Ascent to Heaven in Jewish and Christian Apocalypses* (New York: Oxford University Press, 1993).

47. See A. F. Segal, *Two Powers in Heaven: Early Rabbinic Reports About Christianity and Gnosticism* (Leiden: Brill, 1977); J. Fossum, *The Name of God and the Angel of the Lord* (Tübingen: Mohr, 1985); C. Rowland, *The Open Heaven*, esp. 94ff.;

L. W. Hurtado, *One God, One Lord: Early Christian Devotion and Ancient Jewish Monotheism* (London: SCM, 1988).

48. M. Lieb, *The Visionary Mode* (Ithaca, N.Y.: Cornell University Press, 1991); D. Halperin, *The Faces of the Chariot.*

49. *1 Enoch* 14:8-25, trans. E. Isaac, in *The Old Testament Pseudepigrapha,* vol.1, ed. J. H. Charlesworth (New York: Doubleday, 1983).

50. Translation from G. Vermes, *The Dead Sea Scrolls in English* (Harmondsworth: Penguin, 1961) 228. See C. Newsom, *The Songs of the Sabbath Sacrifice* (Atlanta: Scholars Press, 1985).

51. *Apocalypse of Abraham* 18:1-14, trans. R. Rubinkiewicz, in *The Old Testament Pseudepigrapha,* vol.1.

52. Thoroughly explored in L. Stuckenbruck, *Angel Veneration and Christology* (Tübingen: Mohr, 1995).

53. *Apocalypse of Abraham* 11:1-4, trans. R. Rubinkiewicz, in *The Old Testament Pseudepigrapha,* vol. 1.

54. Vision of the angel in *Joseph and Aseneth* 14:4-11, trans. C. Burchard, in *The Old Testament Pseudepigrapha,* vol. 2, ed. J. H. Charlesworth (New York: Doubleday, 1985).

55. M. Stone, *Fourth Ezra,* Hermeneia (Minneapolis: Fortress, 1990).

56. M. Knibb, "Apocalyptic and Wisdom in 4 Ezra," *Journal for the Study of Judaism* 13 (1982) 56-74.

57. Note the similarities with Ludwig Wittgenstein's understanding of religion as outlined by Ray Monk, *Ludwig Wittgenstein: The Duty of Genius* (London: Vintage, 1990) 409-10.

58. D. Brady, *The Contribution of British Writings Between 1560–1830 to the Interpretation of Revelation 13:16-18* (Tübingen: Mohr, 1983).

59. See the surveys in A. Wainwright, *Mysterious Apocalypse* (Nashville: Abingdon, 1993); E. B. Allo, *L'Apocalypse de Saint Jean* (Paris: Lecoffre, 1921); W. Bousset, *Die Offenbarung Johannis* (Göttingen: 1906); R. H. Charles, *Studies in the Apocalypse* (Edinburgh: T & T Clark, 1910); G. Maier, *Die Offenbarung Johannis und die Kirche* (Tübingen: Mohr, 1981).

60. Survey in R. Bauckham, *The Climax of Prophecy* (Edinburgh: T & T Clark, 1993) chap. 3.

61. K. Wengst, *Pax Romana and the Peace of Jesus Christ* (London: SCM, 1988) 65-66.

62. On Luke and apocalyptic traditions, see S. Garrett, *The Demise of the Devil* (Minneapolis: Fortress, 1989) 128; M. E. Boismard, "Rapprochements littéraires l'évangile de Luc et l'Apocalypse," in J. Schmid and A. Vögtle, *Synoptische Studien* (Munich: Mohr, 1953) 53-63.

63. See further G. Bornkamm, "The Revelation of God's Wrath," in *Early Christian Experience* (London: SCM, 1969) 47-70.

64. L. D. Hurst, *The Epistle to the Hebrews: Its Background of Thought* (Cambridge: Cambridge University Press, 1990) 199.

65. See the survey in C. Rowland, *Christian Origins* (London: SPCK, 1985) 285ff.; G.B.Caird, *New Testament Theology* (Oxford: Oxford University Press, 1994) 250-56; A. L. Moore, *The Parousia in the New Testament* (Leiden: E. J. Brill, 1966); R. Bauckham, *Aufstieg und Niedergang der römischen Welt* (Berlin: de Gruyter, 1972) 2:28.3.

66. E.g., *Pss. Sol.* 17:24-25; *1 Enoch* 46:5-6; 90:37; 4 Ezra 7:29; 12:32; *Syr. Baruch* 29:3; 39:7; 72:2; *Sib. Or.* iii. 652ff.; *T. Levi* 2:11; 4QFlor; 1QS 9:11).

67. See R. Funk, "The Apostolic Parousia: Form and Significance," in W. R. Farmer, C. F. D. Moule, and R. Niebuhr, *Christian History and Interpretation* (Cambridge: Cambridge University Press, 1967) 249ff.

68. See R. Bauckham, "The Delay of the Parousia," *Tyndale Bulletin* 31 (1980) 3-36.

69. B. Daley, *The Hope of the Early Church* (Cambridge: Cambridge University Press, 1991); C. Helms, "The Apocalypse in the Early Church, Christ, Eschaton, and the Millennium" (D. Phil. diss., Oxford University, 1991).

70. Justin *Dialogue with Trypho* 80.

71. Irenaeus *Against Heresies* V.26.1–36.3.

72. Irenaeus *Against Heresies* , III.23.7

73. Irenaeus *Against Heresies* , V.28.3.

74. Irenaeus *Against Heresies* , V.30.3.

75. Hippolytus *Antichrist* 61.

76. Hippolytus *Antichrist,* 12.

77. Hippolytus *Antichrist,* 25ff.

78. Origen *On Prayer* 27:13.

79. Origen *Commentary on John* 1.27.97.

80. Origen *Commentary on John* , 10.35.22.

81. Victorinus *Commentary on the Book of Revelation,* 102:16ff.

82. Victorinus *Commentary on the Book of Revelation,* 46ff.

83. Victorinus *Commentary on the Book of Revelation*, 66.

84. Victorinus *Commentary on the Book of Revelation*, 82.

85. Victorinus *Commentary on the Book of Revelation*, 120.

86. Victorinus *Commentary on the Book of Revelation*, 110.

87. Victorinus *Commentary on the Book of Revelation*, 128.

88. Victorinus *Commentary on the Book of Revelation*, 152.

89. K. Steinhauser, *The Apocalypse Commentary of Tyconius* (Frankfurt: Lang, 1987).

90. See P. Fredriksen, "Tyconius and Augustine on the Apocalypse," in *The Apocalypse in the Middle Ages*, ed. R. Emmerson and B. McGinn (Ithaca, N.Y.: Cornell University Press, 1992) 20-37.

91. Augustine *The City of God* 20.

92. Augustine *The City of God*, 6:3.

93. See Eusebius *Ecclesiastical History* X.9; *Oration* XVI.3-8.

94. Emmerson and McGinn, *The Apocalypse in the Middle Ages*; H. Lee, M. Reeves, and G. Silano, *Western Mediterranean Prophecy: The School of Joachim of Fiore and the Fourteenth Century Breviloquium* (Toronto: Pontifical Institute of Medieval Studies, 1989).

95. D. Burr, *Olivi's Peaceable Kingdom: A Reading of the Apocalypse Commentary* (Philadelphia: University of Pennsylvania Press, 1993).

96. See N. Cohn, *The Pursuit of the Millennium* (London: Paladin, 1984).

97. K. Firth, *The Apocalyptic Tradition in Reformation Britain, 1530–1645* (Oxford: Oxford University Press, 1979); C. Hill, *The Antichrist in Seventeenth Century England*, rev. ed. (London: Verso, 1990); C. Hill, *The English Bible and the Seventeenth Century Revolution* (London: Penguin, 1993).

98. Martin Luther, *Preface to the New Testament*, 12ff.

99. See R. Bauckham, *Tudor Apocalypse: Sixteenth Century Apocalypticism, Millenarianism, and the English Reformation* (Oxford: Sutton Courtenay, 1978) 41ff.

100. Firth, *The Apocalyptic Tradition in Reformation Britain*, 13.

101. Firth, *The Apocalyptic Tradition in Reformation Britain*, 171.

102. Edinburgh 1579. See also Hill, *The English Bible and the Seventeenth Century Revolution*, 56-62. The notes were influenced by Bullinger's sermons and Bale's writing, see Firth, *The Apocalyptic Tradition in Reformation Britain*, 122-24. See also Bauckham, *Tudor Apocalypse*, 45-48.

103. On the interpretation of these verses, see R. L. Petersen, *Preaching in the Last Days: The Theme of "Two Witnesses" in the Sixteenth and Seventeenth Centuries* (London: Oxford University Press, 1993) 199.

104. Hill, *The English Bible and the Seventeenth Century Revolution* , 64.

105. F. E. Brightman, *The English Rite* (London: Rivingtons, 1915) 1:51.

106. See Bauckham, *Tudor Apocalypse*, 54-90; Firth, *The Apocalyptic Tradition in Reformation Britain*, 32-68.

107. P. Matheson, *The Collected Works of Thomas Muentzer* (Edinburgh: T & T Clark, 1988).

108. Hans Hut, "On the Mystery of Baptism," in D. Liechty, *Early Anabaptist Spirituality* (London: SPCK, 1994) 64; and on anabaptism in England, I. B. Horst, *The Radical Brethren* (Nieuwkoop: de Graaf, 1972).

109. K. Deppermann, *Melchior Hoffmann* (Edinburgh: T & T Clark, 1987).

110. Cf. M. Walzer, *Exodus and Revolution* (New York: HarperCollins, 1985) 120-22.

111. On millenarian apocalypticism, see Cohn, *The Pursuit of the Millennium.*

112. W. Klaassen, *Living at the End of the Ages: Apocalyptic Expectation in the Radical Reformation* (Lanham, Md.: University Press of America, 1992).

113. K. Firth, *The Apocalyptic Tradition in Reformation Britain, 1530–1645*, 240-46.

114. Quoted in Firth, *The Apocalyptic Traditon*, 221.

115. C. Burdon, *The Apocalypse in England 1700–1834: Revelation Unravelling* (London: Macmillan, 1997).

116. See C. Hill, *The World Turned Upside Down* (London: Penguin, 1972); C. Hill, *The English Bible and the Seventeenth Century Revolution* (London: Penguin, 1993); Firth, *The Apocalyptic Tradition*, 242.

117. On Winstanley and his relationship to radical interpretation of Scripture, see C. Rowland, *Radical Christianity: A Reading of Recovery*

(Oxford: Polity, 1988). The millenarian tradition is evident in early American exegesis. See R. Bloch, *Visionary Republic, Millennial Themes in American Thought 1756–1800* (Cambridge: Cambridge University Press, 1985).

118. See C. Hill, *A Turbulent Seditious and Fractious People: John Bunyan and His Church* (Oxford: Oxford University Press, 1989).

119. Albrecht Bengel, *Gnomon Novi Testamenti,* 1026 on Rev 1:1, quoted in John Wesley, *Explanatory Notes Upon the New Testament,* 2:313. See also the important attempt to make contemporary the message of Revelation in J. G. Herder, *Maran Atha,* English trans. (London, 1821), discussed by Burdon, *The Apocalypse in England,* 85-87.

120. See M. H. Abrams, *Natural Supernaturalism, Tradition and Revolution in Romantic Literature* (New York: Norton, 1973) 47; M. Butler, *Romantics Rebels and Reactionaries* (Oxford: Oxford University Press, 1981).

121. Burdon, *The Apocalypse in England 1700–1834.*

122. E. Shaffer, *"Kubla Khan" and the Fall of Jerusalem* (Cambridge: Cambridge University Press, 1975).

123. See D. V. Erdman, *Blake: Prophet Against Empire,* 3rd ed. (Princeton: Princeton University Press, 1977).

124. J. Mee, *Dangerous Enthusiasm* (Oxford: Oxford University Press, 1992) 211.

125. Hal Lindsey, *The Late, Great Planet Earth* (London: Lakeland) 1971. According to *US News and World Report* (Dec. 13, 1997) 69, this book and its sequels had phenomenal sales: 40 million copies.

126. A. Mojtabai, *Blessed Assurance* (Boston: Houghton Mifflin) 1987; P. Boyer, *When Time Shall Be No More: Prophecy Belief in Modern American Culture* (Cambridge, Mass.: Harvard University Press, 1992); D. Thompson, *The End of Time: Faith and Fear in the Shadow of the Millennium* (London: Minerva, 1997).

127. M. Goulder, *A Tale of Two Missions* (London: SCM, 1994).

128. F. Engels, *Marx and Engels: Basic Writings on Politics and Philosophy,* ed. L. Feuer (London: Fontana, 1959).

129. J. M. Ford, *Revelation,* AB 38 (New York: Doubleday, 1975).

130. A. Farrer, *A Rebirth of Images: The Making of St. John's Apocalypse* (Westminster: Dacre, 1949); *The Revelation of St. John the Divine* (Oxford: Oxford University Press). Farrer's work is used in a judicious way by J. Sweet, *Revelation* (London: SCM, 1979).

131. E.g., J. C. Beker, *Paul the Apostle: The Triumph of God in Life and Thought* (Edinburgh: T & T Clark, 1980); E. Käsemann, *Commentary on Romans* (London: SCM, 1980).

132. On the apocalyptic character of the Qumran writings, see J. J. Collins, *Apocalypticism and the Dead Sea Scrolls* (London: Routledge, 1997).

133. A. Schweitzer, *The Quest of the Historical Jesus* (London: A. & C. Black, 1931).

134. R. A. Kraft and G. Nickelsburg, *Early Judaism and Its Modern Interpreters* (Philadelphia: Fortress, 1986); J. M. Schmidt, *Die jüdische Apokalyptik* (Neukirchen: Neukirchener Verlag, 1969).

135. P. L. Esler, *The First Christians in Their Social Worlds* (London: Routledge, 1995).

136. P. Hanson, *The Dawn of Apocalyptic* (Philadelphia: Fortress, 1974).

137. See John Gager, *Kingdom and Community* (Englewood Cliffs, N.J.: Prentice Hall, 1975).

138. N. Cohn, *Europe's Inner Demons* (London: Paladin, 1976).

139. S. Hall, "Religious Ideologies and Social Movements in Jamaica," in R. Bobock and K. Thompson, *Religion and Ideology* (Manchester: Manchester University Press, 1985).

140. A. Y. Collins, *Crisis and Catharsis* (Philadelphia: Westminster, 1984); C. G. Jung, *Answer to Job* (London: Routledge, 1984); E. Drewermann, *Tiefenpsychologie und Exegesis. Band II: Vision, Weissagung, Apokalypse Geschichte Gleichnis* (Olten: Walter, 1985) 541-91.

141. A. Boesak, *Comfort and Protest* (Edinburgh: T & T Clark, 1987).

142. P. Richard, *Apocalypse* (Maryknoll, N.Y.: Orbis, 1995).

143. J. Ellul, *Apocalypse: The Book of Revelation* (New York: Seabury, 1977).

144. W. Stringfellow, *Conscience and Obedience* (Waco, Tex.: Word, 1977); *An Ethic for Christians and Other Aliens in a Strange Land* (Waco, Tex.: Word, 1973). Stringfellow's work is a precursor of Walter Wink's work on the principalities and powers. See W. Wink, *Engaging the Powers* (Philadelphia: Fortress, 1992).

145. *Bíblia Sagrada* (São Paulo: 1990).

146. C. Mesters, "The Use of the Bible in Christian Communities of the Common People," in *The Bible and Liberation*, ed. N. Gottwald (Maryknoll, N.Y.: Orbis, 1983) 119-33; C. Mesters, *Defenseless Flower* (London: CIIR, 1989).

147. C. Hill, *The English Bible and the Seventeenth Century Revolution.*

148. See G. B. Caird, *A Commentary on the Revelation of Saint John the Divine* (London: A. & C. Black, 1984).

150. See R. K. Emmerson and B. McGinn, *The Apocalypse in the Middle Ages* (Ithaca: Cornell University Press, 1992); M. R. James, *The Apocalypse in Art* (London: Oxford University Press, 1931); F. van der Meer, *Apocalypse: Visions from the Book of Revelation in Western Art* (London: Thames and Hudson, 1978); R. M. Wright, *Art and Antichrist in Medieval Europe* (Manchester: 1996). See also the use of Kip Gresham's prints of scenes from Revelation in C. Rowland, *Revelation* (London: Epworth, 1993).

151. See *William Blake's Illuminated Books*, 6 vols., ed. David Bindman (London: Tate Gallery Publications/William Blake Trust) 1991–1995.

152. William Blake, *The Four Zoas*, in *Blake: Complete Writings*, ed. G. Keynes (London: Oxford University Press, 1966) 263-382.

153. William Blake, *Jerusalem,* plate 5, ll. 18-20, in *Blake: Complete Writings*, 623.

154. William Blake, Letter to Dr. Trusler, 23 August 1799, in *Blake: Complete Writings*, 793.

155. William Blake, "Auguries of Innocence," ll. 1-2, in Blake: Complete Writings, 431.

156. William Blake, *The Laocoön*, in *Blake: Complete Writings*, 777.

157. William Blake, Letter to Dr. Trusler, 23 August 1799, in *Blake: Complete Writings*, 794.

158. See the essays in M. Bull, *Apocalypse Theory* (Oxford: Blackwell, 1995).

159. D. H. Lawrence, *Apocalypse* (London: Penguin, 1960).

160. Jacques Derrida, "Of an Apocalyptic Tone Recently Adopted in Philosophy," *Semeia* 23 (1982) 63-97.

161. K. Barth, *The Epistle to the Romans* (London: A. & C. Black, 1933) 19. See further B. McCormack, *Karl Barth's Critically Realistic Dialectical Theology* (Oxford: Oxford University Press, 1995).

162. K. Barth, *Church Dogmatics* I/2 (Edinburgh: T & T Clark, 1961) 28ff.

163. E. Bloch, *The Principle of Hope*, trans. N. Plaice, S. Plaice, and P. Knight (Oxford: Basil Blackwell, 1986). For an introduction to Bloch's thought, see W. Hudson, *The Marxist Philosophy of Ernst Bloch* (London: Macmillan, 1982).

164. In Ernst Bloch, *Atheism in Christianity*, trans. J. T. Swann (New York: Herder and Herder, 1972).

165. Bloch, *The Principle of Hope*, 502.

166. Bloch, *The Principle of Hope*,, 1274.

167. Bloch, *The Principle of Hope*,, 509-15. On the links, see C. Rowland, *Radical Christianity: A Reading of Recovery* (Oxford: Polity, 1988).

168. See Walter Benjamin, "Theses on the Philosophy of History," in *Illuminations* (London: Collins Fontana, 1970).

169. R. Wiggerhaus, *The Frankfurt School* (Oxford: Polity, 1994).

170. D. Biale, *Gershom Scholem: Kabbalah and Counter-History* (Cambridge, Mass.: Harvard University Press, 1982).

171. J. Moltmann, *Theology of Hope* (London: SCM, 1975).

172. See L. Boff, *Jesus Christ Liberator* (London: SPCK, 1980).

173. E. Schüssler Fiorenza, *Revelation: Vision of a Just World* (Edinburgh: T & T Clark, 1993) 139. On the language of Revelation, see D. Barr, "The Apocalypse of John as Oral Enactment," *Int.* 40 (1986) 243-56; G. B. Caird, *The Language and Imagery of the Bible* (London: Duckworth, 1980).

174. I am grateful to James Grenfell, Alan Kreider, and Rebekah Rowland for comments on earlier drafts of this survey and for help with proofreading and the checking of references.

ABBREVIATIONS
AND
CHARTS, ILLUSTRATIONS,
AND MAPS

ABBREVIATIONS

GENERAL

BCE	Before the Common Era
CE	Common Era
c.	circa
cent.	century
cf.	compare
chap(s).	chapter(s)
d.	died
Dtr	Deuteronomistic historian
esp.	especially
fem.	feminine
f(f).	and following
HB	Hebrew Bible
lit.	literally
l(l).	line(s)
LXX	Septuagint
MS(S)	manuscript(s)
mg.	margin
masc.	masculine
MT	Masoretic Text
n(n).	note(s)
neut.	neuter
NT	New Testament
OG	Old Greek
OL	Old Latin
OT	Old Testament
par(s).	parallel(s)
pl(s).	plate(s)
sing.	singular
SP	Samaritan Pentateuch
v(v).	verse(s)
Vg	Vulgate
\\	between Scripture references indicates parallelism

BIBLE TRANSLATIONS

ASV	American Standard Version
CEV	Contemporary English Version
CSB	Catholic Study Bible
GNB	Good News Bible
JB	Jerusalem Bible
KJV	King James Version

NAB	New American Bible
NCB	New Century Bible
NEB	New English Bible
NIV	New International Version
NJB	New Jerusalem Bible
NKJV	New King James Version
NRSV	New Revised Standard Version
REB	Revised English Bible
RSV	Revised Standard Version
TLB	The Living Bible
TNK	Tanakh

Biblical Books (with the Apocrypha)

Gen	Nah	1–4 Kgdms	John
Exod	Hab	Add Esth	Acts
Lev	Zeph	Bar	Rom
Num	Hag	Bel	1–2 Cor
Deut	Zech	1–2 Esdr	Gal
Josh	Mal	4 Ezra	Eph
Judg	Ps (Pss)	Jdt	Phil
1–2 Sam	Job	Ep Jer	Col
1–2 Kgs	Prov	1–4 Macc	1–2 Thess
Isa	Ruth	Pr Azar	1–2 Tim
Jer	Cant	Pr Man	Titus
Ezek	Eccl	Sir	Phlm
Hos	Lam	Sus	Heb
Joel	Esth	Tob	Jas
Amos	Dan	Wis	1–2 Pet
Obad	Ezra	Matt	1–3 John
Jonah	Neh	Mark	Jude
Mic	1–2 Chr	Luke	Rev

Pseudepigraphical and Early Patristic Books

Apoc. Ab.	*Apocalypse of Abraham*
Apoc. Adam	*Apocalypse of Adam*
2 Apoc. Bar.	Syriac *Apocalypse of Baruch*
3 Apoc. Bar.	Greek *Apocalypse of Baruch*
Apoc. Mos.	*Apocalypse of Moses*
As. Mos.	*Assumption of Moses*
Ascen. Isa.	*Ascension of Isaiah*
Barn.	*Barnabas*
1–2 Clem.	*1–2 Clement*
Did.	*Didache*
1 Enoch	Ethiopic Book of *Enoch*
2 Enoch	Slavonic Book of *Enoch*
3 Enoch	Hebrew Book of *Enoch*
Ep. Arist.	*Epistle of Aristeas*
Gos. Pet.	*Gospel of Peter*

Herm. *Sim.*	Shepherd of Hermas, *Similitude*
Ign. *Eph.*	Ignatius, *To the Ephesians*
Ign. *Magn.*	Ignatius, *To the Magnesians*
Ign. *Phld.*	Ignatius, *To the Philadelphians*
Ign. *Pol.*	Ignatius, *To Polycarp*
Ign. *Rom.*	Ignatius, *To the Romans*
Ign. *Smyrn.*	Ignatius, *To the Smyrnaeans*
Ign. *Trall.*	Ignatius, *To the Trallians*
Jub.	*Jubilees*
P. Oxy.	*Oxyrynchus Papyri.* Edited by B. P. Grenfell and A. S. Hunt.
Pss. Sol.	*Psalms of Solomon*
Sib. Or.	*Sibylline Oracles*
T. Benj.	*Testament of Benjamin*
T. Dan	*Testament of Dan*
T. Iss.	*Testament of Issachar*
T. Job	*Testament of Job*
T. Jud.	*Testament of Judah*
T. Levi	*Testament of Levi*
T. Naph.	*Testament of Naphtali*
T. Reu.	*Testament of Reuben*
T. Sim.	*Testament of Simeon*

Dead Sea Scrolls and Related Texts

CD	Cairo Genizah text of the *Damascus Document*
DSS	Dead Sea Scrolls
8Ḥev XIIgr	Greek Scroll of the Minor Prophets from Naḥal Ḥever
Q	Qumran
1Q, 2Q, 3Q, etc.	Numbered caves of Qumran yielding written material followed by abbreviation of biblical or apocryphal book (e.g., 1Q pHab) or numbered document (e.g., 1Q7)
1Q28b	Appendix b *(Rule of the Blessings)* to 1QS
1QH^{a}	*Hodayot^{a} (Thanksgiving Hymns^{a})*
1QM	*Milḥamah (War Scroll)*
1QpHab	*Pesher Habakkuk*
1QS	*Serek Hayaḥad (Rule of the Community, Manual of Discipline)*
1QS^{a}	Appendix a *(Rule of the Congregation)* to 1QS
1QS^{b}	Appendix b *(Rule of the Blessings)* to 1QS
4Q175	*Testimonia* (4QTest)
4Q246	*Apocryphon of Daniel* (Aramaic Apocalypse)
4Q298	*Cryptic A: Words of the Sage to the Sons of Dawn*
4Q385^{b}	4QApocryphon of Jeremiah^{c}
4Q389^{a}	4QApocryphon of Jeremiah^{e}
4Q390	4QPseudo-Moses^{e}
4Q394	*Miqsat Maʿaśê ha- Torah^{a}* (4QMMT^{a})
4Q416	*Sapiential Work Ab*
4Q521	*Messianic Apocalypse*
4Q5504Qproto-Esther $^{a\text{-}f}$	ProtoEsther, Aramaic, copies to
4QFlor (MidrEschat^{a})	*Florilegium* (or *Midrash on Eschatology^{a}*)
4QMMT	*Halakhic Letter*

4QpaleoDeutr	Copy of Deuteronomy in paleo-Hebrew script
4QpaleoExod[m]	Copy of Exodus in paleo-Hebrew script
4QpNah	*Nahum Pesher*
4QpPss[a]	*Psalm Pesher A*
4QprNab ar	*Prayer of Nabonidus*
4QPs37	*Psalms Scroll*
4QpsDan	Pseudo-Daniel
4Qsam[a]	First copy of Samuel
4QTob	Copy of Tobit
11QMelch	*Melchizedek*
11QpHab	A fragment of the Habakkuk scroll
11QPs[a]	*Psalms Scroll*[a]
11QTemple	*Temple Scroll*
11QtgJob	*Targum of Job*

Orders and Tractates in Mishnaic and Related Literature

To distinguish between the same-named tractates in the Mishna, Tosepta, Babylonian Talmud, and Jerusalem Talmud, *m., t., b.,* or *y.* precedes the title of the tractate.

ʾAbot	*ʾAbot*
ʾArak.	*ʾArakin*
B. Bat.	*Baba Batra*
B. Men	*Baba Meniʿa*
B. Qam.	*Baba Qamma*
Ber.	*Berakot*
Dem.	*Demai*
Git.	*Giṭṭin*
Ḥag.	*Ḥagigah*
Hor.	*Horayot*
Ḥul.	*Ḥullin*
Ketub.	*Ketubbot*
Maʿaś.	*Maʿaśerot*
Meg.	*Megillah*
Menaḥ.	*Menaḥot*
Mid.	*Middot*
Moʾed Qaṭ.	*Moʾed Qaṭan*
Ned.	*Nedarim*
Pesaḥ.	*Pesaḥim*
Qidd.	*Qiddušin*
Šabb.	*Šabbat*
Sanh.	*Sanhedrin*
Shekal	*Pesahim Shekalim*
Soïa	*Soïa*
Sukk.	*Sukka*
Taʿan.	*Taʿanit*
Tg. Neof.	*Targum Neofiti*
Yad.	*Yadayim*
Yoma	*Yoma (= Kippurim)*

Targumic Material

Tg. Esth. I, II	*First or Second Targum of Esther*
Tg. Neb.	*Targum of the Prophets*

Other Rabbinic Works

ʾAbot R. Nat.	*ʾAbot de Rabbi Nathan*
Pesiq. Rab.	*Pesiqta Rabbati*
Rab.	*Rabbah* (following abbreviation of biblical book—e.g., Gen. Rab. = Genesis Rabbah)
Sipra	*Sipra*
Song Rab.	*Song of Songs Rabbah*

Names of Nag Hammadi Tractates

Ap. John	*Apocryphon of John*
Apoc. Adam	*Apocalypse of Adam*
Ep. Pet. Phil.	*Letter of Peter to Philip*
Exeg. Soul	*Exegesis on the Soul*
Gos. Phil.	*Gospel of Philip*
Gos. Truth	*Gospel of Truth*

Greek Manuscripts and Ancient Versions

Papyrus Manuscripts

𝔓1	Third-century Greek Papyrus manuscript of the Gospels
𝔓29	Third- or fourth-century Greek Papyrus manuscript of Acts
𝔓33	Sixth-century Greek Papyrus manuscript of Acts
𝔓37	Third- or fourth-century Greek Papyrus manuscript of the Gospels
𝔓38	Fourth-century Greek Papyrus manuscript of Acts
𝔓45	Third-century Greek Papyrus manuscript of the Gospels
𝔓46	Third-century Greek Papyrus manuscript of the Gospels
𝔓47	Third-century Greek Papyrus manuscript of the Gospels
𝔓48	Third-century Greek Papyrus manuscript of Acts
𝔓52	Second-century Greek Papyrus manuscript of John 18:31-33, 37-38
𝔓58	Sixth-century Greek Papyrus manuscript of Acts
𝔓64	Third-century Greek Papyrus fragment of Matthew
𝔓66	Third-century Greek Papyrus manuscript of the Gospels
𝔓67	Third-century Greek Papyrus fragment of Matthew
𝔓69	Late second-century Greek Papyrus manuscript of the Gospel of Luke
𝔓75	Third-century Greek Papyrus manuscript of the Gospels

Lettered Uncials

א	Codex Sinaiticus, fourth-century manuscript of LXX, NT, *Epistle of Barnabas*, and *Shepherd of Hermas*
A	Codex Alexandrinus, fifth-century manuscript of LXX, NT, *1 & 2 Clement*, and *Psalms of Solomon*

B	Codex Vaticanus, fourth-century manuscript of LXX and parts of the NT
C	Codex Ephraemi, fifth-century manuscript of parts of LXX and NT
D	Codex Bezae, fifth-century bilingual (Greek and Latin) manuscript of the Gospels and Acts
G	Ninth-century manuscript of the Gospels
K	Ninth-century manuscript of the Gospels
L	Eighth-century manuscript of the Gospels
W	Washington Codex, fifth-century manuscript of the Gospels
X	Codex Monacensis, ninth- or tenth-century miniscule manuscript of the Gospels
Z	Sixth-century manuscript of Matthew
Θ	Koridethi Codex, ninth-century manuscript of the Gospels
Y	Athous Laurae Codex, eighth- or ninth-century manuscript of the Gospels (incomplete), Acts, The Catholic and Pauline Epistles, and Hebrews

Numbered Uncials

058	Fourth-century fragment of Matthew 18
074	Sixth-century fragment of Matthew
078	Sixth-century fragment of Matthew, Luke, and John
0170	Fifth- or sixth-century uncial manuscript of Matthew
0181	Fourth- or fifth-century partial manuscript of Luke 9:59–10:14

Numbered Minuscules

33	Tenth-century manuscript of the Gospels
174	Eleventh-century manuscript of the Gospels
565	Ninth-century miniscule manuscript of the Gospels
700	Eleventh-century miniscule manuscript of the Gospels
892	Ninth-century miniscule manuscript of the Gospels

Ancient Versions

bo	The Bohairic (Memphitic) Coptic Version
bo^{mss}	Some manuscripts in the Bohairic tradition
bo^{pt}	Some manuscripts in the Bohairic tradition
d	The Latin text of Codex Bezae
e	Codex Palatinus, fifth-century Latin manuscript of the Gospels
ff^{2}	Old Latin manuscript, fifth-century translation of the Gospels
Ir^{lat}	The Latin translation of Iraneaus
latt	The whole Latin tradition (including the Vulgate)
mae	Middle Egyptian
sa	The Sahidic (Thebaic) Coptic Version
sy	The Syriac Version
sy^{s}	The Sinaitic Syriac Version

Other Abbreviations

pc	A few other manuscripts
f^{1}	Family 1: miniscule manuscripts belonging to the Lake Group (1, 118, 131, 209, 1582)
f^{13}	Family 13: miniscule manuscripts belonging to the Ferrar Group (13, 69, 124, 174, 230, 346, 543, 788, 826, 828, 983, 1689, 1709)
a*	The original reading of Codex Sinaiticus
a^{1}	The first corrector of Codex Sinaiticus

a^2	The second corrector of Codex Sinaiticus
D*	The original reading of Codex Bezae
D^2	The second corrector (c. fifth century) of Codex Bezae
𝔐	The Majority text (the mass of later manuscripts)
C^2	The corrected text of Codex Ephraemi
700*	The original reading of manuscript 700
NA^{27}	*Novum Testamentum Graece*, Nestle-Aland, 27th ed.
UBS^4	*The Greek New Testament*, United Bible Societies, 4th ed.

Periodicals, Reference Works, and Serials

AB	Anchor Bible
ABD	*Anchor Bible Dictionary.* Edited by D. N. Freedman. 6 vols. New York, 1992
ABR	*Australian Biblical Review*
ABRL	Anchor Bible Reference Library
ACNT	Augsburg Commentaries on the New Testament
AcOr	*Acta orientalia*
AfO	*Archiv für Orientforschung*
AfOB	Archiv für Orientforschung: Beiheft
AGJU	Arbeiten zur Geschichte des antiken Judentums und des Urchristentums
AJP	*American Journal of Philology*
AJSL	*American Journal of Semitic Languages and Literature*
AJT	*American Journal of Theology*
AnBib	Analecta biblica
ANEP	*The Ancient Near East in Pictures Relating to the Old Testament.* Edited by J. B. Pritchard. Princeton, 1954
ANET	*Ancient Near Eastern Texts Relating to the Old Testament.* Edited by J. B. Pritchard. 3rd ed. Princeton, 1969
ANF	*The Ante-Nicene Fathers*
ANRW	*Aufstieg und Niedergang der römischen Welt: Geschichte und Kultur Roms im Spiegel der neueren Forschung.* Edited by H. Temporini and W. Haase. Berlin, 1972–
ANTC	Abingdon New Testament Commentaries
ANTJ	Arbeiten zum Neuen Testament und Judentum
APOT	*Apocrypha and Pseudepigrapha of the Old Testament.* Edited by R. H. Charles. 2 vols. Oxford, 1913
ASNU	Acta seminarii neotestamentici upsaliensis
ATANT	Abhandlungen zur Theologie des Alten und Neuen Testaments
ATD	Das Alte Testament Deutsch
ATDan	Acta theological danica
Aug	*Augustinianum*
BA	*Biblical Archaeologist*
BAGD	Bauer, W., W. F. Arndt, F. W. Gingrich, and F. W. Danker. *Greek-English Lexicon of the New Testament and Other Early Christian Literature.* 2nd ed. Chicago, 1979
BAR	*Biblical Archaeology Review*
BASOR	*Bulletin of the American Schools of Oriental Research*
BBB	Bonner biblische Beiträge
BBET	Beiträge zur biblischen Exegese und Theologie
BBR	*Bulletin for Biblical Research*

BDAG — Bauer, W., F. W. Danker, W. F. Arndt, and F. W. Gingrich. *Greek-English Lexicon of the New Testament and Other Early Christian Literature.* 3rd ed. Chicago, 2000

BDB — Brown, F., S. R. Driver, and C. A. Briggs. *A Hebrew and English Lexicon of the Old Testament.* Oxford, 1907

BDF — Blass, F., A. Debrunner, and R. W. Funk. *A Greek Grammar of the New Testament and Other Early Christian Literature.* Chicago, 1961

BEATAJ — Beiträge zur Erforschung des Alten Testaments und des antiken Judentum

BETL — Bibliotheca ephemeridum theologicarum lovaniensium

BEvT — Beiträge zur evangelischen Theologie

BHS — *Biblia Hebraica Stuttgartensia.* Edited by K. Elliger and W. Randolph. Stuttgart, 1983

BHT — Beiträge zur historischen Theologie

Bib — *Biblica*

BibInt — *Biblical Interpretation*

BibOr — Biblica et orientalia

BJRL — *Bulletin of the John Rylands University Library of Manchester*

BJS — Brown Judaic Studies

BK — *Bibel und Kirche*

BKAT — Biblischer Kommentar, Altes Testament. Edited by M. Noth and H. W. Wolff

BLS — Bible and Literature Series

BN — *Biblische Notizen*

BNTC — Black's New Testament Commentaries

BR — *Biblical Research*

BSac — *Bibliotheca sacra*

BSOAS — *Bulletin of the School of Oriental and African Studies*

BT — *The Bible Translator*

BTB — *Biblical Theology Bulletin*

BVC — *Bible et vie chrétienne*

BWA(N)T — Beiträge zur Wissenschaft vom Alten (und Neuen) Testament

BZ — *Biblische Zeitschrift*

BZAW — Beihefte zur Zeitschrift für die alttestamentliche Wissenschaft

BZNW — Beihefte zur Zeitschrift für die neutestamentliche Wissenschaft

CAD — *The Assyrian Dictionary of the Oriental Institute of the University of Chicago.* Chicago, 1956–

CB — *Cultura bíblica*

CBC — Cambridge Bible Commentary

CBQ — *Catholic Biblical Quarterly*

CBQMS — Catholic Biblical Quarterly Monograph Series

ConBNT — Coniectanea neotestamentica or Coniectanea biblica: New Testament Series

ConBOT — Coniectanea biblica: Old Testament Series

CP — *Classical Philology*

CRAI — Comptes rendus del l'Académie des inscriptions et belles-lettres

CRINT — Compendia rerum iudaicarum ad Novum Testamentum

CTM — *Concordia Theological Monthly*

DJD — Discoveries in the Judaean Desert

EB — Echter Bibel

EI — *Encyclopaedia of Islam.* 9 of 13 projected vols. 2nd ed. Leiden, 1954–

EKKNT — Evangelisch-katholischer Kommentar zum Neuen Testament

Enc — *Encounter*

EncJud	*Encyclopaedia Judaica.* 16 vols. Jerusalem, 1972
EPRO	Etudes préliminairies aux religions orientales dans l'empire romain
ErIsr	*Eretz-Israel*
EstBib	*Estudios bíblicos*
ETL	*Ephemerides theologicae lovanienses*
ETS	Erfurter theologische Studien
EvQ	*Evangelical Quarterly*
EvT	*Evangelische Theologie*
ExAud	*Ex auditu*
ExpTim	*Expository Times*
FAT	Forschungen zum Alten Testament
FB	Forschung zur Bibel
FBBS	Facet Books, Biblical Series
FFNT	Foundations and Facets: New Testament
FOTL	Forms of the Old Testament Literature
FRLANT	Forschungen zur Religion und Literatur des Alten und Neuen Testaments
FTS	Frankfurter Theologische Studien
GBS.OTS	Guides to Biblical Scholarship. Old Testament Series
GCS	Die griechische christliche Schriftsteller der ersten [drei] Jahrhunderte
GKC	*Gesenius' Hebrew Grammar.* Edited by E. Kautzsch. Translated by A. E. Cowley. 2nd ed. Oxford, 1910
GNS	*Good News Studies*
GTA	Göttinger theologischer Arbeiten
HAL	Koehler, L., W. Baumgartner, and J. J. Stamm. *Hebräisches und aramäisches Lexikon zum Alten Testament.* Fascicles 1–5, 1967–1995 (KBL3). ET: *HALOT*
HAR	*Hebrew Annual Review*
HAT	Handbuch zum Alten Testament
HBC	*Harper's Bible Commentary.* Edited by J. L. Mays et al. San Francisco, 1988
HBT	*Horizons in Biblical Theology*
HDB	*Hastings Dictionary of the Bible*
HDR	Harvard Dissertations in Religion
HeyJ	*Heythrop Journal*
HNT	Handbuch zum Neuen Testament
HNTC	Harper's New Testament Commentaries
HR	*History of Religions*
HSM	Harvard Semitic Monographs
HSS	Harvard Semitic Studies
HTKNT	Herders theologischer Kommentar zum Neuen Testament
HTR	*Harvard Theological Review*
HTS	Harvard Theological Studies
HUCA	*Hebrew Union College Annual*
IB	*Interpreter's Bible.* Edited by G. A. Buttrick et al. 12 vols. New York, 1951–1957
IBC	Interpretation: A Bible Commentary for Teaching and Preaching
IBS	*Irish Biblical Studies*
ICC	International Critical Commentary
IDB	*The Interpreter's Dictionary of the Bible.* Edited by G.A. Buttrick. 4 vols. Nashville, 1962

IDBSup	*Interpreter's Dictionary of the Bible: Supplementary Volume.* Edited by K. Crim. Nashville, 1976
IEJ	*Israel Exploration Journal*
Int	*Interpretation*
IRT	Issues in Religion and Theology
ITC	International Theological Commentary
JAAR	*Journal of the American Academy of Religion*
JAL	Jewish Apocryphal Literature Series
JANESCU	*Journal of the Ancient Near Eastern Society of Columbia University*
JAOS	*Journal of the American Oriental Society*
JBL	*Journal of Biblical Literature*
JETS	*Journal of the Evangelical Theological Society*
JJS	*Journal of Jewish Studies*
JNES	*Journal of Near Eastern Studies*
JNSL	*Journal of Northwest Semitic Languages*
JPS	Jewish Publication Society
JPSV	Jewish Publication Society Version
JQR	*Jewish Quarterly Review*
JR	*Journal of Religion*
JRH	*Journal of Religious History*
JSJ	*Journal for the Study of Judaism in the Persian, Hellenistic, and Roman Periods*
JSNT	*Journal for the Study of the New Testament*
JSNTSup	Journal for the Study of the New Testament: Supplement Series
JSOT	*Journal for the Study of the Old Testament*
JSOTSup	Journal for the Study of the Old Testament: Supplement Series
JSP	*Journal for the Study of the Pseudepigrapha*
JSPTSS	Journal of the Study of Pentecostal Theology Supplement Series
JSS	*Journal of Semitic Studies*
JTC	*Journal for Theology and the Church*
JTS	*Journal of Theological Studies*
KAT	Kommentar zum Alten Testament
KEK	Kritisch-exegetischer Kommentar über das Neue Testament (Meyer-Kommentar)
KPG	Knox Preaching Guides
LCL	Loeb Classical Library
LTQ	*Lexington Theological Quarterly*
MNTC	Moffatt New Testament Commentary
NA^{27}	*Novum Testamentum Graece*, Nestle-Aland, 27th ed.
NCBC	New Century Bible Commentary
NHS	Nag Hammadi Studies
NIB	*The New Interpreter's Bible*
NICNT	New International Commentary on the New Testament
NICOT	New International Commentary on the Old Testament
NIGTC	New International Greek Testament Commentary
NJBC	*The New Jerome Biblical Commentary.* Edited by R. E. Brown et al. Englewood Cliffs, 1990
NovT	*Novum Testamentum*
NovTSup	Supplements to Novum Testamentum
NPNF	*Nicene and Post-Nicene Fathers,* Series 1 and 2

NTC	New Testament in Context
NTD	Das Neue Testament Deutsch
NTG	New Testament Guides
NTS	*New Testament Studies*
NTTS	New Testament Tools and Studies
OBC	Oxford Bible Commentary
OBO	Orbis biblicus et orientalis
OBT	Overtures to Biblical Theology
OIP	Oriental Institute Publications
Or	*Orientalia* (NS)
OTG	Old Testament Guides
OTL	Old Testament Library
OTM	Old Testament Message
OTP	*Old Testament Pseudepigrapha.* Edited by J. H. Charlesworth. 2 vols. New York, 1983
OtSt	*Oudtestamentische Studiën*
PAAJR	*Proceedings of the American Academy of Jewish Research*
PEQ	*Palestine Exploration Quarterly*
PGM	*Papyri graecae magicae: Die griechischen Zauberpapyri.* Edited by K. Preisendanz. Berlin, 1928
PTMS	Pittsburgh Theological Monograph Series
QD	Quaestiones disputatae
RANE	Records of the Ancient Near East
RB	*Revue biblique*
ResQ	*Restoration Quarterly*
RevExp	*Review and Expositor*
RevQ	*Revue de Qumran*
RevScRel	*Revue des sciences religieuses*
RSR	*Recherches de science religieuse*
RTL	*Revue théologique de Louvain*
SAA	State Archives of Assyria
SBB	Stuttgarter biblische Beiträge
SBL	Society of Biblical Literature
SBLDS	Society of Biblical Literature Dissertation Series
SBLMS	Society of Biblical Literature Monograph Series
SBLRBS	Society of Biblical Literature Resources for Biblical Study
SBLSCS	Society of Biblical Literature Septuagint and Cognate Studies
SBLSP	*Society of Biblical Literature Seminar Papers*
SBLSS	Society of Biblical Literature Semeia Studies
SBLSymS	Society of Biblical Literature Symposium Series
SBLWAW	Society of Biblical Literature Writings from the Ancient World
SBM	Stuttgarter biblische Monographien
SBS	Stuttgarter Bibelstudien
SBT	Studies in Biblical Theology
SEÅ	*Svensk exegetisk årsbok*
SJLA	Studies in Judaism in Late Antiquity
SJOT	*Scandinavian Journal of the Old Testament*
SJT	*Scottish Journal of Theology*
SKK	Stuttgarter kleiner Kommentar
SNTSMS	Society for New Testament Studies Monograph Series

SOTSMS	Society for Old Testament Study Monograph Series
SP	Sacra pagina
SR	*Studies in Religion*
SSN	Studia semitica neerlandica
Str-B	Strack, H. L., and P. Billerbeck. *Kommentar zum Neuen Testament aus Talmud und Midrasch.* 6 vols. Munich, 1922–6161
SUNT	Studien zur Umwelt des Neuen Testaments
SVTP	Studia in Veteris Testamenti pseudepigrapha
TB	Theologische Bücherei: Neudrucke und Berichte aus dem 20. Jahrhundert
TD	*Theology Digest*
TDNT	*Theological Dictionary of the New Testament.* Edited by G. Kittel and G. Friedrich. Translated by G. W. Bromiley. 10 vols. Grand Rapids, 1964–1976
TDOT	*Theological Dictionary of the Old Testament.* Edited by G. J. Botterweck and H. Ringgren. Translated by J. T. Willis, G. W. Bromiley, and D. E. Green. 8 vols. Grand Rapids, 1974–
THKNT	Theologischer Handkommentar zum Neuen Testament
ThTo	*Theology Today*
TLZ	*Theologische Literaturzeitung*
TOTC	Tyndale Old Testament Commentaries
TQ	*Theologische Quartalschrift*
TS	Texts and Studies
TS	*Theological Studies*
TSK	*Theologische Studien und Kritiken*
TSSI	*Textbook of Syrian Semitic Inscriptions.* J. C. L. Gibson. Oxford, 1971–1982
TynBul	*Tyndale Bulletin*
TZ	*Theologische Zeitschrift*
UBS	United Bible Societies
UBS[4]	*The Greek New Testament*, United Bible Societies, 4th ed.
UF	*Ugarit-Forschungen*
USQR	*Union Seminary Quarterly Review*
UUA	Uppsala Universitetsårskrift
VC	*Vigiliae christianae*
VT	*Vetus Testamentum*
VTSup	Vetus Testamentum Supplements
WA	*Weimar Ausgabe.* (Weimer ed.). M. Luther
WBC	Word Biblical Commentary
WBT	*Word Biblical Themes*
WMANT	Wissenschaftliche Monographien zum Alten und Neuen Testament
WTJ	*Westminster Theological Journal*
WUNT	Wissenschaftliche Untersuchungen zum Neuen Testament
ZAH	*Zeitschrift für Althebräistik*
ZAW	*Zeitschrift für die alttestamentliche Wissenschaft*
ZNW	*Zeitschrift für die neutestamentliche Wissenschaft und die Kunde de älteren Kirche*
ZTK	*Zeitschrift für Theologie und Kirche*

Index of Charts, Illustrations, and Maps

Charts

Illustrations

Maps

NOTES

Notes

Notes